LOCAL AND METROPOLITAN AREA NETWORKS, FIFTH EDITION

An in-depth presentation of the technology and architecture of local and metropolitan area networks. Covers topology, transmission media, medium access control, standards, internetworking, and network management. Provides an up-to-date coverage of LAN/MAN systems, including Fast Ethernet, ATM LANs, Fibre Channel and wireless LANs.

NETWORK AND INTERNETWORK SECURITY: PRINCIPLES AND PRACTICE

A tutorial and survey on network security technology. Each of the basic building blocks of network security, including conventional and public-key cryptography, authentication, and digital signatures, are covered. In addition methods for countering hackers and viruses are explored. The book covers important network security applications, including PGP, PEM, Kerberos, and SNMPv2 security.

ISDN AND BROADBAND ISDN, with FRAME RELAY AND ATM: THIRD EDITION

An in-depth presentation of the technology and architecture of integrated services digital networks (ISDN). Covers the integrated digital network (IDN), ISDN services, architecture, signaling system no. 7 (SS7) and detailed coverage of the ITU-T standards. This new edition also provides detailed coverage of protocols and congestion control strategies for both frame relay and ATM.

BUSINESS DATA COMMUNICATIONS, THIRD EDITION

A comprehensive presentation of data communications and telecommunications from a business perspective. Covers voice, data, image, and video communications and applications technology and includes a number of case studies.

HIGH-SPEED NETWORKS:
TCP/IP and ATM Design Principles

William Stallings

Prentice Hall
Upper Saddle River, New Jersey 07458

Library of Congress Cataloging-in-Publication Data

Stallings, William.
    High-speed networks : TCP / IP and ATM design principles / William
  Stallings
      p. cm.
    Includes bibliographical references and index.
    ISBN 0-13-525965-7
    1. TCP / IP (Computer network protocol)   2. Asynchronous transfer
mode.   3. Computer networks.   I. Title.
TK5105.585.S73   1998
004.6 ' 5—dc21   97-30397
                                    CIP

Publisher: Alan Apt
Editor-in-Chief: Marcia Horton
Editor: Laura Steele
*Assistant Vice President of Production
  and Manufacturing*: David W. Riccardi
Production Manager: Bayani Mendoza de Leon
Production Editor: Rose Kernan
Manufacturing Buyer: Julia Meehan

Creative Director: Paula Maylahn
Art Director: Heather Scott
Cover Designer: Heather Scott
Copy Editor: Patricia Daly
Editorial Assistant: Toni Chavez
Compositor: Preparé/Emilcomp

© 1998 by Prentice-Hall, Inc.
Simon & Schuster / A Viacom Company
Upper Saddle River, New Jersey 07458

The authors and publisher of this book have used their best efforts in preparing this book. These efforts include the development, research, and testing of the theories and programs to determine their effectiveness. The author and publisher make no warranty of any kind, expressed or implied, with regard to these programs or the documentation contained in this book. The author and publisher shall not be liable in any event for incidental or consequential damages in connection with, or arising out of, the furnishing, performance, or use of these programs.

Printed in the United States of America

10 9 8 7 6 5 4 3 2 1

ISBN 0-13-525965-7

Prentice-Hall International (UK) Limited, *London*
Prentice-Hall of Australia Pty. Limited, *Sydney*
Prentice-Hall Canada, Inc., *Toronto*
Prentice-Hall Hispanoamericana, S. A., *Mexico*
Prentice-Hall of India Private Limited, *New Delhi*
Prentice-Hall of Japan, Inc., *Tokyo*
Simon & Schuster Asia Pte. Ltd., *Singapore*
Editora Prentice-Hall do Brasil, Ltda., *Rio de Janeiro*

To A.T.S.,
who is the epitome of je ne sais quoi
and to her constant companion
Geoffroi

CONTENTS

PART SEVEN   COMPRESSION, 469

FOREWORD

In todays fast-paced world of networking and telecommunication, it is a challenge to find, in one place a masterful collection of all the relevant technologies and concepts. It must be complete and have clear and insightful overviews that are brought down to earth with deep, easy to understand technical explanations.

I have always thought this to be an impossible task. But guess what, Bill Stallings has done it! In "High Speed and Gigabit Networking", you will find a definitive explanation of virtually every aspect related to this massive and important topic. He explains everything from self-similarity to ATM traffic management with the smoothness and case of salesperson while maintaining the technical depth and brilliance of a scholar. His accuracy and attention to detail are unsurpassed; his breadth and vision are illuminating.

You will use and treasure this book from the moment you open its cover. Whether used a reference for the practitioner, classroom material for the student or to fortify an existing technical career, this book provides knowledge and insight in a single self-contained volume which you will come to rely on and appreciate.

I hope this says it all. But no matter. With or without my words, this formidable book will speak for itself.

Dr. Stephen M. Walters
Past President & Chairman of the Board, The ATM Forum
Principal and Fellow, Bellcore

PREFACE

This book aims at helping to disentangle from an immense mass of material the crucial issues and cardinal decisions. Throughout I have set myself to explain faithfully and to the best of my ability what happened and why.

—*The World Crisis,* **Winston Churchill**

BACKGROUND

High-speed networks now dominate both the wide-area network (WAN) and local area network (LAN) markets. In the WAN market, two related trends have appeared. Public and private data networks have evolved from packet-switching networks in the 10s and 100s of kbps, to frame relay networks operating at up to 2 Mbps, and now to asynchronous transfer mode (ATM) networks operating at 155 Mbps or more. For the Internet and private corporate internets, data rates have also soared, with one noteworthy milestone being the construction of a 155-Mbps backbone in 1996.

For many years, the most common LAN was the 10-Mbps shared Ethernet. Then came the switched Ethernet, which offers a dedicated 10 Mbps to each end system. This was followed by Fast Ethernet at 100 Mbps and now Gigabit Ethernet. At the same time, ATM LANs with speeds from 25 Mbps to 155 Mbps have appeared.

This rapid introduction of high-speed networks has spurred the development of new applications and has in turn been driven by the popularity of those applications. Key driving forces have been the increasing use of still image and video data in applications and the popularity of the World Wide Web.

OBJECTIVES

High-speed networks, including gigabit networks, form the focus of the book. Design issues related to two types of networks occupy our attention: internets based on the Internet Protocol (IP) and the entire TCP/IP protocol suite, and ATM (asynchronous transfer mode) networks. These two networking technologies dominate the high-speed scene, and share many common design approaches.

The objective of this book is to provide an up-to-date survey of developments in this area. Central problems that confront the network designer are the need to support multimedia and real-time traffic, the need to control congestion, and the need to provide different levels of Quality of Service (QoS) to different applications.

INTENDED AUDIENCE

This book is intended for both a professional and an academic audience. For the professional interested in this field, the book serves as a basic reference volume and is suitable for self study.

As a textbook, it is suitable for an advanced undergraduate or graduate course. The book treats a number of advanced topics and provides a brief survey of the required elementary topics. After Parts I and II, the Parts are relatively independent. Fewer Parts could be covered for a shorter course, and the Parts can be covered in any order.

PLAN OF THE BOOK

The book is divided into seven parts:

I **Protocol and Network Fundamentals:** Provides a brief survey of fundamental principles, with coverage of TCP/IP, internetworking, and packet switching. Network congestion, which is a key concern throughout the book, is examined.

II **High-Speed Networks:** Provides an overview of ATM networks and high-speed LANs.

III **Performance Modeling and Estimation:** The modeling of traffic flow is important both for network design and configuration and for the request of network services. This part provides a tutorial on the use of queuing analysis to model throughput, delay, and buffer requirements. There is increasing evidence that much of the traffic on high-speed networks is self-similar, for which the traditional queuing analysis does not apply. The nature of self-similar traffic, and modeling approaches, are examined.

IV **End-System Traffic Management:** Discusses end-to-end performance parameters and techniques used by TCP to achieve high throughput and to manage congestion. Real-time transport issues are also discussed.

V **Network Traffic Management:** Within an internet or an ATM network, techniques are needed to control congestion and to provide the desired QoS to active applications. This part surveys those techniques.

VI **Internet Routing:** Covers the major approaches to routing, including distance-vector, link-state, and path-vector routing, and examines multicast routing, resource reservation, and IP switching.

VII **Compression:** Covers both lossless and lossy compression techniques.

In addition, the book includes an extensive glossary, a list of frequently-used acronyms, and a bibliography. Each chapter includes problems, suggestions for further reading, and pointers to relevant web sites.

INTERNET SERVICES FOR INSTRUCTORS AND STUDENTS

There is a web page for this book that provides support for students and instructors. The page includes links to relevant sites, transparency masters of figures in the book in PDF (Adobe Acrobat) format, and sign-up information for the book's internet mailing list. The web page is at http://www.shore.net/~ws/HsNet.html.

An Internet mailing list has been set up so that instructors using this book can exchange information, suggestions, and questions with each other and with the author.

As soon as typos or other errors are discovered, an errata list for this book will be available at http://www.shore.net/~ws.

ACKNOWLEDGMENTS

This book has benefited from review by numerous experts in the field and academics, who gave generously of their time and expertise. The following people reviewed all or a large part of the manuscript: Ketil Albertsen (Trondheim College of Engineering), Chase Bailey (Cisco Systems), Michael S. Borella (DePaul University), Gregory Brewster (DePaul University), Doug Jacobson (Iowa State), Matthew Mutka (Michigan State University), J. Mark Pullen (George Mason University), Pradip Srimani (Colorado State University), Anujan Varma (Univ of California, Santa Cruz), Stephen Walters (Bellcore).

In addition, I was extremely fortunate to have reviews of individual chapters by "subject-area gurus", including **self similar traffic**: Ron Addie (University of Southern Queensland), Vern Paxson (Lawrence Berkeley Laboratory), Bo Ryu (Hughes Research Laboratories), and Walter Willinger (AT&T Labs-Research);

TCP congestion control: Sally Floyd (Lawrence Berkeley Laboratory) and Janey Hoe (Mckinsey); **internet congestion control** and ISA, Fred Baker (Cisco Systems) and David Isacoff (); **ATM congestion and traffic control**: Chien Fang (Cisco Systems) and Rohit Goyal (Ohio State University); **internet routing and multicasting**, Deborah Estrin (University of Southern California) and David D. Ward (Ascend Communications); **IP switching**: Larry Lang (Ipsilon Networks); **compression**: Michael R. Bastian (Brigham Young University), Wilson C. Chung (PictureTel Corp), and Nasir Memon (Northern Illinois University); **fractal compression**: Michael Barnsley (Iterated Systems) and Edward R. Vrscay (University of Waterloo).

Also, I would like to acknowledge those who contributed homework problems: Ahmed A-G Helmy (University of Southern California) and Franklin Mendivil (University of Waterloo)

With all this assistance, little remains for which I can take full credit. However, I am proud to say that, with no help whatsoever, I selected all of the quotations.

CHAPTER 1

INTRODUCTION

If the reader is to understand this tale and the point of view from which it is told, he should follow the author's mind in each principal sphere of causation. He must not only be acquainted with the military and naval situations as they existed at the outbreak of war, but with the events which led up to them. He must be introduced to the Admirals and to the Generals; he must study the organization of the Fleets and Armies and the outlines of their strategy by sea and land; he must not shrink even from the design of ships and cannon; he must extend his view to the groupings and slow-growing antagonisms of modern States; he must contract it to the humbler but unavoidable warfare of parties and the interplay of political forces and personalities.

—The World Crisis, **Winston Churchill**

The subject matter of this field ranges over a broad territory: from details such as the treatment of a single packet or cell in a queue at a router or switch to general-purpose techniques for reserving network resources for a given type of traffic; from the definition of the characteristics of a flow of data to methods of compressing data to reduce the network burden. A glance at the table of contents shows that these and related topics will occupy us in this book's 18 chapters.

The central theme we address is the need to carry large volumes of traffic with different quality-of-service requirements over networks operating at very high data rates. The types of network facilities that serve as platforms for addressing the relevant design issues are IP-based internets and ATM networks.[1]

---

[1] We use the term *IP-based internet* to refer to any set of networks interconnected by routers using the Internet protocol (IP) and that carry traffic using the TCP/IP (transmission control protocol/Internet protocol) protocol suite. ATM (asynchronous transfer mode) networks make use of the ATM and related protocols.

In both types of networks, internets and ATM networks, dramatic changes are taking place. In the case of internets, the volume of traffic carried has increased enormously and the character of that traffic has expanded to include multimedia and real-time traffic. In the case of ATM, its native high data rate has attracted not only voice and video traffic but, increasingly, bursty traffic based on TCP/IP. To the technical mind, such rapid and unprecedented changes present a host of interesting design problems in the areas of protocols, congestion control, and traffic characterization and management. It is to such minds that this book addresses itself.

On the other hand, to the corporate information systems potentate or to the end user, interest focuses on satisfying the needs of applications. While this is not a management book, much less a book directed at end users, we can illuminate the requirements for high-speed networks and traffic management by dwelling briefly on the requirements generated by users. That is the purpose of this chapter.

The chapter begins with a look at the trends that have appeared in the evolution of IP-based internets and ATM networks. Then we discuss some of the driving factors that create the requirements for high-speed, high-capacity networks with quality-of-service (QoS) guarantees. Next, the types of services provided by IP-based internets and ATM networks are discussed. Following these stirring accounts, the main body of the chapter closes with a concise outline of the remainder of the book.

The appendix to this chapter lists Internet- and Web-based resources that may be of use to readers and instructors.

1.1   A BRIEF NETWORKING HISTORY

Recent years have seen the development of a number of new protocols and techniques for both IP-based internets and ATM networks. These are briefly reviewed in Section 1.2. First, in this section, we look at some of the factors driving these new developments.

The Growth of the Internet and the World Wide Web

The dominating factor in the development of new protocols and mechanisms for data communications and computer networking is the growth in the Internet. This growth, in turn, has been dominated by the growth of the World Wide Web (WWW), or Web for short. It is doubtful if anyone, anywhere, who uses computer equipment of any sort remains ignorant of these momentous developments. The Internet and the Web, and the applications spun off therefrom, have transformed the way businesses use computing resources and the way in which individuals use personal computers.

The Internet

Today's Internet can be traced back to the Arpanet, which began as a modest experiment in what was then the new technology of packet switching (Table 1.1). Arpanet was first deployed in 1969 with just four packet-switching nodes, used to interconnect a handful of host computers and terminals. The first links interconnecting the nodes were operated at a mere 50 kbps. Funded by the Advanced Research Projects Agency (ARPA) in the U.S. Department of Defense (DoD),

TABLE 1.1   CHRONOLOGY OF INTERNET EVOLUTION

Year	Event
1966	ARPA packet-switching experimentation
1969	First Arpanet nodes operational
1972	Distributed e-mail invented
1973	For non-U.S. computer linked to Arpanet
1975	Arpanet transitioned to Defense Communications Agency
1980	TCP/IP experimentation begins
1981	New host added every 20 days
1983	TCP/IP swithover complete
1986	NSFnet backbone created
1990	Arpanet retired
1991	Gopher introduced
1991	WWW invented
1992	Mosaic introdced
1995	Internet backbone privatized
1996	OC-3 (155 Mbps) backbone built

Arpanet was intended as a vehicle to explore packet-switching technology and protocols that could be used for cooperative, distributed computing.

Some of the early applications developed for the ARPANET offered new functionality. The first two important applications were TELNET and FTP. TELNET provided a lingua franca for remote computer terminals. When the ARPANET was introduced, each different computer system needed a different terminal. The TELNET application provided a common denominator terminal. If software were written for each type of computer to support the "TELNET terminal," then one terminal could interact with all computer types. The File Transport Protocol (FTP) offered a similar open functionality. FTP allowed the transparent transfer of files from one computer to the other over the network. This is not as trivial as it may sound, because various computers have different word sizes, store their bits in different orders, and use different word formats.

Although TELNET and FTP were (and are) useful, the first "killer app" for ARPANET was electronic mail. Before ARPANET there were electronic mail systems, but they were all single computer systems. In 1972, Ray Tomlinson of Bolt Beranek and Newman (BBN) wrote the first package to provide distributed mail service across a computer network using multiple computers. Already by 1973, an ARPA study had found that three quarters of all ARPANET traffic was e-mail [HAFN96]. E-mail was so useful that ARPANET attracted more users, necessitating the addition of more nodes and the use of higher-speed links. Thus, a trend was established that persists to this day.

As ARPANET grew, it attracted not only government and academic researchers as users but also "operational people" who had an actual mission to perform within DoD. Network configuration and management became important issues, as did the reliability and availability of the network. Accordingly, control of ARPANET was transferred in 1975 from the research funding agency ARPA to the Defense Communications Agency.

The technology was so successful that ARPA applied the same packet-switching technology to tactical radio communication (Packet Radio) and to satellite communication (SATNET). Because the three networks operated in very different communication environments, the appropriate values for certain parameters, such as maximum packet size, were different in each case. Faced with the dilemma of integrating these networks, Vint Cerf and Bob Kahn of ARPA started to develop methods and protocols for *internetworking*; that is, communicating across arbitrary, multiple, packet-switched networks. They published a very influential paper in May of 1974 [CERF74] outlining their approach to a transmission control protocol. The proposal was refined and details filled in by the ARPANET community, with major contributions from participants from European Networks, such as Cyclades (France) and EIN, eventually leading to the TCP and IP protocols, which, in turn, formed the basis for what eventually became the TCP/IP protocol suite. This provided the foundation for the Internet, with ARPANET being just one of a number of interconnected networks. In 1982–1983, ARPANET converted from its original NCP protocol to TCP/IP. Many networks then were connected using this technology throughout the world. Nevertheless, use of the ARPANET was generally restricted to ARPA contractors.

The ARPANET and Internet technologies were too useful to remain confined to the defense community. In 1980–1981, the National Science Foundation (NSF) extended support to other computer science research groups with CSNET; in 1986, NSF extended Internet support to all the disciplines of the general research community with the NSFNET backbone. Originally, NSFNET was designed to interconnect six NSF-funded supercomputer centers across the country and the centers to supercomputer users nationwide. Eventually, NSF offered interconnection through its backbone to regional packet-switched networks across the country. In 1990 the ARPANET was shut down.

The World Wide Web

In the Spring of 1989, at CERN (the European Laboratory for Particle Physics), Tim Berners–Lee proposed the idea of a distributed hypermedia technology to facilitate the international exchange of research findings using the Internet. Almost exactly two years later a prototype World Wide Web was developed at CERN using the NeXT computer as a platform. By the end of 1991, CERN released a *line-oriented browser* or reader to a limited population. But the really explosive growth of the technology came with the development at the first *graphically oriented browser*, Mosaic, developed at the NCSA Center at the University of Illinois by Mark Andreasson and others in 1992. Two million copies of Mosaic were delivered over the Internet in a short period of time. Within a few short years, the characteristic Web addresses, the URLs, became ubiquitous. One cannot read a newspaper or watch TV without seeing the addresses everywhere. Figure 1.1 illustrates the exponential growth of the Web.

Just as e-mail triggered rapid growth in ARPANET, so the Web has triggered explosive growth in the Internet. Figure 1.2 shows this dramatic rise. Today, the number of hosts connected to Internet networks exceeds 10 million, the number of users is in the tens of millions, and the number of countries with Internet access is in the hundreds. The sheer number of users dictates ever-higher capacities on the

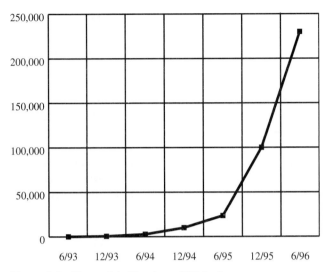

Figure 1.1   Figure 1.1 Number of Web sites.
SOURCE: Matthew Gray of MIT
(http://www.mit.edu:8001/people/mkgray/net).

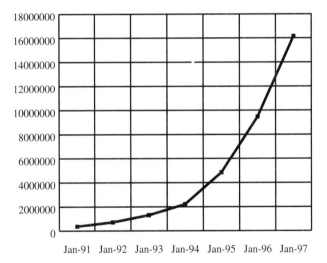

Figure 1.2   Number of Internet hosts.
SOURCE: Network Wizards (http://www.nw.com).

Internet. But more significantly, the nature of the traffic, which increasingly consists of graphics and real-time traffic, places great burdens on the Internet.

The growth of the Internet and the evolution in the nature of its traffic is mirrored in countless corporate networks, which have evolved from simply leased-line or packet-switching links between sites to elaborate private networks supporting intranet applications and tied to the Internet. Thus, the performance demands placed on the Internet are reflected in these private networks, and the protocols and techniques discussed in this book apply to both.

The Arrival of ATM

A network development of perhaps equal importance to the evolution of TCP/IP technology is that of ATM. As with TCP/IP and the Internet, an interesting history can be told. The briefest of summaries is provided herewith.

The early public telephone and telecommunications networks were based on analog switching and transmission technology and on circuit switching. These features persisted for many decades. Eventually, however, these network began to evolve to use digital, computerized switches and digital transmission technology, although still based on circuit switching. Such networks are referred to as integrated digital networks (IDNs), reflecting the integration of switching and transmission using digital techniques. This idea of an IDN was proposed as early as 1959 [VAUG59]. Implementation soon followed. The first digital T-carrier system was introduced into commercial service by AT&T in 1962, and the first large-scale time-division digital switch, the Western Electric 4ESS, was introduced in 1976.

The evolution of public telephone networks from analog to digital was driven by the need to provide economic voice communications. The resulting IDN was also well suited to meet the growing variety of digital data service needs. Thus it came to pass that the IDN combined the coverage of the geographically extensive telephone network with the data-carrying capacity of digital data networks in a structure called the **integrated services digital network** (ISDN). In this latter context, the *integrated* of ISDN refers to the simultaneous carrying of digitized voice and a variety of data traffic on the same digital transmission links and by the same digital exchanges. The key to ISDN is the small marginal cost for offering data services on the digital telephone network, with no cost or performance penalty for voice services already carried on the IDN.

ISDN and Frame Relay

The development of ISDN has been governed by a set of recommendations issue by ITU-T.[2] These recommendations, or standards, were first issued in 1984, with more complete versions issued in later years.

It is enlightening to look at the history of ITU-T's interest in ISDN. In 1968, CCITT established Special Study Group D (forerunner of today's Study Group XVIII, which has ISDN responsibility within ITU-T) to look at a variety of issues related to the use of digital technology in public telephone networks. At each plenary assembly, the study group was given assignments for the next four-year study period. The first and principal question assigned over each period is shown in Table 1.2. The titles of the first question reflect the evolution of ITU-T interest. The focus shifts from digital technology to IDNs to ISDNs.

Even during the first period listed in Table 1.2, there was a vision of an ISDN. Recommendation G.702, issued in 1972, contained the following definition of an ISDN: "an integrated digital network in which the same digital switches and digital paths are used to establish connections for different services; for example, tele-

---

[2] The International Telecommunication Union Telecommunication Standardization Sector. This body was formerly known as CCITT (Consultative Committee on International Telegraphy and Telephony). The new acronym is 20% shorter, but alas the new name is 22% longer.

TABLE 1.2   QUESTION 1 AS ASSIGNED TO SPECIAL
STUDY GROUP D (1969–1976) AND TO STUDY GROUP
XVIII (1977–1992)

Study Period	Title of Question 1
1969–1972	Planning of digital systems
1973–1976	Planning of digital systems and integration of services
1977–1980	Overall aspects of an ISDN
1981–1984	General network aspects of an ISDN
1985–1988	General Question on ISDN
1989–1992	General aspects of ISDN

phony, data." At that point, there was no information on the type of network that could integrate digital switches and paths, or how the network could integrate various services. Nevertheless, it was a recognition of the evolution that could occur using digital technology.

By the 1977–1980 study period, CCITT recognized that the evolution toward a digital network was under way and was more important than the standardization of individual digital systems and equipment. Thus the focus was on the integration aspects of the digital network and on the integration of services on an IDN. Two key developments that emerged during this study period were the following:

- The integration of services is based on providing a standardized user-network interface (UNI) that allows the user to request various services through a uniform set of protocols.
- An ISDN will evolve from the digital telephone network.

At the end of this period, the first ISDN standard emerged; G.705 was simply a general statement of principles and objectives for ISDN. As the next period began (1981–1984), ISDN was declared the major concern of CCITT. A set of recommendations, called the I series, was published at the end of this period. This initial set was incomplete and, in some cases, internally inconsistent. Nevertheless, the specification of ISDN by 1984 was sufficient for manufacturers and service providers to begin to develop ISDN-related equipment and to demonstrate ISDN-related services and networking configurations.

By 1988, the I series recommendations were sufficiently detailed to make preliminary ISDN implementation possible. ISDN came to full fruition and widespread deployment only in the early to mid-1990s.

The most noteworthy technical achievement of the ISDN effort was the development of specifications for frame relay. Frame relay is a streamlined form of packet switching suitable for use in higher-speed networks, up to about 2 Mbps. Although frame relay was initially standardized in the context of ISDN, it quickly outgrew that context and became popular as the basis for a number of public and private network offerings. Frame relay today enjoys a strong presence in a number of non-ISDN contexts.

Broadband ISDN

In 1988, as part of its I series of recommendations on ISDN, CCITT issued the first two recommendations relating to B-ISDN: I.113, *Vocabulary of terms for broadband aspects of ISDN*, and I.121, *Broadband aspects of ISDN*. These documents represented the level of consensus reached among the participants concerning the nature of the future B-ISDN, as of late 1988. They provided a preliminary description and a basis for future standardization and development work. Some of the important notions developed in these documents are presented in Table 1.3. Table 1.4 lists the factors that are guiding ITU-T work on B-ISDN.

Note the reliance of B-ISDN on ATM. Like frame relay, ATM is a streamlined form of packet switching suitable for use in higher-speed networks. ATM uses fixed-size packets, called cells, and achieves even greater efficiencies than frame relay. ATM can be used at speeds in the hundreds of megabits per second and even in the gigabits per second range.

The decision to use ATM as the transfer mode for B-ISDN is a remarkable one. The result is that B-ISDN is a packet-based network, both at the user-network interface and in terms of its internal switching mechanism. Although I.121 states that B-ISDN will support circuit-mode applications, this is done over a packet-based transport mechanism. Thus, ISDN, which began as an evolution from the circuit-switching telephone network, has evolved into a packet-switching network as it takes on broadband services.

TABLE 1.3 NOTEWORTHY STATEMENTS IN I.113 AND I.121

Broadband: A service or a system requiring transmission channels capable of supporting rates greater than the primary rate.
The term B-ISDN is used for convenience in order to refer to and emphasize the broadband aspects of ISDN. The intent, however, is that there be one comprehensive notion of an ISDN that provides broadband and other ISDN services.
Asynchronous transfer mode (ATM) is the transfer mode for implementing B-ISDN and is independent of the means of transport at the physical layer.
B-ISDN will be based on the concepts developed for ISDN and may evolve by progressively incorporating directly into the network additional B-ISDN functions enabling new and advanced services.
Since the B-ISDN is based on overall ISDN concepts, the ISDN access reference configuration is also the basis for the B-ISDN reference configuration.

TABLE 1.4 FACTORS GUIDING ITU-T WORK ON B-ISDN (I.121)

The emerging demand for broadband services
The availability of high-speed transmission, switching, and signal-processing technologies
The improved data- and image-processing capabilities available to the user
The advances in software application processing in the computer and telecommunications industries
The need to integrate interactive and distribution services
The need to integrate both circuit- and packet-transfer mode into one universal broadband network
The need to provide flexibility in satisfying the requirements of both user and operator
The need to cover broadband aspects of ISDN in ITU-T recommendations

Since 1988, the work within ITU-T has been guided by the concepts outlined in Tables 1.3 and 1.4. The result has been the publication of numerous recommendations in the I series that specifically relate to B-ISDN.

Mention should be made at this point of the ATM Forum, which is playing a crucial role in the development of ATM standards. In the ITU and the constituent member bodies from the participating countries, the process of developing standards is characterized by wide participation by government, users, and industry representatives, and by consensus decision making. This process can be quite time consuming. While ITU-T has streamlined its efforts, the delays involved in developing standards are particularly significant in the area of B-ISDN, which is dominated by the rapidly evolving ATM technology. Because of the strong level of interest in ATM technology, the ATM Forum was created with the goal of accelerating the development of ATM standards. The ATM Forum has seen more active participation from computing vendors than has been the case in ITU-T. Because the forum works on the basis of majority rule rather than consensus, it has been able to move rapidly to define some of the needed details for the implementation of ATM. This effort, in turn, has fed into the ITU-T standardization effort.

ATM

Just as frame relay is a technology developed as part of the ISDN effort and now widely used in non-ISDN applications, so ATM is a technology developed as part of the B-ISDN effort and now widely used in non-B-ISDN applications. Three principal market segments exist for ATM technology:

- **Public network infrastructure:** This corresponds to B-ISDN and consists of public telecommunications networks that support public telephony, CATV, and WAN services.

- **ATM LAN:** ATM can be used in the LAN setting in several ways. A single ATM switch or a network of ATM switches can serve as a backbone network in a local setting to interconnect a variety of traditional LANs (e.g., Ethernet). Alternatively, end systems such as servers and high-performance workstations can be directly connected to a local ATM network.

- **ATM WAN:** This market segment includes enterprise networks operating over leased lines, privately owned infrastructure such as optical fiber and wireless links, or links provided as virtual private networks by a public network operator.

As Figure 1.3 illustrates, the LAN market has emerged as a commercially viable sector for ATM-based equipment. This has been driven by the need for high-speed, low-cost support within the local area, as discussed in Section 1.2. Public infrastructure and ATM WAN segments have been slower to mature, due to competition from frame relay and the enormous cost of transitioning from existing configuration. Both these segments are beginning to emerge as major factors in the networking market.

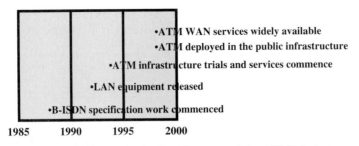

Figure 1.3   Milestones in the Development of the ATM Market.
SOURCE: ATM Forum.

1.2   THE NEED FOR SPEED AND QUALITY OF SERVICE

Momentous changes in the way corporations do business and process information have been driven by changes in networking technology and at the same time have driven those changes. It is hard to separate chicken and egg in this field. Similarly, the use of the Internet by both businesses and individuals reflects this cyclic dependency: The availability of new image-based services on the Internet (i.e., the Web) has resulted in an increase in the total number of users and the traffic volume generated by each user. This, in turn, has resulted in a need to increase the speed and efficiency of the Internet. On the other hand, it is only such increased speed that makes the use of Web-based applications palatable to the end user.

In this section, we survey some of the end-user factors that fit into this equation. We begin with the need for high-speed LANs in the business environment, because this need has appeared first and has forced the pace of networking development. Then we look at business WAN requirements. Finally, we offer a few words about the effect of changes in commercial electronics on network requirements.

The Emergence of High-speed LANs

Personal computers and microcomputer workstations began to achieve widespread acceptance in business computing in the early 1980s and have now achieved virtually the status of the telephone: They are an essential tool for office workers. Until relatively recently, office LANs provided basic connectivity services—connecting personal computers and terminals to mainframes and midrange systems that ran corporate applications, and providing workgroup connectivity at the departmental or divisional level. In both cases, traffic patterns were relatively light, with an emphasis on file transfer and electronic mail. The LANs that were available for this type of workload, primarily Ethernet and token ring, are well suited to this environment.

In the 1990s, two significant trends have altered the role of the personal computer and therefore the requirements on the LAN:

1. The speed and computing power of personal computers has continued to enjoy explosive growth. In 1988, a 16-megahertz 80286 platform with 2 megabytes of RAM was considered a high-end system. In the latter part of the 1990s, a more typical system is a Pentium or PowerPC processor in the hundreds of megahertz with built-in RAM of 64 megabytes or more and internal

disk capacity in the gigabytes. These more powerful platforms support graphics-intensive applications and ever more elaborate graphical user interfaces to the operating system.

2. MIS (management information systems) organizations have recognized the LAN as a viable and essential computing platform, resulting in the focus on network computing. This trend began with client-server computing, which has become a dominant architecture in the business environment, and the more recent Web-focused intranet trend. Both of these approaches involve the frequent transfer of potentially large volumes of data in a transaction-oriented environment.

The effect of these trends has been to increase the volume of data to be handled over LANs and, because applications are more interactive, to reduce the acceptable delay on data transfers. The earlier generation of 10-Mbps Ethernets and 16-Mbps token rings are simply not up to the job of supporting these requirements.

The following are examples of requirements that call for higher-speed LANs:

- **Centralized server farms:** In many applications, there is a need for user, or client, systems to be able to draw huge amounts of data from multiple centralized servers, called server farms. An example is a color publishing operation, in which servers typically contain tens of gigabytes of image data that must be downloaded to imaging workstations. As the performance of the servers themselves has increased, the bottleneck has shifted to the network. Switched Ethernet alone would not solve this problem because of the limit of 10 Mbps on a single link to the client.

- **Power workgroups:** These groups typically consist of a small number of cooperating users who need to draw massive data files across the network. Examples are a software development group that runs tests on a new software version, or a computer-aided design (CAD) company that regularly runs simulations of new designs. In such cases, large amounts of data are distributed to several workstations, processed, and updated at very high speed for multiple iterations.

- **High-speed local backbone:** As processing demand grows, LANs proliferate at a site, and high-speed interconnection is necessary.

Corporate Wide Area Networking Needs

As recently as the early 1990s, there was an emphasis in many organizations on a centralized data processing model. In a typical environment, there might be significant computing facilities at a few regional offices, consisting of mainframes or well-equipped midrange systems. These centralized facilities could handle most corporate applications, including basic finance, accounting, and personnel programs, as well as many of the business-specific applications. Smaller, outlying offices (e.g., a bank branch) could be equipped with terminals or basic personal computers linked to one of the regional centers in a transaction-oriented environment.

This model began to change in the early 1990s, and the change accelerated through the mid-1990s. Many organizations have dispersed their employees into multiple smaller offices. There is a growing use of telecommuting. Most significant, the nature of the application structure has changed. First client-server computing and, more recently, intranet computing have fundamentally restructured the organizational data processing environment. There is now much more reliance on personal computers, workstations, and servers and much less use of centralized mainframe and midrange systems. Furthermore, the virtually universal deployment of graphical user interfaces to the desktop enables the end user to exploit graphic applications, multimedia, and other data-intensive applications. In addition, most organizations require access to the Internet. When a few clicks of the mouse can trigger huge volumes of data, traffic patterns have become more unpredictable while the average load has risen.

All of these trends means that more data must be transported off premises and into the wide area. It has long been accepted that in the typical business environment, about 80% of the traffic remains local and about 20% traverses wide area links. But this rule no longer applies to most companies, with a greater percentage of the traffic going into the WAN environment [COHE96]. This traffic flow shift places a greater burden on LAN backbones and, of course, on the WAN facilities used by a corporation. Thus, just as in the local area, changes in corporate data traffic patterns are driving the creation of high-speed WANs.

Digital Electronics

The rapid conversion of consumer electronics to digital technology is having an impact on both the Internet and corporate intranets. As these new gadgets come into view and proliferate, they will dramatically increase the amount of image and video traffic to be carried by networks.

Two noteworthy examples of this trend are shown in Figure 1.4, which shows the projected growth in the production of digital video disks and digital still cameras.

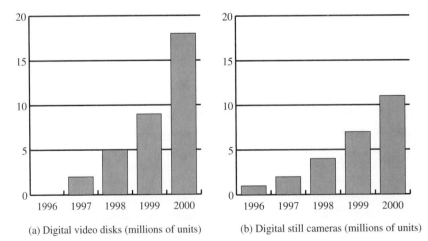

(a) Digital video disks (millions of units)   (b) Digital still cameras (millions of units)

Figure 1.4   Projected worldwide production of digital video and image equipment.
SOURCE: Business Week, November 25, 1996.

Digital Video Disk

With the capacious digital video disk (DVD), the electronics industry has at last found an acceptable replacement for the analog VHS video tape. The DVD will replace the videotape used in videocassette recorders (VCRs) and, more important for this discussion, replace the CD-ROM in personal computers and servers. The DVD takes video into the digital age. It delivers movies with picture quality that out-shines laser disks, and it can be randomly accessed like audio CDs, which DVD machines can also play. Vast volumes of data can be crammed onto the disk, currently seven times as much as a CD-ROM. With DVD's huge storage capacity and vivid quality, PC games will become more realistic and educational software will incorporate more video. Following in the wake of these developments will be a new crest of traffic over the Internet and corporate intranets, as this material is incorporated into Web sites.

A related product development is the digital camcorder. Although relatively unknown in the United States (at the time of this writing), this product already looms large in Japan. This product will make it easier for individuals and companies to make digital video files to be placed on corporate and Internet Web sites, again adding to the traffic burden.

Digital Still Camera

Although the digital still camera has been around for about 15 years, it is only now beginning to take off because prices have dropped to reasonable levels. As yet, quality does not approach that of film, but the convenience for use in networks is unsurpassed. An individual can take a picture of a loved one or pet and zip it right onto a Web page. Companies can quickly develop on-line product catalogs with full-color pictures of every product. Thus, we can expect to see a dramatic growth in the amount of on-line image and video traffic in coming years.

1.3 ADVANCED TCP/IP AND ATM NETWORKS

In the trade press, one frequently finds references to the "battle between IP and ATM." Some writers declare that one will be the ultimate victor, others that the other will be victorious. On the IP side, supporters say that ATM is overexpensive, overcomplicated, and overdue. Instead, corporate networkers will use Ethernet LAN switches to deliver high capacity for workgroups and servers, and rely on enhanced IP-based internets to prioritize time-sensitive traffic and provide enough capacity for all.

On the ATM side, supporters claim that installed ATM is worth the wait and will be the networking equivalent of nirvana. ATM provides efficient high-speed service that is scaleable to virtually any data rate, and seamless desktop-to-desktop connections can be created across ATM LANs and WANs.

This book is based on the premise that both ATM and IP have a long future ahead of them. It seems unlikely that network managers will abandon the huge investment in the installed base of IP-based equipment and software. On the other hand, there is tremendous momentum behind ATM.

In the remainder of this section, we provide a brief overview of some of the important themes related to these two networking technologies.

IP-based Internets

The dominant computer networking paradigm is internetworking, embodied both in the mammoth Internet and in countless smaller corporate internets. Four key technologies have played a role in the evolution of internetworking:

- **TCP and IP:** The original protocol for internetworking, developed as part of the ARPANET research, combined logic for routing through an internet with end-to-end control. The critical point in this protocol design effort came with the split into two protocols: IP for internet routing and delivery, and TCP for reliable end-to-end transport. For applications that do not need reliable delivery, the more efficient UDP (user datagram protocol) can be used on top of IP. Now, for real-time traffic a new protocol, RTP (real-time transport protocol), can be used on top of IP. The flexibility and generality of the TCP/IP model have been a major factor in its dominance.
- **Dynamic routing:** Dynamic routing performs two vital functions: It allows dynamic route discovery, so that end systems and routers do not have to be preconfigured with all possible routes between end systems and reconfigured with each change in topology; and it allows route adjustment in the face of congestion and failure, resulting in efficient load balancing. While routing technology has evolved (e.g., faster hardware to do route table lookups, and more clever techniques to cope with huge routing tables), the basic approach has not changed much over the past 20 years. Dynamic routing enables the construction of large, evolving networks of networks and gives users tremendous flexibility.
- **Packet switching:** The research on TCP/IP and internetworking can be traced back to the ARPA-sponsored research on packet switching. Many of the concepts used in IP-based internets, including end-to-end protocols and dynamic routing, were first developed for packet-switching networks. For wide area data networks, packet switching remains the dominant technology.
- **Ethernet:** As packet switching has dominated wide area data networking, the Ethernet dominates local area networking. The original experimental Ethernet operated at 3 Mbps over coaxial cable. This remarkable scheme now operates over twisted pair and optical fiber as well as coaxial cable. It was released commercially at 10 Mbps and then was scaled up first to 100 Mbps and now 1 Gbps. Most internet configurations involve Ethernet networks.

A final point about the preceding list: Ethernet is in large part responsible for the success of the TCP/IP protocol suite. In the late 1970s and early 1980s, TCP/IP was confined principally to the U.S. Department of Defense and its contractors and related academic research institutions. The rest of the world was hailing the development of the Open Systems Interconnection (OSI) protocol model and the suite of protocols being specified as international standards within this model. But during this period, TCP/IP broke out of the military environment and spread rapidly into the commercial market. The motivation was that TCP/IP was a mature, working set of protocols that provided interoperability and a high level of functionality, whereas the OSI protocols were still evolving and largely unproven in field conditions. The vehicle for this breakout was Ethernet: Many LAN equipment vendors began including TCP/IP in their products, which were then marketed not just to the U.S. military but to commercial customers. The success of Ethernet helped guarantee the success of TCP/IP.

But times change and new requirements develop. The Internet and corporate internets are now faced with the need to support multimedia and real-time traffic. In response to these needs, a radical change in internet architecture is emerging from the mists: the Integrated Services Architecture (ISA). ISA involves upgrading router hardware to support real-time traffic, and it involves a number of new protocols:

- **IPv6:** The new version of IP was driven by a need to expand Internet address space, but it provides features that are essential to ISA.
- **RSVP:** The Resource ReSerVation Protocol enables users to reserve capacity on an internet and to specify the requirements of the traffic, in terms of desired throughput and delay characteristics.
- **RTP:** The Real-time Transport Protocol provides mechanisms for delivering video, audio, and other real-time traffic over an internet so that it can be reproduced effectively at the destination.
- **Multicast routing protocols:** In many instances, multimedia and other real-time traffic is transmitted to multiple destinations simultaneously—multicast. Several new dynamic routing protocols have been developed to deal with multicast routing.

Using these new protocols, an ISA-based internet is capable of effectively handling both traditional "bursty" traffic and multimedia and real-time traffic.

ATM Networks

Commercial acceptance of ATM networks has been slow in coming, but the technology now seems to be permanently out of the woods and into the meadows. Among the key technical ingredients needed for successful ATM networking and now in place are the following:

- **Internal signaling:** Signaling System Number 7 (SS7), developed by CCITT as part of the IDN and ISDN effort, provides a set of protocols by which an ATM-based network can be managed effectively. SS7 includes mechanisms for defining, setting up, and tearing down logical connections for managing network resources.
- **External signaling:** The user-network interface for ATM networks includes mechanisms for setting up and tearing down connections. The protocol enables the user to define the expected traffic characteristics and to request network services at a particular QoS level.
- **Physical layer specification:** ATM is designed to operate in the hundreds of megabits per second and higher. A powerful physical-layer transmission specification is needed to support such data rates. Most prominent among these is

the ITU-T specification known as SDH (synchronous digital hierarchy); its equivalent in the United States is referred to as SONET (synchronous optical network). The mapping from ATM layer data transfer to the SDH/SONET layer has been developed.

- **ATM adaptation:** ATM is a general-purpose transfer service that can support a variety of data transfer services and upper-layer protocols. The key to this support is an ATM adaptation layer (AAL) that maps various upper protocols and services onto the ATM layer.

A milestone in the development of ATM was the release of version 3.1 of the ATM Forum UNI specification in 1994 [ATM94]. This specification involved the participation of hundreds of companies and provides sufficient detail to serve as the basis for implementation. In addition to defining UNI signaling and ATM logical connections, this specification provides a detailed description of techniques for characterizing and managing traffic, including the leaky bucket algorithm.

Just as the Internet has faced new requirements, so have ATM networks. ATM has been successful in supporting the needs of real-time and multimedia traffic, but until recently little was available to provide effective support for the kind of traffic for which the Internet excels: bursty traffic using TCP or UDP. To address these needs, the ATM Forum issued version 4.0 of its Traffic Management Specification in 1996 [ATM96]. This specification defines two new services, with the unrevealing names of available bit rate (ABR) and unspecified bit rate (UBR), together with protocol mechanisms for defining and managing the traffic for these services. Thus, ATM is now capable of providing a complete service to users, covering a wide variety of traffic types.

1.4   OUTLINE OF THIS BOOK

This section contains a brief synopsis of the remainder of this book.

Protocol and Network Fundamentals

Part One reviews some basic concepts in computer networking. Chapter 2 is concerned with network protocols, particularly the TCP/IP protocol suite. The chapter also traces the operation of TCP/IP in an internetworking environment. Chapter 3 provides a survey of data networks, including X.25 packet-switching networks and frame relay networks, together with a discussion of congestion.

The reader with a good background in computer networks may safely skip most of Part One, but is urged to read the section on congestion.

High-speed Networks

Part Two provides a survey of high-speed networks. Chapter 4 is a tutorial in ATM networks. The chapter discusses the key mechanism at the ATM layer and looks at the services provided by ATM and the use of the AAL to implement those services.

Although the focus of this book is on TCP/IP-based internetworking and on ATM networks, an introduction to high-speed LANs is useful. This is provided in

Chapter 5, which focuses on the two most important types of high-speed LANs: high-speed versions of Ethernet, and switched LANs based on ATM.

Performance Modeling and Estimation

Performance modeling and estimation is important in two ways. First, given a characterization of the expected load on a network, the analyst can determine the data rates and buffer capacities needed in the network. Second, users can characterize expected data traffic when making resource reservations for network service. Part Three begins, in Chapter 6, with an overview of basic concepts of probability and stochastic processes that are used in the remainder of Part Three. Chapter 7 provides a tutorial on the most widely used technique for modeling and estimation: queuing analysis. The formulas from queuing analysis used in performance modeling generally assume that traffic is Poisson in nature. However, it has been shown that much of the traffic expected on high-speed networks is self-similar, or fractal, in nature. The implications of this result are explored in Chapter 8.

Part Three is the most mathematically advanced portion of the book, and the reader with a lack of either time or interest could safely skip Chapter 6 and could quickly skim through Chapters 7 and 8 to get a feel for the conclusions drawn.

End–system Traffic Management

The focus of Part Four is the use of transport-level protocols, especially TCP, to make efficient, fair use of a network or internet and to control congestion. Chapter 9 introduces the key parameters of propagation delay, data rate, and throughput in the simple context of link-level flow control protocols. In this context, the relationships among parameters are seen clearly. Chapter 10 looks at transport-level protocols. Congestion control techniques implemented as part of TCP are examined, and the performance of TCP across an ATM network is explored. A real-time transport protocol is also described.

Network Traffic Management

On their own, TCP and other end-to-end protocols can only treat a network or internet as a black box and attempt to deduce the state of congestion in the network or internet. Part Five looks at the protocols and mechanisms that are used internal to a network or internet to control congestion and support various levels of quality of service. Chapter 11 examines the approaches taken in IP-based internets, and Chapter 12 looks at ATM networks.

Internet Routing

Part Six examines the key role played by routing protocols in the operation of internets. Historically, routing has been used as a technique for (1) minimizing the delay experienced by an application by finding the lowest-delay path through an internet, and (2) balancing the load within the internet to minimize overall delay and to avoid congestion. More recently, the use of routing to satisfy QoS requirements has emerged.

Chapter 13 provides a quick overview of relevant concepts of graph theory and least-cost path discovery. Chapter 14 looks at a variety of routing protocols intended to handle unicast, or point-to-point traffic. Chapter 15 deals with multicast traffic and the use of resource reservation. The important new concept of IP switching is also discussed in this chapter.

Compression

As quickly as capacity in networks and internets increases, so does the demand placed on those networks. Part Seven examines a technique that is complementary to the traffic and congestion management techniques discussed in earlier parts: compression. Compression can help ease the traffic burden by reducing the volume of traffic required to support a given application. Chapter 16 provides a brief overview of relevant concepts from information theory and relates these to compression.

Compression techniques fall into two great categories: lossless, suitable for file and message applications; and lossy, suitable for voice and video applications. These are covered in Chapters 17 and 18, respectively.

APPENDIX 1A   INTERNET AND WEB RESOURCES

There are a number of resources available on the Internet and the Web to support this book and to help one keep up with developments in this field.

Web Sites for This Book

A special Web page has been set up for this book at http://www.shore.net/~ws/HsNet.html. The site includes the following:

- Links to other Web sites, including the sites listed in this book, provide a gateway to relevant resources on the Web.
- On-line transparency masters are provided of most of the figures in the book in PDF (Adobe Acrobat) format.
- I also hope to include links to home pages for courses based on the book; these pages may be useful to other instructors in providing ideas about how to structure the course.

As soon as any typos or other errors are discovered, an errata list for this book will be available at http://www.shore.net/~ws. The file will be updated as needed. Please e-mail any errors that you spot to ws@shore.net. Errata sheets for my other books are at the same Web site, as well as discount ordering information for the books.

Other Web Sites

There are numerous Web sites that provide some sort of information related to the topics of this book. Here is a sample:

- http://www.nwfusion.com: A good starting point for information and links to resources about data communications and networking.

- http://www.internic.net/ds/dspg01.html: Maintains archives that relate to the Internet and Internet Engineering Task Force (IETF) activities. Includes keyword-indexed library of Request for Comments (RFCs) and draft documents as well as many other documents related to the Internet and related protocols.
- http://guide.sbanetweb.com: Links to over 1000 hardware and software vendors who currently have World Wide Web (WWW) sites, as well as a list of thousands of computer and networking companies in a Phone Directory.
- http://www.specialty.com/hiband: Links to magazine articles and both vendor and academic white papers on high-speed links and networks. Also links to high-speed vendors and related organizations.
- http://www.comsoc.org: Good way to keep up on conferences, publications, etc. from the IEEE Communications Society.
- http://www.acm.org/sigcomm: Good way to keep up on conferences, publications, etc. from the ACM Special Interest Group on Communications.

In subsequent chapters, pointers to more specific Web sites can be found in the "Recommended Reading" section.

USENET Newsgroups

A number of USENET newsgroups are devoted to some aspect of data communications and networking. As with virtually all USENET groups, there is a high noise to signal ratio, but it is worth experimenting to see if any meet your needs. Here is a sample:

- comp.dcom.cell-relay: Covers ATM and ATM LANs.
- comp.protocols.tcp-ip: Covers the TCP/IP protocol suite.
- comp.compression.research: Covers lossless and lossy compression.
- sci.nonlinear: Covers all aspects of nonlinear phenomenon, including self-similarity and fractals.

PART ONE

Protocol and Network Fundamentals

ISSUES FOR PART ONE

The purpose of Part One is to provide a background and context for the remainder of this book. The fundamental concepts of computer-communication protocols and data networks are presented.

ROAD MAP FOR PART ONE

Chapter 2: Protocols and the TCP/IP Suite

Data network communication and distributed applications rely on underlying communications software that is independent of application and relieves the application of much of the burden of reliably exchanging data. This communications software is organized into a protocol architecture, the most important incarnation of which is the TCP/IP protocol suite. Chapter 2 introduces the concept of a protocol architecture and provides an overview of TCP/IP. Another architecture, the OSI reference model, is briefly described. Finally, the concept of internetworking and the use of TCP/IP to achieve internetworking are discussed.

Chapter 3: Data Networks

Chapter 3 provides an overview of data networks, beginning with a discussion of packet-switching networks and the X.25 interface protocol commonly associated with packet-switching networks. Next, a streamlined type of packet-switching network, the frame relay network, is described. Finally, there is a discussion of congestion control in data networks, a topic that will occupy our attention for much of this book.

CHAPTER 2

PROTOCOLS AND THE TCP/IP SUITE

To destroy communication completely, there must be no rules in common between transmitter and receiver—neither of alphabet nor of syntax.

—On Human Communication, Colin Cherry

W e begin this chapter by introducing the concept of a layered protocol architecture. We then examine the most important such architecture, the TCP/IP protocol suite. TCP/IP is an Internet-based concept and is the framework for developing a complete range of computer communication standards. Virtually all computer vendors now provide support for this architecture. Another well-known architecture is the OSI reference model. OSI is a standardized architecture that is often used to describe communications functions, but that is now rarely implemented.

Following a discussion of protocol architectures, the important concept of internetworking is examined. Inevitably, an organization will require the use of more than one communication network. Some means of interconnecting these networks is required, and this raises issues that relate to the protocol architecture.

2.1   THE NEED FOR A PROTOCOL ARCHITECTURE

When computers, terminals, and/or other data processing devices exchange data, the procedures involved can be quite complex. Consider, for example, the transfer of a file between two computers. There must be a data path between the two computers, either directly or via a communication network. But more is needed. Typical tasks to be performed include the following:

1. The source system must either activate the direct data communication path or inform the communication network of the identity of the desired destination system.
2. The source system must ascertain that the destination system is prepared to receive data.
3. The file transfer application on the source system must ascertain that the file management program on the destination system is prepared to accept and store the file for this particular user.
4. If the file formats used on the two systems are incompatible, one or the other system must perform a format translation function.

It is clear that there must be a high degree of cooperation between the two computer systems. Instead of implementing the logic for this as a single module, the task is broken up into subtasks, each of which is implemented separately. In a protocol architecture, the modules are arranged in a vertical stack. Each layer in the stack performs a related subset of the functions required to communicate with another system. It relies on the next lower layer to perform more primitive functions and to conceal the details of those functions. It provides services to the next higher layer. Ideally, layers should be defined so that changes in one layer do not require changes in other layers.

Of course, it takes two to communicate, so the same set of layered functions must exist in two systems. Communication is achieved by having the corresponding, or *peer*, layers in two systems communicate. The peer layers communicate by means of formatted blocks of data that obey a set of rules or conventions known as a *protocol*. The key features of a protocol are as follows:

- **Syntax:** Concerns the format of the data blocks.
- **Semantics:** Includes control information for coordination and error handling.
- **Timing:** Includes speed matching and sequencing.

2.2   THE TCP/IP PROTOCOL ARCHITECTURE

TCP/IP is a result of protocol research and development conducted on the experimental packet-switched network, ARPANET, funded by the Defense Advanced Research Projects Agency (DARPA), and is generally referred to as the TCP/IP protocol suite. This protocol suite consists of a large collection of protocols that have been issued as Internet standards by the Internet Architecture Board.

TCP/IP Layers

There is no official TCP/IP protocol model, as there is in the case of OSI. However, based on the protocol standards that have been developed, we can organize the communication task for TCP/IP into five relatively independent layers:

- Application layer
- Host-to-host, or transport layer
- Internet layer
- Network access layer
- Physical layer.

The **physical layer** covers the physical interface between a data transmission device (e.g., workstation, computer) and a transmission medium or network. This layer is concerned with specifying the characteristics of the transmission medium, the nature of the signals, the data rate, and related matters.

The **network access layer** is concerned with the exchange of data between an end system and the network to which it is attached. The sending computer must provide the network with the address of the destination computer, so that the network may route the data to the appropriate destination. The sending computer may wish to invoke certain services, such as priority, that might be provided by the network. The specific software used at this layer depends on the type of network to be used; different standards have been developed for circuit switching, packet switching (e.g., X.25), local area networks (e.g., Ethernet), and others. Thus it makes sense to separate those functions having to do with network access into a separate layer. By doing this, the remainder of the communications software, above the network access layer, need not be concerned about the specifics of the network to be used. The same higher-layer software should function properly regardless of the particular network to which the computer is attached.

The network access layer is concerned with access to and routing data across a network for two end systems attached to the same network. In those cases where two devices are attached to different networks, procedures are needed to allow data to traverse multiple interconnected networks. This is the function of the **internet layer**. The internet protocol (IP) is used at this layer to provide the routing function across multiple networks. This protocol is implemented not only in the end systems but also in routers. A router is a processor that connects two networks and whose primary function is to relay data from one network to the other on its route from the source to the destination end system.

Regardless of the nature of the applications that are exchanging data, there is usually a requirement that data be exchanged reliably. That is, we would like to be assured that all the data arrive at the destination application and that the data arrive in the same order in which they were sent. As we shall see, the mechanisms for providing reliability are essentially independent of the nature of the applications. Thus, it makes sense to collect those mechanisms in a common layer shared by all applications; this is referred to as the **host-to-host layer,** or **transport layer**. The transmission control protocol (TCP) is the most commonly used protocol to provide this functionality.

Finally, the **application layer** contains the logic needed to support the various user applications. For each different type of application, such as file transfer, a separate module is needed that is peculiar to that application.

TCP and UDP

For most applications running as part of the TCP/IP protocol architecture, the transport layer protocol is TCP. TCP provides a reliable connection for the transfer of data between applications.

Figure 2.1a shows the header format for TCP, which is a minimum of 20 octets, or 160 bits. The Source Port and Destination Port fields identify the applications at the source and destination systems that are using this connection.[1] The Sequence Number, Acknowledgment Number, and Window fields provide flow control and error control. The checksum is a 16-bit frame check sequence used to detect errors in the TCP segment. The significance of these fields is discussed in detail in Chapter 10.

In addition to TCP, there is one other transport-level protocol that is in common use as part of the TCP/IP protocol suite: the user datagram protocol (UDP). UDP provides a connectionless service for application-level procedures; it does not guarantee delivery, preservation of sequence, or protection against duplication.

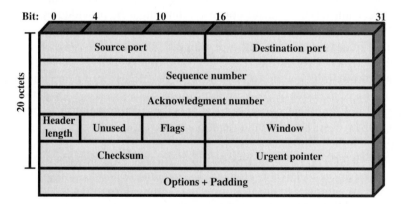

(a) TCP header

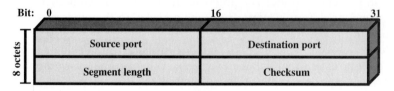

(b) UDP header

Figure 2.1   TCP and UDP headers.

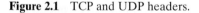

[1] The term *port* corresponds roughly to the term *service access point* (SAP) used in OSI-related documents.

UDP enables a procedure to send messages to other procedures with a minimum of protocol mechanism. Some transaction-oriented applications make use of UDP; one example is SNMP (Simple Network Management Protocol), the standard network management protocol for TCP/IP networks. Because it is connectionless, UDP has very little to do. Essentially, it adds a port-addressing capability to IP. This is best seen by examining the UDP header, shown in Figure 2.1b.

IP and IPv6

For decades, the keystone of the TCP/IP protocol architecture has been the IP. Figure 2.2a shows the IP header format, which is a minimum of 20 octets, or 160 bits. The header includes 32-bit source and destination addresses. The Header Checksum field is used to detect errors in the header to avoid misdelivery. The Protocol field indicates whether TCP, UDP, or some other higher-layer protocol is using IP.

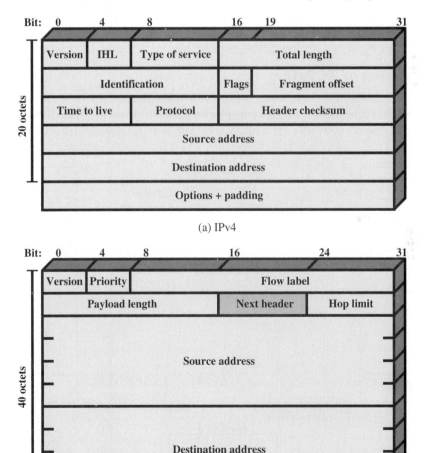

(a) IPv4

(b) IPv6

Figure 2.2   IP headers.

The Flags and Fragment Offset fields are used in the fragmentation and reassembly process, in which a single IP datagram is divided into multiple IP datagrams on transmission and then reassembled at the destination.

In 1995, the Internet Engineering Task Force, which develops protocol standards for the Internet, issued a specification for a next-generation IP, known then as IPng. This specification was turned into a standard in 1996 known as IPv6. IPv6 provides a number of functional enhancements over the existing IP (known as IPv4), designed to accommodate the higher speeds of today's networks and the mix of data streams, including graphic and video, that are becoming more prevalent. But the driving force behind the development of the new protocol was the need for more addresses. The current IP uses a 32-bit address to specify a source or destination. With the explosive growth of the Internet and of private networks attached to the Internet, this address length became insufficient to accommodate all systems needing addresses. As Figure 2.2b shows, IPv6 includes 128-bit source and destination address fields. Ultimately, all installations using TCP/IP are expected to migrate from the current IP to IPv6, but this process will take many years if not decades.

The details of IPv4 and IPv6 are discussed in Chapter 11.

Operation of TCP/IP

Figure 2.3 indicates how these protocols are configured for communications. To make clear that the total communications facility may consist of multiple networks, the constituent networks are usually referred to as *subnetworks*. Some sort of net-

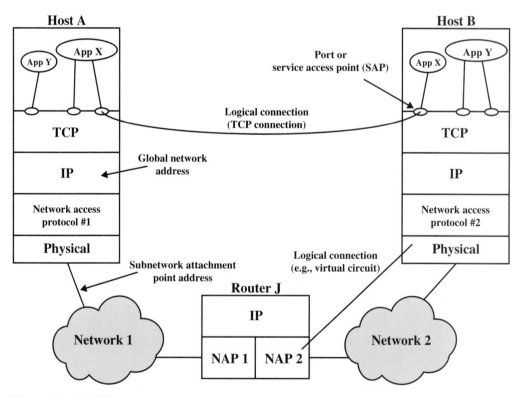

Figure 2.3 TCP/IP concepts.

work access protocol, such as the Ethernet logic, is used to connect a computer to a subnetwork. This protocol enables the host to send data across the subnetwork to another host or, in the case of a host on another subnetwork, to a router. IP is implemented in all end systems and routers. It acts as a relay to move a block of data from one host, through one or more routers, to another host. TCP is implemented only in the end systems; it keeps track of the blocks of data to assure that all are delivered reliably to the appropriate application.

For successful communication, every entity in the overall system must have a unique address. Actually, two levels of addressing are needed. Each host on a subnetwork must have a unique global internet address; this allows the data to be delivered to the proper host. This address is used by IP for routing and delivery. Each application within a host must have an address that is unique within the host; this allows the host-to-host protocol (TCP) to deliver data to the proper process. These latter addresses are known as ports.

Let us trace a simple operation. Suppose that a process, associated with port 1 at host A, wishes to send a message to another process, associated with port 2 at host B. The process at host A hands the message down to TCP with instructions to send it to host B, port 2. TCP hands the message down to IP with instructions to send it to host B. Note that IP need not be told the identity of the destination port. All it needs to know is that the data are intended for host B. Next, IP hands the message down to the network access layer (e.g., Ethernet logic) with instructions to send it to router J (the first hop on the way to host B).

To control this operation, control information as well as user data must be transmitted, as suggested in Figure 2.4. Let us say that the sending process generates a block of data and passes this to TCP. TCP may break this block into smaller pieces to make it more manageable. To each of these pieces, TCP appends control

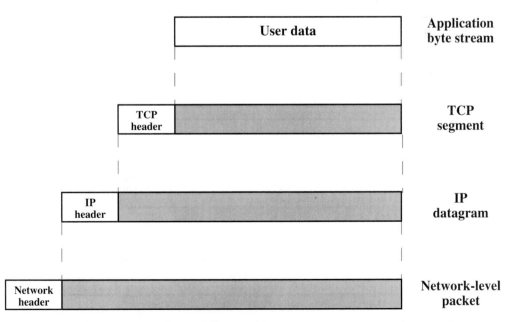

Figure 2.4   Protocol data units in the TCP/IP architecture.

information in the TCP header (Figure 2.1a), forming a *TCP segment*. The control information is to be used by the peer TCP protocol entity at host B. Examples of items that are included in this header are as follows:

- **Destination port:** When the TCP entity at host B receives the segment, it must know to whom the data are to be delivered.
- **Sequence number:** TCP sequentially numbers the segments that it sends to a particular destination port, so that if they arrive out of order, the TCP entity at host B can reorder them.
- **Checksum:** The sending TCP includes a code that is a function of the contents of the remainder of the segment. The receiving TCP performs the same calculation and compares the result with the incoming code. A discrepancy results if there has been some error in transmission.

Next, TCP hands each segment over to IP, with instructions to transmit it to host B. These segments must be transmitted across one or more subnetworks and relayed through one or more intermediate routers. This operation, too, requires the use of control information. Thus IP appends a header of control information (Figure 2.2) to each segment to form an *IP datagram*. An example of an item stored in the IP header is the destination host address (in this example, host B).

Finally, each IP datagram is presented to the network access layer for transmission across the first subnetwork in its journey to the destination. The network access layer appends its own header, creating a packet, or frame. The packet is transmitted across the subnetwork to router J. The packet header contains the information that the subnetwork needs to transfer the data across the subnetwork. Examples of items that may be contained in this header include the following:

- **Destination subnetwork address:** The subnetwork must know to which attached device the packet is to be delivered.
- **Facilities requests:** The network access protocol might request the use of certain subnetwork facilities, such as priority.

At router J, the packet header is stripped off and the IP header examined. On the basis of the destination address information in the IP header, the IP module in the router directs the datagram out across subnetwork 2 to host B. To do this, the datagram is again augmented with a network access header.

When the data are received at host B, the reverse process occurs. At each layer, the corresponding header is removed, and the remainder is passed on to the next higher layer, until the original user data are delivered to the destination process.

TCP/IP Applications

A number of applications have been standardized to operate on top of TCP. We mention three of the most common here.

The **simple mail transfer protocol (SMTP)** provides a basic electronic mail facility. It provides a mechanism for transferring messages among separate hosts. Features of SMTP include mailing lists, return receipts, and forwarding. The SMTP protocol does not specify the way in which messages are to be created; some local editing or native electronic mail facility is required. Once a message is created, SMTP accepts the message and makes use of TCP to send it to an SMTP module on another host. The target SMTP module will make use of a local electronic mail package to store the incoming message in a user's mailbox.

The **file transfer protocol (FTP)** is used to send files from one system to another under user command. Both text and binary files are accommodated, and the protocol provides features for controlling user access. When a user wishes to engage in file transfer, FTP sets up a TCP connection to the target system for the exchange of control messages. This allows user ID and password to be transmitted, and it allows the user to specify the file and file actions desired. Once a file transfer is approved, a second TCP connection is set up for the data transfer. The file is transferred over the data connection, without the overhead of any headers or control information at the application level. When the transfer is complete, the control connection is used to signal the completion and to accept new file transfer commands.

TELNET provides a remote logon capability, which enables a user at a terminal or personal computer to logon to a remote computer and function as if directly connected to that computer. The protocol was designed to work with simple scroll-mode terminals. TELNET is actually implemented in two modules: User TELNET interacts with the terminal I/O module to communicate with a local terminal. It converts the characteristics of real terminals to the network standard and vice versa. Server TELNET interacts with an application, acting as a surrogate terminal handler so that remote terminals appear as local to the application. Terminal traffic between User and Server TELNET is carried on a TCP connection.

Internet Standards

Many of the protocols that make up the TCP/IP protocol suite have been standardized or are in the process of standardization. By universal agreement, an organization known as the Internet Architecture Board (IAB) is responsible for the development and publication of these standards, which are published in a series of documents called Requests for Comments (RFCs).

This subsection provides a brief description of the way in which standards for the TCP/IP protocol suite are developed.

The Internet and Internet Standards

The Internet is a large collection of interconnected networks all of which use the TCP/IP protocol suite. The Internet began with the development of ARPANET, and the subsequent support by the Defense Advanced Research Projects Agency (DARPA) for the development of additional networks to support military users and government contractors.

The IAB is the coordinating committee for Internet design, engineering, and management. Areas covered include the operation of the Internet itself, and the standardization of protocols used by end systems on the Internet for interoperability. The IAB has two principal subsidiary task forces: the Internet Engineering Task Force (IETF), and the Internet Research Task Force (IRTF). The actual work of these task forces is carried out by working groups. Membership in a working group is voluntary; any interested party may participate.

The IETF is responsible for publishing the RFCs, which are the working notes of the Internet research and development community. A document in this series may address virtually any topic related to computer communications, and may be anything from a meeting report to the specification of a standard.

The final decision of which RFCs become Internet standards is made by the IAB, on the recommendation of the IETF. To become a standard, a specification must meet the following criteria:

- Be stable and well-understood
- Be technically competent
- Have multiple, independent, and interoperable implementations with substantial operational experience
- Enjoy significant public support
- Be recognizably useful in some or all parts of the Internet.

The key difference between these criteria and those used for international standards is the emphasis on operational experience.

The Standardization Process

The current Internet standardization process is defined in RFC 2026.[2] Figure 2.5 shows the series of steps, called the *standards track*, that a specification goes

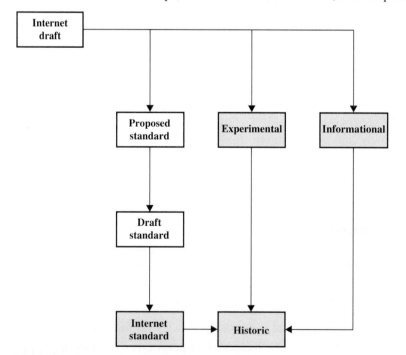

Figure 2.5 Internet standards and nonstandards tracks.

---

[2] RFC 2026. *The Internet Standards Process—Revision 3.* October 1996.

through to become a standard. The steps involve increasing amounts of scrutiny and testing. At each step, the IETF must make a recommendation for advancement of the protocol, and the IAB must ratify it.

The white boxes in the diagram represent temporary states, which should be occupied for the minimum practical time. However, a document must remain a proposed standard for at least six months and a draft standard for at least four months to allow time for review and comment. The gray boxes represent long-term states that may be occupied for years.

The initial step for all RFCs is publication as an Internet Draft. This is a draft version of a document that is made available for informal review. Such documents are readily available on the Internet, which contributes to an open process of review and revision. An Internet Draft may go through many revisions before it is finally published as an RFC.

For a specification that is on the standards track, the entry-level maturity is Proposed Standard. A Proposed Standard is generally stable, has resolved known design choices, is believed to be well understood, has received significant community review, and appears to enjoy enough community interest to be considered valuable.

For a Proposed Standard to advance to Draft Standard, there must be at least two independent and interoperable implementations from different code bases and there must be sufficient operational experience. A Draft Standard is considered a final specification, and changes are typically only made to solve specific new problems.

After some period of review, if a Draft Standard meets all the aforementioned criteria, it may be elevated to the Internet Standard level. An Internet Standard is characterized by a high degree of technical maturity and by a consensus that the specified protocol or service provides significant benefit to the Internet community. At this point, the specification is assigned an STD number as well as an RFC number. Finally, when a protocol becomes obsolete, it is assigned to the Historic status.

There are several additional designations that do not form part of the standards track. A protocol or other specification that is not considered ready for standardization may be published as an experimental RFC. After further work, the specification may be resubmitted for the standards track.

An Informational RFC is published to provide generally useful information to the Internet community.

2.3 THE OSI PROTOCOL ARCHITECTURE

The OSI reference model was developed by the International Organization for Standardization (ISO) as a model for a computer protocol architecture and as a framework for developing protocol standards. It consists of seven layers:

- Application
- Presentation
- Session
- Transport

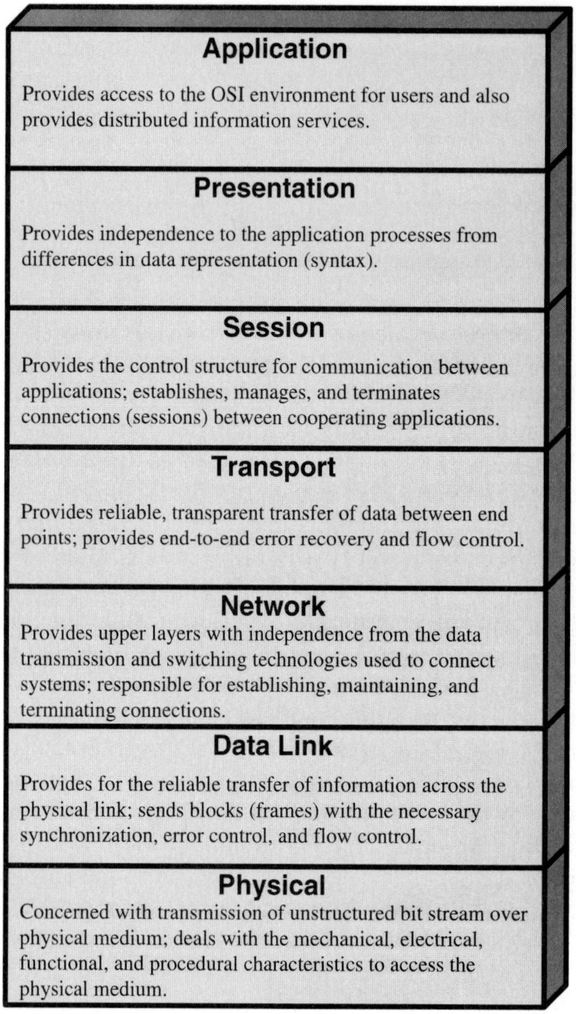

Application

Provides access to the OSI environment for users and also provides distributed information services.

Presentation

Provides independence to the application processes from differences in data representation (syntax).

Session

Provides the control structure for communication between applications; establishes, manages, and terminates connections (sessions) between cooperating applications.

Transport

Provides reliable, transparent transfer of data between end points; provides end-to-end error recovery and flow control.

Network

Provides upper layers with independence from the data transmission and switching technologies used to connect systems; responsible for establishing, maintaining, and terminating connections.

Data Link

Provides for the reliable transfer of information across the physical link; sends blocks (frames) with the necessary synchronization, error control, and flow control.

Physical

Concerned with transmission of unstructured bit stream over physical medium; deals with the mechanical, electrical, functional, and procedural characteristics to access the physical medium.

Figure 2.6 The OSI layers.

- Network
- Data Link
- Physical.

Figure 2.6 illustrates the OSI model and provides a brief definition of the functions performed at each layer. The intent of the OSI model is that protocols be developed to perform the functions of each layer.

The designers of OSI assumed that this model and the protocols developed within this model would come to dominate computer communications, eventually replacing proprietary protocol implementations and rival multivendor models such as TCP/IP. This has not happened. Although many useful protocols have been developed in the context of OSI, the overall seven-layer model has not flourished. Instead, the TCP/IP architecture has come to dominate. There are a number of reasons for this outcome. Perhaps the most important is that the key TCP/IP protocols were mature and well tested at a time when similar OSI protocols were in the development stage. When businesses began to recognize the need for interoperability across networks, only TCP/IP was available and ready to go. Another reason is that the OSI model is unnecessarily complex, with seven layers to accomplish what TCP/IP does with fewer layers.

Figure 2.7 illustrates the layers of the TCP/IP and OSI architectures, showing roughly the correspondence in functionality between the two. The figure also suggests common means of implementing the various layers.

2.4 INTERNETWORKING

In most cases, LAN or WAN is not an isolated entity. An organization may have more than one type of LAN at a given site to satisfy a spectrum of needs. An organization may have multiple LANs of the same type at a given site to accommodate performance or security requirements. And an organization may have LANs at various sites and need them to be interconnected via for WANs central control of distributed information exchange.

An interconnected set of networks, from a user's point of view, may appear simply as a larger network. However, if each of the constituent networks retains its identity, and special mechanisms are needed for communicating across multiple networks, then the entire configuration is often referred to as an **internet**, and each of the constituent networks as a **subnetwork**. These terms are briefly defined in Table 2.1. The most important example of an internet is referred to simply as the Internet. As the Internet has evolved from its modest beginnings as a research-oriented

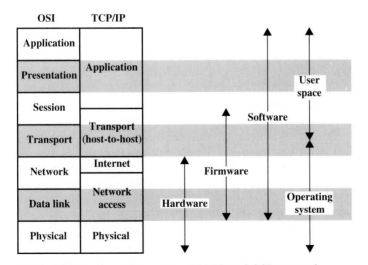

Figure 2.7 A comparison of the TCP/IP and OSI protocol architectures.

TABLE 2.1 INTERNETWORKING TERMS

Communication Network
A facility that provides a data transfer service among devices attached to the network.

Internet
A collection of communication networks interconnected by bridges and/or routers.

Intranet
A corporate internet that provides the key Internet applications, especially the World Wide Web. An intranet operates within the organization for internal purposes and can exist as an isolated, self-contained internet, or may have links to the Internet.

Subnetwork
Refers to a constituent network of an internet. This avoids ambiguity because the entire internet, from a user's point of view, is a single network.

End System (ES)
A device attached to one of the subnetworks of an internet that is used to support end-user applications or services.

Intermediate System (IS)
A device used to connect two subnetworks and permit communication between end systems attached to different subnetworks.

Bridge
An IS used to connect two LANs that use similar LAN protocols. The bridge acts as an address filter, picking up packets from one LAN that are intended for a destination on another LAN and passing those packets on. The bridge does not modify the contents of the packets and does not add anything to the packet. The bridge operates at layer 2 of the OSI model.

Router
An IS used to connect two subnetworks that may or may not be similar. The router employs an internet protocol present in each router and each end system of the network. The router operates at layer 3 of the OSI model.

packet-switching network, it has served as the basis for the development of internetworking technology and as the model for private internets within organizations. These latter are also referred to as **intranets**.

Each constituent subnetwork in an internet supports communication among the devices attached to that subnetwork; these devices are referred to as **end systems** (ESs). In addition, subnetworks are connected by devices referred to in the ISO documents as **intermediate systems** (ISs). ISs provide a communication path and perform the necessary relaying and routing functions so that data can be exchanged between devices attached to different subnetworks in the internet.

Two types of ISs of particular interest are bridges and routers. The differences between them have to do with the types of protocols used for the internetworking logic. In essence, a **bridge** operates at layer 2 of the OSI seven-layer architecture and acts as a relay of frames between like networks. A **router** operates at layer 3 of the OSI architecture and routes packets between potentially different networks. Both the bridge and the router assume that the same upper-layer protocols are in use.

The roles and functions of routers were introduced in the context of the IP earlier in this chapter. However, because of the importance of routers in the overall networking scheme, it is worth providing additional comment in this section.

Routers

Internetworking among dissimilar subnetworks is achieved by using routers to interconnect the subnetworks. Essential functions that the router must perform include the following:

1. Provide a link between networks.
2. Provide for the routing and delivery of data between processes on end systems attached to different networks.
3. Provide these functions in such a way as not to require modifications of the networking architecture of any of the attached subnetworks.

The third point implies that the router must accommodate a number of differences among networks, such as the following:

- **Addressing schemes:** The networks may use different schemes for assigning addresses to devices. For example, an IEEE 802 LAN uses either 16-bit or 48-bit binary addresses for each attached device; an X.25 public packet-switching network uses 12-digit decimal addresses (encoded as 4 bits per digit for a 48-bit address). Some form of global network addressing must be provided, as well as a directory service.
- **Maximum packet sizes:** Packets from one network may have to be broken into smaller pieces to be transmitted on another network, a process known as *segmentation*. For example, Ethernet imposes a maximum packet size of 1500 bytes; a maximum packet size of 1000 bytes is common on X.25 networks. A packet that is transmitted on an Ethernet system and picked up by a router for retransmission on an X.25 network may have to be fragmented into two smaller ones.
- **Interfaces:** The hardware and software interfaces to various networks differ. The concept of a router must be independent of these differences.
- **Reliability:** Various network services may provide anything from a reliable end-to-end virtual circuit to an unreliable service. The operation of the routers should not depend on an assumption of network reliability.

The preceding requirements are best satisfied by an internetworking protocol, such as IP, that is implemented in all end systems and routers.

Internetworking Example

Figure 2.8 depicts a configuration that we will use to illustrate the interactions among protocols for internetworking. In this case, we focus on a server attached to a frame relay WAN and a workstation attached to an IEEE 802 LAN, with a router connecting the two networks. The router will provide a link between the server and the workstation that enables these end systems to ignore the details of the intervening networks.

Figures 2.9 through 2.11 outline typical steps in the transfer of a block of data, such as a file or a Web page, from the server, through an internet, and ultimately to an application in the workstation. In this example, the message passes through just

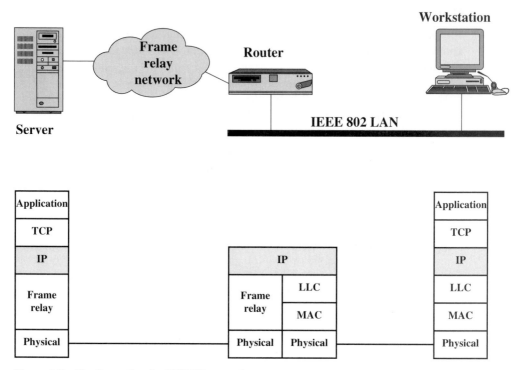

Figure 2.8   Configuration for TCP/IP example.

one router. Before data can be transmitted, the application and transport layers in the server establish, with the corresponding layer in the workstation, the applicable ground rules for a communication session. These include character code to be used, error-checking method, and the like. The protocol at each layer is used for this purpose and then is used in the transmission of the message.

2.5 RECOMMENDED READING

For the reader interested in greater detail on TCP/IP, there are two three-volume works that are more than adequate. The works by Comer and Stevens have become classics and are considered definitive [COME95, COME94a, COME94b]. The works by Stevens and Wright are equally worthwhile and more detailed with respect to protocol operation [STEV94, STEV96, WRIG95]. A more compact and very useful reference work is [MURP95], which covers the spectrum of TCP/IP-related protocols in a technically concise but thorough fashion, including coverage of some protocols not found in the other two works.

COME94a   Comer, D., and Stevens, D. *Internetworking with TCP/IP, Volume II: Design, Implementation, and Internals.* Upper Saddle River, NJ: Prentice Hall, 1994.

COME94b   Comer, D., and Stevens, D. *Internetworking with TCP/IP, Volume III: Client-Server Programming and Applications.* Upper Saddle River, NJ: Prentice Hall, 1994.

COME95   Comer, D. *Internetworking with TCP/IP, Volume I: Principles, Protocols, and Architecture.* Upper Saddle River, NJ: Prentice Hall, 1995.

1. Preparing the data. The application protocol prepares a block of data for transmission. For example, an e-mail message (SMTP), a file (FTP), or a block of user input (TELNET).

2. Using a common syntax. If necessary, the data are converted to a form expected by the destination. This may include a different character code, the use of encryption, and/or compression.

3. Segmenting the data. TCP may break the data block into a number of segments, keeping track of their sequence. Each TCP segment includes a header containing a sequence number and a frame check sequence to detect errors.

4. Duplicating segments. A copy is made of each TCP segment, in case the loss or damage of a segment necessitates retransmission. When an acknowledgment is received from the other TCP entity, a segment is erased.

5. Fragmenting the segments. IP may break a TCP segment into a number of datagrams to meet size requirements of the intervening networks. Each datagram includes a header containing a destination address, a frame check sequence, and other control information.

6. Framing. A frame relay header and trailer is added to each IP datagram. The header contains a connection identifier and the trailer contains a frame check sequence.

Peer-to-peer dialogue. Before data are sent, the sending and receiving applications agree on format and encoding and agree to exchange data.

Peer-to-peer dialogue. The two TCP entities agree to open a connection.

Peer-to-peer dialogue. Each IP datagram is forwarded through networks and routers to the destination system.

Peer-to-peer dialogue. Each frame is forwarded through the frame relay network.

7. Transmission. Each frame is transmitted over the medium as a sequence of bits.

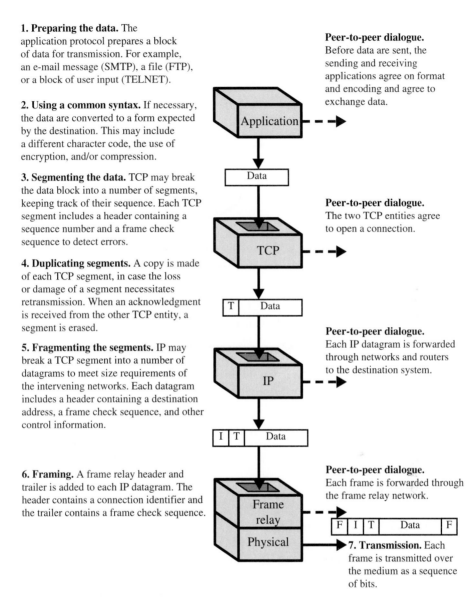

Figure 2.9 Operation of TCP/IP: Action at sender.

MURP95 Murphy, E.; Hayes, S.; and Enders, M. *TCP/IP: Tutorial and Technical Overview.* Upper Saddle River: NJ: Prentice Hall, 1995.

STEV94 Stevens, W. *TCP/IP Illustrated, Volume 1: The Protocols.* Reading, MA: Addison-Wesley, 1994.

STEV96 Stevens, W. *TCP/IP Illustrated, Volume 3: TCP for Transactions, HTTP, NNTP, and the UNIX(R) Domain Protocol.* Reading, MA: Addison-Wesley, 1996.

WRIG95 Wright, G., and Stevens, W. *TCP/IP Illustrated, Volume 2: The Implementation.* Reading, MA: Addison-Wesley, 1995.

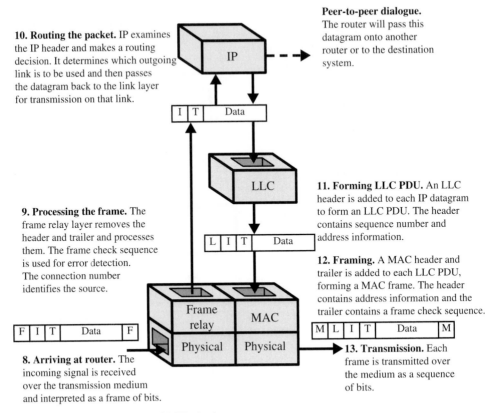

10. Routing the packet. IP examines the IP header and makes a routing decision. It determines which outgoing link is to be used and then passes the datagram back to the link layer for transmission on that link.

Peer-to-peer dialogue. The router will pass this datagram onto another router or to the destination system.

11. Forming LLC PDU. An LLC header is added to each IP datagram to form an LLC PDU. The header contains sequence number and address information.

9. Processing the frame. The frame relay layer removes the header and trailer and processes them. The frame check sequence is used for error detection. The connection number identifies the source.

12. Framing. A MAC header and trailer is added to each LLC PDU, forming a MAC frame. The header contains address information and the trailer contains a frame check sequence.

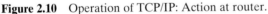

8. Arriving at router. The incoming signal is received over the transmission medium and interpreted as a frame of bits.

13. Transmission. Each frame is transmitted over the medium as a sequence of bits.

Figure 2.10   Operation of TCP/IP: Action at router.

2.6   PROBLEMS

2.1 List the major disadvantages with the layered approach to protocols.

2.2 Using the OSI architecture as a baseline, design an architecture with eight layers and make a case for it. Design one with six layers and make a case for that.

2.3 Two blue armies are each poised on opposite hills preparing to attack a single red army in the valley. The red army can defeat either of the blue armies separately but will fail to defeat both blue armies if they attack simultaneously. The blue armies communicate via an unreliable communications system (a foot soldier). The commander with one of the blue armies would like to attack at noon. His problem is this: If he sends a message to the other blue army, ordering the attack, he cannot be sure it will get through. He could ask for acknowledgment, but that might not get through. Is there a protocol that the two blue armies can use to avoid defeat?

2.4 A broadcast network is one in which a transmission from any one attached station is received by all other attached stations over a shared medium. Examples are a bus-topology local area network, such as Ethernet, and a wireless radio network. Discuss the need or lack of need for a network layer (OSI layer 3) in a broadcast network.

2.5 In Figure 2.4, exactly one protocol data unit (PDU) in layer N is encapsulated in a PDU at layer $(N - 1)$. It is also possibile to the break one N-level PDU into multiple

20. Delivering the data. The application performs any needed transformations, including decompression and decryption, and directs the data to the appropriate file or other destination.

19. Reassembling user data. If TCP has broken the user data into multiple segments, these are reassembled and the block is passed up to the application.

18. Processing the TCP segment. TCP removes the header. It checks the frame check sequence and acknowledges if there is a match and discards for mismatch. Flow control is also performed.

17. Processing the IP datagram. IP removes the header. The frame check sequence and other control information are processed.

16. Processing the LLC PDU. The LLC layer removes the header and processes it. The sequence number is used for flow and error control.

15. Processing the frame. The MAC layer removes the header and trailer and processes them. The frame check sequence is used for error detection.

14. Arriving at destination. The incoming signal is received over the transmission medium and interpreted as a frame of bits.

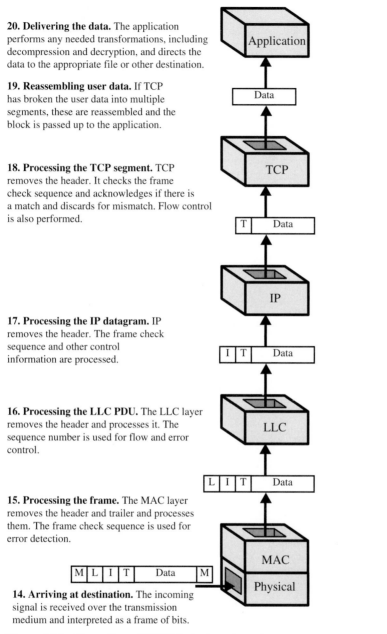

Figure 2.11 Operation of TCP/IP: Action at receiver.

$(N - 1)$-level PDUs (segmentation) or to group multiple N-level PDUs into one $(N - 1)$-level PDU (blocking).
  a. In the case of segmentation, is it necessary that each $(N - 1)$-level segment contain a copy of the N-level header?
  b. In the case of blocking, is it necessary that each N-level PDU retain its own header, or can the data be consolidated into a single N-level PDU with a single N-level header?

CHAPTER 3

DATA NETWORKS

At St. Paul's a great throng crammed the platform. She saw a sea of faces, each stamped with a kind of purposeful, hungry urgency, a determination to get into this train. As before, when she was on the Northern Line, she thought there must be some rule, some operating law, that would stop more than a limited, controlled number getting in. Authority would appear and stop it.

—*King Solomon's Carpet,* Barbara Vine (Ruth Rendell)

This chapter provides an overview of some basic principles of data networks. We begin with a description of packet-switching networks, introducing the fundamental concepts of datagrams and virtual circuits. Next, we review the X.25 packet-switching interface standard. Then we look at frame relay networks, which make use of a streamlined packet-switching mechanism. Finally, we explore the concept of congestion in data networks.

3.1 PACKET-SWITCHING NETWORKS

Around 1970, research began on a new form of architecture for long-distance digital data communications: packet switching. Although the technology of packet switching has evolved substantially since that time, it is remarkable that (1) the basic technology of packet switching is fundamentally the same today as it was in the early-1970s networks, and (2) packet switching remains one of the few effective technologies for long-distance data communications.

The two newest WAN technologies, frame relay and ATM, are essentially variations on the basic packet-switching approach. In this chapter, we provide an overview of the original packet-switching design, which is still in widespread use, and frame relay; ATM is discussed in the next chapter.

We will see that many of the advantages of packet switching (flexibility, resource sharing, robustness, responsiveness) come with a cost. The packet-switching network is a distributed collection of packet-switching nodes. In the ideal, all packet-switching nodes would always know the state of the entire network. Unfortunately, because the nodes are distributed, there is always a time delay between a change in status in one portion of the network and the knowledge of that change elsewhere. Furthermore, there is overhead involved in communicating status information. As a result , a packet-switching network can never perform "perfectly," and elaborate algorithms are used to cope with the time delay and overhead penalties of network operation.

Basic Operation

The long-haul circuit-switching telecommunications network was originally designed to handle voice traffic, and the majority of traffic on these networks continues to be voice. A key characteristic of circuit-switching networks is that resources within the network are dedicated to a particular call. For voice connections, the resulting circuit will enjoy a high percentage of utilization because, most of the time, one party or the other is talking. However, as circuit-switching networks began to be used increasingly for data connections, two shortcomings became apparent:

- In a typical terminal-to-host data connection, much of the time the line is idle. Thus, with data connections, a circuit-switching approach is inefficient.
- In a circuit-switching network, the connection provides for transmission at a constant data rate. Thus, each of the two devices that are connected must transmit and receive at the same data rate as the other. This limits the utility of the network in interconnecting a variety of host computers and terminals.

With packet switching, data are transmitted in short blocks, called packets. A typical upper bound on packet length is 1000 octets (bytes). If a source has a longer message to send, the message is broken up into a series of packets (Figure 3.1). Each

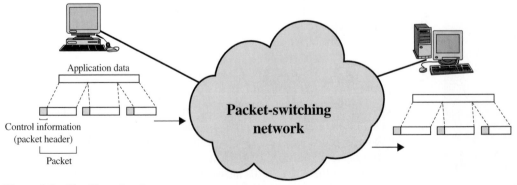

Figure 3.1 The Use of packets.

packet contains a portion (or all for a short message) of the user's data plus some control information. The control information, at a minimum, includes the information that the network requires to be able to route the packet through the network and deliver it to the intended destination. At each node en route, the packet is received, stored briefly, and passed on to the next node.

Figure 3.2 illustrates the basic operation. A transmitting computer or other device sends a message as a sequence of packets (Figure 3.2a). Each packet includes control information indicating the destination station (computer, terminal, etc.). The packets are initially sent to the node to which the sending station attaches. As each

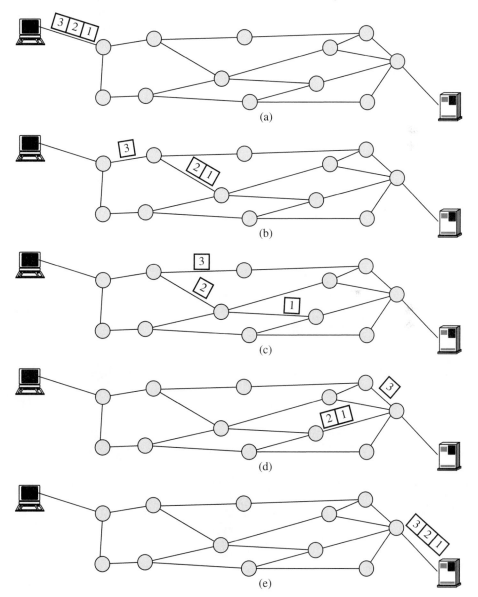

Figure 3.2   Packet switching: Datagram approach.

packet arrives at this node, it stores the packet briefly, determines the next leg of the route, and queues the packet to go out on that link. When the link is available, each packet is transmitted to the next node (Figure 3.2b). All of the packets eventually work their way through the network and are delivered to the intended destination.

Figure 3.3 depicts a simple packet-switching network. Consider a packet to be sent from station A to station E. The packet will include control information that indicates that the intended destination is E. The packet is sent from station A to node 4. Node 4 stores the packet, determines the next leg of the route (say, 5), and queues the packet to go out on that link (the 4–5 link). When the link is available, the packet is transmitted to node 5, which will forward the packet to node 6, and finally to E. This approach has a number of advantages over circuit switching:

- Line efficiency is greater, because a single node-to-node link can be dynamically shared by many packets over time. The packets are queued up and transmitted as rapidly as possible over the link. By contrast, with circuit switching, time on a node-to-node link is preallocated using synchronous time-division multiplexing. Much of the time, such a link may be idle because a portion of its time is dedicated to a connection that is idle.

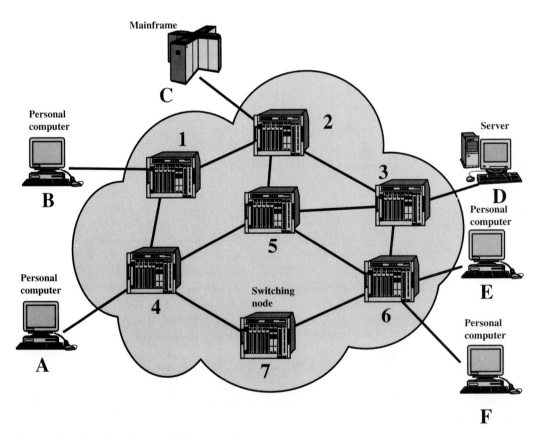

Figure 3.3 Simple packet-switching network.

- A packet-switching network can carry out data-rate conversion. Two stations of different data rates can exchange packets, because each connects to its node at its proper data rate.
- When traffic becomes heavy on a circuit-switching network, some calls are blocked; that is, the network refuses to accept additional connection requests until the load on the network decreases. On a packet-switching network, packets are still accepted, but delivery delay increases.
- Priorities can be used. Thus, if a node has a number of packets queued for transmission, it can transmit the higher-priority packets first. These packets will therefore experience less delay than lower-priority packets.

Packet switching also has disadvantages relative to circuit-switching:

- Each time a packet passes through a packet-switching node it incurs a delay not present in circuit switching. At a minimum, it incurs a transmission delay equal to the length of the packet in bits divided by the incoming channel rate in bits per second; this is the time it takes to absorb the packet into an internal buffer. In addition, there may be a variable delay due to processing and queuing in the node.
- Because the packets between a given source and destination may vary in length, may take different routes, and may be subject to varying delays in the switches they encounter, the overall packet delay can vary substantially. This phenomenon, called *jitter*, may not be desirable for some applications (for example, in real-time applications including telephone voice and real-time video).
- To route packets through the network, overhead information including the address of the destination and often sequencing information must be added to each packet, which reduces the communication capacity available for carrying user data. This is not needed in circuit switching once the circuit is set up.
- More processing is involved in the transfer of information using packet switching than in circuit switching at each node. In the case of circuit switching, there is virtually no processing at each switch once the circuit is set up.

Switching Technique

A station has a message to send through a packet-switching network that is of greater length than the maximum packet size. It therefore breaks the message up into packets and sends these packets, one at a time, to the network. A question arises as to how the network will handle this stream of packets as it attempts to route them through the network and deliver them to the intended destination. Two approaches are used in contemporary networks: datagram and virtual circuit.

In the datagram approach, each packet is treated independently, with no reference to packets that have gone before. This approach is illustrated in Figure 3.2. Each node chooses the next node on a packet's path, taking into account information received from neighboring nodes on traffic, line failures, and so on. So the packets, each with the same destination address, do not all follow the same route (Figure 3.2c), and they may arrive out of sequence at the exit point. In this example, the exit node restores the packets to their original order before delivering them to the destination. In some datagram networks, it is up to the destination rather than the exit node to do the reordering. Also, it is possible for a packet to be destroyed in the net-work. For example, if a packet-switching node crashes momentarily, all of its queued packets may be lost. Again, it is up to either the exit node or the destination to detect the loss of a packet and decide how to recover it. In this technique, each packet, treated independently, is referred to as a datagram.

In the virtual circuit approach, a preplanned route is established before any packets are sent. Once the route is established, all the packets between a pair of communicating parties follow this same route through the network. This is illus-trated in Figure 3.4. Because the route is fixed for the duration of the logical con-nection, it is somewhat similar to a circuit in a circuit-switching network and is

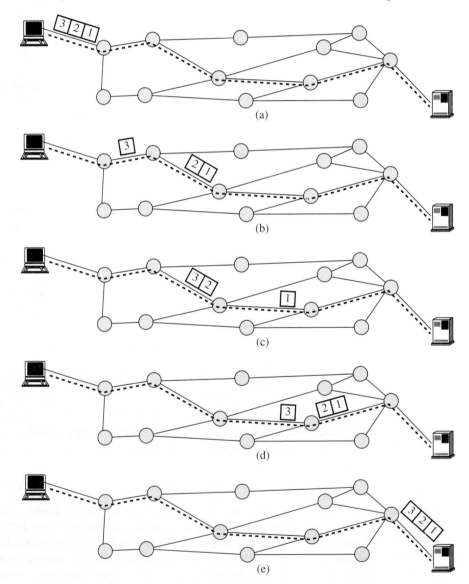

Figure 3.4   Packet switching: Virtual-circuit approach.

referred to as a virtual circuit. Each packet now contains a virtual circuit identifier as well as data. Each node on the preestablished route knows where to direct such packets; no routing decisions are required. At any time, each station can have more than one virtual circuit to any other station and can have virtual circuits to more than one station.

So the main characteristic of the virtual circuit technique is that a route between stations is set up prior to data transfer. Note that this does not mean that this is a dedicated path, as in circuit switching. A packet is still buffered at each node and queued for output over a line. The difference from the datagram approach is that, with virtual circuits, the node need not make a routing decision for each packet. It is made only once for all packets using that virtual circuit.

If two stations wish to exchange data over an extended period of time, there are certain advantages to virtual circuits. First, the network may provide services related to the virtual circuit, including sequencing and error control. Sequencing refers to the fact that, because all packets follow the same route, they arrive in the original order. Error control is a service that assures not only that packets arrive in proper sequence, but that all packets arrive correctly. For example, if a packet in a sequence from node 4 to node 6 fails to arrive at node 6, or arrives with an error, node 6 can request a retransmission of that packet from node 4. Another advantage is that packets should transit the network more rapidly with a virtual circuit; it is not necessary to make a routing decision for each packet at each node.

One advantage of the datagram approach is that the call setup phase is avoided. Thus, if a station wishes to send only one or a few packets, datagram delivery will be quicker. Another advantage of the datagram service is that it is more flexible. For example, if congestion develops in one part of the network, incoming datagrams can be routed away from the congestion. With the use of virtual circuits, packets follow a predefined route, and thus it is more difficult for the network to adapt to congestion. A third advantage is that datagram delivery is inherently more reliable. With the use of virtual circuits, if a node fails, all virtual circuits that pass through that node are lost. With datagram delivery, if a node fails, subsequent packets may find an alternate route that bypasses that node.

Most currently available packet-switching networks make use of virtual circuits for their internal operation. To some degree, this reflects a historical motivation to provide a network that presents a service as reliable (in terms of sequencing) as a circuit-switching network. There are, however, several providers of private packet-switching networks that make use of datagram operation. From the user's point of view, there should be very little difference in the external behavior based on the use of datagrams or virtual circuits. If a manager is faced with a choice, other factors, such as cost and performance, should probably take precedence over whether the internal network operation is datagram or virtual circuit.

Routing

Two related functions, congestion control and routing, are essential to the operation of a packet-switching network. Congestion control is discussed in Section 3.4; here we say a few words about routing.

In virtually all packet-switching networks, some sort of adaptive routing technique is used. That is, the routing decisions that are made change as conditions on the network change. The principal conditions that influence routing decisions are the following:

- **Failure:** When a node or trunk fails, it can no longer be used as part of a route.
- **Congestion:** When a particular portion of the network is heavily congested, it is desirable to route packets around rather than through the area of congestion.

For adaptive routing to be possible, information about the state of the network must be exchanged among the nodes. There is a tradeoff here between the quality of the information and the amount of overhead. The more information that is exchanged, and the more frequently it is exchanged, the better will be the routing decisions that each node makes. On the other hand, this information is itself a load on the network, causing a performance degradation.

3.2 X.25

One technical aspect of packet-switching networks remains to be examined: the interface between attached devices and the network. The almost universally used standard for this purpose is X.25.

X.25 is an ITU-T[1] standard that specifies an interface between a host system and a packet-switching network. The functionality of X.25 is specified on three levels:

- Physical level
- Link level
- Packet level.

The physical level deals with the physical interface between an attached station (computer, terminal) and the link that attaches that station to the packet-switching node. It makes use of the physical-level specification in a standard known as X.21, but in many cases other standards, such as EIA-232, are substituted. The link level provides for the reliable transfer of data across the physical link by transmitting the data as a sequence of frames. The link-level standard is referred to as LAPB (Link Access Protocol—Balanced). LAPB is a subset of HDLC, which is described in Chapter 9.

The packet level provides a *virtual circuit* service. This service enables any subscriber to the network to set up logical connections, called virtual circuits, to other subscribers. An example is shown in Figure 3.5 (compare Figure 3.3). In this example, station A has a virtual circuit connection to C; station B has two virtual circuits established, one to C and one to D; and stations E and F each have a virtual circuit connection to D.

In this context, the term *virtual circuit* refers to the logical connection between two stations through the network; this is perhaps best termed an external virtual circuit. Earlier, we used the term *virtual circuit* to refer to a specific preplanned route

---

[1] The International Telecommunication Union Telecommunication Standardization Sector.

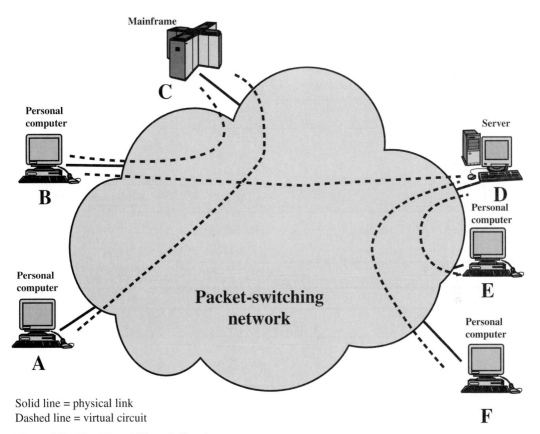

Solid line = physical link
Dashed line = virtual circuit

Figure 3.5 The Use of Virtual Circuits.

through the network between two stations; this could be called an internal virtual circuit. Typically, there is a one-to-one relationship between external and internal virtual circuits. However, it is also possible to employ X.25 with a datagram-style network. What is important for an external virtual circuit is that there is a logical relationship, or logical channel, established between two stations, and all of the data associated with that logical channel are considered as part of a single stream of data between the two stations. For example, in Figure 3.5, station D keeps track of data packets arriving from three different workstations (B, E, F) on the basis of the virtual circuit number associated with each incoming packet.

Figure 3.6 illustrates the relationship between the levels of X.25. User data are passed down to X.25 level 3, which appends control information as a header, creating a packet. This control information serves several purposes, including the following:

1. Identifying by number a particular virtual circuit with which this data is to be associated
2. Providing sequence numbers that can be used for flow and error control on a virtual circuit basis.

The entire X.25 packet is then passed down to the LAPB entity, which appends control information at the front and back of the packet, forming a LAPB

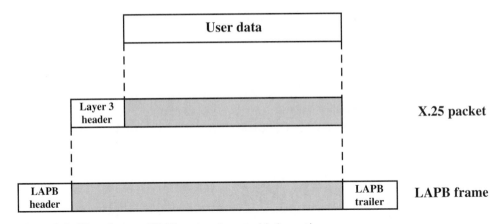

Figure 3.6   User data and X.25 protocol control information.

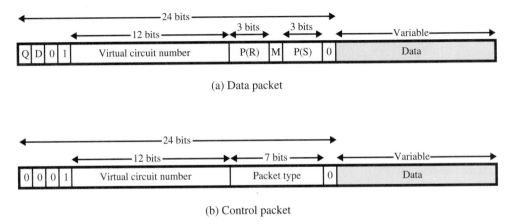

(a) Data packet

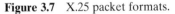

(b) Control packet

Figure 3.7   X.25 packet formats.

frame. Again, the control information in the frame is needed for the operation of the LAPB protocol.

Figure 3.7 shows the packet formats used in X.25. For user data, the data are broken up into blocks of some maximum size, and a 24-bit header is appended to each block to form a *data packet*. The header includes a 12-bit virtual circuit number (expressed as a 4-bit group number and an 8-bit channel number). The P(S) and P(R) fields support the functions of flow control and error control on a virtual circuit basis, in a fashion similar to flow and error control at the link level in such protocols as LAPB and HDLC. The send sequence number, P(S), is used to number all outgoing data packets sequentially on a particular virtual circuit. The receive sequence number, P(R), is an acknowledgment of packets received on that virtual circuit.

In addition to transmitting user data, X.25 must transmit control information related to the establishment, maintenance, and termination of virtual circuits. Control information is transmitted in a *control packet*. Each control packet includes the virtual circuit number; the packet type, which identifies the particular control function; and additional control information related to that function. For example, a Call Request packet includes the following additional fields:

- **Calling DTE address length (4 bits):** Length of the corresponding address field in 4-bit units.
- **Called DTE address length (4 bits):** Length of the corresponding address field in 4-bit units.
- **DTE addresses (variable):** The calling and called DTE addresses.
- **Facility length:** Length of the facility field in octets.
- **Facilities:** A sequence of facility specifications. Each specification consists of an 8-bit facility code and zero or more parameter codes. An example of a facility is reverse charging.

3.3   FRAME RELAY NETWORKS

The traditional approach to packet switching makes use of X.25, which not only determines the user-network interface but also influences the internal design of the network. Three key features of the X.25 approach are as follows:

- Call control packets, used for setting up and clearing virtual circuits, are carried on the same channel and same virtual circuit as data packets. In effect, inband signaling is used.
- Multiplexing of virtual circuits takes place at layer 3.
- Both layer 2 and layer 3 include flow control and error control mechanisms.

This approach results in considerable overhead. Figure 3.8a indicates the flow of data across a packet-switching network through just three nodes between source and destination.[2] Data are taken from the source device and stored to make retransmission possible. The data are organized as a sequence of blocks. For each block, an X.25 header is added to form a packet. Then routing calculations are made. Finally, the packet is enclosed in a LAPB frame by adding a LAPB header and trailer. The frame is then transmitted over a data link to the next packet-switching node. The node performs flow and error control functions at the data link layer, which involves sending an acknowledgment back across the link and may require retransmission. Then the node removes the data link layer fields to examine the packet header for routing purposes. This entire process is repeated at each hop across the network.

All of this overhead may be justified when there is a significant probability of error on any of the links in the network. But this approach is not appropriate for modern digital communication facilities. Today's networks employ reliable digital transmission technology over high-quality, reliable transmission links, many of which are optical fiber. In addition, with the use of optical fiber and digital transmission, high data rates can be achieved. In this environment, the overhead of X.25 is not only unnecessary, but degrades the effective utilization of the available high data rates.

---

[2] To simplify the picture, the processing between each end system and the packet-switching node to which it is attached is ignored.

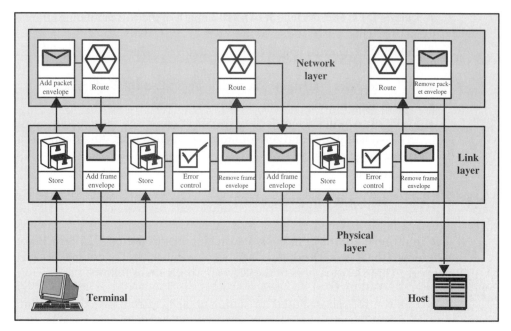

(a) Packet switching

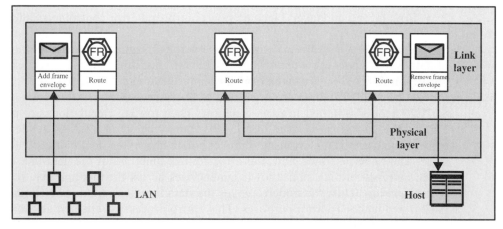

(b) Frame relay

Figure 3.8   Packet switching and frame relay operation.

Frame relay is designed to eliminate much of the overhead that X.25 imposes on end-user systems and on the packet-switching network. The key differences between frame relay and a conventional X.25 packet-switching service are as follows:

- Call control signaling is carried on a separate logical connection from user data. Thus, intermediate nodes need not maintain state tables or process messages relating to call control on an individual per-connection basis.

- Multiplexing and switching of logical connections take place at layer 2 instead of layer 3, eliminating one entire layer of processing.
- There is no hop-by-hop flow control and error control. End-to-end flow control and error control are the responsibility of a higher layer, if employed at all.

Figure 3.8b indicates the operation of frame relay, in which a single user data frame is sent from source to destination through three frame relay nodes. This frame contains the addressing information necessary to route the data through the frame relay network. No flow or error control is performed between frame relay nodes.

Let us consider the advantages and disadvantages of this approach. The principal potential disadvantage of frame relay, compared to X.25, is that we have lost the ability to do link-by-link flow and error control. (Although frame relay does not provide end-to-end flow and error control, this is easily provided at a higher layer.) In X.25, multiple virtual circuits are carried on a single physical link, and LAPB is available at the link level for providing reliable transmission from the source to the packet-switching network and from the packet-switching network to the destination. In addition, at each hop through the network, the link control protocol can be used for reliability. With the use of frame relay, this hop-by-hop link control is lost. However, with the increasing reliability of transmission and switching facilities, this is not a major disadvantage.

The advantage of frame relay is that we have streamlined the communications process. The protocol functionality required at the user-network interface is reduced, as is the internal network processing. As a result, lower delay and higher throughput can be expected. Studies indicate an improvement in throughput using frame relay, compared to X.25, of an order of magnitude or more [HARB92]. The ITU-T Recommendation I.233 indicates that frame relay is to be used at access speeds up to 2 Mbps. Recently, however, frame relay service at even higher data rates has become available.

Frame Relay Architecture

Figure 3.9 compares the protocol make-up of frame relay with that of X.25. As we discussed earlier, X.25 involves three layers of functionality. The physical layer is concerned with the details of the transmission medium and the transmission of bits at a given data rate using a particular signal encoding (e.g., EIA-232). The LAPB protocol provides a reliable data link control protocol across a link. The packet level is used to define virtual circuits. The relationship between LAPB and the packet level is illustrated in Figure 3.10a. Between the subscriber device (DTE—data terminal equipment) and the packet-switching node to which it is attached (DCE—data circuit-terminating equipment), an LAPB protocol is used to assure reliable transfer of frames. Each frame contains a packet that includes a virtual circuit number in its header (Figure 3.7). Thus, a number of different virtual circuits can be supported through the LAPB "pipe." As Figure 3.10a also shows, these virtual circuits can have different routes through the network going to different destinations. Thus, a subscriber can maintain a number of virtual circuits to different other subscribers on the network.

In contrast, frame relay involves the physical layer and a data link control protocol known as LAPF (Link Access Protocol for Frame Mode Bearer Services). In

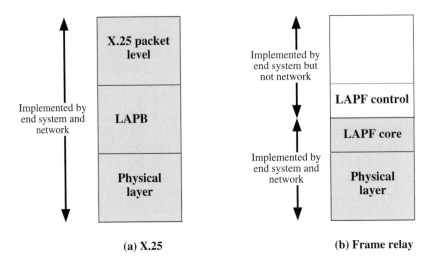

(a) X.25   (b) Frame relay

Figure 3.9   Comparison of X.25 and frame relay protocol stacks.

fact, there are two versions of LAPF defined. All frame relay networks involve the implementation of the **LAPF core** protocol on all subscriber systems and on all frame relay nodes. LAPF core provides a minimal set of data link control functions, consisting of the following:

- Frame delimiting, alignment, and transparency
- Frame multiplexing/demultiplexing using the address field
- Inspection of the frame to ensure that it consists of an integer number of octets prior to zero bit insertion or following zero bit extraction
- Inspection of the frame to ensure that it is neither too long or too short
- Detection of transmission errors
- Congestion control functions.

Above this, the user may choose to select additional data link or network-layer end-to-end functions. One possibility is known as the **LAPF control** protocol. LAPF control is not part of the frame relay service, but may be implemented only in the end systems to provide flow and error control.

The frame relay service using LAPF core has the following properties for the transmission of data:

- Preservation of the order of frame transfer from one edge of the network to the other
- A small probability of frame loss.

As with X.25, frame relay involves the use of logical connections, in this case called virtual connections rather than virtual circuits. Figure 3.10b emphasizes that the frames transmitted over these virtual connections are not protected by a data link control pipe with flow and error control.

Another difference between X.25 and frame relay is that the latter devotes a separate virtual connection to call control. The setting up and tearing down of vir-

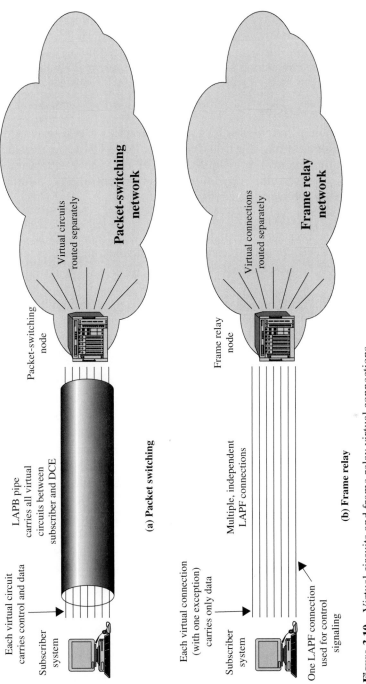

Each virtual circuit carries control and data

Subscriber system

LAPB pipe carries all virtual circuits between subscriber and DCE

Packet-switching node

Virtual circuits routed separately

Packet-switching network

(a) Packet switching

Each virtual connection (with one exception) carries only data

Subscriber system

One LAPF connection used for control signaling

Multiple, independent LAPF connections

Frame relay node

Virtual connections routed separately

Frame relay network

(b) Frame relay

Figure 3.10 Virtual circuits and frame relay virtual connections.

tual connections is done over this permanent control-oriented virtual connection. This is the same principle as the common-channel signaling technique used in ISDN.

The frame relay architecture significantly reduces the amount of work required of the network. User data are transmitted in frames with virtually no processing by the intermediate network nodes, other than to check for errors and to route based on connection number. A frame in error is simply discarded, leaving error recovery to higher layers.

User Data Transfer

The operation of frame relay for user data transfer is best explained by beginning with the frame format, illustrated in Figure 3.11. The format is similar to that of other data link control protocols, such as HDLC and LAPB, with one omission: there is no control field. In traditional data link control protocols, the control field is used for the following functions:

- Part of the control field identifies the frame type. In addition to a frame for carrying user data, there are various control frames. These carry no user data but are used for various protocol control functions, such as setting up and tearing down logical connections.

- The control field for user data frames includes send and receive sequence numbers. The send sequence number is used to number each transmitted frame sequentially. The receive sequence number is used to provide a positive or negative acknowledgment to incoming frames. The use of sequence numbers allows the receiver to control the rate of incoming frames (flow control)

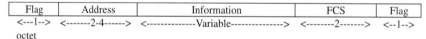

Flag	Address	Information	FCS	Flag
<---1-->	<-------2-4------>	<--------------Variable---------------->	<--------2------->	<--1-->
octet				

(a) Frame format

8	7	6	5	4	3	2	1
Upper DLCI						C/R	EA 0
Lower DLCI			FECN	BECN	DE	EA 1

(b) Address field—2 octets (default)

8	7	6	5	4	3	2	1
Upper DLCI						C/R	EA 0
DLCI			FECN	BECN	DE	EA 0
DLCI							EA 0
Lower DLCI or DL-CORE control					D/C	EA 1

(d) Address field—4 octets

8	7	6	5	4	3	2	1
Upper DLCI						C/R	EA 0
DLCI			FECN	BECN	DE	EA 0
Lower DLCI or DL-CORE control					D/C	EA 1

(c) Address field—3 octets

E	Address field extension bit
C/R	Command/response bit
FECN	Forward explicit congestion notification
BECN	Backward explicit congestion notification
DLCI	Data link congestion identifier
D/C	DLCI or DL-CORE control indicator
DE	Discard eligibility

Figure 3.11 LAPF-core formats.

and to report missing or damaged frames, which can then be retransmitted (error control).

The lack of a control field in the frame relay format means that the process of setting up and tearing down connections must be carried out on a separate channel at a higher layer of software. It also means that it is not possible to perform flow control and error control.

The flag and frame check sequence (FCS) fields function as in HDLC. The flag field is a unique pattern that delimits the start and end of the frame. The FCS field is used for error detection. On transmission, the FCS checksum is calculated and stored in the FCS field. On reception, the checksum is again calculated and compared to the value stored in the incoming FCS field. If there is a mismatch, then the frame is assumed to be in error and is discarded.

The information field carries higher-layer data. The higher-layer data may be either user data or call control messages, as explained in the next subsection.

The address field has a default length of 2 octets and may be extended to 3 or 4 octets. It carries a data link connection identifier (DLCI) of 10, 17, or 24 bits. The DLCI serves the same function as the virtual circuit number in X.25: It allows multiple logical frame relay connections to be multiplexed over a single channel.

The length of the address field, and hence of the DLCI, is determined by the address field extension (EA) bits. The C/R bit is application specific and not used by the standard frame relay protocol. The remaining bits in the address field have to do with congestion control.

Frame Relay Call Control

The actual details of the call control procedure for frame relay depend on the context of its use. The standards that have been developed assume the use of frame relay over ISDN. When frame relay is used over a point-to-point link between a pair of bridges or routers, a simpler protocol may suffice. Here, we summarize the essential elements of frame relay call control.

As with X.25, frame relay supports multiple connections over a single link. In the case of frame relay, these are called data link connections, and each has a unique DLCI. Data transfer involves the following stages:

1. Establish a logical connection between two end points, and assign a unique DLCI to the connection.
2. Exchange information in data frames. Each frame includes a DLCI field to identify the connection.
3. Release the logical connection.

The establishment and release of a logical connection is accomplished by the exchange of messages over a connection dedicated to call control, with DLCI = 0. A frame with DLCI = 0 contains a call control message in the information field. At a minimum, four message types are needed: SETUP, CONNECT, RELEASE, and RELEASE COMPLETE.

Either side may request the establishment of a logical connection by sending a SETUP message. The other side, upon receiving the SETUP message, must reply with a CONNECT message if it accepts the connection; otherwise it responds with a RELEASE COMPLETE message. The side sending the SETUP message may assign the DLCI by choosing an unused value and including this value in the SETUP message. Otherwise, the DLCI value is assigned by the accepting side in the CONNECT message.

Either side may request to clear a logical connection by sending a RELEASE message. The other side, upon receipt of this message, must respond with a RELEASE COMPLETE message.

3.4   CONGESTION IN DATA NETWORKS AND INTERNETS

A key design issue that must be confronted with data networks, such as packet-switching, frame relay, and ATM networks, and with internets is that of congestion control. Indeed, congestion control is one of the central themes of this book. Much of Parts Four and Five are devoted to this topic, and it is also addressed in Part Six.

The phenomenon of congestion is a complex one, as is the subject of congestion control. In very general terms, congestion occurs when the number of packets[3] being transmitted through a network begins to approach the packet-handling capacity of the network. The objective of congestion control is to maintain the number of packets within the network below the level at which performance falls off dramatically.

To understand the issues involved in congestion control, we need to look at some results from queuing theory. This topic is explored in detail in Chapter 7, but the crucial point can be stated briefly. In essence, a data network or internet is a network of queues. At each node (data network switch, internet router), there is a queue of packets for each outgoing channel. If the rate at which packets arrive and queue up exceeds the rate at which packets can be transmitted, the queue size grows without bound and the delay experienced by a packet goes to infinity. Even if the packet arrival rate is less than the packet transmission rate, queue length will grow dramatically as the arrival rate approaches the transmission rate. As a rule of thumb, when the line for which packets are queuing becomes more than 80% utilized, the queue length grows at an alarming rate. This growth in queue length means that the delay experienced by a packet at each node increases. Further, since the size of any queue is finite, as queue length grows, eventually the queue must overflow.

Effects of Congestion

Consider the queuing situation at a single packet switch or router, such as is illustrated in Figure 3.12. Any given node has a number of I/O ports[4] attached to it: one or more to other nodes, and zero or more to end systems. On each port, packets arrive and depart. We can consider that there are two buffers at each port, one to

---

[3] In this section we use the term *packet* in a broad sense, to include packets in a packet-switching network, frames in a frame relay network, cells in an ATM network, or IP datagrams in an internet.

[4] In the case of a switch of a packet-switching, frame relay, or ATM network, each I/O port connects to a transmission link that connects to another node or end system. In the case of a router of an internet, each I/O port connects to either a direct link to another node or to a subnetwork.

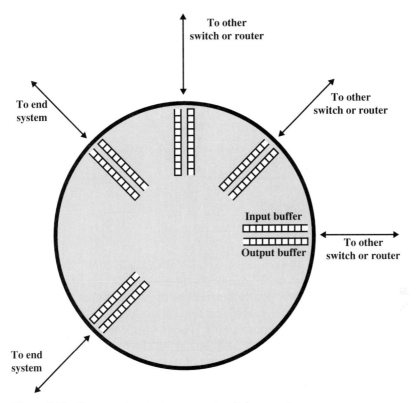

To other
switch or router

To end
system

To other
switch or router

Input buffer

Output buffer

To other
switch or router

To end
system

Figure 3.12   Input and output queues at switch or router.

accept arriving packets, and one to hold packets that are waiting to depart. In practice, there might be two fixed-size buffers associated with each port, or there might be a pool of memory available for all buffering activities. In the latter case, we can think of each port having two variable-size buffers associated with it, subject to the constraint that the sum of all buffer sizes is a constant.

In any case, as packets arrive, they are stored in the input buffer of the corresponding port. The node examines each incoming packet, makes a routing decision, and then moves the packet to the appropriate output buffer. Packets queued for output are transmitted as rapidly as possible; this is, in effect, statistical time-division multiplexing. Now, if packets arrive too fast for the node to process them (make routing decisions) or faster than packets can be cleared from the outgoing buffers, then eventually packets will arrive for which no memory is available.

When such a saturation point is reached, one of two general strategies can be adopted. The first such strategy is simply to discard any incoming packet for which there is no available buffer space. The alternative is for the node that is experiencing these problems to exercise some sort of flow control over its neighbors so that the traffic flow remains manageable. But, as Figure 3.13 illustrates, each of a node's neighbors is also managing a number of queues. If node 6 restrains the flow of packets from node 5, this causes the output buffer in node 5 for the port to node 6 to fill up. Thus, congestion at one point in the network can quickly propagate throughout a region or all of the network. While flow control is indeed a powerful tool, we need to use it in such a way as to manage the traffic on the entire network.

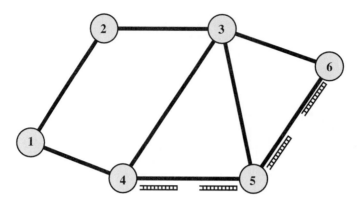

Figure 3.13 Interaction of queues.

Ideal Performance

Figure 3.14 suggests the ideal goal for network utilization. The top graph plots the steady-state total throughput (number of packets delivered to destination end systems) through the network as a function of the offered load (number of packets transmitted by source end systems), both normalized to the maximum theoretical throughput of the network. For example, if a network consists of a single node with two 1-Mbps links, then the theoretical capacity of the network is 2 Mbps, consisting of a 1-Mbps flow in each direction. In the ideal case, the throughput of the network increases to accommodate load up to an offered load equal to the full capacity of the network; then normalized throughput remains at 1.0 at higher input loads. Note, however, what happens to the end-to-end delay experienced by the average packet even with this assumption of ideal performance. At negligible load, there is some small constant amount of delay that consists of the propagation delay through the network from source to destination plus processing delay at each node. As the load on the network increases, queuing delays at each node are added to this fixed amount of delay. When the load exceeds the network capacity, delay becomes infinite in the steady state.

Here is a simple intuitive explanation of why delay must go to infinity. Suppose that each node in the network is equipped with buffers of infinite size and suppose that the input load exceeds network capacity. Under ideal conditions, the network will continue to sustain a normalized throughput of 1.0. Therefore, the rate of packets leaving the network is 1.0. Because the rate of packets entering the network is greater than 1.0, internal queue sizes grow. In the steady state, with input greater than output, these queue sizes grow to infinity and therefore queuing delays grow to infinity.

It is important to grasp the meaning of Figure 3.14 before looking at real-world conditions. This figure represents the ideal, but unattainable, goal of all traffic and congestion control schemes. No scheme can exceed the performance depicted in Figure 3.14.

You will sometimes see the term *power* used in network performance literature. Power is defined as the ratio of throughput to delay, and this is depicted for the ideal case in the bottom graph of Figure 3.14. It has been shown that, typically, a network configuration and congestion control scheme that results in higher

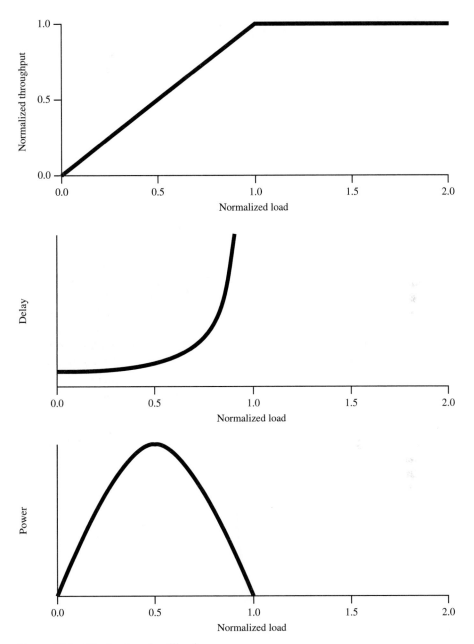

Figure 3.14   Ideal network utilization.

throughput also results in higher delay [JAIN91], and that power is a concise metric that can be used to compare different schemes.

Practical Performance

The ideal case reflected in Figure 3.14 assumes infinite buffers and no overhead related to packet transmission or congestion control. In practice, buffers are finite, leading to buffer overflow, and attempts to control congestion consume network capacity in the exchange of control signals.

Let us consider what happens in a network with finite buffers if no attempt is made to control congestion or to restrain input from end systems. The details will, of course, differ depending on network configuration and on the statistics of the presented traffic. However, the graphs in Figure 3.15 depict the devastating outcome in general terms.

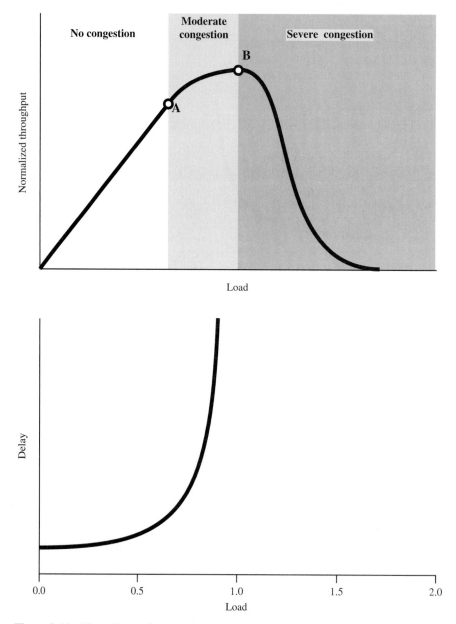

Figure 3.15   The effects of congestion.

At light loads, throughput and hence network utilization increases as the offered load increases. As the load continues to increase, a point is reach (point A in the plot) beyond which the throughput of the network increases at a rate slower than the rate at which offered load is increased. This is due to network entry into a moderate congestion state. In this region, the network continues to cope with the load, although with increased delays. The departure of throughput from the ideal is accounted for by a number of factors. For one thing, the load is unlikely to be uniformly spread throughout the network. Therefore, while some nodes may experience moderate congestion, others may be experiencing severe congestion and may need to discard traffic. In addition, as the load increases, the network will attempt to balance the load by routing packets through areas of lower congestion. For the routing function to work, an increased number of routing messages must be exchanged between nodes to alert each other to areas of congestion; this overhead reduces the capacity available for data packets.

As the load on the network continues to increase, the queue lengths of the various nodes continue to grow. Eventually, a point is reached (point B in the plot) beyond which throughput actually drops with increased offered load. The reason for this is that the buffers at each node are of finite size. When the buffers at a node become full, it must discard packets. Thus, the sources must retransmit the discarded packets in addition to new packets. This only exacerbates the situation: As more and more packets are retransmitted, the load on the system grows, and more buffers become saturated. While the system is trying desperately to clear the backlog, users are pumping old and new packets into the system. Even successfully delivered packets may be retransmitted because it takes too long, at a higher layer (e.g., transport layer) to acknowledge them: The sender assumes the packet did not get through and retransmits. Under these circumstances, the effective capacity of the system is virtually zero.

Congestion Control

Much of this book is devoted to a study of various techniques for controlling congestion. To give context to this discussion, Figure 3.16 provides a general depiction of important congestion control techniques.

Backpressure

We have already made reference to backpressure as a technique for congestion control. This technique produces an effect similar to backpressure in fluids flowing down a pipe. When the end of a pipe is closed (or restricted), the fluid pressure backs up the pipe to the point of origin, where the flow is stopped (or slowed).

Backpressure can be exerted on the basis of links or logical connections. Referring again to Figure 3.13, if node 6 becomes congested (buffers fill up), then node 6 can slow down or halt the flow of all packets from node 5 (or node 3, or both nodes 5 and 3). If this restriction persists, node 5 will need to slow down or halt traffic on its incoming links. This flow restriction propagates backward (against the flow of data traffic) to sources, which are restricted in the flow of new packets into the network.

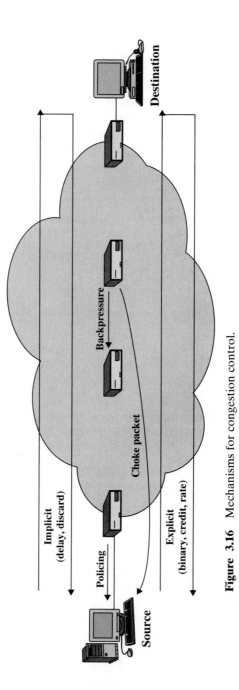

Figure 3.16 Mechanisms for congestion control.

Backpressure can be selectively applied to logical connections, so that the flow from one node to the next is only restricted or halted on some connections, generally the ones with the most traffic. In this case, the restriction propagates back along the connection to the source.

Backpressure is of limited utility. It can be used in a connection-oriented network that allows hop-by-hop (from one node to the next) flow control. X.25-based packet-switching networks typically provide this feature. However, neither frame relay nor ATM has any capability for restricting flow on a hop-by-hop basis. In the case of IP-based internets, there are essentially no built-in facilities for regulating the flow of data from one router to the next along a path through the internet.

Choke Packet

A choke packet is a control packet generated at a congested node and transmitted back to a source node to restrict traffic flow. An example of a choke package is the ICMP (Internet Control Message Protocol) Source Quench packet. Either a router or a destination end system may send this message to a source end system, requesting that it reduce the rate at which it is sending traffic to the internet destination. On receipt of a source quench message, the source host should cut back the rate at which it is sending traffic to the specified destination until it no longer receives source quench messages. The source quench message can be used by a router or host that must discard IP datagrams because of a full buffer. In that case, the router or host will issue a source quench message for every datagram that it discards. In addition, a system may anticipate congestion and issue source quench messages when its buffers approach capacity. In that case, the datagram referred to in the source quench message may well be delivered. Thus, receipt of a source quench message does not imply delivery or nondelivery of the corresponding datagram.

The choke package is a relatively crude technique for controlling congestion. More sophisticated forms of explicit congestion signaling are discussed below.

Implicit Congestion Signaling

When network congestion occurs, two things may happen: (1) The transmission delay for an individual packet from source to destination increases, so that it is noticeably longer than the fixed propagation delay; and (2) packets are discarded. If a source is able to detect increased delays and packet discards, then it has implicit evidence of network congestion. If all sources are able to detect congestion and reduce flow on the basis of congestion, then the network congestion will be relieved. Thus, congestion control on the basis of implicit signaling is the responsibility of end systems and does not require action on the part of network nodes.

Implicit signaling is an effective congestion control technique in connectionless, or datagram, configurations, such as IP-based internets. In such cases, there are no logical connections through the internet on which flow can be regulated. However, between the two end systems, logical connections are established at the TCP level. TCP includes mechanisms for acknowledging receipt of TCP segments and for regulating the flow of data between source and destination on a TCP connection. TCP congestion control techniques based on the ability to detect increased delay and segment loss are discussed in detail in Chapter 10.

Implicit signaling can also be used in connection-oriented networks. For example, in frame relay networks, the LAPF control protocol includes facilities similar to those of TCP for flow and error control. LAPF control is capable of detecting lost frames and adjusting the flow of data accordingly.

Explicit Congestion Signaling

It is desirable to use as much of the available capacity in a network as possible but still react to congestion in a controlled and fair manner. This is the purpose of explicit congestion avoidance techniques. In general terms, for explicit congestion avoidance, the network alerts end systems to growing congestion within the network and the end systems take steps to reduce the offered load to the network.

Typically, explicit congestion control techniques operate over connection-oriented networks and control the flow of packets over individual connections. Explicit congestion-signaling approaches can work in one of two directions:

- **Backward:** Notifies the source that congestion avoidance procedures should be initiated where applicable for traffic in the opposite direction of the received packet. It indicates that the packets that the user transmits on this logical connection may encounter congested resources. Backward information is transmitted either by altering bits in a data packet headed for the source to be controlled or by transmitting separate control packets to the source.
- **Forward:** Notifies the user that congestion avoidance procedures should be initiated where applicable for traffic in the same direction as the received packet. It indicates that this packet, on this logical connection, has encountered congested resources. Again, this information may be transmitted either as altered bits in data packets or in separate control packets. In some schemes, when a forward signal is received by an end system, it echoes the signal back along the logical connection to the source. In other schemes, the end system is expected to exercise flow control upon the source end system at a higher layer (e.g., TCP).

We can divide explicit congestion-signaling approaches into three general categories:

- **Binary:** A bit is set in a data packet as it is forwarded by the congested node. When a source receives a binary indication of congestion on a logical connection, it reduces its traffic flow.
- **Credit based:** These schemes are based on providing an explicit credit to a source over a logical connection. The credit indicates how many octets or how many packets the source may transmit. When the credit is exhausted, the source must await additional credit before sending additional data. Credit-based schemes are common for end-to-end flow control, in which a destination system uses credit to prevent the source from overflowing the destination buffers, but credit-based schemes have also been considered for congestion control.
- **Rate based:** These schemes are based on providing an explicit data-rate limit to the source over a logical connection. The source may transmit data at a rate up to the set limit. To control congestion, any node along the path of the con-

nection can reduce the data-rate limit in a control message to the source. A rate-based scheme for ATM networks is described in Chapter 12.

Traffic Management

There are a number of issues related to congestion control that might be included under the general category of traffic management. In its simplest form, congestion control is concerned with efficiently using a network at high load. The various mechanisms discussed in the previous section can be applied as the situation arises, without regard to the particular source or destination affected. When a node is saturated and must discard packets, it can apply some simple rule, such as discard the most recent arrival. However, other considerations can be used to refine the application of congestion control techniques and discard policy. We briefly introduce several of those areas here. All of these topics are examined in depth later in this book.

Fairness

As congestion develops, flows of packets between sources and destinations will experience increased delays and, with high congestion, packet losses. In the absence of other requirements, we would like to assure that the various flows suffer from congestion equally. To simply discard on a last-in-first-discarded basis may not be fair. As an example of a technique that might promote fairness, a node can maintain a separate queue for each logical connection or for each source-destination pair. If all of the queue buffers are of equal length, then the queues with the highest traffic load will suffer discards more often, allowing lower-traffic connections a fair share of the capacity.

Quality of Service

We might wish to treat different traffic flows differently. For example, as [JAIN92] points out, some applications, such as voice and video, are delay sensitive but loss insensitive. Others, such as file transfer and electronic mail, are delay insensitive but loss sensitive. Still others, such as interactive graphics or interactive computing applications, are delay sensitive and loss sensitive. Also, different traffic flows have different priorities; for example, network management traffic, particularly during times of congestion or failure, is more important than application traffic.

It is particularly important during periods of congestion that traffic flows with different requirements be treated differently and provided a different QoS. For example, a node might transmit higher-priority packets ahead of lower-priority packets in the same queue. Or a node might maintain different queues for different QoS levels and give preferential treatment to the higher levels.

Reservations

One way to avoid congestion and also to provide assured service to applications is to use a reservation scheme. Such a scheme is an integral part of ATM networks. When a logical connection is established, the network and the user enter into a traffic contract, which specifies a data rate and other characteristics of the traffic flow. The network agrees to give a defined QoS as long as the traffic flow is within contract parameters; excess traffic is either discarded or handled on a best-effort basis, subject to discard. If the current outstanding reservations are such that the network resources are inadequate to meet the new reservation, then the new reservation is denied. A similar type of scheme has now been developed for IP-based internets.

One aspect of a reservation scheme is traffic policing (Figure 3.16). A node in the network, typically the node to which the end system attaches, monitors the traffic flow and compares it to the traffic contract. Excess traffic is either discarded or marked to indicate that it is liable to discard or delay.

3.5 RECOMMENDED READING

The literature on packet switching is enormous. Books with good treatments of this subject include [SPOH93], [BERT92], and [SPRA91]. There is also a large body of literature on performance; good summaries are to be found in [STUC85], [SCHW77], and [KLEI76].

A more in-depth treatment of the frame relay can be found in [STAL95].

[YANG95] is a comprehensive survey of congestion control techniques. [JAIN90] and [JAIN92] provide excellent discussions of the requirements for congestion control, the various approaches that can be taken, and performance considerations.

BERT92   Bertsekas, D., and Gallager, R. *Data Networks.* Englewood Cliffs, NJ: Prentice Hall, 1992.

JAIN90   Jain, R. "Congestion Control in Computer Networks: Issues and Trends." *IEEE Network Magazine*, May 1990.

JAIN92   Jain, R. "Myths About Congestion Management in High-Speed Networks." *Internetworking: Research and Experience*, Volume 3, 1993.

KLEI76   Kleinrock, L. *Queuing Systems, Volume II: Computer Applications.* New York: Wiley, 1976.

SCHW77   Schwartz, M. *Computer-Communication Network Design and Analysis.* Englewood Cliffs, NJ: Prentice Hall, 1977.

SPOH93   Spohn, D. *Data Network Design.* New York: McGraw-Hill, 1994.

SPRA91   Spragins, J., Hammond, J., and Pawlikowski, K. *Telecommunications Protocols and Design.* Reading, MA.: Addison-Wesley, 1991.

STAL95   Stallings, W. *ISDN and Broadband ISDN, with Frame Relay and ATM.* Upper Saddle River, NJ: Prentice Hall, 1995.

STUC85   Stuck, B., and Arthurs, E. *A Computer Communications Network Performance Analysis Primer.* Englewood Cliffs, NJ: Prentice Hall, 1985.

YANG95   Yang, C., and Reddy, A. "A Taxonomy for Congestion Control Algorithms in Packet Switching Networks." *IEEE Network*, July/August 1995.

Recommended Web sites:

- http://www.frforum.com: Web site of the Frame Relay Forum, which is leading the effort to expand the functionality of frame relay networks
- http://www.mot.com/MIMS/ISG/tech/frame-relay/resources.html: Exhaustive source of information on frame relay

3.6 PROBLEMS

3.1 Explain the flaw in the following logic: Packet switching requires control and address bits to be added to each packet. This causes considerable overhead in packet switching. In circuit switching, a transparent circuit is established. No extra bits are needed.

a. Therefore, there is no overhead in circuit switching.
b. Because there is no overhead in circuit switching, line utilization must be more efficient than in packet switching.

3.2 Define the following parameters for a switching network:

N = number of hops between two given end systems

L = message length in bits

B = data rate, in bits per second (bps), on all links

P = fixed packet size

H = overhead (header) bits per packet

S = call setup time (circuit switching or virtual circuit) in seconds

D = propagation delay per hop in seconds

a. For $N = 4, L = 3200, B = 9600, P = 1024, H = 16, S = 0.2, D = 0.001$, compute the end-to-end delay for circuit switching, virtual circuit packet switching, and datagram packet switching. Assume that there are no acknowledgments. Ignore processing delay at the nodes.
b. Derive general expressions for the three techniques of part (a), taken two at a time, showing the conditions under which the delays are equal.

3.3 What value of P, as a function of N, L, and H, results in minimum end-to-end delay across a datagram network? Assume that L is much larger than P, and D is zero.

3.4 Consider a packet-switching network of N nodes, connected by the following topologies:
a. Star: One central node has no attached station; all other nodes attach to the central node.
b. Loop: Each node connects to two other nodes to form a closed loop.
c. Fully connected: Each node is directly connected to all other nodes.
For each case, give the average number of hops between stations.

3.5 Consider a binary tree topology for a packet-switching network. The root node connects to two other nodes. All intermediate nodes connect to one node in the direction toward the root, and two in the direction away from the root. At the bottom are nodes with just one link back toward the root. If there are $2^N - 1$ nodes, derive an expression for the mean number of hops per packet for large N, assuming that trips between all node pairs are equally likely.

3.6 There is no error detection mechanism (frame check sequence) in X.25. Isn't this needed to assure that all of the packets are delivered properly?

3.7 When an X.25 DTE and the DCE to which it attaches both decide to put a call through at the same time, a call collision occurs and the incoming call is canceled. When both sides try to clear the same virtual circuit simultaneously, the clear collision is resolved without canceling either request; the virtual circuit in question is cleared. An X.25 Reset packet provides a facility for recovering from an error by reinitializing a virtual circuit; this means that the sequence numbers on both ends are reset to zero. Do you think that simultaneous resets are handled like call collisions or clear collisions? Why?

3.8 In X.25, why is the virtual circuit number used by one station of two communicating stations different from the virtual circuit number used by the other station? After all, it is the same full-duplex virtual circuit.

3.9 A proposed congestion control technique is known as isarithmic control. In this method, the total number of frames in transit is fixed by inserting a fixed number of permits into the network. These permits circulate at random through the frame relay network. Whenever a frame handler wants to relay a frame just given to it by an

attached user, it must first capture and destroy a permit. When the frame is delivered
to the destination user by the frame handler to which it attaches, that frame handler
reissues the permit. List three potential problems with this technique.

3.10 Consider the frame relay network depicted in Figure 3.17. C is the capacity of a link in
frames per second. Node A presents a constant load of 0.8 frames per second destined
for A'. Node B presents a load λ destined for B'. Node S has a common pool of buffers
that it uses for traffic both to A' and B'. When the buffer is full, frames are discarded
and are later retransmitted by the source user. S has a throughput capacity of 2. Plot
the total throughput (i.e., the sum of A–A' and B–B' delivered traffic) as a function of
λ. What fraction of the throughput is A–A' traffic for λ > 1?

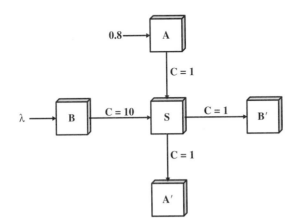

Figure 3.17   Network of nodes.

3.11 In IPv4, each router that handles a datagram decrements the time-to-live (TTL) field in
the header (Figure 2.2a) by the number of seconds that the datagram remains at the
router, or by 1 if the time is less than one second. When a router receives a datagram
whose TTL is 1, it may not forward the datagram but must discard it; if a destination end
system receives such a datagram, it may deliver it to the IP user. If a datagram remains
at a router for a longer period of time than the incoming TTL, it must be discarded.

Now consider a router with an infinite buffer in steady-state overload: The
packet arrival rate exceeds the rate at which packets can be transmitted. The router
employs no congestion control techniques other than discard. What can you say about
the number or proportion of packets flowing through this router that will successfully
reach their destination?

High-speed Networks

ISSUES FOR PART TWO

The original experimental Ethernet operated at 3 Mbps. Shortly after the commercial Ethernet was introduced, a variant known as StarNet was developed, which operated at 1 Mbps over twisted pair. There were also a number of other 1-Mbps twisted-pair LANs. A popular competitor of Ethernet was the 4-Mbps token ring with, again, a 1-Mbps option. In the realm of WANs, a trunk speed of 56 kbps between packet-switching nodes was once quite common. Today, these data rates seems as quaint as they are ineffective.

A variety of factors, including increased desktop computing power, greater reliance on graphically oriented applications, and ease of access to multimedia content, have driven the need for networks of greater and greater capacity. This need is reflected both in LANs, which must support an increasingly dense population of personal computers and workstations as well as a growing reliance on servers, and in WANs, which must support high-volume corporate and personal traffic over a variety of network configurations. Part Two summarizes some of the underlying high-speed network technologies.

ROAD MAP FOR PART TWO

Chapter 4: Asynchronous Transfer Mode

The dominant network technology for very-high-speed wide area networking is ATM. Chapter 4 begins with a description of the key elements of ATM, including its protocol architecture, the use of logical connections, and the ATM cell structure. Then the types of services offered by ATM are described. Finally, the important AAL, by which higher-layer protocols are mapped onto ATM, is explained.

Chapter 5: High-speed LANs

High-speed LANs have emerged as a critical element of corporate informa-tion systems. Such LANs are needed not only to provide an on-premises back-bone for linking departmental LANs, but to support the high-performance requirements of graphics-based client-server and intranet applications.

For most applications, Fast Ethernet and the emerging Gigabit Ether-net technologies dominate corporate high-speed LAN choices. These sys-tems involve the least risk and cost for managers for a number of reasons, including compatibility with the existing large Ethernet installed base, matu-rity of the basic technology, and compatibility with existing network man-agement and configuration software.

A more powerful and flexible approach is afforded by the ATM LAN. This type of LAN extends ATM technology and protocols from the wide area environment to the corporate site. Such LANs are attractive because of ATM's ability to carry an integrated flow of voice, image, video, and data traffic, and because of the seamless connection to the increasingly available ATM WANs. Cost and the fact that this is a newer technology than Ether-net have slowed the introduction of the ATM LAN.

CHAPTER 4

ASYNCHRONOUS TRANSFER MODE

One man had a vision of railways that would link all the mainline railroad termini. His name was Charles Pearson and, though born the son of an upholsterer, he became Solicitor to the city of London. There had previously been a plan for gaslit subway streets through which horse-drawn traffic could pass. This was rejected on the grounds that such sinister tunnels would become lurking places for thieves. Twenty years before his system was built, Pearson envisaged a line running through "a spacious archway," well-lit and well-ventilated.

His was a scheme for trains in a drain.

—*King Solomon's Carpet*, Barbara Vine (Ruth Rendell)

Asynchronous transfer mode, also known as cell relay, is similar in concept to frame relay. Both frame relay and ATM take advantage of the reliability and fidelity of modern digital facilities to provide faster packet switching than X.25. ATM is even more streamlined than frame relay in its functionality and can support data rates several orders of magnitude greater than frame relay.

In addition to their technical similarities, ATM and frame relay have similar histories. Frame relay was developed as part of the work of ISDN, but is now finding wide application in private networks and other non-ISDN applications, particularly in bridges and routers. ATM was developed as part of the work on broadband ISDN, but is used in non-ISDN environments, where very high data rates are required.

We begin with a discussion of the details of the ATM scheme, including protocol architecture, logical connections, and cell structure. Then we examine the important concept of the AAL.

Before proceeding, we should note that specifications for ATM have been developed by both the ITU-T standardization body and the ATM Forum. ITU-T is primarily concerned with developing ATM standards as part of the broadband ISDN standardization effort, whereas the ATM Forum is interested in a broad range of ATM applications. The ATM Forum is a nonprofit international industry consortium; its role and that of ITU-T in the making of ATM specifications are discussed in Section 1.1. Unless otherwise noted, the material in this book is based on the most recent ATM Forum documents, which include Version 3.1 of the User-Network Interface Specification [ATM94] and Version 4.0 of the Traffic Management Specification [ATM96].

4.1 ATM PROTOCOL ARCHITECTURE

ATM is in some ways similar to packet switching using X.25 and to frame relay. Like packet switching and frame relay, ATM involves the transfer of data in discrete chunks. Also, like packet switching and frame relay, ATM allows multiple logical connections to be multiplexed over a single physical interface. In the case of ATM, the information flow on each logical connection is organized into fixed-size packets called cells.

ATM is a streamlined protocol with minimal error and flow control capabilities. This reduces the overhead of processing ATM cells and reduces the number of overhead bits required with each cell, thus enabling ATM to operate at high data rates. Further, the use of fixed-size cells simplifies the processing required at each ATM node, again supporting the use of ATM at high data rates.

The standards issued for ATM by ITU-T are based on the protocol architecture shown in Figure 4.1, which illustrates the basic architecture for an interface between user and network. The physical layer involves the specification of a transmission medium and a signal-encoding scheme. The data rates specified at the physical layer include 155.52 Mbps and 622.08 Mbps. Other data rates, both higher and lower, are possible.

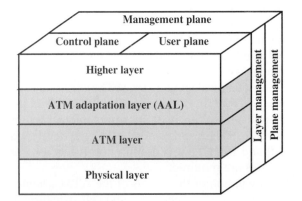

Figure 4.1 ATM protocol architecture.

Two layers of the protocol architecture relate to ATM functions. There is an ATM layer common to all services that provides packet transfer capabilities, and an AAL that is service dependent. The ATM layer defines the transmission of data in fixed-size cells and also defines the use of logical connections. The use of ATM creates the need for an adaptation layer to support information transfer protocols not based on ATM. The AAL maps higher-layer information into ATM cells to be transported over an ATM network and then collects information from ATM cells for delivery to higher layers.

The protocol reference model consists of three separate planes:

- **User plane:** Provides for user information transfer, along with associated controls (e.g., flow control, error control).
- **Control plane:** Performs call control and connection control functions.
- **Management plane:** Includes plane management, which performs management functions related to a system as a whole and provides coordination between all the planes, and layer management, which performs management functions relating to resources and parameters residing in its protocol entities.

4.2 ATM LOGICAL CONNECTIONS

Logical connections in ATM are referred to as virtual channel connections (VCCs). A VCC is analogous to a virtual circuit in X.25 or a data link connection in frame relay; it is the basic unit of switching in an ATM network. A VCC is set up between two end users through the network, and a variable-rate, full-duplex flow of fixed-size cells is exchanged over the connection. VCCs are also used for user-network exchange (control signaling) and network-network exchange (network management and routing).

For ATM, a second sublayer of processing has been introduced that deals with the concept of virtual path (Figure 4.2). A virtual path connection (VPC) is a bundle of VCCs that have the same end points. Thus, all of the cells flowing over all of the VCCs in a single VPC are switched along the same path.

The virtual path concept was developed in response to a trend in high-speed networking in which the control cost of the network is becoming an increasingly higher proportion of the overall network cost. The virtual path technique helps contain the control cost by grouping connections sharing common paths through the network into a single unit. Network management actions can then be applied to a small number of groups of connections instead of a large number of individual connections.

Figure 4.2   ATM connection relationships.

Several advantages can be listed for the use of virtual paths:

- **Simplified network architecture:** Network transport functions can be separated into those related to an individual logical connection (virtual channel) and those related to a group of logical connections (virtual path).
- **Increased network performance and reliability:** The network deals with fewer, aggregated entities.
- **Reduced processing and short connection setup time:** Much of the work is done when the virtual path is set up. By reserving capacity on a virtual path connection in anticipation of later call arrivals, new virtual channel connections can be established by executing simple control functions at the end points of the virtual path connection; no call processing is required at transit nodes. Thus, the addition of new virtual channels to an existing virtual path involves minimal processing.
- **Enhanced network services:** The virtual path is used internal to the network but is also visible to the end user. Thus, the user may define closed user groups or closed networks of virtual channel bundles.

Figure 4.3 suggests in a general way the call establishment process using virtual channels and virtual paths. The process of setting up a virtual path connection is decoupled from the process of setting up an individual virtual channel connection:

- The virtual path control mechanisms include calculating routes, allocating capacity, and storing connection state information.
- To set up a virtual channel, there must first be a virtual path connection to the required destination node with sufficient available capacity to support the virtual channel, with the appropriate quality of service. A virtual channel is set up by storing the required state information (virtual channel/virtual path mapping).

The terminology of virtual paths and virtual channels used in the standards is a bit confusing and is summarized in Table 4.1. Whereas most of the network-layer protocols that we deal with in this book relate only to the user-network interface, the concepts of virtual path and virtual channel are defined with reference to both the user-network interface and the internal network operation.

Virtual Channel Connection Uses

The end points of a VCC may be end users, network entities, or an end user and a network entity. In all cases, cell sequence integrity is preserved within a VCC: that is, cells are delivered in the same order in which they are sent. Let us consider examples of the three uses of a VCC:

- **Between end users:** Can be used to carry end-to-end user data; can also be used to carry control signaling between end users, as explained later in this chapter. A VPC between end users provides them with an overall capacity; the VCC organization of the VPC is up to the two end users, provided that the set of VCCs does not exceed the VPC capacity.

TABLE 4.1 VIRTUAL PATH/VIRTUAL CHANNEL TERMINOLOGY

Virtual Channel (VC)	A generic term used to describe unidirectional transport of ATM cells associated by a common unique identifier value.
Virtual Channel Link	A means of unidirectional transport of ATM cells between a point where a VCI value is assigned and the point where that value is translated or terminated.
Virtual Channel Identifier (VCI)	A unique numerical tag that identifies a particular VC link for a given VPC.
Virtual Channel Connection (VCC)	A concatenation of VC links that extends between two points where ATM service users access the ATM layer. VCCs are provided for the purpose of user-user, user-network, or network-network information transfer. Cell sequence integrity is preserved for cells belonging to the same VCC.
Virtual Path	A generic term used to describe unidirectional transport of ATM cells belonging to virtual channels that are associated by a common unique identifier value.
Virtual Path Link	A group of VC links, identified by a common value of VPI, between a point where a VPI value is assigned and the point where that value is translated or terminated.
Virtual Path Identifier (VPI)	Identifies a particular VP link.
Virtual Path Connection (VPC)	A concatenation of VP links that extends between the point where the VCI values are assigned and the point where those values are translated or removed (i.e., extending the length of a bundle of VC links that share the same VPI). VPCs are provided for the purpose of user-user, user-network, or network-network information transfer.

- **Between an end user and a network entity:** Used for user-to-network control signaling, as discussed later. A user-to-network VPC can be used to aggregate traffic from an end user to a network exchange or network server.
- **Between two network entities:** Used for network traffic management and routing functions. A network-to-network VPC can be used to define a common route for the exchange of network management information.

Virtual Path/Virtual Channel Characteristics

ITU-T Recommendation I.150 lists the following as characteristics of virtual channel connections:

- **Quality of service:** A user of a VCC is provided with a QoS specified by parameters such as cell loss ratio (ratio of cells lost to cells transmitted) and cell delay variation.
- **Switched and semipermanent virtual channel connections:** A switched VCC is an on-demand connection, which requires call-control signaling for setup and tearing down. A semipermanent VCC is one that is of long duration and is set up by configuration or network management action.
- **Cell sequence integrity:** The sequence of transmitted cells within a VCC is preserved.
- **Traffic parameter negotiation and usage monitoring:** Traffic parameters can be negotiated between a user and the network for each VCC. The input of cells to the VCC is monitored by the network to ensure that the negotiated parameters are not violated.

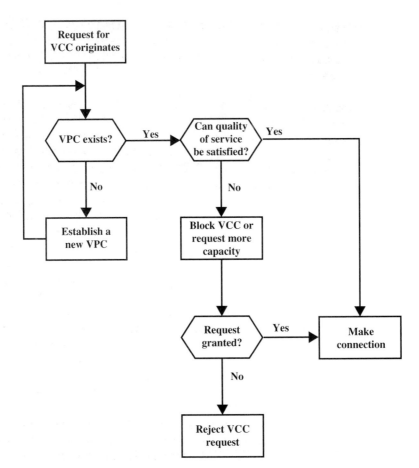

Figure 4.3 Call establishment using virtual paths.

The types of traffic parameters that can be negotiated include average rate, peak rate, burstiness, and peak duration. The network may use a number of strategies to deal with congestion and to manage existing and requested VCCs. At the crudest level, the network may simply deny new requests for VCCs to prevent congestion. Additionally, cells may be discarded if negotiated parameters are violated or if congestion becomes severe. In an extreme situation, existing connections might be terminated.

I.150 also lists characteristics of VPCs. The first four characteristics listed are identical to those for VCCs. That is, quality of service, switched and semipermanent VPCs, cell sequence integrity, and traffic parameter negotiation and usage monitoring are all also characteristics of a VPC. There are a number of reasons for this duplication. First, it provides some flexibility in how the network service manages the requirements placed on it. Second, the network must be concerned with the overall requirements for a VPC, and within a VPC may negotiate the establishment of virtual channels with given characteristics. Finally, once a VPC is set up, it is possible for the end users to negotiate the creation of new VCCs. The VPC characteristics impose a discipline on the choices that the end users may make.

In addition, a fifth characteristic is listed for VPCs:

- **Virtual channel identifier restriction within a VPC:** One or more virtual channel identifiers, or numbers, may not be available to the user of the VPC, but may be reserved for network use. Examples include VCCs used for network management.

Control Signaling

In ATM, a mechanism is needed for the establishment and release of VPCs and VCCs. The exchange of information involved in this process is referred to as control signaling, and it takes place on separate connections from those that are being managed.

For VCCs, I.150 specifies four methods for providing an establishment/release facility. One or a combination of these methods will be used in any particular network:

1. **Semipermanent VCCs** may be used for user-to-user exchange. In this case, no control signaling is required.
2. If there is no preestablished call control signaling channel, then one must be set up. For that purpose, a control signaling exchange must take place between the user and the network on some channel. Hence we need a permanent channel, probably of low data rate, that can be used to set up VCCs that can be used for call control. Such a channel is called a **metasignaling channel** because the channel is used to set up signaling channels.
3. The metasignaling channel can be used to set up a VCC between the user and the network for call control signaling. This **user-to-network signaling virtual channel** can then be used to set up VCCs to carry user data.
4. The metasignaling channel can also be used to set up a **user-to-user signaling virtual channel**. Such a channel must be set up within a preestablished VPC. It can then be used to allow the two end users, without network intervention, to establish and release user-to-user VCCs to carry user data.

For VPCs, three methods are defined in I.150:

1. A VPC can be established on a **semipermanent** basis by prior agreement. In this case, no control signaling is required.
2. VPC establishment/release may be **customer controlled**. In this case, the customer uses a signaling VCC to request the VPC from the network.
3. VPC establishment/release may be **network controlled**. In this case, the network establishes a VPC for its own convenience. The path may be network-to-network, user-to-network, or user-to-user.

4.3 ATM CELLS

The asynchronous transfer mode makes use of fixed-size cells consisting of a 5-octet header and a 48-octet information field. There are several advantages to the use of small, fixed-size cells. First, the use of small cells may reduce queuing delay for a high-priority cell, because it waits less if it arrives slightly behind a lower-priority cell that has gained access to a resource (e.g., the transmitter). Second, it appears that fixed-size cells can be switched more efficiently, which is important for the very high data rates of ATM. With fixed-size cells, it is easier to implement the switching mechanism in hardware.

Header Format

Figure 4.4a shows the cell header format at the user-network interface. Figure 4.4b shows the header format internal to the network. Internal to the network, the generic flow control field, which performs local functions, is not retained. Instead, the virtual path identifier field is expanded from 8 to 12 bits. This allows support for an expanded number of VPCs internal to the network, to include those supporting subscribers and those required for network management.

Because the **generic flow control (GFC) field** does not appear in the cell header internal to the network, it can be used for control of cell flow only at the local user-network interface. The details of its application are for further study. The field

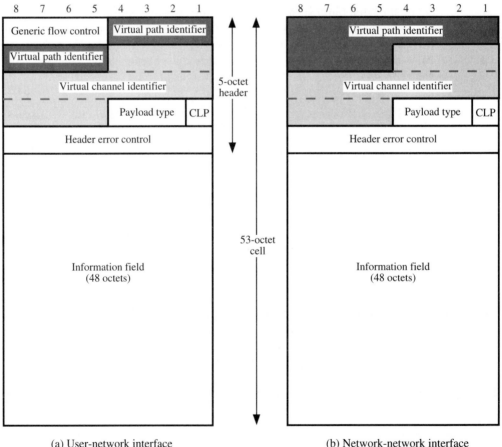

(a) User-network interface   (b) Network-network interface

Figure 4.4 ATM Cell Format.

TABLE 4.2 PAYLOAD TYPE (PT) FIELD CODING

PT Coding	Interpretation		
0 0 0	User data cell,	congestion not experienced,	SDU type = 0
0 0 1	User data cell,	congestion not experienced,	SDU type = 1
0 1 0	User data cell,	congestion experienced,	SDU type = 0
0 1 1	User data cell,	congestion experienced,	SDU type = 1
1 0 0	OAM segment associated cell		
1 0 1	OAM end-to-end associated cell		
1 1 0	Resource management cell		
1 1 1	Reserved for future function		

SDU = Service Data Unit. OAM = Operations, Administration, and Maintenance.

could be used to assist the customer in controlling the flow of traffic for different qualities of service. One candidate for the use of this field is a multiple-priority level indicator to control the flow of information in a service-dependent manner. In any case, the GFC mechanism is intended to alleviate short-term overload conditions in the network.

The **virtual path identifier** (VPI) constitutes a routing field for the network. It is 8 bits at the user-network interface and 12 bits at the network-network interface, allowing for more virtual paths to be supported within the network. The **virtual channel identifier** (VCI) is used for routing to and from the end user. Thus, it functions much as a service access point.

The **payload type** (PT) field indicates the type of information in the information field. Table 4.2 shows the interpretation of the PT bits. A value of 0 in the first bit indicates user information; that is, information from the next higher layer. In this case, the second bit indicates whether congestion has been experienced; the third bit, known as the service data unit (SDU) type bit[1], is a 1-bit field that can be used to discriminate two types of ATM SDUs associated with a connection. The term SDU refers to the 48-octet payload of the cell. The interpretation of this bit depends on context.

A value of 1 in the first bit of the payload type field indicates that this cell carries network management or maintenance information. This indication allows the insertion of network-management cells into a user's VCC without impacting the user's data. Thus, it can provide inband control information.

The **cell loss priority** (CLP) is used to provide guidance to the network in the event of congestion. A value of 0 indicates a cell of relatively higher priority, which should not be discarded unless no other alternative is available. A value of 1 indicates that this cell is subject to discard within the network. The user might employ this field so that extra cells (beyond the negotiated rate) may be inserted into the network, with a CLP of 1, and delivered to the destination if the network is not congested. The network may set this field to 1 for any data cell that is in violation of an agreement concerning traffic parameters between the user and the network. In this case, the switch that does the setting realizes that the cell exceeds the agreed traffic

---

[1] In ITU-T documents, this is referred to as the ATM-user-to-ATM-user (AAU) indication bit; the meaning is the same.

parameters but that the switch is capable of handling the cell. At a later point in the network, if congestion is encountered, this cell has been marked for discard in preference to cells that fall within agreed traffic limits.

Header Error Control

Each ATM cell includes an 8-bit header error control (HEC) field that is calculated based on the remaining 32 bits of the header. The polynomial used to generate the code is $X^8 + X^2 + X + 1$. In most existing protocols that include an error control field, such as HDLC and LAPB, the data that serve as input to the error code calculation are, in general, much longer than the size of the resulting error code. This allows for error detection. In the case of ATM, the input to the calculation is only 32 bits, compared to 8 bits for the code. The fact that the input is relatively short allows the code to be used not only for error detection but, in some cases, for actual error correction. This is because there is sufficient redundancy in the code to recover from certain error patterns.

Figure 4.5 depicts the operation of the HEC algorithm at the receiver. At initialization, the receiver's error correction algorithm is in the default mode for single-bit error correction. As each cell is received, the HEC calculation and comparison is performed. As long as no errors are detected, the receiver remains in error correction mode. When an error is detected, the receiver will correct the error if it is a single-bit error or will detect that a multibit error has occurred. In either case, the receiver now moves to detection mode. In this mode, no attempt is made to correct errors. The reason for this change is a recognition that a noise burst or other event might cause a sequence of errors, a condition for which the HEC is insufficient for error correction. The receiver remains in detection mode as long as errored cells are received. When a header is examined and found not to be in error, the receiver switches back to correction mode. The flowchart of Figure 4.6 shows the consequence of errors in the cell header.

The error protection function provides both recovery from single-bit header errors and a low probability of the delivery of cells with errored headers under bursty error conditions. The error characteristics of fiber-based transmission systems appear to be a mix of single-bit errors and relatively large burst errors. For some transmission systems, the error correction capability, which is more time-consuming, might not be invoked.

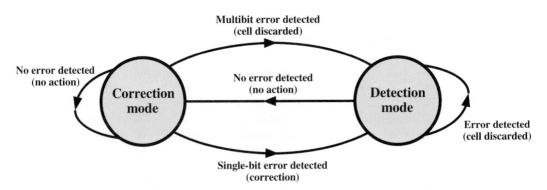

Figure 4.5   HEC operation at receiver.

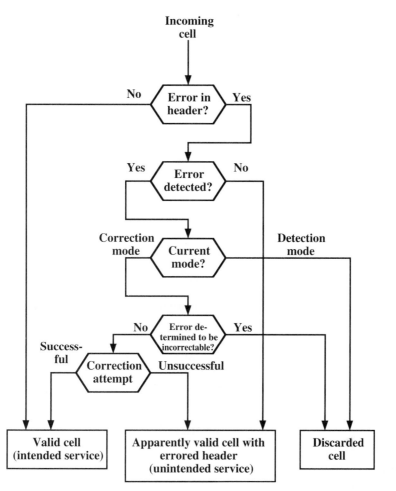

Figure 4.6 Effect of error in cell header.

Figure 4.7, based on one in ITU-T I.432, indicates how random bit errors impact the probability of occurrence of discarded cells and valid cells with errored headers when HEC is employed.

4.4 ATM SERVICE CATEGORIES

An ATM network is designed to be able to transfer many different types of traffic simultaneously, including real-time flows such as voice, video, and bursty TCP flows. Although each such traffic flow is handled as a stream of 53-octet cells traveling through a virtual channel, the way in which each data flow is handled within the network depends on the characteristics of the traffic flow and the requirements of the application. For example, real-time video traffic must be delivered within minimum variation in delay.

We examine the way in which an ATM network handles different types of traffic flows in Chapter 12. In this section, we summarize ATM service categories, which

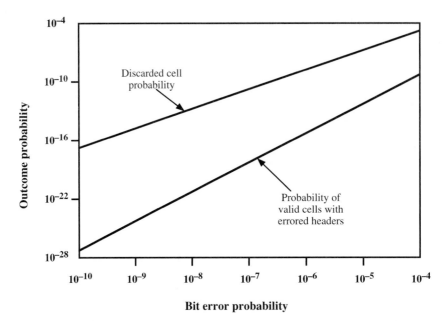

Figure 4.7 Impact of random bit errors on HEC performance.

are used by an end system to identify the type of service required. The following service categories have been defined by the ATM Forum:

- **Real-time service**
  - Constant bit rate (CBR)
  - Real-time variable bit rate (rt-VBR)
- **Non-real-time service**
  - Non-real-time variable bit rate (nrt-VBR)
  - Available bit rate (ABR)
  - Unspecified bit rate (UBR)

Real-time Services

The most important distinction among applications concerns the amount of delay and the variability of delay, referred to as jitter, that the application can tolerate. Real-time applications typically involve a flow of information to a user that is intended to reproduce that flow at a source. For example, a user expects a flow of audio or video information to be presented in a continuous, smooth fashion. A lack of continuity or excessive loss results in significant loss of quality. Applications that involve interaction between people have tight constraints on delay. Typically, any delay above a few hundred milliseconds becomes noticeable and annoying. Accordingly, the demands in the ATM network for switching and delivery of real-time data are high.

Constant Bit Rate

The CBR service is perhaps the simplest service to define. It is used by applications that require a fixed data rate that is continuously available during the connection lifetime and a relatively tight upper bound on transfer delay. CBR is commonly used for uncompressed audio and video information. Example of CBR applications include

- Videoconferencing
- Interactive audio (e.g., telephony)
- Audio/video distribution (e.g., television, distance learning, pay-per-view)
- Audio/video retrieval (e.g., video-on-demand, audio library).

Real-time Variable Bit Rate

The rt-VBR category is intended for time-sensitive applications; that is, those requiring tightly constrained delay and delay variation. The principal difference between applications appropriate for rt-VBR and those appropriate for CBR is that rt-VBR applications transmit at a rate that varies with time. Equivalently, an rt-VBR source can be characterized as somewhat bursty. For example, we shall see in Chapter 18 that the standard approach to video compression results in a sequence of image frames of varying sizes. Because real-time video requires a uniform frame transmission rate, the actual data rate varies.

The rt-VBR service allows the network more flexibility than CBR. The network is able to multiplex a number of connections statistically over the same dedicated capacity and still provide the required service to each connection.

Non-real-time Services

Non-real-time services are intended for applications that have bursty traffic characteristics and do not have tight constraints on delay and delay variation. Accordingly, the network has greater flexibility in handling such traffic flows and can make greater use of statistical multiplexing to increase network efficiency.

Non-real-time Variable Bit Rate

For some non-real-time applications, it is possible to characterize the expected traffic flow so that the network can provide substantially improved QoS in the areas of loss and delay. Such applications can use the nrt-VBR service. With this service, the end system specifies a peak cell rate, a sustainable or average cell rate, and a measure of how bursty or clumped the cells may be. With this information, the network can allocate resources to provide relatively low delay and minimal cell loss.

The nrt-VBR service can be used for data transfers that have critical response-time requirements. Examples include airline reservations, banking transactions, and process monitoring.

Unspecified Bit Rate

At any given time, a certain amount of the capacity of an ATM network is consumed in carrying CBR and the two types of VBR traffic. Additional capacity is available for one or both of the following reasons: (1) Not all of the total resources have been committed to CBR and VBR traffic, and (2) the bursty nature of VBR traffic means that at some times less than the committed capacity is being used. All of this unused capacity could be made available for the UBR service. This service is suitable for applications that can tolerate variable delays and some cell losses, which is typically true of TCP-based traffic. With UBR, cells are forwarded on a first-in-first-out (FIFO) basis using the capacity not consumed by other services; both delays and variable losses are possible. No initial commitment is made to a UBR source and no feedback concerning congestion is provided; this is referred to as a **best-effort service**. Examples of UBR applications include

- Text/data/image transfer, messaging, distribution, retrieval
- Remote terminal (e.g., telecommuting).

Available Bit Rate

Bursty applications that use a reliable end-to-end protocol such as TCP can detect congestion in a network by means of increased round-trip delays and packet discarding. This was discussed briefly in the previous chapter (e.g., see Figure 3.16) and is described in detail in Chapter 10. However, TCP has no mechanism for causing the resources within the network to be shared fairly among many TCP connections. Further, TCP does not minimize congestion as efficiently as is possible using explicit information from congested nodes within the network.

To improve the service provided to bursty sources that would otherwise use UBR, the ABR service has been defined. An application using ABR specifies a peak cell rate (PCR) that it will use and a minimum cell rate (MCR) that it requires. The network allocates resources so that all ABR applications receive at least their MCR capacity. Any unused capacity is then shared in a fair and controlled fashion among all ABR sources. The ABR mechanism uses explicit feedback to sources to assure that capacity is fairly allocated. Any capacity not used by ABR sources remains available for UBR traffic.

An example of an application using ABR is LAN interconnection. In this case, the end systems attached to the ATM network are routers.

Figure 4.8 suggests how a network allocates resources during a steady-state period of time (no additions or deletions of virtual channels).

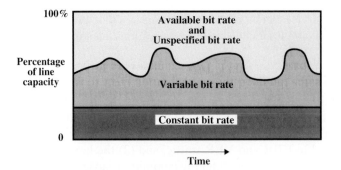

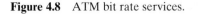

Figure 4.8   ATM bit rate services.

4.5 ATM ADAPTATION LAYER

The use of ATM creates the need for an adaptation layer to support information transfer protocols not based on ATM. Two examples are PCM (pulse code modulation) voice and LAPF. PCM voice is an application that produces a stream of bits from a voice signal. To employ this application over ATM, it is necessary to assemble PCM bits into cells for transmission and to read them out on reception in such a way as to produce a smooth, constant flow of bits to the receiver. LAPF is the standard data link control protocol for frame relay. In a mixed environment, in which frame relay networks interconnect with ATM networks, a convenient way of integrating the two is to map LAPF frames into ATM cells; this will usually mean segmenting one LAPF frame into a number of cells on transmission and reassembling the frame from cells on reception. By allowing the use of LAPF over ATM, all of the existing frame relay applications and control-signaling protocols can be used on an ATM network.

AAL Services

ITU-T I.362 lists the following general examples of services provided by AAL:

- Handling of transmission errors
- Segmentation and reassembly, to enable larger blocks of data to be carried in the information field of ATM cells
- Handling of lost and misinserted cell conditions
- Flow control and timing control.

To minimize the number of different AAL protocols that must be specified to meet a variety of needs, ITU-T has defined four classes of service that cover a broad range of requirements (Table 4.3). The classification is based on whether a timing relationship must be maintained between source and destination, whether the application requires a constant bit rate, and whether the transfer is connection oriented or connectionless. An example of a class A service is circuit emulation. In this case, a constant bit rate, which requires the maintenance of a timing relation, is used and the transfer is connection oriented. An example of a class B service is variable-bit-rate video, such as might be used in a videoconference. Here, the application is connection oriented and timing is important, but the bit rate varies depending on the amount of activity in the scene. Classes C and D correspond to data transfer applications. In both cases, the bit rate may vary and no particular timing relationship is required; differences in data rate are handled by the end systems using buffers. The data transfer may be either connection oriented (class C) or connectionless (class D).

AAL Protocols

To support these various classes of service, a set of protocols at the AAL level have been defined. The AAL layer is organized in two logical sublayers: the convergence sublayer (CS) and the segmentation and reassembly sublayer (SAR). The convergence sublayer provides the functions needed to support specific applications using AAL. Each AAL user attaches to AAL at a service access point (SAP), which is simply the address of the application. This sublayer is thus service dependent.

TABLE 4.3   SERVICE CLASSIFICATION FOR AAL

	Class A	Class B	Class C	Class D
Timing relation between source and destination	Required		Not required	
Bit rate	Constant	Variable		
Connection mode	Connection oriented			Connectionless
AAL Protocol	Type 1	Type 2	Type 3/4	
			Type 5	

The SAR sublayer is responsible for packaging information received from CS into cells for transmission and unpacking the information at the other end. As we have seen, at the ATM layer, each cell consists of a 5-octet header and a 48-octet information field. Thus, SAR must pack any SAR headers and trailers plus CS information into 48-octet blocks.

Initially, ITU-T defined one protocol type for each class of service, named Type 1 through Type 4. Actually, each protocol type consists of two protocols, one at the CS sublayer and one at the SAR sublayer. More recently, types 3 and 4 were merged into a Type 3/4, and a new type, Type 5, was defined. Table 4.3 shows which services are supported by which types, and Table 4.4 lists the currently defined functional details of the four types. In all of these cases, a block of data from a higher layer is encapsulated into a protocol data unit (PDU) at the CS sublayer. In fact, this sublayer is referred to as the common part convergence sublayer (CPCS), leaving open the possibility that additional, specialized functions may be performed at the CS level. The CPCS PDU is then passed to the SAR sublayer, where it is broken up into payload blocks. Each payload block can fit into a SAR-PDU, which has a total length of 48 octets. Each 48-octet SAR-PDU fits into a single ATM cell.

Figure 4.9 shows the formats of the PDUs at the SAR level except for Type 2, which has not yet been defined.

AAL Type 1

For Type 1 operation, we are dealing with a constant bit rate source. In this case, the only responsibility of the SAR protocol is to pack the bits into cells for transmission and unpack them at reception. Each block is accompanied by a sequence number so that errored PDUs can be tracked. The sequence number protection field is an error code for error detection and possibly correction on the sequence number field.

No CS PDU has been defined for Type 1. The functions of the CS sublayer for Type 1 primarily have to do with clocking and synchronization, and a separate CS header is not needed.

AAL Type 2

The remainder of the protocol types (2, 3/4, and 5) deal with variable-bit rate information. Type 2 is intended for analog applications, such as video and audio,

TABLE 4.4 ATM Adaptation Layer Protocol Types

	Services Provided	Overall Functions	SAR Functions	CS Functions
Type 1	• Transfer of SDUs with constant bit rate (CBR) • Transfer of timing information between source and destination • Transfer of structure information between source and destination • Indication of lost or errored information not recovered by type 1	• Segmentation and reassembly • Handling of cell delay variation • Handling of cell payload assembly delay • Handling of lost and misinserted cells • Source clock frequency recovery at destination • Recovery of the source data structure at the receiver • Monitoring and handling of PCI bit errors • Monitoring of user information for bit errors and possible corrective action	• Mapping between CS-PDU and SAR-PDU • Indication of existence of CS function • Sequence numbering • Error protection	• Handling of cell delay variation • Handling of lost and misinserted cells • For some services, clock recovery at the receiver • Transfer of structure information • Forward error correction for high-quality video and audio • Reporting of end-to-end performance status
Type 2	• Transfer of SDUs with variable bit rate (VBR) • Transfer of timing information between source and destination • Indication of lost or errored information not recovered by type 2	• Segmentation and reassembly • Handling of cell delay variation • Handling of lost and misinserted cells • Source clock frequency recovery at destination • Recovery of the source data structure at the receiver • Monitoring and handling of header and trailer bit errors • Monitoring of user information for bit errors and possible corrective action	For further study	For further study
Type 3/4	• Message mode service • Streaming mode service • Assured operation • Nonassured operation		• Segmentation and reassembly • Error detection • Sequence integrity • Multiplexing	• Error detection and handling • Indication of buffer allocation size
Type 5	• Message mode service • Streaming mode service • Assured operation • Nonassured operation		• Segmentation and reassembly • Handling of congestion information • Handling of loss priority information	• Error detection and handling • Padding • Handling of congestion information • Handling of loss priority information

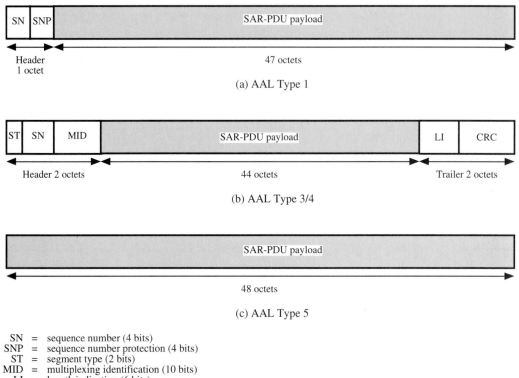

SN = sequence number (4 bits)
SNP = sequence number protection (4 bits)
ST = segment type (2 bits)
MID = multiplexing identification (10 bits)
LI = length indication (6 bits)
CRC = cyclic redundancy check (10 bits)

Figure 4.9   Segmentation and reassembly (SAR) protocol data units (PDUs).

that require timing information but do not require a constant bit rate. An initial specification for the Type 2 protocols (SAR and CS) has been withdrawn, and the current version of I.363 simply lists the services and functions shown in Table 4.4.

AAL Type 3/4

The initial specifications of AAL Type 3 and AAL Type 4 were very similar in terms of PDU format and functionality. Accordingly, it was decided within ITU-T to combine the two into a single protocol specification at the SAR and CS sub-layers, known as Type 3/4.

The types of service provided by AAL Type 3/4 can be characterized along two dimensions:

1. The service may be connectionless or connection oriented. In the former case, each block of data presented to the SAR layer (SAR service data unit, or SDU) is treated independently. In the latter case, it is possible to define multiple SAR logical connections over a single ATM connection.

2. The service may be message mode or streaming mode. Message mode service transfers framed data. Thus, any of the OSI-related protocols and applications would fit into this category. In particular, LAPD or frame relay would be message mode. A single block of data from the layer above AAL is transferred

in one or more cells. Streaming-mode service supports the transfer of low-speed continuous data with low delay requirements. The data are presented to AAL in fixed-size blocks that may be as small as one octet. One block is transferred per cell.

The Type 3/4 AAL provides its data transfer service by accepting blocks of data from the next higher layer and transmitting each to a destination AAL user. Since the ATM layer limits data transfer to a cell payload of 48 octets, the AAL layer must provide, at minimum, a segmentation and reassembly function.

The approach taken by Type 3/4 AAL is depicted in Figure 4.10. A block of data from a higher layer, such as a PDU, is encapsulated into a PDU at the CPCS sublayer. The CPCS PDU is then passed to the SAR sublayer, where it is broken up into 44-octet payload blocks. Each payload block can fit into a SAR-PDU, which includes a header and a trailer for a total length of 48 octets. Each 48-octet SAR-PDU fits into a single ATM cell.

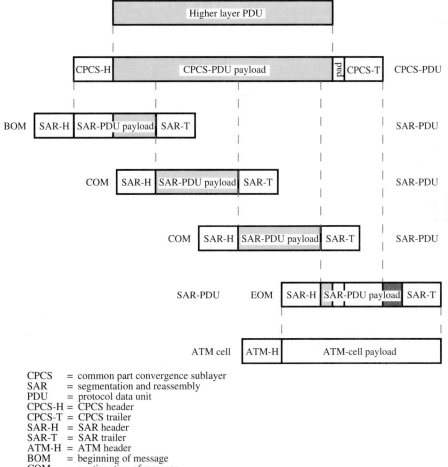

CPCS   = common part convergence sublayer
SAR   = segmentation and reassembly
PDU   = protocol data unit
CPCS-H = CPCS header
CPCS-T = CPCS trailer
SAR-H   = SAR header
SAR-T   = SAR trailer
ATM-H   = ATM header
BOM   = beginning of message
COM   = continuation of message
EOM   = end of message

Figure 4.10 Example of AAL 3/4 transmission.

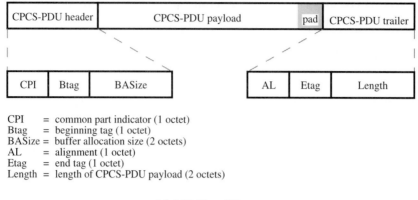

CPI   = common part indicator (1 octet)
Btag   = beginning tag (1 octet)
BASize = buffer allocation size (2 octets)
AL   = alignment (1 octet)
Etag   = end tag (1 octet)
Length = length of CPCS-PDU payload (2 octets)

(a) AAL Type 3/4

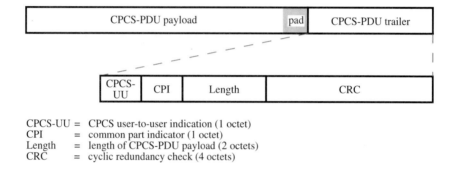

CPCS-UU = CPCS user-to-user indication (1 octet)
CPI   = common part indicator (1 octet)
Length = length of CPCS-PDU payload (2 octets)
CRC   = cyclic redundancy check (4 octets)

(b) AAL Type 5

Figure 4.11   CPCS PDUs.

To understand the functioning of the two sublayers within AAL Type 3/4, let us look at the respective PDUs. The CPCS-PDU is shown in Figure 4.11a. The header consists of three fields:

- **Common part indicator (1 octet):** Indicates the interpretation of the remaining fields in the CPCS-PDU header. Currently, only one interpretation is defined.
- **Beginning tag (1 octet):** A number associated with a particular CPCS-PDU. The same value appears in the Btag field in the header and the Etag field in the trailer. The sender changes the value for each successive CPCS-PDU, enabling the receiver to associate correctly the header and trailer of each CPCS-PDU.
- **Buffer allocation size (2 octets):** Indicates to the receiving peer entity the maximum buffer size required for reassembly of the CPCS-SDU (service data unit). For message mode, the value is equal to the CPCS-PDU payload length. For streaming mode, the value is greater than or equal to the CPCS-PDU payload length.

The payload from the next higher layer is padded out so that the trailer begins on a 32-bit boundary. The CPCS-PDU trailer contains these fields:

- **Alignment (1 octet):** A filler octet whose only purpose is to make the length of the CPCS-PDU equal to 32 bits.
- **End tag (1 octet):** Used with the Btag field in the header.
- **Length (2 octets):** Length of the CPCS-PDU payload field.

Thus, the purpose of the CPCS layer is to alert the receiver that a block of data is coming in segments and that buffer space must be allocated for that reassembly. This enables the receiving CPCS function to verify the correct reception of the entire CPCS PDU.

Figure 4.9b shows the format for the Type 3/4 SAR PDU. Information from the next higher layer, the CS, arrives in blocks referred to as SAR SDUs. Each SDU is transmitted in one or more SAR PDUs. Each SAR PDU, in turn, is transmitted in a single ATM cell. The SAR-PDU header fields are used for the process of segmenting SDUs on transmission and reassembling them on reception:

- **Segment type:** There are four types of SAR-PDUs. A single sequence message (SSM) contains an entire SAR-SDU. If the SAR-SDU is segmented into two or more SAR-PDUs, the first SAR-PDU is the beginning of message (BOM), the last SAR-PDU is the end of message (EOM), and any intermediate SAR-PDUs are continuation of message (COM).
- **Sequence number:** Used in reassembling an SAR-SDU to verify that all of the SAR-PDUs have been received and concatenated properly. A value of the sequence number is set in the BOM and incremented for each successive COM and the EOM for a single SAR-SDU.
- **Message identifier:** This is a unique identifier associated with the set of SAR-PDUs that carry a single SAR-SDU. Again, this number is needed to ensure proper reassembly.

The SAR-PDU trailer contains the following fields:

- **Length indication:** Indicates the number of octets from the SAR-SDU that occupy the segmentation unit of the SAR-PDU. The number has a value between 4 and 44 octets, in multiples of 4. The value will always be 44 for BOM and COM SAR-PDUs. It is a lesser number in an SSM if the SAR-SDU is less than 44 octets in length. It is a lesser number in an EOM if the length of the SAR-SDU is not an integer multiple of 44 octets in length, necessitating the use of a partially filled EOM. In that case, the remainder of the SAR-PDU payload is padded.
- **CRC:** This is a 10-bit cyclic redundancy check (CRC) on the entire SAR-PDU.

A distinctive feature of AAL 3/4 is that it can multiplex different streams of data on the same virtual ATM connection (VCI/VPI). For the connection-oriented service, each logical connection between AAL users is assigned a unique message identifier (MID) value. Thus, the cell traffic from up to 2^{10} different AAL connections can be multiplexed and interleaved over a single ATM connection. For the connectionless service, the MID field can be used to communicate a unique identifier associated with each connectionless user and, again, traffic from multiple AAL users may be multiplexed.

AAL Type 5

AAL Type 5 is becoming increasingly popular, especially in ATM LAN applications. This protocol was introduced to provide a streamlined transport facility for higher-layer protocols that are connection oriented. If it is assumed that the higher layer takes care of connection management and that the ATM layer produces minimal errors, then most of the fields in the SAR and CPCS PDUs are not necessary. For example, with connection-oriented service, the MID field is not necessary. This field is used in AAL 3/4 to multiplex different streams of data on the same virtual ATM connection (VCI/VPI). In AAL 5, it is assumed that higher-layer software takes care of such multiplexing.

Type 5 was introduced to

- Reduce protocol processing overhead
- Reduce transmission overhead
- Ensure adaptability to existing transport protocols.

Figures 4.9c and 4.11b show the SAR-PDU and CPCS-PDU formats for Type 5. Compared to Type 3/4, we have the following amounts of overhead:

Type 3/4	Type 5
8 octets per AAL-SDU	8 octets per AAL-SDU
4 octets per ATM cell	0 octets per ATM cell

To understand the operation of Type 5, let us begin with the CPCS level. The CPCS-PDU (Figure 4.11b) includes a trailer with the following fields:

- **CPCS user-to-user indication (1 octet):** Used to transfer user-to-user information transparently.
- **Common part indicator (1 octet):** Indicates the interpretation of the remaining fields in the CPCS-PDU trailer. Currently, only one interpretation is defined.
- **Length (2 octets):** Length of the CPCS-PDU payload field.
- **Cyclic redundancy check (4 octets):** Used to detect bit errors in the CPCS-PDU.

Note that the Buffer Allocation Size facility has been eliminated. If it is felt necessary for the receiver to preallocate a buffer to do reassembly, this information must be passed at a higher layer. In fact, many higher-layer protocols set or negotiate a maximum PDU size; this information can be used by the receiver to allocate buffers. A 32-bit CRC protects the entire CPCS-PDU, whereas for AAL Type 3/4, a 10-bit CRC is provided for each SAR-PDU. The Type 5 CRC provides strong protection against bit errors. In addition, [WANG92] shows that the 32-bit CRC provides robust detection of cell misordering, a fault condition that might be possible under network failure conditions.

The payload from the next higher layer is padded out so that the entire CPCS-PDU is a multiple of 48 octets. The SAR-PDU consists simply of 48 octets of payload carrying a portion of the CPCS-PDU. The lack of protocol overhead has several implications:

1. Because there is no sequence number, the receiver must assume that all SAR-PDUs arrive in the proper order for reassembly. The CRC field in the CPCS-PDU is intended to verify that.

2. The lack of MID field means that it is not possible to interleave cells from different CPCS-PDUs. Therefore, each successive SAR-PDU carries a portion of the current CPCS-PDU or the first block of the next CPCS-PDU. To distinguish between these two cases, the ATM-SDU type bit in the payload type field of the ATM cell header is used (Figure 4.4). A CPCS-PDU consists of zero or more consecutive SAR-PDUs with the SDU type bit set to 0 followed immediately by an SAR-PDU with the SDU type bit set to 1.

3. The lack of a length indication field means that there is no way for the SAR entity to distinguish between CPCS-PDU octets and filler in the last SAR-PDU. Therefore, there is no way for the SAR entity to find the CPCS-PDU trailer in the last SAR-PDU. To avoid this situation, it is required that the CPCS-PDU payload be padded out so that the last bit of the CPCS trailer occurs as the last bit of the final SAR-PDU.

Figure 4.12 shows an example of AAL 5 transmission. The CPCS-PDU, including padding and trailer, is divided into 48-octet blocks. Each block is transmitted in a single ATM cell.

4.6 RECOMMENDED READING

[GORA95], [MCDY95], [HAND94], and [PRYC96] provide in-depth coverage of ATM. The virtual path/virtual channel approach of ATM is examined in [SATO90], [SATO91], and [BURG91].

[GARR96] provides a rationale for the ATM service categories and discusses the traffic management implications of each. [ARMI93] and [SUZU94] discuss AAL and compare types 3/4 and 5.

ARMI93   Armitage, G., and Adams, K. "Packet Reassembly During Cell Loss." *IEEE Network*, September 1993.

BURG91   Burg, J., and Dorman, D. "Broadband ISDN Resource Management: The Role of Virtual Paths." *IEEE Communications Magazine*, September 1991.

GARR96   Garrett, M. "A Service Architecture for ATM: From Applications to Scheduling." *IEEE Network*, May/June 1996.

GORA95   Goralski, W. *Introduction to ATM Networking.* New York: McGraw-Hill, 1995.

HAND94   Handel, R., Huber, N., and Schroder, S. *ATM Networks: Concepts, Protocols, Applications.* Reading, MA: Addison-Wesley, 1994.

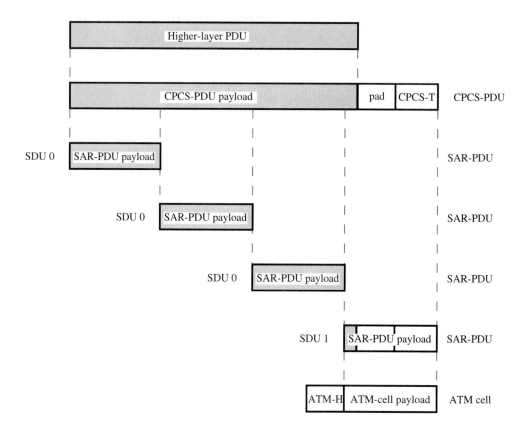

CPCS	= common part convergence sublayer
SAR	= segmentation and reassembly
PDU	= protocol data unit
CPCS-T	= CPCS trailer
ATM-H	= ATM header
SDU	= service data unit type bit

Figure 4.12 Example of AAL 5 transmission.

MCDY95 McDysan, D., and Spohn, D. *ATM: Theory and Application.* New York: McGraw-Hill, 1995.

PRYC96 Prycker, M. *Asynchronous Transfer Mode: Solutions for Broadband ISDN.* New York: Ellis Horwood, 1996.

SATO90 Sato, K., Ohta, S., and Tokizawa, I. "Broad-band ATM Network Architecture Based on Virtual Paths." *IEEE Transactions on Communications,* August 1990.

SATO91 Sato, K., Ueda, H., and Yoshikai, M. "The Role of Virtual Path Crossconnection." *IEEE LTS,* August 1991.

SUZU94 Suzuki, T. "ATM Adaptation Layer Protocol." *IEEE Communications Magazine,* April 1994.

Recommended Web sites:

- http://www.atmforum.com: The Web site of the ATM Forum, which is leading the effort to expand the functionality of ATM networks.

- http://cell-relay.indiana.edu/cell-relay: Contains archives of the cell-relay mailing list, links to numerous ATM-related documents, and links to many ATM-related Web sites.

4.7 PROBLEMS

4.1 One method of transmitting ATM cells is as a continuous stream of cells, with no framing imposed; therefore, the transmission is simply a stream of bits, with all bits being part of cells. Because there is no external frame, some other form of synchronization is needed. This can be achieved using the HEC function. The requirement is to assure that the receiver knows the beginning and ending cell boundaries and does not drift with respect to the sender. Draw a state diagram for the use of the HEC to achieve cell synchronization, and explain its functionality.

4.2 Although ATM does not include any end-to-end error detection and control functions on the user data, it is provided with an HEC field to detect and correct header errors. Let us consider the value of this feature. Suppose that the bit error rate of the transmission system is B. If errors are uniformly distributed, then the probability of an error in the header is

$$\frac{h}{h+1} \times B$$

and the probability of error in the data field is

$$\frac{i}{h+i} \times B$$

where h is the number of bits in the header and i is the number of bits in the data field.

a. Suppose that errors in the header are not detected and not corrected. In that case, a header error may result in a misrouting of the cell to the wrong destination; therefore, i bits will arrive at an incorrect destination, and i bits will not arrive at the correct destination. What is the overall bit error rate $B1$? Find an expression for the multiplication effect on the bit error rate: $M1 = B1/B$.

b. Now suppose that header errors are detected but not corrected. In that case, i bits will not arrive at the correct destination. What is the overall bit error rate $B2$? Find an expression for the multiplication effect on the bit error rate: $M2 = B2/B$.

c. Now suppose that header errors are detected and corrected. What is the overall bit error rate $B3$? Find an expression for the multiplication effect on the bit error rate: $M3 = B3/B$.

d. Plot $M1$, $M2$, and $M3$ as a function of header length for $i = 48 \times 8 = 384$ bits. Comment on the results.

4.3 One key design decision for ATM was whether to use fixed- or variable-length cells. Let us consider this decision from the point of view of efficiency. We can define transmission efficiency as

$$N = \frac{\text{Number of information octets}}{\text{Number of information octets} + \text{Number of overhead octets}}$$

a. Consider the use of fixed-length packets. In this case the overhead consists of the header octets. Define

L = Data field size of the cell in octets

H = Header size of the cell in octets

X = Number of information octets to be transmitted as a single message

Derive an expression for N. *Hint*: The expression will need to use the operator $\lceil \cdot \rceil$, where $\lceil Y \rceil$ = the smallest integer greater than or equal to Y.

b. If cells have variable length, then overhead is determined by the header, plus the flags to delimit the cells or an additional length field in the header. Let Hv = additional overhead octets required to enable the use of variable-length cells. Derive an expression for N in terms of X, H, and Hv.

c. Let $L = 48$, $H = 5$, and $Hv = 2$. Plot N versus message size for fixed- and variable-length cells. Comment on the results.

4.4 Another key design decision for ATM is the size of the data field for fixed-size cells. Let us consider this decision from the point of view of efficiency and delay.

a. Assume that an extended transmission takes place so that all cells are completely filled. Derive an expression for the efficiency N as a function of H and L.

b. Packetization delay is the delay introduced into a transmission stream by the need to buffer bits until an entire packet is filled before transmission. Derive an expression for this delay as a function of L and the data rate R of the source.

c. Common data rates for voice coding are 32 kbps and 64 kbps. Plot packetization delay as a function of L for these two data rates; use a left-hand y-axis with a maximum value of 2 ms. On the same graph, plot transmission efficiency as a function of L; use a right-hand y-axis with a maximum value of 100%. Comment on the results.

4.5 Suppose that AAL 3/4 is being used and that the receiver is in an idle state (no incoming cells). Then a block of user data is transmitted as a sequence of SAR-PDUs.

a. Suppose that the BOM SAR-PDU is lost. What happens at the receiving end?

b. Suppose that one of the COM SAR-PDUs is lost. What happens at the receiving end?

c. Suppose that 16 consecutive COM SAR-PDUs are lost. What happens at the receiving end?

d. Suppose that a multiple of 16 consecutive COM SAR-PDUs are lost. What happens at the receiving end?

4.6 Again using AAL 3/4, suppose that the receiver is in an idle state and that two blocks of user data are transmitted as two separate sequences of SAR-PDUs.

a. Suppose that the EOM SAR-PDU of the first sequence is lost. What happens at the receiving end?

b. Suppose that the EOM SAR-PDU of the first sequence and the BOM SAR-PDU of the second sequence are both lost. What happens at the receiving end?

4.7 Suppose that AAL 5 is being used and that the receiver is in an idle state (no incoming cells). Then a block of user data is transmitted as a sequence of SAR-PDUs.

a. Suppose that a single bit error in one of the SAR-PDUs occurs. What happens at the receiving end?

b. Suppose that one of the cells with SDU type bit = 0 is lost. What happens at the receiving end?

c. Suppose that one of the cells with SDU type bit = 1 is lost. What happens at the receiving end?

CHAPTER 5

HIGH-SPEED LANS

The whole of this operation is described in minute detail in the official British Naval History, and should be studied with its excellent charts by those who are interested in its technical aspect. So complicated is the full story that the lay reader cannot see the wood for the trees. I have endeavored to render intelligible the broad effects.

—The World Crisis, **Winston Churchill**

After a decade or more of gradual refinement and evolution in LAN products, recent years have seen rapid changes in the technology, design, and commercial applications for LANs. A major feature of this evolution is the introduction of a variety of new schemes for high-speed local networking. Although the focus of this book is on high-speed IP-based internets and ATM networks, it is useful to have some feel for the type of demand created by high-speed LANs on both internets and ATM networks.

To keep pace with the changing local networking needs of business, a number of approaches to high-speed LAN design have become commercial products. The most important of these are the following:

- **Fast Ethernet and Gigabit Ethernet:** The extension of 10-Mbps CSMA/CD (carrier sense multiple access with collision detection) to higher speeds is a logical strategy because it tends to preserve the investment in existing systems.
- **ATM LAN:** The extension of ATM from wide area networking into the LAN arena is attractive because of the ease of interconnection of ATM LANs and WANs.

TABLE 5.1 CHARACTERISTICS OF SOME HIGH-SPEED LANS

	Fast Ethernet	Gigabit Ethernet	ATM LAN
Data Rate	100 Mbps	1 Gbps	25 Mbps–1.2 Gpbs
Transmission Media	UTP, STP optical fiber	Optical fiber	UTP, STP, optical fiber
Access Method	CSMA/CD	CSMA/CD	Switched
Supporting Standard	IEEE 802.3	IEEE 802.3	ATM Forum

UTP = unshielded twisted pair, STP = shielded twisted pair.

Table 5.1 lists some of the characteristics of these approaches. The remainder of this chapter fills in some of the details.

5.1 FAST ETHERNET AND GIGABIT ETHERNET

The most widely used high-speed LANs today are based on Ethernet and were developed by the IEEE 802.3 standards committee. A family of 100-Mbps LANs known as Fast Ethernet currently dominate the high-speed LAN market. A more recent entry is Gigabit Ethernet. Before looking at these high-speed LANs, we provide a brief overview of the original 10-Mbps Ethernet and introduce the concept of switched LANs.

Classical Ethernet

Ethernet was originally developed by Xerox and subsequently used as the basis for a family of LAN standards by the IEEE 802.3 committee. Classical Ethernet operates at 10 Mbps over a bus topology LAN using the CSMA/CD medium access control protocol. In this subsection, we introduce the concepts of bus LANs and CSMA/CD operation.

Bus Topology LAN

In a bus topology LAN, all stations attach, through appropriate hardware interfacing known as a tap, directly to a linear transmission medium, or bus. Full-duplex operation between the station and the tap allows data to be transmitted onto the bus and received from the bus. A transmission from any station propagates the length of the medium in both directions and can be received by all other stations. At each end of the bus is a terminator, which absorbs any signal, removing it from the bus.

Two problems present themselves in this arrangement. First, because a transmission from any one station can be received by all other stations, there needs to be some way of indicating for whom the transmission is intended. Second, a mechanism is needed to regulate transmission. To see the reason for this, consider that if two stations on the bus attempt to transmit at the same time, their signals will overlap and become garbled. Or consider that one station decides to transmit continuously for a long period of time, blocking the access of other users.

To solve these problems, stations transmit data in small blocks, known as frames. Each frame consists of a portion of the data that a station wishes to transmit, plus a frame header that contains control information. Each station on the bus

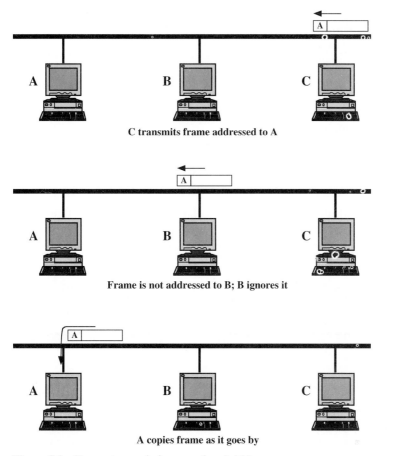

C transmits frame addressed to A

Frame is not addressed to B; B ignores it

A copies frame as it goes by

Figure 5.1   Frame transmission on a bus LAN.

is assigned a unique address, or identifier, and the destination address for a frame is included in its header.

Figure 5.1 illustrates the scheme. In this example, station C wishes to transmit a frame of data to A. The frame header includes A's address. As the frame propagates along the bus, it passes B. B observes the address and ignores the frame. A, on the other hand, sees that the frame is addressed to itself and therefore copies the data from the frame as it goes by.

So the frame structure solves the first problem mentioned previously: It provides a mechanism for indicating the intended recipient of data. It also provides the basic tool for solving the second problem, the regulation of access. In particular, the stations take turns sending frames in some cooperative fashion, as explained in the next subsection.

CSMA/CD

The simplest form of medium access control for a bus LAN is CSMA/CD. With CSMA/CD, a station wishing to transmit first listens to the medium to determine if another transmission is in progress (carrier sense). If the medium is idle, the station may transmit. It may happen that two or more stations attempt to transmit at about the same time. If this happens, there will be a collision; the data from both transmissions will be garbled and not received successfully. Thus, a procedure is needed that specifies what a station should do if the medium is found busy and what it should do if a collision occurs:

1. If the medium is idle, transmit.
2. If the medium is busy, continue to listen until the channel is idle, and then transmit immediately.
3. If a collision is detected during transmission, immediately cease transmitting.
4. After a collision, wait a random amount of time, and then attempt to transmit again (repeat from step 1).

Figure 5.2 illustrates the technique. The upper part of the figure shows a bus LAN layout. The remainder of the figure depicts activity on the bus at four succes-

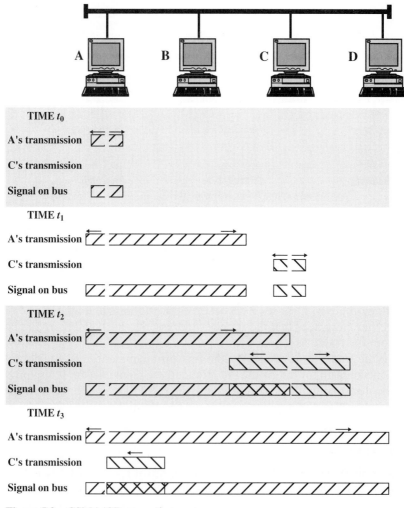

Figure 5.2 CSMA/CD operation.

sive instants in time. At time t_0, station A begins transmitting a packet addressed to D. At t_1, both B and C are ready to transmit. B senses a transmission and so defers. C, however, is still unaware of A's transmission and begins its own transmission. When A's transmission reaches C, at t_2, C detects the collision and ceases transmission. The effect of the collision propagates back to A, where it is detected some time later, t_3, at which time A ceases transmission.

To maintain stability, the amount of delay employed in step 4 is determined by a technique known as **binary exponential backoff**. A station will attempt to transmit repeatedly in the face of repeated collisions, but after each collision, the mean value of the random delay is doubled. After 16 unsuccessful attempts, the station gives up and reports an error. Thus, as congestion increases, stations back off by larger and larger amounts to reduce the probability of collision.

The advantage of CSMA/CD is its simplicity. It is easy to implement the logic required for this protocol. Furthermore, there is little to go wrong in the execution of the protocol. For example, if for some reason a station fails to detect a collision, the worst that can happen is that it continues to transmit its frame, wasting some time on the medium. Once the transmission is over, the algorithm continues to function as before.

IEEE 802.3 Medium Options at 10 Mbps

The IEEE 802.3 committee has defined a number of alternative physical configurations. This is both good and bad. On the good side, the standard has been responsive to evolving technology. On the bad side, the customer, not to mention the potential vendor, is faced with a bewildering array of options. However, the committee has been at pains to ensure that the various options can be easily integrated into a configuration that satisfies a variety of needs. Thus, the user that has a complex set of requirements may find the flexibility and variety of the 802.3 standard to be an asset.

To distinguish the various implementations that are available, the committee has developed a concise notation:

`<data rate in Mbps> <signaling method> <maximum segment length in hundreds of meters>`

In this subsection, we consider the two most important options that operate at 10 Mbps, the rate of the original commercial Ethernet; higher-speed options are discussed in later subsections. The alternatives are as follows:

- 10BASE5
- 10BASE-T

Note that 10BASE-T does not quite follow the notation: "T" stands for twisted pair.

10BASE5 Medium Specification

10BASE5 is the original 802.3 medium specification and is based directly on Ethernet. 10BASE5 specifies the use of 50- Ω coaxial cable bus and uses Manchester digital signaling[1]. The maximum length of a cable segment is set at 500 m. The

---

[1] This is a form of digital signaling that guarantees at least one signal transition during each bit time.

length of the network can be extended by the use of repeaters. A repeater is transparent to the link level; as it does no buffering, it does not isolate one segment from another. So, for example, if two stations on different segments attempt to transmit at the same time, their transmissions will collide. To avoid looping, only one path of segments and repeaters is allowed between any two stations. The standard allows a maximum of four repeaters in the path between any two stations, extending the effective length of the medium to 2.5 km.

10BASE-T Medium Specification

By sacrificing some distance, it is possible to develop a 10-Mbps LAN using the unshielded twisted-pair medium. Such wire is often found prewired in office buildings as excess telephone cable and can be used for LANs. Such an approach is specified in the 10BASE-T specification. The 10BASE-T specification defines a star-shaped topology. A simple system consists of a number of stations connected to a central point, referred to as a multiport repeater, via two twisted pairs. The central point accepts input on any one line and repeats it on all of the other lines.

Stations attach to the multiport repeater via a point-to-point link. Ordinarily, the link consists of two unshielded twisted pairs. Because of the high data rate and the poor transmission qualities of unshielded twisted pair, the length of a link is limited to 100 m. As an alternative, an optical fiber link may be used. In this case, the maximum length is 500 m.

In the simplest 10BASE-T arrangement, the central element of the star is an active element, referred to as the **hub**. Each station is connected to the hub by two twisted pairs (transmit and receive). The hub acts as a repeater: When a single station transmits, the hub repeats the signal on the outgoing line to each station. Note that although this scheme is physically a star, it is logically a bus: A transmission from any one station is received by all other stations, and if two stations transmit at the same time there will be a collision.

Multiple levels of hubs can be cascaded in a hierarchical configuration. Figure 5.3 illustrates a two-level configuration. There is one **header hub** (HHUB) and one

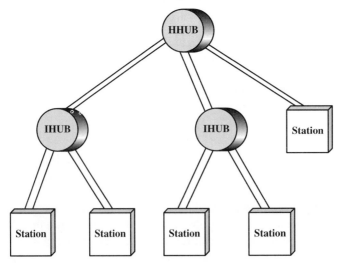

Figure 5.3   Two-level twisted-pair star topology.

or more **intermediate hubs** (IHUB). Each hub may have a mixture of stations and other hubs attached to it from below. This layout fits well with building wiring practices. Typically, there is a wiring closet on each floor of an office building, and a hub can be placed in each one. Each hub could service the stations on its floor.

Hubs and Switches

We have used the term *hub* in the context of the 10BASE-T standard, but this term is used to refer to a number of different types of devices. The most important distinction is between the shared-medium hub and the switched LAN hub.

To clarify the distinction among types of hubs, let us consider Ethernet-style LANs. Figure 5.4a shows a typical bus layout of a traditional 10-Mbps Ethernet. A bus is installed that is laid out so that all the devices to be attached are in reasonable proximity to a point on the bus. A transmission from any one station is propagated along the length of the bus and may be received by all other stations. In the figure, station B is transmitting. This transmission goes from B, across the lead from B to the bus, along the bus in both directions, and along the access lines of each of the other attached stations. In this configuration, all the stations must share the total capacity of the bus, which is 10 Mbps.

A shared-medium hub, such as specified by 10BASE-T, has a central hub, often in a building wiring closet. A star wiring arrangement is used to attach the stations to the hub. In this arrangement, a transmission from any one station is received by the hub and retransmitted on all of the outgoing lines. Therefore, to avoid collision, only one station can transmit at a time. Again, the total capacity of the LAN is the same as that of the access lines from each station (namely, 10 Mbps). The shared-medium hub has several advantages over the simple bus arrangement. For example, it exploits standard building wiring practices in the layout of cable. In addition, the hub can be configured to recognize a malfunctioning station that is jamming the network and to cut that station out of the network. Figure 5.4b illustrates the operation of a shared-medium hub. Here again, station B is transmitting. This transmission goes from B, across the transmit line from B to the hub, and from the hub along the receive lines of each of the other attached stations.

To achieve greater performance, a new form of hub, known as a switching hub, was introduced. In this case, the central hub acts as a switch, much as a packet switch or circuit switch. An incoming frame from a particular station is switched to the appropriate output line to be delivered to the intended destination. At the same time, other unused lines can be used for switching other traffic. Figure 5.4c shows an example in which B is transmitting a frame to A and at the same time C is transmitting a frame to D. So, in this example, the current throughput on the LAN is 20 Mbps, although each individual device is limited to 10 Mbps. The switching hub has several attractive features:

1. No change is required to the software or hardware of the attached devices to convert a bus LAN or a shared-medium LAN to a switching-hub LAN. In the case of a CSMA/CD LAN, each attached device continues to use the CSMA/CD protocol to access the LAN. From the point of view of the attached devices, nothing has changed in the access logic.

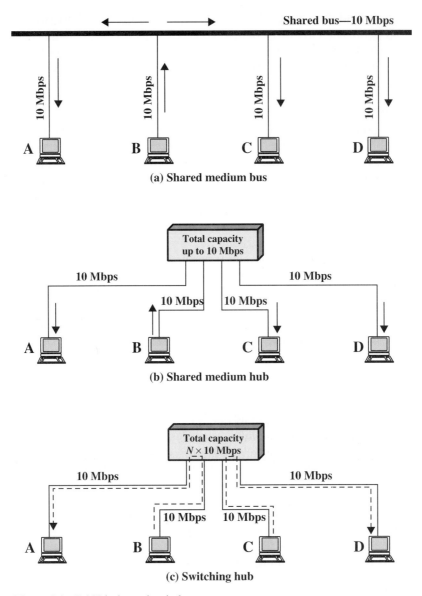

Figure 5.4 LAN hubs and switches.

2. Each attached device has a dedicated capacity equal to that of the entire original LAN, assuming that the hub has sufficient capacity to keep up with all attached devices. For example, in Figure 5.4c, if the hub can sustain a throughput of 20 Mbps, each attached device appears to have a dedicated capacity for either input or output of 10 Mbps.

3. The switching hub scales easily. Additional devices can be attached to the hub by increasing the capacity of the hub correspondingly.

Two types of switching hubs are available as commercial products:

- **Store-and-forward switch:** The hub accepts a frame on an input line, buffers it briefly, and then routes it to the appropriate output line.
- **Cut-through switch:** The hub takes advantage of the fact that the destination address appears at the beginning of the MAC (medium access control) frame. The hub begins repeating the incoming frame onto the appropriate output line as soon as the hub recognizes the destination address.

The cut-through switch yields the highest possible throughput but at some risk of propagating bad frames, because the switch is not able to check the CRC prior to retransmission. The store-and-forward switch involves a delay between sender and receiver but boosts the overall integrity of the network.

The discussion in this section has been in terms of Ethernet hubs and switched Ethernet LANs. However, the principle applies to any type of LAN, including token ring. The type of LAN is determined by the medium access control protocol employed on the access lines between hub and station.

Fast Ethernet

Fast Ethernet refers to a set of specifications developed by the IEEE 802.3 committee to provide a low-cost, Ethernet-compatible LAN operating at 100 Mbps. The blanket designation for these standards is 100BASE-T. The committee defined a number of alternatives to be used with different transmission media.

Figure 5.5 shows the terminology used in labeling the specifications and indicates the media used. All of the 100BASE-T options use the IEEE 802.3 MAC protocol and frame format. 100BASE-X refers to a set of options that use two physical links between nodes; one for transmission and one for reception. 100BASE-TX makes use of shielded twisted pair (STP) or high-quality (Category

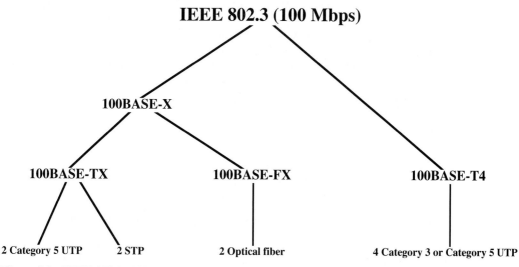

Figure 5.5   IEEE 802.3 100BASE-T options.

5) unshielded twisted pair (UTP). 100BASE-FX uses optical fiber. For all of these schemes the distance involved between hubs and stations is on the order of a maximum of 100 to 200 m.

In many buildings, any of the 100BASE-X options requires the installation of new cable. To minimize costs for buildings that do not have the required cable in place, 100BASE-T4 defines a lower-cost alternative that can use Category 3, voice grade UTP in addition to the higher-quality Category 5 UTP.[2] To achieve the 100-Mbps data rate over lower-quality cable, 100BASE-T4 dictates the use of four twisted-pair lines between nodes, with the data transmission making use of three pairs in one direction at a time.

For all the 100BASE-T options, the topology is similar to that of 10BASE-T—namely, a star-wire topology.

100BASE-X

For all of the transmission media specified under 100BASE-X, a unidirectional data rate of 100 Mbps is achieved transmitting over a single link (single twisted pair, single optical fiber). For all these media, an efficient and effective signal encoding scheme is required. The one chosen is referred to as 4B/5B-NRZI. This encoding technique is more efficient than the Manchester technique used for 10-Mbps Ethernet and is therefore desirable at the higher data rate.

The 100BASE-X designation includes two physical medium specifications: one for twisted pair, known as 100BASE-TX, and one for optical fiber, known as 100-BASE-FX. 100BASE-TX makes use of two pairs of twisted-pair cable, one pair used for transmission and one for reception. Both STP and Category 5 UTP are allowed. 100BASE-FX makes use of two optical fiber cables, one for transmission and one for reception.

100BASE-T4

100BASE-T4 is designed to produce a 100-Mbps data rate over lower-quality Category 3 cable, thus taking advantage of the large installed base of Category 3 cable in office buildings. The specification also indicates that the use of Category 5 cable is optional.

For 100BASE-T4 using voice-grade Category 3 cable, it is not reasonable to expect to achieve 100 Mbps on a single twisted pair. Instead, 100BASE-T4 specifies that the data stream to be transmitted is split into three separate data streams, each with an effective data rate of $33\frac{1}{3}$ Mbps. Four twisted pair are used. Data are transmitted using three pairs and received using three pairs. Thus, two of the pairs must be configured for bidirectional transmission.

---

[2] Category 3 twisted pair is standard telephone wire, which has limited data rate capability. Category 5 is intended to operate at much higher data rates. A key difference between Category 3 and Category 5 cable is the number of twists in the cable per unit distance. Category 5 is much more tightly twisted, typically 3 to 4 twists per inch compared to 3 to 4 twists per foot for Category 3. The tighter twisting is more expensive but provides much better performance than Category 3.

Configuration and Operation

In its simplest form, a 100BASE-T network is configured in a star-wire topology, with all stations connected directly to a central point referred to as a multiport repeater. In this configuration, the repeater has the responsibility for detecting collisions, rather than the attached stations. The repeater functions as follows:

- A valid signal appearing on any single input is repeated on all output link.
- If two inputs occur at the same time, a jam signal is transmitted on all links.

The term *collision domain* is used to define a single CSMA/CD network. This means that if two stations transmit at the same time, a collision will occur. Stations separated by a simple multiport repeater are within the same collision domain, whereas stations separated by a bridge are in different collision domains. Figure 5.6 illustrates this difference. The bridge operates in a store-and-forward fashion and therefore participates in two CSMA/CD algorithms, one for each of the two collision domains that it connects.

The 100BASE-T standard defines two types of repeaters. A Class I repeater can support unlike physical media segments, such as 100BASE-T4 and 100BASE-TX. In this case, there is likely to be increased internal delay in the repeater to handle the conversion from one signaling scheme to another. Therefore, only a single Class I repeater is used in a collision domain. A Class II repeater is limited to a single physical media type, and there may be two Class II repeaters used in a single collision domain.

Full-duplex Operation

A traditional Ethernet is half duplex: A station can either transmit or receive a frame, but it cannot do both simultaneously. With full-duplex operation, a station can transmit and receive simultaneously. If a 100-Mbps Ethernet ran in full duplex mode, the theoretical transfer rate would become 200 Mbps.

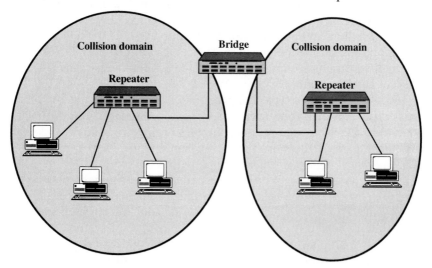

Figure 5.6   100BASE-T collision domains.

Several changes are needed to operate in full-duplex mode. The attached stations must have full-duplex rather than half-duplex adapter cards. The central point in the star wire cannot be a simple multiport repeater but rather must be a switched hub. In this case each station constitutes a separate collision domain. In fact, there are no collisions and the CSMA/CD algorithm is no longer needed. However, the same 802.3 MAC frame format is used and the attached stations can continue to execute the CSMA/CD algorithm, even though no collisions can ever be detected.

Mixed Configuration

One of the strengths of the Fast Ethernet approach is that it readily supports a mixture of existing 10-Mbps LANs and newer 100-Mbps LANs. An example of what can be accomplished is shown in Figure 5.7, in which the 100-Mbps technology is used as a backbone LAN. Many of the stations attach to 10-Mbps hubs using the 10BASE-T standard. These hubs are, in turn, connected to switching hubs that conform to 100BASE-T and that can support both 10-Mbps and 100-Mbps links. Additional high-capacity workstations and servers attach directly to these 10/100 switches. These mixed-capacity switches are, in turn, connected to 100-Mbps hubs using 100-Mbps links. The 100-Mbps hubs provide a building backbone and are also connected to a router that provides connection to an outside WAN.

Gigabit Ethernet

In late 1995, the IEEE 802.3 committee formed a High-speed Study Group to investigate means for conveying packets in Ethernet format at speeds in the gigabits per second range. Since that time, there has been considerable work on the development of the Gigabit Ethernet concept.

The strategy for Gigabit Ethernet is the same as that for Fast Ethernet. While defining a new medium and transmission specification, Gigabit Ethernet retains the CSMA/CD protocol and Ethernet format of its 10-Mbps and 100-Mbps predecessors. It is compatible with 100BASE-T and 10BASE-T, preserving a smooth migration path. As more organizations move to 100BASE-T, putting huge traffic loads on backbone networks, demand for Gigabit Ethernet has intensified.

The medium and transmission specification for Gigabit Ethernet calls for the use of optical fiber over relatively short distances, although UTP, STP, and coaxial cable configurations are also allowed. Table 5.2 compares Gigabit Ethernet with Ethernet and Fast Ethernet.

Figure 5.8 shows a typical application of Gigabit Ethernet. A 1-Gbps switching hub provides backbone connectivity for central servers and high-speed workgroup hubs. Each workgroup hub supports both 1-Gbps links, to connect to the backbone hub and to support high-performance workgroup servers, and 100-Mbps links, to support high-performance workstations, servers, and 100-Mbps hubs.

The success of both Fast Ethernet and Gigabit Ethernet highlights the importance of network management concerns in choosing a network technology. ATM, explored next, may be a technically superior choice for a high-speed backbone because of its flexibility and scalability. However, the Ethernet alternatives offer compatibility with existing installed LANs, network management software, and applications. This compatibility has accounted for the survival of a 20-year-old technology (CSMA/CD) in today's fast-evolving network environment.

TABLE 5.2   COMPARISON OF ETHERNET, FAST ETHERNET, AND GIGABIT ETHERNET

	Ethernet 10BASE-T	Fast Ethernet 100base-X	Gigabit Ethernet
Data Rate	10 Mbps	100 Mbps	1 Gbps
Category 5 UTP	100 m	100 m	25–100 m
STP/Coaxial Cable	500 m	100 m	25–100 m
Multimode Fiber	2 km	400 m (half duplex) 2 km (full duplex)	500 m
Single-Mode Fiber	25 km	20 km	2 km

5.2   ATM LANS

A document on customer premises networks jointly prepared by Apple, Bellcore, Sun, and Xerox [ABSX92] identifies three generations of LANs:

- **First generation:** Typified by the CSMA/CD and token ring LANs. The first generation provided terminal-to-host connectivity and supported client-server architectures at moderate data rates.
- **Second generation:** Typified by the 100-Mbps Fiber Distributed Data Interface (FDDI), an optical token ring LAN. The second generation responds to the need for backbone LANs and for support of high-performance workstations.
- **Third generation:** Typified by ATM LANs. The third generation is designed to provide the aggregate throughputs and real-time transport guarantees that are needed for multimedia applications.

Typical requirements for a third generation LAN include the following:

1. Support multiple, guaranteed classes of service. A live video application, for example, may require a guaranteed 2-Mbps connection for acceptable performance, while a file transfer program can utilize a "background" class of service.
2. Provide scalable throughput that is capable of growing both per-host capacity (to enable applications that require large volumes of data in and out of a single host) and aggregate capacity (to enable installations to grow from a few to several hundred high-performance hosts).
3. Facilitate the interworking between LAN and WAN technology.

ATM is ideally suited to these requirements. Using virtual paths and virtual channels, multiple classes of service are easily accommodated, either in a preconfigured fashion (semipermanent connections) or on demand (switched connections). ATM is easily scalable by adding more ATM switching nodes and using

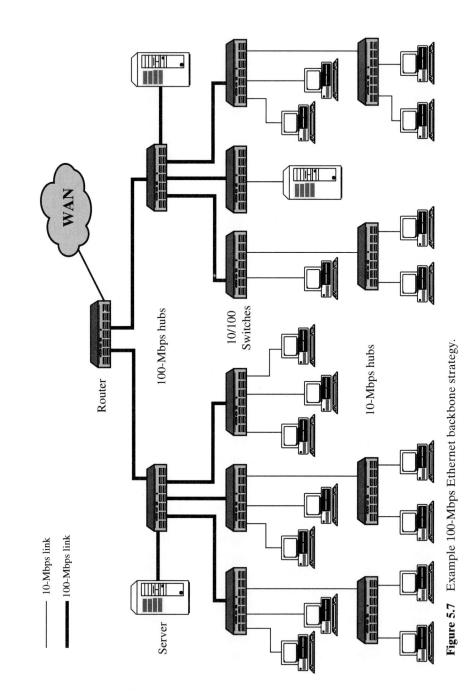

Figure 5.7 Example 100-Mbps Ethernet backbone strategy.

Router

WAN

10-Mbps link

100-Mbps link

100-Mbps hubs

10/100 Switches

10-Mbps hubs

Server

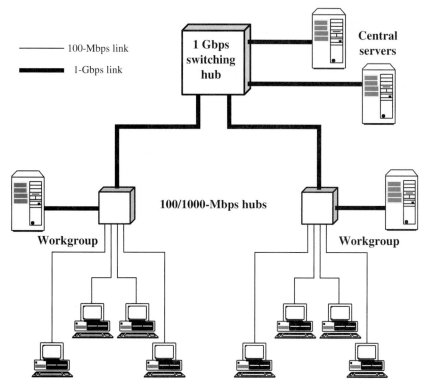

Figure 5.8   Example gigabit Ethernet configuration.

higher (or lower) data rates for attached devices. Finally, with the increasing acceptance of cell-based transport for wide area networking, the use of ATM for a premises network enables seamless integration of LANs and WANs.

The term *ATM LAN* has been used by vendors and researchers to apply to a variety of configurations. At the very least, an ATM LAN implies the use of ATM as a data transfer protocol somewhere within the local premises. Among the possible types of ATM LANs are the following:

- **Gateway to ATM WAN:** An ATM switch acts as a router and traffic concentrator for linking a premises network complex to an ATM WAN.
- **Backbone ATM switch:** Either a single ATM switch or a local network of ATM switches interconnect other LANs.
- **Workgroup ATM:** High-performance multimedia workstations and other end systems connect directly to an ATM switch.

These are all "pure" configurations. In practice, a mixture of two or all three of these types of networks is used to create an ATM LAN.

Figure 5.9 shows an example of a backbone ATM LAN that includes links to the outside world. In this example, the local ATM network consists of four switches interconnected with high-speed point-to-point links running at the standardized ATM rates of 155 Mbps and 622 Mbps. On the premises, there are three other LANs,

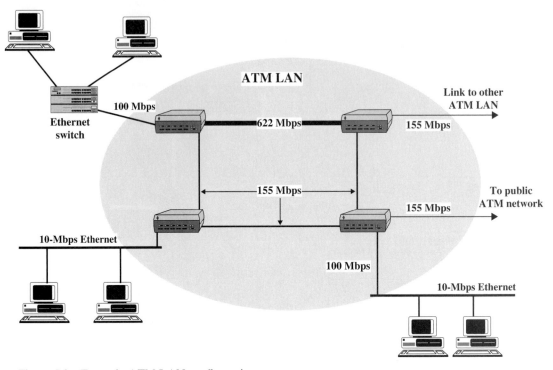

Figure 5.9 Example ATM LAN configuration.

each of which has a direct connection to one of the ATM switches. The data rate from an ATM switch to an attached LAN conforms to the native data rate of that LAN. For example, the connection to the 100BASE-T network is at 100 Mbps. Thus, the switch must include some buffering and speed conversion capability to map the data rate from the attached LAN to an ATM data rate. The ATM switch must also perform some sort of protocol conversion from the MAC protocol used on the attached LAN to the ATM cell stream used on the ATM network. A simple approach is for each ATM switch that attaches to a LAN to function as a bridge or router.

An ATM LAN configuration such as that shown in Figure 5.9 provides a relatively painless method for inserting a high-speed backbone into a local environment. As the on-site demand rises, it is a simple matter to increase the capacity of the backbone by adding more switches, increasing the throughput of each switch, and increasing the data rate of the trunks between switches. With this strategy, the load on individual LANs within the premises can be increased and the number of LANs can grow.

However, this simple backbone ATM LAN does not address all of the needs for local communications. In particular, in the simple backbone configuration, the end systems (workstations, servers, etc.) remain attached to shared-media LANs with the limitations on data rate imposed by the shared medium.

A more advanced and more powerful approach is to use ATM technology in a hub. Figure 5.10 suggests the capabilities that can be provided with this approach. Each ATM hub includes a number of ports that operate at different data rates and

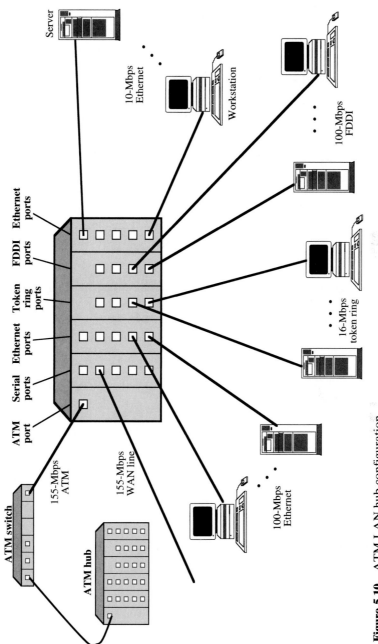

Figure 5.10 ATM LAN hub configuration.

use different protocols. Typically, such a hub consists of a number of rack-mounted modules, with each module containing ports of a given data rate and protocol.

The key difference between the ATM hub shown in Figure 5.10 and the ATM nodes depicted in Figure 5.9 is the way in which individual end systems are handled. Notice that in the ATM hub, each end system has a dedicated point-to-point link to the hub. Each end system includes the communications hardware and software to interface to a particular type of LAN, but in each case, the LAN contains only two devices: the end system and the hub. For example, each device attached to a 10-Mbps Ethernet port operates using the CSMA/CD protocol at 10 Mbps. However, because each end system has its own dedicated line, the effect is that each system has its own dedicated 10-Mbps Ethernet. Therefore, each end system can operate at close to the maximum 10-Mbps data rate.

The use of a configuration such as that of either Figure 5.9 or 5.10 has the advantage that existing LAN installations and LAN hardware, so-called legacy LANs, can continue to be used while ATM technology is introduced. The disadvantage is that the use of such a mixed-protocol environment requires the implementation of some sort of protocol conversion capability. A simpler approach, but one that requires that end systems be equipped with ATM capability, is to implement a "pure" ATM LAN.

One issue that was not addressed in our discussion so far has to do with the interoperability of end systems on a variety of interconnected LANs. End systems attached directly to one of the legacy LANs implement the MAC layer appropriate to that type of LAN. End systems attached directly to an ATM network implement the ATM and AAL protocols. As a result, there are three areas of compatibility to consider:

1. Interaction between an end system on an ATM network and an end system on a legacy LAN
2. Interaction between an end system on a legacy LAN and an end system on another legacy LAN of the same type (e.g., two IEEE 802.3 networks)
3. Interaction between an end system on a legacy LAN and an end system on another legacy LAN of a different type (e.g., an IEEE 802.3 network and an IEEE 802.5 network).

A variety of approaches are possible to meet these requirements. In essence, what is involved is the use of a bridge plus protocol mapping between various MAC layers and mapping between MAC formats and ATM cells. For details, see [STAL97b].

5.3   RECOMMENDED READING

[STAL97] covers in greater detail all of the LAN systems discussed in this chapter. A superb management-oriented treatment of high-speed LANs is [SAUN96], which provides practical guidance on selection, configuration, and performance issues.

[JOHN96] is an exhaustive treatment of Fast Ethernet, emphasizing the technical details. [BREY95] covers both switched 10-Mbps Ethernet and Fast Ethernet, with more emphasis on practical installation issues and providing a comparison with competing technologies.

[KAVA95] and [NEWM94] are good survey articles on LAN ATM architecture and configurations.

BREY95   Breyer, R., and Riley, S. *Switched and Fast Ethernet: How It Works and How to Use It.* Emeryville, CA: Ziff-Davis Press, 1995.

JOHN96   Johnson, H. *Fast Ethernet: Dawn of New Network.* Upper Saddle River, NJ: Prentice Hall, 1996.

KAVA95   Kavak, N. "Data Communication in ATM Networks." *IEEE Network,* May/June 1995.

NEWM94   Newman, P. "ATM Local Area Networks." *IEEE Communications Magazine,* March 1994.

SAUN96   Saunders, S. *The McGraw-Hill High-Speed LANs Handbook.* New York: McGraw-Hill, 1996.

STAL97   Stallings, W. *Local and Metropolitan Area Networks, 5th ed.* Upper Saddle River, NJ: Prentice Hall, 1997.

Useful Web sites:

- http://www.iol.unh.edu: University of New Hampshire site for equipment testing for ATM, Fast Ethernet, and other LANs.

- http://www.gigabit-ethernet.org: The Gigabit Ethernet Alliance is an open forum whose purpose is to promote industry cooperation in the development of Gigabit Ethernet.

5.4   PROBLEMS

5.1   Consider a bus LAN with a number of equally spaced stations with a data rate of 10 Mbps and a bus length of 1 km.

   a.   What is the mean time to send a frame of 1000 bits to another station, measured from the beginning of transmission to the end of reception? Assume a propagation speed of 200 m/μs.

   b.   If two stations begin to transmit at exactly the same time, their packets will interfere with each other. If each transmitting station monitors the bus during transmission, how long before it notices an interference, in seconds? In bit times?

5.2   Repeat Problem 5.1 for a data rate of 100 Mbps.

5.3   A disadvantage of the contention approach for LANs is the capacity wasted due to multiple stations attempting to access the channel at the same time. Suppose that time is divided into discrete slots with each of N stations attempting to transmit with probability p during each slot. What fraction of slots are wasted due to multiple simultaneous transmission attempts?

5.4   A simple medium access control protocol would be to use a fixed-assignment time-division multiplexing (TDM) scheme. Each station is assigned one time slot per cycle for transmission. For a bus LAN, assume that the length of each slot is the time to transmit 100 bits plus the end-to-end propagation delay. Stations monitor all time slots for reception. Assume a propagation time of 2×10^8 m/s. What are the limitations, in terms of number of stations and throughput per station, for a 1-km, 10-Mbps baseband bus?

5.5 The binary exponential backoff algorithm is defined by IEEE 802 as follows:

> The delay is an integral multiple of slot time. The number of slot times to delay before the nth retransmission attempt is chosen as a uniformly distributed random integer r in the range $0 < r < 2^K$, where $K = \min(n, 10)$.

Slot time is roughly twice the round-trip propagation delay. Assume that two stations always have a frame to send. After a collision, what is the mean number of retransmission attempts before one station successfully retransmits?

Performance Modeling and Estimation

ISSUES FOR PART THREE

The reader is no doubt anxious to move on to the vital topics of traffic management, routing, and compression, which are the justification for this work. However, the point of all the algorithms and protocols we will discuss is to deal with traffic through networks and internets. It behooves us to have some understanding of how to characterize such traffic and the performance implications of various traffic patterns. Thus Part Three.

Key to the design of high-performance networks is the ability to model and estimate performance parameters. The designer needs to be able to estimate future traffic volume and characteristics on the basis of observed traffic. The statistical characteristics of a traffic flow affect a wide variety of design and configuration issues, including routing protocols, resource reservation protocols, queuing disciplines used at routers and ATM switches, and buffer sizes. Further, the user needs to be able to characterize planned traffic flow in order to make intelligent reservation decisions.

A number of parameters are important in characterizing data traffic flow:

- **Throughput characteristics:**
  - Average rate: The average load provided by a source is key in determining the amount of resources to be allocated to that source. The average rate expresses the flow that can be sustained by the source over an extended period of time.
  - Peak rate: This parameter tells the network what type of surge traffic must be coped with, either by dedicating data-rate capacity or by allocating sufficient buffer space to smooth out the surges.
  - Variability: Peak rate is one measure of variability; a more direct measure is the variance of the throughput. Variability measures the burstiness of a source and is an indication of the extent to which statistical multiplexing can be used for the purpose of efficiency.

- **Delay characteristics:**
  - Transfer delay: This measures the delay imposed by the network on data transferring from a source to a destination. A maximum transfer delay can also be a requirement expressed by an application.
  - Delay variation: The amount of variation in transfer delay is an important parameter for real-time applications, in which the data displayed at the destination must appear at a smooth continuous rate matching the rate generated at the source.

These and similar parameters have profound effects on network configuration and protocol design. To make effective decisions, the data traffic flow must be modeled reliably.

Queuing analysis provides a simple, tractable means of obtaining useful results to guide the design and sizing of networks. For decades, queuing analysis based on a Poisson traffic assumption has been the constant companion of the network performance analyst. Then, to an unsuspecting world, there emerged from the dim recesses of Boston University and Bellcore a startling result: In at least some cases, data traffic is not Poisson but is self-similar, or fractal, in nature. Faced with such traffic, the performance of a network does not obey the tidy formulas of queuing analysis but produces greater delays and lower throughputs. Since the original discovery, the results have been confirmed numerous times on a variety of traffic types. All of these issues are explored in Part Three.

ROAD MAP FOR PART THREE

Chapter 6: Overview of Probability and Stochastic Processes

This chapter provides an overview of concepts relevant to Part Three. For some readers, this material constitutes a review and refresher. For others, the chapter provides enough background to enable understanding of the discussion in Chapters 7 and 8.

The first part of the chapter provides an overview of essential concepts in probability and random variables; the emphasis is on fundamental principles with wide applicability. The remainder of the chapter deals with stochastic processes. The concept of stochastic processes is introduced and then specific processes relevant to the discussion in Chapter 8 are summarized.

Chapter 7: Queuing Analysis

An important technique that should be available to anyone interested in data communications and computer networking is queuing analysis. Many design areas in these fields, as well as many other areas of computer science, can be represented by a queuing model. Queuing analysis enables the analyst to develop quickly an approximate characterization of the behavior of a system under a range of loads.

The purpose of Chapter 7 is to give the reader the basic tools for performing queuing analysis. The emphasis is on (1) understanding the assumptions underlying queuing analysis, and (2) presenting the formulas that apply in various situations. The chapter covers single and multiserver queues and networks of queues.

Chapter 8: Self-similar Traffic

Although the queuing analysis covered in Chapter 7 has been and remains not only useful but essential for the network and protocol designer, a number of recent studies indicate that much of the traffic on high-speed networks does not exhibit the random character required for the queuing theory equations to be valid. Rather, such traffic has a self-similar, or fractal, character. Chapter 8 introduces and explains the concept of self-similarity. It then applies this concept to data traffic and examines the performance implications.

CHAPTER **6**

OVERVIEW OF PROBABILITY AND STOCHASTIC PROCESSES

The comparatively late rise of the theory of probability shows how hard it is to grasp, and the many paradoxes show clearly that we, as humans, lack a well grounded intuition in this matter.

In probability theory there is a great deal of art in setting up the model, in solving the problem, and in applying the results back to the real world actions that will follow.

—*The Art of Probability,* Richard Hamming

Before setting out on our exploration of queuing analysis and self-similar traffic, some background on probability and stochastic processes needs to be reviewed. The reader familiar with these topics can safely skip this chapter.

The chapter begins with an introduction to some elementary concepts from probability theory and random variables; this material is needed for Chapter 7, on queuing analysis. Following this, we look at stochastic processes, which are important to an understanding of the discussion in Chapter 8, on self-similar traffic.

6.1 PROBABILITY

We give here the barest outline of probability theory, but enough to support the rest of this chapter.

Definitions of Probability

Probability is concerned with the assignment of numbers to events. The probability $P(A)$ of an event A is a number that corresponds to the likelihood that the event A will occur. Generally, we talk of performing an experiment and obtaining an outcome. The event A is a particular outcome or set of outcomes, and a probability is assigned to that event.

It is difficult to get a firm grip on the concept of probability. Different applications of the theory present probability in different lights. In fact, there are a number of different definitions of probability. We highlight three here.

Axiomatic Definition

A formal approach to probability is to state a number of axioms that define a probability measure and, from them, derive laws of probability that can be used to perform useful calculations. The axioms are simply assertions that must be accepted. Once the axioms are accepted, it is possible to prove each of the laws.

The axioms and laws make use of the following concepts from set theory. The certain event Ω is the event that occurs in every experiment; it consists of the universe, or **sample space**, of all possible outcomes. The union $A \cup B$ of two events A and B is the event that occurs when either A or B or both occur. The intersection $A \cap B$, also written AB, is the event that occurs when both events A and B occur. The events A and B are mutually exclusive if the occurrence of one of them excludes the occurrence of the other. The event $\overline{A}$ is the event that occurs when A does not occur. These concepts are easily visualized with Venn diagrams, such as those shown in Figure 6.1. In each diagram, the shaded part corresponds to the expression below the diagram. Parts (c) and (d) correspond to cases in which A and B are not mutually exclusive; that is, some outcomes are defined as part of both events A and B. Parts (e) and (f) correspond to cases in which A and B are mutually exclusive. Note that in these cases, the intersection of the two events is the null set.

The common set of axioms used to define probability are as follows:

1. $0 \leq P(A) \leq 1$ for each event A
2. $P(\Omega) = 1$
3. $P(A \cup B) = P(A) + P(B)$ if A and B are mutually exclusive

Axiom 3 can be extended to many events. For example, $P(A \cup B \cup C) = P(A) + P(B) + P(C)$ if A, B, and C are mutually exclusive. Note that the axioms do not say anything about how probabilities are to be assigned to individual outcomes or events.

Based on these axioms, many laws can be derived. Here are some of the most important:

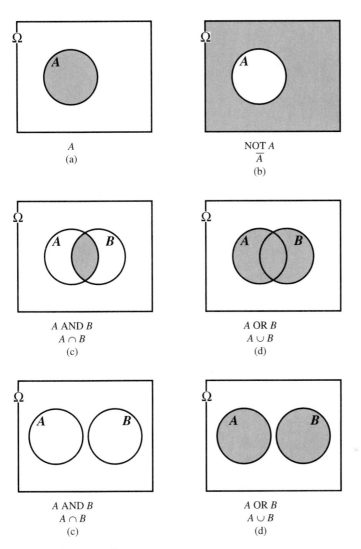

Figure 6.1   Venn diagrams.

$$P(\overline{A}) = 1 - P(A)$$

$$P(A \cap B) = 0 \text{ if } A \text{ and } B \text{ are mutually exclusive}$$

$$P(A \cup B) = P(A) + P(B) - P(A \cap B)$$

$$P(A \cup B \cup C) = P(A) + P(B) + P(C)$$
$$- P(A \cap B) - P(A \cap C) - P(B \cap C) + P(A \cap B \cap C)$$

As an example, consider the throwing of a single die. This has six possible outcomes. The certain event is the event that occurs when any of the six die faces is on top. The union of the events {even} and {less than three} is the event {1 or 2 or 4 or 6}; the intersection of these events is the event {2}. The events {even} and {odd} are mutually exclusive. If we assume that each of the six outcomes is equally likely and assign a probability of 1/6 to each outcome, it is easy to see that the three axioms are satisfied. We can apply the laws of probability as follows:

$$\text{Pr}\{\text{even}\} = \text{Pr}\{2\} + \text{Pr}\{4\} + \text{Pr}\{6\} = 1/2$$

$$\text{Pr}\{\text{less than three}\} = \text{Pr}\{1\} + \text{Pr}\{2\} = 1/3$$

$$\text{Pr}[\{\text{even}\} \cup \{\text{less than three}\}] = \text{Pr}\{\text{even}\} + \text{Pr}\{\text{less than three}\} - \text{Pr}\{2\}$$

$$1/2 + 1/3 - 1/6 = 2/3$$

Relative Frequency Definition

The relative frequency approach uses the following definition of probability. Perform an experiment a number of times; each time is called a *trial*. For each trial, observe whether the event A occurs. Then the probability $P(A)$ of an event A is the limit:

$$P(A) = \lim_{n \to \infty} \frac{n_A}{n}$$

where n is the number of trials and n_A is the number of occurrences of A.

For example, one could toss a coin many times. If the ratio of heads to total tosses hovers around 0.5 after a very large number of tosses, then we can assume that this is a fair coin, with equal probability of heads and tails.

Classical Definition

The classical definition of probability is as follows:

$$P(A) = \frac{N_A}{N}$$

where N is the total number of possible outcomes, provided that all outcomes are equally likely, and N_A is the number of outcomes in which event A occurs.

For example, if we throw one die, then N is 6 and there are three outcomes that correspond to the event {even}; hence $P\{\text{even}\} = 3/6 = 0.5$. Here's a more complicated example: We roll two dice and want to determine the probability p that the sum is 7. You could consider the number of different sums that could be produced $(2, 3, \ldots, 12)$, which is 11, and conclude that the probability is 1/11. This is incorrect. We need to consider equally likely outcomes. For this purpose, we need to consider each combination of die faces, and we must distinguish between the first and second die. For example, the outcome $(3, 4)$ must be counted separately from the outcome $(4, 3)$. With this approach, there are 36 equally likely outcomes, and the favorable outcomes are the six pairs $(1, 6)$, $(2, 5)$, $(3, 4)$, $(4, 3)$, $(5, 2)$, $(6, 1)$. Thus, $p = 6/36 = 1/6$.

Conditional Probability and Independence

We often want to know a probability that is conditional on some event. The effect of the condition is to remove some of the outcomes from the sample space. For example, we might ask the question, What is the probability of getting a sum of 8 on the roll of two die, if we know that the face of at least one die is an even number? We can reason as follows: Because one die is even and the sum is even, the second die must show an even number. Thus there are three equally likely successful outcomes—(2, 6), (4, 4), and (6, 2)—out of a total set of possibilities of {36 − (both faces odd)} = 36 − 3 × 3 = 27. The resulting probability is 3/27 = 1/9.

Formally, the conditional probability of an event A assuming the event B has occurred, denoted by $P(A|B)$, is defined as the ratio

$$P(A|B) = \frac{P(AB)}{P(B)}$$

where we assume $P(B)$ is not zero.

In our example, A = {sum of 8} and B = {at least one die even}. The quantity $P(AB)$ encompasses all of those outcomes in which the sum is 8 and at least one die is even. As we have seen, there are three such outcomes. Thus, $P(AB) = 3/36 = 1/12$. A moment's thought should convince you that $P(B) = 3/4$. We can now calculate:

$$P(A|B) = \frac{1/12}{3/4} = \frac{1}{9}$$

which agrees with our previous reasoning.

Two events A and B are called independent if $P(AB) = P(A)P(B)$. It can easily be seen that if A and B are independent, then $P(A|B) = P(A)$ and $P(B|A) = P(B)$.

Bayes' Theorem

We close this section with one of the most important results from probability theory, known as Bayes' theorem. First we need to state the total probability formula. Given a set of mutually exclusive events $E_1, E_2, ..., E_n$, such that the union of these events covers all possible outcomes and an arbitrary event A, then it can be shown that

$$P(A) = \sum_{i=1}^{n} P(A|E_i)P(E_i) \tag{6.1}$$

Bayes' theorem may be stated as follows:

$$P(E_i|A) = \frac{P(A|E_i)P(E_i)}{P(A)} = \frac{P(A|E_i)P(E_i)}{\sum_{i=1}^{n} P(A|E_i)P(E_i)}$$

Bayes' theorem is used to calculate "posterior odds"; that is, the probability that something really is the case, given evidence in favor of it. For example, suppose we are transmitting a sequence of zeroes and ones over a noisy transmission line. Let $S0$ and $S1$ be the events a zero is sent at a given time and a one is sent, respectively, and $R0$ and $R1$ be the events that a zero is received and a one is received. Suppose we know the probabilities of the source—namely, $P(S1) = p$ and $P(S0) = 1 - p$. Now the line is observed to determine how frequently an error occurs when a one is sent and when a zero is sent, and the following probabilities are calculated: $P(R0|S1) = p_a$ and $P(R1|S0) = p_b$. If a zero is received, we can then calculate the conditional probability of an error—namely, the conditional probability that a one was sent given that a zero was received—using Bayes' theorem:

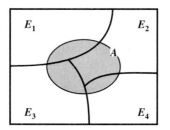

Figure 6.2 Illustration of total probability and Bayes' theorem.

$$P(S1|R0) = \frac{p_a p}{p_a p + (1 - p_b)(1 - p)}$$

Figure 6.2 illustrates the concepts of total probability and Bayes' Theorem.

6.2 RANDOM VARIABLES

A random variable is a mapping from the set of all possible events under consideration to the real numbers. That is, a random variable associates a real number with each event. This concept is sometimes expressed in terms of an experiment with many possible outcomes; a random variable assigns a value to each such outcome. A random variable is **continuous** if it takes on a noncountably infinite number of distinct values. A random variable is **discrete** if it takes on a finite or countably infinite number of values

Distribution and Density Functions

A continuous random variable X can be described by either its **distribution function** $F(x)$ or **density function** $f(x)$:

Distribution function: $F(x) = \Pr[X \leq x]$ $F(-\infty) = 0;$ $F(\infty) = 1$

Density function: $f(x) = \dfrac{d}{dx} F(x)$ $F(x) = \displaystyle\int_{-\infty}^{x} f(y)\, dy$ $\displaystyle\int_{-\infty}^{\infty} f(y)\, dy = 1$

For a discrete random variable, its probability distribution is characterized by

$$P_X(k) = \Pr[X = k] \qquad \sum_{\text{all } k} P_X(k) = 1$$

We are often concerned with some characteristic of a random variable rather than the entire distribution, such as the mean value

$$E[X] = \mu_X = \int_{-\infty}^{\infty} x f(x)\, dx \quad \text{Continuous case}$$

$$E[X] = \mu_X = \sum_{\text{all } k} k \Pr[x = k] \quad \text{Discrete case}$$

Other useful measures are as follows:

$$E[X^2] = \int_{-\infty}^{\infty} x^2 f(x)dx \quad \text{Continuous case}$$

Second moment:

$$E[X^2] = \sum_{\text{all } k} k^2 \Pr[x = k] \quad \text{Discrete case}$$

Variance: $\quad\quad\quad\quad \text{Var}[X] = E[(X - \mu_X)^2] = E[X^2] - \mu_X^2$

Standard deviation: $\quad \sigma_X = \sqrt{\text{Var}[X]}$

The variance and standard deviation are measures of the dispersion of values around the mean. It is easy to show that for a constant a

$$E[aX] = aE[X]; \quad \text{Var}[aX] = a^2 \text{Var}[X]$$

The mean is known as a first-order statistic; the second moment and variance are second-order statistics. Higher-order statistics can also be derived from the probability density function.

For any two random variables X and Y, we have.

$$E[X + Y] = E[X] + E[Y]$$

Important Distributions

Several distributions that play an important role in queuing analysis are described next.

Exponential Distribution

The exponential distribution with parameter λ ($\lambda > 0$) is given by (Figures 6.3a and 6.3b)

$$F(x) = 1 - e^{-\lambda x} \quad \text{Distribution}$$
$$f(x) = \lambda e^{-\lambda x} \quad\quad \text{Density}$$
$$x \geqslant 0$$

The exponential distribution has the interesting property that its mean is equal to its standard deviation:

$$E[X] = \sigma_X = \frac{1}{\lambda}$$

When used to refer to a time interval, such as a service time, this distribution is sometimes referred to as a random distribution. This is because, for a time interval that has already begun, each time at which the interval may finish is equally likely.

This distribution is important in queuing theory because we can often assume that the service time of a server in a queuing system is exponential. In the case of telephone traffic, the service time is the time for which a subscriber engages the equipment of interest. In a packet-switching network, the service time is the transmission time and is therefore proportional to the packet length. It is difficult to give a sound theoretical reason why service times should be exponential, but the fact is

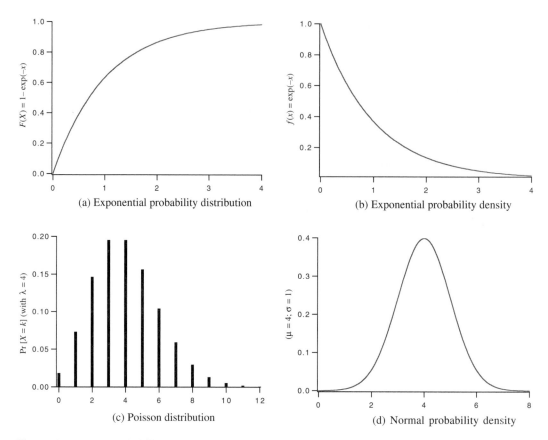

Figure 6.3 Some probability functions.

that in most cases they are very nearly exponential. This is good news because it simplifies the queuing analysis immensely.

Poisson Distribution

Another important distribution is the Poisson distribution (Figure 6.3c) with parameter λ ($\lambda > 0$), which takes on values at the points 0, 1, ...:

$$\Pr[X = k] = \frac{\lambda^k}{k!} e^{-\lambda} \qquad k = 0, 1, 2 \dots$$

$$E[X] = \text{Var}[X] = \lambda$$

If $\lambda < 1$, then $\Pr[X = k]$ is maximum for $k = 0$. If $\lambda > 1$ but not an integer, then $\Pr[X = k]$ is maximum for the largest integer smaller than λ; if λ is a positive integer, then there are two maxima at $k = \lambda$ and $k = \lambda - 1$.

The Poisson distribution is also important in queuing analysis because we must assume a Poisson arrival pattern to be able to develop the queuing equations. Fortunately, the assumption of Poisson arrivals is usually valid.

The way in which the Poisson distribution can be applied to arrival rate is as follows. If items arrive at a queue according to a Poisson process, this may be expressed as

$$\Pr[k \text{ items arrive in time interval } T] = \frac{(\lambda T)^k}{k!} e^{-\lambda T}$$

Expected number of items to arrive in time interval $T = \lambda T$

Mean arrival rate, in items per second $= \lambda$

Arrivals occurring according to a Poisson process are often referred to as random arrivals. This is because the probability of arrival of an item in a small interval is proportional to the length of the interval and is independent of the amount of elapsed time since the arrival of the last item. That is, when items are arriving according to a Poisson process, an item is as likely to arrive at one instant as any other, regardless of the instants at which the other customers arrive.

Another interesting property of the Poisson process is its relationship to the exponential distribution. If we look at the times between arrivals of items T_a (called the interarrival times), then we find that this quantity obeys the exponential distribution

$$\Pr[T_a < t] = 1 - e^{-\lambda t}$$

$$E[T_a] = \frac{1}{\lambda}$$

Thus, the mean interarrival time is the reciprocal of the arrival rate, as one would expect.

Normal Distribution

The normal distribution with parameters λ and σ ($\mu > 0$) has the following density function (Figure 6.3d):

$$f(x) = \frac{1}{\sigma \sqrt{2\pi}} e^{-(x-\mu)^2/2\sigma^2}$$

with

$$E[X] = \mu$$
$$\text{Var}[X] = \sigma^2$$

Under general conditions, the sum (or average) of a large number of independent random variables has approximately a normal distribution. This result is known as the central limit theorem and plays a key role in statistics.

Multiple Random Variables

With two or more random variables, we are often concerned whether variations in one are reflected in the other. This subsection defines some important measures of dependence.

In general, the statistical characterization of multiple random variables requires a definition of their joint probability density function or joint probability distribution function:

Distribution:
$$F(x_1, x_2, \ldots, x_n) = \Pr[X_1 \leqslant x_1, X_2 \leqslant x_2, \ldots, X_n \leqslant x_n]$$

Density:
$$f(x_1, x_2, \ldots, x_n) = \frac{\partial^n}{\partial x_1 \partial x_2 \ldots \partial x_n} F(x_1, x_2, \ldots, x_n)$$

Discrete distribution: $P(x_1, x_2, \ldots, x_n) = \Pr[X_1 = x_1, X_2 = x_2, \ldots, X_n = x_n]$

For any two random variables X and Y, we have

$$E[X + Y] = E[X] + E[Y]$$

Two random variables X and Y are called (statistically) *independent* if $F(x, y) = F(x)F(y)$, and therefore $f(x, y) = f(x)f(y)$. If the random variables X and Y are discrete, then they are independent if $P(x, y) = P(x)P(y)$.

For independent random variables, the following relationships hold:

$$E[XY] = E[X] \times E[Y]$$

$$Var[X + Y] = Var[X] + Var[Y]$$

The *covariance* of two random variables X and Y is defined as follows:

$$Cov(X, Y) = E[(X - \mu_X)(Y - \mu_Y)] = E(XY) - E[X]E[Y]$$

If the variances of X and Y are finite, then their covariance is finite but may be positive, negative, or zero.

For finite variances of X and Y, the *correlation coefficient* of X and Y is defined as

$$r(X, Y) = \frac{Cov(X, Y)}{\sigma_X \sigma_Y} \tag{6.2}$$

We can think of this as a measure of the linear dependence between X and Y, normalized to be relative to the amount of variability in X and Y. The following relationship holds:

$$-1 \leqslant r(X, Y) \leqslant 1$$

It is said that X and Y are positively correlated if $r(X, Y) > 0$, that X and Y are negatively correlated if $r(X, Y) < 0$, and that X and Y are uncorrelated if $r(X, Y) = 0$. If X and Y are independent random variables, then they are uncorrelated and $r(X, Y) = 0$. However, it is possible for X and Y not to be independent yet still be uncorrelated.

The correlation coefficient provides a measure of the extent to which two random variables are linearly related. If the joint distribution of X and Y is relatively concentrated around a straight line in the xy-plane that has a positive slope, then $r(X, Y)$ will typically be close to 1. This indicates that a movement in X will be matched by a movement of relatively similar magnitude and direction in Y. If the joint distribution of X and Y is relatively concentrated around a straight line that has a negative slope, then $r(X, Y)$ will typically be close to -1.

The following relationship is easily demonstrated:

$$Var(X + Y) = Var(X) + Var(Y) + 2Cov(X, Y)$$

If X and Y have the same variance σ^2, then the preceding can be rewritten as

$$\text{Var}(X + Y) = 2\sigma^2(1 + r(X, Y))$$

If X and Y are uncorrelated ($r = 0$), then $\text{Var}(X + Y) = 2\sigma^2$. These results easily generalize. Consider a set of random variables $X_1, ..., X_N$, such that each has the same variance σ^2. Then

$$\text{Var}\left(\sum_{i=1}^{N} X_i\right) = N\sigma^2\left(1 + \sum\sum_{i \neq j} r(i, j)\right)$$

where $r(i, j)$ is shorthand for $r(X_i, X_j)$. Using the relationship $\text{Var}(X/N) = \text{Var}(X)/N^2$, we can develop an equation for the variance of the sample mean of a set of random variables:

$$\overline{X} = \frac{1}{N}\sum_{i=1}^{N} X_i$$

$$\text{Var}(\overline{X}) = \frac{\sigma^2}{N}\left(1 + \sum\sum_{i \neq j} r(i, j)\right)$$

If the X_i are mutually independent, then we have $\text{Var}(\overline{X}) = \sigma^2/N$.

6.3 STOCHASTIC PROCESSES

A stochastic process, also called a *random process*, is a family of random variables $\{\mathbf{x}(t), t \in T\}$ indexed by a parameter t over some index set T. Typically, the index set is interpreted as the time dimension, and $\mathbf{x}(t)$ is a function of time. Another way to say this is that a stochastic process is a random variable that is a function of time. A **continuous-time stochastic process** is one in which t varies continuously, typically over the nonnegative real line $\{\mathbf{x}(t), 0 \leq t < \infty\}$, although sometimes over the entire real line; whereas a **discrete-time stochastic process** is one in which t takes on discrete values, typically the positive integers $\{\mathbf{x}(t), t = 1, 2, ...\}$, although in some cases the range is the integers from $-\infty$ to $+\infty$.

Recall that a random variable is defined as a function that maps the outcome of an experiment into a given value. With that in mind, the expression $\mathbf{x}(t)$ can be interpreted in several ways:

1. A family of time functions (t variable; all possible outcomes)
2. A single time function (t variable; one outcome)
3. A random variable (t fixed; all possible outcomes)
4. A single number (t fixed; one outcome).

The specific interpretation of $\mathbf{x}(t)$ is usually clear from the context.

A word about terminology: A **continuous-value stochastic process** is one in which the random variable $\mathbf{x}(t)$ with t fixed (case 3 in the previous list) takes on continuous values, whereas a **discrete-value stochastic process** is one in which the random variable at any time t takes on a finite or countably infinite number of values.

A continuous-time stochastic process may be either continuous value or discrete value, and a discrete-time stochastic process may be either continuous value or discrete value.

As with any random variable, $\mathbf{x}(t)$ for a fixed value of t can be characterized by a probability distribution and a probability density. For continuous-value stochastic processes, these functions take the following form:

Distribution function: $F(x; t) = \Pr[\mathbf{x}(t) < x]$ $F(-\infty; t) = 0;$ $F(\infty; t) = 1$

Density function: $f(x; t) = \dfrac{\partial}{\partial x} F(x; t)$ $F(x; t) = \displaystyle\int_{-\infty}^{x} f(y; t)\,dy$ $\displaystyle\int_{-\infty}^{\infty} f(y; t)\,dy = 1$

For discrete-value stochastic processes

$$P_{\mathbf{x}(t)}(k) = \Pr[\mathbf{x}(t) = k] \qquad \sum_{\text{all } k} P_{\mathbf{x}(t)}(k) = 1$$

A full statistical characterization of a stochastic process must take into account the time variable. Using the first interpretation in the previous list, a stochastic process $\mathbf{x}(t)$ is a noncountable infinity of random variables, one for each t. To specify fully the statistics of the process, we would need to specify the joint probability density function of the variables $\mathbf{x}(t_1)$, $\mathbf{x}(t_2)$, ..., $\mathbf{x}(t_n)$ for all values of n $(1 \leq n < \infty)$ and all possible sampling times $(t_1, t_2, ..., t_n)$. For our purposes, we need not pursue this topic.

First- and Second-order Statistics

The mean and variance of a stochastic process are defined in the usual way:

$$E[\mathbf{x}(t)] = \mu(t) = \int_{-\infty}^{\infty} x f(x; t)\,dx \quad \text{Continuous-value case}$$

$$E[\mathbf{x}(t)] = \mu(t) = \sum_{\text{all } k} k \Pr[x(t) = k] \quad \text{Discrete-value case}$$

$$E[\mathbf{x}^2(t)] = \int_{-\infty}^{\infty} x^2 f(x; t)\,dx \quad \text{Continuous-value case}$$

$$E[\mathbf{x}^2(t)] = \sum_{\text{all } k} k^2 \Pr[x(t) = k] \quad \text{Discrete-value case}$$

$$\text{Var}[\mathbf{x}(t)] = \sigma^2_{\mathbf{x}(t)} = E[(\mathbf{x}(t) - \mu(t))^2] = E[\mathbf{x}^2(t)] - \mu^2(t)$$

Note that, in general, the mean and variance of a stochastic process are functions of time.

An important concept for our discussion is the *autocorrelation function* $R(t_1, t_2)$, which is the joint moment of the random variables $\mathbf{x}(t_1)$ and $\mathbf{x}(t_2)$:

$$R(t_1, t_2) = E[\mathbf{x}(t_1)\mathbf{x}(t_2)]$$

As with the correlation function for two random variables introduced earlier, the autocorrelation is a measure of the relationship between the two time instances of a stochastic process. A related quantity is the *autocovariance*:

$$C(t_1, t_2) = E[(\mathbf{x}(t_1)] - \mu(t_1)(\mathbf{x}(t_2) - \mu(t_2))] = R(t_1, t_2) - \mu(t_1)\mu(t_2) \qquad (6.3)$$

Note that the variance of $\mathbf{x}(t)$ is given by

$$\text{Var}[\mathbf{x}(t)] = C(t, t) = R(t, t) - \mu^2(t)$$

Finally, the *correlation coefficient* (see Equation 6.2) of $\mathbf{x}(t_1)$ and $\mathbf{x}(t_2)$ is called the normalized autocorrelation function of the stochastic process and can be expressed as

$$\rho(t_1, t_2) = \frac{E[(x(t_1) - \mu(t_1)), (x(t_2) - \mu(t_2))]}{\sigma_1 \sigma_2} \tag{6.4}$$

$$= \frac{C(t_1, t_2)}{\sigma_1 \sigma_2}$$

Unfortunately, some texts and some of the literature refer to $\rho(t_1, t_2)$ as the autocorrelation function, so the reader must beware.

Stationary Stochastic Processes

In general terms, a *stationary stochastic process* is one in which the probability characteristics of the process do not vary as a function of time. There are several different precise definitions of this concept, but the one of most interest here is the concept of *wide sense stationary*. A process is stationary in the wide sense (or weakly stationary) if its expected value is a constant and its autocorrelation function depends only on the time difference:

$$E[x(t)] = \mu$$
$$R(t, t + \tau) = R(t + \tau, t) = R(\tau) = R(-\tau) \quad \text{for all } t$$

From these equalities, the following can be derived:

$$\text{Var}[\mathbf{x}(t)] = R(t, t) - \mu^2(t) = R(0) - \mu^2$$
$$C(t, t + \tau) = R(t, t + \tau) - \mu(t)\mu(t + \tau) = R(\tau) - \mu^2 = C(\tau)$$

An important characteristic of $R(\tau)$ is that it measures the degree of dependence of one time instant of a stochastic process on other time instants. If $R(\tau)$ goes to zero exponentially fast as τ becomes large, then there is little dependence of one instant of a stochastic process on instants far removed in time. Such a process is called a short memory process. Whereas if $R(\tau)$ remains substantial for large values of τ (decays to zero at a slower than exponential rate), the stochastic process is a long memory process.

Spectral Density

The power spectrum (or spectral density) of a stationary random process is the Fourier transform of its autocorrelation function:

$$S(w) = \int_{-\infty}^{\infty} R(\tau)e^{-jw\tau} d\tau$$

where w is the frequency in radians ($w = 2\pi f$) and $j = \sqrt{-1}$.

For a deterministic time function, the spectral density gives the distribution frequency of the power of the signal. For a stochastic process, $S(w)$ is the average density of power in the frequency components of $\mathbf{x}(t)$ in the neighborhood of w. Recall that one interpretation of $\mathbf{x}(t)$ is that of a single time function (t variable; one outcome). For that interpretation, the time function, as with any time function, is made up of a summation of frequency components, and its spectral density gives the relative power contributed by each component. If we view $\mathbf{x}(t)$ as a family of time functions (*t* variable; all possible outcomes), then the spectral density gives the average power in each frequency component, averaged over all possible time functions $\mathbf{x}(t)$.

The Fourier inversion formula gives the time function in terms of its Fourier transform:

$$R(\tau) = \frac{1}{2\pi} \int_{-\infty}^{\infty} S(w)e^{jw\tau} dw$$

With $\tau = 0$, the preceding yields

$$\frac{1}{2\pi} \int_{-\infty}^{\infty} S(w) dw = R(0) = E[|\mathbf{x}(t)|^2]$$

Thus, the total area under $S(w)/2\pi$ equals the average power of the process $\mathbf{x}(t)$. Also note that:

$$S(0) = \int_{-\infty}^{\infty} R(\tau) d\tau$$

$S(0)$ represents the direct-current (dc) component of the power spectrum and corresponds to the integral of the autocorrelation function. This component will be finite only if $R(\tau)$ decays as $\tau \to \infty$ sufficiently rapidly for the integral of $R(\tau)$ to be finite.

We can also express the power spectrum for a stochastic process that is defined at discrete points in time (discrete-time stochastic process). In this case, we have

$$S(w) = \sum_{k=-\infty}^{\infty} R(k)e^{-jkw} \qquad S(0) = \sum_{k=-\infty}^{\infty} R(k)$$

Again, $S(0)$ represents the dc component of the power spectrum and corresponds to the infinite sum of the autocorrelation function. This component will be finite only if $R(\tau)$ decays as $\tau \to \infty$ sufficiently rapidly for the summation to be finite.

Table 6.1 shows some interesting correspondences between the autocorrelation function and the power spectral density.

Independent Increments

A continuous-parameter stochastic process $\{\mathbf{x}(t), 0 \leq t < \infty\}$ is said to have independent increments if $\mathbf{x}(0) = 0$ and, for all choices of indexes $t_0 < t_1 < \ldots < t_n$, the n random variables

$$\mathbf{x}(t_1) - \mathbf{x}(t_0), \mathbf{x}(t_2) - \mathbf{x}(t_1), \ldots, \mathbf{x}(t_n) - \mathbf{x}(t_{n-1})$$

are independent. Thus, the amount of "movement" in a stochastic process in one time interval is independent of the movement in any other non-overlapping time

TABLE 6.1 AUTOCORRELATION FUNCTIONS AND SPECTRAL DENSITIES

Stationary Random Process	Autocorrelation Function	Power Spectral Density
$X(t)$	$R_X(\tau)$	$S_X(w)$
$aX(t)$	$a^2 R_X(\tau)$	$a^2 S_X(w)$
$X'(t)$	$-d^2 R_X(\tau)/d\tau^2$	$w^2 S_X(w)$
$X^{(n)}(t)$	$(-1)^n d^{2n} R_X(\tau)/d\tau^{2n}$	$w^{2n} S_X(w)$
$X(t)\exp(jw_0 t)$	$\exp(jw_0\tau) R_X(\tau)$	$S_X(w - w_0)$

interval. The process is said to have stationary independent increments if, in addition, $\mathbf{x}(t_2 + h) - \mathbf{x}(t_1 + h)$ has the same distribution as $\mathbf{x}(t_2) - \mathbf{x}(t_1)$ for all choices of $t_2 > t_1$ and every $h > 0$.

Two properties of processes with stationary independent increments are noteworthy. If $\mathbf{x}(t)$ has stationary independent increments and $E[\mathbf{x}(t)] = \mu(t)$ is a continuous function of time, then $\mu(t) = a + bt$, where a and b are constants. Also, if $Var[\mathbf{x}(t) - \mathbf{x}(0)]$ is a continuous function of time, then for all s, $Var[\mathbf{x}(s + t) - \mathbf{x}(s)] = \sigma^2 t$, where σ^2 is a constant.

Two processes that play a central role in the theory of stochastic processes, the Brownian motion process and the Poisson process, have independent increments. A brief introduction to both follows.

Brownian Motion Process

Brownian motion is the random movement of microscopic particles suspended in a liquid or gas caused by collisions with molecules of the surrounding medium. This physical phenomenon is the basis for the definition of the Brownian motion stochastic process, also known as the Wiener process and the Wiener-Levy process.

Let us consider the function $B(t)$ for a particle in Brownian motion as denoting the displacement from a starting point in one dimension after time t. Consider the net movement of the particle in a time interval (s, t), which is long compared to the time between impacts. The quantity $B(t) - B(s)$ can be viewed as the sum of a large number of small displacements. By the central limit theorem, we can assume that this quantity has a normal probability distribution.

If we assume that the medium is in equilibrium, it is reasonable to assume that the net displacement depends only on the length of the time interval and not on the time at which the interval begins. That is, the probability distribution of $B(t) - B(s)$ should be the same as $B(t + h) - B(s + h)$ for any $h > 0$. Finally, if the motion of the particle is due entirely to frequent random collisions, then the net displacements in non-overlapping time intervals should be independent and therefore $B(t)$ has independent increments.

With the foregoing reasoning in mind we define a Brownian motion process $B(t)$ as one that satisfies the following conditions:

1. $\{B(t), 0 \leqslant t < \infty\}$ has stationary independent increments.
2. For every $t > 0$, the random variable $B(t)$ has a normal distribution.
3. For all $t > 0$, $E[B(t)] = 0$.
4. $B(0) = 0$.

The probability density of a Brownian motion process has the form

$$f_B(x, t) = \frac{1}{\sigma\sqrt{2\pi t}} \, e^{-(x - \mu(t))^2/2\sigma^2 t}$$

We have assumed that $\mu(t) = 0$ and, for simplicity, let us normalize to $\sigma = 1$. Then the equation becomes

$$f_B(x, t) = \frac{1}{\sqrt{2\pi t}} \, e^{-x^2/2t}$$

From this we have

$$\text{Var}[B(t)] = t; \quad \text{Var}[B(t) - B(s)] = |t - s|$$

Another important quantity is the autocorrelation of $B(t)$, expressed as $R_B(t_1, t_2)$. We derive this quantity in the following way. First, observe that for $t_4 > t_3 > t_2 > t_1$

$$E[(B(t_4) - B(t_3))(B(t_2) - B(t_1))] = E[B(t_4) - B(t_3)] \times E[B(t_2) - B(t_1)]$$
$$= (E[B(t_4)] - E[B(t_3)]) \times (E[B(t_2)] - E[B(t_1)])$$
$$= (0 - 0) \times (0 - 0) = 0$$

The first line of the preceding equation is true because the two intervals are non-overlapping and therefore the quantities $(B(t_4) - B(t_3))$ and $(B(t_2) - B(t_1))$ are independent due to the assumption of independent increments. Recall that for independent random variables X and Y, $E[XY] = E[X]E[Y]$. Now consider the two intervals $(0, t_1)$ and (t_1, t_2) for $0 < t_1 < t_2$. These are nonoverlapping intervals, so

$$0 = E[(B(t_2) - B(t_1))(B(t_1) - B(0))]$$
$$= E[(B(t_2) - B(t_1))B(t_1)]$$
$$= E[B(t_2)B(t_1)] - E[B^2(t_1)]$$
$$= E[B(t_2)B(t_1)] - \text{Var}[B(t_1)]$$
$$= E[B(t_2)B(t_1)] - t_1$$

Therefore,

$$R_B(t_1, t_2) = E[B(t_1)B(t_2)] = t_1 \quad \text{where } t_1 < t_2$$

In general, then, the autocorrelation of $B(t)$ can be expressed as $R_B(t, s) = \min[t, s]$. Because $B(t)$ has zero mean, the autocovariance is the same as the autocorrelation. Thus $C_B(t, s) = \min[t, s]$.

A useful interpretation of a Brownian motion process is the following. Suppose that X is a normally distributed random variable with zero mean and unit variance:

$$f(x) = \frac{1}{\sqrt{2\pi}} e^{-x^2/2}$$

Then define the stochastic process $B(t)$ as follows:

$$B(t) = X\sqrt{t}$$

That is, the value of $B(t)$ at time t is equal to the value of the random variable X multiplied by the square root of the time interval. For a given value of t, $B(t)$ is a normally distributed random variable with zero mean. For any random variable X and constant a, it is true that $\text{Var}(aX) = a^2\text{Var}(x)$. Therefore, $\text{Var}[B(t)] = \text{Var}[X\sqrt{t}] = (\sqrt{t})^2\text{Var}[X] = t$. Therefore, $B(t)$ is a Brownian motion process.

Another way to visualize the Brownian motion process is as the limit of a discrete process. Suppose you are constructing a graph of a function of discrete time based on selecting random numbers with a normal distribution. Each successive y-value is obtained by adding the random number to the y-coordinate of the previous point. Successive *t*-axis points are uniformly spaced (e.g., 1, 2, 3, ...). This would be a discrete-time function that approximates Brownian motion. If we divide the time axis more finely and select the random numbers with proportionately smaller variances, we improve the approximation. In the limit, this becomes a continuous-time Brownian motion process.

Poisson and Related Processes

Recall that for random arrivals in time, we have the Poisson distribution

$$\Pr[k \text{ items arrive in time interval } T] = \frac{(\lambda T)^k}{k!} e^{-\lambda T}$$

We can define a **Poisson counting process** $\{N(t), t \geq 0\}$ as follows:

1. $N(t)$ has stationary independent increments.
2. $N(0) = 0$.
3. For $0 < t_1 < t_2$, the quantity $N(t_2) - N(t_1)$ equals the number of points in the interval (t_1, t_2) and is Poisson distributed with mean $\lambda(t_1 - t_2)$.

Then we have the following probability functions for $N(t)$:

$$\Pr[N(t) = k] = \frac{(\lambda t)^k}{k!} e^{-\lambda t}$$

$$E[N(t)] = \text{Var}[N(t)] = \lambda t$$

Clearly, $N(t)$ is not stationary because its mean is a function of time. Every time function of this stochastic process (one outcome) is of an increasing staircase form with steps equal to 1, occurring at the random points t_i. Figure 6.4a gives an example of $N(t)$ for a specific outcome.

A stationary process related to the Poisson counting process is the **Poisson increment process**. For a Poisson counting process $N(t)$ with mean λt and for a constant L ($L > 0$), we can define the Poisson increment process $X(t)$ as follows:

$$X(t) = \frac{N(t + L) - N(t)}{L}$$

$X(t)$ equals k/L, where k is the number of points in the interval $(t, t + L)$. The increment process derived from the counting process in Figure 6.4a is shown in Figure 6.4b. The following relationship holds:

$$E[X(t)] = \frac{1}{L} E[N(t + L)] - \frac{1}{L} E[N(t)] = \lambda$$

With a constant mean, $X(t)$ is a wide-sense stationary process and therefore has an autocorrelation function of a single variable, $R(\tau)$. It can be shown that this function is

$$R(\tau) = \begin{cases} \lambda^2 & |\tau| > L \\ \lambda^2 + \dfrac{\lambda^2}{L}\left(1 - \dfrac{|\tau|}{L}\right) & |\tau| < L \end{cases} \tag{6.5}$$

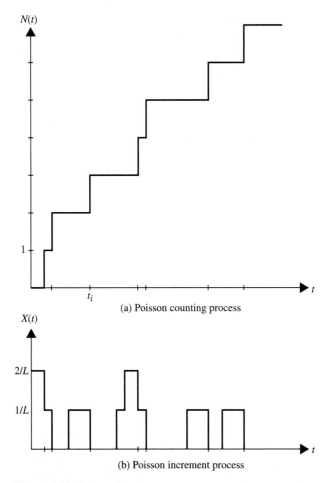

(a) Poisson counting process

(b) Poisson increment process

Figure 6.4 Poisson Processes.

Thus, the correlation is greatest if the two time instants are within the interval length of each other, and it is a small constant value for greater time differences.

Ergodicity

For a stochastic process $\mathbf{x}(t)$, there are two types of "averaging" functions that can be performed: ensemble averages and time averages.

First, consider *ensemble averages*. For a constant value of t, $\mathbf{x}(t)$ is a single random variable with a mean, variance, and other distributional properties. For a given constant value C of t, the following measures exist:

$$E[\mathbf{x}(C)] = \mu_{\mathbf{x}}(C) = \int_{-\infty}^{\infty} x \mathrm{f}(x; C)\,dx \quad \text{Continuous-value case}$$

$$E[\mathbf{x}(C)] = \mu_{\mathbf{x}}(C) = \sum_{\text{all } k} k \Pr[\mathbf{x}(C) = k] \quad \text{Discrete-value case}$$

$$\text{Var}[\mathbf{x}(C)] = \sigma_{\mathbf{x}(C)}^2 = E[(\mathbf{x}(C) - \mu_{\mathbf{x}}(C))^2] = E[\mathbf{x}(C)^2] - \mu_{\mathbf{x}}^2(C)$$

Each of these quantities is calculated over all values of $\mathbf{x}(t)$ for all possible outcomes. For a given random variable, the set of all possible outcomes is called an *ensemble*, and hence these are referred to as ensemble averages.

For time averages, consider a single outcome of $\mathbf{x}(t)$. This is a single deterministic function of t. Looking at $\mathbf{x}(t)$ in this way, we can consider what is the average value of the function over time. This *time average* is generally expressed as follows:

$$M_T = \frac{1}{2T} \int_{-T}^{T} \mathbf{x}(t)\,dt \quad \text{Continuous-time case}$$

$$M_T = \frac{1}{T} \sum_{t=1}^{T} \mathbf{x}(t) \quad \text{Discrete-time case}$$

Note that M_T is a random variable because the calculation of M_T for a single time function is a calculation for a single outcome.

In general terms, a stationary process is said to be *ergodic* if time averages equal ensemble averages. Because $E[\mathbf{x}(t)]$ is a constant for a stationary process, we have

$$E[M_T] = E[\mathbf{x}(t)] = \mu$$

A stationary process is said to be ergodic if

$$\lim_{T \to \infty} \text{Var}(M_T) = 0$$

In words, as the time average is taken over larger and larger time intervals, the value of the time average tends to the ensemble average.

The conditions under which a stochastic process is ergodic are beyond the scope of this book, but the assumption is generally made. Indeed, the assumption of ergodicity is essential to almost any mathematical model used for stationary stochastic processes. The practical importance of ergodicity is that in most cases, one does not have access to the ensemble of outcomes of a stochastic process or even to more than one outcome. Thus, the only means of obtaining estimates of the probabilistic parameters of the stochastic process is to analyze a single time function over a long period of time.

6.4 RECOMMENDED READING

There is a huge collection of books, dating back to the seventeenth century, on probability and random processes. My personal favorite is [HAMM91]; it is both a very practical book on the application of probability and an enlightening treatment of the philosophy of probability. A good book for self-study is [GOLD87]; it contains numerous problems with worked-out solutions.

There are also many books on stochastic processes. My personal favorite is [PAPO91]; this book has remained consistently excellent through multiple editions stretching back to 1965. Another good book, suitable for self-study, is [GRIM92]; it contains a number of problems, and a solutions manual is available from the publisher.

GOLD87   Goldberg, S. *Probability: An Introduction.* New York: Dover, 1987.

GRIM92   Grimmett, G., and Stirzaker, D. *Probability and Random Processes.* Oxford: Oxford University Press, 1992.

HAMM91   Hamming, R. *The Art of Probability: For Scientists and Engineers.* Reading, MA: Addison-Wesley, 1991.

PAPO91   Papoulis, A. *Probability, Random Variables, and Stochastic Processes.* New York: McGraw-Hill, 1991.

6.5   PROBLEMS

6.1   You are asked to play a game in which I hide a prize in one of three boxes while you are out of the room. When you return, you have to guess which box hides the prize. There are two stages to the game. First, you indicate one of the three boxes as your choice. As soon as you do that, I open the lid of one of the other two boxes and I will always open an empty box. I can do this because I know where the prize is hidden. At this point the prize must be in the box that you have chosen or in the other unopened box. You are now free to stick with your original choice or to switch to the other unopened box. You win the prize if your final selection is the box containing the prize. What is your best strategy? Should you (a) stay with your original choice, (b) switch to the other box, or (c) do either because it does not matter?

6.2   A patient has a test for some disease that comes back positive (indicating that he has the disease). You are told that
   • The accuracy of the test is 87% (i.e., if a patient has the disease, 87% of the time the test yields the correct result).
   • The incidence of the disease in the population is 1%.
Given that the test is positive, how probable is it that the patient really has the disease?

6.3   A taxicab was involved in a fatal hit-and-run accident at night. Two cab companies, the Green and the Blue, operate in the city. You are told that
   • 85% of the cabs in the city are Green and 15% are Blue.
   • A witness identified the cab as Blue.
The court tested the reliability of the witness under the same circumstances that existed on the night of the accident and concluded that the witness was correct in identifying the color of the cab 80% of the time. What is the probability that the cab involved in the incident was Blue rather than Green?

6.4   The birthday paradox is a famous problem in probability that can be stated as follows: What is the minimum value of K such that the probability is greater than 0.5 that at least two people in a group of K people have the same birthday? Ignore February 29 and assume that each birthday is equally likely. We will do the problem in two parts.
   a. Define $Q(K)$ as the probability that there are no duplicate birthdays in a group of K people. Derive a formula for $Q(K)$. *Hint*: First determine the number of different ways N that we can have K values with no duplicates.
   b. Define $P(K)$ as the probability that there is at least one duplicate birthday in a group of K people. Derive this formula. What is the minimum value of K such that $P(K) > 0.5$? It may help to plot $P(K)$.

6.5   A pair of fair dice is thrown. Let X be the maximum of the two numbers that comes up.
   a. Find the distribution of X.
   b. Find the expectation $E[X]$, the variance $Var[X]$, and the standard deviation σ_X.

6.6   A player tosses a fair die. If a prime number greater than one appears, he wins that number of dollars, but if a nonprime number appears, he loses that number of dollars.
   a. Denote the player's gain or loss on one toss by the random variable X. Enumerate the distribution of X.
   b. Is the game fair?

6.7 In the carnival game known as chuck-a-luck, a player pays an amount E as an entrance fee, selects a number between one and six, and then rolls three dice. If all three dice show the number selected, the player is paid four times the entrance fee; if two dice show the number, the player is paid three times the entrance fee; and if only one die shows the number, the player is paid twice the entrance fee. If the selected number does not show up, the player is paid nothing. Let X denote the player's gain in a single play of this game, and assume that the dice are fair.
   a. Determine the probability function of X.
   b. Compute $E[X]$.

6.8 The mean and variance of X are 50 and 4, respectively. Evaluate
   a. the mean of X^2
   b. the variance and standard deviation of $2X + 3$
   c. the variance and standard deviation of $-X$.

6.9 The random variable R represents a resistor and is uniform between 900 and 1100 Ω. Find the probability that R is between 950 and 1050.

6.10 Show that, all other things being equal, the greater the correlation coefficient of two random variables, the greater the variance of their sum and the less the variance of their difference.

6.11 Suppose that X and Y each have only two possible values, 0 and 1. Prove that if X and Y are uncorrelated, then they are also independent.

6.12 An artificial example of a stochastic process is a deterministic signal $\mathbf{x}(t) = g(t)$. Determine the mean, variance, and autocorrelation of $\mathbf{x}(t)$.

6.13 Suppose that $\mathbf{x}(t)$ is a stochastic process with

$$\mu(t) = 3 \quad R(t_1, t_2) = 9 + 4e^{-0.2|t_1 - t_2|}$$

Determine the mean, variance, and covariance of the following random variables $Z = \mathbf{x}(5)$ and $W = \mathbf{x}(8)$.

6.14 Let $\{\mathbf{Z_n}\}$ be a set of uncorrelated real-valued random variables, each with a mean of 0 and a variance of 1. Define the moving average

$$\mathbf{Y_n} = \sum_{i=0}^{K} a_i \mathbf{Z_{n-i}}$$

for constants $\alpha_0, \alpha_1, ..., \alpha_K$. Show that $\mathbf{Y}$ is stationary and find its autocovariance function.

6.15 Let $\mathbf{X_n} = \mathbf{A}\cos(n\lambda) = \mathbf{B}\sin(n\lambda)$, where $\mathbf{A}$ and $\mathbf{B}$ are uncorrelated random variables, each with a mean of 0 and a variance of 1. Show that $\mathbf{X}$ is stationary with a spectrum containing exactly one point.

CHAPTER 7

QUEUING ANALYSIS

Again and again the forecasts both of the military and of the naval Intelligence Staffs were vindicated to the wonder of friends and the chagrin of foes.

— ***The World Crisis,*** **Winston Churchill**

In the field of data communications and computer networking, you frequently need to predict the effects of some change in load or design. For example, an organization supports a number of terminals, personal computers, and workstations on a 16-Mbps token ring LAN. Another department in the same building is to be cut over onto the network. Can the existing LAN handle the increased workload, or would it be better to provide a second LAN with a bridge between the two?

There are other cases in which no facility exists but, on the basis of expected demand, a system design needs to be created. For example, a department intends to equip all its personnel with a PC and configure these onto a LAN with a file server. Based on experience elsewhere in the company, you can estimate the load each PC generates and estimate the required capacity of the LAN and the file server. In each case, the concern is system performance. In an interactive or real-time application, that usually means a concern for response time. In other cases, throughput is the principal issue.

To make performance projections, some sort of prediction tool is needed. For networking and communications problems—and indeed for many other practical, real-world problems—analytic models based on queuing theory can often provide the needed answers.

The number of questions that can be addressed with a queuing analysis is endless and touches on virtually every area discussed in this book. The ability to make such an analysis is an essential tool for those involved in this field.

Although the theory of queuing is mathematically complex, the application of queuing theory to the analysis of performance is in many cases remarkably straightforward. A knowledge of elementary statistical concepts (means and standard deviations) and a basic understanding of the applicability of queuing theory is all that is required. Armed with these, the analyst can often make a queuing analysis on the back of an envelope using readily available queuing tables, or using simple computer programs that occupy only a few lines of code.

This chapter provides a practical guide to queuing analysis. A subset, although a very important subset, of the subject is addressed.

7.1   HOW QUEUES BEHAVE; A SIMPLE EXAMPLE

Before getting into the details of queuing analysis, let us look at a crude example that will give some feel for the topic. Consider a Web server that is capable of handling an individual request in an average of 1 ms. In fact, to make things simple, assume that the server handles each request in exactly 1 ms. Now, if the rate of arriving requests is one per millisecond (1000/s), then it seems sensible to state that the server can keep up with the load.

Suppose that the requests arrive at a uniform rate of exactly one request each millisecond. When a request comes in, the server immediately handles the request. Just as the server completes the current request, a new request arrives and the server goes to work again.

Now let's take a more realistic approach and suppose that the average arrival rate for requests is one per millisecond but that there is some variability. During any given 1-ms period, there may be no requests, or one, or multiple requests, but the average is still one per millisecond. Again, common sense would seem to indicate that the server could keep up. During busy times, when lots of requests bunch up, the server can store outstanding requests in a buffer. Another way of putting this is to say that arriving requests enter a queue to await service. During quiet times, the server can catch up and clear the buffer. In this case, the interesting design issue would seem to be: How big should the buffer be?

Tables 7.1 through 7.3 give a very rough idea of the behavior of this system. In Table 7.1, we assume an arrival rate of 500 requests/s, which is half the capacity of the server. The entries in the table show the number of requests that arrive each second, the number of requests served during that second, and the number of outstanding requests waiting in the buffer at the end of the second. After 50 seconds, the table shows an average buffer contents of 43 requests, with a peak of over 600 requests. In Table 7.2, the arrival rate is increased to 95% of the server's capacity—namely, 950 requests/s—and the average buffer contents rises to 1859. This seems a

TABLE 7.1   QUEUE BEHAVIOR WITH NORMALIZED ARRIVAL RATE OF 0.5

Time	Input	Output	Queue	Time	Input	Output	Queue
0	0	0	0	26	190	190	0
1	88	88	0	27	500	500	0
2	796	796	0	28	96	96	0
3	1627	1000	627	29	943	943	0
4	51	678	0	30	105	105	0
5	34	34	0	31	183	183	0
6	966	966	0	32	447	447	0
7	714	714	0	33	542	542	0
8	1276	1000	276	34	166	166	0
9	494	769	0	35	165	165	0
10	933	933	0	36	490	490	0
11	107	107	0	37	510	510	0
12	241	241	0	38	877	877	0
13	16	16	0	39	37	37	0
14	671	671	0	40	163	163	0
15	643	643	0	41	104	104	0
16	812	812	0	42	42	42	0
17	262	262	0	43	291	291	0
18	218	218	0	44	645	645	0
19	1378	1000	378	45	363	363	0
20	507	885	0	46	134	134	0
21	15	15	0	47	920	920	0
22	820	820	0	48	1507	1000	507
23	1253	1000	253	49	598	1000	105
24	307	559	0	50	172	277	0
25	540	540	0	**Average**	499	499	43

little surprising: The arrival rate has gone up by less than a factor of 2, but the average buffer contents has gone up by more than a factor of 40. In Table 7.3, the arrival rate is increased slightly, to 99% of capacity, which yields an average buffer contents of 2583. Thus, a tiny increase in arrival rate results in an increase of almost 40% in the average buffer contents.

What this crude example suggests is that the behavior of a system with a queue may not accord with our intuition.

7.2   WHY QUEUING ANALYSIS?

It is often necessary to make projections of performance on the basis of existing load information or on the basis of estimated load for a new environment. A number of approaches are possible:

1. Do an after-the-fact analysis based on actual values.
2. Make a simple projection by scaling up from existing experience to the expected future environment.
3. Develop an analytic model based on queuing theory.
4. Program and run a simulation model.

TABLE 7.2 QUEUE BEHAVIOR WITH NORMALIZED ARRIVAL RATE OF 0.95

Time	Input	Output	Queue	Time	Input	Output	Queue
0	0	0	0	26	361	1000	3255
1	167	167	0	27	950	1000	3205
2	1512	1000	512	28	182	1000	2387
3	3091	1000	2604	29	1792	1000	3179
4	97	1000	1701	30	200	1000	2378
5	65	1000	765	31	348	1000	1726
6	1835	1000	1601	32	849	1000	1575
7	1357	1000	1957	33	1030	1000	1605
8	2424	1000	3382	34	315	1000	921
9	939	1000	3320	35	314	1000	234
10	1773	1000	4093	36	931	1000	165
11	203	1000	3296	37	969	1000	134
12	458	1000	2754	38	1666	1000	800
13	30	1000	1784	39	70	871	0
14	1275	1000	2059	40	310	310	0
15	1222	1000	2281	41	198	198	0
16	1543	1000	2824	42	80	80	0
17	498	1000	2322	43	553	553	0
18	414	1000	1736	44	1226	1000	226
19	2618	1000	3354	45	690	915	0
20	963	1000	3317	46	255	255	0
21	29	1000	2346	47	1748	1000	748
22	1558	1000	2904	48	2863	1000	2611
23	2381	1000	4285	49	1136	1000	2748
24	583	1000	3868	50	327	1000	2074
25	1026	1000	3894	**Average**	948	907	1859

Option 1 is no option at all: We will wait and see what happens. This leads to unhappy users and to unwise purchases. Option 2 sounds more promising. The analyst may take the position that it is impossible to project future demand with any degree of certainty. Therefore, it is pointless to attempt some exact modeling procedure. Rather, a rough-and-ready projection will provide ballpark estimates. The problem with this approach is that the behavior of most systems under a changing load is not what one would intuitively expect, as Section 7.1 suggests. If there is an environment in which there is a shared facility (e.g., a network, a transmission line, a time-sharing system), then the performance of that system typically responds in an exponential way to increases in demand.

Figure 7.1 is a typical example. The upper line shows what typically happens to user response time on a shared facility as the load on that facility increases. The load is expressed as a fraction of capacity. Thus, if we are dealing with a bridge that is capable of processing and forwarding 1000 frames per second, then a load of 0.5 represents transfer of 500 frames per second, and the response time is the amount of time it takes to retransmit any incoming frame. The lower line is a simple projection[1] based on a knowledge of the behavior of the system up to a load of 0.5. Note

---

[1] In fact, the lower line is based on fitting a third-order polynomial to the data available up to a load of 0.5.

TABLE 7.3   QUEUE BEHAVIOR WITH NORMALIZED ARRIVAL RATE OF 0.99

Time	Input	Output	Queue	Time	Input	Output	Queue
0	0	0	0	26	376	1000	4445
1	174	174	0	27	990	1000	4435
2	1576	1000	576	28	190	1000	3625
3	3221	1000	2798	29	1867	1000	4492
4	101	1000	1899	30	208	1000	3700
5	67	1000	966	31	362	1000	3062
6	1913	1000	1879	32	885	1000	2947
7	1414	1000	2292	33	1073	1000	3020
8	2526	1000	3819	34	329	1000	2349
9	978	1000	3797	35	327	1000	1676
10	1847	1000	4644	36	970	1000	1646
11	212	1000	3856	37	1010	1000	1656
12	477	1000	3333	38	1736	1000	2392
13	32	1000	2365	39	73	1000	1465
14	1329	1000	2693	40	323	1000	788
15	1273	1000	2967	41	206	994	0
16	1608	1000	3574	42	83	83	0
17	519	1000	3093	43	576	576	0
18	432	1000	2525	44	1277	1000	277
19	2728	1000	4253	45	719	996	0
20	1004	1000	4257	46	265	265	0
21	30	1000	3287	47	1822	1000	822
22	1624	1000	3910	48	2984	1000	2805
23	2481	1000	5391	49	1184	1000	2990
24	608	1000	4999	50	341	1000	2330
25	1069	1000	5068	**Average**	988	942	2583

that while things appear rosy when the simple projection is made, performance on the system will in fact collapse beyond a load of about 0.8 to 0.9.

Thus, a more exact prediction tool is needed. Option 3 is to make use of an analytic model, which is one that can be expressed as a set of equations that can be solved to yield the desired parameters (response time, throughput, etc.). For computer, operating-system, and networking problems, and indeed for many practical real-world problems, analytic models based on queuing theory provide a reasonably good fit to reality. The disadvantage of queuing theory is that a number of simplifying assumptions must be made to derive equations for the parameters of interest.

The final approach is a simulation model. Here, given a sufficiently powerful and flexible simulation programming language, the analyst can model reality in great detail and avoid making many of the assumptions required of queuing theory. However, in most cases, a simulation model is not needed or at least is not advisable as a first step in the analysis. For one thing, both existing measurements and projections of future load carry with them a certain margin of error. Thus, no matter how good the simulation model, the value of the results are limited by the quality of the input. For another, despite the many assumptions required of queuing theory, the results that are produced often come quite close to those that would be produced by a more careful simulation analysis. Furthermore, a queuing analysis

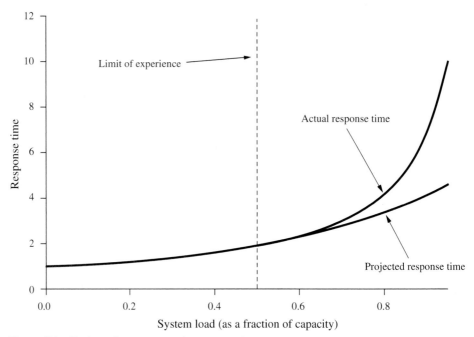

Figure 7.1 Projected versus actual response time.

can literally be accomplished in a matter of minutes for a well-defined problem, whereas simulation exercises can take days, weeks, or longer to program and run.

Accordingly, it behooves the analyst to master the basics of queuing theory.

7.3 QUEUING MODELS

The Single-server Queue

The simplest queuing system is depicted in Figure 7.2. The central element of the system is a server, which provides some service to items. Items from some population of items arrive at the system to be served. If the server is idle, an item is served

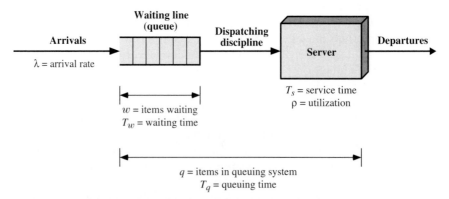

Figure 7.2 Queuing system structure and parameters for single-server queue.

immediately. Otherwise, an arriving item joins a waiting line.[2] When the server has completed serving an item, the item departs. If there are items waiting in the queue, one is immediately dispatched to the server.

Queue Parameters

Figure 7.2 also illustrates some important parameters associated with a queuing model. Items arrive at the facility at some average rate (items arriving per second) λ. At any given time, a certain number of items will be waiting in the queue (zero or more); the average number waiting is w, and the mean time that an item must wait is T_w. T_w is averaged over all incoming items, including those that do not wait at all. The server handles incoming items with an average service time T_s; this is the time interval between the dispatching of an item to the server and the departure of that item from the server. Utilization ρ is the fraction of time that the server is busy, measured over some interval of time. Finally, two parameters apply to the system as a whole. The average number of items in the system, including the item being served (if any) and the items waiting (if any), is q; and the average time that an item spends in the system, waiting and being served, is T_q.

If we assume that the capacity of the queue is infinite, then no items are ever lost from the system; they are just delayed until they can be served. Under these circumstances, the departure rate equals the arrival rate. As the arrival rate, which is the rate of traffic passing through the system, increases, the utilization increases and with it, congestion. The queue becomes longer, increasing waiting time. At $\rho = 1$, the server becomes saturated, working 100% of the time. Thus, the theoretical maximum input rate that can be handled by the system is

$$\lambda_{max} = \frac{1}{T_s}$$

However, queues become very large near system saturation, growing without bound when $\rho = 1$. Practical considerations, such as response time requirements or buffer sizes, usually limit the input rate for a single server to 70–90% of the theoretical maximum.

Illustration of Key Features

It is helpful to have an illustration of the processes involved in queuing. Figure 7.3 shows an example realization of a queuing process, with the total number of items in the system plotted against time. The shaded areas represent time periods in which the server is busy. On the time axis are marked two types of events: the arrival of item j at time A_j and the completion of service of item j at time D_j, when the item departs the system. The time that item j spends in the system is $T_j = D_j - A_j$; the actual service time for item j is denoted by S_j.

In this example, T_1 is composed entirely of the service time S_1 for the first item, because when item 1 arrives the system is empty and it can go straight into service. T_2 is composed of the time that item 2 waits for service $(D_1 - A_2)$ plus its service time S_2. Similarly, $T_3 = (D_3 - A_3) = (D_3 - D_2) + (D_2 - A_3) = S_3 + (D_2 - A_3)$.

---

[2] The waiting line is referred to as a queue in some treatments in the literature; it is also common to refer to the entire system as a queue. Unless otherwise noted, we use the term *queue* to mean "waiting line."

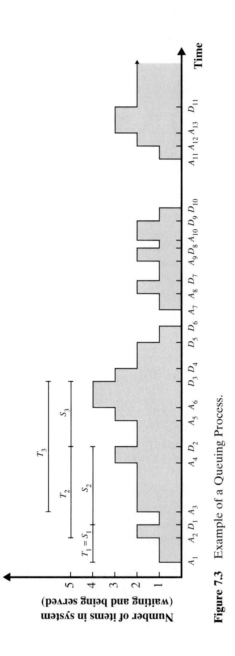

Figure 7.3 Example of a Queuing Process.

154

Model Characteristics

Before deriving any analytic equations for the queuing model, certain key characteristics of the model must be chosen. The following are the typical choices, usually reasonable in a data communications context:

- **Item population:** We assume an infinite population. This means that the arrival rate is not altered by the loss of population. If the population is finite, then the population available for arrival is reduced by the number of items currently in the system; this would typically reduce the arrival rate proportionally. Networking and server problems can usually be handled with an infinite-population assumption.

- **Queue size:** We assume an infinite queue size. Thus, the queue can grow without bound. With a finite queue, items can be lost from the system; that is, if the queue is full and additional items arrive, some items must be discarded. In practice, any queue is finite, but in many cases, this makes no substantive difference to the analysis. We address this issue briefly later in this chapter.

- **Dispatching discipline:** When the server becomes free, and if there is more than one item waiting, a decision must be made as to which item to dispatch next. The simplest approach is first in, first out (FIFO), also known as first come, first served (FCFS); this discipline is what is normally implied when the term *queue* is used. Another possibility is last in, first out (LIFO). One that you might encounter in practice is a dispatching discipline based on service time. For example, a LAN bridge may dispatch packets on the basis of shortest first (to generate the most outgoing packets) or longest first (to minimize processing time relative to transmission time). Unfortunately, a discipline based on service time is very difficult to model analytically. A more common possibility is dispatching on the basis of priority, which is discussed later.

Table 7.4 summarizes the notation that is used in Figure 7.2 and introduces some other useful parameters. In particular, we are often interested in the variability of various parameters, and this is neatly captured in the standard deviation.

TABLE 7.4   NOTATION USED IN THIS CHAPTER

λ	=	mean number of arrivals per second
T_s	=	mean service time for each arrival
σ_{T_s}	=	standard deviation of service time
ρ	=	utilization; fraction of time facility is busy
u	=	traffic intensity
Q	=	number of items in system (waiting and being served)
q	=	mean number of items in system (waiting and being served)
T_Q	=	time an item spends in system
T_q	=	mean time an item spends in system (queuing time)
σ_q	=	standard deviation of q
σ_{T_q}	=	standard deviation of T_q
w	=	mean number of items waiting to be served
T_w	=	mean time an item spends waiting for service
T_d	=	mean waiting time for items that have to wait (not including items with waiting time = 0)
σ_W	=	standard deviation of w
N	=	number of servers
$m_x(r)$	=	the rth percentile; that value of r below which x occurs r percent of the time

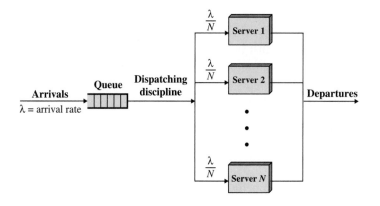

(a) Multiserver queue

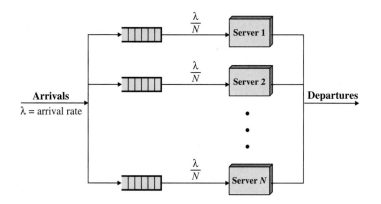

(b) Multiple single-server queues

Figure 7.4 Multiserver Versus Multiple Single-Server Queues.

The Multiserver Queue

Figure 7.4a shows a generalization of the simple model we have been discussing for multiple servers, all sharing a common queue. If an item arrives and at least one server is available, then the item is immediately dispatched to that server. It is assumed that all servers are identical; thus, if more than one server is available, it makes no difference which server is chosen for the item. If all servers are busy, a queue begins to form. As soon as one server becomes free, an item is dispatched from the queue using the dispatching discipline in force.

With the exception of utilization, all of the parameters illustrated in Figure 7.2 carry over to the multiserver case with the same interpretation. If we have N identical servers, then ρ is the utilization of each server, and we can consider $N\rho$ to be the utilization of the entire system; this latter term is often referred to as the traffic intensity u. Thus, the theoretical maximum utilization is $N \times 100\%$, and the theoretical maximum input rate is

$$\lambda_{max} = \frac{N}{T_s}$$

The key characteristics typically chosen for the multiserver queue correspond to those for the single-server queue. That is, we assume an infinite population and an infinite queue size, with a single infinite queue shared among all servers. For our purposes, unless otherwise stated, the dispatching discipline is FIFO. For the multi-server case, if all servers are assumed to be identical, the selection of a particular server for a waiting item has no effect on service time.

By way of contrast, Figure 7.4b shows the structure of multiple single-server queues. As we shall see, this apparently minor change in structure has a significant impact on performance.

Basic Queuing Relationships

To proceed much further, we are going to have to make some simplifying assumptions. These assumptions risk making the models less valid for various real-world situations. Fortunately, in many cases, the results will be sufficiently accurate for planning and design purposes.

There are, however, some relationships that are true in the general case, and these are illustrated in Table 7.5. By themselves, these relationships are not particularly helpful, although they can be used to answer a few basic questions. Here's an example taken from [MOLL89]. Consider a spy from Burger King trying to figure out how many people are inside the McDonald's across the way. He cannot sit inside the McDonald's all day, so he has to arrive at an answer just based on observing the traffic in and out of the building. Over the course of the day, he observes that on average 32 customers per hour go into the restaurant. He notes certain people and finds that on average a customer stays inside 12 minutes. Using Little's formula, the spy deduces that there are on average 6.4 customers in McDonald's at any given time (6.4 = 32 customers/hour × 0.2 hour/customer).

It would be useful at this point to gain an intuitive grasp of the equations in Table 7.5. For the equation $\rho = \lambda T_s$, consider that for an arrival rate of λ the average time between arrivals is $1/\lambda = T$. If T is less than T_s, then during a time interval T, the server is only busy for a time T_s for a utilization of $T_s/T = \lambda T_s$. Similar reasoning applies in the multiserver case to yield $\rho = (\lambda T_s)/N$.

Little's formula is less easy to visualize. Consider the experience of a single item arriving. When the item arrives, it will find on average w items waiting ahead of it. When the item leaves the queue behind it to be serviced, it will leave behind

TABLE 7.5 SOME BASIC QUEUING RELATIONSHIPS

General		Single Server	Multiserver
$q = \lambda T_q$	Little's formula	$\rho = \lambda T_s$	$\rho = \dfrac{\lambda T_s}{N}$
$w = \lambda T_w$	Little's formula	$q = w + \rho$	$u = \lambda T_s = \rho N$
$T_q = T_w + T_s$			$q = w + N\rho$

on average the same number of items in the queue—namely, w. This is in accord with saying that the average number waiting is w. Further, the average time that the item was waiting for service is T_w. Since items arrive at a rate of λ, we can reason that in the time T_w, a total of λT_w items must have arrived. Thus $w = \lambda T_w$. Similar reasoning can be applied to the relationship $q = \lambda T_q$.

Turning to the last equation in the first column In Table 7.5, it is easy to observe that the time that an item spends in the system is the sum of the time waiting for service plus the time being served. Thus, on average, $T_q = T_w + T_s$. The last equations in the second and third columns are easily justified. At any time, the number of items in the system is the sum of the number of items waiting for service plus the number of items being served. For a single server, the average number of items being served is ρ. Therefore, $q = w + \rho$ for a single server. Similarly, $q = w + N\rho$ for N servers.

Assumptions

The fundamental task of a queuing analysis is as follows: Given the following information as input:

- Arrival rate
- Service time

provide as output information concerning

- Items waiting
- Waiting time
- Items queued
- Queuing time.

What specifically would we like to know about these outputs? Certainly we would like to know their average values (w, T_w, q, T_q). In addition, it would be useful to know something about their variability. Thus, the standard deviation of each would be useful (σ_q, σ_{T_q}, σ_w, σ_{T_w}). Other measures may also be useful. For example, to design a buffer associated with a bridge or multiplexer, it might be useful to know for what buffer size the probability of overflow is less than 0.001. That is, what is the value of N such that $\Pr[\text{items waiting} < N] = 0.999$?

To answer such questions in general requires complete knowledge of the probability distribution of the arrival rate and service time. Furthermore, even with that knowledge, the resulting formulas are exceedingly complex. Thus, to make the problem tractable, we need to make some simplifying assumptions.

The most important of these assumptions is that the arrival rate obeys the Poisson distribution, which is equivalent to saying that the interarrival times are exponential, which is equivalent to saying that the arrivals occur randomly and independent of one another. This assumption is almost invariably made. Without it, most queuing analysis is impractical. With this assumption, it turns out that many useful results can be obtained if only the mean and standard deviation of the arrival rate and service time are known. Matters can be made even simpler and more detailed results can be obtained if it is assumed that the service time is exponential or constant.

A convenient notation has been developed for summarizing the principal assumptions that are made in developing a queuing model. The notation is $X/Y/N$, where X refers to the distribution of the interarrival times, Y refers to the distribution of service times, and N refers to the number of servers. The most common distributions are denoted as follows:

G = general independent arrivals or service times

M = negative exponential distribution

D = deterministic arrivals or fixed-length service

Thus, M/M/1 refers to a single-server queuing model with Poisson arrivals and exponential service times.

7.4 SINGLE-SERVER QUEUES

Table 7.6a provides some equations for single-server queues that follow the M/G/1 model. That is, the arrival rate is Poisson and the service time is general. Making use of a scaling factor A, the equations for some of the key output variables are straightforward. Note that the key factor in the scaling parameter is the ratio of the standard deviation of service time to the mean. No other information about the service time is needed. Two special cases are of some interest. When the standard deviation is equal to the mean, the service time distribution is exponential (M/M/1). This is the simplest case, and the easiest one for calculating results. Table 7.6b shows the simplified versions of equations for the standard deviation of q and T_q, plus some other parameters of interest. The other interesting case is a standard deviation of service time equal to zero; that is, a constant service time (M/D/1). The corresponding equations are shown in Table 7.6c.

Figures 7.5 and 7.6 plot values of average queue size and queuing time versus utilization for three values of σ_{T_s}/T_s. Note that the poorest performance is exhibited by the exponential service time, and the best by a constant service time. Usually, one can consider the exponential service time to be a worst case. An analysis based on this assumption will give conservative results. This is nice, because tables are available for the M/M/1 case and values can be looked up quickly.

What value of σ_{T_s}/T_s is one likely to encounter? We can consider four regions:

- **Zero:** This is the rare case of constant service time. For example, if all transmitted messages are of the same length, they would fit this category.
- **Ratio less than 1:** Because this ratio is better than the exponential case, using M/M/1 tables will give queue sizes and times that are slightly larger than they should be. Using the M/M/1 model would give answers on the safe side. An

TABLE 7.6   FORMULAS FOR SINGLE-SERVER QUEUES

Assumptions:
1. Poisson arrival rate.
2. Dispatching discipline does not give preference to items based on service times.
3. Formulas for standard deviation assume first-in, first-out dispatching.
4. No items are discarded from the queue.

(a) General Service Times (M/G/1)	**(b) Exponential Service Times (M/M/1)**	**(c) Constant Service Times (M/D/1)**

(a) General Service Times (M/G/1)

$$A = \frac{1}{2}\left[1 + \left(\frac{\sigma_{T_s}}{T_s}\right)^2\right]$$

$$q = \rho + \frac{\rho^2 A}{1 - \rho}$$

$$w = \frac{\rho^2 A}{1 - \rho}$$

$$T_q = T_s + \frac{\rho T_s A}{1 - \rho}$$

$$T_w = \frac{\rho T_s A}{1 - \rho}$$

(b) Exponential Service Times (M/M/1)

$$q = \frac{\rho}{1 - \rho} \qquad w = \frac{\rho^2}{1 - \rho}$$

$$T_q = \frac{T_s}{1 - \rho} \qquad T_w = \frac{\rho T_s}{1 - \rho}$$

$$\sigma_q = \frac{\sqrt{\rho}}{1 - \rho} \qquad \sigma_{T_q} = \frac{T_s}{1 - \rho}$$

$$\Pr[Q = N] = (1 - \rho)\rho^N$$

$$\Pr[Q \leq N] = \sum_{i=0}^{N}(1 - \rho)\rho^i$$

$$\Pr[T_Q \leq t] = 1 - e^{-(1-\rho)t/T_s}$$

$$m_{T_q}(r) = T_q \times \ln\left(\frac{100}{100 - r}\right)$$

$$m_{T_w}(r) = \frac{T_w}{\rho} \times \ln\left(\frac{100\rho}{100 - r}\right)$$

(c) Constant Service Times (M/D/1)

$$q = \frac{\rho^2}{2(1 - \rho)} + \rho$$

$$w = \frac{\rho^2}{2(1 - \rho)}$$

$$T_q = \frac{T_s(2 - \rho)}{2(1 - \rho)}$$

$$T_w = \frac{\rho T_s}{2(1 - \rho)}$$

$$\sigma_q = \frac{1}{1 - \rho}\sqrt{\rho - \frac{3\rho^2}{2} + \frac{5\rho^3}{6} - \frac{\rho^4}{12}}$$

$$\sigma_{T_q} = \frac{T_s}{1 - \rho}\sqrt{\frac{\rho}{3} - \frac{\rho^2}{12}}$$

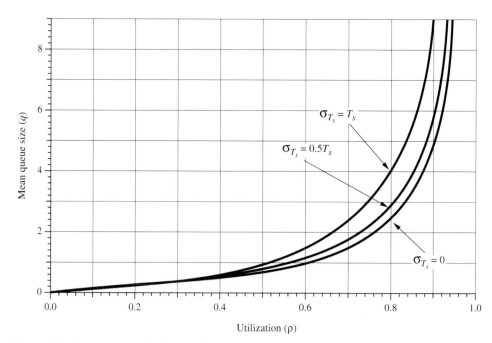

Figure 7.5   Mean queue size for single-server queue.

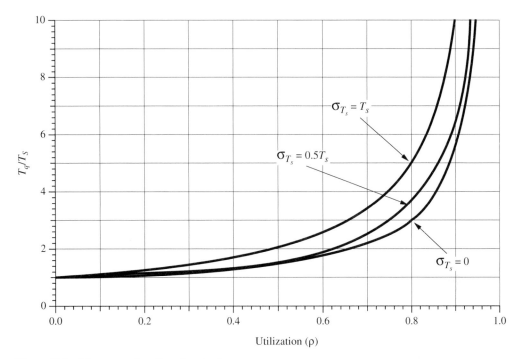

Figure 7.6 Mean queuing time for single-server queue.

example of this category might be a data entry application for a particular form.

- **Ratio close to 1:** This is a common occurrence and corresponds to exponential service time. That is, service times are essentially random. Consider message lengths to a computer terminal: A full screen might be 1920 characters, with message sizes varying over the full range. Airline reservations, file lookups on inquires, shared LAN, and packet-switching networks are examples of systems that often fit this category.

- **Ratio greater than 1:** If you observe this, you need to use the M/G/1 model and not rely on the M/M/1 model. A common occurrence of this is a bimodal distribution, with a wide spread between the peaks. An example is a system that experiences many short messages, many long messages, and few in between.

The same consideration applies to the arrival rate. For a Poisson arrival rate, the interarrival times are exponential, and the ratio of standard deviation to mean is 1. If the observed ratio is much less than one, then arrivals tend to be evenly spaced (not much variability), and the Poisson assumption will overestimate queue sizes and delays. On the other hand, if the ratio is greater than 1, then arrivals tend to cluster and congestion becomes more acute.

7.5 MULTISERVER QUEUES

Table 7.7 lists formulas for some key parameters for the multiserver case. Note the restrictiveness of the assumptions. Useful congestion statistics for this model have been obtained only for the case of M/M/N, where the exponential service times are identical for the N servers.

Note the presence of the Erlang C function in nearly all of the equations. This is the probability that all servers are busy at a given instant; equivalently, this is the probability that the number of items in the system (waiting and being served) is greater than or equal to the number of servers. The equation has the form

$$C(N, u) = \frac{1 - K}{1 - \rho K}$$

where K is known as the Poisson ratio function because it is a probability; its value is always between zero and one. As can be seen, this quantity is a function of the number of servers and the utilization. Unfortunately, this expression turns up frequently in queuing calculations and is not easy to compute. Tables of values are

TABLE 7.7 FORMULAS FOR MULTISERVER QUEUES (M/M/N)

Assumptions:
1. Poisson arrival rate.
2. Exponential service times.
3. All servers equally loaded.
4. All servers have same mean service time.
5. First-in, first-out dispatching.
6. No items are discarded from the queue.

$$K = \frac{\sum_{I=0}^{N-1} \frac{(N\rho)^I}{I!}}{\sum_{I=0}^{N} \frac{(N\rho)^I}{I!}} \quad \text{Poisson ratio function}$$

$$\text{Erlang } C \text{ function} = \text{Probability that all servers are busy} = C = \frac{1 - K}{1 - \rho K}$$

$$q = C\frac{\rho}{1 - \rho} + N\rho \qquad W = C\frac{\rho}{1 - \rho}$$

$$T_q = \frac{C}{N}\frac{T_s}{1 - \rho} + T_s \qquad T_W = \frac{C}{N}\frac{T_s}{1 - \rho}$$

$$\sigma_{T_q} = \frac{T_s}{N(1 - \rho)}\sqrt{C(2 - C) + N^2(1 - \rho)^2}$$

$$\sigma_W = \frac{1}{1 - \rho}\sqrt{C\rho(1 + \rho - C\rho)}$$

$$\Pr[T_W > t] = Ce^{-N(1-\rho)t/T_s}$$

$$m_{T_w}(r) = \frac{T_s}{N(1 - \rho)}\ln\left(\frac{100C}{100 - r}\right)$$

$$T_d = \frac{T_s}{N(1 - \rho)}$$

readily found, or a computer program must be used. Note that for a single-server system, this equation simplifies to $C(1, u) = \rho$.

7.6 EXAMPLES

Let us look at a few examples to get some feel for the use of these equations.

Database Server

Consider a LAN with 100 personal computers and a server that maintains a common database for a query application. The average time for the server to respond to a query is 0.6 seconds, and the standard deviation is estimated to equal the mean. At peak times, the query rate over the LAN reaches 20 queries per minute. We would like to answer the following questions:

- What is the average response time ignoring line overhead?
- If a 1.5-second response time is considered the maximum acceptable, what percent growth in message load can occur before the maximum is reached?
- If 20% more utilization is experienced, will response time increase by more or less than 20%?

Assume an M/M/1 model, with the database server being the server in the model. We ignore the effect of the LAN, assuming that its contribution to the delay is negligible. Facility utilization is calculated as

$$\rho = \lambda T_s$$
$$= (20 \text{ arrivals per minute})(0.6 \text{ seconds per transmission})/$$
$$(60 \text{ seconds/minute})$$
$$= 0.2$$

The first value, average response time, is easily calculated:

$$T_q = T_s/(1 - \rho)$$
$$= 0.6/(1 - 0.2) = 0.75 \text{ seconds}$$

The second value is more difficult to obtain. Indeed, as worded, there is no answer because there is a nonzero probability that some instances of response time will exceed 1.5 seconds for any value of utilization. Instead, let us say that we would like 90% of all responses to be less than 1.5 seconds. Then, we can use the equation from Table 7.6b:

$$m_{T_q}(r) = T_q \times \ln(100/(100 - r))$$

$$m_{T_q}(90) = T_q \times \ln(10) = \frac{T_s}{1 - \rho} \times 2.3 = 1.5 \text{ seconds}$$

We have $T_s = 0.6$. Solving for ρ yields $\rho = 0.08$. In fact, utilization would have to decline from 20% to 8% to put 1.5 seconds at the 90th percentile.

The third part of the question is to find the relationship between increases in load versus response time. Because a facility utilization of 0.2 is down in the flat part of the curve, response time will increase more slowly than utilization. In this case, if facility utilization increases from 20% to 40%, which is a 100% increase, the value of T_q goes from 0.75 seconds to 1.0 second, which is an increase of only 33%.

Calculating Percentiles

Consider a configuration in which packets are sent from computers on a LAN to systems on other networks. All of these packets must pass through a router that connects the LAN to a wide area network and hence to the outside world. Let us look at the traffic from the LAN through the router. Packets arrive with a mean arrival rate of five per second. The average packet length is 144 octets, and it is assumed that packet length is exponentially distributed. Line speed from the router to the wide area network is 9600 bps. The following questions are asked:

1. What is the mean queuing time in the router?
2. How many packets are in the router, including those waiting for transmission and the one currently being transmitted (if any), on the average?
3. Same question as (2), for the 90th percentile.
4. Same question as (2), for the 95th percentile.

$$\lambda = 5 \text{ packets/second}$$
$$T_s = (144 \text{ octets} \times 8 \text{ bits/octet})/9600 \text{ bps} = 0.12 \text{ second}$$
$$\rho = \lambda T_s = 5 \times 0.12 = 0.6$$
$$T_q = T_s/(1 - \rho) = 0.3 \text{ second} \qquad \text{Mean queuing time}$$
$$q = \rho/(1 - \rho) = 1.5 \text{ packets} \qquad \text{Mean queue length}$$

To obtain the percentiles, we use the equation from Table 7.6b:

$$\Pr[Q = N] = (1 - \rho)\rho^N$$

To calculate the rth percentile of queue size, we write the preceding equation in cumulative form:

$$\frac{r}{100} = \sum_{k=0}^{m_q(r)} (1 - \rho)\rho^k = 1 - \rho^{1 + m_q(r)}$$

Here $m_q(r)$ represents the maximum number of packets in the queue expected r percent of the time. That is, $m_q(r)$ is that value below which q occurs r percent of the time. In the form given, we can determine the percentile for any queue size. We wish to do the reverse: Given r, find $m_q(r)$. So, taking the logarithm of both sides,

$$m_q(r) = \frac{\ln\left(1 - \dfrac{r}{100}\right)}{\ln \rho} - 1$$

If $m_q(r)$ is fractional, take the next higher integer; if it is negative, set it to zero. For our example, $\rho = 0.6$ and we wish to find $m_q(90)$ and $m_q(95)$:

$$m_q(r) = \frac{\ln\left(1 - \frac{r}{100}\right)}{\ln\rho} - 1$$

Thus, 90% of the time there are fewer than four packets in the queue, and 95% of the time there are fewer than five packets. If we were designing to a 95th percentile criterion, a buffer would have to be provided to store at least five packets.

A Multiserver Problem [3]

An engineering firm provides each of its analysts with a personal computer, all of which are hooked up over a LAN to a database server. In addition, there is an expensive, standalone graphics workstation that is used for special-purpose design tasks. During the course of a typical eight-hour day, 10 engineers will make use of the workstation and spend an average of 30 minutes at a session.

Single-server Model

The engineers complain to their manager that the wait for using the workstation is long, often an hour or more, and are asking for more workstations. This surprises the manager since the utilization of the workstation is only 5/8 ($10 \times 1/2 = 5$ hours out of 8). To convince the manager, one of the engineers performs a queuing analysis. The engineer makes the usual assumptions of an infinite population, random arrivals, and exponential service times, none of which seem unreasonable for rough calculations. Using the equations in Tables 7.5 and 7.6b, the engineer gets

$$T_w = \frac{\rho T_s}{1 - \rho} = 50 \text{ minutes} \qquad \text{Average time an engineer spends waiting for the workstation}$$

$$m_{T_w}(90) = \frac{T_w}{\rho} \times \ln(10\rho) = 146.6 \text{ minutes} \qquad \text{90th percentile waiting time}$$

$$\lambda = \frac{10}{8 \times 60} = 0.021 \text{ engineers/minute} \qquad \text{Arrival rate of engineers}$$

$$w = \lambda T_w = 1.0416 \text{ engineers} \qquad \text{Average number of engineers waiting}$$

These figures show that indeed the engineers do have to wait an average of almost an hour to use the workstation and that in 10% of the cases, an engineer has to wait well over two hours. Even if there is a significant error in the estimate (say, 20%), the waiting time is still far too long. Furthermore, if an engineer can do no useful work while waiting for the workstation, then a little over one engineer-day is being lost.

Multiserver Model

The engineers have convinced the manager of the need for more workstations. They would like the mean waiting time not to exceed 10 minutes, with the 90th percentile value not to exceed 15 minutes. This concerns the manager, who reasons that

---

[3] This example is based on one that originally appeared in [ALLE80].

if one workstation results in a waiting time of 50 minutes, then five workstations will be required to get the average down to 10 minutes.

The engineers set to work to determine how many workstations are required. There are two possibilities: Put additional workstations in the same room as the original one (multiserver queue) or scatter the workstations to various rooms on various floors (multiple single-server queues). First, we look at the multiserver case and consider the addition of a second workstation in the same room. Let's assume that the addition of the new workstation, which reduces waiting time, does not affect the arrival rate (10 engineers per day). Then the available service time is 16 hours in an 8-hour day with a demand of 5 hours (10 engineers $\times$ 0.5 hours), giving a utilization of 5/16 = 0.3125. Using the equations in Table 7.7,

$$C(2, u) = C(2, 0.625) = 0.1488 \qquad \text{Probability both servers are busy}$$

$$T_w = \frac{CT_s}{N(1 - \rho)} = 3.247 \text{ minutes} \qquad \begin{array}{l}\text{Average time an engineer spends}\\ \text{waiting for a workstation}\end{array}$$

$$m_{T_w}(90) = \frac{T_s}{2(1 - \rho)} \ln(10C) = 8.67 \text{ minutes} \quad \text{90th percentile waiting time}$$

$$w = \lambda T_w = 0.07 \text{ engineers} \qquad \text{Average number of engineers waiting}$$

With this arrangement, the probability that an engineer that wishes to use a workstation must wait is less than 0.15 and the average wait is just a little over three minutes, with the 90th-percentile wait of under nine minutes. Despite the manager's doubts, the multiserver arrangement with two workstations easily meets the design requirement.

All of the engineers are housed on two floors of the building, so the manager wonders whether it might be more convenient to place one workstation on each floor. If we assume that the traffic to the two workstations is about evenly split, then there are two M/M/1 queues, each with a λ of five engineers per eight-hour day. This yields

$$\rho = \lambda T_s = 0.3125 \qquad \text{Utilization of one server}$$

$$T_w = \frac{\rho T_s}{1 - \rho} = 13.64 \text{ minutes} \qquad \begin{array}{l}\text{Average time an engineer spends}\\ \text{waiting for the workstation}\end{array}$$

$$m_{T_w}(90) = \frac{T_w}{\rho} \times \ln(10\rho) = 49.73 \text{ minutes} \quad \text{90th percentile waiting time}$$

$$w = \lambda T_w = 1.142 \text{ engineers} \qquad \text{Average number of engineers waiting}$$

This performance is significantly worse than the multiserver model and does not meet the design criteria. Table 7.8 summarizes the results and also shows the results for four and five separate workstations. Note that to meet the design goal, five separate workstations are needed compared to only two multiserver workstations.

Although you may not be an expert in queuing theory, you now know enough to be annoyed when you have to wait in a line at a multiple single-server queue facility.

TABLE 7.8   SUMMARY OF CALCULATIONS FOR MULTISERVER EXAMPLE

Workstations	System	ρ	T_w	$m\,T_w(90)$
1	M/M/1	0.625	50.00	146.61
2	M/M/2	0.3125	3.25	8.67
2	M/M/1's	0.3125	13.64	49.73
4	M/M/1's	0.15625	5.56	15.87
5	M/M/1's	0.125	4.29	7.65

7.7 QUEUES WITH PRIORITIES

So far we have considered queues in which items are treated in a first-come, first-served basis. There are many cases in both networking and operating-system design in which it is desirable to use priorities. Priorities may be assigned in a variety of ways. For example, priorities may be assigned on the basis of traffic type. If it turns out that the average service time for the various traffic types is identical, then the overall equations for the system are not changed, although the performance seen by the different traffic classes will differ.

An important case is one in which priority is assigned on the basis of average service time. Typically, items with shorter expected service times are given priority over items with longer service times. For example, a packet-switching network may give priority to shorter packets so that they are not delayed behind long packets. With this kind of scheme, performance is improved for higher-priority traffic.

Table 7.9 shows the formulas that apply when we assume two priority classes with different service times for each class. These results are easily generalized to any number of priority classes.

To see the effects of the use of priority, let us consider a simple of example of a data stream consisting of a mixture of long and short packets being transmitted by

TABLE 7.9   FORMULAS FOR SINGLE-SERVER QUEUES
WITH TWO PRIORITY CATEGORIES

Assumptions:
1. Poisson arrival rate.
2. Priority 1 items are serviced before priority 2 items.
3. First-in, first-out dispatching for items of equal priority.
4. No item is interrupted while being served.
5. No items leave the queue (lost calls delayed).

(a) General Formulas

$$\lambda = \lambda_1 + \lambda_2$$

$$\rho_1 = \lambda_1 T_{s1}; \quad \rho_2 = \lambda_2 T_{s2}$$

$$\rho = \rho_1 + \rho_2$$

$$T_s = \frac{\lambda_1}{\lambda} T_{s1} + \frac{\lambda_2}{\lambda} T_{s2}$$

$$T_q = \frac{\lambda_1}{\lambda} T_{q1} + \frac{\lambda_2}{\lambda} T_{q2}$$

(b) Exponential Service Times

$$w_1 = \frac{\rho_1 (\rho_1 T_{s1} + \rho_2 T_{s2})}{T_{s1}(1 - \rho_1)}$$

$$w_2 = w_1 \frac{\lambda_2}{\lambda_1 (1 - \rho)}$$

$$T_{q1} = T_{s1} + \frac{\rho_1 T_{s1} + \rho_2 T_{s2}}{1 - \rho_1}$$

$$T_{q2} = T_{s2} + \frac{T_{q1} - T_{s1}}{1 - \rho}$$

a packet-switching node and that the rate of arrival of the two types of packets is equal. Suppose that both packets have lengths that are exponentially distributed and that the long packets have a mean packet length of 10 times the short packets. In particular, let us assume a 64-kbps transmission link and that the mean packet lengths are 80 and 800 octets. Then the two service times are 0.01 and 0.1 seconds. Also assume that the arrival rate for each type is eight packets per second. So that the shorter packets are not held up by the longer packets, let us assign the shorter packets a higher priority. Then

$$\rho_1 = 8 \times 0.01 = 0.08 \quad \rho_2 = 8 \times 0.1 = 0.8 \quad \rho = 0.88$$

$$T_{q1} = 0.01 + \frac{0.08 \times 0.01 \times 0.8 \times 0.1}{1 - 0.08} = 0.098 \text{ seconds}$$

$$T_{q2} = 0.1 + \frac{0.098 - 0.01}{1 - 0.88} = 0.833 \text{ seconds}$$

$$T_q = 0.5 \times 0.098 + 0.5 \times 0.833 = 0.4655 \text{ seconds}$$

So we see that the higher-priority packets get considerably better service than the lower-priority packets.

7.8 NETWORKS OF QUEUES

In a distributed environment, isolated queues are unfortunately not the only problem presented to the analyst. Often, the problem to be analyzed consists of several interconnected queues. Figure 7.7 illustrates this situation, using nodes to represent queues and the interconnecting lines to represent traffic flow.

Two elements of such a network complicate the methods shown so far:

- The partitioning and merging of traffic, as illustrated by nodes 1 and 5, respectively, in the figure
- The existence of queues in tandem, or series, as illustrated by nodes 3 and 4.

No exact method has been developed for analyzing general queuing problems that have the aforementioned elements. However, if the traffic flow is Poisson and the service times are exponential, an exact and simple solution exists. In this section, we first examine the two elements listed previously, and then present the approach to queuing analysis.

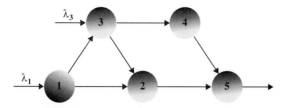

Figure 7.7   Example of a network of queues.

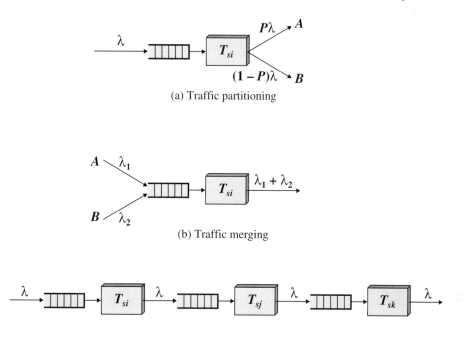

(a) Traffic partitioning

(b) Traffic merging

(c) Simple tandem queue

Figure 7.8   Elements of queuing networks.

Partitioning and Merging of Traffic Streams

Suppose that traffic arrives at a queue with a mean arrival rate of λ, and that there are two paths, A and B, by which an item may depart (Figure 7.8a). When an item is serviced and departs the queue, it does so via path A with probability P and via path B with probability $(1 - P)$. In general, the traffic distribution of streams A and B will differ from the incoming distribution. However, if the incoming distribution is Poisson, then the two departing traffic flows also have Poisson distributions, with mean rates of $P\lambda$ and $(1 - P)\lambda$.

A similar situation exists for traffic merging (Figure 7.8b). If two Poisson streams with mean rates of λ_1 and λ_2 are merged, the resulting stream is Poisson with a mean rate of $\lambda_1 + \lambda_2$.

Both of these results generalize to more than two departing streams for partitioning and more than two arriving streams for merging.

Queues in Tandem

Figure 7.8c is an example of a set of single-server queues in tandem: The input for each queue except the first is the output of the previous queue. Assume that the input to the first queue is Poisson. Then, if the service time of each queue is exponential and the queues are of infinite capacity, the output of each queue is a Poisson stream statistically identical to the input. When this stream is fed into the next queue, the delays at the second queue are the same as if the original traffic had bypassed the first queue and fed directly into the second queue. Thus, the queues are independent and may be analyzed one at a time. Therefore, the mean total delay for the tandem system is equal to the sum of the mean delays at each stage.

This result can be extended to the case where some or all of the nodes in tandem are multiserver queues.

Jackson's Theorem

Jackson's theorem can be used to analyze a network of queues. The theorem is based on three assumptions:

1. The queuing network consists of m nodes, each of which provides an independent exponential service.
2. Items arriving from outside the system to any one of the nodes arrive with a Poisson rate.
3. Once served at a node, an item goes (immediately) to one of the other nodes with a fixed probability, or out of the system.

Jackson's theorem states that in such a network of queues, each node is an independent queuing system, with a Poisson input determined by the principles of partitioning, merging, and tandem queuing. Thus, each node may be analyzed separately from the others using the M/M/1 or M/M/N model, and the results may be combined by ordinary statistical methods. Mean delays at each node may be added to derive system delays, but nothing can be said about the higher moments of system delays (e.g., standard deviation).

Jackson's theorem appears attractive for application to packet-switching networks. One can model the packet-switching network as a network of queues. Each packet represents an individual item. We assume that each packet is transmitted separately and, at each packet-switching node in the path from source to destination, the packet is queued for transmission on the next length. The service at a queue is the actual transmission of the packet and is proportional to the length of the packet.

The flaw in this approach is that a condition of the theorem is violated: namely, it is not the case that the service distributions are independent. Because the length of a packet is the same at each transmission link, the arrival process to each queue is correlated to the service process. However, Kleinrock [KLEI76] has demonstrated that, because of the averaging effect of merging and partitioning, assuming independent service times provides a good approximation.

Application to a Packet-switching Network[4]

Consider a packet-switching network consisting of nodes interconnected by transmission links, with each node acting as the interface for zero or more attached systems, each of which functions as a source and destination of traffic. The external workload that is offered to the network can be characterized as

$$\gamma = \sum_{j=1}^{N} \sum_{k=1}^{N} \gamma_{jk}$$

where

---

[4] This discussion is based on the development in [MOLL89].

γ = total workload in packets per second

γ_{jk} = workload between source j and destination k

N = total number of sources and destinations

Because a packet may traverse more than one link between source and destination, the total internal workload will be higher than the offered load:

$$\lambda = \sum_{i=1}^{L} \lambda_i$$

where

λ = total load on all of the links in the network

λ_i = load on link i

L = total number of links

The internal load will depend on the actual path taken by packets through the network. We will assume that a routing algorithm is given such that the load on the individual links λ_i can be determined from the offered load γ_{jk}. For any particular routing assignment, we can determine the average number of links that a packet will traverse from these workload parameters. Some thought should convince you that the average length for all paths is given by

$$E[\text{number of links in a path}] = \frac{\lambda}{\gamma}$$

Our objective is to determine the average delay T experienced by a packet through the network. For this purpose, it is useful to apply Little's formula (Table 7.5). For each link in the network, the average number of items waiting and being served for that link is given by

$$q_i = \lambda_i T_{qi}$$

where T_{qi} is the yet-to-be-determined queuing delay at each queue. Suppose that we sum these quantities. That would give us the average total number of packets waiting in all of the queues of the network. It turns out that Little's formula works in the aggregate as well.[5] Thus, the number of packets waiting and being served in the network can be expressed as γT. Combining the two,

$$T = \frac{1}{\gamma} \sum_{i=1}^{L} \lambda_i T_{qi}$$

To determine the value of T, we need to determine the values of the individual delays, T_{qi}. Because we are assuming that each queue can be treated as an independent M/M/1 model, this is easily determined:

$$T_{qi} = \frac{T_{si}}{1 - \rho_i} = \frac{T_{si}}{1 - \lambda_i T_{si}}$$

---

[5] In essence, this statement is based on the fact that the sum of the averages is the average of the sums.

The service time T_{si} for link i is just the product of the data rate on the link, in bits per second (R_i) and the average packet length in bits (M). Then

$$T_{qi} = \frac{\dfrac{M}{R_i}}{1 - \dfrac{M\lambda_i}{R_i}} = \frac{M}{R_i - M\lambda_i}$$

Putting all of the elements together, we can calculate the average delay of packets sent through the network:

$$T = \frac{1}{\gamma} \sum_{i=1}^{L} \frac{M\lambda_i}{R_i - M\lambda_i}$$

7.9 OTHER QUEUING MODELS

In this chapter, we have concentrated on one type of queuing model. There are in fact a number of models, based on two key factors:

- The manner in which blocked items are handled
- The number of traffic sources.

When an item arrives at a server and finds that server busy, or arrives at a multiple-server facility and finds all servers busy, that item is said to be blocked. Blocked items can be handled in a number of ways. First, the item can be placed in a queue awaiting a free server. This policy is referred to in the telephone traffic literature as *lost calls delayed*, although in fact the call is not lost. Alternatively, no queue is provided. This, in turn, leads to two assumptions about the action of the item. The item may wait some random amount of time and then try again; this is known as *lost calls cleared*. If the item repeatedly attempts to gain service, with no pause, it is referred to as *lost calls held*. The lost calls delayed model is the most appropriate for most computer and data communications problems. Lost calls cleared is usually the most appropriate in a telephone switching environment.

The second key element of a traffic model is whether the number of sources is assumed to be infinite or finite. For an infinite source model, there is assumed to be a fixed arrival rate. For the finite source case, the arrival rate will depend on the number of sources already engaged. Thus, if each of L sources generates arrivals at a rate λ/L, then when the queuing facility is unoccupied, the arrival rate is λ. However, if K sources are in the queuing facility at a particular time, then the instantaneous arrival rate at that time is $\lambda(L - K)/L$. Infinite source models are easier to deal with. The infinite source assumption is reasonable when the number of sources is at least 5 to 10 times the capacity of the system.

7.10 ESTIMATING MODEL PARAMETERS

To perform a queuing analysis, we need to estimate the values of the input parameters, specifically the mean and standard deviation of the arrival rate and service time. If we are contemplating a new system, these estimates may have to be based on judgment and an assessment of the equipment and work patterns likely to prevail. However, it will often be the case that an existing system is available for examination. For example, a collection of terminals, personal computers, and host computers are interconnected in a building by direct connection and multiplexers, and it is desired to replace the interconnection facility with a local area network. To be able to size the network, it is possible to measure the load currently generated by each device.

Sampling

The measurements that are taken are in the form of samples. A particular parameter (for example, the rate of packets generated by a terminal or the size of packets) is estimated by observing the number of packets generated during a period of time.

The most important quantity to estimate is the mean. For many of the equations in Tables 7.6 and 7.7, this is the only quantity that need be estimated. The estimate is referred to as the sample mean $\overline{X}$, and is calculated as follows:

$$\overline{X} = \frac{1}{N} \sum_{i=1}^{N} X_i$$

where

N = sample size
X_i = ith sample

It is important to note that the sample mean is itself a random variable. For example, if you take a sample from some population and calculate the sample mean, and do this a number of times, the calculated values will differ. Thus, we can talk of the mean and standard deviation of the sample mean, or even of the entire probability distribution of the sample mean. To distinguish the concepts, it is common to refer to the probability distribution of the original random variable X as the *underlying distribution* and the probability distribution of the sample mean $\overline{X}$ as the *sampling distribution of the mean*.

The remarkable thing about the sample mean is that its probability distribution tends to the normal distribution as N increases for virtually all underlying distributions. The assumption of normality breaks down only if N is very small or if the underlying distribution is highly abnormal.

The mean and variance of $\overline{X}$ are as follows:

$$E[\overline{X}] = \mu$$

$$Var[\overline{X}] = \frac{\sigma_X^2}{N}$$

Thus, if a sample mean is calculated, its expected value is the same as that of the underlying random variable and the variability of the sample mean around this

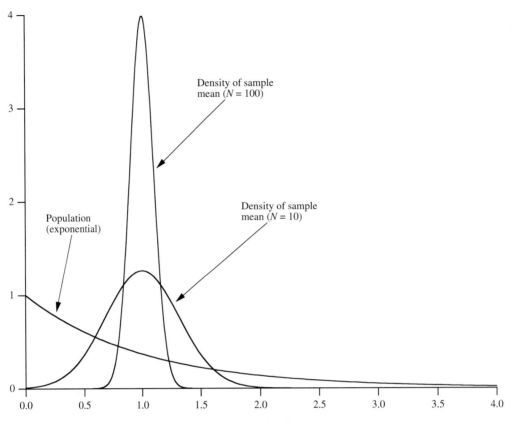

Figure 7.9 Sample means for an exponential distribution.

expected value decreases as N increases. These characteristics are illustrated in Figure 7.9. The figure shows an underlying exponential distribution with mean value $\mu = 1$. This could be the distribution of service times of a server or of the interarrival times of a Poisson arrival process. If a sample of size 10 is used to estimate the value of μ, then the expected value is indeed μ, but the actual value could easily be off by as much as 50%. If the sample size is 100, the spread among possible calculated values is considerably tightened, so that we would expect the actual sample mean for any given sample to be much closer to μ.

The sample mean as defined previously can be used directly to estimate the service time of a server. For arrival rate, one can observe the interarrival times for a sequence of N arrivals, calculate the sample mean, and then calculate the estimated arrival rate. An equivalent and simpler approach is to use the following estimate:

$$\bar{\lambda} = \frac{N}{T}$$

where N is the number of items observed in a period of time of duration T.

For much of queuing analysis, it is only an estimate of the mean that is required. But for a few important equations, an estimate of the variance of the

TABLE 7.10   STATISTICAL PARAMETERS

	Population	Sample Mean	Sample Variance
Random variable	X	$\overline{X} = \dfrac{1}{N} \sum_{i=1}^{N} X_i$	$S^2 = \dfrac{1}{N-1} \sum_{i=1}^{N} (X_i - \overline{X})^2$
Expected value	$E[X] = \mu$	$E[\overline{X}] = \mu$	$E[S^2] = \sigma_X^2$
Variance	$Var[X] = E[(X - \mu)^2] = \sigma_X^2$	$Var[\overline{X}] = \dfrac{\sigma_X^2}{N}$	

N = sample size, X_i = i th sample.

underlying random variable σ_X^2 is also needed. The sample variance is calculated as follows:

$$S^2 = \frac{1}{N-1} \sum_{i=1}^{N} (X_i - \overline{X})^2$$

The expected value of S^2 has the desired value:

$$E[S^2] = \sigma_X^2$$

The variance of S^2 depends on the underlying distribution and is, in general, difficult to calculate. However, as you would expect, the variance of S^2 decreases as N increases.

Table 7.10 summarizes the concepts discussed in this section.

Sampling Errors

When we estimate values such as the mean and standard deviation on the basis of a sample, we leave the realm of probability and enter that of statistics. This is a complex topic that will not be explored here, except to provide a few comments.

The probabilistic nature of our estimated values is a source of error, known as sampling error. In general, the greater the size of the sample taken, the smaller the standard deviation of the sample mean or other quantity, and therefore the closer that our estimate is likely to be to the actual value. By making certain reasonable assumptions about the nature of the random variable being tested and the randomness of the sampling procedure, one can in fact determine the probability that a sample mean or sample standard deviation is within a certain distance from the actual mean or standard deviation. This concept is often reported with the results of a sample. For example, it is common for the result of an opinion poll to include a comment such as "The result is within 5% of the true value with a confidence (probability) of 99%."

There is, however, another source of error, which is less widely appreciated among nonstatisticians: bias. For example, if an opinion poll is conducted and only members of a certain socioeconomic group are interviewed, the results are not necessarily representative of the entire population. In a communications context, sampling done during one time of day may not reflect the activity at another time of day. If we are concerned with designing a system that will handle the peak load that is likely to be experienced, then we should observe the traffic during the time of day that is most likely to produce the greatest load.

7.11 RECOMMENDED READING

A good practical reference is [TANN95]; it provides detailed guidance for the application of queuing analysis plus a number of worked-out examples. The book also contains a disk with an extensive library of subroutines in Pascal for calculating the characteristics of many queuing situations. [MART93] provides a good overview of queuing theory and contains a number of graphs and tables that can be used to perform quick queuing analyses.

For those who wish to delve more deeply into queuing theory, a host of books is available. Some of the more worthwhile ones are the following. A good text that covers queuing theory and its application to computers and communications is [MOLL89]. [STUC85] is an excellent treatment that focuses on data communications and networking. The classic treatment of queuing theory for computer applications, with a detailed discussion of computer networks, is found in [KLEI75] and [KLEI76].

A good elementary introduction to statistics is [PHIL92]. For a more detailed and rigorous treatment, there are numerous texts; one that is particularly well-suited for self-study is [BULM79]. The U.S. government publishes two excellent guides to the practical application of statistics. [NBS63], which is still available, contains tables, formulas, and examples that aid in determining the proper procedure for estimating values from samples and in evaluating the results. [LURI94] contains detailed step-by-step procedures for performing various statistical tests, as well as a certain amount of tutorial information on the procedures.

BULM79 Bulmer, M. *Principles of Statistics.* New York: Dover, 1979.

KLEI75 Kleinrock, L. *Queueing Systems, Volume I: Theory.* New York: Wiley, 1975.

KLEI76 Kleinrock, L. *Queueing Systems, Volume II: Computer Applications.* New York: Wiley, 1976.

LURI94 Lurie, D., and Moore, R. *Applying Statistics.* U.S. Nuclear Regulatory Commission Report NUREG-1475. (Available from the Government Printing Office, GPO Stock Number 052-020-00390-4.)

MART93 Martine, R. *Basic Traffic Analysis.* Englewood Cliffs, NJ: Prentice Hall, 1993.

MOLL89 Molloy, M. *Fundamentals of Performance Modeling.* New York: Macmillan, 1989.

NBS63 National Bureau of Standards. *Experimental Statistics.* NBS Handbook 91, 1963. (Available from the Government Printing Office, GPO Stock Number 003-003-00135-0.)

PHIL92 Phillips, J. *How to Think About Statistics.* New York: Freeman, 1992.

STUC85 Stuck, B. and Arthurs, E. *A Computer and Communications Network Performance Analysis Primer.* Englewood Cliffs, NJ: Prentice Hall, 1985.

TANN95 Tanner, M. *Practical Queueing Analysis.* New York: McGraw-Hill, 1995.

7.12 PROBLEMS

7.1 Section 7.3 provided an intuitive argument to justify Little's formula. Develop a similar argument to justify the relationship $w = \lambda T_w$.

7.2 Figure 7.3 shows the number of items in a system as a function of time. This can be viewed as the difference between an arrival process and a departure process, of the form $n(t) = a(t) - d(t)$.

  a. On one graph, show the functions $a(t)$ and $d(t)$ that produce the $n(t)$ shown in Figure 7.3.

  b. Using the graph from (a), develop an intuitive argument to justify Little's formula. *Hint:* Consider the area between the two step functions, computed first by adding vertical rectangles and second by adding horizontal rectangles.

7.3 The owner of a shop observes that on average 18 customers per hour arrive and there are typically 8 customers in the shop. What is the average length of time each customer spends in the shop?

7.4 A simulation program of a multiprocessor system starts running with no jobs in the queue and ends with no jobs in the queue. The simulation program reports the average number of jobs in the system over the simulation run as 12.356, the average arrival rate as 25.6 jobs per minute, and the average delay for a job of 7.34 minutes. Was the simulation correct?

7.5 Section 7.3 provided an intuitive argument to justify the single-server relationship $\rho = \lambda T_s$. Develop a similar argument to justify the multiserver relationship $\rho = \lambda T_s / M$.

7.6 If an M/M/1 queue has arrivals at a rate of two per minute and serves at a rate of four per minute, how many customers are found in the system on average? How many customers are found in service on average?

7.7 What is the utilization of an M/M/1 queue that has four people waiting on average?

7.8 At an ATM machine in a supermarket, the average length of a transaction is two minutes, and on average, customers arrive to use the machine once every five minutes. How long is the average time that a person must spend waiting and using the machine? What is the 90th percentile of queuing time? On average, how many people are waiting to use the machine? Assume M/M/1.

7.9 Messages arrive at random to be sent across a communications link with a data rate of 9600 bps. The link is 70% utilized, and the average message length is 1000 octets. Determine the average waiting time for constant-length messages and for exponentially distributed length messages.

7.10 Messages of three different sizes flow through a message switch. Seventy percent of the messages take 1 ms to serve, 20 percent take 3 ms, and 10 percent take 10 ms. Calculate the average time spent in the switch and the average number of messages in the switch when messages arrive at an average rate of (a) one per 3 ms, (b) one per 4 ms, and (c) one per 5 ms.

7.11 Messages arrive at a switching center for a particular outgoing communications line in a Poisson manner with a mean arrival rate of 180 messages per hour. Message length is distributed exponentially with a mean length of 14,400 characters. Line speed is 9600 bps.
   a. What is the mean waiting time in the switching center?
   b. How many messages will be waiting in the switching center for transmission on the average?

7.12 Often inputs to a queuing system are not independent and random but occur in clusters. Mean waiting delays are greater for this type of arrival pattern than for Poisson arrivals. This problem demonstrates the effect with a simple example. Assume that items arrive at a queue in fixed-size batches of M items. The batches have a Poisson arrival distribution with mean rate λ/M, yielding a customer arrival rate of λ. For each item, the service time is T_s with a standard deviation of service time of σ_{T_s}.
   a. If we treat the batches as large-size items, what is the mean and variance of batch service time? What is the mean batch waiting time?
   b. What is the mean waiting time for service for an item once its batch begins service? Assume that an item may be in any of the M positions in a batch with equal probability. What is the total mean waiting time for an item?
   c. Verify the results of (b) by showing that for $M = 1$, the results reduce to the $M/G/1$ case. How do the results vary for values of $M > 1$?

7.13 Consider a single queue with a constant service time of four seconds and a Poisson input with mean rate of 0.20 items per second.

    a. Find the mean and standard deviation of queue size.

    b. Find the mean and standard deviation of queuing time.

7.14 Consider a frame relay node that is handling a Poisson stream of incoming frames to be transmitted on a particular 1-Mbps outgoing link. The stream consists of two types of frames. Both types of frames have the same exponential distribution of frame length with a mean of 1000 bits.

    a. Assume that priorities are not used. The combined arrival rate of frame of both types is 800 frames/second. What is the mean queuing time (T_q) for all frames?

    b. Now assume that the two types are assigned different priorities, with the arrival rate of type 1 equal 200 frames/second and the arrival rate of type 2 equal 600 frames/second. Calculate the mean queuing time for type 1, type 2, and overall.

    c. Repeat (b) for $\lambda_1 = \lambda_2 = 400$ frames/second.

    d. Repeat (b) for $\lambda_1 = 600$ frames/second and $\lambda_2 = 200$ frames/second.

7.15 The multilink protocol is part of X.25; a similar facility is used in IBM's System Network Architecture (SNA). With MLP, a set of data links exists between two nodes and is used as a pooled resource for transmitting packets, regardless of virtual circuit number. When a packet is presented to MLP for transmission, any available link can be chosen for the job. For example, if two LANs at different sites are connected by a pair of bridges, there may be multiple point-to-point links between the bridges to increase throughput and availability. The MLP approach requires extra processing and frame overhead compared to a simple link protocol. A special MLP header is necessary for the protocol. An alternative is to assign each of the arriving packets to the queue for a single outgoing link in round-robin fashion. This would simplify processing, but what kind of effect would it have on performance? Let us consider a concrete example. Suppose that there are five 9600-bps links connecting two nodes, that the average packet size is 100 octets with an exponential distribution, and that packets arrive at a rate of 48 per second.

    a. For a single-server design, calculate ρ and T_q.

    b. For a multiserver design, it can be calculated that the Erlang C function has a value of 0.554. Determine T_q.

7.16 A supplement to the X.25 packet-switching standard is a set of standards for a packet assembler-disassembler (PAD), defined in standards X.3, X.28, and X.29. A PAD is used to connect asynchronous terminals to a packet-switching network. Each terminal attached to a PAD sends characters one at a time. These are buffered in the PAD and then assembled into an X.25 packet, which is transmitted to the packet-switching network. The buffer length is equal to the maximum data field size for an X.25 packet. A packet is formed from assembled characters and transmitted whenever the buffer is full, a special control character such as a carriage return is received, or when a timeout occurs. For this problem, we ignore the last two conditions. Figure 7.10 illustrates the queuing model for the PAD. The first queue models the delay for characters waiting to be put into a packet; this queue is completely emptied when it is filled. The second queue models the delay waiting to transmit packets. Use the following notation:

    λ = Poisson input rate of characters from each terminal

    C = Rate of transmission on the output channel in characters per second

    M = Number of data characters in a packet

    H = Number of overhead characters in a packet

    K = Number of terminals

    a. Determine the average waiting time for a character in the input queue.

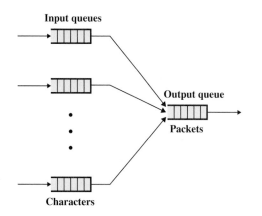

Input queues

Output queue

Packets

Characters

Figure 7.10 Queuing model for a packet assembler/disassembler (PAD).

b. Determine the average waiting time for a packet in the output queue.
c. Determine the average time spent by a character from when it leaves the terminal to when it leaves the PAD. Plot the result as a function of normalized load.

7.17 A fraction P of the traffic from a single exponential server is fed back into the input as shown in Figure 7.11. In the figure, Λ denotes the system throughput, which is the output rate from the server.

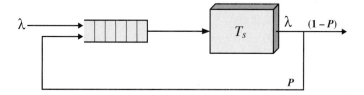

λ

T_s

λ $(1 - P)$

P

Figure 7.11 Feedback queue.

a. Determine the system throughput, server utilization, and mean queuing time for one pass through the server.
b. Determine the mean number of passes that an item makes through the system and the mean total time spent in the system.

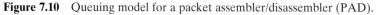

CHAPTER 8

SELF-SIMILAR TRAFFIC

I conceived and developed a new geometry of nature and implemented its use in a number of diverse fields. It describes many of the irregular and fragmented patterns around us, and leads to full-fledged theories, by identifying a family of shapes I call fractals. The most useful fractals involve chance and both their regularities and their irregularities are statistical. Also, the shapes described here tend to be scaling, implying that the degree of their irregularity and/or fragmentation is identical at all scales.

—*The Fractal Geometry of Nature,* Benoit Mandelbrot

The queuing analysis presented in Chapter 7 has been tremendously useful to network designers and systems analysts in doing capacity planning and performance prediction. However, in many real-world cases, it has been found that the predicted results from a queuing analysis differ substantially from the actual observed performance. Recall that the validity of queuing analysis depends on the Poisson nature of the data traffic. In recent years, a number of studies have demonstrated that for some environments, the traffic pattern is self-similar rather than Poisson.

Self-similarity is a concept related to two others that have received much publicity: fractals and chaos theory. We begin this chapter with a description of the phenomenon of self-similarity. Next, we look specifically at self-similar data traffic, including evidence for its existence and its key characteristics. The next section looks at the performance implications of this type of traffic as compared to Poisson traffic. Then techniques for modeling self-similar traffic and estimating key parameters are discussed. An important parameter in all of these discussions, the Hurst parameter, is described in an appendix to this chapter.

The discussion in this chapter makes use of concepts from the field of stochastic processes. For the reader not familiar with this area, a brief overview is provided in Section 6.3.

8.1 SELF-SIMILARITY

Suppose that you are monitoring a 1-Mbps frame relay line and fixed-length frames of 4000 bits are being transmitted, so that the transmission time of each frame is 4 ms. The following arrival times are recorded at the receiver (the time at which the first bit of each frame arrives):

0	8	24	32	72	80	96	104	216	224	240	248	288	296	312	320
648	656	672	680	720	728	744	752	864	872	888	896	936	944	960	968

That is, the first frame arrives at $t = 0$ ms, the second at $t = 8$ ms, and so on.

It is difficult to discern any pattern or statistical properties. However, the traffic does seem bursty, as you would expect for data traffic. Some of the arrival times are clustered together, and there are some gaps. The largest gap is 328 ms from time 320 to 648, but there are some smaller gaps as well, including numerous gaps of 40 ms or more, the equivalent of 10 frame times or more. Suppose that we aggregate the traffic and consider a cluster to be any group of frames in which there are no gaps greater than five frame times (20 ms), and we record the start time of each cluster. Then we have

0	72	216	288	648	720	864	936

The gaps between clusters are of uneven length, but it is still difficult to observe a pattern. Let's try a greater degree of aggregation. Define a cluster as any group of frames in which there are no gaps greater than 10 frame times (40 ms). Then we have arrival times as follows:

0	216	648	864

In this case the gaps are 216, 432, 216. The pattern is two clusters with a gap between, followed by a larger gap, followed again by two clusters with the smaller gap between. Now go back and look at the previous aggregation into eight clusters, and we see this pattern repeated. The first four arrival times follow the pattern of (arrival, short gap, arrival, long gap, arrival, short gap, arrival), as do the last four arrival times. Looking back at the original data set of 32 arrivals, we see this same pattern repeated eight times. Thus, we have a pattern that appears in the raw data and again at different levels of aggregation. That is, the time sequence exhibits the same pattern regardless of the degree of resolution. This is the essence of self-similarity.

Self-similarity is such an important concept that, in a way, it is surprising that only recently has it been applied to data communications traffic analysis. The ubiquity of self-similarity was emphasized in a memorable statement by Manfred Schroeder [SCHR91]:

> The unifying concept underlying fractals, chaos, and power laws is self-similarity. Self-similarity, or invariance against changes in scale or size, is an attribute of many laws of nature and innumerable phenomena in the world around us. Self-similarity is, in fact, one of the decisive symmetries that shape our universe and our efforts to comprehend it.

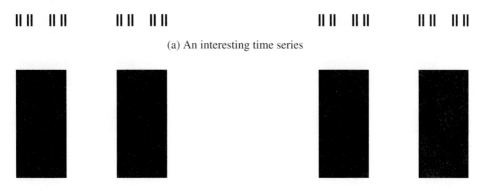

(a) An interesting time series

(b) Aggregated time series

Figure 8.1 Self-similar time series.

A phenomenon that is self-similar looks the same or behaves the same when viewed at different degrees of "magnification" or different scales on a dimension. The dimension can be space (length, width) or time. In this chapter, we are concerned with time series and stochastic processes that exhibit self-similarity with respect to time. The next section makes the scaling operation with respect to time precise.

The pattern discussed in this section is easier to see in a picture. Figure 8.1a depicts the sequence of frame arrivals over time. Each vertical line represents one frame, with a width proportional to 4 ms, the time it takes a receiver to absorb an entire frame, from first bit to last. Figure 8.1b shows the data aggregated into four large clusters; the height and width of the vertical lines in the aggregated sequence are in proportion to the scale of the aggregation. In this figure, it is easy to see that the pattern of (arrival, short gap, arrival, long gap, arrival, short gap, arrival) appears at different resolutions of the data.

This made-up example is derived from the Cantor set, a famous construct that appears in virtually every book on chaos, fractals, and nonlinear dynamics. Figure 8.2 illustrates the construction of the Cantor set, which obeys the following rules:

1. Begin with the closed interval [0, 1], represented by a line segment.
2. Remove the middle third of the line.
3. For each succeeding step, remove the middle third of the lines created by the preceding step.

This is essentially a recursive process that can be more precisely defined as follows. Let S_i represent the Cantor set after i levels of recursion. Then

$$S_0 = [0, 1]$$

$$S_1 = [0, 1/3] \cup [2/3, 1]$$

$$S_2 = [0, 1/9] \cup [2/9, 1/3] \cup [2/3, 7/9] \cup [8/9, 1]$$

and so on.

If we think of the Cantor line as being a time line, then each successive step magnifies the time scale by a factor of 3. Note that at every step, the left (and right)

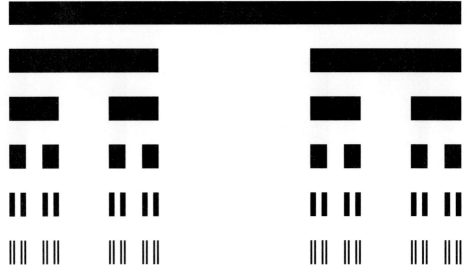

Figure 8.2   A Cantor set to five levels of recursion.

portion of the set is an exact replica of the full set in the preceding step. The Cantor set reveals two properties seen in all self-similar phenomena:

1. It has structure at arbitrarily small scales. If we magnify part of the set repeatedly, we continue to see a complex pattern of points separated by gaps of various sizes. Like a complicated spy thriller, with "wheels within wheels," the process seems unending. In contrast, when we look at a smooth, continuous curve under repeated magnification, it becomes more and more featureless.

2. The structures repeat. A self-similar structure contains smaller replicas of itself at all scales. For example, at every step, the left (and right) portion of the Cantor set is an exact replica of the full set in the preceding step.

These properties do not hold indefinitely for real phenomena. At some point under magnification, the structure and the similarity break down. But over a large range of scales, many phenomena exhibit self-similarity.

Although ours is a simple made-up example, we can gain some insights into self-similar data traffic from its study. Perhaps the most striking feature, from the point of view of network performance, is the persistence of clustering. With Poisson traffic, clustering occurs in the short-term (small time scale) but smoothes out over the long term.[1] We can design a system of servers and queues with buffers in the expectation of such long-term smoothness. The implication is that, because things smooth out over the long run, only modest-sized buffers are needed; a queue may build up in the short run, but over a longer period the buffers are cleared out. How-

---

[1] To be more specific, clustering occurs on a preferred time scale determined by the mean interarrival time of the Poisson events. The notion of *short term* is relative.

ever, if the bursty behavior is itself bursty—that is, the clusters are clustered—then queue sizes may build up more than would be expected from a Poisson traffic stream. This leads to the observation that traditional queuing analysis, which assumes Poisson traffic, may not accurately predict the performance of self-similar traffic. We will see that there is evidence to support this observation.

8.2 SELF-SIMILAR DATA TRAFFIC

The type of self-similarity described in Section 8.1 might be termed exact self-similarity: A given pattern is reproduced exactly at different scales. This exact self-similarity can be constructed for a deterministic time series. However, data traffic is best viewed as a stochastic process, and we can only talk of statistical self-similarity.[2]

An analogy might be useful here. A deterministic periodic signal is characterized by an invariance with respect to time translation: The signal is identical if translated in time by multiples of the period. For example, for the deterministic periodic function $g(t)$ with period T

$$g(t) = g(t + aT) \qquad a = 0, \pm 1, \pm 2 \dots$$

In contrast, for a stationary stochastic process, the statistics of the process are invariant to time translations: The mean is independent of time and the autocorrelation function depends only on a time difference.

A deterministic self-similar signal is invariant to changes in scale. For a stochastic process, we can say that the statistics of the process do not change with a change in the time scale. Both qualitatively and quantitatively, the process lacks a characteristic scale: Average behavior of the process in the short-term is the same as it is in the long term. Such nondeterministic self-similarity is quite common in both natural and human-made phenomena; it is seen in natural landscapes, in the distribution of earthquakes, in ocean waves, in turbulent flow, in the fluctuations in the stock market, and in the pattern of errors and data traffic on communication channels.

Figure 8.3a is an example of a self-similar stochastic process. Note that the time function is not exactly reproduced at different time scales, but that the waves at different time scales resemble each other. Contrast this with Figure 8.3b, which shows an instance of a typical stationary random process. In this case we see that at higher levels of magnification, the function has different characteristics, becoming choppier and more irregular. Put the opposite way, as we look at longer time scales, the signal seems to exhibit less fluctuation and be more regular.

In this section, we present some definitions of self-similar stochastic processes and then comment on some examples reported in the literature and discuss rationales for this phenomenon.

---

[2] An exception is a continuous stream of fixed-size blocks of data, such as an ATM cell stream carrying uncompressed video at a constant cell rate. The more typical case is one in which there is an average data rate of cells or packets but there is some variation around that average.

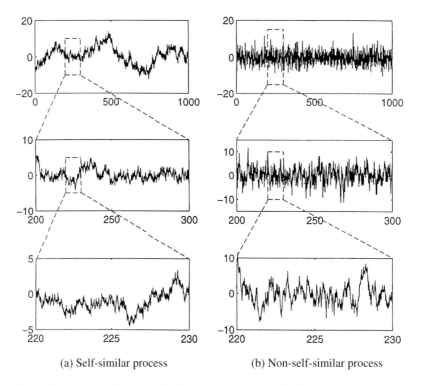

(a) Self-similar process   (b) Non-self-similar process

Figure 8.3 Comparison of self-similar and non-self-similar stochastic processes [WORN96].

Self-similar stochastic processes have been defined in a number of ways in the literature. This section reviews some of the most important approaches. It is perhaps easiest to grasp the concept by looking at continuous-time stochastic processes, which we do first. We then turn to discrete-time stochastic processes, which are more broadly relevant to our discussion.[3]

Continuous-time Definition

A common definition of self-similar stochastic processes (e.g., see [WORN96]) is based on a direct scaling of the continuous time variable, as follows. A stochastic process $\mathbf{x}(t)$ is statistically self-similar with parameter H ($0.5 \leq H \leq 1$) if for any real $a > 0$, the process $a^{-H}\mathbf{x}(at)$ has the same statistical properties as $\mathbf{x}(t)$. This relationship may be expressed by the following three conditions:

---

[3] A continuous-time stochastic process is one in which t varies continuously, whereas a discrete-time stochastic process is one in which t takes on only discrete values; see Section 6.3 for a discussion.

1. $E[\mathbf{x}(t)] = \dfrac{E[\mathbf{x}(at)]}{a^H}$ Mean

2. $Var[\mathbf{x}(t)] = \dfrac{Var[\mathbf{x}(at)]}{a^{2H}}$ Variance

3. $R_{\mathbf{x}}(t, s) = \dfrac{R_{\mathbf{x}}(at, as)}{a^{2H}}$ Autocorrelation

The parameter H, known as the Hurst parameter, or the self-similarity parameter, is a key measure of self-similarity. More precisely, H is a measure of the persistence of a statistical phenomenon and is a measure of the length of the long-range dependence of a stochastic process. A value of $H = 0.5$ indicates the absence of self-similarity. The closer H is to 1, the greater the degree of persistence or long-range dependence.[4]

As an example based on this definition, we consider the fractional Brownian motion (FBM) process, which is a generalization of the familiar Brownian motion process (defined in Section 6.3). A detailed derivation of this process is beyond the scope of this chapter. However, a brief introduction is worthwhile because the FBM process is frequently used in the analysis of self-similar data traffic.

An FBM process $B_H(t)$ can be defined as follows:

$$B_H(t) = Xt^H \quad (t > 0; 0.5 \leqslant H < 1)$$

where X is a normally distributed random variable with zero mean and variance 1, and H is a parameter of the process. Thus, the value of the process at time t is equal to the value of the random variable X multiplied by the time interval raised to the power H. For a given value of t, $B_H(t)$ is equal to a constant times the normal random variable X. Therefore, $B_H(t)$ is a normally distributed random variable with zero mean. Note that for $H = 1/2$ this conforms to the definition of a Brownian motion process.

We have $E[B_H(t)] = 0$ because $E[X] = 0$. Also, for any random variable X and constant a, $Var(aX) = a^2 Var(X)$. Therefore, $Var[B_H(t)] = Var[t^H X] = t^{2H}$. These observations again show that for $H = 0.5$, the FBM process reduces to an ordinary Brownian motion process.

The probability density of a Brownian motion process has the form

$$f_{B_H}(x, t) = \dfrac{1}{\sqrt{2\pi t^{2H}}} e^{-x^2/2t^{2H}}$$

It can be shown that this process has stationary increments and that

$$Var[B_H(t) - B_H(s)] = E[(B_H(t) - B_H(s))^2] = |t - s|^2$$

An important quantity of interest is the autocorrelation of $B_H(t)$, expressed as $R_{B_H}(t, s) = E[B_H(t)B_H(s)]$. This value can be derived in the following way. First, observe that

$$E[(B_H(t) - B_H(s))^2] = E[B_H^2(t) + B_H^2(s) - 2B^H(t)B_H(s)]$$

---

[4] These concepts will become clear later in the chapter. H is described in more detail in the appendix to this chapter.

Rearranging,

$$E[B_H(t)B_H(s)] = \frac{1}{2}(E[B_H^2(t)] + E[B_H^2(s)] - E[(B_H(t) - B_H(s))^2])$$

$$= \frac{1}{2}(\text{Var}[B_H(t)] + \text{Var}[B_H(s)] - \text{Var}[B_H(t) - B_H(s)])$$

$$= \frac{1}{2}(t^{2H} + s^{2H} - |t - s|^{2H})$$

Again, this reduces to the autocorrelation of a Brownian motion process for $H = 0.5$.

To see that the FBM process is self-similar, we must show that it satisfies the three conditions listed previously. Consider the process $B_H(at)$, where $B_H(t)$ is the FBM process just defined. Then $B_H(at) = X(at)^H$, and it is easily seen that $E[B_H(at)] = a^H E[B_H(at)] = 0$, satisfying the first condition. $\text{Var}[B_H(at)] = \text{Var}[X(at)^H] = (at)^{2H}\text{Var}[X] = (at)^{2H}$. Therefore, $\text{Var}[B_H(t)] = \text{Var}[B_H(at)]/a^{2H}$, satisfying the second condition listed.

The third condition listed is also satisfied:

$$R_{B_H}(at, as) = \frac{1}{2}((at)^{2H} + (as)^{2H} - |at - as|^{2H})$$

$$= \frac{a^{2H}}{2}(t^{2H} + s^{2H} - |t - s|^{2H})$$

$$= a^{2H}R_{B_H}(t, s)$$

A striking difference between a Brownian motion process and an FBM process is that the former has independent and uncorrelated intervals, while the latter has infinitely long-run correlations. This can be clearly demonstrated by considering the correlation between past increments and future increments. Consider the correlation between the increment from $-t$ to 0 and the increment from 0 to t:

$$E[(B_H(0) - B_H(-t))(B_H(t) - B_H(0))] = E[-B_H(-t)B_H(t)]$$

$$= -\frac{1}{2}((-t)^{2H} + t^{2H} - |-t - t|^{2H})$$

$$= \frac{1}{2}(2t)^{2H} - t^{2H}$$

Note that for $H = 0.5$, the correlation of past and future increments vanishes, as required for the Brownian motion process, which has independent increments. However, for $H > 0.5$, we have the noteworthy feature of **persistence**. In this case, if for some time in the past we have a positive increment (i.e., an increase), then on average there will be a positive increment in the future. Therefore, an increasing (or decreasing) trend in the past implies an increasing (or decreasing) trend in the future. This correlation applies for arbitrarily large values of t, and the strength of the correlation increases with larger values of H.

This persistence behavior is in conflict with what is normally assumed about stochastic phenomenon. Some processes, such as Brownian motion, have independent increments. For many other processes, while we may accept that events may be correlated when separated by a small amount of time Δt, we assume that they definitely become uncorrelated as $\Delta t \to \infty$.

We now turn to a set of more or less equivalent formulations of self-similarity for stationary time series, which have been used in analyzing data traffic. In all of these cases, we are concerned with a stochastic process that is defined at discrete points in time, so that the stochastic process $X(t)$ is defined as $\{\mathbf{x}_t, t = 0, 1, 2, ...\}$.

Discrete-time Definition

For a stationary time series $\mathbf{x}$, we define the m-aggregated time series $\mathbf{x}^{(m)} = \{\mathbf{x}_k^{(m)}, k = 0, 1, 2, ...\}$ by summing the original time series over nonoverlapping, adjacent blocks of size m. This may be expressed as

$$\mathbf{x}_k^{(m)} = \frac{1}{m} \sum_{i=km-(m-1)}^{km} \mathbf{x}_i$$

For example, $\mathbf{x}^{(3)}$ is defined as

$$\mathbf{x}_k^{(3)} = \frac{\mathbf{x}_{3k-2} + \mathbf{x}_{3k-1} + \mathbf{x}_{3k}}{3}$$

One way of viewing the aggregated time series is as a technique for compressing the time scale. We can consider $\mathbf{x}^{(1)}$ to be the highest magnification or highest resolution possible for this time series. The process $\mathbf{x}^{(3)}$ is the same process reduced in magnification by a factor of 3. By averaging over each set of three points, we lose the fine detail available at the highest magnification. If the statistics of the process (mean, variance, correlation, etc.) are preserved with compression, then we are dealing with a self-similar process.

We can also view each point in the series $\mathbf{x}^{(m)}$ as a time average of the process x. For an ergodic process (see Section 6.3), a time average should equal an ensemble average, and the variance of the time average should go to zero relatively quickly as m becomes large. This does not happen for a self-similar process; the variance does go to zero but does so more slowly than for a stationary ergodic process. Let us make these statements more precise.

A process $\mathbf{x}$ is said to be **exactly self-similar** with parameter β ($0 < \beta < 1$) if for all $m = 1, 2, ...$ we have

$$\mathrm{Var}(\mathbf{x}^{(m)}) = \frac{\mathrm{Var}(\mathbf{x})}{m^\beta} \qquad \text{Variance}$$

$$\mathrm{R}_{x^{(m)}}(k) = \mathrm{R}_{\mathbf{x}}(k) \qquad \text{Autocorrelation}$$

The parameter β can be shown to be related to the Hurst parameter, defined earlier, as $H = 1 - (\beta/2)$. For a stationary, ergodic process, $\beta = 1$ and the variance of the time average decays to zero at the rate of $1/m$. For a self-similar process, the variance of the time average decays more slowly.

A weaker condition is the following: A process $\mathbf{x}$ is said to be **asymptotically self-similar** if for all k large enough

$$\text{Var}(\mathbf{x}^{(m)}) = \frac{\text{Var}(\mathbf{x})}{m^{\beta}} \qquad \text{Variance}$$

$$R_{x^{(m)}}(k) \to R_x(k) \quad as \quad m \to \infty \quad \text{Autocorrelation}$$

Thus, with this definition of self-similarity, the autocorrelation[5] of the aggregated process has the same form as the original process. This would suggest that the degree of variability, or burstiness, would be the same at different time scales.

An interesting feature of the preceding definitions is that the autocorrelation of the aggregated self-similar process does not go to zero as $m \to \infty$. This is in contrast to stochastic processes typically used for packet data models, which have the following relationship:

$$R^{(m)}(\tau) \to 0 \quad as \quad m \to \infty$$

An autocorrelation function $R(\tau)$ that is equal to zero is consistent with white noise (i.e., a purely random stochastic process with a uniform power spectrum). Figure 8.3 provides useful intuition on this point. In Figure 8.3b, as the level of aggregation increases (m increases), the process increasingly resembles white noise. In contrast, in Figure 8.3a, all the plots have a similar structure that is distinctly different from white noise.

Another interesting feature of the preceding definitions is that the variance of $\mathbf{x}^{(m)}$ decreases more slowly than $1/m$ as $m \to \infty$; that is, it decreases proportional to $1/m^{\beta}$. For stochastic processes typically used for packet data models, the variance decreases proportional to $1/m$. This latter rate of decrease is easily seen by considering that $\mathbf{x}^{(m)}$ is a time average and, for an ergodic process, is statistically equivalent to a sample mean with sample size m. As was shown in Chapter 6, the variance of the sample mean is equal to the variance of the underlying random variable divided by m. However, for a self-similar process, aggregating by a factor of m is not quite the same thing as taking a sample mean with sample size m because of the persistence of statistical properties across time scales.

Long-range Dependence

One of the most significant properties of self-similar processes is referred to as long-range dependence. This property is defined in terms of the behavior of the autocovariance[6] $C(\tau)$ as τ increases.

For many processes, the autocovariance rapidly decays with τ. For example, for the Poisson increment process with increment L and mean λ (defined in Section 6.3), the autocovariance for values of $\tau > L$ is (see Equation 6.5):

$$C(\tau) = R(\tau) - \lambda^2 = \lambda^2 - \lambda^2 = 0$$

---

[5] See Section 6.3 for a definition of autocorrelation.

[6] Some of the properties of self-similar processes are most clearly stated in terms of the autocorrelation $R(\tau)$, while others are best expressed in terms of the autocovariance $C(\tau) = R(\tau) - \mu^2$, where $\mu = E[\mathbf{x}(t)]$. Unfortunately, in the literature on self-similar data traffic, the term *autocorrelation* is sometimes used to mean autocovariance and is sometimes used to mean a normalized autocovariance called the correlation coefficient (see Equation 6.4). It is up to the reader to take care in these cases.

In general, a **short-range dependent** process satisfies the condition that its autocovariance decays at least as fast as exponentially:

$$C(k) \frown a^{|k|} \quad as \ |k| \to \infty, \quad 0 < a < 1$$

where $\frown$ denotes that the expressions on the two sides are asymptotically proportional to each other.

The types of data traffic models typically considered in the literature employ only short-range dependent processes. Using the equality

$$\sum_{k=0}^{\infty} x^k = \frac{1}{1-x} \quad |x| < 1$$

we can observe that $\sum_k C(k)$ is finite.

In contrast, a **long-range dependent** process has a hyperbolically decaying autocovariance:

$$C(k) \frown |k|^{-\beta} \quad as \ |k| \to \infty, \quad 0 < \beta < 1$$

where β is the same parameter defined earlier and is related to the Hurst parameter as $H = 1 - (\beta/2)$. In this case, $\sum_k C(k) = \infty$.

Long-range dependence intuitively reflects the persistence phenomenon in self-similar processes—namely, the existence of clustering and bursty characteristics at all time scales.

Spectral Density

An equivalent formulation of long-range dependence can be stated in the frequency domain. Specifically, the power spectral density obeys a power law near the origin:

$$S(w) \frown \frac{1}{|w|^{\gamma}} \quad as \ w \to 0, \ 0 < \gamma < 1$$

As was discussed in Section 6.3, the spectral density for a discrete-time stochastic process is defined as follows:

$$S(w) = \sum_{k=-\infty}^{\infty} R(k)e^{-j2kw} \quad S(0) = \sum_{k=-\infty}^{\infty} R(k)$$

It can be shown that $\gamma = 1 - \beta = 2H - 1$.

In contrast, short-range dependent process are characterized by a spectral density that remains finite as $w \to 0$. This occurs when $\gamma = 0$ or, equivalently, $H = 0.5$. In terms of the autocorrelation function, an infinite value of $S(0)$ results if the values of $R(k)$ do not decay sufficiently rapidly for large k to form a finite sum.

This formulation can be useful in testing for self-similarity.

Heavy-tailed Distributions

The three preceding formulations of self-similar data traffic, in terms of aggregated time series, long-range dependence, and power spectra, provide equivalent definitions. A somewhat different characterization is in terms of heavy-tailed distributions. In essence, it is possible to define self-similar stochastic processes with such distributions, although the class of processes so defined is more inclusive than the preceding formulations. One attraction of the heavy-tailed distribution approach is that it leads to manageable simulation models. In this subsection we provide a brief overview.

Heavy-tailed distributions can be used to characterize probability densities that describe traffic processes such as packet interarrival times and burst lengths. The distribution of a random variable X is said to be heavy tailed if

$$1 - F(x) = \Pr[X > x] \frown \frac{1}{x^\alpha} \qquad \text{as } x \to \infty, \ 0 < \alpha$$

In general, a random variable with a heavy-tailed distribution exhibits a high or even infinite variance.

The simplest heavy-tailed distribution is the Pareto distribution with parameters k and α $(k, \alpha > 0)$, with density and distribution functions

$$\text{f}(x) = F(x) = 0 \qquad (x \leq k)$$

$$\text{f}(x) = \frac{\alpha}{k} \left(\frac{k}{x}\right)^{\alpha+1} \qquad F(x) = 1 - \left(\frac{k}{x}\right)^\alpha \qquad (x > k; \alpha > 0)$$

and a mean value

$$E[X] = \frac{\alpha}{\alpha - 1} k \qquad (\alpha > 1)$$

The parameter k specifies the minimum value that the random variable can take. The parameter α determines the mean and variance of the random variable: If $\alpha \leq 2$, then the distribution has infinite variance, and if $\alpha \leq 1$, it has infinite mean and variance. Figure 8.4 compares the Pareto and exponential density functions on a log-linear scale. Note that on this scale the exponential density function is a straight line, reflecting the exponential decay of the distribution. The tail of the Pareto distribution decays much more slowly than exponential; hence the term *heavy tail*.

The Pareto distribution has been observed in a wide variety of phenomena from the social and physical sciences and from communications. A brief discussion can be found in [PAXS95].

Examples of Self-similar Data Traffic

Since 1993, a number of studies reported in the literature have documented that the pattern of data traffic is well modeled by self-similar processes in a wide variety of real-world networking situations. This subsection presents a sampling of these reports and attempts to shed light on the causes of self-similarity.

Ethernet Traffic

The seminal paper in the study of self-similar data traffic is "On the Self-similar Nature of Ethernet Traffic" [LELA93], subsequently revised and expanded in [LELA94]. Although a few prior papers had provided informal descriptions of data traffic behavior that turn out to be well described by self-similar processes, no one

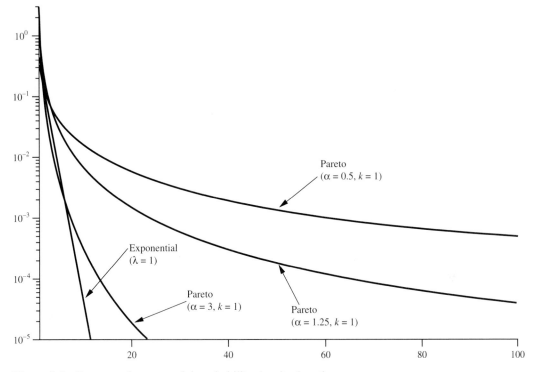

Figure 8.4   Pareto and exponential probability density functions.

had introduced the key notion of self-similarity.[7] This paper shattered the illusion that straightforward queuing analysis using the Poisson traffic assumption is adequate to model all network traffic. Using a massive amount of data and careful statistical analysis, the paper made the point that, for Ethernet traffic, a new modeling and analysis approach is required. This paper triggered a flood of research on the subject. Month by month, new papers have appeared that confirm the presence of self-similarity in other types of data traffic.

The original paper reports the results of a detailed, high-resolution (time accuracy of 20 µs) collection of Ethernet traffic measurements conducted between 1989 and 1992. The data consist of four sets of traffic measurements, each representing between 20 and 40 consecutive hours of Ethernet traffic and consisting of a total of well over 100 million packets. The data were collected from various Ethernet LANs at Bellcore.

The left column of Figure 8.5 shows plots of the number of packets per unit time for a measurement set from 1989, which consists of over 27 hours of continuous monitoring of the Ethernet traffic. The first plot shows the entire 27-hour run, using a time unit of 100 seconds, for a plot with 1000 data points. Each subsequent plot is obtained from the previous one by increasing the time resolution by a factor of 10 and displaying a randomly chosen subinterval (indicated by a darker shade).

---

[7] The fractal pioneer Mandelbrot had long ago demonstrated the self-similar nature of errors in transmission lines [MAND65], but no one had thought to apply this type of analysis to the data traffic itself.

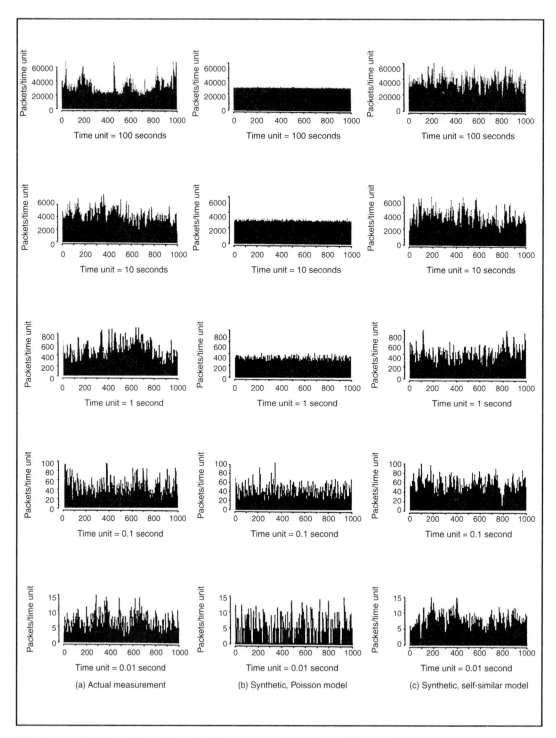

Figure 8.5   Comparison of actual and synthetic Ethernet traffic [WILL97].

Thus the second plot covers a period of approximately 2.7 hours, the third 0.27 hours, and so on. Looked at from the other direction, as we move up from the bottom of the first column of plots, a data point in a plot is formed by averaging over the corresponding 10 data points from the next lower plot.

Several interesting observations can be made about these data. With the possible exception of the first plot, all of the plots look similar to one another in a distributional sense.[8] That is, all of the plots involve a fair amount of burstiness. Thus, Ethernet traffic tends to look the same at large scales (hours, minutes) and at small scales (seconds, milliseconds). Further, note that there is no natural "length" to bursts. At every time scale, bursts consist of bursty subperiods separated by less bursty subperiods. This self-similar character is dramatically different from what is observed in voice telephone traffic and from stochastic models traditionally used in data network analysis and design.

To see the contrast, consider the middle column of Figure 8.5. This set of plots was generated in the same fashion as the Ethernet plots, but using synthetic traffic data. The data were generated using a Poisson model comparable to the real data in terms of average packet size and arrival rate. At high resolution (time unit = 0.1 seconds) the traffic is quite bursty, as would be expected. As the data are aggregated over increasingly long time scales, the traffic pattern smoothes out. This is what would be expected from a stationary, ergodic stochastic process such as defined with a Poisson model. Each level of aggregation represents the taking of a sequence of nonoverlapping sample means with a sample size of 10. Therefore, we would expect the variance in the data to be reduced by a factor of 10 for each level of aggregation. The resulting visual distinction between the left and middle columns is striking.

Based on a variety of statistical tests, the authors estimated that the Ethernet traffic was self-similar with a Hurst parameter H of 0.9. The right column of Figure 8.5 provides visual confirmation of this analysis. These plots were generated with a self-similar traffic model with $H = 0.9$. The plots show the same general character as those of the real Ethernet traffic.

One is naturally interested in why such results occur. The reasoning behind traditional queuing modeling used in traffic analysis has been that when data from a number of sources are combined, such as would occur on a LAN or with multiplexing, then the combined statistics of the various sources have the types of characteristics assumed for queuing analysis. The authors of the Ethernet report showed that there is a way of modeling the Ethernet traffic that (1) produces results similar to actual Ethernet traffic, (2) requires very few parameters to define, and (3) is physically plausible.

The approach used, and analyzed at length in [WILL97], is to model Ethernet traffic as being generated by the superposition of many Pareto-like ON/OFF sources. Each such source alternates between an ON period, in which a burst of packets is transmitted, and an OFF, or idle, period. If we assume that the periods are characterized by independent, identically distributed random variables and that each source is governed by the same distributions, then it is a tractable (but difficult) matter to determine the behavior of the superposition or multiplexing of multiple

---

[8] The differences in the character of the first plot can perhaps be accounted for on the basis of time-of-day effects.

such sources. In fact, this approach can be used to generate traffic that corresponds to traditional traffic models. The key element is to use a finite-variance distribution, such as exponential or geometric, to characterize the length of the ON and OFF periods. As we have seen, such models do not reflect the real Ethernet traffic.

What the Bellcore researchers did was to model the ON/OFF time periods with distributions with infinite variance, in particular using the Pareto distribution with parameter α between 1 and 2. As was mentioned, in this range, the random variable has a finite mean and an infinite variance. [WILL97] demonstrates that the superposition of many Pareto-distributed ON/OFF sources results in self-similar traffic with Hurst parameter $H = (3 - \alpha)/2$. Note that for $1 < \alpha < 2$, we have $0.5 < H < 1$, which is the range for self-similarity. For the Ethernet traffic under study, the analysts found that individual sources had a typical α of 1.2, which results in self-similar traffic with $H = 0.9$.

[WILL97] demonstrates that a heavy-tailed distribution such as Pareto reflects the actual behavior of an individual Ethernet source. Intuitively, the high or infinite variance of a heavy-tailed distribution exhibits extreme variability and therefore variability on all time scales. An application or a workstation will typically generate traffic in bursts with idle periods in between. With a high-variance distribution, the range of time intervals involved can be very wide, with lots of very short bursts, many long bursts, and some very long bursts. Mandelbrot, the mathematician who coined the term *fractal*, referred to this characteristic as the **Noah effect** in reference to the Biblical passage (Genesis 7:11–12): "In the six hundredth year of Noah's life, the windows of heaven were opened, and the rain was upon the earth forty days and forty nights."

World Wide Web Traffic

[CROV96] reports on a study of Web traffic that involved over half a million requests for Web documents. The data were collected from 37 workstation-based Web browsers in the Boston University Computer Science Department. The methodology used was similar to that of the Ethernet study just discussed. The study showed that the traffic pattern generated by the browsers was self-similar. The analysts modeled each Web browser as an ON/OFF source and found that the data fit very well to a Pareto distribution. For various measurement sets, the analysts found Pareto distributions with α ranging from 1.16 to 1.5.

The analysts for this study did some additional testing to attempt to explain the self-similar behavior. They looked at the size of the WWW transfers from servers back to browsers and found that the tail of the distribution followed a Pareto-type distribution. The authors hypothesize that Web traffic reflects a random selection of files for transfer. In particular, if users selected files for transfer by following links without regard to the size of the file being transferred, the size of transfer might represent essentially random samples from the distribution of Web files. Digging further, the analysts found that indeed files available via the Web over the Internet have a size distribution that is heavy tailed. This makes some sense because although there are plenty of small files out on the Internet, there are also plenty of large and very large files as well. One example of a file type that contributes very large files is the multimedia file, which is increasingly popular on the Web.

Signaling System Number 7 Traffic

The study reported in [DUFF94] looked at the control signaling traffic generated on digital telecommunications networks. The control signal protocol is Signaling System Number 7 (SS7), used on ISDN and other digital networks. The study encompassed about 170 million signaling messages collected from a variety of different working SS7-controlled networks. SS7 is a common-channel signaling protocol that is used by the internal switching nodes of a telecommunications network for the exchange of control messages. Control functions include setting up routes for connections through the network, maintaining and terminating connections, and sending traffic and error status alerts.

The study showed clearly that traditional Poisson-based models were inadequate to account for SS7 behavior. As in the two studies just discussed, this study found that self-similar traffic models provided a better fit. Further, with the control signaling data available, the authors were also able to study the traffic pattern of actual calls and, in particular, to look at call duration. Here, the data revealed that these call durations were best characterized by a heavy-tailed distribution.

TCP, FTP, and TELNET Traffic

[PAXS95] reports on a study of wide area TCP traffic, together with studies of FTP and TELNET traffic carried over TCP connections. The following general conclusions were reached:

1. Commonly used Poisson models seriously underestimate the burstiness of TCP traffic over a wide range of time scales.
2. For interactive TELNET traffic, *connection* arrivals are well-modeled as Poisson. However, the Poisson assumption for *packet* arrivals—namely, exponentially distributed interarrival times—significantly underestimates the burstiness of the traffic.
3. For bulk transfer, performed by FTP, the traffic structure again differs markedly from Poisson. As with the TELNET data, FTP session arrivals correspond well to the Poisson model but data connections have a much burstier arrival rate. In addition, the distribution of the number of bytes in each burst has a heavy upper tail.

Variable Bit Rate Video

A number of studies have shown that digitized video of the type that is transmitted over ATM networks and the Internet is self-similar. For example, [GARR94] performed an experiment on two hours of video using the movie *Star Wars* as the source. The video was encoded using the JPEG standard (described in Part VII of this book). The result was a data stream consisting of variable-length frames, with one data frame for each video frame. The variable length of the frames is due to the nature of the compression/encoding algorithm. It is this variability in frame length that gives rise to a stochastic process.

The result of the analysis is that the video transmission exhibits a self-similar character and that the frame length conforms to a Pareto distribution, at least in the tail of the distribution. The authors show how the high variability relates to the action in the film. In essence, the film contains scenes with little action, scenes with quite a bit of action, and scenes that are heavy on special effects with a great deal of rapid movement. All of this can be related to a heavy-tailed distribution of the encoded video.

In a broader study, [BERA95] looked at 20 different VBR sequences, generated by a number of different codecs and covering a wide range of different scenes, including the *Star Wars* sequence just discussed. The analysis showed that long-range dependence is an inherent feature of VBR video traffic, independent of codecs used and scene recorded.

Deterministic Data Transfer

An intriguing study reported in [DEAN96] looked at a generalized token-passing network that could be used to model a token ring or token bus LAN. The authors used deterministic data sources and varied the total load on the network by varying the amount of load generated by each source. Remarkably, for moderately complex networks (a few hundred elements), the data traffic is self-similar. The authors conclude that in a network with a number of protocol interactions between remote sources and destinations, the underlying protocols govern the dynamics of data traffic flow to produce self-similar behavior.

8.3 PERFORMANCE IMPLICATIONS OF SELF-SIMILARITY

The good news about the prevalence of self-similar data traffic is that today's high-speed computers and networks enable us to rapidly collect and analyze sufficient data to determine the existence of self-similarity in a given environment and to estimate its parameters. The bad news is that self-similarity has a profound impact on performance.

Ethernet/ISDN Analysis

We begin with the results of studies reported in [ERRA96] and [ERRA94] by researchers at Bellcore. The study used the Ethernet data discussed in Section 8.2 and repeated the analysis with a set of ISDN data that consisted of over 100,000 data packets. In both cases, the actual packet delay as a function of utilization was plotted. In addition, the parameters necessary for a queuing analysis were measured from the trace data and plugged into the queuing formulas.

Figure 8.6 is representative of the results achieved. The agreement between actual waiting time and the estimated waiting time obtained using conventional queuing theory is very poor. With traditional queuing analysis, the effective capacity of a server is about 80%, whereas for the actual data expected delay begins to increase sharply in the 50—60% range. Qualitatively similar results were obtained for every ISDN and Ethernet data set examined by the researchers.

Ethernet Data

In their key paper on Ethernet traffic [LELA94] and in related papers, the researchers addressed the problem of the performance implications of self-similar-

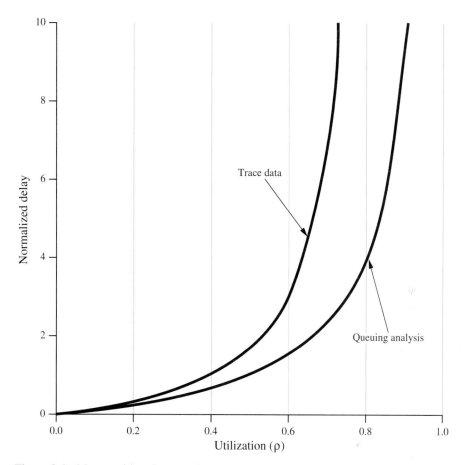

Figure 8.6   Mean waiting time results.

ity. One important discovery was that the higher the load on the Ethernet, the higher the estimated Hurst parameter H or, equivalently, the higher the degree of self-similarity. This result is vital because it is precisely at high loads that performance issues become most relevant.

An equally important result of the Ethernet analysis was the inadequacy of traditional queuing models to predict performance. For example, a common assumption concerning data traffic is that multiplexing a large number of independent traffic streams results in a Poisson process. [WILL94] points out that this assumption and the resulting queuing analysis led ATM switch vendors to produce first-generation switches with small buffers (10–100 cells). When these switches were deployed in the field and exposed to real traffic, cell losses far beyond those expected were experienced and resulted in a redesign of the switches. The analysis in [LELA94] shows that if the input is self-similar, then increased delays and increased buffer size requirements will be experienced in any multiplexing of self-similar streams. This applies to switches, such as ATM, frame relay, and 100BASE-T switches; to WAN routers; to shared-medium LANs, such as Ethernet; and to statistical multiplexers.

Storage Model with Self-similar Input

The two analyses discussed so far were based on comparing actual trace data to models based on Poisson assumptions. In this subsection, we look at an influential paper by Norros [NORR94] that attempts to develop reliable analytic models of self-similar behavior. This paper has inspired a number of subsequent modeling efforts and is representative of many such approaches.

Norros used the FBM process (described in Section 8.2) as a building block. Norros then developed a workload model based on FBM processes and an infinite buffer with constant service times. The mathematical development in the paper is beyond the scope of this discussion, but one simple result is representative of the performance implications developed in the paper. Under certain assumptions, the storage or buffer requirement q as a function of the mean utilization ρ obeys

$$q = \frac{\rho^{1/2(1-H)}}{(1 - \rho)^{H/(1-H)}}$$

where H is the Hurst parameter. For $H = 0.5$, this relationship simplifies to $q = \rho/(1 - \rho)$, which is the classic queuing result of a system with exponential interarrival times and exponential service times (M/M/1). For a system with constant service times (M/D/1), the classic queuing result is

$$q = \frac{\rho}{1 - \rho} - \frac{\rho^2}{2(1 - \rho)}$$

Figure 8.7 plots the results for $H = 0.9$ and 0.75 and compares these to the M/M/1 and M/D/1 cases (compare the delay time results in Figure 8.6). As can be seen, the buffer requirements begin to explode at lower levels of utilization for higher degrees of long-range dependence (higher values of H). This has an obvious consequence for buffer design: If high levels of utilization are required, drastically larger buffers are needed for self-similar traffic than would be predicted based on classical queuing analysis.

The Applicability of Self-similar Traffic Models

A number of studies, some of which have been cited in this section, point to a self-similar traffic pattern in many network environments. The question arises as to how prevalent such traffic patterns are and under what conditions performance analysis is critically dependent on taking self-similarity into account. This is currently an active area of research. This chapter contains references to a number of papers that demonstrate the relevance of self-similarity under a variety of conditions. However, the reader should keep in mind that this does not mean that traditional queuing analysis is now irrelevant.

As an example of the lack of consensus on the scope of applicability of the self-similar model, a session at the 1995 SIGMETRICS conference considered this point [ERRA95]. The results reported in that session clearly demonstrate that self-similar effects are relevant in some networking environments and do not significantly affect performance in other environments. Other papers reflect this spectrum of relevance. For example, [RYU96] provides evidence that one can ignore the self-similarity of VBR traffic over ATM networks in dimensioning buffers. [LIVN93]

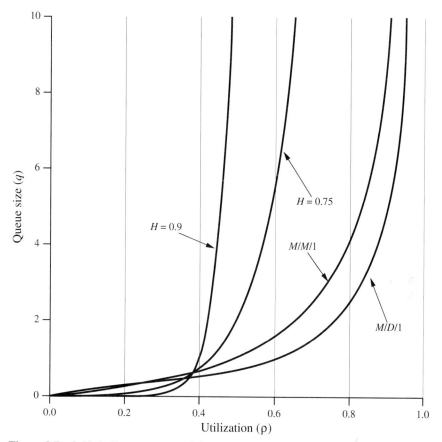

Figure 8.7   Self-similar storage model.

demonstrates that in many cases, the presence of self-similarity in either interarrival times or service times can have a dramatic impact on queuing performance. [GROS96] suggest that capturing or estimating self-similarity parameters for data traffic is sometimes relevant and sometimes not.

   An insight that may prove to be critical is provided in [RYU97]. The authors draw a distinction between self-similarity at the application level and at the network level. Application-level self-similar traffic originates from a source that exhibits self-similarity over a wide range of time scales without any interaction with the network; in other words, the self-similarity is inherent in the data traffic source. A good example of this is VBR video traffic. Network-level self-similar traffic exhibits self-similarity over a wide range of time scales as a result of numerous interactions with the network (or internet); TCP-based traffic is a good example. This distinction is important for several reasons. First, as mentioned in the preceding paragraph, Ryu argues elsewhere that the self-similarity of VBR traffic can often be ignored in dimensioning buffers, and provides some analytical and empirical arguments to support this assertion. Thus, application-level self-similar traffic, at least in some cases, may be treated differently than network-level self-similar traffic. Second, because the traffic behavior of application-level self-similar traffic remains largely independent of the network conditions under which it is sent, this traffic can be effectively managed in the context of admission control and resource allocation subject to QoS guarantees. On the other hand, network-level self-similar traffic changes its behavior depending on congestion status, retransmission scheme (different TCP version), number of concurrent users, request file size (for Web), FTP file size, and so on. This makes it difficult to perform traffic engineering effectively on such sources. How important this distinction between network-level and application-level is in practice is a subject of ongoing research.

8.4 MODELING AND ESTIMATION OF SELF-SIMILAR DATA TRAFFIC

A number of approaches have been taken to determine whether a given time series of actual data is self-similar and, if so, to estimate the self-similarity parameter H. This section summarizes some of the more common approaches taken.

Variance–time Plot

Recall that for the aggregated time series $\mathbf{x}^{(m)}$ of a self-similar process, the variance obeys the following for large m:

$$\mathrm{Var}\,(\mathbf{x}^{(m)}) \backsim \frac{\mathrm{Var}\,(\mathbf{x})}{m^{\beta}}$$

where the self-similarity parameter $H = 1 - (\beta/2)$. This can be rewritten as

$$\log[\mathrm{Var}\,(\mathbf{x}^{(m)})] \sim \log[\mathrm{Var}(\mathbf{x})] - \beta \log(m)$$

Because $\log[\mathrm{Var}\,(\mathbf{x})]$ is a constant independent of m, if we plot $\mathrm{Var}(\mathbf{x}^{(m)})$ versus m on a log-log graph, the result should be a straight line with a slope of $-\beta$. The plot is easily generated[9] from a data series $\mathbf{x}(t)$ by generating the aggregate process at different levels of aggregation m and then computing the variance. A number of researchers have done this [e.g., CROV96, LELA94] and have found that the experimental results do fall on a negatively sloping straight line. It is then a straightforward matter to estimate H. Slope values between -1 and 0 suggest self-similarity.

R/S Plot

For a stochastic process $\mathbf{x}(t)$ defined at discrete time instances $\{\mathbf{x}_t, t = 0, 1, 2, ...\}$, the rescaled range of $\mathbf{x}(t)$ over a time interval N is defined as the ratio R/S:

$$\frac{R}{S} = \frac{\max_{1 \leq j \leq N}\left[\sum_{k=1}^{j}(X_k - M(N))\right] - \max_{1 \leq j \leq N}\left[\sum_{k=1}^{j}(X_k - M(N))\right]}{\sqrt{\frac{1}{N}\sum_{j=1}^{N}(X_k - M(N))^2}}$$

where $M(N)$ is the sample mean over the time period N:

---

[9] Of course, if we are plotting actual data, we have to use the sample variance rather than the actual variance.

$$M(N) = \frac{1}{N}\sum_{j=1}^{N} X_j$$

The numerator in this ratio is a measure of the range of the process and the denominator is the sample standard deviation. This ratio is examined in the appendix to this chapter. For a self-similar process, the ratio has the following characteristic for large N:

$$R/S \frown (N/2)^H \qquad \text{with } H > 0.5$$

This can be rewritten as

$$\log[R/S] \frown H\log(N) - H\log(2)$$

If we plot $\log[R/S]$ versus N on a log-log graph, the result should fit a straight line with slope H. Again, this analysis has been performed on a number of data sets with results that fit a straight line.

Whittle's Estimator

The variance-time plot and the R/S plot are heuristic or "eyeballing" methods and should be treated as such. That is, they should not be used to obtain point estimates of H, but to get a rough idea whether a given data set is consistent with self-similar features ($H > 0.5$) or whether it falls within the realm of traditional short-range dependent models ($H \approx 0.5$). We now turn to an estimator that offers more statistical rigor but that requires that certain assumptions about the underlying data are satisfied. To begin, we need to present an estimator of power spectral density.

The Periodogram

A classic problem in stochastic process theory is the estimation of the power spectrum $S(w)$ of a stationary process $\mathbf{x}(t)$ in terms of a single realization of a finite segment of the process. That is, we have only one sample of $\mathbf{x}(t)$ covering a finite period of time. As was stated in Section 6.3, for a discrete-time stationary stochastic process, the autocorrelation and spectral density are defined as

$$R(k) = E[\mathbf{x}(t)\mathbf{x}(t+k)] \qquad S(w) = \sum_{k} R(k)e^{-jwk}$$

If we assume that the process is ergodic in correlation (time averages equal ensemble averages), then we can estimate the autocorrelation function by

$$\hat{R}_N(k) = \frac{1}{N}\sum_{n=0}^{N-1} X(n+k)X(n)$$

Since the spectral density $S(w)$ is the Fourier Transform of the autocorrelation function $R(k)$, one might hope that a Fourier operation on the estimate of the autocorrelation function would produce a good estimate of the spectral density. This is in fact the case under certain reasonable conditions.

The spectral density of a stochastic process $\mathbf{x}(t)$ defined at discrete time instances $\{\mathbf{x}_t, t = 0, 1, 2, \ldots\}$ can be estimated by a Fourier series operation over a time period N, as follows:

$$I_N(w) = \frac{1}{2\pi N} \left| \sum_{k=1}^{N} \mathbf{x}_k e^{jkw} \right|^2$$

This estimator is referred to in the literature as a **periodogram**, or intensity function.[10]

Estimating *H*

Suppose that we assume that the observed time series is from a self-similar stochastic process with parameter H and that a particular form, such as the fractional Brownian motion process, is chosen. Then the spectral density of the chosen process, can be expressed as $S(w, H)$, where the form of the density is known but the parameter H is unknown. Then it can be shown that H can be estimated by finding the value of H that minimizes the following expression:

$$\int_{-\pi}^{\pi} \frac{I_N(w)}{S(w, H)} \, dw$$

This is known as the Whittle estimator and is discussed at length in [BERA94]. If the sequence $\{\mathbf{x}_k\}$ has length N, then the preceding integral is readily converted to a discrete summation over the frequencies $w = 2\pi/N, 4\pi/N, ..., 2\pi$. An advantage of this approach is that it produces not only an estimate of H but a sample variance, so that confidence intervals can be computed. This is possible because the estimator is asymptotically normal. The sample variance is expressed as

$$\mathrm{Var}(\hat{H}) = 4\pi \left[\int_{-\pi}^{\pi} \left(\frac{\partial \log S(w)}{\partial H} \right)^2 dw \right]^{-1}$$

The Whittle estimator serves a different purpose than the variance-time plot and the R/S plot. Those two techniques are used to test whether a time series if self-similar and if so to obtain a rough estimate H. The Whittle estimator assumes that the time series is a self-similar process of a particular form and provides an estimate of H with confidence intervals.

8.5   RECOMMENDED READING

The topic of self-similarity is related to both fractals and chaos theory, and numerous books abound. [SCHR91] is a fascinating book devoted to self-similarity and its manifestations in fractals, chaos, and many other areas.

The volume of literature on self-similar data traffic is exploding, and only a few key papers are mentioned here. [LELA94] is one of the most important networking papers of the decade and launched this new examination of data traffic performance. [WILL94], from the same authors, is an informal discussion of the importance of self-similar traffic modeling. [PAXS95] provides a solid analysis of TCP-based self-similar traffic and includes a number

---

[10]   Most texts on stochastic processes treat periodograms but discuss only a continuous-time formulation. For the interested reader, good discussions of a discrete-time formulation are found in [BOX94] and [STAR94].

of useful appendixes on underlying mathematical concepts of general interest in self-similar traffic modeling. [ERRA96] focuses on the impact of self-similarity on queuing performance and provides a good overview of the issues and modeling techniques involved.

[FEDE88] includes a detailed analysis of the Hurst parameter and the R/S ratio, plus a good treatment of fractional Brownian motion processes. [NORR95] discusses the application of fractional Brownian motion to the analysis of data traffic.

ERRA96   Erramilli, A., Narayan, O., and Willinger, W. "Experimental Queueing Analysis with Long-range Dependent Packet Traffic." *IEEE/ACM Transactions on Networking*, April 1996.

FEDE88   Feder. J. *Fractals*. New York: Plenum Press, 1988.

LELA94   Leland, W., Taqqu, M., Willinger, W., and Wilson, D. "On the Self-similar Nature of Ethernet Traffic (Extended Version)." *IEEE/ACM Transactions on Networking*, February 1994.

NORR95   Norros, I. "On the Use of Fractional Brownian Motion in the Theory of Connectionless Networks." *IEEE Journal on Selected Areas in Communications*, August 1995.

PAXS95   Paxson, V., and Floyd, S. "Wide Area Traffic: The Failure of Poisson Modeling." *IEEE/ACM Transactions on Networking*, June 1995.

SCHR91   Schroeder, M. *Fractals, Chaos, Power Laws: Minutes from an Infinite Paradise.* New York: Freeman, 1991.

WILL94   Willinger, W., Wilson, D., Wilson, D., and Taqqu, M. "Self-similar Traffic Modeling for High-speed Networks." *ConneXions*, November 1994.

8.6 PROBLEMS

8.1 What is the length of a Cantor set after N iterations?

8.2 Show that the Cantor set consists of all points in the interval [0, 1] that have no 1's in their base-3 expression.

8.3 In what sense is this sequence self-similar?

$$… 1/8, 1/4, 1/2, 1, 2, 4, 8, …$$

8.4 Show that if X has a Pareto distribution with parameters k and α, then the random variable $Y = \ln(X/k)$ has an exponential distribution with parameter α.

8.5 The continuous-time definition of a self-similar stochastic process described in Section 8.2 included equations that relate $E[\mathbf{x}(t)]$ to $E[\mathbf{x}(at)]$ and relate $\text{Var}[\mathbf{x}(t)]$ to $\text{Var}[\mathbf{x}(at)]$.
  a. Show the equations for $H = 1$ and $H = 0.5$ and comment on the results.
  b. Rewrite the equations to relate $E[\mathbf{x}(at)]$ to $E[a\mathbf{x}(t)]$ and relate $\text{Var}[\mathbf{x}(at)]$ to $\text{Var}[a\mathbf{x}(t)]$.
  c. Show the equations from (b) for $H = 1$ and $H = 0.5$ and comment on the results.

APPENDIX 8A   THE HURST SELF-SIMILARITY PARAMETER

Throughout this chapter, we have made use of the Hurst parameter H as a convenient measure of the self-similarity of a stochastic process. This parameter was named after H. E. Hurst, who spent a lifetime studying the Nile and other rivers and the problems related to water storage [HURS65]. Among other things, Hurst discovered that water levels of the Nile River over an 800-year period obeyed a self-similar pattern. This appendix provides some background on the development of H.

Hurst, a hydrologist, made a study of the long-term water flow characteristics of various rivers. He observed that some rivers (the Rhine, for example) had reasonably mild fluctuations. Others, such as the Nile, presented a very different picture. Hurst noted that the long-term and short-term characteristics of the Nile were similar. In the short term, as one might expect, there were year-to-year fluctuations in the level of the Nile. One might also expect that these fluctuations would tend to average out so that over the long run, the level of the Nile would stay within a fairly narrow range, with good and bad times coming close together. This is not the case for the Nile. In the long term, long periods of drought were followed by long periods in which there were floods nearly every year. Mandelbrot has labeled this phenomenon the **Joseph effect**, in reference to the Biblical passage: (Genesis 41:29–30): "Joseph said unto Pharaoh, There come seven years of great plenty throughout all the land of Egypt; and there shall arise after them seven years of famine." This is perhaps not the best term, because the long-term behavior showed no such regularity. Rather, there was no persisting cycle in the data at any time scale.

Hurst addressed the problem of designing an ideal reservoir to regulate the flow of the Nile based on the given record of observed flow. An ideal reservoir is one that provides a constant outflow equal to the average inflow and that never overflows and never empties. For this design, we need to get some measure of the variability of the water flow. Suppose that measurements are taken at one-year intervals. Define the following:

X_j = Inflow during year j ($1 \leq j \leq N$); this is the time series under study

$M(N)$ = Constant yearly outflow, based on observation of N years of historical data

L_j = Reservoir level at end of year j ($1 \leq j \leq N$)

N = Number of years of observation

Figure 8.8 illustrates these quantities. On the basis of the record of N years, we would like to know the maximum and minimum levels that the reservoir experiences ($L_{max}(N), L_{min}(N)$) and the range $R(N) = L_{max}(N) - L_{min}(N)$.

Given a knowledge of the inflow values over the period of interest, the desired quantities are easily calculated:

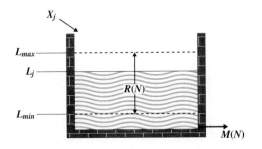

Figure 8.8   Illustration of parameters for Hurst analysis.

$$M(N) = \frac{1}{N} \sum_{j=1}^{N} X_j$$

$$L_j = \sum_{k=1}^{j} X_k - jM(N)$$

$$R(N) = \max_{1 \leq j \leq N} L_j - \min_{1 \leq j \leq N} L_j$$

In words, $M(N)$ is the average inflow over N years, L_j is equal to the total inflow over the first j years minus the total outflow over those years, and $R(N)$ is the difference between the highest and lowest values of L_j over those years. As should be clear, the range depends on the time interval N and is a nondecreasing function of N. Note that this range parameter R is not the same as the range of the time series X_j, which is expressed as

$$\text{Range}(X, N) = \max_{1 \leq j \leq N} X_j - \min_{1 \leq j \leq N} X_j$$

Instead, we can view L_j as the accumulated amount by which the time series has departed from the mean up to time j. Thus, R is in a sense a better measure of the variability of X about its mean.

Hurst examined a number of different phenomena and developed a normalized, dimensionless measure to characterize variability, R/S, where S is the sample variance:

$$S = \sqrt{\frac{1}{N} \sum_{j=1}^{N} (X_j - M(N))^2}$$

In a sense, both R and S measure the variability of the data; R "looks" at the data linearly, whereas S is based on the squared data. Hurst referred to this ratio as the **rescaled range**.

Hurst found that for many natural phenomena, including river discharges, mud sediments, and tree rings, the ratio R/S as a function of N is well described by the following empirical relation for large N:

$$R/S \sim (N/2)^H \qquad \text{with } H > 0.5$$

It is easy to verify this visually by plotting the value of R/S calculated for different values of N on a log-log plot (log R/S versus log N). For many sets of data, Hurst found that the data points fell on a straight line; the slope of the line is H by the preceding formula.

It can be shown that for any short-range dependent process, R/S becomes asymptotically proportional to $N^{1/2}$.; that is, $H = 0.5$. However, Hurst found many phenomena with values of H ranging from 0.7 to 0.9. The larger values of H suggest a higher degree of persistent variability in the data.

End-system Traffic Management

ISSUES FOR PART FOUR

The primary motivation, indeed the sole motivation, for moving to higher-speed networks and internets is to support more traffic: more end systems, and higher data rates for applications at the end systems. Unfortunately, the interaction between the protocols in the end systems and the traffic management mechanisms in the networks and routers can result in gross under-utilization of a high-speed network. For example, [COME95a] reports on a measurement of FTP with surprising results. When transferring a 4.4-megabyte data file between two hosts connected to the same 10-Mbps Ethernet, FTP reports a mean throughput of 1.313 Mbps. Using the same software and computers to transfer the file across a 100-Mbps ATM path produced a mean throughput of only 0.366 Mbps. Here we have a situation in which network capacity is increased by a factor of 10 and throughput drops by a factor of almost 4!

The key to understanding this problem is in the traffic control mechanisms using by end-to-end transport-level protocols such as TCP. TCP is the most commonly used transport protocol for data transfer, supporting such applications as file transfer, electronic mail, remote terminal access, Web access, and client-server applications. TCP is an end-to-end protocol that treats the intervening network or internet as a black box; it has no direct means of determining the condition of the network but must deduce network conditions on the basis of its dialogue with other end systems.[1]

Two end systems communicating via TCP employ a flow control mechanism with two key features: (1) As data are received at a destination, the destination returns acknowledgments to the sender, and (2) each acknowledgment is accompanied with an indication of how much additional data the destination is prepared to receive. This mechanism was designed to enable the destination to control the flow of data from the source so as to avoid overloading the destination, but this same mechanism is also used as a means of net-

---

[1] There are a few exceptions, such as the ATM ABR service, discussed in Chapter 11.

work congestion control. If a source fails to receive an acknowledgment to a segment of data, it will eventually time out and retransmit that segment. However, the source has no way of knowing whether the unacknowledged segment has been discarded by the network or has simply been excessively delayed but eventually reaches the destination. In the either case, the source should reduce its rate of transmission because a lost or delayed segment is evidence of network congestion; but in the second case, TCP should not retransmit the segment because this would unnecessarily add to the congestion.

Thus, in any network or internet configuration, end systems have only a crude tool for assessing network congestion and reacting to it. But the importance of congestion control increases dramatically with the data rate of the network, for two reasons:

1. The only feedback that a TCP source has to any transmission is delayed by the round-trip time from source to destination. At higher speeds, the source has transmitted a huge number of additional bits before receiving that feedback. Thus, if congestion has developed, by the time a source has evidence of that congestion, it has already worsened the problem by many bits.

2. High-speed network traffic spikes can be enormous, especially if the traffic has a self-similar profile. Thus, congestion can arise quickly and be sustained so that many segments must be dropped by the network before the sources react to the problem. In such a situation, the black box is in danger of becoming a black hole, sucking up all incoming segments and delivering few.

To achieve greater performance out of high-speed networks, end systems must regulate their flow of data to efficiently use network resources without overloading the system, which results in congestion and throughput collapse. This is the focus of Part Four.

ROAD MAP FOR PART FOUR

Chapter 9: Link-level Flow and Error Control

The tool that is available to transport-level protocols, such as TCP, for assessing network conditions and regulating their flow of traffic is a sliding-window flow control mechanism. This mechanism is very similar to one used in data link control protocols such as HDLC. To clarify the nature of this mechanism and how it depends on key factors such as data rate and propagation delay, it is best to first examine flow control at the data link layer, where fewer variables are involved. This we do in Chapter 9.

Chapter 10: Transport-level Traffic Control

In Chapter 10, transport-level traffic management is examined. The chapter explains the TCP flow control mechanism and then shows how it is also used for congestion control. The subtle relationship between TCP and ATM is also explored. Finally, a transport-level protocol designed for multicast, real-time traffic, known as RTP, is examined.

CHAPTER 9

LINK-LEVEL FLOW AND ERROR CONTROL

I had throughout the greatest misgivings of an impulsive offensive by the French that was not based on calm calculations of numbers, distances, and times.

—*The World Crisis,* **Winston Churchill**

The fundamental mechanisms that determine the performance of communication links, networks, and internetworks are flow control and error control. Throughout this book, there are discussions of techniques for dealing with congestion and achieving high levels of utilization based on controlling the flow of protocol data units from sources and through intermediate systems. Intimately associated with flow control techniques is the need to recover from the loss of PDUs due to transmission errors or the discard of packets in the face of congestion.

In designing high-speed networks and internetworks, it is therefore essential to understand the performance implications of flow and error control techniques. These techniques are implemented at the link level, in some network-level protocols such as X.25, at the transport level, and in some application-level protocols.

It turns out to be extraordinarily difficult to model the performance of flow and error control techniques. The simplest case is that of a link control protocol operating between two devices connected by a point-to-point link. Here we need only be concerned with a constant propagation delay between the two devices, a constant data rate, a probabilistic error rate, and perhaps the statistical characteristics of the traffic. Even in this simple case, which has been analyzed in published studies as far back as the early 1960s, papers are still being published that present new results (e.g., [ZORZ96]). When we deal with flow and error control across a network or internetwork (e.g., at the TCP level), analysis is vastly more complex and must take into account variable propagation delay, variable data rate, the effects of congestion produced by other traffic sources entering the network, the effects of dynamic routing decisions, relative priorities among multiple logical connections, and other factors. Yet it is critical to get some handle on flow and error control performance at layers above the link level to design the details of the flow and error control mechanisms in such protocols as TCP.

Because of the importance of this topic, we devote a chapter to analyzing the performance of link-level flow and error control mechanisms. It is possible in this relatively simple context to draw some conclusions about the impact of various factors on flow and error control performance. These conclusions provide insight that can guide our assessment and design of flow and error control mechanisms at higher protocol layers.

The chapter begins with a brief overview of the concepts of flow and error control. Then the basic mechanisms used in virtually all link-level protocols are described. Finally, some straightforward performance results are presented. The insight gained from these performance results will be useful in our discussion in Chapter 10.

9.1   THE NEED FOR FLOW AND ERROR CONTROL

Flow Control

Flow control is a protocol mechanism that enables a destination entity to regulate the flow of PDUs sent by a source entity. Flow control limits the amount or rate of data that is sent. The destination system may need to limit the flow for one of several reasons, including the following:

1. As each PDU arrives, the destination must do a certain amount of processing of the PDU header. The source may attempt to send PDUs faster than the destination can process them.

2. The destination protocol entity may buffer the incoming data for delivery to a higher-level protocol user. If that user is slow in retrieving the data, the buffer may fill up and the destination may need to limit or temporarily halt the flow from the source.

3. The destination may buffer the incoming data for retransmission on another I/O port (e.g., in the case of a bridge or router, or a packet-switching node) and may need to limit the incoming flow to match the outgoing flow.

The first two reasons come into play between end systems, either at the link level (two end systems connected by a direct link) or across a network. The final case deals with the forwarding of PDUs across a switched network (e.g., via packet-switched nodes) or across an internetwork (e.g., via bridges or routers).

Flow control can be exercised at a number of protocol levels. The effect is indicated in Figure 9.1. One example of this would be the case of a number of X.25 virtual circuits (level 3) multiplexed over a data link using LAPB (which is X.25 level 2). Another example would be the multiplexing of multiple TCP connections over an HDLC link. Flow control is exercised along each logical connection at the higher level independently of the flow control on the other connections. The total traffic on all of the connections is subjected to further flow control at the lower level.

Further complicating the study of flow control is that fact that it can be employed in various contexts, as suggested in Figure 9.2. The figure indicates two end systems connected through a network or internetwork. In the case of a network, the intermediate systems are individual network nodes, such as packet, frame relay, or ATM switches. In the case of an internetwork, the intermediate systems are typically routers. We now briefly consider the relationship between the protocol level of flow control and the scope across which flow control is exercised.

Hop Scope

Between intermediate systems that are directly connected, flow control can be exercised at the link level. For example, in the case of adjacent packet-switching nodes, LAPB is used. Each packet-switching node buffers incoming packets and routes them on the appropriate outgoing link. To assure that its buffers do not overflow, it can use LAPB flow control to limit the volume of incoming traffic. Link-level flow control can also be used between directly connected routers in an

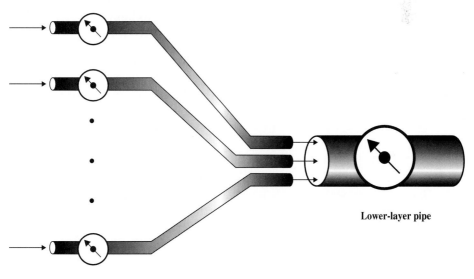

Lower-layer pipe

Higher-layer pipes

Figure 9.1   Flow control at multiple protocol layers.

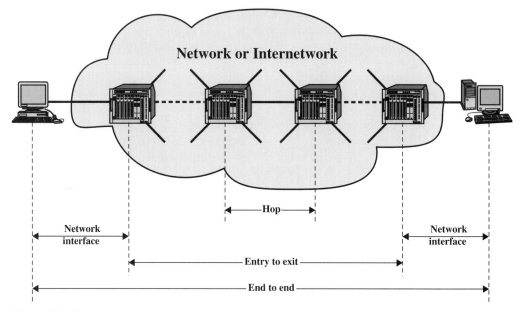

Figure 9.2   Flow control scope.

internetwork. Again, a router may use a link-level protocol such as HDLC to limit the volume of incoming datagrams to avoid buffer overflow.

Network Interface

A link-level protocol is also often used across the interface link between an end system and a network or internetwork. Again, in the case of an X.25 packet-switching network, LAPB enables the network to limit the total flow of packets from an end system into the network. In other networks, such as frame relay and ATM network, no flow control is exercised at the link level.

Flow control can also occur at a network protocol layer across the network interface. In this case, flow control is exercised for individual logical connections. The most common example of this is X.25. When the D bit in the packet header is set to zero, flow control is exercised between the end system and the network on each individual virtual circuit.

Entry to Exit

Some networks provide a form of flow control between entry and exit nodes for logical connections, such as virtual circuits. The objective in this context is to regulate input traffic so as to avoid the overflow of buffers at the exit point. The details of this mechanism are transparent to end users but may affect the flow of data across the network interface.

End to End

Flow control can be exercised on logical connections between end systems. Here the objective is for the receiving end system to regulate incoming flow so as to avoid buffer overflow and to satisfy application requirements. TCP provides such end-to-end flow control over individual TCP connections between end systems. End-to-end flow control can also be exercised on an X.25 virtual circuit basis when the D bit in the packet header is set to one.

End-to-end flow control at the data link layer is also frequently employed. Examples include the following:

- In a circuit-switched or ATM network, if a link control protocol such as HDLC is implemented in the end systems, then it operates end to end.
- Logical link control (LLC) operating across a LAN is exercised between end systems. In this case, the flow control operates over logical connections between end systems.
- The LAPF (Link Access Procedure for Frame Mode Bearer Services) control protocol enables the use of flow control mechanisms over logical connections between end systems across a frame relay network.

In the LLC and LAPF cases, the propagation delay between end systems is variable, and hence the analysis presented in Section 9.3 does not apply.

Error Control

Error control techniques are used to recover from the loss or damage of PDUs in transit between source and destination. Typically, error control involves error detection, based on a frame check sequence (FCS), and PDU retransmission. Error control and flow control are implemented together in a single mechanism that regulates the flow of PDUs and determines when one or more PDUs need to be retransmitted. Thus, error control, as with flow control, is a function that is performed at various protocol levels.

9.2 LINK CONTROL MECHANISMS

Three techniques are in common use for flow and error control at the link level: stop and wait, Go-Back-N, and selective reject. The latter two are special cases of the sliding-window technique. We examine all of these mechanisms in this section.

In the discussion that follows, we assume two end systems connected by a direct link. The source system wishes to send a message or block of data to the destination. Rather than send the data in a single block, it is broken up into a sequence of frames. This is done for one or more of the following reasons:

- The buffer size of the receiver may be limited.
- The longer the transmission, the more likely that there will be an error, necessitating retransmission of the entire frame. With smaller frames, errors are detected sooner, and a smaller amount of data needs to be retransmitted.
- On a shared medium, such as a LAN, it is usually desirable not to permit one station to occupy the medium for an extended period, thus causing long delays at the other sending stations.

Stop and Wait

The simplest form of flow control, known as stop-and-wait flow control, works as follows. A source entity transmits a frame. After reception, the destination entity indicates its willingness to accept another frame by sending back an acknowledgment to the frame just received. The source must wait until it receives the acknowledgment before sending the next frame. The destination can thus stop the flow of data by simply withholding acknowledgment.

The stop-and-wait scheme must take into account two types of errors. First, the frame that arrives at the destination could be damaged; that is, one or more bits have been altered. To enable the receiver to detect this error, the link control frame includes a frame check sequence, typically the cyclic redundancy check (CRC). If an error is detected, the receiver discards the frame. To account for this possibility, the source station is equipped with a timer. After a frame is transmitted, the source station waits for an acknowledgment. If no acknowledgment is received by the time that the timer expires, then the same frame is sent again. Note that this method requires that the transmitter maintain a copy of a transmitted frame until an acknowledgment is received for that frame.

The second sort of error is a damaged acknowledgment. Consider the following situation. Station A sends a frame. The frame is received correctly by station B, which responds with an acknowledgment (ACK). The ACK is damaged in transit and is not recognizable by A, which will therefore time out and resend the same frame. This duplicate frame arrives and is accepted by B. B has therefore accepted two copies of the same frame as if they were separate. To avoid this problem, data frames are alternately labeled with 0 or 1, and positive acknowledgments are of the form ACK0 and ACK1. The convention for the use of ACK0 and ACK1 is as follows: An ACK0 acknowledges receipt of a frame numbered 1 and indicates that the receiver is ready for a frame numbered 0; an ACK1 acknowledges receipt of a frame numbered 0 and indicates that the receiver is ready for a frame numbered 1.

The use of error detection, timers, acknowledgments, and retransmissions is referred to as automatic repeat request (ARQ); thus, the protocol we have been discussing is referred to as stop-and-wait ARQ. These same ARQ techniques show up in all link level flow and error control techniques.

Figure 9.3 gives an example of the use of stop-and-wait ARQ, showing the transmission of a sequence of frames from source A to destination B. This is a vertical-time sequence diagram. It has the advantages of showing time dependencies and illustrating the correct send-receive relationship. Each arrow represents a single frame transiting a data link between two stations. The data are sent in a sequence of frames with each frame containing a portion of the data and some control information. The time it takes for a station to emit all of the bits of a frame onto the medium is the transmission time; this is proportional to the length of the frame. The propagation time is the time it takes for a bit to traverse the link between source and destination.

The figure shows the two types of errors described previously. The third frame transmitted by A is lost or damaged and therefore no ACK is returned by B. A times out and retransmits the frame. Later, A transmits a frame labeled 1 but the ACK0 for that frame is lost. A times out and retransmits the same frame. When B receives two frames in a row with the same label, it discards the second frame but sends back an ACK0 to each.

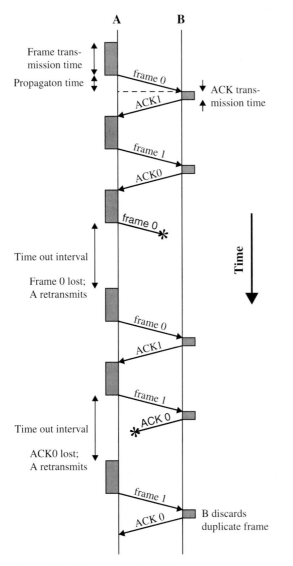

Figure 9.3 Stop-and-wait ARQ.

The stop-and-wait technique is rarely used because of its inefficiency. The source of this inefficiency is that only one frame at a time can be in transit. If the propagation time is long relative to the transmission time, then the line will be idle most of the time. This effect is illustrated in Figure 9.4. The sequence of events is as follows:

1. At time $t = 0$, station A begins to transmit a frame.
2. The transmission time for the frame is T_{frame}. Thus, at $t = T_{frame}$, the last bit of the frame has just been transmitted. If the propagation time from A to B is

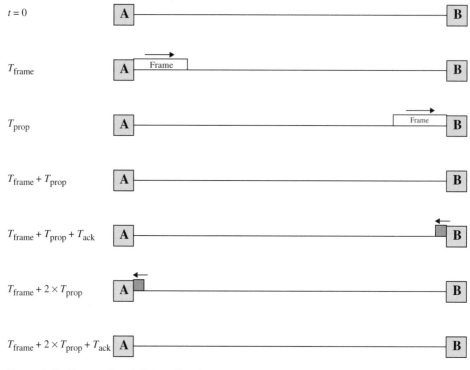

Figure 9.4 Stop-and-wait link utilization.

greater than T_{frame}, then at this time all of the bits of the frame are on the link in transit.

3. The propagation time from A to B is T_{prop}. At $t = T_{prop}$, the first bit of the frame has just arrived at B and the remaining bits are coming in behind on the link.

4. At $t = T_{frame} + T_{prop}$, the entire frame has been absorbed by B.

5. Assume that B immediately sends an acknowledgment and that the processing time between receiving the frame and sending the ACK is negligible. The transmission time for the ACK is T_{ack}. Then by $t = T_{frame} + T_{prop} + T_{ack}$, the entire ACK has been transmitted. The ACK, represented by a shaded block in the figure, is typically much shorter than a data frame.

6. At $t = T_{frame} + 2 \times T_{prop}$, the first bit of the ACK has just arrived at A and the remaining bits are coming in behind on the link.

7. At $t = T_{frame} + 2 \times T_{prop} + T_{ack}$, the entire ACK has been absorbed by A.

In this scenario, it is clear that the line is underutilized. Assuming no errors, A would be capable of sending frames at a rate of $1/T_{frame}$. But because of the need to wait for an acknowledgment, the maximum rate is reduced to $1/(T_{frame} + 2 \times T_{prop} + T_{ack})$. If T_{prop} is large relative to T_{frame}, then this is a substantial reduction in potential throughput.

Sliding-window Techniques

The essence of the problem described so far is that only one frame at a time can be in transit. In situations where the bit length of the link (represented by T_{prop}) is greater than the frame length (represented by T_{frame}), serious inefficiencies result. Efficiency can be greatly improved by allowing multiple frames to be in transit at the same time.

Let us examine how this might work for two stations, A and B, connected via a full-duplex link. Station B allocates buffer space for n frames. Thus, B can accept n frames, and A is allowed to send n frames without waiting for any acknowledgments. To keep track of which frames have been acknowledged, each is labeled with a sequence number. B acknowledges a frame by sending an acknowledgment that includes the sequence number of the next frame expected. This acknowledgment also implicitly announces that B is prepared to receive the next n frames, beginning with the number specified. This scheme can also be used to acknowledge multiple frames. For example, B could receive frames 2, 3, and 4, but withhold acknowledgment until frame 4 has arrived. By then returning an acknowledgment with sequence number 5, B acknowledges frames 2, 3, and 4 at one time. A maintains a list of sequence numbers that it is allowed to send, and B maintains a list of sequence numbers that it is prepared to receive. Each of these lists can be thought of as a *window* of frames. The operation is referred to as sliding-window flow control.

Because the sequence number to be used occupies a field in the frame, it is clearly of bounded size. For example, for a 3-bit field, the sequence number can range from 0 to 7. Accordingly, frames are numbered modulo 8; that is, after sequence number 7, the next number is 0. In general, for a k-bit field the range of sequence numbers is 0 through $2^k - 1$, and frames are numbered modulo 2^k. With this in mind, Figure 9.5 is a useful way of depicting the sliding-window process. It assumes the use of a 3-bit sequence number. The shaded rectangle indicates the frames that may be sent; in this figure, the sender may transmit five frames, beginning with frame 0. Each time a frame is sent, the shaded window shrinks; each time an acknowledgment is received, the shaded window grows. Frames between the vertical bar and the shaded window have been sent but not yet acknowledged. As we shall see, the sender must buffer these frames in case they need to be retransmitted.

The actual window size need not be the maximum possible size for a given sequence number length. For example, using a 3-bit sequence number, a window size of 4 could be configured for the stations using the sliding-window flow control protocol.

An example is shown in Figure 9.6. The example assumes a 3-bit sequence number field and a maximum window size of seven frames. Initially, A and B have windows indicating that A may transmit seven frames, beginning with frame 0 (F0). After transmitting three frames (F0, F1, F2) without acknowledgment, A has shrunk its window to four frames and maintains a copy of the three transmitted frames. The window indicates that A may transmit four frames, beginning with frame number 3. B then transmits an RR (receive ready) 3, which means[1] "I have received all frames up through frame number 2 and am ready to receive frame number 3; in fact, I am

---

[1] The RR is a separate control frame. Most data link control protocols also allow for *piggybacked acknowledgments*. Each data frame includes not only a sequence number for that frame but also an acknowledgement sequence number that serves the same function as the RR frame. Thus, in a full-duplex exchange of data frames, separate RR frames are rarely used.

prepared to receive seven frames, beginning with frame number 3." With this acknowledgment, A is back up to permission to transmit seven frames, still beginning with frame 3; also, A may discard the buffered frames that have now been acknowledged. A proceeds to transmit frames 3, 4, 5, and 6. B returns RR 4, which acknowledges F3, and allows transmission of F4 through F2. By the time this RR reaches A, it has already transmitted F4, F5, and F6, and therefore A may only open its window to permit sending four frames beginning with F7.

Two sliding-window techniques are found in link control protocols: go-back-N ARQ and selective-reject ARQ; these differ in the way that errors are handled.

Go-back-N ARQ

The form of error control based on sliding-window flow control that is most commonly used is called go-back-N ARQ. In go-back-N ARQ, a station may send a series of frames sequentially numbered modulo some maximum value. While no errors occur, the destination will acknowledge incoming frames with an RR frame. If the destination station detects an error in a frame, it sends a negative acknowledgment (REJ = reject) for that frame. The destination station will discard that frame and all future incoming frames until the frame in error is correctly received. Thus, the source station, when it receives a REJ, must retransmit the frame in error plus all succeeding frames that were transmitted in the interim.

Consider that station A is sending frames to station B. After each transmission, A sets an acknowledgment timer for the frame just transmitted. Suppose that A has just transmitted frame i. The go-back-N technique takes into account the following contingencies:

1. **Damaged frame.** There are three subcases:
   a. B detects an error and has previously successfully received frame $(i - 1)$. B sends REJ i, indicated that frame i is rejected. When A receives the REJ, it must retransmit frame i and all subsequent frames that it has transmitted since the original transmission of frame i.
   b. Frame i is lost in transit. A subsequently sends frame $(i + 1)$. B receives frame $(i + 1)$ out of order and sends a REJ i. A must retransmit frame i and all subsequent frames.
   c. Frame i is lost in transit and A does not soon send additional frames. B receives nothing and returns neither an RR nor a REJ. When A's timer expires, it transmits an RR frame that includes a bit known as the P bit, which is set to 1. B interprets the RR frame with a P bit of 1 as a command that must be acknowledged by sending an RR indicating the next frame that it expects. When A receives the RR, it retransmits frame i.

2. **Damaged RR.** There are two subcases:
   a. B receives frame i and sends RR $(i + 1)$, which is lost in transit. Because acknowledgments are cumulative (e.g., RR 6 means that all frames through 5 are acknowledged), it may be that A will receive a subsequent

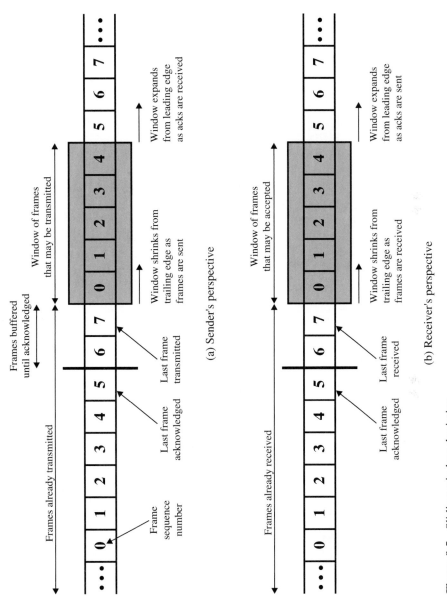

Figure 9.5 Sliding-window depiction.

222

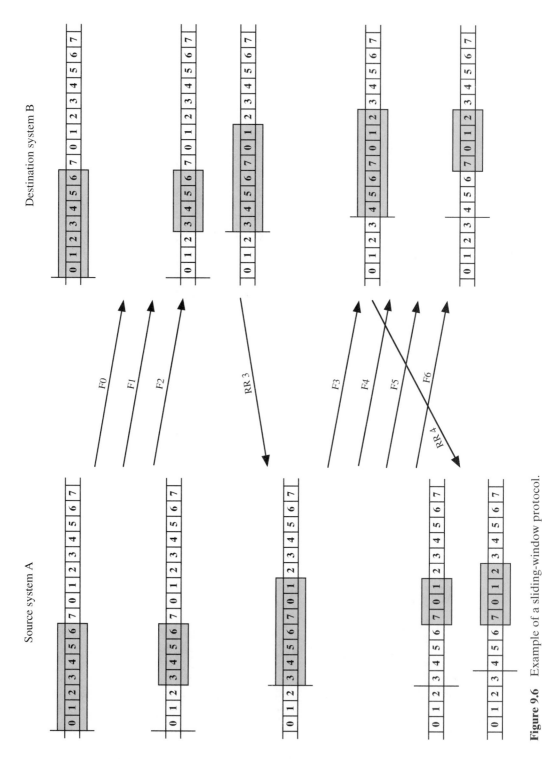

Figure 9.6 Example of a sliding-window protocol.

RR to a subsequent frame and that it will arrive before the timer associated with frame *i* expires.

   b. If A's timer expires, it transmits an RR command as in Case 1c. It sets another timer, called the P-bit timer. If B fails to respond to the RR command, or if its response is damaged, then A's P-bit timer will expire. At this point, A will try again by issuing a new RR command and restarting the P-bit timer. This procedure is tried for a number of iterations. If A fails to obtain an acknowledgment after some maximum number of attempts, it initiates a reset procedure.

3. Damaged REJ. If a REJ is lost, this is equivalent to Case 1c.

Figure 9.7a is an example of the frame flow for go-back-N ARQ. Because of the propagation delay on the line, by the time that an acknowledgment (positive or negative) arrives back at the sending station, it has already sent at least one additional frame beyond the one being acknowledged. In this example, frame 4 is damaged. Frames 5 and 6 are received out of order and are discarded by B. When frame 5 arrives, B immediately sends a REJ 4. When the REJ is received to frame 4, not only frame 4 but frames 5 and 6 must be retransmitted. Note that the transmitter must keep a copy of all unacknowledged frames.

Selective-reject ARQ

With selective-reject ARQ, the only frames retransmitted are those that receive a negative acknowledgment, in this case called SREJ, or those that time out. Figure 9.7b illustrates this scheme. When frame 5 is received out of order, B sends a SREJ 4, indicating that frame 4 has not been received. However, B continues to accept incoming frames and buffers them until a valid frame 4 is received. At that point, B can place the frames in the proper order for delivery to higher-layer software.

Selective reject would appear to be more efficient than go-back-N, because it minimizes the amount of retransmission. On the other hand, the receiver must maintain a buffer large enough to save post-SREJ frames until the frame in error is retransmitted, and must contain logic for reinserting that frame in the proper sequence. The transmitter, too, requires more complex logic to be able to send a frame out of sequence. Because of such complications, select-reject ARQ is much less widely used than go-back-N ARQ.

9.3   ARQ PERFORMANCE

In this section, we examine some of the performance issues related to the use of ARQ techniques over a point-to-point link. The section begins with stop-and-wait ARQ. Then we define an important parameter, generally called *a*, that captures the essence of the performance characteristics of a data link. Use of this parameter simplifies the presentation of go-back-N and selective-reject performance.

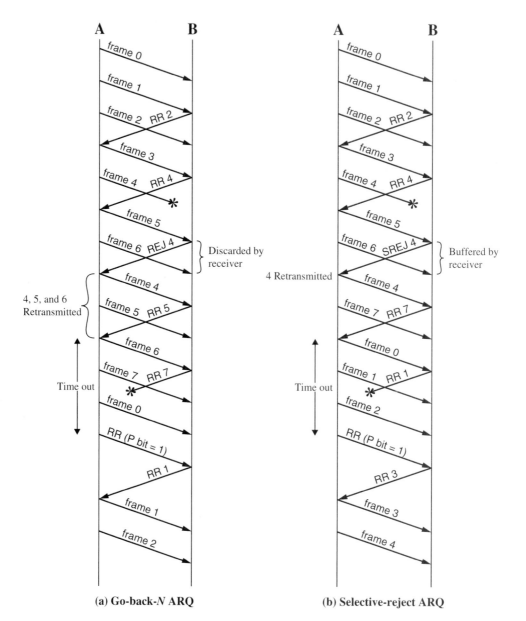

Figure 9.7 Sliding-Window ARQ Protocols.

Stop-and-wait ARQ

We look first at the performance of stop-and-wait flow control under the assumption of no errors, and then take into account errors.

Error-free Stop-and-wait

We wish to determine the maximum rate at which frames can be transmitted over a line using stop-and-wait flow control, assuming no errors. Suppose that a long message is to be sent from A to B as a sequence of frames $f_1, f_2, ..., f_n$, in the following fashion:

- A sends f_1.
- B sends an acknowledgment.
- A sends f_2.
- B sends an acknowledgment.
  ⋮
- A sends f_n.
- B sends an acknowledgment.

The total time to send the data can be expressed as nT, where T is the time to send one frame, receive an acknowledgment, and be ready to send the next frame. We can express T as follows:

$$T = T_{frame} + T_{prop} + T_{proc} + T_{ack} + T_{prop} + T_{proc}$$

where (see Figure 9.4)

T_{frame} = time to transmit a frame (time for the transmitter to send out all of the bits of the frame)

T_{prop} = propagation time between A and B (either direction)

T_{proc} = processing time at each station to react to an incoming event

T_{ack} = time to transmit an acknowledgment

Let us assume that the processing time is relatively negligible and that the acknowledgment frame is very small compared to a data frame, both of which are reasonable assumptions. Further assume a fixed frame size. Then stop-and-wait flow control allows data to be transmitted at the rate of one frame every T seconds, with T approximated as

$$T = T_{frame} + 2T_{prop}$$

The throughput, therefore, can be expressed as $1/T = 1/(T_{frame} + 2T_{prop})$ frames per second. For purposes of comparison, it is desirable to express throughput as a normalized quantity. If a frame can be transmitted in T_{frame} seconds, then the actual data rate on the link is $1/T_{frame}$ frames per second. Thus, the normalized throughput S can be expressed as

$$S = \frac{1/(T_{frame} + 2T_{prop})}{1/T_{frame}} = \frac{T_{frame}}{T_{frame} + 2T_{prop}} \tag{9.1}$$

If this derivation is not clear, consider the following. Let the data rate, in bits per second, on the link be R and the length of a frame, in bits, be L. Then the throughput on the link, in bits per second, is (L bits/frame) $\times$ ($1/T$ frames per second) = $L/(T_{frame} + 2T_{prop})$. To normalize throughput, we divide the throughput on the line, in bits per second, by the actual data rate:

$$S = \frac{L/(T_{frame} + 2T_{prop})}{R}$$

Substituting $T_{frame} = L/R$, we get Equation 9.1. It is useful to define the parameter $a = T_{prop}/T_{frame}$. Then,

$$S = \frac{1}{1 + 2a} \tag{9.2}$$

This is the maximum possible normalized throughput on the link using stop and wait. Because the frame contains overhead bits, effective throughput is lower. The parameter a is constant if both T_{prop} and T_{frame} are constants, which is typically the case: Fixed-length frames are often used for all except the last frame in a sequence, and the propagation delay is constant for point-to-point links.

Stop-and-wait ARQ with Errors

Refer back to Figure 9.4. The time required to transmit a frame successfully is $(T_{frame} + 2T_{prop})$. Now suppose that a frame is lost or that its ACK is lost and that two transmission attempts are required for successful transmission. In this case, the time for transmission of the frame is

$$T = T_{frame} + \text{Timeout} + T_{frame} + 2T_{prop}$$

To simplify the derivation, assume that the timeout value is equal to twice the propagation delay. That is, if a station does not receive an acknowledgment within twice the propagation delay, it will retransmit the frame. In fact, a slightly longer timeout value must be used to account for processing time at the destination, but our approximation is reasonable. Thus, for a frame that must be transmitted twice, the time required is

$$T = 2(T_{frame} + 2T_{prop})$$

In general, if a frame suffers $(x - 1)$ consecutive failures so that it must be transmitted x times for successful delivery, then the time required is $x(T_{frame} + 2T_{prop})$. Defining N_x to be the average number of times each frame must be transmitted, then the average time to transmit a frame successfully is:

$$T = N_x(T_{frame} + 2T_{prop})$$

Using the same derivation as before, we arrive at a normalized throughput of

$$S = \frac{T_{frame}}{N_x(T_{frame} + 2T_{prop})} = \frac{1}{N_x(1 + 2a)} \tag{9.3}$$

A simple expression for N_x can be derived by considering the probability P that a single frame is in error. If we assume that ACKs are never in error, the probability that it will take exactly k attempts to transmit a frame successfully is the probability of $(k - 1)$ unsuccessful attempts followed by one successful attempt. The probability of this occurring is just the product of the probability of the individual events occurring:

$$\Pr[\text{exactly } k \text{ attempts}] = \Pr[(k - 1) \text{ unsuccessful attempts}] \times \Pr[\text{successful attempt}]$$
$$= P^{k-1} \times (1 - P)$$

Therefore,[2]

$$N_x = \mathrm{E}[\text{transmissions}] = \sum_{i=1}^{\infty} (i \times \Pr[i \text{ transmissions}])$$

$$= \sum_{i=1}^{\infty} (i P^{i-1}(1-P)) = \frac{1}{1-P}$$

Substituting into Equation 9.3 yields the following formula for stop-and-wait throughput:

> **Stop and Wait:** $S = \dfrac{1-P}{1+2a}$

The Parameter *a*

In the preceding discussion, the parameter *a* was defined as follows:

$$a = \frac{\text{Propagation time}}{\text{Transmission time}} \qquad (9.4)$$

This parameter is very useful in assessing the performance of various link control schemes and provides an insight into the factors affecting performance. We can cast Equation 9.4 in a different form with the following variables:

d = Distance of the link between two stations.

V = Velocity of propagation of the signal along the link. For unguided transmission through air or space, V is the speed of light, 3×10^8 m/s. For guided transmission, V is approximately the speed of light for optical fiber and about 0.67 times the speed of light for copper media.

L = Length of a link control frame in bits; for now, we assume a constant length.

R = Data rate on the link, in bits per second.

The propagation time is equal to the distance d of the link divided by the velocity of propagation V. The transmission time is equal to the length of the frame in bits L divided by the data rate R. Therefore,

$$a = \frac{d/V}{L/R} = \frac{Rd}{VL}$$

Thus, for fixed-length frames and a fixed distance between stations, a is proportional to the data rate times the length of the medium. A useful way of looking at a is that it represents the length of the medium in bits $(R \times d/V)$ compared to the frame length (L).

With this interpretation in mind, Figure 9.8 illustrates Equation 9.2. In this figure, transmission time is normalized to 1 and hence the propagation time, by Equation 9.4, is a. For the case of $a > 1$, the link's bit length is greater than that of the

---

[2] This derivation uses the equality

$$\sum_{i=1}^{\infty} (i X^{i-1}) = \frac{1}{(1-X)^2} \qquad \text{for } (-1 < X < 1).$$

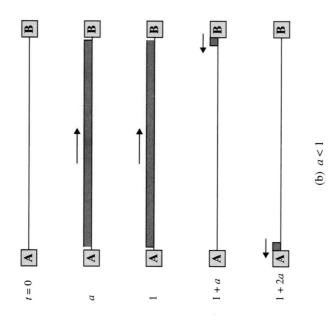

(a) $a > 1$

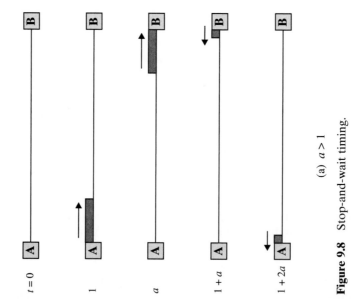

(b) $a < 1$

Figure 9.8   Stop-and-wait timing.

frame; this is shown in Figure 9.8a, which essentially reproduces Figure 9.4 but ignores ACK transmission time. Station A begins transmitting a frame at time 0. At $t = 1$, A completes transmission. At $t = a$, the leading edge of the frame reaches the receiving station B. At $t = 1 + a$, B has received the entire frame and immediately transmits a small acknowledgment frame. This acknowledgment arrives back at A at $t = 1 + 2a$. Total elapsed time is $1 + 2a$. Hence, the rate at which frames can be transmitted is $1/(1 + 2a)$. The same result is achieved with $a < 1$, as illustrated in Figure 9.8b.

Let us consider a few examples. First, consider a WAN using ATM, with the two stations a thousand kilometers apart. The standard ATM frame size (called a cell) is 424 bits, and one of the standardized data rates is 155.52 Mbps. Thus, transmission time equals $424/(155.52 \times 10^6) = 2.7 \times 10^{-6}$ s. If we assume an optical fiber link, then the propagation time is $(10^6 \text{ m})/(3 \times 10^8 \text{ m/s}) = 0.33 \times 10^{-2}$ s. Thus, $a = (0.33 \times 10^{-2})/(2.7 \times 10^{-6}) = 1222$, and normalized throughput is only $1/2445 = 0.0004$!

At the other extreme, in terms of distance, is the LAN. Distances range from 0.1 to 10 km, with data rates of 10 Mbps to 1 Gbps; higher data rates tend to be associated with shorter distances. Using a value of $V = 2 \times 10^8$ m/s, a frame size of 1000 bits, and a data rate of 10 Mbps, the value of a is in the range of 0.005 to 0.5. This yields a normalized throughput in the range of 0.5 to 0.99. For a 100-Mbps LAN, given the shorter distances, comparable utilizations are possible.

We can see that LANs are typically quite efficient, whereas high-speed WANs are not. As a final example, let us consider digital data transmission via modem over a voice-grade line. A typical data rate is 28.8 kbps. Again, let us consider a 1000-bit frame. The link distance can be anywhere from a few tens of meters to thousands of kilometers. If we pick, say, as a short distance $d = 1000$ m, then $a = (28,800 \text{ bps} \times 1000 \text{ m})/(2 \times 10^8 \text{ m/s} \times 1000 \text{ bits}) = 1.44 \times 10^{-4}$, and normalized throughput is effectively 1.0. Even in a long-distance case, such as $d = 5000$ km, we have $a = (28,800 \times 5 \times 10^6)/(2 \times 10^8 \times 1000 \text{ bits}) = 0.72$ and normalized throughput equals 0.4.

Table 9.1 gives some values of a. The first (gray) band of rows might be found with an ISDN link of 64 kbps. The distance of 35,863 km corresponds to a satellite link. The second (white) band of rows are typical of frame relay network links, and the final (gray) band correspond to LAN links.

Stop-and-wait Revisited

Both parts of Figure 9.8 (a and b) consist of a sequence of snapshots of the transmission process over time. In both cases, the first three snapshots show the process of transmitting a frame containing data, and the last two snapshots shows the return of a small acknowledgment frame. Note that for $a > 1$, the line is always underutilized; and even for $a < 1$, the line is inefficiently utilized. In essence, for very high data rates, for very long distances between sender and receiver, stop-and-wait flow control provides inefficient line utilization.

To see the effect of a on normalized throughput, we can plot $S = (1 - P)/(1 + 2a)$. Although the value of S depends on P, fortunately P appears only in the expression $(1 - P)$, so that P will have no noticeable affect on the result over a wide range of values of P. We arbitrarily choose $P = 10^{-3}$.

Figure 9.9 shows the performance of stop-and-wait ARQ as a function of a. For values of $a > 1$, throughput is severely degraded. For values of $a > 10$, stop and

TABLE 9.1   SOME VALUES OF *a*

Data Rate (Mbps)	Frame Size (bits)	Distance (km)	*a*
0.064	1000	0.1	0.00003
0.064	1000	1	0.0003
0.064	1000	35,863	7.65
0.064	10,000	0.1	0.000003
0.064	10,000	1	0.00003
0.064	10,000	35,863	0.77
1	1000	1	0.005
1	1000	3000	15
1	1000	35,863	119.5
1	10,000	1	0.0005
1	10,000	3000	1.5
1	10,000	35,863	11.95
10	1000	0.05	0.0025
10	1000	0.5	0.025
10	10,000	0.05	0.00025
10	10,000	0.5	0.0025
100	1000	0.1	0.05
100	10,000	0.1	0.005
1000	1000	0.1	0.5
1000	10,000	0.1	0.05

wait is so inefficient that it is useless. Figure 9.9 also illustrates the dependence of *a* on data rate, distance, and frame length.

Sliding–window ARQ

As before, we begin by looking at error-free operation, which is the same for both go-back-N and selective-reject ARQ.

Error-free Sliding-window Flow Control

For sliding-window flow control, the throughput on the line depends on both the window size W and the value of a. For convenience, let us again normalize frame transmission time to a value of 1; thus, the propagation time is a. Figure 9.10 illustrates the efficiency of a full duplex point-to-point line. Station A begins to emit a sequence of frames at time $t = 0$. The leading edge of the first frame reaches station B at $t = a$. The first frame is entirely absorbed by $t = a + 1$. Assuming negligible processing time, B can immediately acknowledge the first frame (ACK1). Let us also assume that the acknowledgment frame is so small that transmission time is negligible. Then the ACK1 reaches A at $t = 2a + 1$. To evaluate performance, we need to consider two cases:

- Case 1: $W \geqslant 2a + 1$. The acknowledgment for frame 1 reaches A before A has exhausted its window. Thus, A can transmit continuously with no pause and normalized throughput is 1.0.
- Case 2: $W < 2a + 1$. A exhausts its window at $t = W$ and cannot send additional frames until $t = 2a + 1$. Thus, normalized throughput is W time units out of a period of $(2a + 1)$ time units.

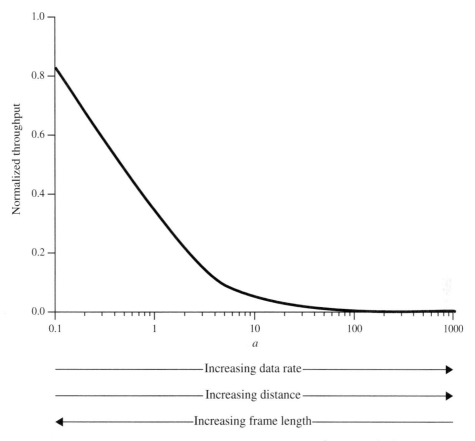

Figure 9.9 Performance of stop-and-wait protocol ($P = 10^{-3}$).

Therefore, we can state that

$$S = \begin{cases} 1 & W \geq 2a + 1 \\ \dfrac{W}{2a + 1} & W < 2a + 1 \end{cases} \tag{9.5}$$

Typically, the sequence number is provided for in an n-bit field and the maximum window size is $W = 2^n - 1$. Figure 9.11 shows the maximum throughput achievable for window sizes of 1, 7, and 127 as a function of a. A window size of 1 corresponds to stop and wait. A window size of 7 (3 bits) is adequate for many applications. A window size of 127 (7 bits) is adequate for larger values of a, such as may be found in high-speed WANs.

Selective-reject ARQ

For the sliding-window protocol, Equation 9.5 applies for error-free operation. For selective-reject ARQ, we can use the same reasoning as applied to stop-and-wait ARQ. That is, the error-free equations must be divided by N_x. Again, $N_x = 1/(1 - P)$. Therefore, we need to multiply the right-hand side of Equation 9.5 by $(1 - P)$. The result is

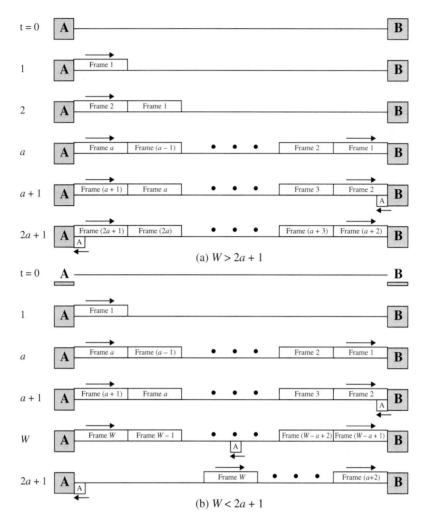

Figure 9.10 Timing of sliding-window protocol.

$$\textbf{Selective reject:}\quad S = \begin{cases} 1 - P & W \geqslant 2a + 1 \\ \dfrac{W(1 - P)}{2a + 1} & W < 2a + 1 \end{cases}$$

Go-back-N ARQ

The same reasoning applies for go-back-N ARQ, but we must be more careful in approximating N_x. Each error generates a requirement to retransmit K frames rather than just one frame. Thus,

$N_x = \mathrm{E}\,[\text{number of transmitted frames to transmit one frame successfully}]$

$$= \sum_{i=1}^{\infty} \mathrm{f}(i)\, P^{i-1}(1 - P)$$

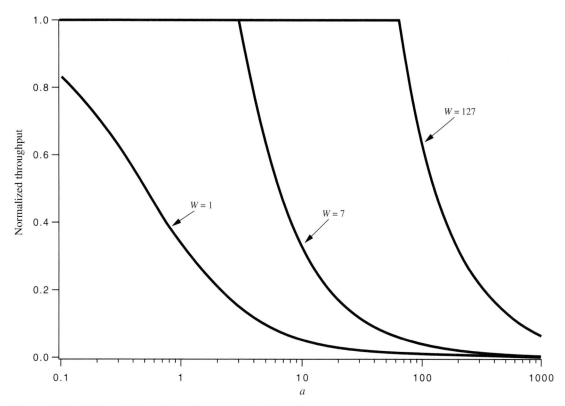

Figure 9.11   Sliding-window throughput as a function of a.

where $f(i)$ is the total number of frames transmitted if the original frame must be transmitted i times. This can be expressed as

$$f(i) = 1 + (i - 1)K$$

$$= (1 - K) + Ki$$

Substituting yields[3]

$$N_x = (1 - K) \sum_{i=1}^{\infty} P^{i-1}(1 - P) + K \sum_{i=1}^{\infty} i P^{i-1}(1 - P)$$

$$= 1 - K + \frac{K}{1 - P}$$

$$= \frac{1 - P + KP}{1 - P}$$

By studying Figure 9.10, the reader should conclude that K is approximately equal to $(2a + 1)$ for $W \geq (2a + 1)$, and $K = W$ for $W < (2a + 1)$. Thus

---

[3] This derivation uses the equality

$$\sum_{i=1}^{\infty} X^{i-1} = \frac{1}{1 - X} \quad \text{for } (-1 < X < 1).$$

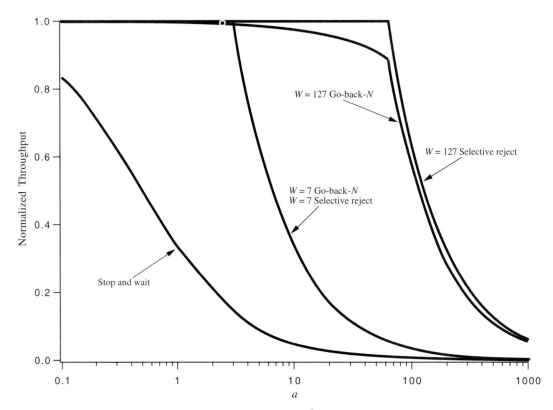

Figure 9.12   ARQ throughput as a function of a $(P = 10^{-3})$.

$$\textbf{Go back N:}\quad S = \begin{cases} \dfrac{1 - P}{1 + 2aP} & W \geqslant 2a + 1 \\[2mm] \dfrac{W(1 - P)}{(2a + 1)(1 - P + WP)} & W < 2a + 1 \end{cases}$$

Note that for $W = 1$, both selective-reject and go-back-N ARQ reduce to stop and wait. Figure 9.12[4] compares these three error control techniques as a function of a for a value of $P = 10^{-3}$. This figure and the equations are only approximations. For example, we have ignored errors in acknowledgment frames and, in the case of go-back-N, errors in retransmitted frames other than the frame initially in error. However, the results do give an indication of the relative performance of the three techniques.

Finally, Figure 9.13 shows the normalized throughput for the three ARQ techniques as a function of window size W for $a = 10$ and $a = 100$.

---

[4] For $N = 7$, the curves for go-back-N and selective reject are so close that they appear to be identical in the figure.

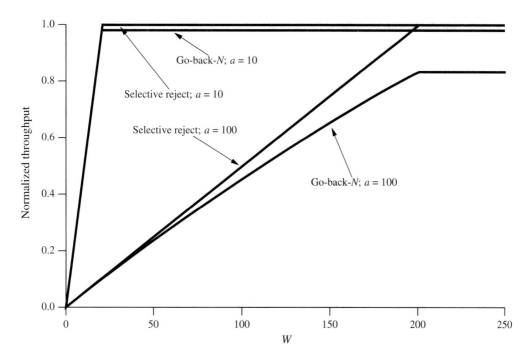

Figure 9.13 ARQ throughput as a function of W ($P = 10^{-3}$).

9.4 RECOMMENDED READING

There is a large body of literature on the performance of ARQ link control protocols. Three classic papers, well worth reading, are [BENE64], [KONH80], and [BUX80]. A readable survey with simplified performance results is [LIN84]. A more recent analysis is [ZORZ96]. Two books with good coverage of link-level performance are [SPRA91] and [WALR91].

BENE64 Benice, R. "An Analysis of Retransmission Systems." *IEEE Transactions on Communication Technology*, December 1964.

BUX80 Bux, W., Kummerle, K., and Truong, H. "Balanced HDLC Procedures: A Performance Analysis." *IEEE Transactions on Communications*, November 1980.

KONH80 Konheim, A. "A Queuing Analysis of Two ARQ Protocols." *IEEE Transactions on Communications*, July 1980.

LIN84 Lin, S., Costello, D., and Miller, M. "Automatic-Repeat-Request Error-Control Schemes." *IEEE Communications Magazine*, December 1984.

SPRA91 Spragins, J., Hammond, J., and Pawlikowski, K. *Telecommunications: Protocols and Design.* Reading, MA: Addison-Wesley, 1991.

WALR91 Walrand, J. *Communication Networks: A First Course.* Homewood, IL: Aksen Associates, 1991.

ZORZ96 Zorzi, M., and Rao, R. "On the Use of Renewal Theory in the Analysis of ARQ Protocols." *IEEE Transactions on Communications*, September 1996.

9.5 PROBLEMS

9.1 Consider a half-duplex point-to-point link using a stop-and-wait scheme.
  a. What is the effect on line utilization of increasing the message size so that fewer messages will be required? Other factors remain constant.
  b. What is the effect on line utilization of increasing the number of frames for a constant message size?
  c. What is the effect on line utilization of increasing frame size?

9.2 A channel has a data rate of 4 kbps and a propagation delay of 20 ms. For what range of frame sizes does stop and wait give an efficiency of at least 50%?

9.3 Consider the use of 1000-bit frames on a 1-Mbps satellite channel with a 270-ms delay. What is the maximum link utilization for
  a. Stop-and-wait flow control?
  b. Continuous flow control with a window size of 7?
  c. Continuous flow control with a window size of 127?
  d. Continuous flow control with a window size of 255?

9.4 In Figure 9.14 frames are generated at node A and sent to node C through node B. Determine the minimum transmission rate required between nodes B and C so that the buffers of node B are not flooded, based on the following:
  • The data rate between A and B is 100 kbps.
  • The propagation delay is 10 μs/mile for both lines.
  • There are full-duplex-lines between the nodes.
  • All data frames are 1000 bits long; ACK frames are separate frames of negligible length.
  • Between A and B, a sliding-window protocol with a window size of 3 is used.
  • Between B and C, stop and wait is used.
  • There are no errors.
  Hint: In order not to flood the buffers of B, the average number of frames entering and leaving B must be the same over a long interval.

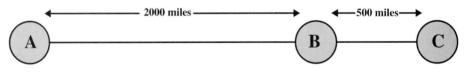

Figure 9.14   Configuration for problem 9.4.

9.5 A channel has a data rate of R bps and a propagation delay of t s/km. The distance between the sending and receiving nodes is L km. Nodes exchange fixed-size frames of B bits. Find a formula that gives the minimum sequence field size of the frame as a function of $R, t, B,$ and L (considering maximum utilization). Assume that ACK frames are negligible in size and that the processing at the nodes is instantaneous.

9.6 Why is it not necessary to have NAK0 and NAK1 for stop-and-wait ARQ?

9.7 Suppose that a selective-reject ARQ is used where $N = 4$. Show, by example, that a 3-bit sequence number is needed.

9.8 Using the same assumptions that are used for Figure 9.12, show line utilization as a function of P, the probability that a single frame is in error for the following error-control techniques:

a. Stop and wait
b. Go-back-N with $N = 7$
c. Go-back-N with $N = 127$
d. Selective reject with $N = 7$
e. Selective reject with $N = 127$

Do all of the preceding for the following values of a: 0.1, 1, 10, 100. Draw conclusions about which technique is appropriate for various ranges of a.

9.9 Out-of-sequence acknowledgment can not be used for selective-reject ARQ. That is, if frame i is rejected by station X, all subsequent I frames and RR frames sent by X must have receive sequence number $N(R) = i$ until frame i is successfully received, even if other frames with send sequence number $N(S) > i$ are successfully received in the meantime. One possible refinement is the following: $N(R) = j$ in a data frame or an RR frame is interpreted to mean that frame $j - 1$ and all preceding frames are accepted except those that have been explicitly rejected using a SREJ frame. Comment on any possible drawback to this scheme.

9.10 The ISO standard for HDLC procedures (ISO 4335) includes the following definitions: (1) an REJ condition is considered cleared upon the receipt of an incoming data frame with an $N(S)$ equal to the $N(R)$ of the outgoing REJ frame; and (2) a SREJ condition is considered cleared upon the receipt of a data frame with an $N(S)$ equal to the $N(R)$ of the SREJ frame. The standard includes rules concerning the relationship between REJ and SREJ frames. These rules indicate what is allowable (in terms of transmitting REJ and SREJ frames) if a REJ condition has not yet been cleared and what is allowable if a SREJ condition has not yet been cleared. Deduce the rules and justify your answer.

9.11 Two stations communicate via a 1-Mbps satellite link with a propagation delay of 270 ms. The satellite serves merely to retransmit data received from one station to another, with negligible switching delay. Using HDLC frames of 1024 bits with 3-bit sequence numbers, what is the maximum possible data throughput (not counting the 48 overhead bits per frame)?

9.12 A World Wide Web server is usually set up to receive relatively small messages from its clients but to transmit potentially very large messages to them. Explain, then, which type of ARQ protocol (selective reject, go-back-N) would provide less of a burden to a particularly popular WWW server.

CHAPTER 10

TRANSPORT PROTOCOLS

"I tell you," went on Syme with passion, "that every time a train comes in I feel that it has broken past batteries of besiegers, and that man has won a battle against chaos. You say contemptuously that when one has left Sloane Square one must come to Victoria. I say that one might do a thousand things instead, and that whenever I really come there I have the sense of hairbreadth escape. And when I hear the guard shout out the word 'Victoria,' it is not an unmeaning word. It is to me the cry of a herald announcing conquest. It is to me indeed 'Victoria'; it is the victory of Adam."

—The Man Who Was Thursday, G. K. Chesterton

To achieve good performance for end systems and for the connecting networks as a whole, the design and implementation of the transport protocol is a vital ingredient. The transport protocol provides an interface between applications and the networking facility that enables the applications to request a desired quality of service. Connection-oriented transport protocols, such as TCP, divide the total flow of application data into disjoint logical streams and may allocate resources differently among those streams. Finally, the transport protocol's policies for transmission and retransmission of data units have a profound impact on the level of congestion in the networking facility.

This chapter examines two important transport protocols and discusses the performance implications of each. TCP is the most widely used transport protocol, employed by the majority of applications that use the TCP/IP protocol suite. We begin with an overview of TCP, focusing on the flow and error control features of the protocol. Then we examine the complex issue of TCP congestion control. This is followed by a discussion of the performance implications of running TCP/IP over ATM. Finally, we look at RTP, which is designed with multimedia applications in mind.

10.1 TRANSMISSION CONTROL PROTOCOL

The current version of TCP is officially defined in RFC 793.[1] A number of enhancements and implementation specifications have been added subsequently. Those that are required for a conformant implementation of TCP as of 1989 are documented in RFC 1122.[2] Since then, a number of additional changes have been documented; these will be referenced as needed.

The section begins with a look at the protocol operation TCP. Then we look at the key issue of TCP retransmission timing. Finally, we discuss certain common implementation options.

Protocol Operation

A good way to begin a description of TCP operation is to examine the TCP header format. Having done so, we provide an overview of TCP mechanisms with special attention to flow and error control.

TCP Header Format

TCP uses only a single type of protocol data unit, called a TCP segment. The header is shown in Figure 10.1. Because one header must serve to perform all protocol mechanisms, it is rather large, with a minimum length of 20 octets. The fields are as follows:

- **Source port (16 bits):** Source TCP user.
- **Destination port (16 bits):** Destination TCP user.

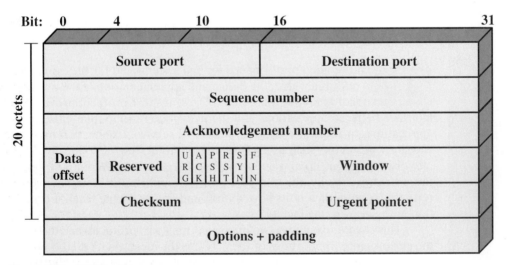

Figure 10.1 TCP header.

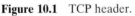

[1] RFC 793, *Transmission Control Protocol*, September 1981.

[2] RFC 1122, *Requirements of Internet Hosts—Communication Layers*, October 1989.

- **Sequence number (32 bits):** Sequence number of the first data octet in this segment except when SYN flag is set. If SYN is set, this field is the initial sequence number (ISN) and the first data octet is ISN + 1.
- **Acknowledgment number (32 bits):** A piggybacked acknowledgment. Contains the sequence number of the next data octet that the TCP entity expects to receive.
- **Data offset (4 bits):** Number of 32-bit words in the header.
- **Reserved (6 bits):** Reserved for future use.
- **Flags (6 bits):**
    URG: Urgent pointer field significant.
    ACK: Acknowledgment field significant.
    PSH: Push function.
    RST: Reset the connection.
    SYN: Synchronize the sequence numbers.
    FIN: No more data from sender.
- **Window (16 bits):** Flow control credit allocation, in octets. Contains the number of data octets beginning with the one indicated in the acknowledgment field that the sender is willing to accept.
- **Checksum (16 bits):** An error detection code.
- **Urgent Pointer (16 bits):** Points to the last octet in a sequence of urgent data. This allows the receiver to know how much urgent data is coming.
- **Options (variable):** Specifies optional features.

Several of the fields in the TCP header warrant further elaboration. The *sequence number* and *acknowledgment number* are bound to octets rather than to entire segments. For example, if a segment contains sequence number 1000 and includes 600 octets of data, the sequence number refers to the first octet in the data field; the next segment in logical order will have sequence number 1600. Thus, TCP is logically stream oriented: It accepts a stream of octets from the user, groups them into segments as it sees fit, and numbers each octet in the stream.

The PUSH and URGENT flags implement two TCP services:

- **Data stream push:** Ordinarily, TCP decides when sufficient data have accumulated to form a segment for transmission. The TCP user can require TCP to transmit all outstanding data up to and including that labeled with a PUSH flag. On the receiving end, TCP will deliver these data to the user in the same manner. A user might request this if it has come to a logical break in the data.
- **Urgent data signaling:** This provides a means of informing the destination TCP user that significant or "urgent" data are in the upcoming data stream. It is up to the destination user to determine appropriate action.

A TCP user (typically an application, such as FTP) issues a SEND command to pass a block of data to TCP, which places the data in a send buffer. If the PUSH flag is set, any outstanding data in the send buffer, including the data that have just been submitted, are immediately sent out in one or more segments, with the last segment marked with the PUSH flag. If the PUSH flag is not set, TCP may hold the data in the send buffer and send the data out in one or more segments as convenient. For example, TCP may wait until more data are submitted in order to send larger, more efficient segments. The user may associate an URGENT flag with the data in a SEND command. In this case, the resulting segment is marked with an URGENT flag.

The data in segments arriving across a connection to a TCP entity are similarly stored in a deliver buffer associated with that connection. If the incoming data are marked with a PUSH flag, that data, together with any data currently in the deliver buffer, are immediately submitted to the destination user in a RECEIVE command. If the incoming data are not marked with a PUSH flag, TCP delivers the data as convenient. For example, TCP may wait until more incoming data accumulate to minimize system interrupts. If the incoming data are marked with an URGENT flag, the user is signaled that urgent data are present.

The *checksum* field applies to the entire segment plus a pseudoheader prefixed to the header at the time of calculation (at both transmission and reception). The pseudoheader includes the following fields from the IP header: source and destination internet address and protocol, plus a segment length field. By including the pseudoheader, TCP protects itself from misdelivery by IP. That is, if IP delivers a segment to the wrong host, even if the segment contains no bit errors, the receiving TCP entity will detect the delivery error. The TCP checksum is calculated as the 16-bit one's complement addition of all 16-bit words in the pseudoheader, TCP header, and TCP segment body. For purposes of computation, the checksum field is itself initialized to a value of zero.

RFC 793 defines only one *option*, maximum segment size. This 16-bit option may only be used in the initial connection request segments; it specifies the maximum segment size, in octets, that will be accepted on this connection. Since the publication of RFC 793, two other options have gained widespread acceptance:

- **Window scale factor:** Ordinarily, the Window field in the TCP header gives a credit allocation in octets. When the window scale option is in use, the value in the Window field is multiplied by a 2^F, where F is the value of the window scale option. The maximum value of F that TCP accepts is 14. This option is only used in the initial connection request segments.

- **Timestamp:** This option actually can be used in any data segment and defines two optional fields. TCP may include a Timestamp Value field in any outgoing segment. When this segment is acknowledged from the other side, the responding TCP includes a Timestamp Echo Reply field with the same value as the Timestamp Value field in the segment being acknowledged. This option provides a way for TCP implementations to continuously monitor the round-trip time of a connection.

TCP Flow Control

As with most protocols that provide flow control, TCP uses a form of sliding-window mechanism. It differs from the mechanism used in many other protocols, such as LLC, HDLC, and X.25, in that it decouples acknowledgment of received data units from the granting of permission to send additional data units.

The flow control mechanism used by TCP[3] is known as a credit allocation scheme. For this scheme, each individual octet of data that is transmitted is considered to have a sequence number. When a TCP entity sends a segment, it includes the sequence number of the first octet in the segment data field. A TCP entity acknowledges an incoming segment with a message of the form (A = i, W = j), with the following interpretation:

- All octets through sequence number $i - 1$ are acknowledged; the next expected octet has sequence number i.
- Permission is granted to send an additional window (W) of j octets of data; that is, the j octets corresponding to sequence numbers i through $i + j - 1$.

Figure 10.2 illustrates the mechanism (compare Figure 9.6). For simplicity, we show data flow in one direction only and assume that 200 octets of data are sent in each segment. Initially, through the connection establishment process, the sending and receiving sequence numbers are synchronized and A is granted an initial credit allocation of 1400 octets, beginning with octet number 1001. After sending 600 octets in three segments, A has shrunk its window to a size of 800 octets (numbers 1601 through 2400). Following receipt of these segments, B acknowledges receipt of all octets through 1601 and issues a credit of 1000 octets. This means that A can send octets 1601 through 2600 (five segments). However, by the time that B's message has arrived at A, A has already sent two segments, containing octets 1601 through 2000 (which was permissible under the initial allocation). Thus, A's remaining credit at this point is only 400 octets (two segments). As the exchange proceeds, A advances the trailing edge of its window each time that it transmits and advances the leading edge only when it is granted credit.

Figure 10.3 shows the view of this mechanism from both the sending and receiving sides (compare Figure 9.5). Typically, both sides take both views because data may be exchanged in both directions (full duplex).

The credit allocation mechanism is quite flexible. For example, consider that the last message issued by B was (A = i, W = j) and that the last octet of data received by B was octet number $i - 1$. Then

- To increase credit to an amount k ($k > j$) when no additional data have arrived, B issues (A = i, W = k).
- To acknowledge an incoming segment containing m octets of data ($m < j$) without granting additional credit, B issues (A = $i + m$, W = $j - m$).

Note that the receiver is not required to immediately acknowledge incoming segments, but may wait and issue a cumulative acknowledgment for a number of segments.

The receiver needs to adopt some policy concerning the amount of data it permits the sender to transmit. The conservative approach is to only allow new segments up to the limit of available buffer space. If this policy were in effect in Figure

---

[3] This same mechanism is used in the ISO standard reliable transport protocol, known as TP4.

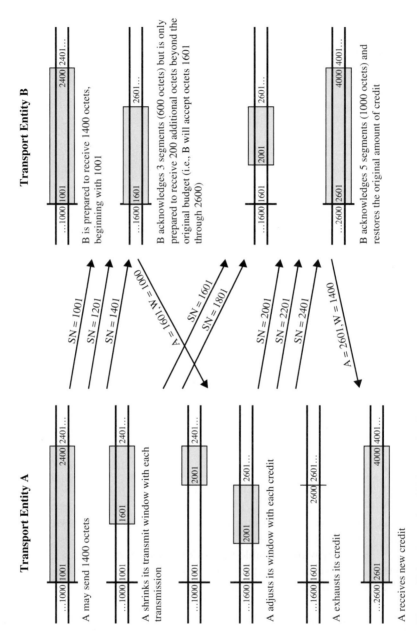

Figure 10.2 Example of TCP credit allocation mechanism.

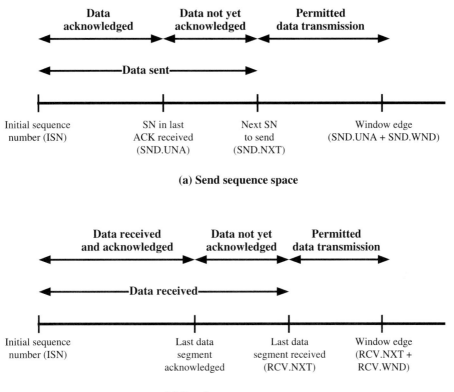

(a) Send sequence space

(b) Receive sequence space

Figure 10.3   Sending and receiving flow control perspectives.

10.2, the first credit message implies that B has 1000 available octets in its buffer, and the second message that B has 1400 available octets.

A conservative flow control scheme may limit the throughput of the transport connection in long-delay situations. The receiver could potentially increase throughput by optimistically granting credit for space it does not have. For example, if a receiver's buffer is full but it anticipates that it can release space for 1000 octets within a round-trip propagation time, it could immediately send a credit of 1000. If the receiver can keep up with the sender, this scheme may increase throughput and can do no harm. If the sender is faster than the receiver, however, some segments may be discarded, necessitating a retransmission. Because retransmissions are not otherwise necessary with a reliable network service (in the absence of internet congestion), an optimistic flow control scheme will complicate the protocol.

Effect of Window Size on Performance

As in the case of sliding-window link control, examined in Chapter 9, we can determine the maximum possible throughput on a TCP connection. As before, throughput depends on the window size, propagation delay, and data rate. In the case of link control protocols, both window size and sequence numbers refer to frames, and the normalized throughput depends on frame size as well as the other factors just mentioned. In the case of TCP, window size and sequence numbers refer to individual octets; accordingly, we need to recast our derivation in a way that does not include segment size.

We use the following notation:

W = TCP window size (octets)

R = Data rate (bps) at TCP source available to a given TCP connection

D = Propagation delay (seconds) between TCP source and destination over a given TCP connection

For simplicity, let us ignore the overhead bits in a TCP segment. Suppose that a source TCP entity begins to transmit a sequence of octets over a connection to a destination. It will take D seconds for the first octet to arrive at the destination and an additional time D for an acknowledgment to return. During that time, the source, if not limited, could transmit a total of $2RD$ bits, or $RD/4$ octets. In fact, the source is limited to window size of W octets until an acknowledgment is received. Accordingly, if $W > RD/4$, the maximum possible throughput can be achieved over this connection. If $W < RD/4$, then the maximum achievable normalized throughput is just the ratio of W to $RD/4$. Thus, the normalized throughput S can be expressed as

$$S = \begin{cases} 1 & W > RD/4 \\ \dfrac{4W}{RD} & W < RD/4 \end{cases} \tag{10.1}$$

Figure 10.4 shows the maximum throughput achievable as a function of the RD product (compare Figure 9.11). The maximum window size is $2^{16} - 1 = 65{,}535$ octets. This should suffice for most applications. For example, the figure shows that the RD product for a 1-Gbps Ethernet with an extent of 100 m is less than 10^3 bits. Even in the case of a T-1 (1.544 Mbps) satellite link, the maximum window size provides good performance. However, one can imagine network connections for which the default window size is inadequate. One example, shown in the figure, is an optical SDH (synchronous digital hierarchy) link operating at 155 Mbps between two distant points. For such cases, the window scale factor can be used to improve potential throughput. The figure shows the use of a window scale factor of 4, which increases the window size to $2^{20} - 1 \approx 10^6$ octets.

Figure 10.4 gives some feel for the performance potential of a TCP connection. However, there are many complicating factors to take into account, including the following:

1. In most cases, a number of TCP connections are multiplexed over the same network interface, so each connection is only allocated a fraction of the available capacity. This reduces R and therefore reduces inefficiency.

2. On the other hand, many TCP connections will involve a hop across multiple networks. In that case, D is the sum of the delays across each network plus the delays at each router along the path. The router delays will often be the biggest contributor to D, especially in times of congestion.

3. The value of R referred to in Equation 10.1 refers to the data rate available to the connection at the source TCP entity. If this data rate is greater than the

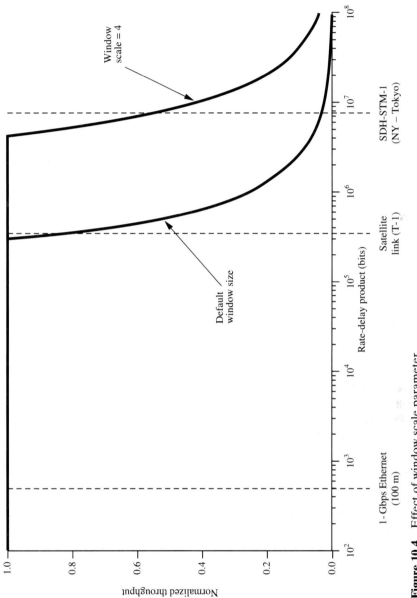

Figure 10.4 Effect of window scale parameter.

data rate encountered on one of the hops from source to destination, then an attempt to transmit at the higher data rate will create a bottleneck en route, increasing D.

4. If any segments are lost and must be retransmitted, throughput is reduced. The magnitude of the impact of lost segments on will depend on the retransmission policy, discussed in the next subsection.

In modern internets, few segments will be lost due to transmission line errors. Rather most segment losses are due to the dropping of packets by congested routers or by congested network switches (e.g., packet switches, frame relay switches). Congestion control is an issue that involves the network or internet as a whole. However, there are measures that can be taken by individual TCP entities to avoid or relieve congestion, and these are discussed in Section 10.2.

Retransmission Strategy

As with link control protocols, TCP must include an error control as well as a flow control scheme. In the case of TCP, there is no explicit negative acknowledgment, such as the REJ or SREJ found in link control protocols. Rather, TCP relies exclusively on positive acknowledgment and retransmission when an acknowledgment does not arrive within a given timeout period.

Two events necessitate the retransmission of a segment. First, the segment may be damaged in transit but nevertheless arrive at its destination. The checksum included with the segment enables the receiving transport entity to detect the error and discard the segment. The more common contingency is that a segment fails to arrive. In either case, the sending transport entity does not know that the segment transmission was unsuccessful.

If a segment does not arrive successfully, no ACK will be issued and a retransmission is in order. To cope with this situation, there must be a timer associated with each segment as it is sent. If the timer expires before the segment is acknowledged, the sender must retransmit.

A key design issue in TCP is the value of the retransmission timer. If the value is too small, there will be many unnecessary retransmissions, wasting network capacity. If the value is too large, the protocol will be sluggish in responding to a lost segment. The timer should be set at a value somewhat longer than the round-trip delay (send segment, receive ACK). Of course, this delay is variable even under constant network load. Worse, the statistics of the delay will vary with changing internet conditions.

Two strategies suggest themselves. A fixed timer value could be used, based on an understanding of the internet's typical behavior. This strategy suffers from an inability to respond to changing network conditions. If the value is set too high, the service will always be sluggish. If it is set too low, a positive feedback condition can develop, in which internet congestion leads to more retransmissions, which increases congestion.

An adaptive scheme has its own problems. Suppose that the TCP entity keeps track of the time taken to acknowledge data segments and sets its retransmission timer based on the average of the observed delays. This value cannot be trusted for three reasons:

- The peer TCP entity may not acknowledge a segment immediately. Recall that we gave it the privilege of cumulative acknowledgments.
- If a segment has been retransmitted, the sender cannot know whether the received ACK is a response to the initial transmission or the retransmission.
- Internet conditions may change suddenly.

The problem admits of no complete solution. There will always be some uncertainty concerning the best value for the retransmission timer. In the next subsection, we look at the time calculation specified in RFC 793. Section 10.2 examines more elaborate strategies for timeout selection.

Adaptive Retransmission Timer

As network or internet conditions change, a static retransmission timer is likely to be either too long or too short. Accordingly, virtually all TCP implementations attempt to estimate the current round-trip delay by observing the pattern of delay for recent segments, and then set the timer to a value somewhat greater than the estimated round-trip delay.

One approach would be simply to take the average of observed round-trip times over a number of segments. If the average accurately predicts future round-trip delays, then the resulting retransmission timer will yield good performance. The simple averaging method can be expressed as follows:

$$\text{ARTT}(K + 1) = \frac{1}{K + 1} \sum_{i=1}^{K+1} \text{RTT}(i) \tag{10.2}$$

where $\text{RTT}(i)$ is the round-trip time observed for the ith transmitted segment, and $\text{ARTT}(K)$ is the average round-trip time for the first K segments.

This expression can be rewritten as follows:

$$\text{ARTT}(K + 1) = \frac{K}{K + 1} \text{ARTT}(K) + \frac{1}{K + 1} \text{RTT}(K + 1) \tag{10.3}$$

With this formulation, it is not necessary to recalculate the entire summation each time.

Note that each term in the summation is given equal weight; that is, each term is multiplied by the same constant $1/(K + 1)$. Typically, we would like to give greater weight to more recent instances because they are more likely to reflect future behavior. A common technique for predicting the next value on the basis of a time series of past values, and the one specified in RFC 793, is exponential averaging.

$$\text{SRTT}(K + 1) = \alpha \times \text{SRTT}(K) + (1 - \alpha) \times \text{RTT}(K + 1) \tag{10.4}$$

where $\text{SRTT}(K)$ is called the smoothed round-trip time estimate. Compare this with Equation 10.3. By using a constant value of α ($0 < \alpha < 1$), independent of the number of past observations, we have a circumstance in which all past values are considered, but the more distant ones have less weight. To see this more clearly, consider the following expansion of Equation 10.4:

$$\text{SRTT}(K + 1) = (1 - \alpha)\text{RTT}(K + 1) + \alpha(1 - \alpha)\text{RTT}(K) + \alpha^2(1 - \alpha)\text{RTT}(K - 1) + \ldots + \\ \alpha^K(1 - \alpha)\text{RTT}(1) + \alpha^{K+1}\text{RTT}(0)$$

Since both α and $(1 - \alpha)$ are less than one, each successive term in the preceding equation is smaller. For example, for $\alpha = 0.8$ the expansion is

$$\mathrm{SRTT}(K + 1) = 0.2\,\mathrm{RTT}(K + 1) + 0.16\,\mathrm{RTT}(K) + 0.128\,\mathrm{RTT}(K - 1) + \ldots$$

The older the observation, the less it is counted in the average.

The size of the coefficient as a function of its position in the expansion is shown in Figure 10.5. The smaller the value of α, the greater the weight given to the more recent observations. For $\alpha = 0.5$, virtually all of the weight is given to the four or five most recent observations, whereas for $\alpha = 0.875$, the averaging is effectively spread out over the ten or so most recent observations. The advantage of using a small value of α is that the average will quickly reflect a rapid change in the observed quantity. The disadvantage is that if there is a brief surge in the value of the observed quantity and it then settles back to some average value, the use of a small value of α will result in jerky changes in the average.

Figure 10.6 compares simple averaging with exponential averaging (for two different values of α). In Figure 10.6a, the observed value begins at 1, grows gradually to a value of 10, and then stays there. In Figure 10.6b, the observed value begins at 20, declines gradually to 10, and then stays there. In both cases, we start out with an estimate of $\mathrm{SRTT}(0) = 0$. Note that exponential averaging tracks changes in process behavior faster than does simple averaging and that the smaller value of α results in a more rapid reaction to the change in the observed value.

Equation 10.4 is used in RFC 793 to estimate the current round-trip time. As was mentioned, the retransmission timer should be set at a value somewhat greater than the estimated round-trip time. One possibility is to use a constant value:

$$\mathrm{RTO}(K + 1) = \mathrm{SRTT}(K + 1) + \Delta$$

where RTO is the retransmission timer (also called the retransmission timeout) and Δ is a constant. The disadvantage of this is that Δ is not proportional to SRTT. For large values of SRTT, Δ is relatively small and fluctuations in the actual RTT will result in unnecessary retransmissions. For small values of SRTT, Δ is relatively large and causes unnecessary delays in retransmitting lost segments. Accordingly, RFC 793 specifies the use of a timer whose value is proportional to SRTT, within limits:

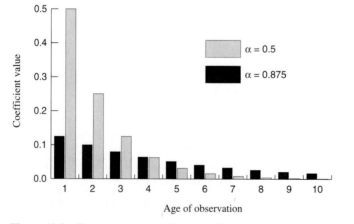

Figure 10.5 Exponential smoothing coefficients.

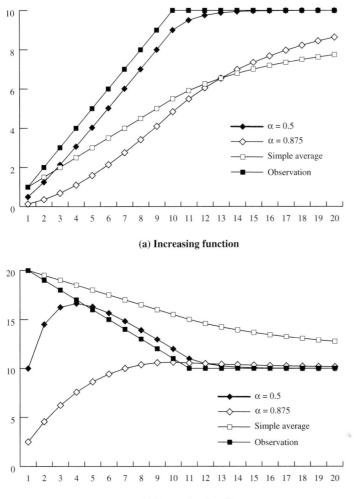

(a) Increasing function

(b) Decreasing function

Figure 10.6   Use of exponential averaging.

$$RTO(K + 1) = \text{MIN}(\text{UBOUND}, \text{MAX}(\text{LBOUND}, \beta \times \text{SRTT}(K + 1)))   \quad (10.5)$$

where UBOUND and LBOUND are prechosen fixed upper and lower bounds on the timer value and β is a constant. RFC 793 does not recommend specific values but does list as "example values" the following: α between 0.8 and 0.9 and β between 1.3 and 2.0.

TCP Implementation Policy Options

The TCP standard provides a precise specification of the protocol to be used between TCP entities. However, certain aspects of the protocol admit several possible implementation options. Although two implementations that choose alternative options will be interoperable, there may be performance implications. The design areas for which options are specified are the following:

- Send policy
- Deliver policy
- Accept policy
- Retransmit policy
- Acknowledge policy.

Send Policy

In the absence of PUSHed data and a closed transmission window, a sending TCP entity is free to transmit data at its own convenience. As data are issued by the user, they are buffered in the transmit buffer. TCP may construct a segment for each batch of data provided by its user or it may wait until a certain amount of data accumulates before constructing and sending a segment. The actual policy will depend on performance considerations. If transmissions are infrequent and large, there is low overhead in terms of segment generation and processing. On the other hand, if transmissions are frequent and small, then the system is providing quick response.

One danger of frequent, small transmission is known as the silly window syndrome, which is discussed in Problems 10.6 and 10.7.

Deliver Policy

In the absence of a PUSH, a receiving TCP entity is free to deliver data to the user at its own convenience. It may deliver data as each in-order segment is received, or it may buffer data from a number of segments in the receive buffer before delivery. The actual policy will depend on performance considerations. If deliveries are infrequent and large, the user is not receiving data as promptly as may be desirable. On the other hand, if deliveries are frequent and small, there may be unnecessary processing both in TCP and in the user software, as well as an unnecessary number of operating-system interrupts.

Accept Policy

When all data segments arrive in order over a TCP connection, TCP places the data in a receive buffer for delivery to the user. It is possible, however, for segments to arrive out of order. In this case, the receiving TCP entity has two options:

- **In order:** Accept only segments that arrive in order; any segment that arrives out of order is discarded.
- **In window:** Accept all segments that are within the receive window.

The in-order policy makes for a simple implementation but places a burden on the networking facility, as the sending TCP must time out and retransmit segments that were successfully received but discarded because of misordering. Furthermore, if a single segment is lost in transit, then all subsequent segments must be retransmitted once the sending TCP times out on the lost segment.

The in-window policy may reduce transmissions but requires a more complex acceptance test and a more sophisticated data storage scheme to buffer and keep track of data accepted out of order.

Retransmit Policy

TCP maintains a queue of segments that have been sent but not yet acknowledged. The TCP specification states that TCP will retransmit a segment if it fails to receive an acknowledgment within a given time. A TCP implementation may employ one of three retransmission strategies:

- **First only:** Maintain one retransmission timer for the entire queue. If an acknowledgment is received, remove the appropriate segment or segments from the queue and reset the timer. If the timer expires, retransmit the segment at the front of the queue and reset the timer.
- **Batch:** Maintain one retransmission timer for the entire queue. If an acknowledgment is received, remove the appropriate segment or segments from the queue and reset the timer. If the timer expires, retransmit all segments in the queue and reset the timer.
- **Individual:** Maintain one timer for each segment in the queue. If an acknowledgment is received, remove the appropriate segment or segments from the queue and destroy the corresponding timer or timers. If any timer expires, retransmit the corresponding segment individually and reset its timer.

The first-only policy is efficient in terms of traffic generated, because only lost segments (or segments whose ACK was lost) are retransmitted. Because the timer for the second segment in the queue is not set until the first segment is acknowledged, however, there can be considerable delays. The individual policy solves this problem at the expense of a more complex implementation. The batch policy also reduces the likelihood of long delays but may result in unnecessary retransmissions.

The actual effectiveness of the retransmit policy depends in part on the accept policy of the receiver. If the receiver is using an in-order accept policy, then it will discard segments received after a lost segment. This fits best with batch retransmission. If the receiver is using an in-window accept policy, then a first-only or individual retransmission policy is best. Of course, in a mixed network of computers, both accept policies may be in use.

Acknowledge Policy

When a data segment arrives that is in sequence, the receiving TCP entity has two options concerning the timing of acknowledgment:

- **Immediate**: When data are accepted, immediately transmit an empty (no data) segment containing the appropriate acknowledgment number.
- **Cumulative**: When data are accepted, record the need for acknowledgment, but wait for an outbound segment with data on which to piggyback the acknowledgment. To avoid long delay, set a window timer; if the timer expires before an acknowledgment is sent, transmit an empty segment containing the appropriate acknowledgment number.

The immediate policy is simple and keeps the sending TCP entity fully informed, which limits unnecessary retransmissions. However, this policy results in extra segment transmissions (namely, empty segments used only to ACK). Furthermore, the policy can increase the load on the network. Consider that a TCP entity receives a segment and immediately sends an ACK. Then the data in the segment are released to the application, which expands the receive window, triggering another empty TCP segment to provide additional credit to the sending TCP entity.

Because of the potential overhead of the immediate policy, the cumulative policy is typically used. Recognize, however, that the use of this policy requires more processing at the receiving end and complicates the task of estimating round-trip delay by the sending TCP entity.

10.2 TCP CONGESTION CONTROL

Congestion in a network or internet creates obvious problems for the end systems: reduced availability and throughput and lengthened response times. Within a switched network, such as a packet-switching or frame relay network, dynamic routing can be used to help alleviate congestion by spreading the load more evenly among the switches and links. Similarly, internet routing algorithms can spread the load among the routers and networks to relieve congestion. However, these measures are only effective for dealing with unbalanced loads and brief surges in traffic. Ultimately, congestion can only be controlled by limiting the total amount of data entering the internet to the amount that the internet can carry. This is the underlying objective of all congestion control mechanisms.

Congestion control in a TCP/IP-based internet is a complex and difficult undertaking whose study has generated numerous research efforts, implementation experiments, and papers over a period of decades. The task is a difficult one because of the following factors:

1. IP is a connectionless, stateless protocol that includes no provision for detecting, much less for controlling congestion.
2. TCP provides only end-to-end flow control and can only deduce the presence of congestion within the intervening internet by indirect means. Further, because delays in a network or internet are variable and may be long (relative to segment size), a TCP entity's knowledge of conditions is unreliable.
3. There is no cooperative, distributed algorithm to bind together the various TCP entities. Therefore, the TCP entities cannot cooperate to maintain a certain total level of flow and, indeed, are more likely to compete selfishly for available resources.

With regard to the connectionless IP environment, the ICMP Source Quench message provides a blunt and crude instrument for restraining source flow but is not an effective means, by itself, for congestion control. RSVP (Resource Reservation Protocol), described in Chapter 15, may in future help to control congestion, but its widespread implementation is a long way off.

The only tool in TCP that relates to network congestion is the sliding-window flow and error control mechanism. This mechanism is designed for the management of end-to-end traffic. However, a number of clever techniques have been developed that enable the use of this mechanism for congestion detection, avoidance, and recovery. This section surveys some of the most important and widely implemented mechanisms. We begin first with a discussion of the relationship between TCP flow and congestion control.

TCP Flow and Congestion Control

In a data link control protocol, the sliding-window flow control technique provides a way for the receiver to pace the sender. The receiver will only acknowledge frames and expand the window to the extent that it has buffer space available. The same pacing effect takes place in TCP: The rate at which a TCP entity can send data is determined by the rate of incoming ACKs to previous segments. However, in the case of TCP, the rate of ACK arrival is determined by the bottleneck in the round-trip path between source and destination, and that bottleneck may be either the destination or the internet.

Figure 10.7a, based on a figure in [JACO88], illustrates a case in which the bottleneck is somewhere in the internet. The configuration is abstracted as a pipe connecting source and destination. The thickness (height) of the pipe is proportional to

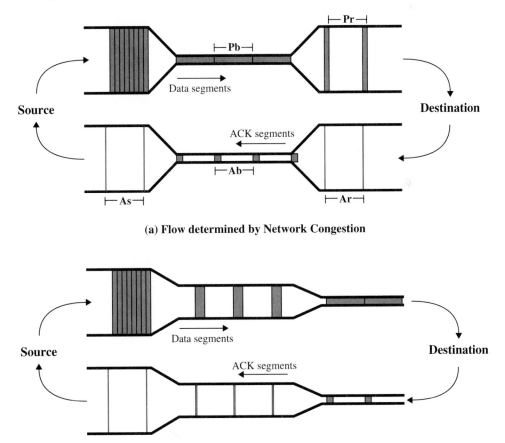

(a) Flow determined by Network Congestion

(b) Flow determined by Destination System

Figure 10.7   TCP Segment Pacing.

the data rate. The source and destination are on high-capacity networks and each can operate at that high capacity. The thinner central portion of the pipe represents a lower-speed link that creates the bottleneck. Each segment is represented by a rectangle whose area is proportional to the number of bits. So when a segment is squeezed into a narrower pipe, it spreads out in time. The time Pb is the minimum segment spacing on the slowest link. As segments arrive at the destination, this spacing is preserved even though the data rate increases, because the interarrival time does not change. Accordingly, the segment spacing at the receiver, Pr, equals Pb. If the destination acknowledges segments as they come in, then the spacing of ACK segments as they leave the receiver is determined by the segment arrival spacing, so that Ar = Pr. Finally, since the time slot Pb is big enough for a data segment, it is big enough for an ACK segment, so Ab = Ar.

The returning ACKs function as pacing signals. In the steady state, after an initial burst, the sender's segment rate will match the arrival rate of the ACKs. Thus, the sender's segment rate is equal to that of the slowest link on the path. In this way, TCP automatically senses the network bottleneck and regulates its flow accordingly. This has been referred to as TCP's *self-clocking* behavior.

This self-clocking behavior works equally well if the bottleneck is at the receiver. Suppose that the receiver can only absorb segments on a given connection slowly, either because of its native processing load or because of the press of incoming segments on other connections. Figure 10.7b represents this case. Here, we assume that the slowest link in the network is relatively wide, about half the data rate of the source, but that the pipe at the destination is narrow. In that case, ACKs will be emitted at a rate equal to the absorption capacity of the destination, and the resulting ACK stream paces the source so that segments arrive only as fast as can be handled.

Figure 10.7 illustrates an important point: The source has no way of knowing whether the pacing rate at which it receives ACKs reflects the status of the internet (congestion control) or the status of the destination (flow control). If ACKs arrive relatively slowly due to network congestion, it might be advisable for the source to transmit segments even more slowly than the ACK pace, to help relieve internet congestion. On the other hand, if the slow pace is due to flow control from the destination, then this pace should dictate the TCP send policy.

The bottleneck along a round-trip path between source and destination can occur in a variety of places and be either logical or physical. Figure 10.8 illustrates the possibilities. In this example, if the sender dedicates its entire LAN capacity to a single TCP connection, then it has a potential throughput of 10 Mbps. In that case the 1.5-Mbps links between each router and the intervening internet become bottlenecks. This is a physical bottleneck, and once a steady state is reached, TCP can efficiently use the available capacity. However, more often the bottleneck will be logical and due to queuing effects at a router, network switch, or the destination. Such queuing delays fluctuate with the overall load, making it difficult to achieve a steady-state flow.

The fluctuations in delays that are inherent in an IP-based internet present a challenge in designing flow policies for TCP sources. If TCP flows are too slow, then the internet is underutilized and throughputs are unnecessarily low. If one or a few TCP sources use excessive capacity, then other TCP flows will be crowded out. If

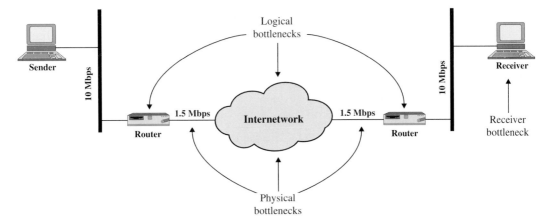

Figure 10.8   Context for TCP flow and congestion control.

many TCP sources use excessive capacity, then segments will be lost in transit, forc-ing retransmission, or ACKs will be excessively delayed, triggering unnecessary retransmissions as sources time out. Furthermore, such retransmission can have a positive feedback effect: As more segments are retransmitted, congestion grows, which increases delays and the number of dropped segments. These effects result in even more retransmissions, which make the problem even worse.

It can be seen, then, that although the TCP sliding-window mechanism is designed for end-to-end flow control, it must be used in a way that takes into account the need for congestion control. Since the publication of RFC 793, a num-ber of techniques have been implemented that are intended to improve TCP con-gestion control characteristics. Table 10.1 lists some of the most popular of these techniques. None of these techniques extend or violate the original TCP standard; rather they represent implementation policies that are within the scope of the TCP specification. The table indicates which of these techniques are mandated in RFC 1122 and also shows which have been implemented in the popular Berkeley version of UNIX. Two successive releases of the Berkeley TCP code, referred to as Tahoe and Reno, are often referenced in the literature on the effects of various TCP con-gestion control techniques.

TABLE 10.1   IMPLEMENTATION OF TCP CONGESTION CONTROL MEASURES

Measure	RFC 1122	TCP Tahoe	TCP Reno
RTT Variance Estimation	✓	✓	✓
Exponential RTO Backoff	✓	✓	✓
Karn's Algorithm	✓	✓	✓
Slow Start	✓	✓	✓
Dynamic Window Sizing on Congestion	✓	✓	✓
Fast Retransmit		✓	✓
Fast Recovery			✓

Retransmission Timer Management

The first three techniques that we examine deal with the calculation of the retransmission timer (RTO). The value of this timer can have a critical effect on TCP's reaction to congestion. The techniques are

- RTT variance estimation
- Exponential RTO backoff
- Karn's algorithm.

RTT Variance Estimation (Jacobson's Algorithm)

The technique specified in the TCP standard, and described in Equations 10.4 and 10.5, enables a TCP entity to adapt to changes in round-trip time. However, it does not cope well with a situation in which the round-trip time exhibits a relatively high variance. [ZHAN86] points out three sources of high variance:

1. If the data rate on the TCP connection is relatively low, then the transmission delay will be relatively large compared to propagation time and the variance in delay due to variance in IP datagram size will be significant. Thus, the SRTT estimator is heavily influenced by characteristics that are a property of the data and not of the network.
2. Internet traffic load and conditions may change abruptly due to traffic from other sources, causing abrupt changes in RTT.
3. The peer TCP entity may not acknowledge each segment immediately because of its own processing delays and because it exercises its privilege to use cumulative acknowledgments.

The original TCP specification tries to account for this variability by multiplying the RTT estimator by a constant factor:

$$\text{RTO}(K + 1) = \beta \times \text{SRTT}(K + 1)$$

where typically a value of $\beta = 2$ is used. In a stable environment, with low variance of RTT, this formulation results in an unnecessarily high value of RTO, and in an unstable environment a value of 2 may be inadequate to protect against unnecessary retransmissions.

A more effective approach is to estimate the variability in RTT values and to use that as input into the calculation of an RTO. One possibility would be to calculate the sample standard deviation (see Chapter 7). However, this involves a square and a square root calculation. A variation measure that is easier to estimate is the mean deviation, defined as:[4]

$$\text{MDEV}(X) = E[|X - E[X]|]$$

As with the estimate of RTT, a simple average could be used to estimate MDEV:

$$\text{AERR}(K + 1) = \text{RTT}(K + 1) - \text{ARTT}(K)$$

---

[4] In [JACO88], Jacobson says that the mean deviation is a more conservative estimate because it is larger than the standard deviation. This is not true in general; however, the mean deviation is a perfectly respectable measure of dispersion.

$$\text{ADEV}(K + 1) = \frac{1}{K + 1} \sum_{i=1}^{K+1} |\text{AERR}(i)|$$

$$= \frac{K}{K + 1} \text{ADEV}(K) + \frac{1}{K + 1} |\text{AERR}(K + 1)|$$

where $\text{ARTT}(K)$ is the simple average defined in Equation 10.2 and $\text{AERR}(K)$ is the sample mean deviation measured at time K.

As with the definition of ARRT, each term in the summation of ADEV is given equal weight; that is, each term is multiplied by the same constant $1/(K + 1)$. Again, we would like to give greater weight to more recent instances because they are more likely to reflect future behavior. Jacobson, who proposed the use of a dynamic estimate of variability in estimating RTT [JACO88], suggests using the same exponential smoothing technique as is used for the calculation of SRTT. The complete algorithm proposed by Jacobson can be expressed as follows:

$$\text{SRTT}(K + 1) = (1 - g) \times \text{SRTT}(K) + g \times \text{RTT}(K + 1)$$

$$\text{SERR}(K + 1) = \text{RTT}(K + 1) - \text{SRTT}(K)$$

$$\text{SDEV}(K + 1) = (1 - h) \times \text{SDEV}(K) + h \times |\text{SERR}(K + 1)| \quad (10.6)$$

$$\text{RTO}(K + 1) = \text{SRTT}(K + 1) + f \times \text{SDEV}(K + 1)$$

As in the RFC 793 definition (Equation 10.4), SRTT is an exponentially smoothed estimate of RTT, with $(1 - g)$ equivalent to α. Now, however, instead of multiplying the estimate SRTT by a constant (Equation 10.5), a multiple of the estimated mean deviation is added to SRTT to form the retransmission timer. Based on his timing experiments, Jacobson proposed the following values for the constants in his original paper [JACO88]:

$$g = 1/8 = 0.125$$
$$h = 1/4 = 0.25$$
$$f = 2$$

After further research [JACO90a], he recommended changing the value of f to 4, and this is the standard value used in current implementations.

Figure 10.9 illustrates the use of Equation 10.6 on the same data set used in Figure 10.6. Once the arrival times stabilize, the variation estimate SDEV declines. The values of RTO for both $f = 2$ and $f = 4$ are quite conservative as long as RTT is changing, but then begin to converge to RTT when it stabilizes.

Experience has shown that Jacobson's algorithm can significantly improve TCP performance. However, it does not stand by itself. Two other factors must be considered:

1. What RTO value should be used on a retransmitted segment? The exponential RTO backoff algorithm is used for this purpose.
2. Which round-trip samples should be used as input to Jacobson's algorithm? Karn's algorithm determines which samples to use.

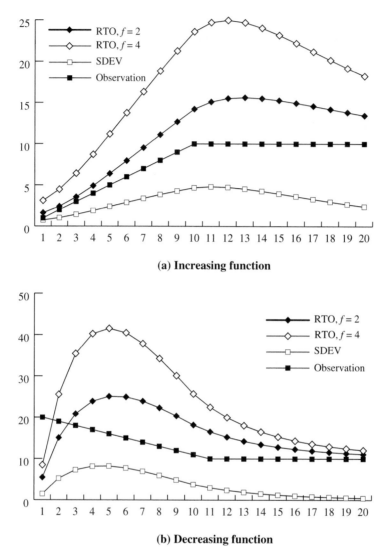

(a) Increasing function

(b) Decreasing function

Figure 10.9 Jacobson's RTO calculation.

Exponential RTO Backoff

When a TCP sender times out on a segment, it must retransmit that segment. RFC 793 assumes that the same RTO value will be used for this retransmitted segment. However, because the timeout is probably due to network congestion, manifested as a dropped packet or a long delay in round-trip time, maintaining the same RTO value is ill advised.

Consider the following scenario. There are a number of active TCP connections from various sources sending traffic into an internet. A region of congestion develops such that segments on many of these connections are lost or delayed past the RTO time of the connections. Therefore, at roughly the same time, many segments will be retransmitted into the internet, maintaining or even increasing the congestion. All of the sources then wait a local (to each connection) RTO time and retransmit yet again. This pattern of behavior could cause a sustained condition of congestion.

A more sensible policy dictates that a TCP source increase its RTO each time the same segment is retransmitted; this is referred to as a *backoff* process. In the scenario of the preceding paragraph, after the first retransmission of a segment on each affected connection, the TCP sources will all wait a longer time before performing a second retransmission. This may give the internet time to clear the current congestion. If a second retransmission is required, each TCP source will wait an even longer time before timing out for a third retransmission, giving the internet an even longer period to recover.

A simple technique for implementing RTO backoff is to multiply the RTO for a segment by a constant value for each retransmission:

$$RTO = q \times RTO \tag{10.7}$$

Equation 10.7 causes RTO to grow exponentially with each retransmission. The most commonly used value of q is 2. With this value, the technique is referred to as *binary exponential backoff*. This is the same technique used in the Ethernet CSMA/CD protocol.

Karn's Algorithm

If no segments are retransmitted, the sampling process for Jacobson's algorithm is straightforward. The RTT for each segment can be included in the calculation. Suppose, however, that a segment times out and must be retransmitted. If an acknowledgment is subsequently received, there are two possibilities:

1. This is the ACK to the first transmission of the segment. In this case, the RTT is simply longer than expected, but is an accurate reflection of network conditions.
2. This is the ACK to the second transmission.

The TCP source cannot distinguish between these two cases. If the second case is true and the TCP entity simply measures the RTT from the first transmission until receipt of the ACK, the measured time will be much too long. The measured RTT will be on the order of the actual RTT plus the RTO. Feeding this false RTT into Jacobson's algorithm will produce an unnecessarily high value of SRTT and therefore RTO. Furthermore, this effect propagates forward a number of iterations, since the SRTT value of one iteration is an input value in the next iteration.

An even worse approach would be to measure the RTT from the *second* transmission to the receipt of the ACK. If this is in fact the ACK to the first transmission, then the measured RTT will be much too small, producing a too low value of SRTT and RTO. This is likely to have a positive feedback effect, causing additional retransmissions and additional false measurements.

Karn's algorithm [KARN91] solves this problem with the following rules:

1. Do not use the measured RTT for a retransmitted segment to update SRTT and SDEV (Equation 10.6).

2. Calculate the backoff RTO using Equation 10.7 when a retransmission occurs.

3. Use the backoff RTO value for succeeding segments until an acknowledgment arrives for a segment that has not been retransmitted.

When an acknowledgment is received to an unretransmitted segment, Jacobson's algorithm is again activated to compute future RTO values.

Window Management

In addition to techniques for improving the effectiveness of the retransmission timer, a number of approaches to managing the send window have been examined. The size of TCP's send window can have a critical effect on whether TCP can be used efficiently without causing congestion. We discuss four techniques found in virtually all modern implementations of TCP[5]:

- Slow start
- Dynamic window sizing on congestion
- Fast retransmit
- Fast recovery.

Slow Start

The larger the send window used in TCP, the more segments that a TCP source can send before it must wait for an acknowledgment. In the ordinary course of events, the self-clocking nature of TCP (see Figure 10.7) paces TCP appropriately. However, when a connection is first initialized, it has no such pacing to guide it.

One strategy that could be followed is for the TCP sender to begin sending from some relatively large window, hoping to approximate the window size that would ultimately be provided by the connection. This is risky because the sender might flood the internet with many segments before it realized from timeouts that the flow was excessive. Instead, some means of gradually expanding the window until pacing takes over is needed.

Jacobson [JACO88] recommends a procedure known as slow start. TCP makes use of a congestion window, measured in segments rather than octets. At any time, TCP transmission is constrained by the following relationship:

$$awnd = \text{MIN}[credit, cwnd] \qquad (10.8)$$

where

$awnd$ = allowed window, in segments. This is the number of segments that TCP is currently allowed to send without receiving further acknowledgments.

$cwnd$ = congestion window, in segments. A window used by TCP during startup and to reduce flow during periods of congestion.

$credit$ = the amount of unused credit granted in the most recent acknowledgment, in segments. When an acknowledgment is received, this value is

---

[5] Documented in RFC 2001, *TCP Slow Start, Congestion Avoidance, Fast Retransmit, and Fast Recovery Algorithms*, January 1997.

calculated as *window/segment size*, where *window* is a field in the incoming TCP segment (the amount of data the peer TCP entity is willing to accept).

When a new connection is opened, the TCP entity initializes *cwnd* = 1. That is, TCP is only allowed to send 1 segment and then must wait for an acknowledgment before transmitting a second segment. Each time an acknowledgment is received, the value of *cwnd* is increased by 1, up to some maximum value.

In effect, the slow-start mechanism probes the internet to make sure that it is not sending too many segments into an already congested environment. As acknowledgments arrive, TCP is able to open up its window until the flow is controlled by the incoming ACKs rather than by *cwnd*.

The term *slow start* is a bit of a misnomer, because *cwnd* actually grows exponentially. When the first ACK arrives, TCP opens *cwnd* to 2 and can send two segments. When these two segments are ACKed, TCP can slide the window 1 segment for each incoming ACK and can increase *cwnd* by 1 for each incoming ACK. Therefore, at this point TCP can send four segments. When these four are ACKed, TCP will be able to send eight segments. Figure 10.10 illustrates this phenomenon. In this example, A is sending 100-octet segments, and after approximately four round-trip times, A is able to fill the pipe with a continuous flow of segments.

Dynamic Window Sizing on Congestion

The slow-start algorithm has been found to work effectively for initializing a connection. It enables the TCP sender to quickly determine a reasonable window size for the connection. Might not the same technique be useful when there is a surge in congestion? In particular, suppose a TCP entity initiates a connection and goes through the slow-start procedure. At some point, either before or after *cwnd* reaches the size of the credit allocated by the other side, a segment is lost (timeout). This is a signal that congestion is occurring. It is not clear how serious the congestion is. Therefore, a prudent procedure would be to reset *cwnd* = 1 and begin the slow-start process all over.

This seems like a reasonable, conservative procedure, but in fact it is not conservative enough. Jacobson [JACO88] points out that "it is easy to drive a network into saturation but hard for the net to recover." In other words, once congestion occurs, it may take a long time for the congestion to clear.[6] Thus, the exponential growth of *cwnd* under slow start may be too aggressive and may worsen the congestion. Instead, Jacobson proposed the use of slow start to begin with, followed by a linear growth in *cwnd*. The rules are as follows. When a timeout occurs

1. Set a slow-start threshold equal to half the current congestion window; that is, set *ssthresh* = *cwnd*/2.

2. Set *cwnd* = 1 and perform the slow-start process until *cwnd* = *ssthresh*. In this phase, *cwnd* is increased by 1 for every ACK received.

3. For *cwnd* ≥ *ssthresh*, increase *cwnd* by one for each round-trip time.

---

[6] Kleinrock refers to this phenomenon as the long-tail effect during a rush-hour period. See Sections 2.7 and 2.10 of [KLEI76] for a detailed discussion.

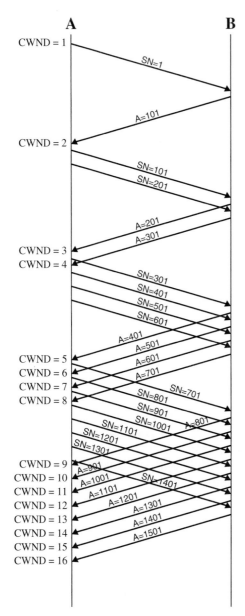

Figure 10.10   Effect of slow start.

Figure 10.11 illustrates the use of slow start. The left half of the figure shows a connection starting up and repeats Figure 10.10. Added to this figure is one final segment that will time out. The behavior after timeout is shown in Figure 10.11b. The value of *ssthresh* is set to 8. Until this threshold is reached, TCP uses the exponential slow-start procedure to expand the congestion window. Afterward, *cwnd* is increased linearly. This behavior is easily seen in Figure 10.12. Note that it takes 11 round-trip times to recover to the *cwnd* level that initially took 4 round-trip times to achieve.

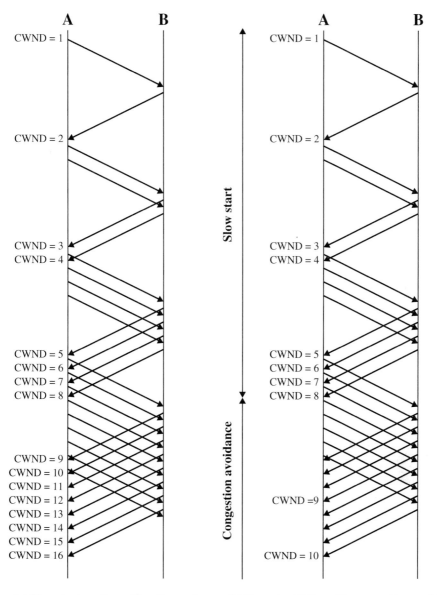

(a) Slow start, ending with a time out **(b) Slow start followed by congestion avoidance**

Figure 10.11 Slow start and congestion avoidance.

Fast Retransmit

The retransmission timer (RTO) that is used by a sending TCP entity to determine when to retransmit a segment will generally be noticeably longer than the actual round-trip time (RTT) that the ACK for that segment will take to reach the sender. Both the original RFC 793 algorithm and the Jacobson algorithm set the value of RTO at somewhat greater than the estimated round-trip time SRTT. Several factors make this margin desirable:

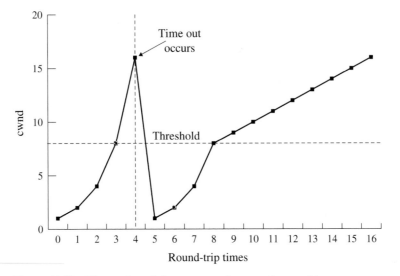

Figure 10.12 Illustration of slow start and congestion avoidance.

1. RTO is calculated on the basis of a prediction of the next RTT, estimated from past values of RTT. If delays in the network fluctuate, then the estimated RTT may be smaller than the actual RTT.

2. Similarly, if delays at the destination fluctuate, the estimated RTT becomes unreliable.

3. The destination system may not ACK each segment but cumulatively ACK multiple segments, while at the same time sending ACKs when it has any data to send. This behavior contributes to fluctuations in RTT.

A consequence of these factors is that if a segment is lost, TCP may be slow to retransmit. If the destination TCP is using an in-order accept policy (see Section 10.1), then many segments may be lost. Even in the much more likely case that the destination TCP is using an in-window accept policy, a slow retransmission can cause problems. To see this, suppose that A transmits a sequence of segments, the first of which is lost. As long as its send window is not empty and RTO does not expire, A can continue to transmit without receiving an acknowledgment. B receives all of these segments except the first. But B must buffer all of these incoming segments until the missing one is retransmitted; it cannot clear its buffer by sending the data to an application until the missing segment arrives. If retransmission of the missing segment is delayed too long, B will have to begin discarding incoming segments.

Jacobson [JACO90b] proposed two procedures, called fast retransmit and fast recovery, that under some circumstances improve on the performance provided by RTO. Fast retransmit takes advantage of the following rule in TCP. If a TCP entity receives a segment out of order, it must immediately issue an ACK for the last in-order segment that was received. TCP will continue to repeat this ACK with each incoming segment until the missing segment arrives to "plug the hole" in its buffer. When the hole is plugged, TCP sends a cumulative ACK for all of the in-order segments received so far.

When a source TCP receives a duplicate ACK, it means that either (1) the segment following the ACKed segment was delayed so that it ultimately arrived out of order, or (2) that segment was lost. In case (1), the segment does ultimately arrive and therefore TCP should not retransmit. But in case (2) the arrival of a duplicate ACK can function as an early warning system to tell the source TCP that a segment has been lost and must be retransmitted. To make sure that we have case (2) rather than case (1), Jacobson recommends that a TCP sender wait until it receives three duplicate ACKs to the same segment (that is, a total of four ACKs to the same segment). Under these circumstances, it is highly likely that the following segment has been lost and should be retransmitted immediately, rather than waiting for a timeout.

Figure 10.13 illustrates the fast retransmit process. A sends a sequence of segments with 200 octets of data in each. Segment 1201 is lost, but A will not normally react to this until a time RTO has elapsed, and will continue to send segments until its window closes. B receives segment 1001 (octets 1001 through 1200) and acknowledges it with an ACK 1201. It then receives segment 1401 (octets 1401 through 1600). Because this segment is out of order, B repeats the ACK 1201 and will continue to repeat it with each incoming segment until segment 1201 arrives. By the time A receives four ACKs to segment 1001, it has sent seven segments beyond segment 1201. A immediately retransmits segment 1201 and then picks up where it left off.

Note that A can assume that segments subsequent to 1201 have been getting through. Otherwise, B would not be receiving the additional segments that trigger the duplicate ACKs.

Fast Recovery

When a TCP entity retransmits a segment using fast retransmit, it knows (or rather assumes) that a segment was lost, even though it has not yet timed out on that segment. Accordingly, the TCP entity should take congestion avoidance measures. One obvious strategy is the slow-start/congestion avoidance procedure used with a timeout occurs. That is, the entity could set $ssthresh$ to $cwnd/2$, set $cwnd = 1$ and begin the exponential slow-start process until $cwnd = ssthresh$, and then increase $cwnd$ linearly. Jacobson [JACO90b] argues that this approach is unnecessarily conservative. As was just pointed out, the very fact that multiple ACKs have returned indicates that data segments are getting through fairly regularly to the other side. So Jacobson proposes a fast recovery technique: Retransmit the lost segment, cut $cwnd$ in half, and then proceed with the linear increase of $cwnd$. This technique avoids the initial exponential slow-start process.

More precisely, the fast recovery technique can be stated as follows:

1. When the third duplicate ACK arrives,
   a. Set $ssthresh = cwnd/2$.
   b. Retransmit the missing segment.
   c. Set $cwnd = ssthresh + 3$.
   The reason for adding 3 to $ssthresh$ is that this accounts for the number of segments that have left the network and that the other end has cached.

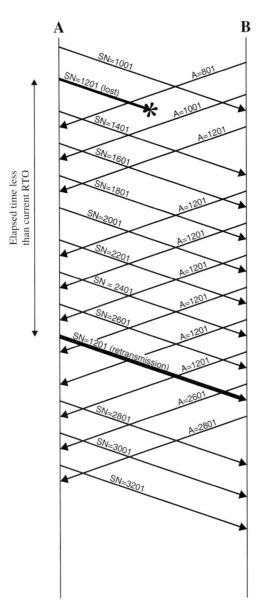

Figure 10.13 Fast retransmit.

2. Each time an additional duplicate ACK (for the same segment) arrives, increment *cwnd* by 1 and transmit a segment if possible. This accounts for the additional segment that has left the network and that triggered the duplicate ACK.

3. When the next ACK arrives that acknowledges new data (i.e., a cumulative acknowledgment of the missing segment plus other later segments), set *cwnd* = *ssthresh*.

An example,[7] from [HOE96], illustrates the operation (Figure 10.14). The *y*-axis in the upper figure represents segment numbers.[8] In the upper figure, each small diamond shape represents a segment transmitted at that time, with the height proportional to the size of the segment. These segments are bounded by two lines: The lower line indicates the last acknowledged sequence number (SND.UNA) and the upper line represents that sequence number plus the send window (SND.UNA + SND.WND).[9] Small tick marks on the bottom bounding line indicate duplicate ACKs. The lower figure shows the value of *cwnd* over the same time frame.

In the early part of this time period, a stable flow is maintained, with a stable window size and a full pipe; during this period *cwnd* remains at a maximum value equal to the receiver's stable credit allocation (10 segments). Just before time 5.43 (circled region), duplicate ACKs for segment 579 begin to arrive. When the third duplicate arrives, segment 580 is retransmitted, and *cwnd* is reduced by half plus three segments. We then enter a region in which the source can transmit one additional segment for each duplicate ACK received. Note that in this region the values of SND.UNA and SND.WND remain constant. In this example, the source is unable to transmit any segments until *cwnd* regains its former value. At this point, the source transmits one segment for each incoming duplicate ACK. As *cwnd* continues to grow, we get an inflated *cwnd* that accounts for cached segments at the destination side. Finally, at just before 5.6 seconds, a cumulative ACK is received for a large number of segments. This ACK arrives in a time RTT from the retransmission of segment 580. This ACK causes *cwnd* to be retracted to *ssthresh*, and the sender then enters the linear congestion avoidance mode.

10.3 PERFORMANCE OF TCP OVER ATM

Until recently, virtually all of the experience in running TCP and IP has been over networks with relatively few features for congestion control and quality of service, such as X.25 WANs and IEEE 802 LANs. Increasingly, however, the TCP/IP protocol stack is being used over ATM networks. Such networks are capable of complex quality-of-service functions and have a wide variety of congestion and traffic control facilities. In addition, ATM uses a small transfer unit, the 53-octet cell, so that TCP segments are fragmented into a number of parts.

The growing use of TCP/IP over ATM has sparked a flood of research on its performance implications. In essence, the issue is how best to manage TCP's segment size, window management, and congestion control policies on the one hand, and ATM's quality-of-service and traffic control policies on the other, to achieve

---

[7] In this example, *cwnd* is expressed in octets rather than segments. To translate to segments, divide *cwnd* by the maximum segment size, which is assumed to be 1024 octets.

[8] To simplify, the segment number of a segment is the closest integer to the highest sequence number in the segment divided by 1024 octets.

[9] See Figure 10.3.

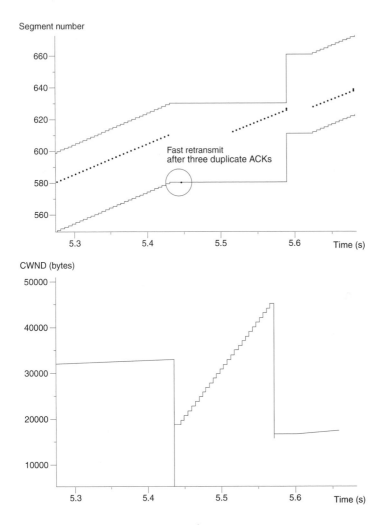

Figure 10.14 Fast recovery example.

high throughput for TCP traffic, fair allocation among various TCP connections, and efficient use of the underlying ATM network. This issue is fiendishly complex because of the many factors involved. Further, the context in which TCP operates over ATM is a factor. TCP/IP can operate end to end over a single ATM network, or there may be one or more ATM LANs and/or ATM WANs along an internetwork route that also involves non-ATM networks.

Because this topic is so complex, and because research is still ongoing with few consensus conclusions so far, we cannot attempt a thorough survey here. Rather, this section introduces some of the design issues involved and summarizes some of the results produced so far. We begin with a basic description of the TCP over ATM environment. Then we look at several mechanisms related to congestion control in ATM networks carrying TCP traffic. We first discuss the case of TCP over UBR, which provides no interaction between the congestion control mechanisms of TCP and ATM. Then we examine TCP over ABR, where the ATM layer is able to signal congestion information to TCP/IP.

Protocol Architecture

The typical implementation of TCP/IP over ATM uses the following protocol stack:

- TCP
- IP
- AAL5
- ATM.

Recall that the ATM Adaptation Layer (AAL) is responsible for mapping each higher-layer protocol data unit into ATM cells. AAL, in turn, consists of two sublayers: a Convergence Sublayer (CS), which provides functions to support specific higher layers, and a Segmentation and Reassembly Sublayer (SAR), which is responsible for packing information from CS into cells and unpacking the information at the other end. Each sublayer may employ headers and/or trailers to perform its functions.

AAL5 is the most commonly used form of AAL to support TCP/IP traffic. In AAL5, there are no overhead bits at the SAR level, which simply segments CS data into 48-octet blocks; and there is a minimal trailer at the CS level, whose principal purpose is to perform a CRC check on the CS block of data.

Figure 10.15 is an example of the relationship among the various layers. In this example, an entire TCP segment is carried in an IP datagram. If necessary, the TCP segment can be fragmented into pieces carried in multiple IP datagrams. However, there must be a one-to-one mapping between an IP datagram and the CS PDU that carries it; that is, each CS PDU carries exactly one IP datagram. The CS PDU includes an 8-octet trailer and any padding required to make the CS PDU an integer multiple of 48 octets.

The CS PDU is segmented into blocks of 48 octets and packed into ATM cells (in this example five cells are required). In each cell except the last, the SDU type bit is set to zero (see Table 4.2). The SDU type bit is set to one in the last cell to signal the SAR sublayer that an entire CS PDU has been delivered.

Figure 10.15 shows the most straightforward and, so far, the most common way of carrying TCP/IP traffic over an ATM network. Variations on this structure are possible, including the partial or complete elimination of the IP layer; these alternatives are described in RFC 1932.[10]

---

[10] RFC 1932, *IP over ATM: A Framework Document*, April 1996.

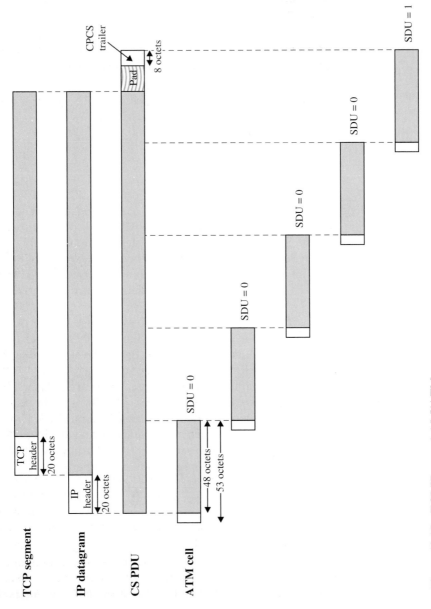

Figure 10.15 TCP/IP over AAL5/ATM.

272

TCP over UBR

In examining the performance of TCP over ATM, we must look at two quite different cases, based on the class of ATM service used: available bit rate (ABR) and unspecified bit rate (UBR). Recall from Chapter 4 that both ABR and UBR are designed to support traditional data traffic applications, as opposed to voice or video. Typically, data traffic is much burstier than voice or video, and a constant or near-constant delivery rate is not required. For the user the concern is one of throughput, while for the network the concern is that bursts of traffic from many users at the same time could overwhelm switches, causing cells to be dropped. ABR is intended for applications in which delay is a concern, such as on-line sessions between a user and a server. UBR is directed at delay-tolerant applications, such as file transfer and electronic mail.

The main practical difference between ABR and UBR is that, in the case of ABR, the network will provide congestion information to the user, enabling the user to reduce or increase the sending rate to achieve high efficiency. No such feedback is provided for UBR, which increases the risk of discarded cells and therefore the amount of traffic that must be retransmitted.

Because the ABR service is relatively new and is considerably more complex than UBR, UBR has been the preferred service for TCP traffic. In this subsection, we look at the performance to be expected in running TCP over a plain UBR service and then look at enhancements to ATM switch functionality that can improve TCP over UBR efficiency.

Performance of Plain UBR

Before looking at performance studies, we can make some obvious deductions about TCP over UBR. In any networking environment, TCP will achieve its maximum possible throughput when no segments are lost and, therefore, no retransmissions are required. In an ATM network, we can only guarantee that no segments will be lost if each ATM switch has buffer capacity equal to the sum of the TCP receive windows for all active TCP connections over the network. The sum of the TCP receive windows defines the total number of octets that may enter the network at a given time; if there is buffer capacity available for that total, then no segments will be lost.

In general, it will not be practical for each ATM switch to have such a huge buffer capacity, especially since the quantity in question (gross receive window size) is dynamic. Thus, we can conclude that the actual buffer capacity at ATM switches is a critical parameter in assessing TCP throughput performance. Other factors come into play, but this is a good place to start.

A striking demonstration of the effect of switch buffer size on TCP performance is reported by Romanow and Floyd [ROMA95]. The authors performed simulations on a simple ATM configuration with the following characteristics:

- Data rate of 141 Mbps.
- End-to-end propagation delay, not counting switch delay, of 6 μs. This results in a TCP pipe of just two cells (round-trip time = four cells).
- IP packet sizes ranging from 512 octets to 9180. A packet size of 512 octets is common in IP networks; 1500 is the maximum packet size for Ethernet; and 9180 is the default for IP over ATM (RFC 1626).

- TCP window sizes ranging from 8 kilobytes to 64 kilobytes.
- ATM switch buffer size per output port ranging from 256 cells to 8000 cells. This range covers most commercial products.
- One-to-one mapping of TCP connections to ATM virtual channels (VCs).
- All TCP sources have an infinite supply of data ready to transmit; thus TCP will drive the network to the maximum that it can, subject to TCP congestion control and window size constraints.

[ROMA95] compares this environment with what the authors refer to as packet TCP. The packet TCP configuration is identical to the ATM configuration just defined except that the unit of transfer is the IP datagram rather than the ATM cell; a packet-switched network that can handle entire IP datagrams without fragmentation is assumed. Figure 10.16a shows the results for packet TCP. Even for small packet-switch buffer size, the throughput achieved is near to the maximum possible. With the short RTT, the TCP sliding-window flow control and congestion control mechanisms succeed in maintaining a very low level of segment retransmissions, resulting in high relative throughput.

Figure 10.16b shows the results for TCP over plain UBR. Whereas packet TCP exhibits throughput that is over 90% for a range of conditions, TCP over plain UBR can yield throughput as low as 34%. The following effects can be observed:

- Smaller switch buffer size reduces throughput; note that this is only slightly the case for packet TCP.
- Larger TCP segment size also reduces throughput.

Other results, not shown in these figures, are as follows:

- Larger TCP receive window size reduces throughput.
- Increased congestion, caused by an increased number of TCP connections (and therefore an increased number of VCs), reduces throughput.

The key to understanding the difference between cell-based and packet-based switching performance is simple. When a single cell must be dropped due to congestion, other cells that are part of the same IP datagram are unusable. Yet the ATM network will forward these useless cells to the destination. Thus, we can make the following observations:

- Smaller buffers increase the probability of dropped cells and therefore of wasted resources due to the transmission of useless cells.
- A larger segment size increases the number of useless cells that are transmitted if a single cell is dropped. Further, a larger segment size results in a more aggressive TCP window increase algorithm, which in the congestion avoidance phase increases window size by one segment per round-trip time.

These results are confirmed in other studies that use different network configurations. For example, [SCIU96] reports on a study involving satellite links with very long RTTs; using TCP over plain UBR, the authors were only able to achieve a utilization of 73%. Both [MOLD95] and [COME95b] report that with a large seg-

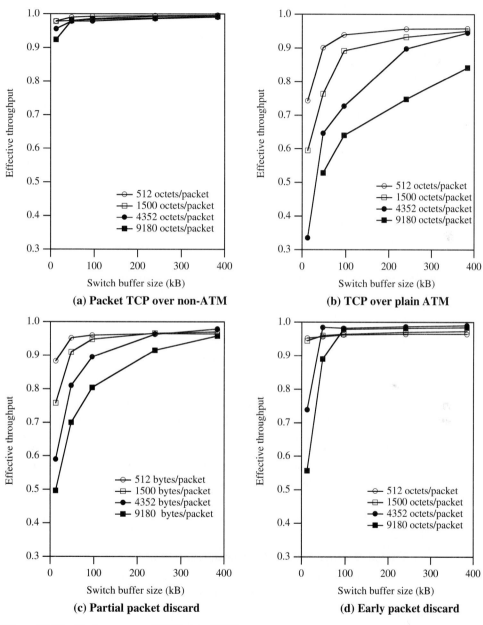

(a) Packet TCP over non-ATM

(b) TCP over plain ATM

(c) Partial packet discard

(d) Early packet discard

Figure 10.16   Performance of TCP over UBR.

ment size, certain combinations of send and receive buffer size can result in dramatic drops in throughput, down to just a few percent of normal. [TIPP95], instead of using a maximum-load simulation, used a self-similar traffic model and confirmed that TCP throughput depends critically on ATM switch buffer size. Finally, [FANG94] reported similar results and demonstrated that as congestion increases, the effect on different TCP connections varies widely, so that there is an unfair allocation of resources.

Partial Packet Discard and Early Packet Discard

The conclusions of all of these studies have led a number of switch vendors to increase ATM switch buffer size. A number of vendors have also been influenced by proposals made in [ROMA95] for two techniques to improve the cell discard behavior. These proposals are referred to as partial packet discard and early packet discard. Both strategies are aimed at reducing the transmission of useless cells.

Partial packet discard (PPD) operates as follows: If a cell from an IP datagram is dropped from a switch buffer, the subsequent cells in that datagram are also discarded. For a switch to recognize, at the ATM level, which cells belong to a given IP datagram, PPD must operate on a per-virtual-channel basis. When a switch discards a cell on a particular VC, it then discards all subsequent cells on that VC until it sees a cell with the SDU type bit set to one in the ATM cell header. This cell marks the end of an AAL5 PDU and therefore the end of an IP datagram. This final cell is not dropped. Because AAL5 does not support the multiplexing of cells from different PDUs, the SDU parameter can be used successfully to delimit IP datagram boundaries.

Figure 10.16c shows the performance of PPD. As can be seen, PPD provides better performance than TCP over plain ATM, but is not as effective as one might wish. Improvement is limited because PPD only discards the "tail end" of a datagram. On average, we can expect that only half of a damaged datagram is discarded with each cell discard. Similar results have been reported in [KAMA96] and [FANG94].

A more effective scheme is **early packet discard (EPD)**. In this case, when a switch buffer reaches a threshold level, but before it is actually required to discard any cells due to buffer overflow, an entire IP datagram is dropped. Thus, when the switch senses that congestion is beginning and that cell discard may soon be necessary, it preemptively discards all of the cells, starting with the first, of an IP datagram. For this purpose, the switch looks for the first incoming cell on a VC with an SDU bit of 0 that immediately follows a cell on the same VC with an SDU bit of 1. This cell marks the beginning of a new datagram, and the discarding begins with this cell. In effect, the EPD strategy emulates a packet-switching network in which entire packets are dropped.

Figure 10.16d shows the performance of EPD, with a threshold set to half the total buffer size. Except for very small buffer sizes, high effective throughput is achieved. Similar results are reported in [FANG95].

The combination of EPD with the TCP congestion control mechanism seems to provide effective throughput for the average TCP connection. EPD has a short-term orientation, anticipating congestion and reacting immediately to drop a packet. Complementing this action is the longer-term orientation of TCP, which reacts to packet loss by backing off and only slowly resuming its former rate of transmission.

EPD with Fair Buffer Allocation

Despite the effectiveness of EPD, a serious problem remains: fairness. When the EPD mechanism is activated, it selects the first available full packet for discard, regardless of which VC (and therefore which TCP connection) is carrying that packet. One might think that, on average, all TCP connections would be equally affected. However, in a number of studies, (e.g., [FANG95], [GOYA97]), EPD has exhibited unfair treatment of TCP connections. There are several apparent causes for this. First, EPD has a bias against connections with shorter IP datagrams. When an ATM switch begins to search for the beginning of a packet for discard, it is more likely to find the beginning of one of the smaller packets first, and might never need to drop cells from connections with larger packets. In addition, EPD exhibits a bias against connections that pass through multiple congested switches, because packets on such connections are vulnerable to EPD more frequently.

A proposed enhancement to EPD to increase fairness is known as fair buffer allocation (FBA); favorable results using EPD with FBA are reported in [FANG95] and [GOYA97]. In essence, FBA works as follows: When EPD is invoked, the switch will choose to discard from the VC that is using more than its fair share of the switch's buffer.

To explain the FBA algorithm, we define the following parameters for a given ATM switch (Figure 10.17):

B = Buffer capacity of the switch, in cells

R = Threshold parameter which triggers packet discard; $R < B$

N = The current number of cells in the buffer; $N \leq B$

$N(i)$ = The current number of cells in the buffer for VC i

V = Number of active VCs; that is, the number of VCs that have at least one cell in the buffer

The following relationship is satisfied:

$$N = \sum_{i=1}^{V} N(i)$$

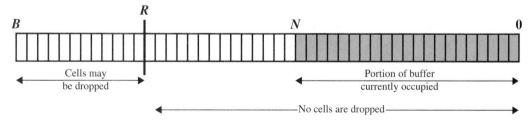

N = Number of cells currently buffered

R = Threshold

B = Buffer size, in cells

Figure 10.17 ATM switch buffer layout for selective drop and fair buffer allocation.

It will help to clarify the FBA mechanism if we first look at a simpler scheme, called selective drop and proposed in [GOYA97]. If there are V active VCs at a switch and N buffered cells, then a fair allocation would be if the same number of cells were buffered for each VC. That is, ideally, there would be N/V cells buffered for each of the active VCs. For each VC, we calculate a weight $W(i)$ as the ratio between the actual number of cells buffered and the ideal number:

$$W(i) = \frac{N(i)}{N/V} = \frac{N(i) \times V}{N}$$

For example, if there are $V = 10$ active VCs but VC 1 has one fifth of the total buffered cells $[(N(i)/N = 0.2]$, then the weight for VC 1 is 2. Any weight greater than one means that the VC has a disproportionate share of buffer resources.

The rule for **selective drop** is based on the following condition:

$$(N > R) \text{ AND } W(i) > Z \tag{10.9}$$

If the buffer occupancy exceeds the threshold, then the next new incoming packet on VC i is dropped if $W(i)$ exceeds a parameter Z. Experiments reported in [GOYA97] showed good results for a value of Z of a little less than one. The following conclusions were reached:

- Selective drop provides improved fairness compared to plain EPD. The dropping of a packet forces the corresponding TCP connection to back off and reduce window size. At the same time, ATM buffer resources are freed up and other TCP connections can increase their window size and throughput. Thus, selective drop works with TCP congestion control to balance loads.
- Fairness and total throughput increase with increased ATM switch buffer size.
- Fairness decreases with increasing number of sources.

Both EPD and selective drop begin to drop cells when a fixed threshold is reached. **Fair buffer allocation** adopts a policy of more aggressive dropping of packets as congestion increases. The rule for FBA is based on the following condition:

$$(N > R) \text{ AND } W(i) > Z \times \left(\frac{B - R}{N - R}\right) \tag{10.10}$$

As with selective drop (Equation 10.9), FBA causes a packet to be dropped from VC i if the condition is met. For FBA, $W(i)$ is compared to a value that increases as congestion increases. If we think of the final $(B - R)$ cell slots in the buffer as a safety zone, then the greater of the fraction of the safety zone that is occupied, the smaller the value to which $W(i)$ is compared. As congestion increases, the switch will begin to drop packets from more and more VCs, exempting only those that have a few buffered cells.

Table 10.2, based on [GOYA97], compares plain UBR, EPD, selective drop, and FBA. The results are based on a simulation of a configuration of 10 TCP sources, all of which go through the same two ATM switches to reach a destination. Each source sends the maximum allowable amount of data in 512-octet segments over a single TCP connection. The end-to-end delay is 15 μs for a LAN configuration and 15 ms for a WAN configuration.

TABLE 10.2   PERFORMANCE OF TCP OVER UBR

(a) Throughput

Config-uration	Number of Sources	Buffer Size (cells)	UBR	EPD	Selective Drop	FBA
LAN	5	1000	0.21	0.49	0.75	0.88
LAN	5	2000	0.32	0.68	0.85	0.84
LAN	5	3000	0.47	0.72	0.90	0.92
LAN	15	1000	0.22	0.55	0.76	0.91
LAN	15	2000	0.49	0.81	0.82	0.85
LAN	15	3000	0.47	0.91	0.94	0.95
WAN	5	12000	0.86	0.90	0.90	0.95
WAN	5	24000	0.90	0.91	0.92	0.92
WAN	5	36000	0.91	0.81	0.81	0.81
WAN	15	12000	0.96	0.92	0.94	0.95
WAN	15	24000	0.94	0.91	0.94	0.96
WAN	15	36000	0.92	0.96	0.96	0.95

(b) Fairness

Config-uration	Number of Sources	Buffer Size (cells)	UBR	EPD	Selective Drop	FBA
LAN	5	1000	0.68	0.57	0.99	0.98
LAN	5	2000	0.90	0.98	0.96	0.98
LAN	5	3000	0.97	0.84	0.99	0.97
LAN	15	1000	0.31	0.56	0.76	0.97
LAN	15	2000	0.59	0.87	0.98	0.96
LAN	15	3000	0.80	0.78	0.94	0.93
WAN	5	12000	0.75	0.94	0.95	0.94
WAN	5	24000	0.83	0.99	0.99	1.00
WAN	5	36000	0.86	1.00	1.00	1.00
WAN	15	12000	0.67	0.93	0.91	0.97
WAN	15	24000	0.82	0.92	0.97	0.98
WAN	15	36000	0.77	0.91	0.89	0.97

Table 10.2a shows the comparative throughput results. The overall normalized throughput is calculated as

$$\text{Throughput} = \frac{\Sigma x_i}{V \times M}$$

where

x_i = throughput of the ith TCP source
V = number of TCP sources (= number of VCs)
M = maximum possible TCP throughput

Table 10.2a shows that FBA is, in general, only slightly better than selective drop. Table 10.2b shows the fairness results, using the following as a measure of fairness:

$$\text{Fairness} = \frac{(\Sigma x_i)^2}{V \times \Sigma(x_i^2)}$$

This is a normalized measure of the dispersion of the values of x_i. The results show that selective drop is considerably fairer than EPD and that FBA is only slightly better than selective drop.

TCP Over ABR

With modest adjustments to switch mechanisms, good performance of TCP over UBR can be achieved. These results have reduced the incentive to make use of the more complex and more expensive ABR service. However, this service has now been fully defined by the ATM Forum and is likely to be increasingly implemented by ATM switch vendors. Accordingly, it is worthwhile to examine the performance implications of TCP over ABR.

The assessment of TCP performance over ABR is even more complex than the TCP-UBR case, and it is difficult to make general conclusions. In this subsection, we highlight some of the design issues involved and report the results of three recent studies.

ABR Effect on TCP Flows

As was discussed in Chapter 4, ABR is in essence a protocol for informing the source about the capacity made available to it by the network (we go into more detail in Chapter 12). For each virtual channel using ABR, a minimum cell rate (MCR) and peak cell rate (PCR) are initially established. The ABR mechanism makes an amount of capacity available to the source that is at least MCR and an additional amount that results from sharing the available capacity among all the active ABR connections. As congestion increases in the network, less capacity is made available to individual VCs and therefore to individual TCP connections.

ABR flow control consists of two modes of operation: binary mode and explicit rate mode. In binary mode, a switch signals the beginning/end of congestion to the source, which can modify its rate of transmission up or down by an incremental amount. In explicit rate mode, an ATM switch employs a control algorithm to allocate capacity among the VCs traversing the switch. The switch then sends explicit rate guidance to each source, which adjusts its rate of transmission accordingly. In both modes, a variety of parameters determine the exact behavior of the ABR algorithm, making performance modeling and analysis difficult.

[KALY97] observes that TCP over ABR traffic operates in two quite different modes: window limited and rate limited. In **window-limited mode**, a TCP source is governed by the TCP flow and congestion control mechanism. When a TCP connection is set up and a VC is assigned, ABR will typically allocate a relatively high rate to the source, only reducing that rate when congestion occurs. Thus, for a time, TCP can send as much data as it can. This rate is therefore determined by the congestion window and the TCP slow-start mechanism. Observe in Figure 10.10 that TCP traffic begins with a short active period (one segment) followed by a long idle period of nearly one RTT and that each RTT, the active period doubles and the idle period contracts until TCP is sending continuously. Up until this point, TCP is likely to be window limited. Once TCP is prepared to send segments continuously, congestion may occur and the connection becomes **rate limited**. The ABR mechanism exerts a backpressure on TCP sources that can reduce the transmission of TCP segments. After one RTT, a reduced rate of segment transmission is reflected in a reduced rate of returning ACKs.

Performance of TCP Over ABR

One of the most comprehensive studies so far of TCP performance over ABR is reported in [FANG97]. The authors examined 15 parameters associated with the ABR algorithm and looked at different switch buffer sizes and network propagation delays. They then compared binary-mode ABR performance with UBR-EPD and UBR-EPD-FBA for both throughput and fairness. Looking at an impressive number of variations of simulation parameters, the authors came to two important conclusions:

1. The performance and fairness of ABR are quite sensitive to some of the ABR parameter settings, and in some cases very poor performance and/or very poor fairness are achieved. This suggests the need for ongoing tuning of ABR parameters in a live network configuration.

2. Overall, ABR does not provide significant performance improvement over the simpler and less expensive UBR-EPD or UBR-EPD-FBA. In fact, for many parameter settings, ABR provides inferior throughput and/or fairness.

Similar conclusions are reported in [SAIT96]. Their study showed that for binary-mode ABR compared to plain UBR, buffer size was a critical parameter; ABR was superior for some buffer sizes while UBR was superior for others. The authors also compared explicit-rate-mode ABR to binary-mode ABR and plain UBR. They found that the explicit rate mode provided better than or equal throughput to binary-mode ABR or plain UBR. However, when a finer granularity is used on the TCP round-trip timer, this advantage is lessened considerably. By using finer granularity, TCP can detect a packet loss more quickly and improve TCP performance over UBR.

Finally, [KALY97] compared plain UBR with explicit-rate-mode ABR. They concluded that the performance depends critically on ATM switch buffer size. However, in the case of ABR, the amount of buffering required does not depend on the number of TCP connections. Instead, ABR switches with buffers equal to a small multiple of the capacity-delay diameter of the network are sufficient to guarantee high throughput. On the other hand, UBR seems to require buffering proportional to the sum of the TCP receive windows of all sources. Note, however, that if small buffers are used in ABR switches, then the queues at the sources may become large.

Overall, the case for using ABR rather than UBR to support TCP traffic is far from clear. Further experience and study are needed.

10.4 REAL-TIME TRANSPORT PROTOCOL

The most widely used transport-level protocol is TCP. Although TCP has proven its value in supporting a wide range of distributed applications, it is not suited for use with real-time distributed applications. By a real-time distributed application, we mean one in which a source is generating a stream of data at a constant rate, and one or more destinations must deliver that data to an application at the same constant rate. Examples of such applications include audio and video conferencing, live video distribution (not for storage but for immediate play), shared workspaces, remote medical diagnosis, telephony, command and control systems, distributed interactive simulations, games, and real-time monitoring. A number of features of TCP disqualify it for use as the transport protocol for such applications:

1. TCP is a point-to-point protocol that sets up a connection between two end points. Therefore, it is not suitable for multicast distribution.
2. TCP includes mechanisms for retransmission of lost segments, which then arrive out of order. Such segments are not usable in most real-time applications.
3. TCP contains no convenient mechanism for associating timing information with segments, which is another real-time requirement.

The other widely used transport protocol, UDP, does not exhibit the first two characteristics in the preceding list but, like TCP, does not provide timing information. By itself, UDP does not provide any general-purpose tools useful for real-time applications.

Although each real-time application could include its own mechanisms for supporting real-time transport, there are a number of common features that warrant the definition of a common protocol. A standards-track protocol designed for this purpose is the real-time transport protocol, defined in RFC 1889.[11]

This section provides an overview of RTP. We begin with a discussion of real-time transport requirements. Next, we examine the philosophical approach of RTP. The remainder of the section is devoted to the two protocols that make up RTP: The first is simply called RTP and is a data transfer protocol; the other is a control protocol known as RTCP (RTP Control Protocol).

The Transport of Real–time Traffic

The widespread deployment of high-speed LANs and WANs and the increase in the line capacity on the Internet and other internets has opened up the possibility of using IP-based networks for the transport of real-time traffic. However, it is important to recognize that the requirements of real-time traffic differ from those of high-speed but non-real-time traffic.

With traditional internet applications, such as file transfer, electronic mail, and client-server applications including the Web, the performance metrics of interest are generally throughput and delay. There is also a concern with reliability, and mechanisms are used to make sure that no data are lost, corrupted, or misordered during transit. By contrast, real-time applications are more concerned with timing issues. In most cases, there is a requirement that data be delivered at a constant rate equal to the sending rate. In other cases, a deadline is associated with each block of data, such that the data are not usable after the deadline has expired.

---

[11] RFC 1889, *RTP: A Transport Protocol for Real-time Applications*, January 1996.

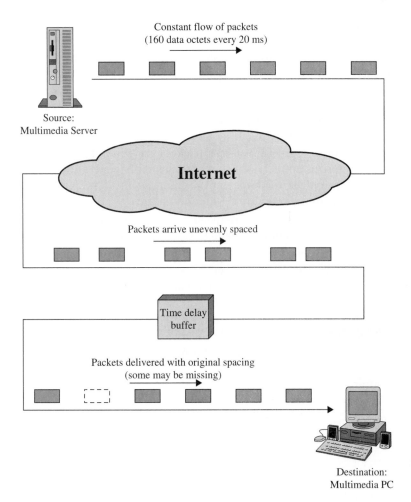

Figure 10.18   Real-time traffic.

Real-time Traffic Characteristics

Figure 10.18 illustrates a typical real-time environment. Here, a server is generating audio to be transmitted at 64 kbps. The digitized audio is transmitted in packets containing 160 octets of data, so that one packet is issued every 20 ms. These packets are passed through an internet and delivered to a multimedia PC, which plays the audio in real time as it arrives. However, because of the variable delay imposed by the internet, the interarrival times between packets are not maintained at a fixed 20 ms at the destination. To compensate for this, the incoming packets are buffered, delayed slightly, and then released at a constant rate to the software that generates the audio.

The compensation provided by the delay buffer is limited. To understand this, we need to define the concept of *delay jitter*, which is the maximum variation in delay experienced by packets in a single session. For example, if the minimum end-to-end delay seen by any packet is 1 ms and the maximum is 6 ms, then the delay jitter is 5 ms. As long as the time delay buffer delays incoming packets by at least 5 ms, then the output of the buffer will include all incoming packets. However, if the buffer delayed packets only by 4 ms, then any incoming packets that had experienced a relative delay of more than 4 ms (an absolute delay of more than 5 ms) would have to be discarded so as not to be played back out of order.

The description of real-time traffic so far implies a series of equal-size packets generated at a constant rate. This is not always the profile of the traffic. Figure 10.19 illustrates some of the common possibilities:

- **Continuous data source:** Fixed-size packets are generated at fixed intervals. This characterizes applications that are constantly generating data, have few redundancies, and are too important to compress in a lossy way. Examples are air traffic control radar and real-time simulations.
- **On/off source:** The source alternates between periods when fixed-size packets are generated at fixed intervals and periods of inactivity. A voice source, such as in telephony or audio conferencing, fits this profile.
- **Variable packet size:** The source generates variable-length packets at uniform intervals. An example is digitized video in which different frames may experience different compression ratios for the same output quality level.[12]

Requirements for Real-time Communication

[ARAS94] lists the following as desirable properties for real-time communication:

- Low jitter
- Low latency
- Ability to easily integrate non-real-time and real-time services

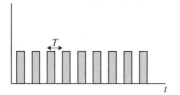

(a) Continuous data source

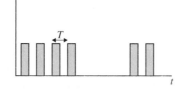

(b) Voice source
with silent intervals

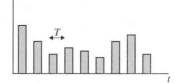

(c) Compressed video source

Figure 10.19   Real-time packet transmission (based on [ARAS94]).

---

[12] See Chapter 18 for a discussion of video compression.

- Adaptability to dynamically changing network and traffic conditions
- Good performance for large networks and large numbers of connections
- Modest buffer requirements within the network
- High effective capacity utilization
- Low overhead in header bits per packet
- Low processing overhead per packet within the network and at the end system.

These requirements are difficult to meet in a wide area IP-based network or internet. Neither TCP nor UDP by itself is appropriate. We will see that RTP provides a reasonable foundation for addressing these issues.

Hard versus Soft Real-time Applications

A distinction needs to be made between hard and soft real-time communication applications. Soft real-time applications can tolerate the loss of some portion of the communicated data, while hard real-time applications have zero loss tolerance. In general, soft real-time applications impose fewer requirements on the network, and it is therefore permissible to focus on maximizing network utilization, even at the cost of some lost or misordered packets. In hard real-time applications, a deterministic upper bound on jitter and high reliability take precedence over network utilization considerations.

RTP is best suited to soft real-time communication. It lacks the necessary mechanisms to support hard real-time traffic.

RTP Protocol Architecture

In RTP, there is close coupling between the RTP functionality and the application-layer functionality. Indeed, RTP is best viewed as a framework that applications can use directly to implement a single protocol. Without the application-specific information, RTP is not a full protocol. On the other hand, RTP imposes a structure and defines common functions so that individual real-time applications are relieved of part of their burden.

RTP follows the principles of protocol architecture design outlined in a paper by Clark and Tennenhouse [CLAR90]. The two key concepts presented in that paper are application-level framing and integrated layer processing.

Application Level Framing

In a traditional transport protocol, such as TCP, the responsibility for recovering from lost portions of data is performed transparently at the transport layer. [CLAR90] lists two scenarios in which it might be more appropriate for recovery from lost data to be performed by the application:

1. The application, within limits, may accept less than perfect delivery and continue unchecked. This is the case for real-time audio and video. For such applications, it may be necessary to inform the source in more general terms about the quality of the delivery rather than to ask for retransmission. If too much data are being lost, the source might move to a lower-quality transmission that places lower demands on the network, increasing the probability of delivery.

2. It may be preferable to have the application rather than the transport protocol provide data for retransmission. This is useful in the following contexts:

   a. The sending application may recompute lost data values rather than
      storing them.

   b. The sending application can provide revised values rather than simply
      retransmitting lost values, or send new data that "fix" the consequences of
      the original loss.

To enable the application to have control over the retransmission function,
Clark and Tennenhouse propose that lower layers, such as presentation and transport, deal with data in units that the application specifies. The application should
break the flow of data into application-level data units (ADUs), and the lower layers must preserve these ADU boundaries as they process the data. The application-
level frame is the unit of error recovery. Thus, if a portion of an ADU is lost in
transmission, the application will typically be unable to make use of the remaining
portions. In such a case, the application layer will discard all arriving portions and
arrange for retransmission of the entire ADU, if necessary.

Integrated Layer Processing

In a typical layered protocol architecture, such as TCP/IP or OSI, each layer
of the architecture contains a subset of the functions to be performed for communications, and each layer must logically be structured as a separate module in end
systems. Thus, on transmission, a block of data flows down through and is sequentially processed by each layer of the architecture. This structure restricts the imple-
menter from invoking certain functions in parallel or out of the layered order to
achieve greater efficiency. Integrated layer processing, as proposed in [CLAR90],
captures the idea that adjacent layers may be tightly coupled and that the imple-
menter should be free to implement the functions in those layers in a tightly coupled manner.

The idea that a strict protocol layering may lead to inefficiencies has been pro-
pounded by a number of researchers. For example, [CROW92] examined the inefficiencies of running a remote procedure call (RPC) on top of TCP and suggested a
tighter coupling of the two layers. They argued that the integrated layer processing
approach is preferable for efficient data transfer.

Figure 10.20 illustrates the manner in which RTP realizes the principle of integrated layer processing. RTP is designed to run on top of a connectionless transport
protocol such as UDP. UDP provides the basic port addressing functionality of the
transport layer. RTP contains further transport-level functions, such as sequencing.
However, RTP by itself is not complete. It is completed by modifications and/or
additions to the RTP headers to include application-layer functionality. The figure
indicates that several different standards for encoding video data can be used in conjunction with RTP for video transmission.

RTP Data Transfer Protocol

We first look at the basic concepts of the RTP data transfer protocol and then examine the protocol header format. Throughout this section, the term *RTP* will refer to
the RTP data transfer protocol.

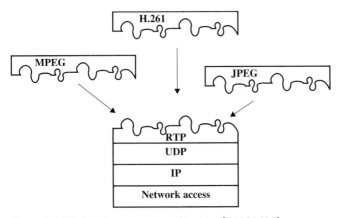

Figure 10.20   RTP protocol architecture [THOM96].

RTP Concepts

RTP supports the transfer of real-time data among a number of participants in a session. A session is simply a logical association among two or more RTP entities that is maintained for the duration of the data transfer. A session is defined by the following:

- **RTP port number:** The destination port address is used by all participants for RTP transfers. If UDP is the lower layer, this port number appears in the Destination Port field (see Figure 2.1) of the UDP header.
- **RTCP port number:** The destination port address is used by all participants for RTCP transfers.
- **Participant IP addresses:** This can either be a multicast IP address, so that the multicast group defines the participants, or a set of unicast IP addresses.

The process of setting up a session is beyond the scope of RTP and RTCP.

Although RTP can be used for unicast real-time transmission, its strength lies in its ability to support multicast transmission. For this purpose, each RTP data unit includes a source identifier that identifies which member of the group generated the data. It also includes a timestamp so that the proper timing can be re-created on the receiving end using a delay buffer. RTP also identifies the payload format of the data being transmitted.

RTP allows the use of two kinds of RTP relays: translators and mixers. First we need to define the concept of relay. A relay operating at a given protocol layer is an intermediate system that acts as both a destination and a source in a data transfer. For example, suppose that system A wishes to send data to system B but cannot do so directly. Possible reasons are that B may be behind a firewall or B may not be able to use the format transmitted by A. In such a case, A may be able to send the data to an intermediate relay R. R accepts the data unit, makes any necessary changes or performs any necessary processing, and then transmits the data to B.

A **mixer** is an RTP relay that receives streams of RTP packets from one or more sources, combines these streams, and forwards a new RTP packet stream to one or more destinations. The mixer may change the data format or simply perform the mixing function. Because the timing among the multiple inputs is not typically synchronized, the mixer provides the timing information in the combined packet stream and identifies itself as the source of synchronization.

An example of the use of a mixer is to combine of a number of on/off sources such as audio. Suppose that a number of systems are members of an audio session and each generates its own RTP stream. Most of the time only one source is active, although occasionally more than one source will be "speaking" at the same time. A new system may wish to join the session, but its link to the network may not be of sufficient capacity to carry all of the RTP streams. Instead, a mixer could receive all of the RTP streams, combine them into a single stream, and retransmit that stream to the new session member. If more than one incoming stream is active at one time, the mixer would simply sum their PCM values. The RTP header generated by the mixer includes the identifier(s) of the source(s) that contributed to the data in each packet.

The **translator** is a simpler device that produces one or more outgoing RTP packet for each incoming RTP packet. The translator may change the format of the data in the packet or use a different lower-level protocol suite to transfer from one domain to another. Examples of translator use include the following:

- A potential recipient may not be able to handle a high-speed video signal used by the other participants. The translator converts the video to a lower-quality format requiring a lower data rate.
- An application-level firewall may prevent the forwarding of IP packets. Two translators are used, one on each side of the firewall, with the outside one funneling all multicast packets received through a secure connection to the translator inside the firewall. The inside translator then sends out RTP packets to a multicast group protected by the firewall.
- A translator can replicate an incoming multicast RTP packet and send it to a number of unicast destinations.

RTP Fixed Header

Each RTP packet includes a fixed header and may also include additional application-specific header fields. Figure 10.21 shows the fixed header. The first 12 octets (shaded portion) are always present and consist of the following fields:

- **Version (2 bits):** Current version is 2.
- **Padding (1 bit):** Indicates whether padding octets appear at the end of the payload. If so, the last octet of the payload contains a count of the number of padding octets. Padding is used if the application requires that the payload be an integer multiple of some length, such as 32 bits.
- **Extension (1 bit):** If set, the fixed header is followed by exactly one extension header, which is used for experimental extensions to RTP.
- **CSRC Count (4 bits):** The number of CSRC identifiers that follow the fixed header.
- **Marker (1 bit):** The interpretation of the marker bit depends on the payload type; it is typically used to indicate a boundary in the data stream. For video,

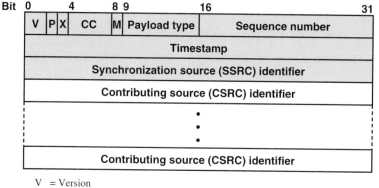

V = Version
P = Padding
X = Extension
CC = CSRC count
M = Marker

Figure 10.21   RTP header.

it is set to mark the end of a frame. For audio, it is set to mark the beginning of a talk spurt.

- **Payload Type (7 bits):** Identifies the format of the RTP payload, which follows the RTP header.
- **Sequence Number (16 bits):** Each source starts with a random sequence number, which is incremented by one for each RTP data packet sent. This allows for loss detection and packet sequencing within a series of packets with the same timestamp. A number of consecutive packets may have the same timestamp if they are logically generated at the same time; an example is several packets belonging to the same video frame.
- **Timestamp (32 bits):** Corresponds to the generation instant of the first octet of data in the payload. The time units of this field depend on the payload type. The values must be generated from a local clock at the source.
- **Synchronization Source Identifier:** A randomly generated value that uniquely identifies the source within a session.

Following the fixed header, there may be one or more of the following field:

- **Contributing Source Identifier:** Identifies a contributing source for the payload. These identifiers are supplied by a mixer.

The Payload Type field identifies the media type of the payload and the format of the data, including the use of compression or encryption. In a steady state, a source should only use one payload type during a session, but may change the payload type in response to changing conditions, as discovered by RTCP. Table 10.3 summarizes the payload types defined in RFC 1890. [13]

---

[13] RFC 1890, *RTP Profile for Audio and Video Conferences with Minimal Control*, January 1996.

TABLE 10.3 PAYLOAD TYPES FOR STANDARD AUDIO
AND VIDEO ENCODINGS (RFC 1890)

0	PCMU audio	16–23	unassigned audio
1	1016 audio	24	unassigned video
2	G721 audio	25	CelB video
3	GSM audio	26	JPEG video
4	unassigned audio	27	unassigned
5	DV14 audio (8 kHz)	28	nv video
6	DV14 audio (16 kHz)	29–30	unassigned video
7	LPC audio	31	H261 video
8	PCMA audio	32	MPV video
9	G722 audio	33	MP2T video
10	L16 audio (stereo)	34–71	unassigned
11	L16 audio (mono)	72–76	reserved
12–13	unassigned audio	77–95	unassigned
14	MPA audio	96–127	dynamic
15	G728 audio		

RTP Control Protocol

The RTP data transfer protocol is used only for the transmission of user data, typically in multicast fashion among all participants in a session. A separate control protocol (RTCP) also operates in a multicast fashion to provide feedback to RTP data sources as well as all session participants. RTCP uses the same underlying transport service as RTP (usually UDP) and a separate port number. Each participant periodically issues an RTCP packet to all other session members. RFC 1889 outlines four functions performed by RTCP:

- **Quality of service and congestion control:** RTCP provides feedback on the quality of data distribution. Because RTCP packets are multicast, all session members can assess how well other members are performing and receiving. Sender reports enable receivers to estimate data rates and the quality of the transmission. Receiver reports indicate any problems encountered by receivers, including missing packets and excessive jitter. For example, an audio-video application might decide to reduce the rate of transmission over low-speed links if the traffic quality over the links is not high enough to support the current rate. The feedback from receivers is also important in diagnosing distribution faults. By monitoring reports from all session recipients, a network manager can tell whether a problem is specific to a single user or more widespread.
- **Identification:** RTCP packets carry a persistent textual description of the RTCP source. This provides more information about the source of data packets than the random SSRC identifier and enables a user to associate multiple streams from different sessions. For example, separate sessions for audio and video may be in progress.
- **Session size estimation and scaling:** To perform the first two functions, all participants send periodic RTCP packets. The rate of transmission of such packets must be scaled down as the number of participants increases. In a session with few participants, RTCP packets are sent at the maximum rate of one

every five seconds. RFC 1889 includes a relatively complex algorithm by which each participant limits its RTCP rate on the basis of the total session population. The objective is to limit RTCP traffic to less than 5% of total session traffic.

- **Session control:** RTCP optionally provides minimal session control information. An example is a participant identification to be displayed in the user interface.

An RTCP transmission consists of a number of separate RTCP packets bundled in a single UDP datagram (or other lower-level data unit). The following packet types are defined in RFC 1889:

- Sender Report (SR)
- Receiver Report (RR)
- Source Description (SDES)
- Goodbye (BYE)
- Application specific.

Figure 10.22 depicts the formats of these packet types. Each type begins with a 32-bit word containing the following fields:

- **Version (2 bits):** Current version is 2.
- **Padding (1 bit):** If set, indicates that this packet contains padding octets and the end of the control information. If so, the last octet of the padding contains a count of the number of padding octets.
- **Count (5 bits):** The number of reception report blocks contained in an SR or RR packet (RC), or the number of source items contained in an SDES or BYE packet.
- **Packet Type (8 bits):** Identifies RTCP packet type.
- **Length (16 bits):** Length of this packet in 32 bit words, minus one.

In addition, the Sender Report and Receiver Report packets contain the following field:

- **Synchronization Source Identifier:** Identifies the source of this RTCP packet.

We now turn to a description of each packet type.

Sender Report

RTCP receivers provide reception quality feedback using a Sender Report or a Receiver Report, depending on whether the receiver is also a sender during this session. Figure 10.22a shows the format of a Sender Report. The Sender Report consists of a **header**, already described, a sender information block, and zero or more reception report blocks. The **sender information block** includes the following fields:

- **NTP Timestamp (64 bits):** The absolute wallclock time when this report was sent; this is an unsigned fixed-point number with the integer part in the first 32 bits and the fractional part in the last 32 bits. This may be used by the

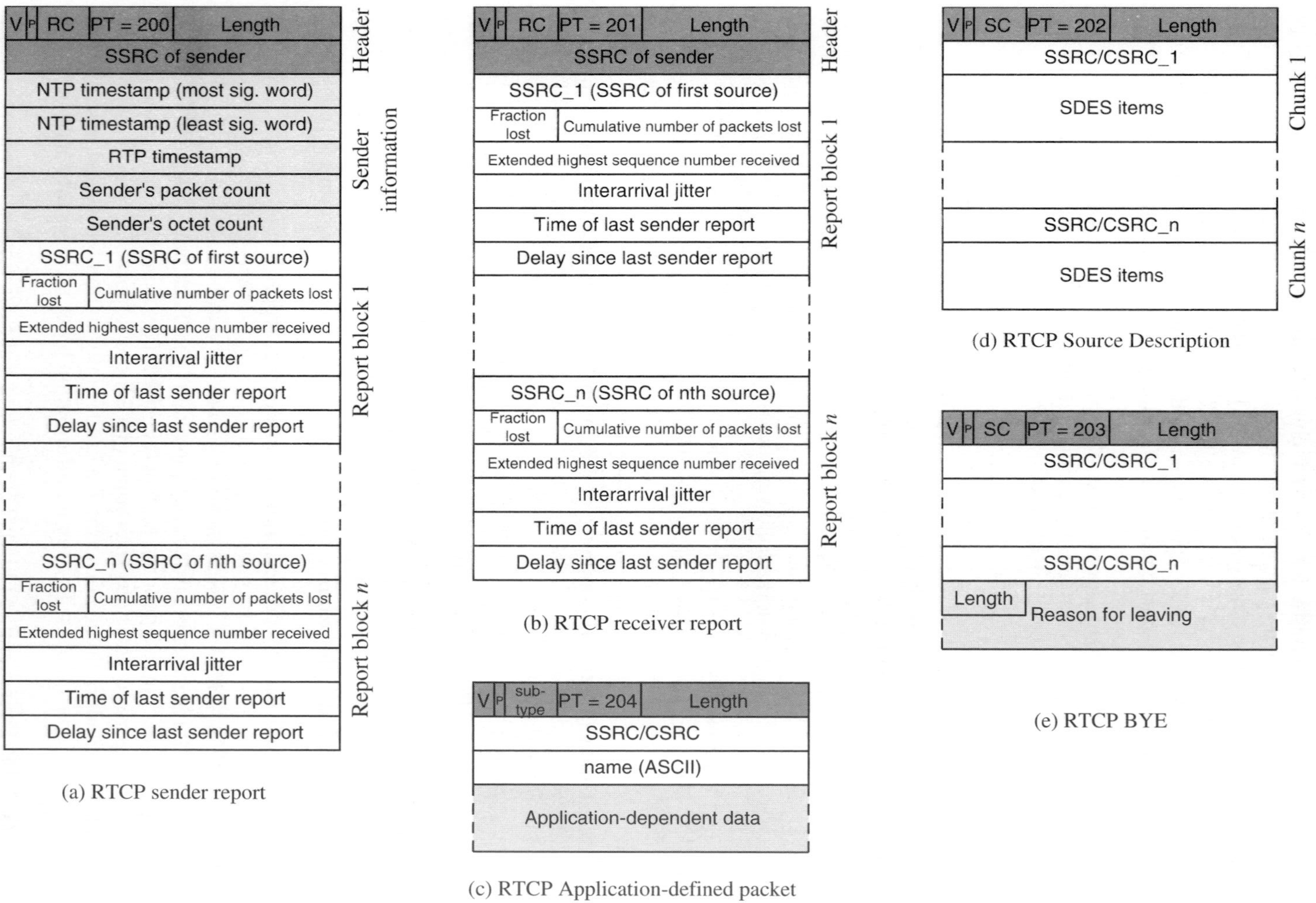

Figure 10.22 RTCP formats.

sender in combination with timestamps returned in receiver reports to measure round-trip time to those receivers.

- **RTP Timestamp (32 bits):** This is a the relative time used to create timestamps in RTP data packets. This lets recipients place this report in the appropriate time sequence with RTP data packets from this source.
- **Sender's Packet Count (32 bits):** Total number of RTP data packets transmitted by this sender so far in this session.
- **Sender's Octet Count (32 bits):** Total number of RTP payload octets transmitted by this sender so far in this session.

Following the sender information block are zero or more **reception report blocks**. One reception block is included for each source from which this participant has received data during this session. Each block includes the following fields:

- **SSRC_n (32 bits):** Identifies the source referred to by this report block.
- **Fraction lost (8 bits):** The fraction of RTP data packets from SSRC_n lost since the previous SR or RR packet was sent.
- **Cumulative number of packets lost (24 bits):** Total number of RTP data packets from SSRC_n lost during this session.
- **Extended highest sequence number received (32 bits):** The least significant 16 bits record the highest RTP data sequence number received from SSRC_n. The most significant 16 bits record the number of times the sequence number has wrapped back to zero.
- **Interarrival jitter (32 bits):** An estimate of the jitter experienced on RTP data packets from SSRC_n, explained later in this chapter.
- **Last SR timestamp (32 bits):** The middle 32 bits of the NTP timestamp in the last SR packet received from SSRC_n. This captures the least significant half of the integer and the most significant half of the fractional part of the timestamp and should be adequate.
- **Delay since last SR (32 bits):** The delay, expressed in units of 2^{-16} seconds, between receipt of the last SR packet from SSRC_n and the transmission of this report block. These last two fields can be used by a source to estimate round-trip time to a particular receiver.

Recall that delay jitter was defined as the maximum variation in delay experienced by packets in a single session. There is no simple way to measure this quantity at the receiver, but it is possible to estimate the average jitter in the following way. At a particular receiver, define the following parameters for a given source:

$S(I)$ = Timestamp from RTP data packet I

$R(I)$ = Time of arrival for RTP data packet I, expressed in RTP timestamp units. The receiver must use the same clock frequency (increment interval) as the source but need not synchronize time values with the source.

$D(I)$ = The difference between the interarrival time at the receiver and the spacing between adjacent RTP data packets leaving the source

$J(I)$ = Estimated average interarrival jitter up to the receipt of RTP data packet I

The value of $D(I)$ is calculated as

$$D(I) = (R(I) - R(I - 1)) - (S(I) - S(I - 1))$$

Thus, $D(I)$ measures how much the spacing between arriving packets differs from the spacing between transmitted packets. In the absence of jitter, the spacings will be the same and $D(I)$ will have a value of 0. The interarrival jitter is calculated continuously as each data packet I is received, according to the formula

$$J(I) = \frac{15}{16}J(I - 1) + \frac{1}{16}|D(I)|$$

$J(I)$ is calculated as an exponential average [14] of observed values of $D(I)$. Only a small weight is given to the most recent observation, so that temporary fluctuations do not invalidate the estimate.

The values in the Sender Report enable senders, receivers, and network managers to monitor conditions on the network as they relate to a particular session. For example, packet loss values give an indication of persistent congestion, while the jitter measures transient congestion. The jitter measure may provide a warning of increasing congestion before it leads to packet loss.

Receiver Report

The format for the Receiver Report (Figure 10.22b) is the same as that for a Sender Report, except that the Packet Type field has a different value and there is no sender information block.

Source Description

The Source Description packet (Figure 10.23d) is used by a source to provide more information about itself. The packet consists of a 32-bit header followed by zero or more chunks, each of which contains information describing this source. Each chunk begins with an identifier for this source or for a contributing source. This is followed by a list of descriptive items. Table 10.4 lists the types of descriptive items defined in RFC 1889.

TABLE 10.4 SDES TYPES (RFC 1889)

Value	Name	Description
0	END	End of SDES list
1	CNAME	Canonical name: unique among all participants within one RTP session
2	NAME	Real user name of the source
3	EMAIL	E-mail address
4	PHONE	Telephone number
5	LOC	Geographic location
6	TOOL	Name of application generating the stream
7	NOTE	Transient message describing the current state of the source
8	PRIV	Private experimental or application-specific extensions

---

[14] For comparison, see Equation 10.4.

Goodbye

The BYE packet indicates that one or more sources are no longer active. This confirms to receivers that a prolonged silence is due to departure rather than network failure. If a BYE packet is received by a mixer, it is forwarded with the list of sources unchanged. The format of the BYE packet consists of a 32-bit header followed by one or more source identifiers. Optionally, the packet may include a textual description of the reason for leaving.

Application-defined Packet

This packet is intended for experimental use for functions and features that are application specific. Ultimately, an experimental packet type that proves generally useful may be assigned a packet type number and become part of the standardized RTCP.

10.5 RECOMMENDED READING

[STAL97] contains a detailed discussion of TCP services and mechanisms. Perhaps the best coverage of the various TCP strategies for flow and congestion control is to be found in [STEV94]. An essential paper for understanding the issues involved is the classic [JACO88].

[COME95a] devotes a chapter to a discussion of the mechanics of running TCP/IP over ATM, including the mapping of IP addresses to ATM addresses and the segmentation of IP datagrams into ATM cells. [ROMA95] is the classic paper on TCP over ATM performance; it introduces the PPD and EPD techniques and evaluates the various factors that affect TCP over UBR throughput. [COME95b] is an illuminating study of TCP over UBR behavior that clearly explains the relationship between TCP flow and congestion control mechanisms and ATM cell discard; another important paper is [PERL95]. [KALY97] is a worthwhile article for understanding the interaction between TCP and ABR.

[THOM96] contains a useful chapter on RTP/RTCP.

COME95a   Comer, D. *Internetworking with TCP/IP, Volume I: Principles, Protocols and Architecture.* Upper Saddle River, NJ: Prentice Hall, 1995.

COME95b   Comer, D.; and Lin, J. "TCP Buffering and Performance Over an ATM Network." *Internetworking: Research and Experience*, March 1995.

JACO88   Jacobson, V. "Congestion Avoidance and Control." *Proceedings, SIGCOMM '88, Computer Communication Review*, August 1988; reprinted in *Computer Communication Review*, January 1995; a slightly revised version is available at ftp.ee.lbl.gov/papers/congavoid.ps.Z.

KALY97   Kalyanaraman, S., et al. "Performance and Buffering Requirements of Internet Protocols over ATM ABR and UBR Services. *IEEE Communications Magazine*, January 1997.

PERL95   Perloff, M., and Reiss, K. "Improvements to TCP Performance in High-Speed ATM Networks." *Communications of the ACM*, February 1995.

ROMA95   Romanow, A., and Floyd. S. "Dynamics of TCP Traffic Over ATM Networks." *IEEE Journal on Selected Areas in Communications*, May 1995.

STAL97   Stallings, W. *Data and Computer Communications, Fifth Edition.* Upper Saddle River, NJ: Prentice-Hall, 1997.

STEV94   Stevens, W. *TCP/IP Illustrated, Volume 1: The Protocols.* Reading, MA: Addison-Wesley, 1994.

THOM96   Thomas, S. *IPng and the TCP/IP Protocols: Implementing the Next Generation Internet.* New York: Wiley, 1996.

Recommended web sites:

- http://www-nrg.ee.lbl.gov: Lawrence Berkeley National Labs Network Research Group. One of the most active groups in the areas covered in this chapter. The site contains many papers and useful pointers.
- http://www.cis.ohio-state.edu/~jain: Raj Jain's home page. This site contains many of his papers on the areas covered in this chapter plus useful pointers.

10.6 PROBLEMS

10.1 Two TCP entities communicate across a reliable network. Let the normalized time to transmit a fixed-length segment equal 1. Assume that the end-to-end propagation delay is 3, and that it takes a time 2 to deliver data from a received segment to the transport user. The sender initially grants a credit of seven segments. The receiver uses a conservative flow control policy and updates its credit allocation at every opportunity. What is the maximum achievable throughput?

10.2 Consider a transport protocol that uses a connection-oriented network service. Suppose that the transport protocol uses a credit allocation flow control scheme, and the network protocol uses a sliding-window scheme. What relationship, if any, should there be between the dynamic window of the transport protocol and the fixed window of the network protocol?

10.3 In a credit flow control scheme such as TCP's, what provision can be made for credit allocations that are lost or misordered in transit?

10.4 Why is the TCP Window Scale option limited to a maximum value of 14?

10.5 One difficulty with the original TCP SRTT estimator is the choice of an initial value . In the absence of any special knowledge of network conditions, the typical approach is to pick an arbitrary value, such as 3 seconds, and hope that this will converge quickly to an accurate value. If this estimate is too small, TCP will perform unnecessary retransmissions. If it is too large, TCP will wait a long time before retransmitting if the first segment is lost. Also, the convergence may be slow, as this problem indicates.
   a. Choose $\alpha = 0.85$ and SRTT(0) = 3 seconds, and assume all measured RTT values = 1 second and no packet loss. What is SRTT(19)? *Hint:* Equation 10.4 can be rewritten to simplify the calculation, using the expression $(1 - \alpha^n)/(1 - \alpha)$.
   b. Now let SRTT(0) = 1 second and assume measured RTT values = 3 seconds and no packet loss. What is SRTT(19)?

10.6 A poor implementation of TCP's sliding-window scheme can lead to extremely poor performance. There is a phenomenon known as the silly window syndrome (SWS), which can easily cause degradation in performance by several factors of 10. As an example of SWS, consider an application that is engaged in a lengthy file transfer, and that TCP is transferring this file in 200-octet segments. The receiver initially provides a credit of 1000. The sender uses up this window with five segments of 200 octets. Now suppose that the receiver returns an acknowledgment to each segment and provides an additional credit of 200 octets for every received segment. From the receiver's point of view, this opens the window back up to 1000 octets. However, from the sender's point of view, if the first acknowledgment arrives after five segments have been sent, a window of only 200 octets becomes available. Assume that at some point, the receiver calculates a window of 200 octets but has only 50 octets to send until it reaches a "push" point. It therefore sends 50 octets in one segment, followed by 150 octets in the next segment, and then resumes transmission of 200-octet segments. What might now happen to cause a performance problem? State the SWS in more general terms.

10.7 TCP mandates that both the receiver and the sender should incorporate mechanisms to cope with SWS.

    a. Suggest a strategy for the receiver. *Hint:* Let the receiver "lie" about how much buffer space is available under certain circumstances. State a reasonable rule of thumb for this.

    b. Suggest a strategy for the sender. *Hint:* Consider the relationship between the maximum possible send window and what is currently available to send.

10.8 Calculate the standard deviation and the mean deviation of the following random variables:

    a. X takes on the values 1, 0, 0, 0 for four equally likely outcomes.

    b. Y takes on the values 1 with probability 0.7 and 0 with probability 0.3.

10.9 In Equation 10.6, rewrite the definition of $SRTT(K + 1)$ so that it is a function of $SERR(K + 1)$. Interpret the result.

10.10 A TCP entity opens a connection and uses slow start. Approximately how many round-trip times are required before TCP can send N segments?

10.11 Although slow start with congestion avoidance is an effective technique for coping with congestion, it can result in long recovery times in high-speed networks, as this problem demonstrates.

    a. Assume a round-trip delay of 60 ms (about what might occur across a continent) and a link with an available bandwidth of 1 Gbps and a segment size of 576 octets. Determine the window size needed to keep the pipe full and the time it will take to reach that window size after a timeout using Jacobson's approach.

    b. Repeat (a) for a segment size of 16 Kilobytes.

10.12 In the discussion of fast retransmit, it is stated that the destination may have to discard some out-of-order segments because its buffer overflows. But doesn't the flow credit issued by the destination control the source's window so that overflow cannot occur?

10.13 In the partial packet discard scheme described in Section 10.3, the final cell in a datagram is not dropped. Why?

10.14 A single video source transmits 30 frames per second, each containing 2 Mb of data. The data experiences a delay jitter of 1 s. What size of delay buffer is required at the destination to eliminate the jitter?

10.15 Argue the effectiveness, or lack thereof, of using RTP as a means of alleviating network congestion for multicast traffic.

10.16 Illustrate how the last two fields in an RTCP SR or RR receiver report block can be used to calculate round-trip propagation time.

PART FIVE

Network Traffic Management

The demands on both IP-based internets and ATM networks are rising both in terms of volume and types of service. IP-based internets were designed for applications that are relatively delay insensitive, can tolerate variations in throughput, and can tolerate packet loss, and they were initially deployed using relatively low-capacity links and supporting a modest demand. Today, IP-based internets are being asked to support high volumes of traffic over high-capacity links, and the traffic mix includes real-time or near-real-time applications that are sensitive to delay and throughput variations and to packet loss. Similarly, ATM networks were designed with a focus on real-time and near-real-time applications, supported through the CBR and VBR services, but today face an increasing demand for service by TCP/IP-based applications with bursty traffic characteristics.

IP-based internets and ATM networks face similar design requirements:

- **Control congestion:** The enemy of any switching network is congestion. It is congestion that prevents the network, be it an ATM network or an IP-based internet, from satisfying its traffic demands in an efficient and responsive manner. If congestion is not controlled, switch or router buffers fill up and packets must be discarded. For applications that can tolerate packet loss, discarding means the packets must be retransmitted, which increases congestion. For applications that are intolerant of packet loss, discarding means reduction in quality of service.
- **Provide low delay:** Delay is minimized when congestion is absent and queue lengths very short. However, to support many applications, network utilization must be relatively high. This suggests at least a degree of congestion and therefore some excess delay.
- **Provide high throughput:** High throughput can be achieved by dedicating capacity. However, to utilize the network efficiently, some amount of statistical multiplexing must be done, which to some extent conflicts with the provision of high throughput.

- **Support QoS:** The provision of different levels of QoS to different traffic flows requires intelligent treatment of packets or cells as they flow through the network.
- **Provide fair service:** Another desirable goal is fairness. In general terms, fairness refers to the provision of an approximately equal amount of capacity to all competing traffic flows with the same QoS.

Although different solutions have been devised to cope with these requirements for IP-based internets and ATM networks, the reader will see a number of similarities and the use of the same design principles in the next two chapters.

ROAD MAP FOR PART FIVE

Chapter 11: Internetwork Traffic Management

Until relatively recently, traffic management by IP routers consisted of dropping packets when buffers became full and letting end-system software, especially TCP, cope with the results. To respond to the new demands on IP-based networks, an elaborate set of mechanisms and protocols are being developed. The umbrella term for this effort is *ISA*. Chapter 11 provides an overview of this architecture, discussing its motivation and functionality. The two important traffic control mechanisms that are part of ISA are also discussed: queuing discipline and packet discard strategy. Two other key elements of ISA are discussed elsewhere: the RTP, in Chapter 10; and Resource ReSerVation Protocol (RSVP), in Chapter 15.

Chapter 11 also includes an overview of the current IP, and the next-generation internet protocol (IPv6).

Chapter 12: Traffic and Congestion Control in ATM Networks

ATM networks are characterized by the use of logical connections (virtual channels and virtual paths) and by traffic contracts that reserve network resources to serve individual connections. A traffic contract specifies the characteristics of the traffic flow to be presented by the source on this connection, plus a requested QoS that the network should provide for this connection. On the basis of the expected traffic pattern and the required QoS, network switches must reserve resources and handle the cell flow to fulfill the traffic contract.

Chapter 12 begins with an overview of the unique requirements for managing cell-based traffic in an ATM network and then looks at the specific parameters (traffic characteristics, QoS parameters) that define a traffic contract. Following this, the overall framework that has been developed for ATM traffic control is explained. The next section examines the traffic control techniques that have been developed for dealing with delay-sensitive traffic (i.e., CBR and VBR). Finally, ATM traffic control techniques to deal with bursty traffic (ABR service) are discussed.

CHAPTER 11

INTERNETWORK TRAFFIC MANAGEMENT

In the Tokyo underground, staff are employed exclusively to collect into baskets sleeves torn from passengers' clothes in the crush and the shoes they have left behind.

—*King Solomon's Carpet,* **Barbara Vine (Ruth Rendell)**

A s the Internet and private internets grow in scale, a host of new demands march steadily into view. Low-volume TELNET conversations are leapfrogged by high-volume client/server applications. To this has more recently been added the tremendous volume of Web traffic, which is increasingly graphics intensive. Now real-time voice and video applications add to the burden.

To cope with these demands, it is not enough to increase internet capacity. Sensible and effective methods for managing the traffic and controlling congestion are needed. This is the focus of this chapter. We begin with an overview of the two extant versions of the internet protocol: IPv4 and IPv6; it is IP that is the primary vehicle for traffic management. Next, we look at an emerging framework for internet traffic management known as ISA. Finally, we discuss important resource allocation and congestion control mechanisms in the areas of queuing discipline and packet discard policy.

11.1 THE INTERNET PROTOCOL

In this section, we look at version 4 of IP, officially defined in RFC 791.[1] Although it is intended that IPv4 will ultimately be replaced by IPv6, it is currently the standard IP used in TCP/IP networks.

The protocol between IP entities is best described with reference to the IP datagram format, shown in Figure 11.1. The fields are as follows:

- **Version (4 bits):** Indicates version number, to allow evolution of the protocol; the value is 4.
- **Internet Header Length (IHL) (4 bits):** Length of header in 32-bit words. The minimum value is five, for a minimum header length of 20 octets.
- **Type of Service (8 bits):** Provides guidance to end-system IP modules and to routers along the datagram's path. Figure 11.2 shows the encoding for this field, as defined in RFC 1349.[2]

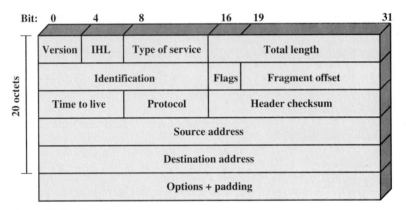

Figure 11.1 IPv4 header.

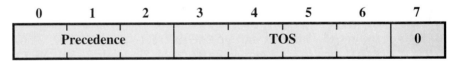

Precedence			TOS				
0	1	2	3	4	5	6	7

Precedence
111	Network control
110	Internetwork control
101	Critical
100	Flash override
011	Flash
010	Immediate
001	Priority
000	Routine

TOS
1000	Minimize delay
0100	Maximize throughput
0010	Maximize reliability
0001	Minimize monetary cost
0000	Normal service

Figure 11.2 IPv4 type of service field.

---

[1] RFC 791, *Internet Protocol*, September 1981.

[2] RFC 1349, *Type of Service in the Internet Protocol Suite*, July 1992.

- **Total Length (16 bits):** Total datagram length, in octets.
- **Identifier (16 bits):** A sequence number that, together with the source address, destination address, and user protocol, is intended to identify a datagram uniquely. Thus, the identifier should be unique for the datagram's source address, destination address, and user protocol for the time during which the datagram will remain in the internet.
- **Flags (3 bits):** Only two of the bits are currently defined. When a datagram is fragmented, the More bit indicates whether this is the last fragment in the original datagram. The Don't Fragment bit prohibits fragmentation when set. This bit may be useful if it is known that the destination does not have the capability to reassemble fragments. However, if this bit is set, the datagram will be discarded if it exceeds the maximum size of an en route subnetwork. Therefore, if the bit is set, it may be advisable to use source routing to avoid subnetworks with small maximum packet size.
- **Fragment Offset (13 bits):** Indicates where in the original datagram this fragment belongs, measured in 64-bit units. This implies that fragments other than the last fragment must contain a data field that is a multiple of 64 bits in length.
- **Time to Live (8 bits):** Specifies how long, in seconds, a datagram is allowed to remain in the internet. Every router that processes a datagram must decrease the TTL by at least one, so the TTL is somewhat similar to a hop count.
- **Protocol (8 bits):** Indicates the next higher-level protocol, which is to receive the data field at the destination.
- **Header Checksum (16 bits):** An error-detecting code applied to the header only. Because some header fields may change during transit (e.g., time to live, segmentation-related fields), this is reverified and recomputed at each router. The checksum field is the 16-bit one's complement addition of all 16-bit words in the header. For purposes of computation, the checksum field is itself initialized to a value of zero.
- **Source Address (32 bits):** Coded to allow a variable allocation of bits to specify the network and the end system attached to the specified network (7 and 24 bits, 14 and 16 bits, or 21 and 8 bits).
- **Destination Address (32 bits):** Same characteristics as source address.
- **Options (variable):** Encodes the options requested by the sending user.
- **Padding (variable):** Used to ensure that the datagram header is a multiple of 32 bits in length.
- **Data (variable):** The data field must be an integer multiple of 8 bits in length. The maximum length of the datagram (data field plus header) is 65,535 octets.

In the remainder of this section, we look at the type-of-service and options fields in more detail.

Type of Service

The **type-of-service (TOS)** field consists of two subfields: a 3-bit precedence subfield and a 4-bit TOS subfield. These subfields serve complementary functions. The TOS subfield provides guidance to the IP entity (in the source or router) on selecting the next hop for this datagram, and the precedence subfield provides guidance about the relative allocation of router resources for this datagram.

TOS Subfield

The TOS field is set by the source system to indicate the type or quality of service that should be provided, if possible, for this datagram. In practice, routers may ignore this subfield. However, if a router implements a TOS capability, there are three possible ways in which the router can respond to the TOS value:

- **Route selection:** A routing decision could be made on the basis of type of service. For example, any datagram requesting minimized delay should not be routed through a subnetwork that includes a satellite link.
- **Subnetwork service:** For the next hop, the router can request a type of service from the subnetwork that most closely matches the requested TOS. A number of networks (e.g., ATM) support some sort of type of service.
- **Queuing discipline:** A router may allow TOS and precedence to affect how queues are handled. For example, a router may give preferential treatment in queues to datagrams requesting minimized delay, or a router might attempt to avoid discarding datagrams that have requested maximized reliability.

Both RFC 1349, which defines the current interpretation of the TOS field, and RFC 1812,[3] which lists requirements for IPv4 routers, focus on the first alternative—namely, the influence of TOS on routing decisions. The way in which a router learns which routes support which TOS is beyond the scope of these specifications. In general, there are two possibilities. First, within a routing domain, a domain administrator could preconfigure the TOS to be associated with different routes. Second, a routing protocol could dynamically monitor the TOS along various routes by monitoring delays, throughputs, and dropped datagrams; OSPF (open shortest path first) is an example of a protocol that supports this capability (see Section 14.3).

When TOS routing is implemented, RFC 1812 specifies the following rules for forwarding a datagram with a nonzero TOS:

1. The router determines all available routes to the destination; if there are none, the datagram is discarded.
2. If one or more routes have the same TOS as the requested TOS, then the router chooses the route with the best metric[4] based on its routing algorithms; this choice is discussed in Part Six of this book.
3. Otherwise, if one or more routes have a TOS = 0 (normal service), then the best of these routes is chosen.
4. Otherwise, the router discards the datagram.

Under this set of rules, a router might actually discard a datagram even though a route is available, because there is no route with either the same TOS or normal ser-

---

[3] RFC 1812, *Requirements for IP Version 4 Routers*, June 1995.

[4] A routing metric is some measure of the "cost" of a particular route. Examples of metrics are the number of subnetwork hops along a route and the total time delay along a route.

TABLE 11.1   RECOMMENDED DEFAULT VALUES FOR TOS FIELD

Protocol	Minimize Delay	Maximize Throughput	Maximize Reliability	Minimize Monetary Cost	Normal Service
TELNET	X				
FTP 　Control 　Data	X	X			
TFTP	X				
SMTP 　Command Phase 　Data Phase	X	X			
Domain Name Service 　UDP Query 　TCP Query 　Zone Transfer	X	X			X
NNTP				X	
ICMP 　Errors 　Requests 　Responses *					X X
Any IGP			X		
EGP					X
SNMP			X		
BOOTP					X

* An ICMP message may be sent with a TOS other than 0000, in which case the response should have the same TOS.

vice. In practice, routing algorithms always support a TOS = 0 route for any destination that is reachable.

Table 11.1 shows the recommended TOS values that should be requested by common protocols.

Precedence Subfield

The precedence field is set to indicate the degree of urgency or priority to be associated with a datagram. The precedence indicator ranges from the highest level of **Network Control** to the lowest level of **Routine**. The Network Control level is intended for use only within a subnetwork. For example, if a subnetwork management entity needs to send control information to a host attached to the same subnetwork, this precedence level would be used and could be supported by actions in the sending IP entity. The **Internetwork Control** level is intended for router-based control messages; an example is the exchange of routing information. The remaining levels have suggestive titles but no precise definition for general use.[5]

Again, in practice, routers may ignore this subfield. As with the TOS subfield, if a router supports the precedence subfield, there are three approaches to responding: route selection, subnetwork service, and queuing discipline. Among routes with equal routing metrics, a particular route may be selected if the router has a smaller queue for that route or if the next hop on that route supports subnetwork precedence or priority (e.g., a token ring network supports priority). Regardless of the route chosen, if the subnetwork on the next hop supports precedence, then that service is invoked.

However, it is intended that the principal effect of the precedence subfield is in relationship to the queuing discipline at the router. The way in which a router deals with precedence is explored in more detail in Section 11.4. Here, we summarize the recommendations in RFC 1812, which fall into two categories:

- **Queue service**
  a. Routers SHOULD implement precedence-ordered queue service. Precedence-ordered queue service means that when a packet is selected for output on a (logical) link, the packet of highest precedence that has been queued for that link is sent.
  b. Any router MAY implement other policy-based throughput management procedures that result in other than strict precedence ordering, but it MUST be configurable to suppress them (i.e., use strict ordering).

- **Congestion control.** When a router receives a packet beyond its storage capacity, it must discard it or some other packet or packets.
  a. A router MAY discard the packet it has just received; this is the simplest but not the best policy.
  b. Ideally, the router should select a packet from one of the sessions most heavily abusing the link, given that the applicable quality-of-service policy permits this. A recommended policy in datagram environments using FIFO queues is to discard a packet randomly selected from the queue. An equivalent algorithm in routers using fair queues is to discard from the longest queue or that using the greatest virtual time (this strategy is explained in Section 11.4). A router MAY use these algorithms to determine which packet to discard.
  c. If precedence-ordered queue service is implemented and enabled, the router MUST NOT discard a packet whose IP precedence is higher than that of a packet that is not discarded.
  d. A router MAY protect packets whose IP headers request the maximize reliability TOS, except where doing so would be in violation of the previous rule.

---

[5] These terms are meaningful in U.S. Department of Defense applications; they are standard defense messaging labels.

e. A router MAY protect fragmented IP packets, on the theory that dropping a fragment of a datagram may increase congestion by causing all fragments of the datagram to be retransmitted by the source.

f. To help prevent routing perturbations or disruption of management functions, the router MAY protect packets used for routing control, link control, or network management from being discarded. Dedicated routers (i.e., routers that are not also general-purpose hosts, terminal servers, etc.) can achieve an approximation of this rule by protecting packets whose source or destination is the router itself.

IPv4 Options

The options field is a variable-length field that, if present, specifies one or more options related to this datagram. The options currently defined are as follows:

- **Security:** Allows a security label to be attached to a datagram.
- **Source routing:** A sequenced list of router addresses that specifies the route to be followed. Routing may be strict (only identified routers may be visited) or loose (other intermediate routers may be visited).
- **Route recording:** A field is allocated to record the sequence of routers visited by the datagram.
- **Timestamping:** The source IP entity and some or all intermediate routers add a timestamp (precision to milliseconds) to the data unit as it goes by.

11.2 IPV6

For decades, the keystone of the TCP/IP protocol architecture has been IPv4. In 1995, the Internet Engineering Task Force issued a specification for a next-generation IP, known then as IPng. This specification was turned into a standard in 1996 known as IPv6. IPv6 provides a number of functional enhancements over the existing IP, designed to accommodate the higher speeds of today's networks and the mix of data streams, including graphic and video, that are becoming more prevalent. But the driving force behind the development of the new protocol was the need for more addresses. The current IP uses a 32-bit address to specify a source or destination. With the explosive growth of the Internet and of private networks attached to the Internet, this address length became insufficient to accommodate all of the systems needing addresses. To meet the need, IPv6 includes 128-bit source and destination address fields.

Ultimately, all of the installations using TCP/IP are expected to migrate from the IPv4 to IPv6, but this process will take many years if not decades.

Table 11.2 lists some of the key defining documents for IPv6. In this section, we will provide an overview, focusing on those aspects that relate to traffic management.

TABLE 11.2 IPV6 RFCs

RFC Number	Title	Date
1752	The Recommendation for the IP Next Generation Protocol	January 1995
1809	Using the Flow Label in IPv6	June 1995
1881	IPv6 Address Allocation Management	December 1995
1883	Internet Protocol, Version 6 Specification	December 1995
1884	IP Version 6 Addressing Architecture	December 1995
1885	Internet Control Message Protocol (ICMPv6) for the Internet Protocol Version 6 (IPv6) Specification	December 1995
1886	DNS Extensions to Support IP Version 6	December 1995
1887	An Architecture for IPv6 Unicast Address Allocation	December 1995
1897	IPv6 Testing Address Allocation	January 1996
1924	A Compact Representation of IPv6 Addresses	April 1996
1933	Transition Mechanisms for IPv6 Hosts and Routers	April 1996

IPv6 Formats

An IPv6 protocol data unit (known as a packet) has the following general form:

IPv6 Header	Extension Header	• • •	Extension Header	Transport-level PDU

←——— 40 octets ———→ ←——————— 0 or more ———————→

The only header that is required is referred to simply as the IPv6 header. This is of fixed size with a length of 40 octets, compared to 20 octets for the mandatory portion of the IPv4 header. The following extension headers have been defined:

- **Hop-by-Hop Options header:** Defines special options that require hop-by-hop processing.
- **Routing header:** Provides extended routing, similar to IPv4 source routing.
- **Fragment header:** Contains fragmentation and reassembly information.
- **Authentication header:** Provides packet integrity and authentication.
- **Encapsulating Security Payload header:** Provides privacy.
- **Destination Options header:** Contains optional information to be examined by the destination node.

The IPv6 standard recommends that, when multiple extension headers are used, the IPv6 headers appear in the following order:

1. IPv6 header: Mandatory, must always appear first.
2. Hop-by-Hop Options header
3. Destination Options header: For options to be processed by the first destination that appears in the IPv6 Destination Address field plus subsequent destinations listed in the Routing Header.

4. Routing header
5. Fragment header
6. Authentication header
7. Encapsulating Security Payload header
8. Destination Options header: For options to be processed only by the final destination of the packet.

Figure 11.3 shows an example of an IPv6 packet that includes an instance of each header. Note that the IPv6 header and each extension header include a Next Header field (except the encapsulating security payload header). This field identifies the type of the immediately following header. If the next header is an extension header, then this field contains the type identifier of that header. Otherwise, this

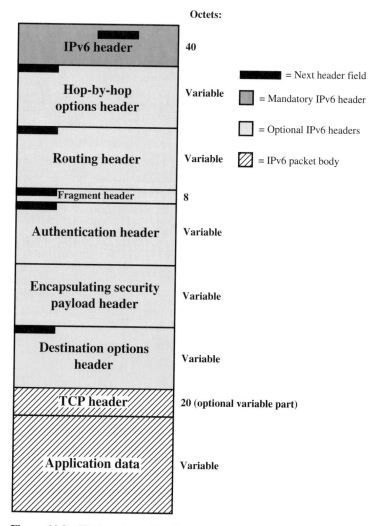

Figure 11.3   IPv6 packet with all extension headers.

field contains the protocol identifier of the upper-layer protocol using IPv6 (typically a transport-level protocol), using the same values as the IPv4 Protocol field. In the figure, the upper-layer protocol is TCP, so the upper-layer data carried by the IPv6 packet consists of a TCP header followed by a block of application data.

We first look at the main IPv6 header and then examine each of the extensions in turn.

IPv6 Header

The IPv6 header has a fixed length of 40 octets, consisting of the following fields (Figure 11.4):

- **Version (4 bits):** Internet Protocol version number; the value is 6.
- **Priority (4 bits):** Priority value, discussed later in this chapter.
- **Flow Label (24 bits):** May be used by a host to label those packets for which it is requesting special handling by routers within a network; discussed later.
- **Payload Length (16 bits):** Length of the remainder of the IPv6 packet following the header, in octets. In other words, this is the total length of all of the extension headers plus the transport-level PDU.
- **Next Header (8 bits):** Identifies the type of header immediately following the IPv6 header; this will either be an IPv6 extension header or a higher-layer header, such as TCP or UDP.
- **Hop Limit (8 bits):** The remaining number of allowable hops for this packet. The Hop Limit is set to some desired maximum value by the source and decremented by 1 by each node that forwards the packet. The packet is discarded if Hop Limit is decremented to zero. This is a simplification over the processing implied the Time-to-Live field of IPv4. The consensus was that the extra effort in accounting for time intervals in IPv4 added no significant value to the protocol. In fact, IPv4 routers, as a general rule, treat the Time-to-Live field as a Hop Limit field.

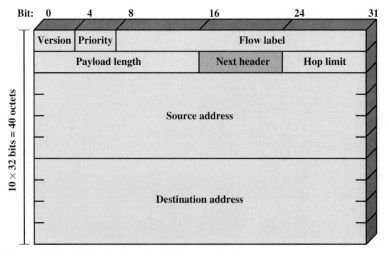

Figure 11.4 IPv6 header.

- **Source Address (128 bits):** The address of the originator of the packet.
- **Destination Address (128 bits):** The address of the intended recipient of the packet. This may not in fact be the intended ultimate destination if a Routing header is present, as explained later.

Although the IPv6 header is longer than the mandatory portion of the IPv4 header (40 octets versus 20 octets), it contains fewer fields (8 versus 12). Thus, routers have less processing to do per header, which should speed up routing.

Priority Field

The 4-bit priority field enables a source to identify the desired transmit and delivery priority of each packet relative to other packets from the same source. In fact, the field enables the source to identify two separate priority-related characteristics of each packet. First, packets are classified as being part of traffic either for which the source is providing congestion control or traffic for which the source is not providing congestion control; and second, packets are assigned one of eight levels of relative priority within each classification. Figure 11.5 illustrates the interpretation of priority-field values.

Congestion-controlled-traffic refers to traffic for which the source "backs off" in response to congestion. An example is the TCP congestion control mechanism, described in Chapter 10.

The nature of congestion-controlled traffic is that it is acceptable for there to be variable amount of delay in the delivery of packets and even for packets to arrive out of order. IPv6 defines the following categories of congestion-controlled traffic, in order of decreasing priority:

- **Internet control traffic:** This is the most important traffic to deliver, especially during times of high congestion. For example, routing protocols such as OSPF and BGP (border gateway protocol) need to receive updates concerning traffic conditions so that they can adjust routes to try to relieve congestion. Management protocols, such as SNMP, need to be able to report congestion to

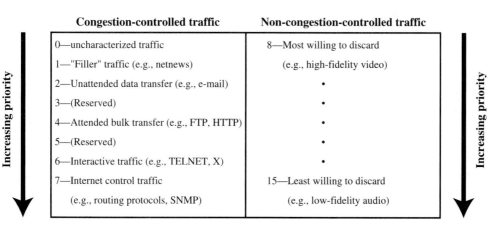

Congestion-controlled traffic	Non-congestion-controlled traffic
0—uncharacterized traffic	8—Most willing to discard
1—"Filler" traffic (e.g., netnews)	(e.g., high-fidelity video)
2—Unattended data transfer (e.g., e-mail)	•
3—(Reserved)	•
4—Attended bulk transfer (e.g., FTP, HTTP)	•
5—(Reserved)	•
6—Interactive traffic (e.g., TELNET, X)	•
7—Internet control traffic	15—Least willing to discard
(e.g., routing protocols, SNMP)	(e.g., low-fidelity audio)

Increasing priority (left) / Increasing priority (right)

Figure 11.5   IPv6 priorities.

network management applications and be able to perform dynamic reconfiguration and to alter performance-related parameters to cope with congestion.

- **Interactive traffic:** After Internet control traffic, the most important traffic to support is interactive traffic, such as on-line user-to-host connections. User efficiency is critically dependent on rapid response time during interactive sessions, so delay must be minimized.

- **Attended bulk transfer:** These are applications that may involve the transfer of a large amount of data and for which the user is generally waiting for the transfer to complete. This category differs from interactive traffic in the sense that the user is prepared to accept a larger amount of delay for the bulk transfer than experienced during an interactive dialogue. A good example of this is FTP. Another example is hypertext transfer protocol (HTTP), which supports Web browser-server interaction.[6]

- **Unattended data transfer:** These are applications that are initiated by a user but that are not expected to be delivered instantly. Generally, the user will not wait for the transfer to be complete, but will go on to other tasks. The best example of this category is electronic mail.

- **Filler traffic:** This is traffic that is expected to be handled in the background when other forms of traffic have been delivered. USENET messages are good examples.

- **Uncharacterized traffic:** If the upper-layer application gives IPv6 no guidance about priority, then the traffic is assigned this lowest-priority value.

Non-congestion-controlled traffic is traffic for which a constant data rate and a constant delivery delay, or at least relatively smooth data rate and delivery delay, are desirable. Examples are real-time video and audio. In these cases, it makes no sense to retransmit discarded packets and it further is important to maintain a smooth delivery flow. Eight levels of priority are allocated for this type of traffic, from the lowest priority 8 (most willing to discard) to the highest priority 15 (least willing to discard). In general, the criterion is how much the quality of the received traffic will deteriorate with the dropping of some packets. For example, low-fidelity audio, such as a telephone voice conversation, would typically be assigned a high priority. The reason is that the loss of a few packets of audio is readily apparent as clicks and buzzes on the line. On the other hand, a high-fidelity video signal contains a fair amount of redundancy and the loss of a few packets will probably not be noticeable; therefore, this traffic is assigned a relatively low priority.

There is no priority relationship implied between the congestion-controlled priorities on the one hand and the non-congestion-controlled priorities on the other hand. Priorities are relative only within each category.

Flow Label

The IPv6 standard defines a flow as a sequence of packets sent from a particular source to a particular (unicast or multicast) destination for which the source

---

[6] In the case of HTTP, the duration of the underlying connection may be too brief for the sender to receive feedback and therefore HTTP may not do congestion control.

desires special handling by the intervening routers. A flow is uniquely identified by the combination of a source address and a nonzero 24-bit flow label. Thus, all packets that are to be part of the same flow are assigned the same flow label by the source.

From the source's point of view, a flow typically will be a sequence of packets that are generated from a single application instance at the source and that have the same transfer service requirements. A flow may comprise a single TCP connection or even multiple TCP connections; an example of the use of multiple TCP connections is a file transfer application, which could have one control connection and multiple data connections. A single application may generate a single flow or multiple flows. An example of the use of multiple flows is multimedia conferencing, which might have one flow for audio and one for graphic windows, each with different transfer requirements in terms of data rate, delay, and delay variation.

From the router's point of view, a flow is a sequence of packets that share attributes that affect how they are handled by the router. These include path, resource allocation, discard requirements, accounting, and security attributes. The router may treat packets from different flows differently in a number of ways, including allocating different buffer sizes, giving different precedence in terms of forwarding, and requesting different quality of service from subnetworks.

There is no special significance to any particular flow label. Instead the special handling to be provided for a packet flow must be declared in some other way. For example, a source might negotiate or request special handling ahead of time from routers by means of a control protocol, or at transmission time by information in one of the extension headers in the packet, such as the Hop-by-Hop Options header. Examples of special handling that might be requested include some sort of nondefault quality of service and some form of real-time service.

In principle, all of a user's requirements for a particular flow could be defined in an extension header and included with each packet. If we wish to leave the concept of flow open to include a wide variety of requirements, this design approach could result in very large packet headers. The alternative, adopted for IPv6, is the flow label, in which the flow requirements are defined prior to flow commencement and a unique flow label is assigned to the flow. In this case, the router must save flow requirement information about each flow.

The following rules apply to the flow label:

1. Hosts or routers that do not support the Flow Label field must set the field to zero when originating a packet, pass the field unchanged when forwarding a packet, and ignore the field when receiving a packet.

2. All packets originating from a given source with the same nonzero Flow Label must have the same Destination Address, Source Address, Priority, Hop-by-Hop Options header contents (if this header is present), and Routing header contents (if this header is present). The intent is that a router can decide how to route and process the packet by simply looking up the flow label in a table and without examining the rest of the header.

3. The source assigns a flow label to a flow. New flow labels must be chosen (pseudo-) randomly and uniformly in the range 1 to $2^{24} - 1$, subject to the restriction that a source must not reuse a flow label for a new flow within the lifetime of the existing flow.

This last point requires some elaboration. The router must maintain information about the characteristics of each active flow that may pass through it, presumably in some sort of table. To forward packets efficiently and rapidly, table lookup must be efficient. One alternative is to have a table with 2^{24} (over 16 million) entries, one for each possible flow label; this imposes an unnecessary memory burden on the router. Another alternative is to have one entry in the table per active flow, include the flow label with each entry, and require the router to search the entire table each time a packet is encountered. This imposes an unnecessary processing burden on the router. Instead, most router designs are likely to use some sort of hash table approach. With this approach a moderate-sized table is used, and each flow entry is mapped into the table using a hashing function on the flow label. The hashing function might simply be the low-order few bits (say 10 or 12) of the flow label or some simple calculation on the 24 bits of the flow label. In any case, the efficiency of the hash approach typically depends on the flow labels being uniformly distributed over their possible range (hence requirement number 3 in the preceding list).

IPv6 Addresses

IPv6 addresses are 128 bits in length. Addresses are assigned to individual interfaces on nodes, not to the nodes themselves.[7] A single interface may have multiple unique unicast addresses. Any of the unicast addresses associated with a node's interface may be used to uniquely identify that node.

The combination of long addresses and multiple addresses per interface enables improved routing efficiency over IPv4. In IPv4, addresses generally do not have a structure that assists routing, and therefore a router may need to maintain a huge table of routing paths. Longer internet addresses allow for aggregating addresses by hierarchies of network, access provider, geography, corporation, and so on. Such aggregation should make for smaller routing tables and faster table lookups. The allowance for multiple addresses per interface would allow a subscriber that uses multiple access providers across the same interface to have separate addresses aggregated under each provider's address space.

IPv6 allows three types of addresses:

- **Unicast:** An identifier for a single interface. A packet sent to a unicast address is delivered to the interface identified by that address.
- **Anycast:** An identifier for a set of interfaces (typically belonging to different nodes). A packet sent to an anycast address is delivered to one of the interfaces identified by that address (the "nearest" one, according to the routing protocols' measure of distance).
- **Multicast**: An identifier for a set of interfaces (typically belonging to different nodes). A packet sent to a multicast address is delivered to all interfaces identified by that address.

---

[7] In IPv6, *a node* is any device that implements IPv6; this includes hosts and routers.

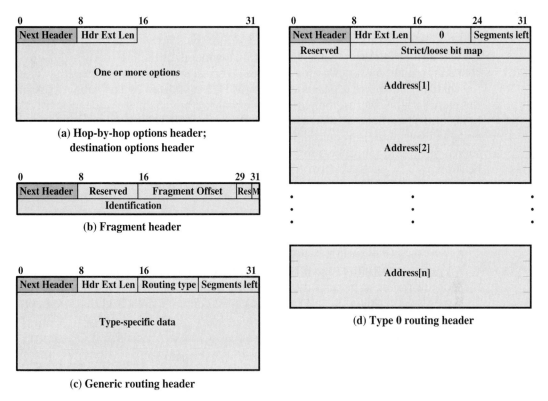

Figure 11.6   IPv6 extension headers.

Hop-by-Hop Options Header

The Hop-by-Hop Options header carries optional information that, if present, must be examined by every router along the path. This header consists of the following (Figure 11.6a):

- **Next Header (8 bits):** Identifies the type of header immediately following this header.
- **Header Extension Length (8 bits):** Length of this header in 64-bit units, not including the first 64 bits.
- **Options:** A variable-length field consisting of one or more option definitions.

In the IPv6 standard, only one option is so far specified: the Jumbo Payload option, used to send IPv6 packets with payloads longer than $2^{16} - 1 = 65,535$ octets. The Option Data field of this option is 32 bits long and gives the length of the packet in octets, excluding the IPv6 header. For such packets, the Payload Length field in the IPv6 header must be set to zero, and there must be no Fragment header. With this option, IPv6 supports packet sizes up to more than 4 billion octets. This facilitates the transmission of large video packets and enables IPv6 to make the best use of available capacity over any transmission medium.

Fragment Header

In IPv6, fragmentation may only be performed by source nodes, not by routers along a packet's delivery path. To take full advantage of the internetworking environment, a node must perform a path discovery algorithm that enables it to learn the smallest maximum transmission unit (MTU) supported by any subnetwork on the path. In other words, the path discovery algorithm enables a node to learn the MTU of the "bottleneck" subnetwork on the path. With this knowledge, the source node will fragment, as required, for each given destination address. Otherwise the source must limit all packets to 576 octets, which is the minimum MTU that must be supported by each subnetwork.

The fragment header consists of the following (Figure 11.6b):

- **Next Header (8 bits):** Identifies the type of header immediately following this header.
- **Reserved (8 bits):** For future use.
- **Fragment Offset (13 bits):** Indicates where in the original packet the payload of this fragment belongs. It is measured in 64-bit units. This implies that fragments (other than the last fragment) must contain a data field that is a multiple of 64 bits long.
- **Res (2 bits):** Reserved for future use.
- **M Flag (1 bit):** 1 = more fragments; 0 = last fragment.
- **Identification (32 bits):** Intended to uniquely identify the original packet. The identifier must be unique for the packet's source address and destination address for the time during which the packet will remain in the internet. All fragments with the same identifier, source address and destination address are reassembled to form the original packet.

Routing Header

The Routing header contains a list of one or more intermediate nodes to be visited on the way to a packet's destination. All routing headers start with a 32-bit block consisting of four 8-bit fields, followed by routing data specific to a given routing type (Figure 11.6c). The four 8-bit fields are as follows:

- **Next Header:** Identifies the type of header immediately following this header.
- **Header Extension Length:** Length of this header in 64-bit units, not including the first 64 bits.
- **Routing Type:** Identifies a particular Routing header variant. If a router does not recognize the Routing Type value, it must discard the packet.
- **Segments Left:** Number of route segments remaining; that is, the number of explicitly listed intermediate nodes still to be visited before reaching the final destination.

The only specific routing header format defined in RFC 1883 is the Type 0 Routing header (Figure 11.6d). In addition to the leading four 8-bit fields, the Type 0 header includes a 24-bit Strict/Loose Bit Map. The bits of the field are considered to be numbered from left to right (bit 0 through bit 23), with each bit corresponding to one segment. Each bit indicates whether the corresponding next destination address must be a neighbor of the preceding address (1 = strict, must be a neighbor; 0 = loose, need not be a neighbor).

When using the Type 0 Routing header, the source node does not place the ultimate destination address in the IPv6 header. Instead, that address is the last address listed in the Routing header (Address[n] in Figure 11.6d), and the IPv6 header contains the destination address of the first desired router on the path. The Routing header will not be examined until the packet reaches the node identified in the IPv6 header. At that point, the packet IPv6 and Routing header contents are updated and the packet is forwarded. The update consists of placing the next address to be visited in the IPv6 header and decrementing the Segments Left field in the Routing header.

Destination Options Header

The Destination Options header carries optional information that, if present, is examined only by the packet's destination node. The format of this header is the same as that of the Hop-by-Hop Options header (Figure 11.6a).

11.3 INTEGRATED SERVICES ARCHITECTURE

Historically, IP-based internets have been able to provide a simple best-effort delivery service to all applications using an internet. Although the IPv4 header is equipped with fields that can specify precedence and type of service, this information has generally been ignored by routers, both in the selection of routes and the treatment of individual packets.

But the needs of users have changed. A company may have spent millions of dollars installing an IP-based internet designed to transport data among LANs, but now finds that new real-time, multimedia, and multicasting applications are not well supported by such a configuration. The only networking scheme designed from day one to support both traditional TCP and UDP traffic and real-time traffic is ATM. However, reliance on ATM means either constructing a second networking infrastructure for real-time traffic or replacing the existing IP-based configuration with ATM, both of which are costly alternatives.

Thus, there is a strong need to be able to support a variety of traffic with a variety of QoS requirements, within the TCP/IP architecture. The RTP, described in Chapter 10, is one component in meeting the need. However, the fundamental requirement is to add new functionality to routers and a means for requesting QoS-based service from internets. To meet this requirement, the IETF is developing a suite of standards under the general umbrella of the Integrated Services Architecture. ISA, which is intended to provide QoS transport over IP-based internets, is defined in overall terms in RFC 1633,[8] while a number of other documents are being

---

[8] RFC 1633, *Integrated Services in the Internet Architecture: An Overview*, July 1994.

developed to fill in the details. Already, a number of vendors have implemented portions of the ISA in routers and end-system software.

This section provides an overview of ISA.

Internet Traffic

Traffic on a network or internet can be divided into two broad categories: elastic and inelastic. A consideration of their differing requirements clarifies the need for an enhanced internet architecture.

Elastic Traffic

Elastic traffic is that which can adjust, over wide ranges, to changes in delay and throughput across an internet and still meet the needs of its applications. This is the traditional type of traffic supported on TCP/IP-based internets and is the type of traffic for which internets were designed. Applications that generate such traffic typically use TCP or UDP as a transport protocol. In the case of UDP, the application will use as much capacity as is available up to the rate that the application generates data. In the case of TCP, the application will use as much capacity as is available up to the maximum rate that the end-to-end receiver can accept data. Also with TCP, traffic on individual connections adjusts to congestion by reducing the rate at which data are presented to the network; this involves the RTT backoff and slow-start mechanisms described in Section 10.2.

Applications that can be classified as elastic include the common applications that operate over TCP or UDP, including file transfer (FTP), electronic mail (SMTP), remote logon (TELNET), network management (SNMP), and Web access (HTTP). However, note that there are differences among the requirements of these applications. For example,

- E-mail is generally quite insensitive to changes in delay.
- When file transfer is done on-line, as it frequently is, the user expects the delay to be proportional to the file size and so is sensitive to changes in throughput.
- With network management, delay is generally not a serious concern. However, if failures in an internet are the cause of congestion, then the need for SNMP messages to get through with minimum delay increases with increased congestion.
- Interactive applications, such as remote logon and Web access, are quite sensitive to delay.

It is important to realize that it is not per-packet delay that is the quantity of interest. As noted in [CLAR95], observation of real delays across the Internet suggest that wide variations in delay do not occur. Because of the congestion control mechanisms in TCP, when congestion develops, delays only increase modestly before the arrival rate from the various TCP connections slow down. Instead, the quality of service perceived by the user relates to the total elapsed time to transfer an element of the current application. For an interactive TELNET-based application, the element may be a single keystroke or single line. For a Web access, the element is a Web page, which could be as little as a few kilobytes or could be substantially larger for an image-rich page. For a scientific application, the element could be many megabytes of data.

For very small elements, the total elapsed time is dominated by the delay time across the internet. However, for larger elements, the total elapsed time is dictated by the sliding-window performance of TCP and is therefore dominated by the throughput achieved over the TCP connection. Thus, for large transfers, the transfer time is proportional to the size of the file and the degree to which the source slows due to congestion.

It should be clear that even if we confine our attention to elastic traffic, a QoS-based internet service could be of benefit. Without such a service, routers are dealing evenhandedly with arriving IP packets, with no concern for the type of application and whether this packet is part of a large transfer element or a small one. Under such circumstances, and if congestion develops, it is unlikely that resources will be allocated in such a way as to meet the needs of all applications fairly. When inelastic traffic is added to the mix, matters are even more unsatisfactory.

Inelastic Traffic

Inelastic traffic is that which does not easily adapt, if at all, to changes in delay and throughput across an internet. The prime example is real-time traffic, which was described in Section 10.4. The requirements for inelastic traffic may include the following:

- **Throughput:** A minimum throughput value may be required. Unlike most elastic traffic, which can continue to deliver data with perhaps degraded service, many inelastic applications absolutely require a given minimum throughput.
- **Delay:** An example of a delay-sensitive application is stock trading; someone who consistently receives later service will consistently act later, and with greater disadvantage.
- **Jitter:** As explained in Section 10.4, the magnitude of delay variation is a critical factor in real-time applications. The larger the allowable delay, the longer the real delay in delivering the data and the greater the size of the delay buffer required at receivers. Real-time interactive applications, such as teleconferencing, may require a reasonable upper bound on jitter.
- **Packet loss:** Real-time applications vary in the amount of packet loss, if any, that they can sustain.

These requirements are difficult to meet in an environment with variable queuing delays and congestion losses. Accordingly, inelastic traffic introduces two new requirements into the internet architecture. First, some means is needed to give preferential treatment to applications with more demanding requirements. Applications need to be able to state their requirements, either ahead of time in some sort of service request function, or on the fly, by means of fields in the IP packet header. The former approach is preferable: It provides more flexibility in stating requirements, and it enables the network to anticipate demands and deny new requests if the required resources are unavailable. This approach implies the use of some sort of resource reservation protocol.

A second requirement in supporting inelastic traffic in an internet architecture is that elastic traffic must still be supported. Inelastic applications typically do not back off and reduce demand in the face of congestion, in contrast to TCP-based applications. Therefore, in times of congestion, inelastic traffic will continue to supply a high load, and elastic traffic will be crowded off the internet. A reservation protocol can help control this situation by denying service requests that would leave too few resources available to handle current elastic traffic.

ISA Approach

The purpose of ISA is to enable the provision of QoS support over IP-based internets. The central design issue for ISA is how to share the available capacity in times of congestion.

For an IP-based internet that provides only a best-effort service, the tools for controlling congestion and providing service are limited. In essence, routers have two mechanisms to work with:

- **Routing algorithm:** Most routing protocols in use in internets allow routes to be selected to minimize delay. Routers exchange information to get a picture of the delays throughout the internet. Minimum-delay routing helps to balance loads, thus decreasing local congestion, and helps to reduce delays seen by individual TCP connections.

- **Packet discard:** When a router's buffer overflows, it discards packets. Typically, the most recent packet is discarded. The effect of lost packets on a TCP connection is that the sending TCP entity backs off and reduces its load, thus helping to alleviate internet congestion.

These tools have worked reasonably well, especially with the refinements in TCP congestion control techniques described in Section 10.2. However, as the discussion in the preceding subsection shows, such techniques are inadequate for the variety of traffic now coming to internets.

ISA is an overall architecture within which a number of enhancements to the traditional best-effort mechanisms are being developed. In ISA, each IP packet can be associated with a flow. RFC 1633 defines a flow as a distinguishable stream of related IP packets that results from a single user activity and requires the same QoS. For example, a flow might consist of one transport connection or one video stream distinguishable by the ISA. A flow differs from a TCP connection in two key particulars: A flow is unidirectional, and there can be more than one recipient of a flow (multicast). Typically, an IP packet is identified as a member of a flow on the basis of source and destination IP addresses and port numbers, and protocol type. The flow identifier in the IPv6 header is not necessarily equivalent to an ISA flow, but in future the IPv6 flow identifier could be used in ISA.

ISA makes use of the following functions to manage congestion and provide QoS transport:

- **Admission control:** For QoS transport (other than default best-effort transport), ISA requires that a reservation be made for a new flow. If the routers collectively determine that there are insufficient resources to guarantee the requested QoS, then the flow is not admitted. The protocol RSVP, discussed in Chapter 15, is used to make reservations.

- **Routing algorithm:** The routing decision may be based on a variety of QoS parameters, not just minimum delay. For example, the routing protocol OSPF, discussed in Chapter 14, can select routes based on QoS.
- **Queuing discipline:** A vital element of the ISA is an effective queuing policy that takes into account the differing requirements of different flows. Queuing policies are discussed in Section 11.4.
- **Discard policy:** A queuing policy determines which packet to transmit next if a number of packets are queued for the same output port. A separate issue is the choice and timing of packet discards. A discard policy can be an important element in managing congestion and meeting QoS guarantees. Discard policies are discussed in Section 11.5.

ISA Components

Figure 11.7 is a general depiction of the implementation architecture for ISA within a router. Below the thick horizontal line are the forwarding functions of the router; these are executed for each packet and therefore must be highly optimized. The remaining functions, above the line, are background functions that create data structures used by the forwarding functions.

The principal background functions are as follows:

- **Reservation protocol:** This protocol is used among routers and between routers and end systems to reserve resources for a new flow at a given level of QoS. The reservation protocol is responsible for maintaining flow-specific state information at the end systems and at the routers along the path of the flow. The RSVP protocol described in Chapter 15 is used for this purpose. The

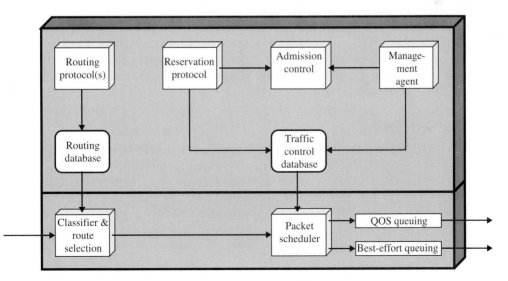

Figure 11.7   Integrated services architecture implemented in router.

reservation protocol updates the traffic control database used by the packet scheduler to determine the service provided for packets of each flow.

- **Admission control:** When a new flow is requested, the reservation protocol invokes the admission control function. This function determines if sufficient resources are available for this flow at the requested QoS. This determination is based on the current level of commitment to other reservations and/or on the current load on the network.

- **Management agent:** A network management agent is able to modify the traffic control database and to direct the admission control module in order to set admission control policies.

- **Routing protocol:** The routing protocol is responsible for maintaining a routing database that gives the next hop to be taken for each destination address and each flow.

These background functions support the main task of the router, which is the forwarding of packets. The two principal functional areas that accomplish forwarding are the following:

- **Classifier and route selection:** For the purposes of forwarding and traffic control, incoming packets must be mapped into classes. A class may correspond to a single flow or to a set of flows with the same QoS requirements. For example, the packets of all video flows or the packets of all flows attributable to a particular organization may be treated identically for purposes of resource allocation and queuing discipline. The selection of class is based on fields in the IP header. Based on the packet's class and its destination IP address, this function determines the next-hop address for this packet.

- **Packet scheduler:** This function manages one or more queues for each output port. It determines the order in which queued packets are transmitted and the selection of packets for discard, if necessary. Decisions are made based on a packet's class, the contents of the traffic control database, and current and past activity on this outgoing port. Part of the packet scheduler's task is that of policing, which is the function of determining whether the packet traffic in a given flow exceeds the requested capacity and, if so, deciding how to treat the excess packets.

ISA Services

ISA service for a flow of packets is defined on two levels. First, a number of general categories of service are provided, each of which provides a certain general type of service guarantees. Second, within each category, the service for a particular flow is specified by the values of certain parameters; together, these values are referred to as a traffic specification (TSpec). Currently, three categories of service are defined:

- Guaranteed
- Controlled load
- Best effort.

An application can request a reservation for a flow for a guaranteed or controlled load QoS, with a TSpec that define the exact amount of service required. If the reservation is accepted, then the TSpec is part of the contract between the data flow and the service. The service agrees to provide the requested QoS as long as the flow's data traffic continues to be described accurately by the TSpec. Packets that are not part of a reserved flow are by default given a best-effort delivery service.

Before looking at the ISA service categories, one general concept should be defined: the token bucket traffic specification. This is a way of characterizing traffic that has three advantages in the context of ISA:

1. Many traffic sources can easily and accurately be defined by a token bucket scheme.
2. The token bucket scheme provides a concise description of the load to be imposed by a flow, enabling the service to determine easily the resource requirement.
3. The token bucket scheme provides the input parameters to a policing function.

A token bucket traffic specification consists of two parameters: a token replenishment rate R and a bucket size B. The token rate R specifies the continually sustainable data rate; that is, over a relatively long period of time, the average data rate to be supported for this flow is R. The bucket size B specifies the amount by which the data rate can exceed R for short periods of time. The exact condition is as follows: During any time period T, the amount of data sent cannot exceed $RT + B$.

Figure 11.8 illustrates this scheme and explains the use of the term *bucket*. The bucket represents a counter that indicates the allowable number of octets of IP data that can be sent at any time. The bucket fills with *octet tokens* at the rate of R (i.e., the counter is incremented R times per second), up to the bucket capacity (up to the maximum counter value). IP packets arrive and are queued for processing. An IP packet may be processed if there are sufficient octet tokens to match the IP data

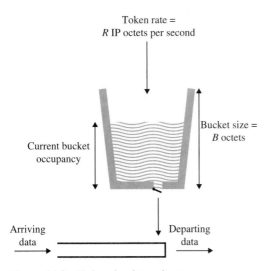

Figure 11.8   Token bucket scheme.

size. If so, the packet is processed and the bucket is drained of the corresponding number of tokens. If a packet arrives and there are insufficient tokens available, then the packet exceeds the TSpec for this flow. The treatment for such packets is not specified in the ISA documents; common actions are relegating the packet to best effort service, discarding the packet, or marking the packet in such a way that it may be discarded in future.

Note that over the long run, the rate of IP data allowed by the token bucket is R. However, if there is an idle or relatively slow period, the bucket capacity builds up, so that at most an additional B octets above the stated rate can be accepted. Thus, B is a measure of the degree of burstiness of the data flow that is allowed.

Guaranteed Service

The key elements of the guaranteed service are as follows:

1. The service provides assured capacity level, or data rate.
2. There is a specified upper bound on the queuing delay through the network. This must be added to the propagation delay, or latency, to arrive at the bound on total delay through the network.
3. There are no queuing losses. That is, no packets are lost due to buffer overflow; packets may be lost due to failures in the network or changes in routing paths.

One category of applications for this service is those that need an upper bound on delay so that a delay buffer can be used for real-time playback of incoming data, and that do not tolerate packet losses because of the degredation in the quality of the output. Another example is applications with hard real-time deadlines.

The guaranteed service is the most demanding service provided by ISA. Because the delay bound is firm, the delay has to be set at a large value to cover rare cases of long queuing delays.

Controlled Load

The key elements of the controlled load service are as follows:

1. The service tightly approximates the behavior visible to applications receiving best-effort service under unloaded conditions.
2. There is no specified upper bound on the queuing delay through the network. However, the service ensures that a very high percentage of the packets do not experience delays that greatly exceed the minimum transit delay (i.e., the delay due to propagation time plus router processing time with no queuing delays).
3. A very high percentage of transmitted packets will be successfully delivered (i.e., almost no queuing loss).

As was mentioned, the risk in an internet that provides QoS for real-time applications is that best-effort traffic is crowded out. This is because best-effort types of applications employ TCP, which will back off in the face of congestion and delays. The controlled load service guarantees that the network will set aside sufficient resources so that an application that receives this service will see a network that responds as if these real-time applications were not present and competing for resources.

The controlled service is useful for applications that have been referred to as adaptive real-time applications [CLAR92]. Such applications do not require an a priori upper bound on the delay through the network. Rather, the receiver measures the jitter experienced by incoming packets and sets the playback point to the minimum delay that still produces a sufficiently low loss rate. For example: video can be adaptive by dropping a frame or delaying the output stream slightly; voice can be adaptive by adjusting silent periods.

11.4 QUEUING DISCIPLINE

An important component of an ISA implementation is the queuing discipline used at the routers. Routers traditionally have used a FIFO queuing discipline, also known as FCFS, at each output port. A single queue is maintained at each output port. When a new packet arrives and is routed to an output port, it is placed at the end of the queue. As long as the queue is not empty, the router transmits packets from the queue, taking the oldest remaining packet next.

There are several drawbacks to the FIFO queuing discipline:

1. No special treatment is given to packets from flows that are of higher priority or are more delay sensitive. If a number of packets from different flows are ready to forward, they are handled strictly in FIFO order.

2. If a number of smaller packets are queued behind a long packet, then FIFO queuing results in a larger average delay per packet than if the shorter packets were transmitted before the longer packet. In general, flows of larger packets get better service.

3. A greedy TCP connection can crowd out more altruistic connections. If congestion occurs and one TCP connection fails to back off, other connections along the same path segment must back off more than they would otherwise have to do.

Fair Queuing

To overcome some of the drawbacks of FIFO queuing, Nagle proposed a scheme called fair queuing (FQ) [NAGL87]. In this scheme, a router maintains multiple queues at each output port. Nagle suggested maintaining one queue for each source (Figure 11.9); it would also be possible to maintain one queue for each flow.

With fair queuing, each incoming packet is placed in the appropriate queue. The queues are serviced in round-robin fashion, taking one packet from each nonempty queue in turn. Empty queues are skipped over.

This scheme is fair in that each busy flow gets to send exactly one packet per cycle. Further, this is a form of load balancing among the various flows. Also note that there is no advantage in being greedy. A greedy flow finds that its queues become long, increasing its delays, whereas other flows are unaffected by this behavior.

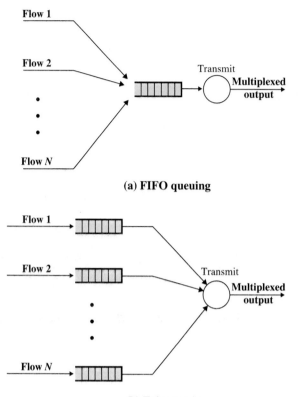

(a) FIFO queuing

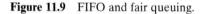

(b) Fair queuing

Figure 11.9 FIFO and fair queuing.

Processor Sharing

A serious drawback to the fair queuing scheme is that short packets are penalized: More capacity goes to flows with longer average packet size compared to flows with shorter average packet size. The reason for this is that each queue transmits one packet per cycle.

This disadvantage is overcome with bit-round fair queuing (BRFQ), which uses packet length as well as flow identification to schedule packets; this technique is described in [DEME90].

To understand BRFQ, let us first consider an ideal policy that is not practical to implement. Set up the multiple queues, as in FQ, but now transmit only one bit from each queue on each round. In this way, longer packets no longer receive an advantage, and each busy source receives exactly the same amount of capacity. In particular, if there are N queues and each of the queues always has a packet to send, then each queue receives exactly $1/N$ of the available capacity.

This bit-by-bit approach is known as processor sharing (PS). To understand what follows, it will be useful to define some terms:

$R(t)$ = number of rounds in the PS service discipline that have occurred up to time t, normalized to the output data rate

$N(t)$ = number of nonempty queues at time t

P_i^α = transmission time for packet i in queue α, normalized to the output data rate

τ_i^α = arrival time for packet i in queue α

S_i^α = value of $R(t)$ when packet i in queue α begins transmission

F_i^α = value of $R(t)$ when packet i in queue α ends transmission

We can think of $R(t)$ as a virtual time, which records the rate of service seen by the packet at the head of a queue. An equivalent definition is

$$R'(t) = \frac{d}{dt} R(t) = \frac{1}{\max[1, N(t)]}$$

As an example, consider three queues with a traffic pattern characterized by the following table:

	Queue α		Queue β		Queue γ
	Packet 1	Packet 2	Packet 1	Packet 2	Packet 1
Real arrival time τ_i	0	2	1	2	3
Transmission time P_i	3	1	1	4	3
Virtual start time S_i	0	3	1	2	3
Virtual finish time F_i	3	4	2	6	5

The values of τ_i and P_i are given; the values of S_i and F_i are determined by the PS queuing policy. The solid lines in Figure 11.10 show the service provided to the three queues. The first packet to arrive at queue α receives one unit of service in the real interval $[0, 1)$, with the virtual time $R(1) = 1$ at the end of that interval. In the real interval $[1, 3)$, bits are being transmitted from two queues, so each receives a service rate of $R' = 1/2$ and accumulates one unit of service in this interval, so that $R(3) = R(1) + 1/2 \times (3 - 1) = 2$. Similarly, in the interval $[3, 9)$, all three queues are active, so each receives service at rate $R' = 1/3$ and accumulates two units of service in this interval. This is enough service for two packets to be completely transmitted from α, one packet from β, and an additional packet from β and one packet from γ to be in progress.

The following recurrence relationships summarize how the PS system evolves in virtual time:

$$F_i^\alpha = S_i^\alpha + P_i^\alpha \tag{11.1}$$
$$S_i^\alpha = \max[F_{i-1}^\alpha, R(\tau_i^\alpha)]$$

Note that from these equations, we can compute a packet's virtual finishing time the moment it arrives. However, we cannot compute the packet's real finishing time on its arrival because the real finishing time depends on future arrivals.

Bit-round Fair Queuing

We wish to transmit entire packets rather than individual bits. BRFQ is designed to emulate a bit-by-bit round-robin discipline. BRFQ is implemented by computing virtual starting and finishing times on the fly as if PS were running. The BRFQ rule

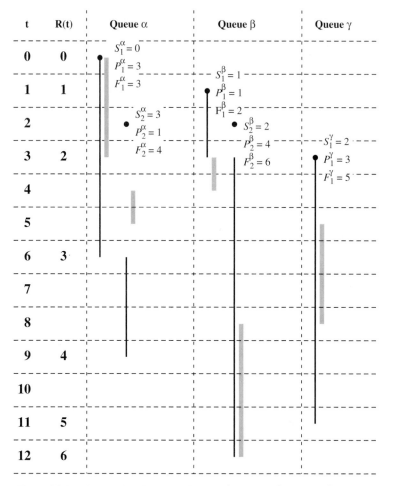

Figure 11.10 Example of PS and BRFQ (based on [GREE92]).

is simply this: Whenever a packet finishes transmission, the next packet sent is the one with the smallest value of F_i^α.

PS and BRFQ are compared in Figure 11.10. The solid lines represent the transmission times under PS, and the gray bars represent BRFQ transmission. Note that the order of transmission of packets, based on either real start time or real finish time, is not exactly the same for BRFQ and PS. Nevertheless, BRFQ gives a good approximation to the performance of PS. In fact, it is demonstrated in [GREE92] that the throughput and average delay experienced by each flow under BRFQ converges to that under PS as time increases.

Figure 11.11a shows timing diagrams of three flows at a router output port. In the first three rows, vertical arrows denote the arrival times of packets, with length proportional to packet size. The packets arriving on flow 1 are twice as long as those on the other flows. The next three rows show the packet transmission times under various queuing disciplines.[9] The shading is provided simply to clarify the relation-

---

[9] We will use the convention that ties are resolved in favor of the flow with the smallest flow number.

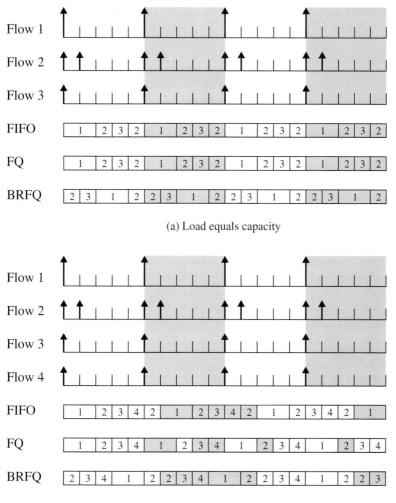

Figure 11.11 Comparison of FIFO and fair queuing.

ship between the arrival timing diagrams and the transmission timing diagrams. In this case, both FIFO and FQ yield the same output pattern. BRFQ provides the same amount of service to all flows as do the other disciplines, but when multiple packets arrive at the same time, preference is given to short packets. Accordingly, flows 2 and 3 experience lower average delay than under FIFO or FQ.

In Figure 11.11b, an additional flow is added, so that the router cannot keep up with the demand. Delays will increase as the queue lengths grow. If all of the sources are well-behaved TCP entities, then the flows will back off and congestion eases. Meanwhile, differences are apparent among the different policies. Under FIFO, the delays experienced by all flows uniformly grow at a rate of one time unit every five time units. With fair queuing, only flow 2 is penalized; all other flows experience no increase in delay. Consequently, the queue for flow 2 is the only one that grows. Eventually, flow 2 will detect the growing delay and back off. In one sense, this is fair, because each flow is allowed to send one packet per cycle. But the demand from flow 1 and flow 2 is in fact identical, and flow 1 gains an advantage because it uses larger packets. BRFQ instead is fair on the basis of amount of data transmitted rather than number of packets transmitted. Like FIFO, BRFQ causes all delays to increase, but in the case of BRFQ, smaller packets are given preference.

Generalized Processor Sharing

BRFQ is an improvement over FQ or FIFO in that it fairly allocates the available capacity among all active flows through a node. However, it is not able to provide different amounts of the capacity to different flows. To support QoS transport, this differential allocation capability is needed. The approach that has received the widest acceptance is an enhancement of BRFQ known as weighted fair queuing (WFQ).[10] Again, it will clarify the description if we first look at a bit-by-bit round robin version.

To take in to account the differing demands of different sources, we can generalize the PS discipline to allow for arbitrary capacity allocations. With GPS, each flow α is assigned a weight ϕ_α that determines how many bits are transmitted from that queue during each round. Thus, if the weight for a given flow is 5, then during each round that the queue is nonempty, 5 bits will be transmitted. Some thought should convince you that we can model this process by modifying Equation 11.1 as follows:

$$F_i^\alpha = S_i^\alpha + \frac{P_i^\alpha}{\phi_\alpha} \tag{11.2}$$

$$S_i^\alpha = \max[F_{i-1}^\alpha, R(\tau_i^\alpha)]$$

In effect, we set the effective packet length to $1/\phi_\alpha$ times the true packet length. It is easy to see that, at any given time, the service rate g_i for a nonempty flow i is

$$g_i = \frac{\phi_i}{\sum_j \phi_j} C \tag{11.3}$$

where the sum is taken over all active queues and C is the outgoing link data rate.

GPS is attractive because it provides a means of responding to different service requests. If a source requests a given service rate g_i for a flow, then the node can grant the request if sufficient capacity is available and can assign the proper weight to guarantee the service. Equally important, GPS provides a way of guaranteeing that delays for a well-behaved flow do not exceed some bound. Consider a set of flows that are defined by, and limited to, the token bucket specification described in Section 11.3, where B_i and R_i are the bucket size and token rate respectively for flow i. Now let the weight assigned to each flow equal the token rate; that is, $\phi_i = R_i$. Then the maximum delay experienced by flow i, D_i, is bounded by

---

[10] The concept of WFQ was first introduced in [DEME90]; it is briefly mentioned in that paper, with no analysis, and the term *WFQ* is not used. The first rigorous analysis of WFQ is reported in [PARE93] and [PARE94], where it is referred to as *packet-by-packet generalized processor sharing* (PGPS).

$$D_i \leq \frac{B_i}{R_i} \tag{11.4}$$

The proof of this is given in [PARE94]; here we give an intuitive argument. Assume a situation in which all of the flows have been low or idle for some time and that all of the buckets are full. Then all of the flows begin to transmit at the maximum rate. The network is configured, by reservation, to handle the maximum rate R_i from each flow. At this rate, tokens are added to the bucket as fast as they are drained. If the node keeps up with the flow, then the queue length at the node will not exceed the bucket size. So the delay experienced by the flow through the node will not exceed the bucket size divided by the token rate, which is Equation 11.4.

Weighted Fair Queuing

Again, we wish to transmit entire packets rather than individual bits. Just as BRFQ emulates the bit-by-bit PS, WFQ emulates the bit-by-bit GPS. The strategy is the same: Whenever a packet finishes transmission, the next packet sent is the one with the smallest value of F_i^α. In this case, Equation 11.2 governs the calculation of F_i^α.

Figure 11.12, based on examples in [ZHAN95], illustrates the action of WFQ and compares it to FIFO. All packets have the same size of 1 and the link speed is 1. The guaranteed rate for connection 1 is 0.5 and the guaranteed rate for the other 10 connections is 0.05. In the upper example, flow 1 sends 11 back-to-back packets starting at time 0 and the other flows send a single packet at time 0. Under FIFO, one packet from each flow is transmitted and then the remaining 10 packets of flow 1.[11] Under WFQ, because the first 10 packets on flow 1 all have PS finish times smaller than packets on other connections, the node will transmit these packets first. In both cases, each flow receives the guaranteed flow rate over the interval of 20 time units, but the relative delays suffered are changed to favor flow 1 in WFQ. The lower part of the example is more revealing. Here, the packets from flow 1 arrive uniformly at the desired rate. Under FIFO, all but the first packet are substantially delayed because of other traffic that should be getting a smaller portion of capacity. WFQ closely approximates giving a uniform and appropriate amount of service to each flow.

It was pointed out the GPS is attractive because it enables a router to assign the appropriate weight to each flow to guarantee service and because it is possible to guarantee an upper bound on delay. These qualities carry over to the WFQ approximation to GPS. In this case, Equation 11.4 must be modified as follows:

$$D_i \leq \frac{B_i}{R_i} + \frac{(K_i - 1)L_i}{R_i} \sum_{m=1}^{K_i} \frac{L_{max}}{C_m} \tag{11.5}$$

where

D_i = maximum delay experienced by flow i

B_i = token bucket size for flow i

R_i = token rate for flow i

---

[11] Note that the same result is achieved with FQ. This is also true in Figure 11.12b.

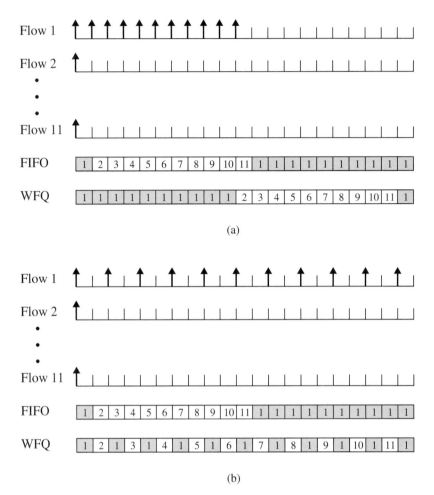

Figure 11.12 Comparison of FIFO and WFQ.

K_i = number of nodes in the path flow i through the internet
L_i = maximum packet size for flow i
L_{max} = maximum packet length for all flows through all nodes on the path of flow i
C_m = outgoing link capacity at node m

The first term carries over from the GPS case and accounts for delay due to bucket size, which is the same as delay due to burstiness. The second term is proportional to the delay experienced at each node for each packet by this flow. The final term reflects the consequence of packet-by-packet rather than bit-by-bit transmission. Again, we give an intuitive explanation. In both BRFQ and WFQ, a packet may leave some time later than it would have under bit-by-bit processing (PS or GPS). The reason is that the node can only choose for transmission among all the packets that have already arrived. If the next packet chosen is relatively large and a small packet arrives during this transmission, it may be that under GPS, this small packet has the earliest finish time and therefore should have been transmitted first under WFQ. Because it did not arrive, it was not transmitted and has to be delayed up to at most the full length of the longest packet that moves through this node.

Equation 11.5 is important in the design of an ISA. It says that there is an easy way to set parameters in a router to guarantee a given rate of service. Further, at this rate, an upper bound on delay can be granted to the user. Finally, [PARE94] shows that the maximum queue size needed at each node is proportional to the maximum delay defined in Equation 11.5; in particular, it approaches $g_i D_i$. Thus, the node can easily determine the resources required to grant a particular reservation.

11.5 RANDOM EARLY DETECTION

Another approach to congestion management in internets is proactive packet discard. In this technique, a router discards one or more incoming packets before the output buffer is completely full, in order to improve the performance of the network. This technique is designed for use on a single FIFO queue and so can be used in any internet architecture. In the context of ISA, proactive packet discard can be exercised on one or more queues for elastic traffic at each router to improve the performance provided to the elastic traffic.

The most important example of proactive packet discard is known as random early detection (RED), introduced in [FLOY93]. RED has already been implemented by a number of vendors. In this section, we look first at the motivation and objectives for RED and then examine its design.

Motivation

When there is a surge of congestion on a network, router buffers fill up and routers begin to drop packets. For TCP traffic, this is a signal to enter the slow start phase, which reduces the load on the network and relieves the congestion. There are two difficulties with this scenario. First, lost packets must be retransmitted, adding to the load on the network and imposing significant delays on the TCP flows. More serious is the phenomenon termed *global synchronization*. With a traffic burst, queues fill up and a number of packets are dropped. The likely result is that many TCP connections are affected and enter slow start. This causes a dramatic drop in network traffic, so that for a time the network is unnecessarily underutilized. Because many TCP connections entered slow start at about the same time, they will come out of slow start at about the same time, causing another big burst and another cycle of feast and famine.

One solution is to use bigger buffers at each router to reduce the probability of dropping packets. This is a bad solution for two reasons. First, as these big buffers fill up, the delays suffered by all connections increase dramatically. Worse, if the traffic is self-similar, which it very well might be, in essence you cannot build buffers big enough: Big bursts arrive one after another so that congestion is sustained and the buffer requirements grow.

A better solution would be to anticipate the onset of congestion and tell one TCP connection at a time to slow down. Then measure the effect of that one slowdown before, if necessary, slowing down another connection. In this fashion, as congestion begins, the brakes are gradually applied to gently reduce traffic load, with minimal impact on TCP connections and without global synchronization. RED provides this solution.

RED Design Goals

[FLOY93] lists the following design goals for RED:

- **Congestion avoidance:** RED is designed to avoid congestion rather than react to it. Thus, RED must detect the onset of congestion to maintain the network in a region of low delay and high throughput.
- **Global synchronization avoidance:** When the onset of congestion is recognized, the router must decide which connection or connections to notify to back off. In current implementations, this notification is implicit and provided by dropping packets. By detecting congestion early and notifying only as many connections as necessary, global synchronization is avoided.
- **Avoidance of bias against bursty traffic:** The onset of congestion is likely to occur with the arrival of a burst of traffic from one or a few sources. This burst adds to the burden already supported at the router. If only arriving packets are selected for dropping, then it is likely that the discard algorithm will be biased against burst sources as compared to smooth sources with the same average traffic.
- **Bound on average queue length:** RED should be able to control the average queue size and therefore control the average delay.

RED Algorithm

In general terms, the RED algorithm performs the following steps for each packet arrival:

```
calculate the average queue size avg
if avg < TH_min
    queue packet
else if TH_min ≤ avg < TH_max
    calculate probability P_a
    with probability P_a
        discard packet
    else with probability 1 - P_a
        queue packet
else if avg ≥ TH_max
    discard packet
```

The algorithm performs two functions each time a new packet arrives at a FIFO output queue. The first step is to compute the average queue length, *avg*. This

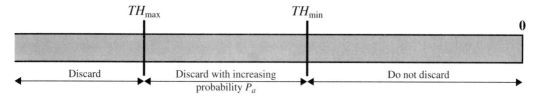

Figure 11.13   RED buffer.

average queue length is compared to two thresholds (Figure 11.13). If *avg* is less than a lower threshold TH_{min}, congestion is assumed to be minimal or nonexistent, and the packet is placed in the queue. If *avg* is greater than an upper threshold TH_{max}, congestion is assume to be serious, and the packet is discarded. If *avg* is between the two thresholds, then we are in an area that might indicate the onset of congestion. In this region, a probability P_a is calculated that depends on the exact value of *avg* and that increases the closer *avg* gets to the upper threshold. When the queue is in this region, the packet is discarded with probability P_a and queued with probability $1 - P_a$.

In essence, the first part of the algorithm (calculate queue size) determines the degree of burstiness to be allowed, and the second part of the algorithm (determine packet discard) determines the frequency of dropped packets given the current level of congestion.

Using Figure 11.14, we now examine the RED algorithm in more detail.

Calculating Average Queue Size

The average queue size is calculated using an exponentially weighted average of previous queue lengths. The **else** clause takes into account periods when the queue is empty by estimating the number *m* of small packets that could have been transmitted by the router during the idle period.

One might ask why an average queue size is used when it would be simpler to use the actual queue size. The purpose of using an average queue size is to filter out transient congestion at the router. The weight w_q determines how rapidly *avg* changes in response to changes in actual queue size. [FLOY93] recommends a quite small value of 0.002. As a result, *avg* lags considerably behind changes in actual queue size. The use of this small weight prevents the algorithm from reacting to short bursts of congestion.

Determining Packet Discard

If *avg* is less than TH_{min}, the incoming packet is queued, and if *avg* is greater than TH_{max}, the incoming packet is automatically discarded. The critical region is for a value of *avg* between the two thresholds. In this region, RED assigns a probability of discard to an incoming packet that depends on two factors:

Initialization:

 $avg \leftarrow 0$

 $count \leftarrow -1$

For each packet arrival

 CALCULATE AVERAGE QUEUE SIZE

  if the queue is not empty (i.e., $q > 0$)

   $avg \leftarrow (1 - w_q)avg + w_q\, q$

  else

   $m \leftarrow \text{f}(time - q\_time)$

   $avg \leftarrow (1 - w_q)^m\, avg$

 DETERMINE PACKET DISCARD

  if $avg < TH_{min}$

   queue packet

   $count \leftarrow -1$

  else if $TH_{min} \leq avg \leq TH_{max}$

   increment $count$

   $P_b \leftarrow P_{max}(avg - TH_{min})/(TH_{max} - TH_{min})$

   $P_a \leftarrow P_b/(1 - count \times P_b)$

   with probability P_a

    discard packet

    $count \leftarrow 0$

   else with probability $1 - P_a$

    queue packet

  else if $avg > TH_{max}$

   discard packet

   $count \leftarrow 0$

When queue becomes empty

 $q\_time \leftarrow time$

Saved Variables:

 avg: average queue size

 q_time: start of queue idle time

 $count$: packets since last discarded packet

Fixed Parameters:

 w_q: queue weight

 TH_{min}: Minimum threshold for queue

 TH_{max}: Maximum threshold for queue

 P_{max}: Maximum value for P_b

Other:

 P_a: current packet- marking probability

 P_b: temporary probability used in calculation

 q: current queue size

 $time$: current time

 $\text{f}(t)$: a linear function of time t

Figure 11.14 RED algorithm.

- The closer avg is to TH_{max}, the higher the probability of discard.
- As long as avg is in the critical range, we keep a *count* of how many consecutive packets escape discard; the higher the value of *count*, the higher the probability of discard.

The steps in the calculation shown in Figure 11.14 make it difficult to figure out exactly what is going on, so a brief discussion is in order. First, a temporary probability value P_b is calculated. This is a value that increases linearly from 0 at $avg = TH_{min}$ to some maximum value P_{max} at $avg = TH_{max}$. This is seen more easily if we define the quantity F:

$$F = \frac{avg - TH_{min}}{TH_{max} - TH_{min}}$$

which is the fraction of the critical region less than avg. Then we have

$$P_b = F \times P_{max} \qquad 0 \leqslant F \leqslant 1$$

Probabilistic phenomena behave in ways that produce clusters. For example, if we flip a fair coin many times, we cannot expect to see a uniform alternating series of heads and tails. Instead, there will be many clusters of all heads, clusters of all tails, clusters of mostly heads, and so on, with a long-term average of 50-50. For the RED algorithm, we would like to space the discards relatively evenly so that a bursty source is not penalized. So, rather than use P_b directly, it is used in the calculation of a second probability P_a, which is the probability used to determine discard. Substituting F into the equation from Figure 11.14, we get the following definition:

$$P_a = \frac{F \times P_{max}}{1 - count \times F \times P_{max}} = \frac{1}{\dfrac{1}{F \times P_{max}} - count}$$

$$= \frac{P_b}{1 - count \times P_b} = \frac{1}{\dfrac{1}{P_b} - count}$$

Figure 11.15 gives some insight into this function. For a given value of $count$, P_a increases gradually from $P_a = 0$ at $avg = TH_{min}$ to the maximum value shown at $avg = TH_{max}$. This is a reasonable design: There is a smooth increase of P_a as the value of avg approaches TH_{max}. But the true nature of the function is revealed if we hold F constant and plot P_a as a function of count. The value of P_a increases slowly and then rises dramatically until it reaches $P_a = 1$ at count $= (1/F \times P_{max}) - 1$. Thus, for most values of $count$, the probability of discard is extremely low and becomes very near to 1 when $count$ becomes very near to its maximum value. The effect of this is to force a more or less uniform spacing of discards. In fact, it can be shown that if we let P_a be the discard probability and X be the number of packets that arrive after a discarded packet until the next packet is discarded, then X is a uniformly distributed random variable from $\{1, 2, ..., 1/P_b\}$:

$$\Pr[X = n] = \begin{cases} F \times P_{max} & 1 \leqslant n \leqslant \dfrac{1}{F \times P_{max}} \\ 0 & n > \dfrac{1}{F \times P_{max}} \end{cases}$$

$$E[X] = \frac{1}{2 \times F \times P_{max}} + \frac{1}{2}$$

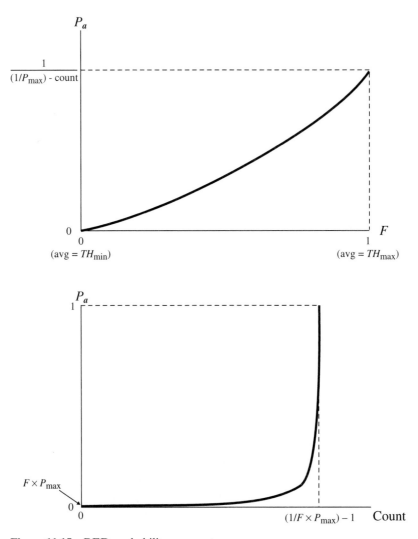

Figure 11.15 RED probability parameter.

As an example, [FLOY93] recommends a value $P_{max} = 0.02$. When the average queue size is halfway between TH_{min} and TH_{max} ($F = 0.5$), roughly one out of 50 (one out of $1/P_{max}$) arriving packets is discarded.

Figure 11.16 shows the results of a simulation [FLOY93] comparing RED to a **drop-tail** policy, which simply drops an arriving packet if the queue is full. At high levels of congestion, RED is superior to drop tail in providing high throughput.

11.6 RECOMMENDED READING

Good coverage of internetworking and IPv4 can be found in [COME95] and [STEV94]. [BRAD96] is a thorough treatment of IPv6-related issues; the book provides a relatively non-technical discussion of the requirements for IPv6 and the history of the IPv6 development.

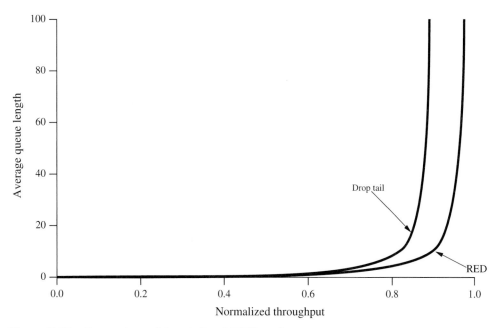

Figure 11.16   Comparison of drop tail and RED performance.

[HUIT96] is a straightforward technical description of the various RFCs that together make up the IPv6 specification; the book provide a discussion of the purpose of various features and of the operation of the protocol.

RFC 1633 is the defining document for the Integrated Services Architecture and provides an excellent overview. [CLAR92] and [CLAR95] provide valuable surveys of the issues involved in internet service allocation for real-time and elastic applications, respectively. [SHEN95] is a masterful analysis of the rationale for a QoS-based internet architecture.

[ZHAN95] is a broad survey of queuing disciplines that can be used in an ISA, including an analysis of FQ and WFQ. [CLAR92] provides an analysis of WFQ and some alternative disciplines. [FLOY97] considers the congestion impacts from an increasing deployment of non-congestion-controlled best-effort traffic (traffic without the TCP congestion control mechanism) and measures that can be taken by routers, including the queuing and packet discard strategies discussed in this chapter.

BRAD96   Bradner, S., and Mankin, A. *IPng: Internet Protocol Next Generation.* Reading, MA: Addison-Wesley, 1996.

CLAR92   Clark, D., Shenker, S., and Zhang, L. "Supporting Real-Time Applications in an Integrated Services Packet Network: Architecture and Mechanism" *Proceedings, SIGCOMM '92*, August 1992.

CLAR95   Clark, D. *Adding Service Discrimination to the Internet.* MIT Laboratory for Computer Science Technical Report, September 1995. Available at http://ana-www.lcs.mit.edu/anaweb/papers.html

COME95   Comer, D. *Internetworking with TCP/IP, Volume I: Principles, Protocols and Architecture.* Upper Saddle River, NJ: Prentice Hall, 1995.

FLOY97   Floyd, S., and Fall, K. "Router Mechanisms to Support End-to-End Congestion Control." *Proceedings, SIGCOMM'97*, 1997.

HUIT96   Huitema, C. *IPv6: The New Internet Protocol.* Upper Saddle River, NJ: Prentice Hall, 1996.

SHEN95   Shenker, S. "Fundamental Design Issues for the Future Internet." *IEEE Journal on Selected Areas in Communications*, September 1995.

STEV94   Stevens, W. *TCP/IP Illustrated, Volume 1: The Protocols.* Reading, MA: Addison-Wesley, 1994.

ZHAN95   Zhang, H. "Service Disciplines for Guaranteed Performance Service in Packet-switching Networks." *Proceedings of the IEEE*, October 1995.

Recommended Web site:

- http://playground.sun.com/pub/ipng/html/ipng-main.html: Contains information about IPv6 and related topics.

11.7 PROBLEMS

11.1 The *identifier, don't fragment identifier,* and *time to live* parameters are generally provided by the source IP user, carried in the IP datagram across the internet to the destination IP entity, but are not delivered to the destination IP user because they are only of concern to IP. For each of these parameters indicate whether it is of concern to the IP entity in the source, the IP entities in any intermediate routers, and the IP entity in the destination end systems. Justify your answer.

11.2 What are the pros and cons of intermediate reassembly of an internet segmented datagram versus reassembly at the final destination?

11.3 What is the header overhead in the IP protocol?

11.4 Describe some circumstances in which it might be desirable to use source routing rather than let the routers make the routing decision.

11.5 Because of segmentation, an IP datagram can arrive in several pieces, not necessarily in the correct order. The IP entity at the receiving end system must accumulate these segments until the original datagram is reconstituted.

    a. Consider that the IP entity creates a buffer for assembling the data field in the original datagram. As assembly proceeds, the buffer will contain blocks of data and "holes" between the data blocks. Describe an algorithm for reassembly based on this concept.

    b. For the algorithm in part (a), it is necessary to keep track of the holes. Describe a simple mechanism for doing this.

11.6 The IP checksum needs to be recalculated at routers because of changes to the IP header, such as the lifetime field. It is possible to recalculate the checksum from scratch. Suggest a procedure that involves less calculation. *Hint:* Suppose that the value in octet k is changed by $Z = \text{new\_value} - \text{old\_value}$; consider the effect of this change on the checksum.

11.7 An IP datagram is to be segmented. Which options in the option field need to be copied into the header of each segment, and which need only be retained in the first segment? Justify the handling of each option.

11.8 Compare the individual fields of the IPv4 header with the IPv6 header. Account for the functionality provided by each IPv4 field by showing how the same functionality is provided in IPv6.

11.9 Justify the recommended order in which IPv6 extension headers appear (i.e., why is the Hop-by-Hop Options header first? Why is the Routing Header before the Fragment header? and so on).

11.10 The IPv6 standard states that if a packet with a nonzero flow label arrives at a router and the router has no information for that flow label, the router should ignore the flow label and forward the packet.

a. What are the disadvantages of treating this event as an error, discarding the packet, and sending an ICMP message?

b. Are there situations in which routing the packet as if its flow label were zero will cause the wrong result? Explain.

11.11 The IPv6 flow mechanism assumes that the state associated with a given flow label is stored in routers, so the routers know how to handle packets that carry that flow label. A design requirement is to flush flow labels that are no longer being used (stale flow label) from routers.

a. Assume that a source always send a control message to all affected routers deleting a flow label when the source finishes with that flow. In that case, how could a stale flow label persist?

b. Suggest router and source mechanisms to overcome the problem of stale flow labels.

11.12 The question arises as to which packets generated by a source should carry nonzero IPv6 flow labels. For some applications, the answer is obvious. Small exchanges of data should have a zero flow label because it is not worth creating a flow for a few packets. Real-time flows should have a flow label; such flows are a primary reason flow labels were created. A more difficult issue is what to do with peers sending large amounts of best-effort traffic (e.g., TCP connections). Make a case for assigning a unique flow label to each long-term TCP connection. Make a case for not doing this.

11.13 The original IPv6 specifications combined the Priority and Flow Label fields into a single 28-bit Flow Label field. This allowed flows to redefine the interpretation of different values of priority. Suggest reasons why the final specification includes the Priority field as a distinct field.

11.14 It is clear that if a router gives preferential treatment to one flow or one class of flows, then that flow or class of flows will receive improved service. It is not as clear that the overall service provided by the internet is improved. This question is intended to illustrate an overall improvement. Consider a network with a single link modeled by an exponential server of rate $T_s = 1$, and consider two classes of flows with Poisson arrival rates of $\lambda_1 = \lambda_2 = 0.25$ and that have utility functions $U_1 = 4 - 2t_{q1}$ and $U_2 = 4 - t_{q2}$, where t_{qi} represents the average queuing delay to class i. Thus, class 1 traffic is more sensitive to delay than class 2. Define the total utility of the network as $V = U_1 + U_2$.

a. Assume that the two classes are treated alike and that FIFO queuing is used. What is V?

b. Now assume a strict priority service, so that packets from class 1 are always transmitted before packets in class 2. What is V? Comment.

11.15 The token bucket scheme places a limit on the length of time at which traffic can depart at the maximum data rate. Let the token bucket be defined by a bucket size b octets and a token arrival rate of r octets/s, and let the maximum output data rate be M octets/s.

a. Derive a formula for S, which is the length of the maximum-rate burst. That is, for how long can a flow transmit at the maximum output rate when governed by a token bucket?

b. What is the value of S for $b = 250$ KB, $r = 2$ MB/s, and $M = 25$ MB/s?

Hint: The formula for S is not so simple as it might appear because more tokens arrive while the burst is being output.

11.16 The GPS queuing discipline described in Section 11.4 can be defined as follows.

Let $S_i(\tau, t)$ be the amount of flow i traffic transmitted in an interval $(\tau, t]$. Then a GPS server is defined as one for which

$$\frac{S_i(\tau, t)}{S_j(\tau, t)} \geq \frac{\phi_i}{\phi_j}, \quad j = 1, 2, \dots, N$$

Validate this definition by showing that Equation 11.3 can be derived from it.

11.17 In the RED algorithm, there are a number of parameters to be set. Let us consider some of the design issues involved.

    a. What is the relationship between the value chosen for TH_{min} and the degree of burstiness of the traffic?

    b. What is the relationship between the value $(TH_{max} - TH_{min})$ and the typical RTT seen by TCP?

CHAPTER 12

TRAFFIC AND CONGESTION CONTROL IN ATM NETWORKS

We were doing very well, up to the kind of sum when a bath is filling at the rate of so many gallons and two holes are letting the water out, and please to say how long it will take to fill the bath, when my mother put down the socks she was darning and clicked her tongue in impatience.

"Filling up an old bath with holes in it, indeed. Who would be such a fool?"

"A sum it is, girl," my father said. "A sum. A problem for the mind."

"Filling the boy with old nonsense," Mama said.

"Not nonsense, Beth," my father said. "A sum, it is. The water pours in and takes so long. It pours out and takes so long. How long to fill? That is all."

"But who would pour water into an old bath with holes?" my mother said. "Who would think to do it, but a lunatic?"

—*How Green Was My Valley,* **Richard Llewellyn**

As is the case with IP-based internets, traffic and congestion control techniques are vital to the successful operation of ATM-based networks. Without such techniques, traffic from user nodes can exceed the capacity of the network, causing buffers of ATM switches to overflow and leading to data losses.

Because of their high speed and small cell size, ATM networks present difficulties in effectively controlling congestion not found in other types of networks, including frame relay and packet-switching networks. The complexity of the problem is compounded by the limited number of overhead bits available for exerting control over the flow of user cells. This area is currently the subject of intense research, and approaches to traffic and congestion control are still evolving. ITU-T has defined a restricted initial set of traffic and congestion control capabilities aiming at simple mechanisms and realistic network efficiency; these are specified in I.371. The ATM Forum has published a somewhat more advanced version of this set in its *Traffic Management Specification Version 4.0* [ATM96]. This chapter focuses on the ATM Forum specifications.

We begin with an overview of the congestion problem and the framework adopted by ITU-T and the ATM Forum. The focus of the mechanisms is on control schemes for delay-sensitive traffic such as voice and video. These schemes are not suited for handling bursty traffic. In the next section we examine traffic control, which refers to the set of actions taken by the network to avoid congestion. Then we examine congestion control, which refers to the set of actions taken by the network to minimize the intensity, spread, and duration of congestion once congestion has already occurred. Finally, we look at the congestion control schemes developed for dealing with bursty traffic, which have been adopted as part of the ABR service.

12.1 REQUIREMENTS FOR ATM TRAFFIC AND CONGESTION CONTROL

The types of traffic patterns imposed on ATM networks, as well as the transmission characteristics of those networks, differ markedly from those of other switching networks. Most packet-switching and frame relay networks carry non-real-time data traffic. Typically, the traffic on individual virtual circuits or frame relay connections is bursty in nature, and the receiving system expects to receive incoming traffic on each connection in a bursty fashion. As a result,

1. The network does not need to replicate the exact timing pattern of incoming traffic at the exit node.
2. Simple statistical multiplexing can be used to accommodate multiple logical connections over the physical interface between user and network. The average data rate required by each connection is less than the burst rate for that connection, and the user-network interface (UNI) need only be designed for a capacity somewhat greater than the sum of the average data rates for all connections.

A number of tools have been developed for control of congestion in packet-switched and frame relay networks, as we have seen. These types of congestion control schemes are inadequate for ATM networks. [GERS91] cites the following reasons:

1. Much of the traffic is not amenable to flow control. For example, voice and video traffic sources cannot stop generating cells even when the network is congested.
2. Feedback is slow due to the drastically reduced cell transmission time compared to propagation delays across the network.
3. ATM networks typically support a wide range of applications requiring capacity ranging from a few kilobits per second to several hundred megabits per sec-

ond. Relatively simple-minded congestion control schemes generally end up penalizing one end or the other of that spectrum.

4. Applications on ATM networks may generate very different traffic patterns (e.g., constant bit rate versus variable bit rate sources). Again, it is difficult for conventional congestion control techniques to handle fairly such variety.

5. Different applications on ATM networks require different network services (e.g., delay-sensitive service for voice and video, and loss-sensitive service for data).

6. The very high speeds in switching and transmission make ATM networks more volatile in terms of congestion and traffic control. A scheme that relies heavily on reacting to changing conditions will produce extreme and wasteful fluctuations in routing policy and flow control.

Two key performance issues that relate to the preceding points are latency/speed effects and cell delay variation, topics to which we now turn.

Latency/Speed Effects

Consider the transfer of ATM cells over a network at a data rate of 150 Mbps. At that rate, it takes $(53 \times 8 \text{ bits})/(150 \times 10^6 \text{ bps}) \approx 3 \times 10^{-6}$ seconds to insert a single cell onto the network. The time it takes to transfer the cell from the source to the destination user will depend on the number of intermediate ATM switches, the switching time at each switch, and the propagation time along all links in the path from source to destination. For simplicity, ignore ATM switching delays and assume propagation at the speed of light. Then, if source and destination are on opposite coasts of the United States, the round-trip propagation delay is about 30×10^{-3} seconds.

With these conditions in place, suppose that source A is performing a long file transfer to destination B and that implicit congestion control is being used (i.e., there are no explicit congestion notifications; the source deduces the presence of congestion by the loss of data). If the network drops a cell due to congestion, B can return a reject message to A, which must then retransmit the dropped cell and possibly all subsequent cells. But by the time the notification gets back to A, it has transmitted an additional N cells, where

$$N = \frac{30 \times 10^{-3} \text{ seconds}}{3 \times 10^{-6} \text{ seconds/cell}} = 10^4 \text{ cells} = 4.24 \times 10^6 \text{ bits}$$

Over 4 megabits of data have been transmitted before A can react to the congestion indication.

This calculation helps to explain why the techniques that are satisfactory for more traditional networks break down when dealing with ATM WANs.

Cell Delay Variation

For an ATM network, voice and video signals can be digitized and transmitted as a stream of cells. A key requirement, especially for voice, is that the delay across the network be short. Generally, this will be the case for ATM networks. As we have discussed, ATM is designed to minimize the processing and transmission overhead internal to the network so that very fast cell switching and routing is possible.

There is another important requirement that to some extent conflicts with the preceding requirement—namely, that the rate of delivery of cells to the destination user must be constant. It is inevitable that there will be some variability in the rate of delivery of cells due both to effects within the network and at the source UNI; we summarize these effects presently. First, let us consider how the destination user might cope with variations in the delay of cells as the transit from source user to destination user.

A general procedure for achieving a constant bit rate is illustrated in Figure 12.1. Let $D(i)$ represent the end-to-end delay experienced by the ith cell. The destination system does not know the exact amount of this delay: There is no time-stamp information associated with each cell and, even if there were, it is impossible to keep source and destination clocks perfectly synchronized. When the first cell on a connection arrives at time $t(0)$, the target user delays the cell an additional amount $V(0)$ prior to delivery to the application. $V(0)$ is an estimate of the amount of cell delay variation that this application can tolerate and that is likely to be produced by the network.

Subsequent cells are delayed so that they are delivered to the user at a constant rate of R cells per second. The time between delivery of cells to the target application (time between the start of delivery of one cell and the start of delivery of the next cell) is therefore $\delta = 1/R$. To achieve a constant rate, the next cell is delayed a variable amount $V(1)$ to satisfy

$$t(1) + V(1) = t(0) + V(0) + \delta$$

So

$$V(1) = V(0) - [t(1) - (t(0) + \delta)]$$

In general,

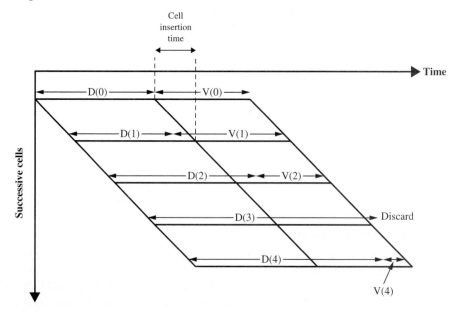

Figure 12.1   Time reassembly of CBR cells.

$$V(i) = V(0) - [t(i) - (t(0) + i \times \delta)]$$

which can also be expressed as

$$V(i) = V(i - 1) - [t(i) - (t(i - 1) + \delta)]$$

If the computed value of $V(i)$ is negative, then that cell is discarded. The result is that data are delivered to the higher layer at a constant bit rate, with occasional gaps due to dropped cells.

The amount of the initial delay $V(0)$, which is also the average delay applied to all incoming cells, is a function of the anticipated cell delay variation. To minimize this delay, a subscriber will therefore request a minimal cell delay variation from the network provider. This leads to a tradeoff: Cell delay variation can be reduced by increasing the data rate at the UNI relative to the load and by increasing resources within the network.

Network Contribution to Cell Delay Variation

One component of cell delay variation is due to events within the network. For packet-switching networks, packet delay variation can be considerable due to queuing effects at each of the intermediate switching nodes and the processing time required to analyze packet headers and perform routing. To a much lesser extent, this is also true of frame delay variation in frame relay networks. In the case of ATM networks, cell delay variations due to network effects are likely to be even less than for frame relay. The principal reasons for this are the following:

1. The ATM protocol is designed to minimize processing overhead at intermediate switching nodes. The cells are fixed size with fixed header formats, and there is no flow control or error control processing required.
2. To accommodate the high speeds of ATM networks, ATM switches have had to be designed to provide extremely high throughput. Thus, the processing time for an individual cell at a node is negligible.

The only factor that could lead to noticeable cell delay variation within the network is congestion. If the network begins to become congested, either cells must be discarded or there will be a buildup of queuing delays at affected switches. Thus, it is important that the total load accepted by the network at any time not be such as to cause congestion.

Cell Delay Variation at the UNI

Even if an application generates data for transmission at a constant bit rate, cell delay variation can occur at the source due to the processing that takes place at the three layers of the ATM model.

Figure 12.2 illustrates the potential causes of cell delay variation. In this example, ATM connections A and B support user data rates of X and Y Mbps, respectively. At the AAL level, data is segmented into 48-octet blocks. Note that on a time diagram, the blocks appear to be of different sizes for the two connections; specifically, the time required to generate a 48-octet block of data, in microseconds, is

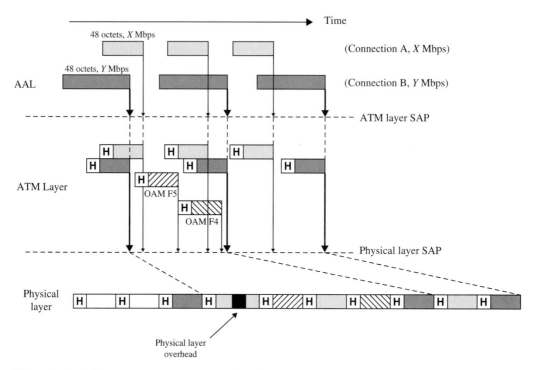

Figure 12.2 Origins of cell delay variation (I.371).

$$\text{Connection A: } \frac{48 \times 8}{X}$$

$$\text{Connection B: } \frac{48 \times 8}{Y}$$

The ATM layer encapsulates each segment into a 53-octet cell. These cells must be interleaved and delivered to the physical layer to be transmitted at the data rate of the physical link. Delay is introduced into this interleaving process: If two cells from different connections arrive at the ATM layer at overlapping times, one of the cells must be delayed by the amount of the overlap. In addition, the ATM layer is generating OAM (operation and maintenance) cells that must also be interleaved with user cells.

At the physical layer, there is opportunity for the introduction of further cell delays. For example, if cells are transmitted in SDH (synchronous digital hierarchy) frames, overhead bits for those frames will be inserted onto the physical link, delaying bits from the ATM layer.

None of the delays just listed can be predicted in any detail, and none follow any repetitive pattern. Accordingly, there is a random element to the time interval between reception of data at the ATM layer from the AAL and the transmission of that data in a cell across the UNI.

12.2 ATM TRAFFIC-RELATED ATTRIBUTES

Recall from Chapter 5 that there are five ATM service categories defined by the ATM Forum:

- **Constant bit rate (CBR):** Requires that a fixed data rate be made available by the ATM provider. The network must ensure that this capacity is available and also polices the incoming traffic on a CBR connection to ensure that the subscriber does not exceed its allocation.
- **Real-time variable bit rate (rt-VBR):** Intended for applications that require tightly constrained delay and delay variation but do not exhibit the fixed data rate of CBR. Rather than a single rate, a VBR connection is defined in terms of a sustained rate for normal use and a faster burst rate for occasional use at peak periods. The faster rate is guaranteed but it is understood that the user will not continuously require this faster rate. In addition, bounds on cell transfer delay and delay variation are specified.
- **Non-real-time variable bit rate (nrt-VBR):** Similar to rt-VBR, except that there is no delay variation bound specified, and a certain low cell loss ratio is allowed.
- **Unspecified bit rate (UBR):** This is a best-effort service. No amount of capacity is guaranteed, and any cells may be discarded.
- **Available bit rate (ABR):** Provides the user with a guaranteed minimum capacity. When additional capacity is available, the user may burst above the minimum rate with minimized risk of cell loss.

These service categories are characterized by a number of ATM attributes that fall into three categories:

- **Traffic descriptors:** Describe the traffic characteristics of a source and of a connection. A network will establish a connection for this source only if sufficient resources are available to support this traffic volume.
- **QoS parameters:** Characterize the performance of an ATM connection in terms of the quality of service that it provides. For a given connection, a user will request a particular QoS.
- **Other:** The only other attribute defined so far is a feedback attribute for ABR.

Table 12.1 lists the ATM attributes and indicates their applicability to each service category.

Traffic Descriptors

The ATM Forum has defined a number of descriptors that characterize the traffic pattern of a flow of cells over an ATM connection. This traffic pattern must be viewed from two different perspectives. First, there is the intrinsic nature of the traffic generated by the source and submitted to the network across the UNI. Second, this flow of cells will be modified inside the network, along the ATM connection, by the variability in delays suffered and by the treatment of cells that do not conform to the source traffic pattern.

TABLE 12.1 ATM SERVICE CATEGORY ATTRIBUTES

Attribute	ATM Layer Service Category				
	CBR	rt-VBR	nrt-VBR	UBR	ABR
Traffic Parameters					
PCR and CDVT (4, 5)	specified			specified(2)	specified(3)
SCR, MBS, CDVT (4, 5)	N/A	specified		N/A	
MCR (4)	N/A				specified
QoS Parameters					
peak-to-peak CDV	specified		unspecified		
maxCTD	specified		unspecified		
CLR (4)	specified			unspecified	(1)
Other Attributes					
Feedback	unspecified				specified

1. CLR is low for sources that adjust cell flow in response to control information. Whether a quantitative value for CLR is specified is network specific.
2. May not be subject to CAC and UPC procedures.
3. Represents the maximum rate at which ABR source may ever send. The actual rate is subject to the control information.
4. These parameters are either explicitly or implicitly specified for PVCs or SVCs.
5. CDVT is not signaled. In general, CDVT need not have a unique value for a connection. Different values may apply at each interface along the path of a connection.

The source characteristics of an ATM flow are captured in a **source traffic descriptor**, which includes the following: peak cell rate (PCR), sustainable cell rate (SCR), maximum burst size (MBS), and minimum cell rate (MCR). Not all of these descriptors are used to characterize all flows (see Table 12.1). The characteristics of an ATM flow over an ATM connection are captured in a **connection traffic descriptor**, which includes the following: the source traffic descriptor, a cell delay variation tolerance (CDVT), and a conformance definition that unambiguously specifies a test for determining whether a given cell on this connection conforms to the source traffic descriptor.

Thus, the structure of the connection traffic descriptor is of this form:

CONNECTION TRAFFIC DESCRIPTOR

Source traffic descriptor
—Peak cell rate (PCR)
—Sustainable cell rate (SCR)
—Maximum burst size (MBS)
—Minimum cell rate (MCR)

Cell delay variation tolerance (CDVT)

Conformance definition

The PCR, SCR, MBS, and MCR descriptors characterize the traffic submitted to the network and are sufficient for the network to make resource allocation decisions. As we have seen, at least a portion of the cell delay variation is caused by the network and therefore cannot be specified by the source, but must be supplied by the network. We now define at each of these descriptors in turn.

Source Traffic Descriptor

The **peak cell rate** defines an upper bound on the traffic that can be submitted by a source on an ATM connection. The PCR is defined in terms of the variable T, the minimum spacing between cells, so that the PCR $= 1/T$. The PCR descriptor is mandatory for CBR and VBR services.

The **sustainable cell rate** defines an upper bound on the average rate of an ATM connection, calculated over a time scale that is large relative to T. SCR is needed to specify a VBR source. It enables the network to allocate resources efficiently among a number of VBR sources without dedicating the amount of resources required to support a constant PCR rate. The SCR descriptor is only useful if SCR $<$ PCR.

The **maximum burst size** is the maximum number of cells that can be sent continuously at the peak cell rate. If cells are presented to the network in clumps equal to the MBS, then the idle gap between clumps must be sufficient so that the overall rate does not exceed the SCR. The SCR and MBS must both be specified for VBR sources.

The **minimum cell rate** is used with the ABR service. It defines the minimum commitment requested of the network; a value of zero can be used. The goal of the ABR service is to provide rapid access to unused network capacity at up to PCR, whenever the capacity is available. The quantity (PCR $-$ MCR) represents an elastic component of data flow for which the network provides only the assurance that this capacity will be shared fairly among the ABR flows.

Connection Traffic Descriptor

In addition to the source traffic descriptor, the connection traffic descriptor includes the CDVT and a conformance definition. The **cell delay variation tolerance** is a measure of the amount of variation in cell delay that is introduced by the network interface (e.g., SDH) and at the UNI. CDVT represents a bound on the delay variability due to the slotted nature of ATM, the physical layer overhead, and ATM layer functions such as cell multiplexing. CDVT is expressed as time variable τ. The interpretation of τ is discussed in Section 12.4. The **conformance definition** is used to specify unambiguously the conforming cells of a connection at the UNI. The network may enforce conformance by dropping or marking cells that exceed the conformance definition. The generic cell rate algorithm (GCRA), described in Section 12.4, is used to define conformance.

QoS Parameters

The following ATM QoS parameters are defined by the ATM Forum:

- Peak-to-peak cell delay variation

- Maximum cell transfer delay (maxCTD)
- Cell loss ratio (CLR).

We need first to define cell transfer delay (CTD), which is the elapsed time between two cell events. Typically, CTD refers to the time between transmission of the last bit of a cell at the source UNI and the receipt of the first bit of a cell at the destination UNI. In general terms, CTD is a variable that typically has a probability density function that looks like that of Figure 12.3. As indicated, there is a minimum delay, called the fixed delay, which includes propagation delay through the physical media, delays induced by the transmission system, and fixed components of switch processing delay. The variable portion of the delay (CDV) is due to buffering and cell scheduling.

With reference to this figure, **maxCTD** defines the maximum requested delay for this connection. A fraction α of all cells will exceed this threshold and must either be discarded or delivered late. The remaining $(1 - \alpha)$ portion are within the requested QoS. The amount of delay experienced by such cells is within the range between the fixed delay and maxCTD; this range is referred to the **peak-to-peak CDV**.

The QoS parameter CDV should not be confused with the traffic contract CDVT. CDV is usually negotiated during connection establishment (for switched virtual connections), whereas CDVT is normally explicitly set at the UNI and is not negotiated. The source traffic has to conform to the CDVT value to be eligible for QoS guarantees; this is checked and enforced by usage parameter control, described

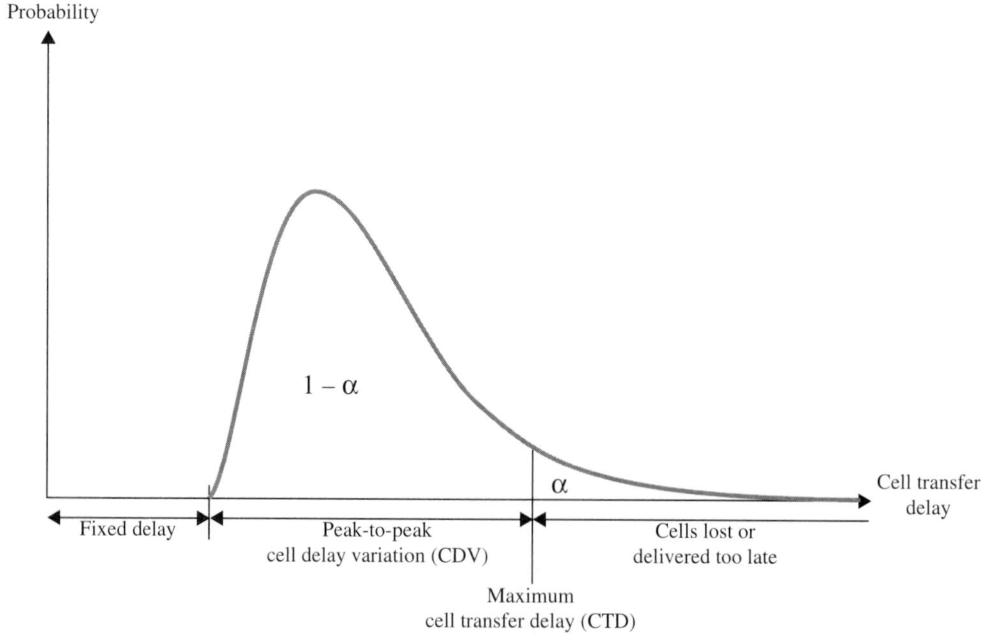

Figure 12.3 Cell transfer delay probability density function (for real-time service categories).

in Section 12.4. The delay variation addressed by CDVT is the variation introduced by the source traffic itself. The network tries to provide the negotiated CDV to the compliant source traffic. This CDV is the difference between the best- and worst-case expected end-to-end cell transfer delay. The best case is equal to the fixed delay. The worst case is equal to maxCTD, incurred as a result of buffering and cell switching. Therefore, CDVT is an upper bound on CDV at the UNI, the latter being only one of several contributing factors to CDV.

Finally, the **cell loss ratio** is simply the ratio of lost cells to total transmitted cells on a connection.

12.3 TRAFFIC MANAGEMENT FRAMEWORK

I.371 lists the following objectives of ATM layer traffic and congestion control:

- ATM layer traffic and congestion control should support a set of ATM layer QoS classes sufficient for all foreseeable network services; the specification of these QoS classes should be consistent with network performance parameters currently under study.
- ATM layer traffic and congestion control should not rely on AAL protocols that are network service specific, nor on higher-layer protocols that are application specific. Protocol layers above the ATM layer may make use of information provided by the ATM layer to improve the utility they can derive from the network.
- The design of an optimum set of ATM layer traffic controls and congestion controls should minimize network and end-system complexity while maximizing network utilization.

To meet these objectives, ITU-T has defined a collection of traffic and congestion control functions that operate across a spectrum of timing intervals. Table 12.2 lists these functions with respect to the response times within which they operate. Four levels of timing are considered:

- **Cell insertion time:** Functions at this level react immediately to cells as they are transmitted.
- **Round-trip propagation time:** At this level, the network responds within the lifetime of a cell in the network and may provide feedback indications to the source.
- **Connection duration:** At this level, the network determines whether a new connection at a given QoS can be accommodated and what performance levels will be agreed to.
- **Long term:** These are controls that affect more than one ATM connection and are established for long-term use.

TABLE 12.2 TRAFFIC CONTROL AND CONGESTION CONTROL FUNCTIONS

Response Time	Traffic Control Functions	Congestion Control Functions
Long Term	• Resource management using virtual paths	
Connection Duration	• Connection admission control (CAC)	
Round-trip Propagation Time	• Fast resource management	• Explicit forward congestion indication (EFCI) • ABR flow control
Cell Insertion Time	• Usage parameter control (UPC) • Priority control • Traffic shaping	• Selective cell discard • Frame discard

The essence of the traffic control strategy is based on (1) determining whether a given new ATM connection can be accommodated and (2) agreeing with the subscriber on the performance parameters that will be supported. In effect, the subscriber and the network enter into a traffic contract: The network agrees to support traffic at a certain level on this connection, and the subscriber agrees not to exceed performance limits. Traffic control functions are concerned with establishing these traffic parameters and enforcing them. Thus, they are concerned with congestion avoidance. If traffic control fails in certain instances, then congestion may occur. At this point, congestion control functions are invoked to respond to and recover from the congestion.

12.4 TRAFFIC CONTROL

ITU-T and the ATM Forum have defined a range of traffic control functions to maintain the QoS of ATM connections. ATM traffic control function refers to the set of actions taken by the network to avoid congestion conditions or to minimize congestion effects. The following functions have been defined:

- Resource management using virtual paths
- Connection admission control
- Usage parameter control
- Selective cell discard
- Traffic shaping.

We examine each of these in turn.

Resource Management Using Virtual Paths

The essential concept behind network resource management is to allocate network resources in such a way as to separate traffic flows according to service characteristics. So far, the only specific traffic control function based on network resource management defined by the ATM Forum deals with the use of virtual paths.

As discussed in Chapter 5, a VPC provides a convenient means of grouping similar VCCs. The network provides aggregate capacity and performance characteristics on the virtual path, and these are shared by the virtual connections. There are three cases to consider:

- **User-to-user application:** The VPC extends between a pair of UNIs. In this case the network has no knowledge of the QoS of the individual VCCs within a VPC. It is the user's responsibility to assure that the aggregate demand from the VCCs can be accommodated by the VPC.
- **User-to-network application:** The VPC extends between a UNI and a network node. In this case the network is aware of the QoS parameters of the VCCs within the VPC and has to accommodate them.
- **Network-to-network application:** The VPC extends between two network nodes. Again, in this case the network is aware of the QoS parameters of the VCCs within the VPC and has to accommodate them.

The QoS parameters that are of primary concern for network resource management are cell loss ratio, maximum cell transfer delay, and peak-to-peak cell delay variation, all of which are affected by the amount of resources devoted to the VPC by the network. If a VCC extends through multiple VPCs, then the performance of that VCC depends on the performances of the consecutive VPCs and on how the connection is handled at any node that performs VCC-related functions. Such a node may be a switch, concentrator, or other network equipment. The performance of each VPC depends on the capacity of that VPC and the traffic characteristics of the VCCs contained within the VPC. The performance of each VCC-related function depends on the switching/processing speed at the node and on the relative priority with which various cells are handled.

Figure 12.4 gives an example. VCCs 1 and 2 experience a performance that depends on VPCs b and c and on how these VCCs are handled by the intermediate nodes. This may differ from the performance experienced by VCCs 3, 4, and 5.

There are a number of alternatives for the way in which VCCs are grouped and the type of performance they experience. If all of the VCCs within a VPC are handled similarly, then they should experience similar expected network performance, in terms of cell loss ratio, cell transfer delay, and cell delay variation. Alternatively, when different VCCs within the same VPC require different QoS, the VPC performance objectives agreed by network and subscriber should be set suitably for the most demanding VCC requirement.

In either case, with multiple VCCs within the same VPC, the network has two general options for allocating capacity to the VPC:

- **Aggregate peak demand:** The network may set the capacity (data rate) of the VPC equal to the total of the peak data rates of all of the VCCs within the

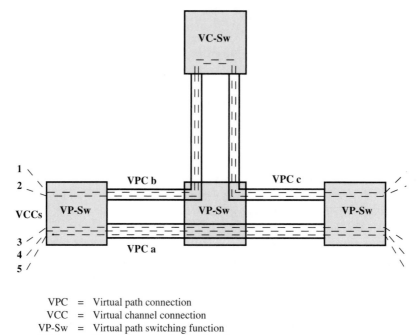

VPC   = Virtual path connection
VCC   = Virtual channel connection
VP-Sw = Virtual path switching function
VC-Sw = Virtual channel switching function

Figure 12.4   Configuration of VCCs and VPCs.

VPC. The advantage of this approach is that each VCC can be given a QoS that accommodates its peak demand. The disadvantage is that most of the time, the VPC capacity will not be fully utilized and therefore the network will have underutilized resources.

- **Statistical multiplexing:** If the network sets the capacity of the VPC to be greater than or equal to the average data rates of all the VCCs but less than the aggregate peak demand, then a statistical multiplexing service is supplied. With statistical multiplexing, VCCs experience greater cell delay variation and greater cell transfer delay. Depending on the size of buffers used to queue cells for transmission, VCCs may also experience greater cell loss ratio. This approach has the advantage of more efficient utilization of capacity and is attractive if the VCCs can tolerate the lower QoS.

When statistical multiplexing is used, it is preferable to group VCCs into VPCs on the basis of similar traffic characteristics and similar QoS requirements. If dissimilar VCCs share the same VPC and statistical multiplexing is used, it is difficult to provide fair access to both high-demand and low-demand traffic streams.

Connection Admission Control

Connection admission control is the first line of defense for the network in protecting itself from excessive loads. In essence, when a user requests a new VPC or VCC, the user must specify (implicitly or explicitly) the service required in both directions for that connection. The request consists of the following:

- Service category (CBR, rt-VBR, nrt-vBR, ABR, UBR)
- Connection traffic descriptor, consisting of
  —Source traffic descriptor (PCR, SCR, MBS, MCR)
  —CDVT
  —Requested conformance definition
- Requested and acceptable value of each QoS parameter (peak-to-peak CDV, maxCTD, CLR).

The network accepts the connection only if it can commit the resources necessary to support that traffic level while at the same time maintaining the agreed QoS of existing connections. By accepting the connection, the network forms a *traffic contract* with the user. Once the connection is accepted, the network continues to provide the agreed QoS as long as the user complies with the traffic contract.

For a given connection (VPC or VCC) the traffic contract parameters may be specified in several ways, as illustrated in Table 12.3. Parameter values may be implicitly defined by default rules set by the network operator. In this case, all connections are assigned the same values, or all connections of a given class are assigned the same values for that class. The network operator may also associate parameter values with a given subscriber and assign these at the time of subscription. Finally, parameter values tailored to a particular connection may be assigned at connection time. In the case of a permanent virtual connection, these values are assigned by the network when the connection is set up. For a switched virtual connection, the parameters are negotiated between the user and the network via a signaling protocol.

Another aspect of the traffic contract that may be requested or assigned for a connection is cell loss priority. A user may request two levels of cell loss priority for an ATM connection; the priority of an individual cell is indicated by the user through the CLP bit in the cell header (Figure 4.4). When two priority levels are used, the traffic parameters for both cell flows must be specified. Typically, this is done by specifying a set of traffic parameters for high-priority traffic (CLP = 0) and a set of traffic parameters for all traffic (CLP = 0 + 1). Based on this breakdown, the network may be able to allocate resources more efficiently.

TABLE 12.3 PROCEDURES USED TO SET VALUES OF TRAFFIC CONTRACT PARAMETERS

	Explicitly Specified Parameters		Implicitly Specified Parameters
	Parameter values set at connection-setup time	Parameter values specified at subscription time	Parameter values set using default rules
	Requested by user/NMS	assigned by network operator	
SVC	signaling	by subscription	network-operator default rules.
PVC	NMS	by subscription	network-operator default rules.

SVC = switched virtual connection, PVC = permanent virtual connection, NMS = network management system.

Usage Parameter Control

Once a connection has been accepted by the Connection Admission Control function, the Usage Parameter Control (UPC) function of the network monitors the connection to determine whether the traffic conforms to the traffic contract. The main purpose of Usage Parameter Control is to protect network resources from an overload on one connection that would adversely affect the QoS on other connections by detecting violations of assigned parameters and taking appropriate actions.

UPC Location

Usage parameter control can be done at both the virtual path and virtual channel levels. Of these, the more important is VPC-level control, because network resources are, in general, initially allocated on the basis of virtual paths, with the virtual path capacity shared among the member virtual channels.

The place at which usage parameter control can be exercised depends on the configuration, as illustrated in Figure 12.5. If the first point of termination of a VCC is a node within the network that performs virtual channel connection related functions (case A), then UPC is performed on incoming cells before the VCC switching function is executed. If a VCC passes through one or more VPC switching points before connection to a VCC switching point within the network (case B), then

1. Usage parameter control is performed on incoming cells on a virtual path basis at the VPC switching points.
2. Usage parameter control is performed on a virtual channel basis at the first point where VCC-related functions are performed.

Finally, if a VCC is connected to a user or another network provider (case C), then this network provides usage parameter control only at the virtual path level.

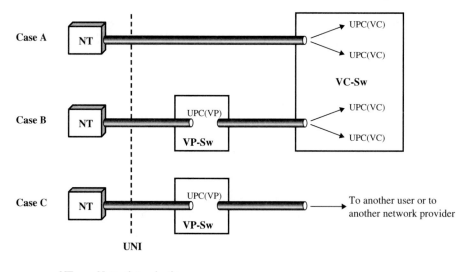

NT   = Network termination
VP-Sw = Virtual path switching function
VC-Sw = Virtual channel switching function

Figure 12.5   Location of the usage parameter control function.

Peak Cell Rate Algorithm

So far, we have discussed usage parameter control in general terms, without specifying how the UPC function determines whether the user is complying with the traffic contract. There are two separate functions encompassed by UPC:

- Control of peak cell rate and the associated CDVT
- Control of sustainable cell rate and the associated burst tolerance.

Let us first consider the peak cell rate and the associated CDVT. In simple terms, a traffic flow is compliant if the peak rate of cell transmission does not exceed the agreed peak cell rate, subject to the possibility of cell delay variation within the agreed bound.

I.371 and the ATM Traffic Management Specification provide an algorithm that (1) serves as an operational definition of the relationship between peak cell rate and CDVT, and (2) can be used for usage parameter control to monitor compliance with the traffic contract.

Figure 12.6 shows two equivalent versions of the algorithm. The algorithm is referred to as the generic cell rate algorithm because it is also used for the sustainable cell rate, as explained later. The algorithm takes two arguments, an increment I and a limit L, and is expressed as GCRA(I, L).

It is useful to examine both versions to gain greater insight into the relationship between the two parameters. Suppose that we have specified a peak cell rate R and a CDVT limit of τ. Then $T = 1/R$ is the interarrival time between cells if there were no CDVT. With CDVT, T is the average interarrival time at the peak rate. The peak cell rate algorithm is therefore expressed as GCRA(T, τ).

Consider the **virtual scheduling algorithm**. The algorithm is initialized with the arrival of the first cell on a connection at time $t_a(1)$. The algorithm updates a theoretical arrival time (TAT), which is a target time for the next cell arrival. If the cell arrives later than the TAT, then it is compliant and the TAT is updated to the arrival time plus T. If the cell arrives earlier than TAT but within τ time units of TAT, then the cell is still considered compliant and TAT is incremented by T. In this latter case, it is permissible for the cell to arrive early because is does so within the CDVT. Finally, if the cell arrives too early (before TAT $- \tau$), then it is outside the CDVT bound and is declared noncompliant; in this case TAT remains unchanged. Figure 12.7a illustrates these three zones.

An example of this algorithm is shown in Figure 12.8. For this figure, the time to insert a single 53-octet cell is δ, and $T = 4.5\delta$. Thus, the peak cell rate is equal to the data rate at the UNI divided by 4.5. For example, if the data rate is 150 Mbps, then the peak cell rate is $150/4.5 = 26.67$ Mbps. Figure 12.8a allows the minimum CDVT ($\tau = \delta/2$), just enough to accommodate the fact that data are transmitted in cells and therefore each arrival time will be an integer multiple of δ, whereas the increment value is on a 0.5 mark. Because of the tight tolerance, the cell arrival time can never drift very far from the TAT.

As the CDVT τ increases, cell arrivals can drift increasingly far from the TAT. More significantly, the potential for cell clumping, which is the phenomenon that will stress network resources, increases. The greatest degree of clumping occurs when it is possible for a source to transmit multiple cells back to back, (i.e., at the

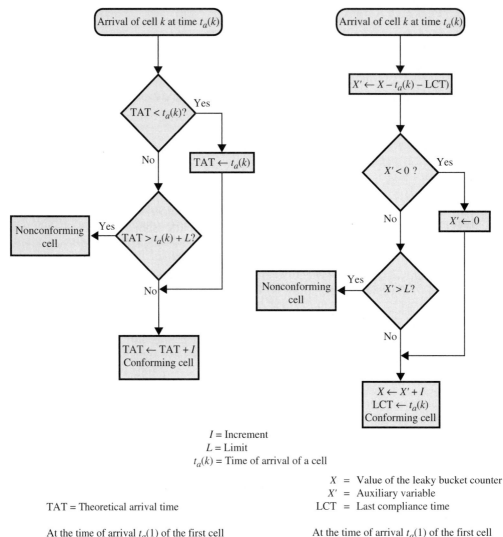

I = Increment
L = Limit
$t_a(k)$ = Time of arrival of a cell

X = Value of the leaky bucket counter
X' = Auxiliary variable
LCT = Last compliance time

TAT = Theoretical arrival time

At the time of arrival $t_a(1)$ of the first cell
of the connection, TAT = $t_a(1)$

At the time of arrival $t_a(1)$ of the first cell
of the connection, $X = 0$ and LCT = $t_a(1)$

(a) Virtual scheduling algorithm

(b) Continuous-state leaky bucket algorithm

Figure 12.6 Equivalent versions of the generic cell rate algorithm—GCRA(I,L).

full link rate). This condition is possible when τ exceeds $T - \delta$. Specifically, for $\tau > T - \delta$, the maximum number N of conforming back-to-back cells equals

$$N = \left\lfloor 1 + \frac{\tau}{T - \delta} \right\rfloor \tag{12.1}$$

where $\lfloor x \rfloor$ stands for the integer part of x. Back-to-back cell clumping is illustrated in Figures 12.8c and 12.8d.

Returning to the flowchart in Figure 12.6a, note that it is not possible to build up credit. If a cell arrives late, meaning that there has been an idle period on this

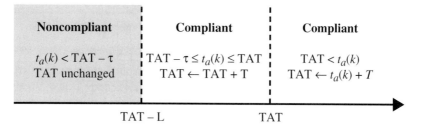

Noncompliant	**Compliant**	**Compliant**
$t_a(k) < \text{TAT} - \tau$	$\text{TAT} - \tau \leq t_a(k) \leq \text{TAT}$	$\text{TAT} < t_a(k)$
TAT unchanged	$\text{TAT} \leftarrow \text{TAT} + T$	$\text{TAT} \leftarrow t_a(k) + T$

TAT – L $\qquad\qquad$ TAT

(a) Virtual scheduling algorithm

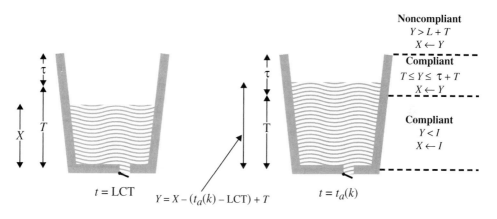

Noncompliant
$Y > L + T$
$X \leftarrow Y$

Compliant
$T \leq Y \leq \tau + T$
$X \leftarrow Y$

Compliant
$Y < I$
$X \leftarrow I$

$t = \text{LCT}$ $\qquad$ $Y = X - (t_a(k) - \text{LCT}) + T$ $\qquad$ $t = t_a(k)$

(b) Continuous-state leaky bucket algorithm

Figure 12.7 Depiction of GCRA(T, τ).

connection, the next value of TAT is set relative to the current arrival, rather than the current value of TAT. If this rule were not followed and TAT were simply incremented by T after every cell arrival, then the occurrence of a long idle period would enable a source to send a long string of cells at the full link rate. This would create a surge not accounted for in the network resource allocation.

The GCRA can also be expressed as a **leaky bucket algorithm**. The basic principle of leaky bucket is depicted in Figure 12.9. The algorithm maintains a running count of the cumulative amount of data sent in a counter X. The counter is decremented at a constant rate of one unit per time unit to a minimum value of zero; this is equivalent to a bucket that leaks at a rate of 1. The counter is incremented by I for each arriving cell, subject to the restriction that the maximum counter value is $I + L$. Any arriving cell that would cause the counter to exceed its maximum is defined as nonconforming; this is equivalent to a bucket with a capacity of $I + L$.

Figure 12.6b shows a leaky bucket algorithm that is equivalent to that of Figure 12.6a. The algorithm defines a finite-capacity bucket that drains at a continuous rate of 1 unit per time unit and whose content is increased by T for each compliant cell. The total capacity of the bucket is $T + \tau$. After the arrival of the kth cell, at $t_a(k)$, the algorithm checks to see if the bucket has overflowed. If so, the cell is nonconforming. If not, the bucket is incremented. The amount of the increment depends on whether the bucket was fully drained between cell arrivals. Figure 12.7b

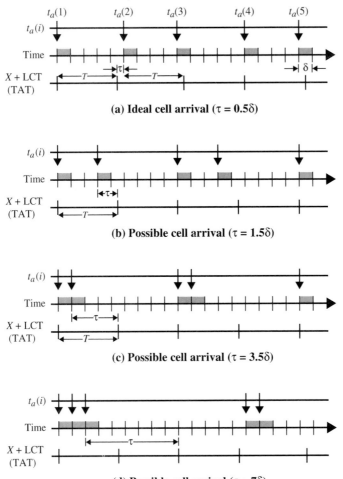

Figure 12.8 Cell arrival at the user-network interface ($T = 4.5\delta$).

illustrates the algorithm; the left part shows the state of the bucket after a cell has been processed, and the right part shows the state of the bucket after a new cell arrives. A review of Figure 12.8 shows that this algorithm is equivalent to that of Figure 12.6a.

Sustainable Cell Rate Algorithm

The sustainable cell rate algorithm (1) serves as an operational definition of the relationship between sustainable cell rate and burst tolerance, and (2) can be used for usage parameter control to monitor compliance with the traffic contract.

The same algorithm that is used to define peak cell rate monitoring is also used to define sustainable cell rate monitoring. In this case, for a sustainable cell rate R_s, $T_s = 1/R_s$ is the interarrival time between cells at that rate if there is no burstiness. The burst tolerance is represented as τ_s. Thus the sustainable cell rate algorithm is expressed as GCRA(T_s, τ_s).

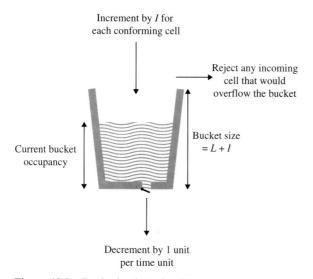

Increment by I for each conforming cell

Reject any incoming cell that would overflow the bucket

Bucket size $= L + I$

Current bucket occupancy

Decrement by 1 unit per time unit

Figure 12.9   Leaky bucket algorithm.

Unlike the CDVT, the burst tolerance is not selected directly. Rather, it is derived from an understanding of the burstiness of the traffic stream. In particular, let T be the time between cells at the peak rate. If the traffic stream is constrained by both a peak cell rate using $\text{GCRA}(T, \tau)$ and a sustainable cell rate $\text{GCRA}(T_s, \tau_s)$, then the maximum burst size MBS that may be transmitted at the peak rate is given by

$$MBS = \left\lfloor 1 + \frac{\tau_s}{T_s - T} \right\rfloor \tag{12.2}$$

In the signaling message, the burst tolerance is conveyed using MBS, which is coded in number of cells. The MBS is then used to derive τ_s, which in turn is used in the GCRA algorithm to monitor the sustainable cell rate. Given the MBS, T, and T_s, then τ_s can be any value in the interval

$$[(MBS - 1)(T_s - T), MBS(T_s - T)] \tag{12.3}$$

For uniformity, the minimum value is used:

$$\tau_s = (MBS - 1)(T_s - T)$$

UPC Actions

The GCRA algorithm, or some similar algorithm, is used by the network to ensure compliance with the negotiated traffic contract. The simplest strategy is that compliant cells are passed along and noncompliant cells are discarded at the point of the UPC function.

When no additional network resource has been allocated to CLP = 1 traffic flow, CLP = 0 cells identified as nonconforming are discarded. If the user has negotiated two levels of cell loss priority for a network, then the situation is more complex. The following rules apply:

1. A cell with CLP = 0 that conforms to the traffic contract for CLP = 0 passes.
2. A cell with CLP = 0 that is noncompliant for (CLP = 0) traffic but compliant for (CLP = 0 + 1) traffic is tagged and passed.
3. A cell with CLP = 0 that is noncompliant for (CLP = 0) traffic and noncompliant for (CLP = 0 + 1) traffic is discarded.
4. A cell with CLP = 1 that is compliant for (CLP = 0 + 1) traffic is passed.
5. A cell with CLP = 1 that is noncompliant for (CLP = 0 + 1) traffic is discarded.

Figure 12.10 illustrates the relationship between the UPC function and the CLP bit. The UPC function first tests the (CLP = 0) flow for compliance and then the combined (CLP = 0 + 1) flow. If the tagging option is used, a noncompliant (CLP = 0) cell is tagged but still considered part of the (CLP = 0 + 1) flow and subjected to the second test.

Selective Cell Discard

Selective cell discard comes into play when the network, at some point beyond the UPC function, discards (CLP = 1) cells. The objective is to discard lower-priority cells to protect the performance for higher-priority cells. Note that the network has no way to discriminate between cells that were labeled as lower priority by the source and cells that were tagged by the UPC function.

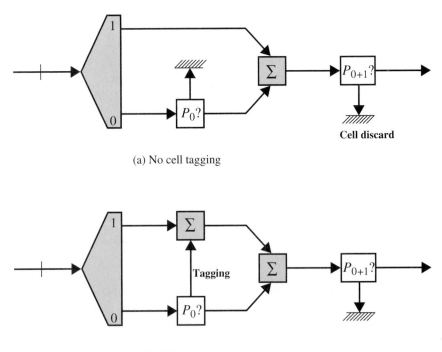

(a) No cell tagging

(b) Cell tagging

$P?$ = Compliance test for parameter P

Figure 12.10 Possible actions of the UPC function.

Traffic Shaping

The GCRA algorithm is referred to as a form of **traffic policing**. Traffic policing occurs when a flow of data is regulated so that cells (or frames or packets) that exceed a certain performance level are discarded or tagged. It may be desirable to supplement a traffic policing policy with a **traffic shaping** policy. Traffic shaping is used to smooth out a traffic flow and reduce cell clumping. This can result in a fairer allocation of resources and a reduced average delay time.

A simple approach to traffic shaping is to use a form of the leaky bucket algorithm known as token bucket. In contrast to the GCRA leaky bucket (Figure 12.9), which simply monitors the traffic and rejects or discards noncompliant cells, a traffic shaping leaky bucket controls the flow of compliant cells.

Figure 12.11 illustrates the basic principle of the token bucket. A token generator produces tokens at a rate of ρ tokens per second and places these in the token bucket, which has a maximum capacity of β tokens. Cells arriving from the source are placed in a buffer with a maximum capacity of K cells. To transmit a cell through the server, one token must be removed from the cell. If the token bucket is empty, the cell is queued waiting for the next token. The result of this scheme is that if there is a backlog of cells and an empty bucket, then cells are emitted at a smooth flow of ρ cells per second with no cell delay variation until the backlog is cleared. Thus, the token bucket smoothes out bursts of cells.

12.5 ABR TRAFFIC MANAGEMENT

The QoS provided for CBR, rt-VBR, and nrt-VBR is based on (1) a traffic contract that specifies the characteristics of the cell flow and (2) UPC performed by the network to enforce the flow. During the connection admission process, the network uses the proposed traffic contract to determine if resources are available for this new connection. If so, and once the connection is established, UPC may discard or tag as lower priority any cell that exceeds the parameters of the traffic contract. There is no feedback to the source concerning congestion. The approach just described is referred to as **open-loop control** because of its lack of feedback.

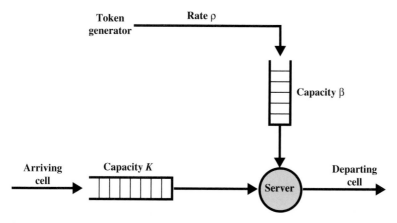

Figure 12.11   Token bucket for traffic shaping.

The open-loop approach is not suited to many data applications. Typical non-real-time applications, such as file transfer, Web access, remote procedure calls, distributed file service, and so on, do not have well-defined traffic characteristics, other than perhaps a peak cell rate. The PCR by itself is not sufficient for the network to allocate resources effectively. Furthermore, such applications can generally tolerate unpredictable delays and time-varying throughput.

Such applications can be handled in one of two ways. One possibility is to allow these applications to share the unused capacity in a relatively uncontrolled fashion. As congestion rises, cells will be lost, and the various sources will back off and reduce their data rate; this style of transmission fits will with TCP's congestion control techniques, discussed in Chapter 11, and this is the mode of operation for the UBR service. This approach is referred to as **best effort**. The disadvantage of the best-effort approach is its inefficiency: Cells are dropped, causing retransmissions.

The other way is to allow a number of sources to share the capacity not used by CBR and VBR but to provide feedback to sources to adjust the load dynamically and thus avoid cell loss and share the capacity fairly. This is referred to as **closed-loop control** because of its use of feedback. This approach is used for ABR.

In this section, we provide an overview of the ABR service and look in some detail at the feedback mechanism used to control cell flow.

ABR Rate Control

[CHEN96] lists the following as the chief characteristics of the ABR service:

1. ABR connections share available capacity. ABR connections have access to the instantaneous capacity unused by CBR/VBR connections. Thus, ABR can increase network utilization without affecting the QoS of CBR/VBR connections.

2. The share of available capacity used by a single ABR connection is dynamic and varies between an agreed MCR and PCR. The MCR assigned to a particular connection may be zero. With a nonzero MCR, the network provides an assurance of minimum throughput; however, a source may transmit at less than a nonzero MCR over any period of time.

3. The network provides feedback to ABR sources so that ABR flow is limited to available capacity. The time delays inherent in providing feedback dictate the use of buffers along a connection's path; the buffers absorb excess traffic generated prior to the arrival of the feedback at the source. Because of the large data rate and relatively large propagation delay through a network, these buffers may be substantial, leading to large delays. Accordingly, the ABR service is appropriate for applications that can tolerate adjustments to their transmission rates and unpredictable cell delays.

4. For ABR sources that adapt their transmission rate to the provided feedback, a low cell loss ratio is guaranteed. This is a major distinction between ABR and UBR.

Feedback Mechanisms

The rate of transmission of cells from a source on an ABR connection is characterized by four parameters:

- **Allowed cell rate (ACR):** The current rate at which the source is permitted to transmit cells. The source may transmit at any rate between zero and ACR.
- **Minimum cell rate (MCR):** The minimum value that ACR may take (i.e., the network will not restrict a source's flow to less than MCR). MCR may, however, be set to zero for a given connection.
- **Peak cell rate (PCR):** The maximum value that ACR may take.
- **Initial cell rate (ICR):** The initial value assigned to ACR.

A source starts out with ACR = ICR and dynamically adjusts ACR based on feedback from the network. Feedback is provided periodically in the form of a sequence of resource management (RM) cells. Each cell contains three fields that provide feedback to the source: a *congestion indication* (CI) bit, a *no increase* (NI) bit, and an *explicit cell rate* (ER) field. The source reacts according to the following rules:

```
if CI = 1
   reduce ACR by an amount proportional to the current ACR but not
   less than MCR
else if NI = 0 increase ACR by an amount proportional to PCR but
   not more than PCR
if ACR > ER set ACR <- max [ER, MCR]
```

Thus, the source first checks the two feedback bits. If an increase is called for, it is a fixed-size increment equal to RIF × PCR, where RIF is a fixed *rate increase factor*. If a decrease is called for, the decrease is exponential by an amount RDF × ACR, where RDF is a *fixed rate decrease* factor. Finally, if ER is smaller than ACR, the source reduces ACR to ER. All of these adjustments are subject to the constraint that ACR varies between the limits of MCR and PCR. The following table summarizes these rules:

NI	CI	Action
0	0	$ACR \leftarrow max[MCR, min[ER, PCR, ACR + RIF \times PCR]]$
0	1	$ACR \leftarrow max[MCR, min[ER, ACR(1 - RDF)]]$
1	0	$ACR \leftarrow max[MCR, min[ER, ACR]]$
1	1	$ACR \leftarrow max[MCR, min[ER, ACR(1 - RDF)]]$

Figure 12.12 illustrates the effect of feedback on ACR. For this example an RIF of 1/16 is used, which is the default value; as can be seen, each increase is by a constant amount. The default value for RDF is also 1/16, but a value of 1/4 is used in Figure 12.12 to highlight the exponential effect of RDF: The amount of the decrease is proportional to the current value of ACR. With linear increase and exponential decrease, the source will slowly increase its rate when there is no evidence of congestion, but at high rates will rapidly decrease its rate when there is indication of congestion.

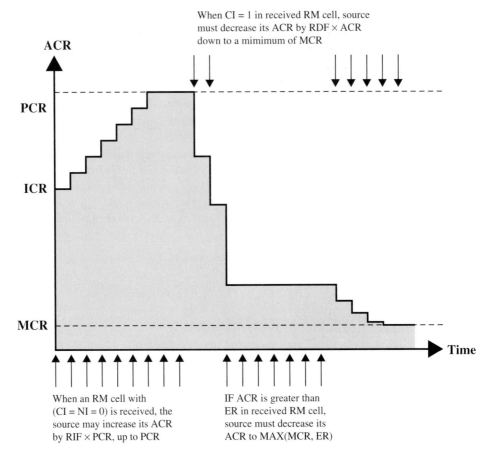

Figure 12.12 Variations in allowed cell rate (based on [SAIT96]).

Cell Flow

Having looked at the way in which a source reacts to feedback, we now describe the way in which feedback is provided. Figure 12.13 illustrates the mechanism. This figure depicts a flow of data in one direction over an ATM connection; a similar flow occurs in the opposite sense for two-way data communication.

Two types of ATM cells flow on an ABR connection: data cells and resource management cells. A source receives a regular sequence of RM cells that provide feedback to enable it to adjust its rate of cell transmission. The bulk of the RM cells are initiated by the source, which transmits one **forward RM (FRM) cell** for every (Nrm − 1) data cells, where Nrm is a preset parameter (usually equal to 32). As each FRM is received at the destination, it is turned around and transmitted back to the source as a **backward RM (BRM) cell**.

Each FRM contains the CI, NI, and ER fields. The source typically sets CI = 0, NI = 0 or 1, and ER equal to some desired transmission rate in the range ICR ≤ ER ≤ PCR. Any of these fields may be changed by an ATM switch or the destination system before the corresponding BRM returns to the source.

An ATM switch has a number of ways to provide rate control feedback to a source:

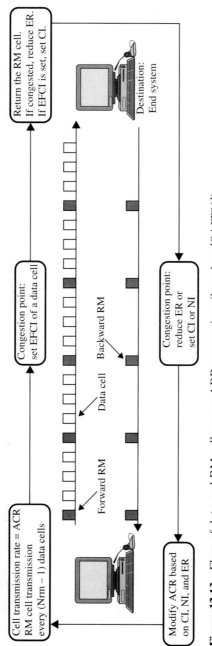

Figure 12.13 Flow of data and RM cells on an ABR connection (based on [SAIT96]).

- **EFCI marking:** The switch may set the EFCI (explicit forward congestion indication) condition in an ATM data cell header (using the payload type field) as it passes in the forward direction. This will cause the destination end system to set the CI bit in a BRM cell.
- **Relative rate marking:** The switch may directly set the CI or NI bit of a passing RM. If the bit is set in an FRM, then that bit will remain set in the corresponding BRM when the turnaround occurs at the destination. More rapid results are achieved by setting one of these bits in a passing BRM. To achieve the most rapid result, a switch may generate a BRM with CI or NI set rather than wait for a passing BRM.
- **Explicit rate marking:** The switch may reduce the value of the ER field of an FRM or BRM.

These actions enable an ATM switch to signal a source that congestion is occurring and to reduce its cell rate. The destination system can also signal congestion. Under normal conditions, a destination system simply converts each incoming FRM to a BRM without changing the NI, CI, or ER fields, except that the CI bit is set if an EFCI signal has been received on the previous data cell. However, if the destination is experiencing congestion, it may set the CI or NI bit, or reduce the ER value when converting an FRM to a BRM.

The first ATM switches to support ABR use the EFCI, NI, and CI bits, providing a simple relative-rate control mechanism. The more complex controls associated with the use of explicit rate constitute a second generation of ABR service.

Note that the general structure of the flow in Figure 12.13 resembles the TCP segment pacing using ACKs (see Figure 10.7). There are two crucial differences. First, ABR feedback controls the rate of transmission of cells whereas TCP feedback controls a window size. Hence, the ABR technique is referred to as *rate control* in contrast to TCP's *credit control*. Second, in ABR, feedback may be provided either by an intermediate ATM switch or the destination, whereas in TCP the feedback is only provided by the destination.

RM Cell Format

Figure 12.14 shows the format of an RM cell. It includes the following elements:

- **Header (5 octets):** The ATM header has PT = 110 to indicate an RM cell. For rate control on a virtual channel, the VPI and VCI are identical to those of data cells on that connection. For rate control on a virtual path, the same VPI is used and VCI = 6.
- **Protocol identifier (1 octet):** Identifies service using this RM cell. For ABR, ID = 1.
- **Message type (1 octet):** Contains the following 1-bit indicators:
    Direction (DIR): FRM (DIR = 0) or BRM (DIR = 1).
    BECN cell (BN): Indicates cell initially generated by source (BN = 0) or by a switch or destination (BN = 1).
    Congestion indication (CI): (CI = 1) indicates congestion.
    No increase (NI): (NI = 1) indicates no additive increase allowed.
    Request/acknowledge (RA): Defined in I.371; not used in ATM Forum ABR.

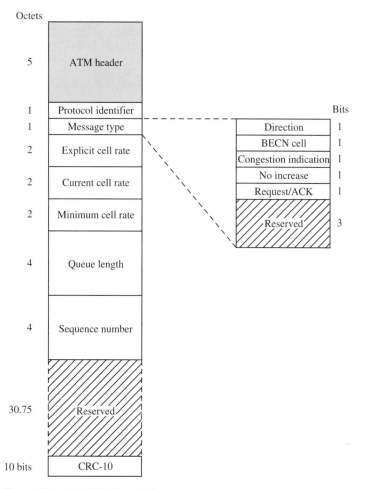

Figure 12.14   ABR RM cell format.

- **Explicit cell rate (2 octets):** Used to limit the source ACR to a specified value.
- **Current cell rate (2 octets):** Set by source to its current ACR. This may be useful to network elements in determining a value for ER.
- **Minimum cell rate (2 octets):** Set by source. May be useful to network elements in allocating capacity among connections.
- **Queue length (4 octets):** Defined in I.371; not used in ATM Forum ABR.
- **Sequence number (4 octets):** Defined in I.371; not used in ATM Forum ABR.
- **CRC-10 (10 bits):** An error detection code that covers the RM payload (entire cell except for header).

Table 12.4 shows the initial values assigned to an RM cell when it is first generated. In addition to the RM fields, there are a number of parameters that control the ABR mechanism; these are defined in Table 12.5.

TABLE 12.4 INITIAL VALUES OF RM CELL FIELDS

Field	If source generated	If switch generated or destination generated
Direction (DIR)	0	1
BECN Cell (BN)	0	1
Congestion Indication (CI)	0	0 or 1
No Increase (NI)	0 or 1	0 or 1
Explicit Cell Rate (ECR)	≤ PCR parameter	any rate value
Current Cell Rate (CCR)	ACR parameter	0
Minimum Cell Rate (MCR)	MCR parameter	0

TABLE 12.5 ABR PARAMETERS

Label	Name	Description	Default
PCR	Peak cell rate	Fixed upper limit on source rate	—
MCR	Minimum cell rate	Lower limit on source rate guaranteed by network	0
ICR	Initial cell rate	Initial value of ACR; rate at which source should send initially and after an idle period	PCR
RIF	Rate increase factor	Amount by which cell transmission rate may increase upon receipt of an RM cell	1/16
Nrm		Maximum number of cells a source may send for each forward RM cell	32
Mrm		Controls allocation of bandwidth between forward RM cells, backward RM cells, and data cells	2
RDF	Rate decrease factor	Multiplicative factor that controls the decrease of cell transmission rate	1/16
ACR	Allowed cell rate	Current upper limit on source rate; adjusted by feedback within the range of MCR to PCR	—
CRM		Number of forward RM cells that may be sent in the absence of received backward RM cells	$2^{19} - 1$
ADTF	ACR decrease time factor	Time allowed between sending RM cells before the rate is decreased to ICR	0.5 ms
Trm		Upper bound on the time between consecutive forward RM cells for an active source	100 ms
FRTT	Fixed round-trip time	Sum of the fixed and propagation delays from source to destination and back	—
TBE	Transient buffer exposure	Negotiated number of cells that source can send initially before first RM cell returns	$2^{24} - 1$
CDF	Cutoff decrease factor	Controls decrease in ACR in combination with CRM	1/16
TCR	Tagged cell rate	Upper limit on rate at which a source may send out-of-rate forward RM cells	10 cells/s

ABR Capacity Allocation

In support of the ABR service, ATM switches must perform two functions:

- **Congestion control:** Because the ABR service is to provide for minimal cell loss, the rate control mechanisms of ABR must be used by switches to limit the rate of arriving packets to that which can be handled by the network. For this purpose, a switch must monitor queue lengths and begin to throttle back rates as the buffers approach capacity.
- **Fair capacity allocation:** An ATM switch should allocate a fair share of its capacity among all connections that pass through this switch point. Therefore, when congestion arises, the switch should throttle back on those connections that are using more than their fair share of the capacity.

These design requirements are similar to those for routers in an IP-based network, as discussed in Sections 11.4 and 11.5. The difference is that in the case of IP routers, the only signals that can be sent to sources are implicit (increasing delay and cell loss), whereas with ABR, explicit signals for rate control can be sent.

Switch algorithms for congestion control and fair capacity allocation fall into two broad categories: binary feedback schemes that use only the EFCI, CI and NI bits, and explicit rate feedback schemes that use the ER field. This is an area of active ongoing research. Here we survey some of the most important schemes proposed in the two categories.

Binary Feedback Schemes

All binary feedback schemes have the same general structure. An ATM switch monitors its buffer utilization on each output port. When congestion approaches, the switch performs a binary notification either by setting the EFCI on a forward data cell or by setting CI or NI on a forward or backward RM. The distinction among different schemes is in the determination of which connection to notify first. We summarize three approaches: single FIFO queue, multiple queues, and fair share notification.

The simplest approach is to dedicate the buffer at each output port to a **single FIFO queue**. When buffer occupancy exceeds a threshold (e.g., 80% of buffer size), the switch begins to issue binary notifications and continues to do so until buffer occupancy falls below the threshold. Notification could be issued by marking the EFCI in each incoming data cell or by setting CI or NI on each passing RM cell. A minor refinement is the use of two thresholds. When queue length increases sufficiently to cross the upper threshold, binary notification begins. Binary notification ceases only when the queue decreases below the lower threshold. This is similar to the operation of a thermostat and prevents frequent on/off transitions.

On the face of it, this approach seems fair, because a connection that has relatively more cells passing through a switch has a greater probability of receiving a binary notification. However, the single FIFO queue may unfairly penalize connections that pass through a number of switches. Suppose that a number of switches in the network are congested. In that case, connections that pass through more switches have a greater probability of receiving a binary notification than connections with comparable traffic but a shorter path.

Fairness can be improved by allocating a **separate queue** to each virtual connection or to each group of VCs. A separate threshold is used on each queue so that at any time, binary notification is provided only to VCs with long queues. In addition to being more fair, this approach has two other advantages. First, because each queue is isolated from the others, a misbehaving source will not affect other VCs. Second, the delay and loss behavior of individual VCs are decoupled, resulting in the potential of giving different QoS to different VCs.

More sophisticated is a technique referred to as selective feedback or intelligent marking. This technique is based on trying to allocate a **fair share** of the capacity dynamically. For example, we can define

$$Fairshare = \frac{\text{Target rate}}{\text{Number of connections}}$$

When congestion occurs, the switch marks cells on any VC which satisfies CCR > *Fairshare*.

Explicit Rate Feedback Schemes

All explicit rate feedback schemes share the following general functions:

1. Compute the fair share of the capacity for each VC that can be supported.
2. Determine the current load, or degree of congestion.
3. Compute an explicit rate (ER) for each connection and send that ER to the source.

In the remainder of this section, we describe the following examples of explicit rate feedback:

- Enhanced proportional rate control algorithm (EPRCA)
- Explicit rate indication for congestion avoidance (ERICA)
- Congestion avoidance using proportional control (CAPC).

For the **EPRCA** scheme, a switch keeps track of the average value of the current load on each connection, which is termed the mean allowed cell rate (MACR):

$$MACR(I) = (1 - \alpha) \times MACR(I - 1) + \alpha \times CCR(I)$$

where $CCR(I)$ is the value of the CCR field in the Ith arriving FRM. This is an exponential average of the kind we have seen a number of times in this book. Typically, $\alpha = 1/16$, so that more weight is given to past values of CCR than the current value. Thus, MACR represents an estimate of the average load passing through the switch at the current time. The objective is this: If congestion occurs, the switch reduces each VC to no more than DPF × MACR, where DPF is a *down pressure factor*. Because all VCs are reduced to the same ER, the throttling is performed fairly. Specifically, when the queue length at an output port exceeds a threshold, all RMs for connections that pass through that port are updated as follows:

$$ER \leftarrow \min[ER, DPF \times MACR]$$

A typical value for DPF is 7/8.

The EPRCA scheme reacts to congestion by lowering the ERs of VCs that are consuming more than their fair share of capacity. The next two schemes are congestion avoidance schemes that attempt to manage the ERs of all connections to avoid the onset of severe congestion. Schemes in this category make adjustments based on a load factor LF defined as follows:

$$LF = \frac{\text{Input rate}}{\text{Target rate}} \tag{12.4}$$

The input rate is measured over a fixed averaging interval, and the target rate is set slightly below the link bandwidth (e.g., 85–90%). When LF > 1, congestion is threatened, and many VCs will have their rates reduced. When LF < 1, there is no congestion and rate reduction is not necessary. Both the ERICA and CAPC schemes make use of LF, and in both cases the objective is to maintain the network at a load LF close to 1.

The **ERICA algorithm** defines the fair share for each connection as follows:

$$Fairshare = \frac{\text{Target rate}}{\text{Number of connections}}$$

The current share used by a particular VC is defined as

$$VCshare = \frac{\text{CCR}}{\text{LF}}$$

This may seem a strange way to calculate share. To clarify, we expand using Equation 12.4:

$$VCshare = \frac{\text{CCR}}{\text{Input rate}} \times \text{Target rate}$$

The first term on the right-hand side says what fraction of the current load passing through this output port is due to this VC. Multiplying this by the target rate indicates the relative amount of the target rate that would be assigned to this VC if we simply adjusted all VC rates up or down so that the total input rate equals the target rate. Rather than adjust all VC rates up or down, ERICA selectively adjusts VC rates so that the total ER allocated to connections equals the target rate and is allocated fairly. This is achieved by using the following allocation:

$$ER = \max[Fairshare, VCshare] \tag{12.5}$$

The effect of this is the following. Under low loads (LF < 1) each VC is assigned an ER greater than its current CCR, with those VCs whose *VCshare* is less than their *Fairshare* receiving a proportionately greater increase. Under high loads (LF > 1), some VCs are assigned an ER greater than their current CCR, and some are assigned a lower ER, done in such a way as to benefit those VCs with the lesser shares.

To get some insight into the behavior of ERICA, consider a case in which congestion is currently low and all connections begin to send at high rates of CCR. ERICA allows all VCs to change their rate to *VCshare*, which aims at bringing the system to an efficient operating point (LF = 1). At this load, if some VCs drop their rate (reduce CCR); then LF drops and individual *VCshare* values increase. However, regardless of load, sources are allowed to send at a rate of at least *Fairshare*. The effect of these rules is that ERICA improves fairness at every step, even under overload conditions [JAIN96b].

Equation 12.5 does not take into account any restrictions placed on a flow by other switches upstream from this switch. No switch is allowed to increase the ER value in an RM, so we must revise the allocation as follows:

$$newER = \min[oldER, \max[\textit{Fairshare}, \textit{VCshare}]] \tag{12.6}$$

where oldER is the value in an incoming RM and newER is the value in the corresponding outgoing RM.

The CAPC algorithm also uses the load factor LF to determine ER assignments. The fair share for each VC is initialized at (target rate)/(number of connections), as in ERICA. Then, with each arriving RM, Fairshare is updated as follows:

    if LF < 1   *Fairshare* ← *Fairshare* × min[ERU, 1 + (1 − LF) × Rup)

    if LF > 1   *Fairshare* ← *Fairshare* × max[ERF, 1 - (LF - 1) × Rdn)

where

   ERU = determines the maximum increase allowed in the allotment of fair share; ERU > 1

   Rup = a slope parameter between 0.025 and 0.1

   ERF = determines the maximum decrease allowed in the allotment of fair share; typically set to 0.5

   Rdn = a slope parameter between 0.2 and 0.8

If the calculated value of Fairshare is lower than the ER value in the RM cell, then the ER field in the RM cell is set to Fairshare.

The CAPC algorithm is simpler to implement than ERICA. However, the algorithm has been shown to exhibit very large rate oscillations if RIF (rate increase factor) is set too high, and can sometimes lead to unfairness [ARUL96].

12.6 RECOMMENDED READING

Although there is a great deal of literature on ATM, there are relatively few good treatments of ATM traffic control and performance. [MCDY95] contains a thorough discussion of ATM traffic control for CBR and VBR. Two excellent treatments of ATM traffic characteristics and performance are [SCHW96] and [PITT96].

[CHEN96] is a good overview of ABR that contrasts this service with CBR and VBR and summarizes the traffic control mechanism. [JAIN96] provides a detailed explanation of the behavior of source and destination systems in transmitting data and RM cells. [ARUL96] is a broad survey of capacity allocations schemes for ABR service. [SAIT96] is a useful discussion of the performance implications of the various elements of the ABR traffic control mechanism. Two other helpful performance analyses are found in [BONO95] and [OSHA95]

ARUL96   Arulambalam, A., Chen, X., and Ansari, N. "Allocating Fair Rates for Available Bit Rate Service in ATM Networks." *IEEE Communications Magazine*, November 1996.

BONO95   Bonomi, F., and Fendick, K. "The Rate-based Flow Control Framework for the Available Bit Rate ATM Service." *IEEE Network*, March/April 1995.

CHEN96   Chen, T., Liu, S., and Samalam, V. "The Available Bit Rate Service for Data in ATM Networks." *IEEE Communications Magazine*, May 1996.

JAIN96   Jain, R. et al. "Source Behavior for ATM ABR Traffic Management: An Explanation. *IEEE Communications Magazine*, November 1996.

MCDY95   McDysan, D., and Spohn, D. *ATM: Theory and Application.* New York: McGraw-Hill, 1995.

OSHA95   Oshaki, H. et al. "Rate-based Congestion Control for ATM Networks." *Computer Communication Review*, April 1995.

PITT96   Pitts, J., and Schormans, J. *Introduction to ATM Design and Performance.* New York: Wiley, 1996.

SAIT96   Saito, J. et al. "Performance Issues in Public ABR Service." *IEEE Communications Magazine*, November 1996.

SCHW96   Schwartz, M. *Broadband Integrated Networks.* Upper Saddle River, NJ: Prentice Hall PTR, 1996.

12.7 PROBLEMS

12.1 **a.** Demonstrate that Equation 12.1 is correct.
  b. Demonstrate that Equation 12.2 is correct.
  c. Demonstrate that Equation 12.3 is correct.

12.2 Show that over any closed interval of length t, the number of cells $N(t)$, that can be emitted with spacing no less than T and still be in conformance with GCRA (T_s, τ_s) is bounded by

$$N(t) \leq \min\left(\left\lfloor 1 + \frac{t + \tau_s}{T_s} \right\rfloor, \left\lfloor 1 + \frac{t}{T} \right\rfloor\right)$$

12.3 For the ERICA algorithm, consider the action at a switch in which each incoming ER value is greater than or equal to the incoming CCR value, so that we may use Equation 12.5 rather than Equation 12.6; this corresponds to a case in which other switches are not restricting flow. List the conditions (e.g., in terms of LF, *Fairshare*, and *VCshare*) under which the ER assigned to a VC is greater than the current CCR and the conditions under which ER < CCR.

PART SIX

Internet Routing

ISSUES FOR PART SIX

The architecture of today's Internet is built on a collection of a small number (a dozen or so at the time of writing) core backbone providers called network service providers (NSPs). Each backbone consists of a packet-switching network running over high-speed lines and a boundary of high-performance routers. The NSPs share traffic at exchange points. Local and regional Internet service providers (ISPs) maintain their own communications facilities of routers and lines and contract with backbone providers to carry their traffic for the long haul.

Private networks owned and operated by businesses typically consist of a number of Ethernet-type LANs interconnected by leased lines or by public or private packet-switching networks. These networks, in turn, have one or more access points into the Internet.

The traffic that the Internet and these private internetworks must carry continues to grow and change. The demand generated by traditional data-based applications, such as electronic mail, usenet news, file transfer, and remote logon, is sufficient to challenge these systems. But the driving factors are the heavy use of the World Wide Web, which demands real-time response, and the increasing use of voice, image, and even video over internetwork architectures.

These internetwork schemes are essentially datagram packet-switching technology with routers functioning as the switches. This technology was not designed to handle voice and video and is straining to meet the demands placed on it. While some foresee the replacement of this conglomeration of Ethernet-based LANs, packet-based WANs, and IP-datagram-based routers with a seamless ATM transport service from desktop to backbone, that day is far off. Meanwhile, the internetworking and routing functions of these networks must be engineered to meet the load.

The performance problems in an internetwork environment are most readily seen on the Internet itself. During at least one period in 1996, some NSPs posted packet loss rates of 30% to 50%, while throughout the year some NSPs experienced losses approaching 30% with some regularity [BRUN96]. A 10% loss is noticeable in service performance, while a 50% loss almost renders the service unusable. Much of the problem can be traced not just to the sheer volume of traffic but also to the poor performance of the routers in maintaining routing tables and in selecting the best routes for a given class of traffic. These problems also show up in private internetworks, particularly when intranet services such as the Web are provided and when Ethernets and packet-switching WANs are used to carry voice and video.

The type of congestion control and traffic policing strategies that have proved effective in ATM networks do not directly carry over to a connectionless, packet-based internetwork architecture. The latter architecture does not rely on end-to-end virtual channels that can be managed in terms of capacity and variability of bit rate. Instead, the key to effective performance management in an packet-based internetwork environment is the router. The router must

1. Have the processing capacity to move IP datagrams through the router at extremely high rates.
2. Have sufficient knowledge of the networked configuration to pick a route that is appropriate to a given class of traffic and to compensate for congestion and failure in the internetwork.
3. Employ a scheme for exchanging routing information with other routers that is effective and does not excessively contribute to the traffic burden.

The first point is addressed in the domain of processor and operating system design and does not concern us here. The remaining points hinge on the routing function and the routing protocol that supports that function. This is the focus of Part Six.

ROAD MAP FOR PART SIX

Chapter 13: Overview of Graph Theory and Least-cost Paths

The central task of a router is to forward IP datagrams along a route that is preferred under some criterion. For this purpose, a routing metric, or cost function, is assigned to each router-to-router hop through the internet for a given type of service. The router must choose a route that minimizes the path cost for a datagram. Chapter 13 presents the algorithms that are typically used to compute this minimum path. The chapter also introduces some elementary concepts in graph theory that are needed to develop the routing algorithms.

Chapter 14: Routing Protocols

To determine a minimum-cost route, a router must have some information about the cost of alternative paths through the internetwork of which it is a part. Chapter 14 looks at important protocols that are used for the acquisition of such routing information.

Chapter 15: Routing for High-speed and Multimedia Traffic

Chapter 15 addresses the challenging issues raised when routers must function in a high-speed environment and must handle multimedia traffic. The chapter examines the concept of multicasting and the use of multicast routing protocols. Then the use of a resource reservation protocol to support the routing function is examined. Finally, the concept of IP switching is explored.

CHAPTER 13

OVERVIEW
OF GRAPH THEORY
AND LEAST-COST PATHS

The map of the London Underground, which can be seen inside every train, has been called a model of its kind, a work of art. It presents the underground network as a geometric grid. The tube lines do not, of course, lie at right angles to one another like the streets of Manhattan. Nor do they branch off at acute angles or form perfect oblongs.

—*King Solomon's Carpet,* **Barbara Vine (Ruth Rendell)**

Communications networks are represented in a natural way by graphs, in which the switches are the vertices of the graph and the communication lines are the edges of the graph. A number of concepts from graph theory are useful in the design of networks and in the development of routing algorithms.

This chapter begins with an introduction to some elementary concepts from graph theory. Following this, we look at two shortest-path algorithms that are used in most network and internet routing protocols.

The discussion in this chapter is necessarily abstract. Although the routing protocols discussed in Chapters 14 and 15 make use of the algorithms described in this chapter to determine specific routes, it is not essential to an understanding of the routing protocols to have a complete understanding of the shortest-path algorithms. Accordingly, the reader may safely skim or even skip this chapter on a first reading.

13.1 ELEMENTARY CONCEPTS OF GRAPH THEORY

A graph $G(V, E)$ consists of a two sets of objects called **vertices** (or nodes) and **edges** (or links), with each edge defined as an unordered pair of vertices. Graphs are depicted by representing the vertices as dots or circles and the edges as lines connecting the vertices. For example, in Figure 13.1a, the set V consists of $\{V_1, V_2, V_3, V_4, V_5, V_6\}$ and the set E consists of $\{(V_1, V_2), (V_1, V_3), (V_1, V_4), (V_2, V_3), (V_2, V_4), (V_3, V_4), (V_3, V_5), (V_3, V_6), (V_4, V_5), (V_5, V_6)\}$. A vertex i is **adjacent** to a vertex j in the vertex set V if (i, j) is an edge in the edge set E. The edge (i, j) is **incident** with the vertices i and j.

The magnitude of a graph is characterized by the number of vertices $|V|$, called the **order** of G, and the number of edges $|E|$, called the **size** of G. The running time of an algorithm performed on a graph is typically measured in terms of these two parameters. In Figure 13.1a, $|V| = 6$ and $|E| = 10$.

A graph can also be represented by an **adjacency matrix**. Number the vertices in some arbitrary manner 1, 2, ..., $|V|$. Then the $|V| \times |V|$ adjacency matrix $A = (a_{ij})$ is defined by:

$$a_{ij} = \begin{cases} 1 & \text{if } (i, j) \in E \\ 0 & \text{otherwise} \end{cases}$$

Figure 13.1b is an example. Note that the matrix is symmetrical about the diagonal from upper left to lower right; this is because an edge is defined as an unordered pair. Hence the edge (V_1, V_2) is the same as the edge (V_2, V_1).

Two edges that are incident on the same pair of vertices are called **parallel edges**. An edge incident on a single vertex is called a **loop**. A graph with neither loops nor parallel edges is called a **simple graph**.

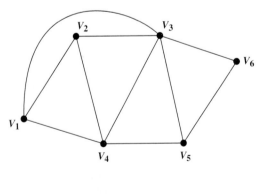

(a) Graph

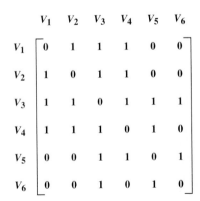

(b) Adjacency matrix

Figure 13.1   Graph with adjacency matrix.

A **path** from vertex i to vertex j is an alternating sequence of vertices and edges beginning with vertex i and ending with vertex j, such that each edge is incident on the preceding and following vertices. In a **simple path**, no vertex and no edge appears more than once in the sequence. In a simple graph, a path may be defined as a sequence of vertices, such that each vertex is adjacent to the preceding and following vertices in the sequence, and no vertex repeats.

The following are the simple paths from V_1 to V_6 in Figure 13.1:

$$V_1, V_2, V_3, V_4, V_5, V_6$$

$$V_1, V_2, V_3, V_5, V_6$$

$$V_1, V_2, V_3, V_6$$

$$V_1, V_2, V_4, V_3, V_5, V_6$$

$$V_1, V_2, V_4, V_5, V_6$$

$$V_1, V_3, V_2, V_4, V_5, V_6$$

$$V_1, V_3, V_4, V_5, V_6$$

$$V_1, V_3, V_5, V_6$$

$$V_1, V_3, V_6$$

$$V_1, V_4, V_2, V_3, V_5, V_6$$

$$V_1, V_4, V_2, V_3, V_6$$

$$V_1, V_4, V_3, V_5, V_6$$

$$V_1, V_4, V_3, V_6$$

$$V_1, V_4, V_5, V_6$$

Of these 14 paths, V_1, V_3, V_6 is the shortest, involving only two edges. In general, the **distance** between two vertices is equal to minimum number of edges in any path connecting them.

A cycle is a path in which the beginning and ending vertices are the same. For example, V_1, V_3, V_4, V_1 is a cycle in the graph of Figure 13.1.

Finally, a graph is connected if there is a path between any two of its vertices.

Digraphs and Weighted Graphs

A directed graph, or **digraph**, $G(V, E)$ consists of a set of vertices V and a set of edges E, with each edge defined as an ordered pair of vertices. Digraphs are depicted by representing the vertices as dots or circles and the edges as lines connecting the vertices, with an arrowhead indicating the direction of the edge. Typically, parallel edges are allowed in digraphs, provided that two parallel edges point in opposite directions. Such digraphs are well suited to represent communication networks, with each directed edge representing the flow of data in one direction between network nodes.

An adjacency matrix can still be used to characterize a digraph, but in this case the matrix will not be symmetric unless each pair of adjacent vertices is connected by a pair of parallel edges.

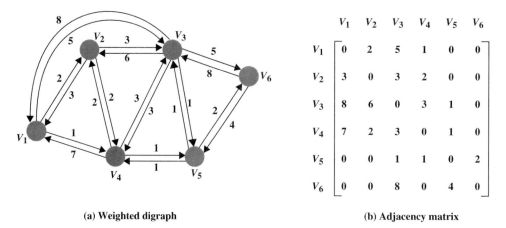

	V_1	V_2	V_3	V_4	V_5	V_6
V_1	0	2	5	1	0	0
V_2	3	0	3	2	0	0
V_3	8	6	0	3	1	0
V_4	7	2	3	0	1	0
V_5	0	0	1	1	0	2
V_6	0	0	8	0	4	0

(a) Weighted digraph   **(b) Adjacency matrix**

Figure 13.2   Weighted digraph with adjacency matrix.

A **weighted graph** or **weighted digraph** is one in which a number is associated with each edge. Figure 13.2a is an example of a weighted digraph.[1] An adjacency matrix $\mathbf{A} = (a_{ij})$ is defined for such a graph as follows:

$$a_{ij} = \begin{cases} w_{ij} & \text{if } (i,j) \in E \\ 0 & \text{otherwise} \end{cases}$$

where w_{ij} is the weight assigned to edge (i,j).

In a weighted graph or digraph, the **length** of a path is the sum of the weights of the edges in the path. Table 13.1 shows the path distances and path lengths for the path from V_1 to V_6 in Figure 13.2. Note that the shortest-distance path (V_1, V_3, V_6) is not the same as the shortest-length path (V_1, V_4, V_5, V_6).

TABLE 13.1   PATH DISTANCES AND LENGTHS FOR PATH FROM V_1 TO V_6 IN FIGURE 13.2

Path	Distance	Length
$V_1, V_2, V_3, V_4, V_5, V_6$	5	11
V_1, V_2, V_3, V_5, V_6	4	8
V_1, V_2, V_3, V_6	3	10
$V_1, V_2, V_4, V_3, V_5, V_6$	5	10
V_1, V_2, V_4, V_5, V_6	4	7
$V_1, V_3, V_2, V_4, V_5, V_6$	5	16
V_1, V_3, V_4, V_5, V_6	4	11
V_1, V_3, V_5, V_6	3	8
V_1, V_3, V_6	2	10
$V_1, V_4, V_2, V_3, V_5, V_6$	5	9
V_1, V_4, V_2, V_3, V_6	4	11
V_1, V_4, V_3, V_5, V_6	4	7
V_1, V_4, V_3, V_6	3	9
V_1, V_4, V_5, V_6	3	4

[1] A weighted graph version of this digraph is frequently used to illustrate routing algorithms. It first appeared in [SCHW80].

Trees

Trees are one of the most widely used subclasses of graphs, and they find many uses in computer science and in networking. The following are equivalent definitions of a tree:

1. A tree is a simple graph satisfying the following: If i and j are vertices in T, there is a unique simple path from i to j.
2. A simple graph of N vertices is a tree if it has $N - 1$ edges and no cycles.
3. A simple graph of N vertices is a tree if it has $N - 1$ edges and is connected.

Figure 13.3 is an example of a tree.

One vertex of a tree may be designated as the root. Typically this is drawn at the top of the diagram. In Figure 13.3, V_1 is the root. Under the root, and at the same level as each other, are placed those vertices adjacent to the root; these are vertices that can be reached from the root on a path of distance 1. Under each of these vertices are placed vertices that are adjacent to vertices on the first level and that can be reached from the root on a path of distance 2. This continues through an arbitrary number of levels. Each vertex other than the root has a single **parent** vertex, which is the adjacent vertex closer to the root. Each vertex has zero or more **child** vertices, which are the adjacent vertices farther from the root. A vertex with no child vertices is called a **leaf**.

For convenience, the root of a tree is referred to as level 0. The vertices immediately under the root are at level 1; these can all be reached from the root on a simple path of length 1. Similarly, the child vertices of the level 1 vertices are at level 2 and can all be reached from the root on a simple path of length 2.

Spanning Tree

Before defining the important concept of a spanning tree, we need the definition of a subgraph. A **subgraph** of a graph G is obtained by selecting a number of edges and vertices from G such that for each edge selected, the two vertices incident on that edge must also be selected. More formally, given a graph $G(V, E)$, the graph $G'(V', E')$ is a subgraph of G if and only if

1. $V' \subseteq V$ and $E' \subseteq E$, and
2. For every edge $e' \in E'$, if e' is incident on v' and w' then $v', w' \in V'$.

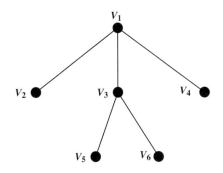

Figure 13.3   A tree.

A subgraph T of a graph G is called a **spanning tree** of G if T is a tree and includes all of the vertices of G. In other words, a spanning tree T is formed from G by removing edges in such a way that all of the cycles of G are removed but connectivity is preserved. As long as we remove one edge at a time, it is automatic that connectivity is preserved. That is, given a graph with at least one cycle, if we remove a single edge from the cycle, thus breaking the cycle, connectivity is still preserved. Repeated application of this rule removes all cycles while retaining connectivity.

Figure 13.3 is a spanning tree of the graph of Figure 13.1a. In general, the spanning tree of a graph is not unique. For example, Figure 13.4 shows two other spanning trees for the graph of Figure 13.1.

Breadth-first Search for a Spanning Tree

Given a graph, we may wish to find a spanning tree for it. This problem has been much studied because automated methods of finding spanning trees may be applied to other problems as well. In particular, one of the most common approaches to finding a spanning tree is known as the breadth-first search (BFS)[2]; we will see in Section 13.2 that Dijkstra's shortest-path routing algorithm is based on the use of BFS.

The idea behind BFS is to process all the vertices on a given level before moving to the next level. In the process, we partition the vertices of the graph into sets of vertices at various levels. Start at any vertex x and assign it to level 0. All vertices adjacent to x are at level 1. Let V_{i1}, V_{i2}, ..., V_{ir} be the vertices at level i. Consider all vertices adjacent to V_{i1} that are not in level 0, 1, 2, ..., i and assign these vertices to level $(i + 1)$. Then consider all vertices adjacent to V_{i2} that are not in level 0, 1, 2, ..., i, $(i + 1)$ and assign these vertices also to level $(i + 1)$. Continue this process until all vertices are examined.

We illustrate this first with an example and then state the algorithm. The example is shown in Figure 13.5 and is based on the graph of Figure 13.1a.

First, an ordering must be selected; we will use the obvious ordering of V_1, V_2, V_3, V_4, V_5, V_6. Next, select the first vertex and label it the root. Let T consist of this single vertex V_1 with no edges. Then add to T each edge (V_1, x) and the vertex x on

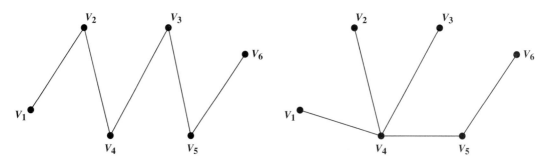

Figure 13.4   Spanning trees for graph of Figure 13.1.

---

[2]   You may think that this is one acronym that we could do without. However, I am aware of at least one paper in the literature on routing that uses this acronym without definition. Now you know what it stands for.

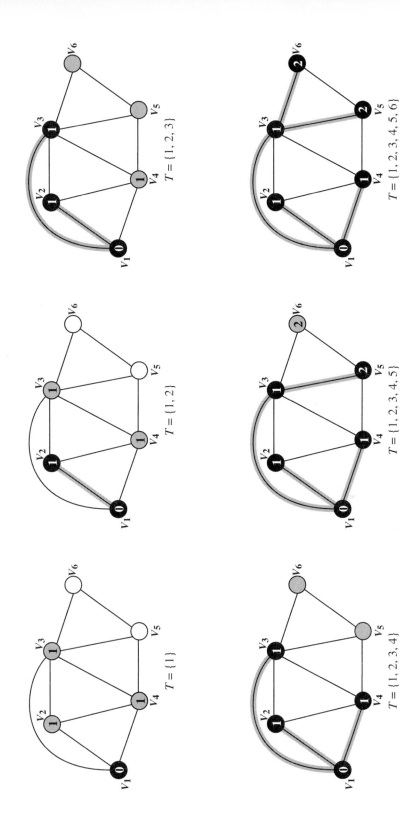

Figure 13.5   Breadth-first search of graph of Figure 13.1.

which it is incident for all vertices not in T, such that no cycle is produced in T. In this case, the edges $(V_1, V_2), (V_1, V_3), (V_1, V_4)$ and the vertices V_2, V_3, V_4 are added to T. This addition constitutes the first level.

Repeat this procedure for all the vertices on level 1 by examining each in order and adding to T:

V_2: None

V_3: Add edges $(V_3, V_5), (V_3, V_6)$ and vertices V_5, V_6

V_4: None

At this point, all vertices have been added. If this were not the case, the procedure would be repeated with level 3 vertices and so on until all vertices had been added.

In Figure 13.5, each vertex that is added to T is colored black as it is added, and each edge is colored gray as it is added. A vertex is discovered the first time that it is encountered during the algorithm and is labeled gray. The gray vertices are a sort of frontier between T and the rest of the graph and constitute the candidates for addition at any point in time. When the algorithm is completed, the shaded edges define the spanning tree.

Here is a more formal definition of the BFS algorithm. The input to the algorithm is a connected graph G with vertices ordered $V_1, V_2, \ldots V_N$, and the output is the spanning tree T. S is a temporary set of vertices.

1. **[Initialization]**. Set S to $\{V_1\}$ and set T to the graph consisting of V_1 and no edges. Designate V_1 as the root of the tree.
2. **[Add edges]**. Process the vertices in S in order. For each vertex x in S, process each adjacent vertex y in G in order; add edge (x, y) and vertex y to T provided that this does not produce a cycle in T. If no edges are added in this step, halt. T is a spanning tree.
3. **[Update S]**. Replace the contents of S with the children in T of S ordered consistent with the original ordering. Go to step 2.

This algorithm will produce a spanning tree rooted at V_1. One happy consequence of the BFS algorithm is that it finds the shortest-path distance from a given source vertex to all other vertices. The **shortest-path distance** $\delta(s, v)$ from vertex s to vertex v is the minimum number of edges in any path from s to v. The formal proof of this assertion is rather long, and the reader is referred to [CORM90] for a clear derivation (it occupies three large pages). But an intuitive argument is easily made. We start with root vertex r in G and construct the BFS spanning tree T. All vertices adjacent to r become part of T at level 1. Clearly, the vertices in this portion of T satisfy the property that T defines the shortest path from each level 1 vertex to r, because all of the paths are of length 1. Now consider a vertex x at level 2 of T. In T, x has a path length of 2 from r. Is it possible that there is a shorter path in G from the root to x? No, because that would mean there is a path in G from r to x of length 1 and that therefore r and x are adjacent. In that case, x would have been included in level 1 of T.

Now we ask the opposite question. In T, only those vertices at level 2 are of length 2 from r. Is it possible that there is some other vertex y in G that is at a level greater than 2 in T but that has a path in G of length 1 or 2 to r? In other words, have we left any vertices out at level 2 of T? Again the answer is no. If there were a path in G of length 1 from r to y, then y is adjacent to r and would have been included in level 1. If there were a path in G of length 2 from r to y, then y must be adjacent to a vertex at level 1 in T and therefore would have been included in level 2 of T.

This line of reasoning can be extended to show that at each level i T includes all those vertices, and only those vertices, whose minimum path distance from r is i.

It is useful to obtain an estimate of the running time of the BFS algorithm. After initialization, each vertex is placed in S exactly once, and hence removed from S exactly once. So the total time devoted to operations involving S is on the order of $|V|$. When a vertex is processed, all of its adjacent vertices are examined, meaning that all of its edges are examined. For an edge leading to a vertex already in T, the algorithm rejects it as a candidate. For other edges, the algorithm must determine if inclusion creates a cycle. Thus, the bulk of the edge processing occurs once per edge and the total processing is on the order of $|E|$. So we can conclude that the processing time of the BFS algorithm is linear with $|V|$ and $|E|$.

13.2 SHORTEST PATH LENGTH DETERMINATION

A packet-switching network (or a frame relay or ATM network) can be viewed in an obvious way as a digraph, with each packet-switching node corresponding to a vertex, and each communications link between nodes corresponding to a pair of parallel edges, each carrying data in one direction. In such a network, a routing decision is needed to transmit a packet from a source node through various links and packet switches to a destination node; this is equivalent to finding a path through the graph.

For an internet, such as the Internet or an intranet, a digraph representation is also appropriate. In this case, each router corresponds to a vertex. If two routers are directly connected to the same network, such as a LAN or WAN, then that two-way connection corresponds to a pair of parallel edges connecting the corresponding vertices. If more than two routers attach to a network, then that network is represented by multiple pairs of parallel edges, one pair to connect each pair of routers attached to the network. In an internet, a routing decision is needed to transmit an IP datagram from a source router through various networks and routers to a destination router; again, this is equivalent to finding a path through the graph.

Virtually all packet-switched networks and all internets base their routing decision on some form of least-cost criterion. If the criterion is to minimize the number of hops, each hop (edge) has a value of 1; this corresponds in graph theoretic terms to finding the **minimum path distance**. More typically, a cost is associated with each hop. The cost may be inversely proportional to the link capacity, proportional to the current load on the link, or some combination. Or the cost may include other criteria, such as the monetary cost of using the hop. In any case, these hop costs are used as input to a least-cost routing algorithm, which can be simply stated as follows:

Given a network of nodes connected by bidirectional links, where each link has a cost associated with it in each direction, define the cost of a path between two nodes as the sum of the costs of the links traversed. For each pair of nodes, find the path with the least cost.

Note that the cost of a link may differ in its two directions. This would be true, for example, if the cost of a hop equaled the length of the queue of datagrams awaiting transmission from each of the two nodes on the hop. This corresponds in graph theoretic terms to finding the **minimum path length** in a weighted digraph.

Most least-cost routing algorithms in use in packet-switched networks and internets are variations of one of two common algorithms, known as Dijkstra's algorithm and the Bellman-Ford algorithm. This section provides a summary of these two algorithms.

Dijkstra's Algorithm

Dijkstra's algorithm [DIJK59] can be stated as follows: Find the shortest paths from a given source vertex to all other vertices by developing the paths in order of increasing path length. The algorithm proceeds in stages. By the kth stage, the shortest paths to the k vertices closest to (least cost away from) the source vertex have been determined; these vertices are in a set T. At stage $(k + 1)$, the vertex not in T that has the shortest path from the source vertex is added to T. As each vertex is added to T, its path from the source is defined. The algorithm can be formally described as follows. Define

N = set of vertices in the network

s = source vertex

T = set of vertices so far incorporated by the algorithm

$w(i, j)$ = link cost from vertex i to vertex j; $w(i, i) = 0$; $w(i, j) = \infty$ if the two vertices are not directly connected; $w(i, j) \geq 0$ if the two vertices are directly connected

$L(n)$ = cost of the least-cost path from vertex s to vertex n that is currently known to the algorithm; at termination, this is the cost of the least-cost path in the graph from s to n.

The algorithm has three steps; steps 2 and 3 are repeated until $T = N$. That is, steps 2 and 3 are repeated until final paths have been assigned to all vertices in the network:

1. **[Initialization]**

   $T = \{s\}$ i.e., the set of vertices so far incorporated consists of only the source vertex.

   $L(n) = w(i, j)$ for $n \neq s$ i.e., the initial path costs to neighboring vertices are simply the link costs.

2. **[Get next vertex]** Find the neighboring vertex not in T that has the least-cost path from vertex s and incorporate that vertex into T: Also incorporate the edge that is incident on that vertex and a vertex in T that contributes to the path. This can be expressed as

$$\text{Find } x \notin T \text{ such that } L(x) = \min_{j \notin T} L(j)$$

Add x to T; add to T the edge that is incident on x and that contributes the least-cost component to $L(x)$—that is, the last hop in the path.

3. **[Update least-cost paths]**

$$L(n) = \min[L(n), L(x) + w(x, n)] \text{ for all } n \notin M$$

If the latter term is the minimum, the path from s to n is now the path from s to x concatenated with the edge from x to n.

The algorithm terminates when all vertices have been added to T. Thus, the algorithm requires $|V|$ iterations. At termination, the value $L(x)$ associated with each vertex x is the cost (length) of the least-cost path from s to x. In addition, T is a spanning tree of the original digraph and defines the least-cost path from s to each other vertex.

One iteration of steps 2 and 3 adds one new vertex to T and defines the least-cost path from s to that vertex. In other words, at each iteration one vertex x is added to T and the value of $L(x)$ at that time is the length of the minimum path from s to x; further, that minimum path is defined by the unique path from s to x within T. That path passes only through vertices that are in T. To see this, consider the following line of reasoning. The vertex x added on the first iteration must be adjacent to s and there must be no other path to x that is lower in cost. If x is not adjacent to s, there would be another vertex adjacent to s that is the first hop on the lowest-cost path to x, and that vertex would have been preferred to x for addition to T. If x is adjacent to s but the path s-x is not the lowest-cost path to x, then there is another vertex y adjacent to s that is on that lowest-cost path and y would have been preferred to x for addition to T. After k iterations, there are k vertices in T, and the least-cost path from s to each of these vertices has been defined. Now consider all possible paths from s to vertices not in T. Among those paths, there is one of least cost that passes exclusively through vertices in T (see Problem 13.9), ending with a direct link from some vertex in T to a vertex not in T. This vertex is added to T and the associated path is defined as the least-cost path for that vertex.

Table 13.2a and Figure 13.6 show the result of applying this algorithm to the graph of Figure 13.2a, using $s = V_1$. The shaded edges define the spanning tree for the graph. The values in each circle are the current estimates of $L(x)$ for each vertex x. A vertex is shaded when it is added to T. Note that at each step the path to each vertex plus the total cost of that path is generated. After the final iteration, the least-cost path to each vertex and the cost of that path have been developed. The same procedure can be used with vertex 2 as source vertex, and so on.

It can be demonstrated [CORM90] that the running time of Dijkstra's algorithm is on the order of $|V|^2$. To see this intuitively, note that there are $|V| - 1$ iterations of the algorithm and that the number of operations performed during each iteration is proportional to $|V|$.

Bellman-Ford Algorithm

The Bellman-Ford algorithm [FORD62] can be stated as follows: Find the shortest paths from a given source vertex subject to the constraint that the paths contain at most one link, then find the shortest paths with a constraint of paths of at most two

TABLE 13.2 EXAMPLE OF LEAST-COST ROUTING ALGORITHMS (USING FIGURE 13.2)

(a) Dijkstra'a Algorithm ($s = 1$)

Iteration	T	$L(2)$	Path	$L(3)$	Path	$L(4)$	Path	$L(5)$	Path	$L(6)$	Path
1	{1}	2	1–2	5	1–3	1	1–4	∞	—	∞	—
2	{1, 4}	2	1–2	4	1–4–3	1	1–4	2	1–4–5	∞	—
3	{1, 2, 4}	2	1–2	4	1–4–3	1	1–4	2	1–4–5	∞	—
4	{1, 2, 4, 5}	2	1–2	3	1–4–5–3	1	1–4	2	1–4–5	4	1–4–5–6
5	{1, 2, 3, 4, 5}	2	1–2	3	1–4–5–3	1	1–4	2	1–4–5	4	1–4–5–6
6	{1, 2, 3, 4, 5, 6}	2	1–2	3	1–4–5–3	1	1–4	2	1–4–5	4	1–4–5–6

(b) Bellman-Ford Algorithm ($s = 1$)

h	$L_h(2)$	Path	$L_h(3)$	Path	$L_h(4)$	Path	$L_h(5)$	Path	$L_h(6)$	Path
0	∞	—	∞	—	∞	—	∞	—	∞	—
1	2	1–2	5	1–3	1	1–4	∞	—	∞	—
2	2	1–2	4	1–4–3	1	1–4	2	1–4–5	10	1–3–6
3	2	1–2	3	1–4–5–3	1	1–4	2	1–4–5	4	1–4–5–6
4	2	1–2	3	1–4–5–3	1	1–4	2	1–4–5	4	1–4–5–6

links, and so on. This algorithm also proceeds in stages. The algorithm can be formally described as follows. Define

s = source vertex

$w(i, j)$ = link cost from vertex i to vertex j; $w(i, i) = 0$; $w(i, j) = \infty$ if the two vertices are not directly connected; $w(i, j) \geq 0$ if the two vertices are directly connected

h = maximum number of links in a path at the current stage of the algorithm

$L_h(n)$ = cost of the least-cost path from vertex s to vertex n under the constraint of no more than h links

The algorithm has the following steps; step 2 is repeated until none of the costs changes:

1. **[Initialization]**

$$L_0(n) = \infty, \text{ for all } n \neq s$$

$$L_h(s) = 0, \text{ for all } h$$

2. **[Update]**
For each successive $h \geq 0$:
For each $n \neq s$, compute

$$L_{h+1}(n) = \min_j [L_h(j) + w(j, n)]$$

Connect n with the predecessor vertex j that achieves the minimum, and eliminate any connection of n with a different predecessor vertex formed during an earlier iteration. The path from s to n terminates with the link from j to n.

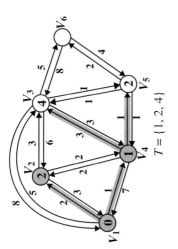

$T = \{1\}$

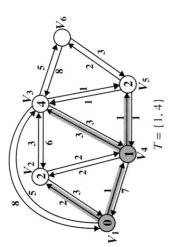

$T = \{1, 4\}$

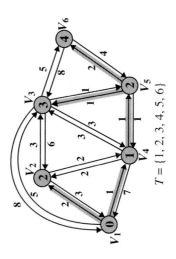

$T = \{1, 2, 4\}$

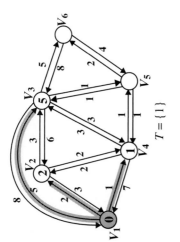

$T = \{1, 2, 4, 5\}$

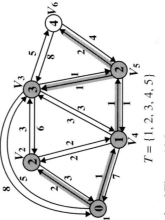

$T = \{1, 2, 3, 4, 5\}$

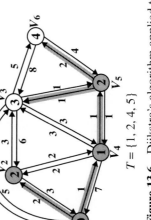

$T = \{1, 2, 3, 4, 5, 6\}$

Figure 13.6 Dijkstra's algorithm applied to graph of Figure 13.2.

395

For the iteration of step 2 with $h = K$, and for each destination vertex n, the algorithm compares potential paths from s to n of length $K + 1$ with the path that existed at the end of the previous iteration. If the previous, shorter, path has less cost, then that path is retained. Otherwise a new path with length $K + 1$ is defined from s to n; this path consists of a path of length K from s to some vertex j, plus a direct hop from vertex j to vertex n. In this case, the path from s to j that is used is the K-hop path for j defined in the previous iteration (see Problem 13.10). At the termination of the algorithm, a spanning tree of the graph has been defined.

Table 13.2b and Figure 13.7 show the result of applying this algorithm to Figure 13.2a, using $s = V_1$. At each step, the least-cost paths with a maximum number of links equal to h are found. After the final iteration, the least-cost path to each vertex and the cost of that path have been developed. The same procedure can be used with vertex 2 as source vertex, and so on. Note that the results agree with those obtained using Dijkstra's algorithm.

It can be demonstrated [CORM90] that the running time of the Bellman-Ford algorithm is on the order of $|V| \times |E|$. To see this intuitively, note that there are $|V| - 1$ iterations of the inner loop of step 2 and that each iteration involves examining the weight on each edge.

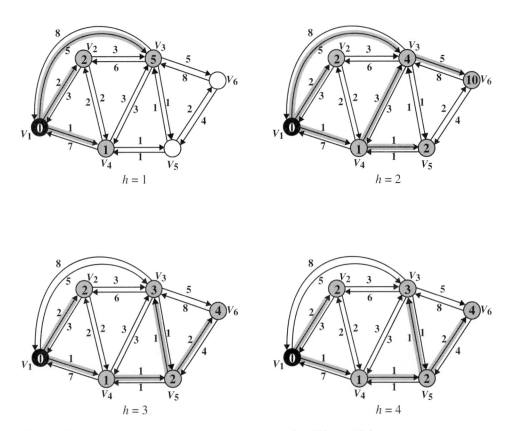

Figure 13.7 Bellman-Ford algorithm applied to graph of Figure 13.2.

Comparison

One interesting comparison can be made between these two algorithms, and it concerns what information needs to be gathered. Consider first the Bellman-Ford algorithm. In step 2, the calculation for vertex n involves knowledge of the link cost to all neighboring vertices to vertex n [i.e., $w(j, n)$] plus the total path cost to each of those neighboring vertices from a particular source vertex s [i.e., $L_h(j)$]. Each vertex can maintain a set of costs and associated paths for every other vertex in the network and exchange this information with its direct neighbors from time to time. Each vertex can therefore use the expression in step 2 of the Bellman-Ford algorithm, based only on information from its neighbors and knowledge of its link costs, to update it costs and paths. On the other hand, consider Dijkstra's algorithm. Step 3 appears to require that each vertex must have complete topological information about the network. That is, each vertex must know the link costs of all links in the network. Thus, for this algorithm, information must be exchanged with all other vertices.

In general, evaluation of the relative merits of the two algorithms should consider the processing time of the algorithms and the amount of information that must be collected from other nodes in the network or internet. The evaluation will depend on the implementation approach and the specific implementation.

A final point: Both algorithms are known to converge under static conditions of topology and link costs and will converge to the same solution. If the link costs change over time, the algorithm will attempt to catch up with these changes. However, if the link cost depends on traffic, which in turn depends on the routes chosen, then a feedback condition exists, and instabilities may result.

13.3 RECOMMENDED READING

[ORE90] and [CHAR77] are two excellent elementary introductions to graph theory; both contain numerous problems with solutions, making them suitable for self-study.

[CORM90] contains a thorough and rigorous treatment of graph algorithms, including a detailed analysis of the shortest-path algorithms discussed in this chapter. [BERT92] also discusses these algorithms in detail.

BERT92   Bertsekas, D., and Gallager, R. *Data Networks.* Upper Saddle River, NJ: Prentice Hall, 1992.

CHAR77   Chartrand, G. *Introductory Graph Theory.* New York: Dover, 1977.

CORM90   Cormen, T., Leiserson, C., and Rivest, R. *Introduction to Algorithms.* Cambridge, MA: MIT Press, 1990.

ORE90   Ore, O., and Wilson, R. *Graphs and Their Uses.* Washington, DC: The Mathematical Association of America, 1990.

13.4 PROBLEMS

13.1 The graph K_n, called the complete graph of on n vertices, has n vertices and every vertex is joined to every other vertex by an edge. Find a formula for the number of edges in K_n.

13.2 Consider the graph with $V = \{a, b, c, d, e, f\}$ and $E = \{(a, b), (a, d), (b, c), (b, e), (c, e), (c, f), (d, e), (e, f)\}$

    a. Draw the graph.

    b. Find all paths from *a* to *f*.

    c. Find the length of the shortest path from *a* to *f*.

13.3 Find all spanning trees of this graph:

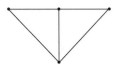

13.4 An edge in *G* is in every spanning tree of *G*. What can you say about the edge?

13.5 Prove that the breadth-first search algorithm is correct. That is, show that this algorithm will produce a spanning tree rooted at V_1.

13.6 Write a breadth-first search algorithm to test whether a graph is connected.

13.7 Show the execution of the breadth-first search algorithm on the graph of Figure 13.8, using the style of Figure 13.5.

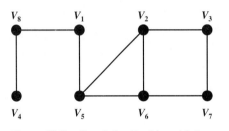

Figure 13.8   Graph for Problem 13.6.

13.8 Dijkstra's algorithm, for finding the least-cost path from a specified vertex *s* to a specified vertex *t*, can be expressed in the following program:

```
for n := 1 to N do
    begin
        L[n] := ∞; final[n] := false; {all vertices are temporarily labeled with ∞}
        pred[n] := 1
    end;
L[s] := 0; final[s] := true;        {vertex s is permanently labeled with 0}
recent := s;                        {the most recent vertex to be permanently labeled is s}
path := true;
{initialization over}
while final[t] = false do
begin
    for n := 1 to N do    {find new label}
        if (w[recent, n] < ∞) AND (NOT final[n]) then
        {for every immediate successor of recent that is not permanently labeled, do}
            begin {update temporary labels}
                newlabel := L[recent] + w[recent,n];
                if newlabel <L[n] then
                        begin L[n] :=  newlabel; pred[n] := recent end
                        {re-label n if there is a shorter path via vertex recent and make
```

```
                    recent the predecessor of n on the shortest path from s}
        end;
     temp := ∞;
   for x := 1 to N do {find vertex with smallest temporary label}
        if (NOT final[x]) AND (L[x] < temp) then
            begin y := x; temp : = L[x] end;
   if temp < ∞ then {there is a path} then
        begin final[y] := true; recent := y end
        {y, the next closest vertex to s gets permanently labeled}
   else begin path := false; final[t] := true end
end
```

In this program, each vertex is assigned a temporary label initially. As a final path to a vertex is determined, it is assigned a permanent label equal to the cost of the path from s. Write a similar program for the Bellman-Ford algorithm. *Hint:* The Bellman-Ford algorithm is often called a label-correcting method, in contrast to Dijkstra's label-setting method.

13.9 In the discussion of Dijkstra's algorithm, it is asserted that at each iteration, a new vertex is added to T and that the least-cost path for that new vertex passes only through vertices already in T. Demonstrate that this is true. *Hint:* Begin at the beginning. Show that the first vertex added to T must have a direct link to the source vertex. Then show that the second vertex to T must either have a direct link to the source vertex or a direct link to the first vertex added to T, and so on. Remember that all link costs are assumed nonnegative.

13.10 In the discussion of the Bellman-Ford algorithm, it is asserted that at the iteration for which $h = K$, if any path of length $K + 1$ is defined, the first K hops of that path form a path defined in the previous iteration. Demonstrate that this is true.

13.11 In step 3 of Dijkstra's algorithm, the least-cost path values are only updated for vertices not yet in T. Is it not possible that a lower-cost path could be found to a vertex already in T? If so, demonstrate by example. If not, provide reasoning as to why not.

13.12 Using Dijkstra's algorithm, generate a least-cost route to all other vertices for vertices 2 through 6 of Figure 13.2. Display the results as in Table 13.2a.

13.13 Repeat Problem 13.12 using the Bellman-Ford algorithm.

13.14 Apply Dijkstra's routing algorithm to the graphs in Figure 13.9. In the figure, the weights between two adjacent nodes are the same in both directions. Provide a table similar to Table 13.2 and a figure similar to Figure 13.6.

13.15 Repeat Problem 13.14 using the Bellman-Ford algorithm.

13.16 Will Dijkstra's algorithm and the Bellman-Ford algorithm always yield the same solutions? Why or why not?

13.17 Both Dijkstra's algorithm and the Bellman-Ford algorithm find the least-cost paths from one vertex to all other vertices. The Floyd-Warshall algorithm finds the least-cost paths between all pairs of vertices together. Define

$N = $ set of vertices in the network

$w(i, j) = $ link cost from vertex i to vertex j; $w(i, i) = 0$; $w(i, j) = \infty$ if the two vertices are not directly connected

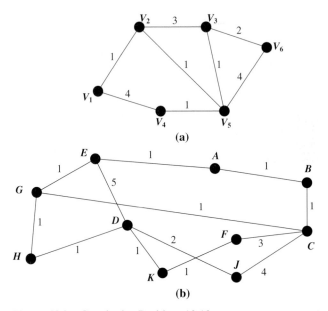

Figure 13.9   Graphs for Problem 13.13.

$L_n(i, j) =$ cost of the least-cost path from vertex i to vertex j with the constraint that only vertices $1, 2, ..., n$ can be used as intermediate vertices on paths

The algorithm has the following steps:
1. Initialize:

$$L_0(i, j) = w(i, j), \text{ for all } i, j, i \neq j$$

2. For $n = 0, 1, ..., N - 1$

$$L_{n+1}(i, j) = \min[L_n(i, j), L_n(i, n + 1) + L_n(n + 1, j)] \quad \text{for all } i \neq j$$

Explain the algorithm in words. Use induction to demonstrate that the algorithm works.

CHAPTER **14**

ROUTING PROTOCOLS

She occupied herself with studying a map on the opposite wall because she knew she would have to change trains at some point. Tottenham Court Road must be that point, an interchange from the black line to the red. This train would take her there, was bearing her there rapidly now, and at the station she would follow the signs, for signs there must be, to the Central Line going westward.

—*King Solomon's Carpet*, Barbara Vine (Ruth Rendell)

Routing protocols are an essential ingredient to the operation of an internet. Internets operate on the basis of routers that forward IP datagrams from router to router on a path from the source host to the destination host. For a router to perform its function, it must have some idea of the topology of the internet and the best route to follow. It is the purpose of the routing protocol to provide the needed information.

We begin this chapter with a discussion of the basic principles of internet routing, including a consideration of routing in high-speed internets. Then we look at four important routing protocols: RIP, OSPF, BGP, and IDRP.

14.1 INTERNET ROUTING PRINCIPLES

One of the most complex and critical aspects of internet design is routing. This section begins with a discussion of the routing mechanism. Then we look at the general architecture of internet routing.

The Routing Function

The routers in an internet perform much the same function as packet-switching nodes (PSNs) in a packet-switching network. Just as the PSN is responsible for receiving and forwarding packets through a packet-switching network, the router is responsible for receiving and forwarding IP datagrams through an internet. For this purpose, the routers of an internet need to make routing decisions based on knowledge of the topology and conditions of the internet.

As we discussed in Chapter 13, the routing decision is based on some form of least-cost criterion. If the criterion is to minimize the number of hops, each hop (edge) has a value of 1. More typically, a cost is associated with each hop. The cost may be inversely proportional to the link capacity, proportional to the current load on the link, or some combination. Or the cost may include other criteria, such as the monetary cost of using the hop. In any case, these hop costs are used as input to a least-cost routing algorithm, such as those described in Chapter 13.

Fixed Routing

In a simple configuration, a fixed routing scheme is possible. For fixed routing, a single, permanent route is configured for each source-destination pair of nodes in the network. The routes are fixed, or at most only change when there is a change in the topology of the network. Thus, the link costs used in designing routes cannot be based on any dynamic variable such as traffic. They could, however, be based on estimated traffic volumes between various source-destination pairs or the capacity of each link.

Consider the configuration of Figure 14.1, consisting of five networks and eight routers. A link cost is associated with the output side of each router for each network. In a fixed routing scheme, this cost might reflect the expected traffic load between a given router and a given attached network. Figure 14.2 suggests how fixed routing might be implemented. Each router maintains a table that has an entry for each network in the configuration. It is not necessary to have an entry for each possible destination host. Typically, an IP address consists of a host portion and a network portion. For purposes of routing, only the network portion is of interest. Once an IP datagram has reached a router attached to the destination network, that router can deliver the datagram to the appropriate destination host on that network.

Each entry in the routing table indicates a destination network and the next router to take for that destination. It is not necessary for a router to store the complete route for each possible destination. Rather, it is sufficient to know, for each destination, the identity of the next node on the route. To see this, suppose that the least-cost route from X to Y begins with the X-A link. Call the remainder of the route R_1; this is the part from A to Y. Define R_2 as the least-cost route from A to Y. If the cost of R_1 is greater than that of R_2, then the X-Y route can be improved by using R_2 instead. If the cost of R_1 is less than R_2, then R_2 is not the least-cost route from A to Y. Therefore, $R_1 = R_2$. Thus, at each point along a route, it is only necessary to know the identity of the next hop, not the entire route. In our example, the route from router F to network 2 begins by going through router H. The route from router H to network 2 goes through router G. Finally, router G is directly attached to network 2. Thus, the complete route from router F to network 2 is F-H-G.

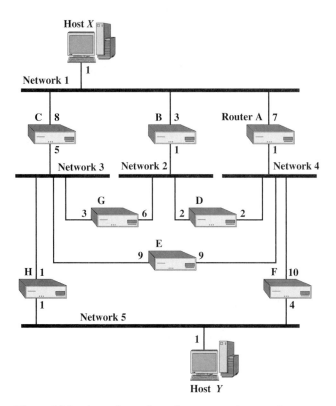

Figure 14.1   A configuration of routers and networks.

Router A Table	
Network	**Router**
1	D
2	D
3	D
4	–
5	F

Router B Table	
Network	**Router**
1	–
2	–
3	G
4	D
5	G

Router C Table	
Network	**Router**
1	–
2	B
3	–
4	A
5	H

Router D Table	
Network	**Router**
1	B
2	–
3	G
4	–
5	F

Router E Table	
Network	**Router**
1	D
2	D
3	–
4	–
5	H

Router F Table	
Network	**Router**
1	H
2	H
3	H
4	–
5	–

Router G Table	
Network	**Router**
1	B
2	–
3	–
4	D
5	H

Router H Table	
Network	**Router**
1	C
2	G
3	–
4	G
5	–

Host X Table	
Network	**Router**
1	–
2	B
3	B
4	A
5	A

Figure 14.2   Routing tables for Figure 14.1.

Such routing tables are required in each router. In addition, it may be desirable to configure routing tables in hosts. If a host is attached to a single network and that network has only one attached router, then a routing table is not needed for that host: All off-network traffic must be directed to the single router. However, if there are multiple routers attached to the network, then the host should have a table that indicates which router to use for each off-network destination. The alternative is to designate a default router, but this is not an optimal solution. Figure 14.2 shows the routing table for host X.

Adaptive Routing

In virtually all internet configurations, the routers employ some sort of adaptive routing technique. With adaptive routing, as conditions in the internet change, the routes used for forwarding datagrams may change. The principal conditions that influence routing decisions are as follows:

- **Failure:** When a network or router fails, it can no longer be used as part of a route.
- **Congestion:** When a particular portion of the internet is heavily congested, it is desirable to route datagrams around rather than through the area of congestion. Thus, the routing strategy can help to avoid, or at least avoid exacerbating, congestion; this is critical in high-speed internets.

There are several drawbacks associated with the use of adaptive routing:

- The routing decision is more complex; therefore, the processing burden on routers increases.
- In most cases, adaptive strategies depend on status information that is collected at one place but used at another. There is a tradeoff here between the quality of the information and the amount of overhead. The more information that is exchanged, and the more frequently it is exchanged, the better will be the routing decisions that each node makes. On the other hand, this information is itself a load on the constituent networks, causing a performance degradation.
- An adaptive strategy may react too quickly, causing congestion-producing oscillation, or too slowly, being irrelevant.
- An adaptive strategy can produce pathologies, such as fluttering and looping.

It is worth elaborating on these last two points. If an adaptive strategy reacts very quickly, minor fluctuations in load in the internet may cause a number of routers to shift traffic to a temporarily less loaded region. This quick reaction, in turn, causes a surge of traffic in the new region, which may result in some of the traffic being rerouted back in the direction it came from. If an adaptive strategy reacts very slowly to changes in load, by the time that routing decisions are made, the load distribution may have changed so markedly that the new routing decisions are inappropriate.

Fluttering refers to rapid oscillations in routing. This can be caused by the router's attempt to do load splitting, or balancing. RFC 1812 describes load split-

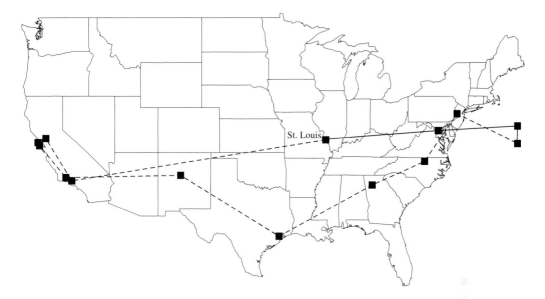

Figure 14.3   Example of fluttering: Routes taken by alternating packets from wust1 (St. Louis, Missouri) to umann (Mannheim, Germany.

ting in the following way[1]: "At the end of the Next-Hop selection process, multiple routes may still remain. The router may retain more than one route and employ a load splitting mechanism to divide traffic among them." Such load splitting can lead to aberrant behavior. An example reported in [PAXS96] is illustrated in Figure 14.3. In this instance, a router in St. Louis split its load for the umann destination between a next hop to Washington, DC (solid; 17 hops to umann), and Anaheim (dotted line; 29 hops). The result was that successive packets bound for umann travel via a radically different route. The [PAXS96] study consisted of observation of Internet traffic at selected locations over several days; a number of instances of fluttering were observed.

A more serious pathology is *looping*, in which packets forwarded by a router eventually return to the router. Routing algorithms are designed to prevent looping, but looping may occur when the internet experiences a change in connectivity and that change is not immediately propagated to all of the other routers. In their observations over three days, [PAXS96] observed 60 instances of looping, some of these lasting several hours and a few lasting more than half a day. Such extremely persistent loops will clearly disrupt traffic for some sources.

Despite their problems, adaptive routing strategies are by far more prevalent than fixed routing, for two reasons:

- An adaptive routing strategy can improve performance, as seen by the network user.
- An adaptive routing strategy can aid in congestion control.

---

[1]   RFC 1812, *Requirements for IP Version 4 Routers*, June 1995.

These benefits may or may not be realized, depending on the soundness of the design and the nature of the load. By and large, adaptive routing is an extraordinarily complex task to perform properly. This accounts for the fact that routing protocols have undergone a continual evolution over the years.

A convenient way to classify adaptive routing strategies is on the basis of information source: local, adjacent nodes, all nodes. An example of an adaptive routing strategy that relies only on local information is one in which a router routes each datagram to the outgoing network for which it has the shortest queue length Q. This would have the effect of balancing the load on outgoing networks. However, some outgoing networks may not be headed in the correct general direction. We can improve matters by also taking into account preferred direction. In this case, each network attached to the router would have a bias B_i for each destination network i. For each incoming datagram headed for network i, the router would choose the outgoing link that minimizes $Q + B_i$. Thus a router would tend to send datagrams in the right direction, with a concession made to current traffic delays.

Adaptive schemes based only on local information are rarely used; such schemes do not exploit information from adjacent routers or more distant routers, which would improve the quality of the routing decisions. Strategies based on information from adjacent routers or all routers are commonly found. Both take advantage of information that each router has about delays and outages that it experiences. Strategies based on information from adjacent routers are called distance-vector algorithms, and strategies based on information from all routers are called link-state algorithms. In either case, a routing protocol is needed for the exchange of information.

A final point: The actual routing mechanism is independent of the type of routing protocol and is independent of whether there is a routing protocol or a fixed routing strategy. Consider Figures 14.1 and 14.2, which were used to illustrate fixed routing. The link costs illustrated in Figure 14.1 can be dynamic costs, which reflect current delays at the corresponding interfaces. The routing tables in Figure 14.2 could be constructed from information provided by a routing protocol rather than configured ahead of time.

Autonomous Systems

To proceed in our discussion of routing protocols, we need to introduce the concept of an **autonomous system**. An autonomous system (AS) exhibits the following characteristics:

1. An AS consists of a group of routers exchanging information via a common routing protocol.
2. An AS is a set of routers and networks managed by a single organization.
3. Except in times of failure, an AS is connected (in a graph-theoretic sense).

A common routing protocol, which we shall refer to as an **interior routing protocol** (IRP), passes routing information between routers within an AS. The protocol used within the AS need not be implemented outside of the system. This flexibility allows IRPs to be custom tailored to specific applications and requirements.

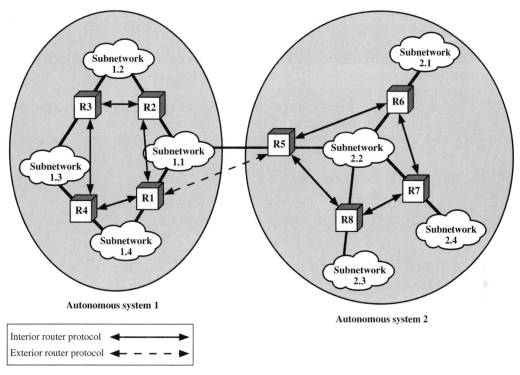

Figure 14.4   Application of exterior and interior routing protocols.

It may happen, however, that an internet will be constructed of more than one AS. For example, all of the LANs at a site, such as an office complex or campus, could be linked by routers to form an AS. This system might be linked through a wide area network to other ASs. The situation is illustrated in Figure 14.4. In this case, the routing algorithms and routing tables used by routers in different ASs may differ. Nevertheless, the routers in one AS need at least a minimal level of information concerning networks outside the system that can be reached. The protocol used to pass routing information between routers in different ASs is referred to as an **exterior routing protocol** (ERP).[2]

We can expect that an ERP will need to pass less information than an IRP, for the following reason. If a datagram is to be transferred from a host in one AS to a host in another AS, a router in the first system need only determine the target AS and devise a route to get into that target system. Once the datagram enters the target AS, the routers within that system can cooperate to deliver the datagram; the ERP is not concerned with, and does not know about, the details of the route followed within the target AS.

In the remainder of this chapter, we look at what are perhaps the most important examples of these two types of routing protocols: the interior routing protocols RIP and OSPF and the exterior routing protocols BGP and IDRP.

---

[2]   In the literature, the terms interior gateway protocol (IGP) and exterior gateway protocol (EGP) are often used for what are referred to here as IRP and ERP. However, because the terms *IGP* and *EGP* also refer to specific protocols, we avoid their use to define the general concepts.

14.2 DISTANCE-VECTOR PROTOCOL: RIP

A relatively simple interior routing protocol is the Routing Information Protocol (RIP).[3] Despite its simplicity, it remains suitable for smaller internets and is still the most widely used routing protocol.

A key feature of RIP is that it uses a technique known as distance-vector routing. We begin with a general description of this technique. Then we show how this technique is adapted for use in RIP. Finally, we define the RIP packet format.

Distance-vector Routing

Distance-vector routing requires that each node (router or host that implements RIP) exchange information with its neighboring nodes. Two nodes are said to be neighbors if they are both directly connected to the same network.

The Algorithm

For purposes of the protocol, each node maintains three vectors. First, each node x maintains a link cost vector of the form

$$\mathbf{W}_x = \begin{bmatrix} w(x, 1) \\ \vdots \\ w(x, M) \end{bmatrix}$$

where M is the number of networks to which node x directly attaches. A link cost $w(x, i)$ is associated with the output side of each node for each attached network i. For example, in the configuration of Figure 14.1, all of the link costs are indicated. Host X attaches to only one network and so has only one link cost, with a value of 1; router A attaches to networks 1 and 4 and has link costs of $w(A, 1) = 7$ and $w(A, 4) = 1$.

Two other vectors are maintained:

$$\mathbf{L}_x = \begin{bmatrix} L(x, 1) \\ \vdots \\ L(x, N) \end{bmatrix} \qquad \mathbf{R}_x = \begin{bmatrix} R(x, 1) \\ \vdots \\ R(x, N) \end{bmatrix}$$

where

$\mathbf{L}_x$ = distance vector for node x

$L(x, j)$ = current estimate of minimum delay from node x to network j

N = number of networks in the configuration

$\mathbf{R}_x$ = next-hop vector for node x

---

[3] Defined in RFC 1058, *Routing Information Protocol*, June 1988. There is a newer version, known as RIP-2, but this was never widely deployed and is not covered in this chapter.

$R(x, j)$ = the next router in the current minimum-delay route from node x to network j

Periodically (every 30 seconds), each node exchanges its distance vector with all of its neighbors. On the basis of all incoming distance vectors, a node x updates both of its vectors as follows:

$$L(x, j) = \underset{y \in A}{\text{Min}}[L(y, j) + w(x, N_{xy})] \tag{14.1}$$

$R(x, j) = y$ using y that minimizes the preceding expression

where

A = set of neighbor nodes for node x

N_{xy} = network that connects node x and router y

Figure 14.5 illustrates the operation of the algorithm, using the network of Figure 14.1. Figure 14.5a shows the routing table for host X at an instant in time that reflects the link costs of Figure 14.1. For each destination network, a path delay is

Destination Network	Next Router $R(X,j)$	Metric $L(X,j)$
1	–	1
2	B	2
3	B	5
4	A	2
5	A	6

B
3
1
4
3
4

C
8
8
5
6
6

A
6
3
2
1
2

(a) Routing table of host X before update

(b) Delay vectors sent to host X from neighbor routers

Destination Network	Next Router $R(X, j)$	Metric $L(X, j)$
1	–	1
2	B	2
3	A	3
4	A	2
5	A	3

(c) Routing table of host X after update

Figure 14.5   Distance-vector algorithm applied to Figure 14.1.

specified, and the next router on the route that produces that delay. At some point, suppose the link costs change (i.e., the observed link delays change) as follows: Both link costs from E become 1, and both link costs from F become 1. Assume that X's neighbors (routers A, B, and C) learn of the change. Each of these nodes updates its distance vector and sends a copy to all of its neighbors, including X (Figure 14.5b). X replaces its current routing table with a new one, based solely on the incoming distance vector and its own estimate of link delay to each of its neighbors. In this case, the link delay to all three neighbors is the same, because all three routers are reached via network 1. The result is shown in Figure 14.5c.

Distributed Bellman-Ford Algorithm

In the example just shown, the algorithm appears to work. To understand why, compare Equation 14.1 with the update step in the Bellman-Ford algorithm defined in Chapter 13. The equation is essentially the same. In essence, the routing algorithm used in RIP is a distributed version of the Bellman-Ford algorithm. This algorithm was used as the original routing algorithm in the ARPANET packet-switching network.

It may help to clarify the nature of the distributed Bellman-Ford algorithm to consider a synchronous version of the algorithm. Suppose that each router x begins with the following assignment:

$$L(x,j) = \begin{cases} w(x,j) & \text{if } x \text{ is directly connected to network } j \\ \infty & \text{otherwise} \end{cases} \qquad (14.2)$$

Then all routers simultaneously exchange their distance vectors and compute Equation 14.1. After computation is complete, all routers again simultaneously exchange their distance vectors and compute Equation 14.1. Each iteration is equivalent to one iteration of step 2 of the Bellman-Ford algorithm (incrementing h by 1) executed in parallel at each node of the graph. Consider a single node s. After the first iteration, it is aware of all shortest-length paths with a distance of at most one hop; after the second iteration, it is aware of all shortest-length paths with a distance of at most two hops; and so on, until all true shortest-length paths from s are found.

It would be difficult to coordinate the activities of all routers so that the algorithm could be executed synchronously. Instead, RIP and all other routing protocol based on distance-vector routing use an asynchronous method. When a node is started up, it initializes itself according to Equation 14.2 and performs an update according to Equation 14.1 after new distance vectors are received from all its neighbors. Every 30 seconds, by its own timer, each router transmits its distance vector to its neighbors. It can be shown that this algorithm is valid; that is, it produces the correct results for each node. If one or more changes occur in link costs in the configuration, then the new shortest-path calculations will converge to the correct answer within a finite time proportional to the number of routers. The derivation is lengthy and can be found in [BERT92].

RIP Details

The preceding general description of a distance-vector routing algorithm ignores some practical details in the distributed operation of the algorithm among a number of cooperating nodes. In this subsection, we look at the details of the algorithm as actually implemented in RIP.

Incremental Update

Equation 14.1 assumes that a node receives distance-vector updates from all of its neighbors within a short window of time and then does a total update based on all of the incoming vectors. This requirement is not practical for several reasons. Because the algorithm operates asynchronously, there is no guarantee that all updates will be received within any given window. Further, RIP packets are sent using UDP, which is an unreliable transport protocol, so that some RIP packets may not arrive.

Therefore, RIP is designed to operate incrementally by updating its routing table after receipt of any individual distance vector. The following rules are obeyed:

1. If the incoming distance vector includes a new destination network, this information is added to the routing table.
2. If the node receives a route with a smaller delay metric to a destination, it replaces the existing route. For example, suppose we have the configuration of Figure 14.1 and the routing table for host X of Figure 14.5a. Now suppose that X receives only one update—namely, the update from B shown in Figure 14.5b. In that case, the only change that is made to X's routing table is to set $L(X, 5)$ = 5 and $R(X, 5) = B$. If the distance vector from A, shown in Figure 14.5b, subsequently arrives, then X's routing table is updated to that of Figure 14.5c.
3. If the node receives an update vector from router R and the node currently has one or more entries in its routing table for which R is the next hop, then all of these entries are updated to reflect the new information from R.

To see the need for the third rule, suppose that Figure 14.5c is the current routing table for X, reflecting the configuration of Figure 14.1, except that the link costs from E are both 1 and the link costs from F are both 1. Now suppose that router F goes down and this is detected by A. Soon A will send a distance vector to X that reports a path distance to network 5 of 3. In this case, it is necessary for X to increase the value of $L(X, 5)$ from 3 to 4.

Topology Changes

In the preceding paragraph we supposed that A became aware that F had failed. How is this possible? The mechanism used in RIP is the following. Every router is supposed to send an update vector to its neighbors every 30 seconds. If a node K has an entry in its routing table for network i with the next hop to router N, and if K receives no updates from N within 180 seconds, it marks the route as invalid. The assumption is made that either router N has crashed or that the network connecting K to N has become unstable. When K hears from any neighbor that has a valid route to i, the valid route replaces the invalid one.

The way in which a route is marked invalid is to set the value of the distance to the route to infinity. In practice, RIP uses a value of 16 to equal infinity, for reasons explained next.

Counting to Infinity Problem

One of the more significant problems with RIP is its slow convergence to a change in topology. Consider the configuration of Figure 14.6, with all link costs equal to one. B maintains a distance to network 5 of 2, with a next hop of D, while A and C both maintain a distance to network 5 of 3, with a next hop to B. Now suppose that router D fails. Then the following scenario could occur:

1. B determines that network 5 is no longer directly reachable and sets its distance count to 4, based on a report from A or C. At the next reporting interval, B advertises this information in distance vectors to A and C.
2. A and C receive this increased distance information from D and increment their reachability information to network 5 to a distance of 5 (4 from B plus 1 to reach B).
3. B receives the distance count of 5 and assumes that network 5 is now a distance 6 away.

This pattern continues until the distance value reaches infinity, which is only 16 in RIP. Once this value is obtained, a node determines that the target network is no longer reachable. With a reporting interval of 30 seconds, this type of condition can take from 8 to 16 minutes to resolve itself.

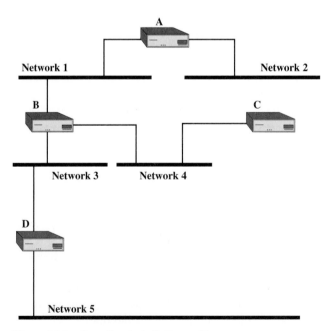

Figure 14.6   Counting to infinity problem.

Split Horizon with Poisoned Reverse

The counting-to-infinity problem is caused by a mutual misunderstanding between B and A (and between C and A). Each thinks that it can reach network 5 via the other. The *split horizon* rule in RIP states that it is never useful to send information about a route back in the direction from which it came, as the router sending you the information is nearer to the destination than you are. The split horizon rule does speed things up; an erroneous route will be eliminated within the interval of the 180-second timeout.

At a small increase in message size, RIP provides even faster response by using the *poisoned reverse*. This rule differs from simple split horizon by sending updates to neighbors with a hop count of 16 for routes learned from those neighbors. If two routers have routes pointing at each other, advertising reverse routes with a metric of 16 breaks the loop immediately.

RIP Packet Format

Figure 14.7 shows the format of a RIP packet. Each packet includes a header with the following fields:

- **Command:** 1 for a request, 2 for a reply. Routing updates are sent as replies whether requested or not. When a node initializes RIP, it broadcasts a RIP request; each router receiving the request immediately sends out a reply.
- **Version:** 1 for the original RIP, 2 for RIP-2.

This header is followed by one or more blocks, each of which gives the path distance to a particular target network. The relevant fields are as follows:

- **IP address:** An IP address that has a nonzero network portion and a zero host portion. This uniquely defines a particular network.
- **Metric:** The path distance from this router to the identified network.

Typically, a link cost of 1 is used, so that the metric is a simple hop count. If larger values of link cost are allowed, then the number of hops that can be measure is correspondingly smaller.

RIP Limitations

RIP continues to be a popular routing protocol because it is simple and because it is well suited to small internets, of which there are many. However, it does have a number of limitations, including the following:

1. As internets grow, destinations that require a metric of more than 15 become unreachable, making RIP unsuitable for large configurations. On the other hand, if larger metrics were allowed, the convergence of the protocol upon initialization or after topology changes can be lengthy.
2. The overly simplistic metric leads to suboptimal routing tables, resulting in packets being sent over slow (or otherwise costly) links when better paths are available.

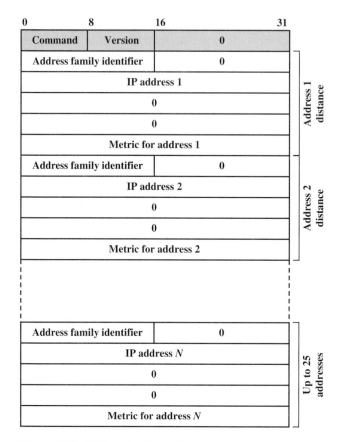

Figure 14.7 RIP packet format.

3. RIP-enabled devices will accept RIP updates from any device. This enables a misconfigured device easily to disrupt an entire configuration.

14.3 LINK-STATE PROTOCOL: OSPF

As the size and speed of the Internet and other internets have increased, the limitations of RIP have eroded its popularity. Although RIP is still widely used, the Open Shortest Path First protocol (OSPF)[4] is now considered the preferred interior routing protocol for TCP/IP-based internets.

Central to the operation of OSPF is the use of link-state routing. We begin with a general description of this technique. Then we show how this technique is adapted for use in OSPF.

---

[4] RFC 1583, *OSFP Version 2*, March 1994.

Link-state Routing

Distance-vector routing requires the transmission of a considerable amount of information by each router. Each router must send a distance vector to all of its neighbors, and that vector contains the estimated path cost to all networks in the configuration. Furthermore, when there is a significant change in a link cost or when a link is unavailable, it may take a considerable amount of time for this information to propagate through the internet. Link-state routing is designed to overcome these drawbacks.

General Description

When a router is initialized, it determines the link cost on each of its network interfaces. The router then advertises this set of link costs to all other routers in the internet topology, not just neighboring routers. From then on, the router monitors its link costs. Whenever there is a significant change (a link cost increases or decreases substantially, a new link is created, an existing link becomes unavailable), the router again advertises its set of link costs to all other routers in the configuration.

Because each router receives the link costs of all routers in the configuration, each router can construct the topology of the entire configuration and then calculate the shortest path to each destination network. Having done this, the router can construct its routing table, listing the first hop to each destination. Because the router has a representation of the entire network, it does not use a distributed version of a routing algorithm, as is done in distance-vector routing. Rather, the router can use any routing algorithm to determine the shortest paths. In practice, Dijkstra's algorithm is used.

Table 14.1 compares distance-vector and link-state routing.

Flooding

Link-state routing uses a simple technique known as flooding. This technique requires no network topology information, and it works as follows. A packet is sent by a source router to every one of its neighbors. At each router, an incoming packet is retransmitted on all outgoing links except for the link on which it arrived. The use of flooding in the configuration of Figure 14.1 is shown in Figure 14.8. After the first transmission, all routers within one hop of the source have received the packet.

TABLE 14.1 A COMPARISON OF ROUTING PHILOSOPHIES

Distance-vector Routing	Link-state Routing
Each router sends routing information to its neighbors.	Each router sends routing information to all other routers.
The information sent is an estimate of its path cost to all networks.	The information sent is the exact value of its link cost to adjacent networks.
Information is sent on a regular periodic basis.	Information is sent when changes occur.
A router determines next-hop information by using the distributed Bellman-Ford algorithm on the received estimated path costs.	A router first builds up a description of the topology of the internet and then may use any routing algorithm to determine next-hop information.

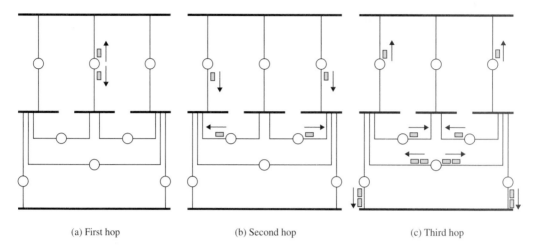

| (a) First hop | (b) Second hop | (c) Third hop |

Figure 14.8   Flooding example.

After the second transmission, all routers within two hops of the source have received the packet, and so on.

Unless something is done to stop the incessant retransmission of packets, the number of packets in circulation just from a single source packet grows without bound. In our example, two packets are generated for the first hop, four packets for the second hop, and twelve packets for the third hop, which in this case is unnecessary. One way to prevent this is for each node to remember the identity of those packets it has already retransmitted. When duplicate copies of the packet arrive, they are discarded. This is the method used in OSPF.

The flooding technique has three remarkable properties:

- All possible routes between source and destination are tried. Thus, no matter what link or node outages have occurred, a packet will always get through if at least one path between source and destination exists.
- Because all routes are tried, at least one copy of the packet to arrive at the destination will have used a minimum-delay route.
- All nodes that are directly or indirectly connected to the source node are visited.

Because of the first property, the flooding technique is highly robust. Because of the second property, flooded information reaches all routers quickly. Because of the third property, all routers receive the information needed to create a routing table.

The principal disadvantage of flooding is the high traffic load that it generates, which is directly proportional to the connectivity of the network.

OSPF Overview

Each router maintains descriptions of the state of its local links to subnetworks, and from time to time transmits updated state information to all of the routers of which it is aware. Every router receiving an update packet must acknowledge it to the sender. Such updates produce a fair amount of routing traffic because the link descriptions, though small, often need to be sent.

Each router maintains a database that reflects the known topology of the configuration. The topology is expressed as a directed graph. The graph consists of the following:

- Vertices, or nodes, of two types:
  — router
  — network, which is, in turn, of two types:
    - transit if it can carry data that neither originates nor terminates on an end system attached to this network
    - stub, if it is not a transit network
- Edges of two types:
  — graph edges that connect two router vertices when the corresponding routers are connected to each other by a direct point-to-point link
  — graph edges that connect a router vertex to a network vertex when the router is directly connected to the network.

Figure 14.9 (based on a figure in RFC 1583) shows an example of a configuration, and Figure 14.10 is the resulting directed graph. The mapping is straightforward:

- Two routers joined by a point-to-point link are represented in the graph as being directly connected by a pair of edges, one in each direction (e.g., routers 6 and 10).

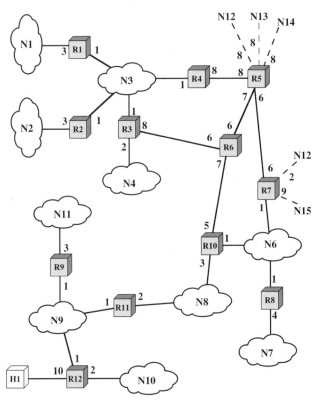

Figure 14.9   A sample autonomous system.

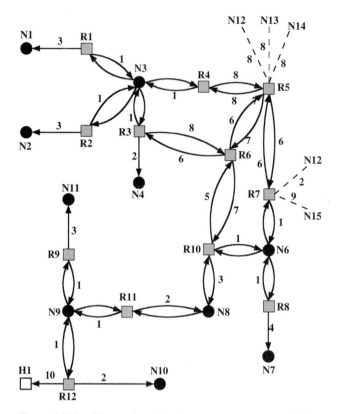

Figure 14.10 Directed graph of autonomous system of Figure 14.9.

- When multiple routers are attached to a network (such as a LAN or packet-switching network), the directed graph shows all routers bidirectionally connected to the network vertex (e.g., routers 1, 2, 3, and 4 all connect to network 3).
- If a single router is attached to a network, the network will appear in the graph as a stub connection (e.g., network 7).
- An end system, called a host, can be directly connected to a router, in which case it is depicted in the corresponding graph (e.g., host 1).
- If a router is connected to other autonomous systems, then the path cost to each network in the other system must be obtained by some exterior routing protocol. Each such network is represented on the graph by a stub and an edge to the router with the known path cost (e.g., networks 12 through 15).

A cost is associated with the output side of each router interface. This cost is configurable by the system administrator. Arcs on the graph are labeled with the cost of the corresponding router output interface. Arcs having no labeled cost have a cost of 0. Note that arcs leading from networks to routers always have a cost of 0.

A database corresponding to the directed graph is maintained by each router. It is pieced together from link state messages from other routers in the internet. Using Dijkstra's algorithm (see Chapter 13), a router calculates the least-cost path

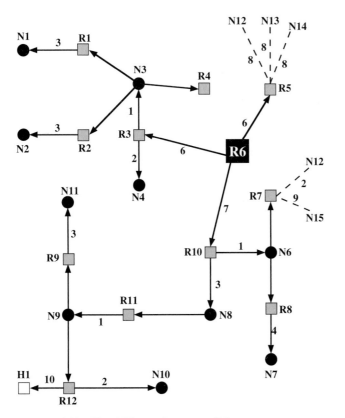

Figure 14.11 The SPF tree for router R6.

to all destination networks. The result for router 6 of Figure 14.9 is shown as a spanning tree in Figure 14.11, with R6 as the root of the tree. The tree gives the entire route to any destination network or host. However, only the next hop to the destination is used in the forwarding process. The resulting routing table for router 6 is shown in Table 14.2. The table includes entries for routers advertising external routes (routers 5 and 7). For external networks whose identity is known, entries are also provided.

Link Costs

The costs associated with each hop, in each direction, are referred to as routing metrics. OSPF provides a flexible routing metric scheme based on the concept of type of service (TOS). These categories are used:

- **Normal (TOS 0):** This is the default routing metric and is assigned by routing administrators to satisfy any administrative policies. The default metric is understood by every router. The values may be assigned arbitrarily. The simplest technique would be to assign a constant value of 1 to every hop, resulting in a minimum-hop calculation. More typically, the metric will be assigned to reflect performance in some way.

TABLE 14.2   ROUTING TABLE FOR RT6

Destination	Next Hop	Distance
N1	RT3	10
N2	RT3	10
N3	RT3	7
N4	RT3	8
N6	RT10	8
N7	RT10	12
N8	RT10	10
N9	RT10	11
N10	RT10	13
N11	RT10	14
H1	RT10	21
RT5	RT5	6
RT7	RT10	8
N12	RT10	10
N13	RT5	14
N14	RT5	14
N15	RT10	17

- **Minimize monetary cost (TOS 2):** This metric can be used if actual monetary costs can be assigned to network use.
- **Maximize reliability (TOS 4):** This metric could be preconfigured or could be based on a recent history of outages or on measured packet error rates.
- **Maximize throughput (TOS 8):** This metric is preconfigured based on the data rate of the interface. Typically, the metric is the duration of a bit in 10-nanosecond units. Thus, a 10-Mbps Ethernet is assigned a value 10, and a 56-kbps link is assigned 1785.
- **Minimize delay (TOS 16):** This is a measure of the transit time or delay through a particular hop. Typically, this consists of propagation delay plus queuing delay at the router and is measured dynamically by each router for each of its network interfaces.

These are the same categories used in the IPv4 TOS field (Figure 11.2). When a router advertises, it provides a link cost for each TOS that is implemented by that router. If a metric for some TOS is not specified, its cost usually defaults to the cost for TOS 0.

Each router may therefore construct up to five distinct routing tables, one for each TOS. In effect, each router generates five spanning trees for the configuration. IP datagrams are then routed on the basis of TOS. Each IP datagram may include a requested TOS. If no request is included in the datagram header, then the default TOS 0 is used for routing.

Areas

To make the complexity of large internets more manageable, OSPF incorporates the concept of area. Any internet can be configured to consist of a backbone and multiple areas, defined as follows:

- **Area:** A collection of contiguous networks and hosts, together with routers having interfaces to any one of the included networks
- **Backbone:** A contiguous collection of networks not contained in any area, their attached routers, and those routers that belong to multiple areas.

Each area runs a separate copy of the basic link-state routing algorithm and thus maintains a topological database and corresponding graph that reflects the topology of just that area. Link-state information is broadcast only to other routers in the same area. This reduces the amount of OSPF traffic considerably in a large internet. If the source and destination of an IP datagram are within the same area, then only intra-area routing is required. In this case, the routing relies solely on the link-state information generated within the area.

If the source and destination of an IP datagram are within different areas, then the routing involves a path consisting of three legs. The first leg of the path is within the source area and the third leg is within the destination area; these two legs use intra-area routing. The second leg of the path requires that the datagram be routed through the backbone from the source area to the destination area. The backbone itself has all of the properties of an area and uses the link-state routing algorithm to perform inter-area routing.

At a top level, OSPF views the internet as having a star configuration. The root or hub is the backbone, and each of the areas is attached to the backbone.

14.4 PATH-VECTOR PROTOCOLS: BGP AND IDRP

The Border Gateway Protocol (BGP) is an exterior routing protocol developed for use in conjunction with internets that employ the TCP/IP protocol suite, although the concepts are applicable to any internet. BGP has become the preferred exterior routing protocol for the Internet.

A key feature of BGP is that it uses a technique known as path-vector routing. We begin with a general description of this technique. Then we look at some of the details of BGP. Finally, we introduce IDRP, which is a follow-on protocol intended for use with IPv6.

Path-vector Routing

Neither a distance-vector protocol, such as used by RIP, nor a link-state protocol, such as used by OSPF, is effective for an exterior routing protocol.

In a distance-vector routing protocol, each router advertises to its neighbors a vector listing each network it can reach, together with a distance metric associated with the path to that network. Each router builds up a routing database on the basis of these neighbor updates, but does not know the identity of intermediate routers and networks on any particular path. There are two problems with this approach for an exterior routing protocol:

1. This distance-vector protocol assumes that all routers share a common distance metric with which to judge router preferences. This may not be the case among

different autonomous systems. If different routers attach different meanings to a given metric, it may not be possible to create stable, loop-free routes.

2. A given autonomous system may have different priorities from other autonomous systems and may have restrictions that prohibit the use of certain other autonomous systems. A distance-vector algorithm gives no information about the autonomous systems that will be visited along a route.

In a link-state routing protocol, each router advertises its link metrics to all other routers. Each router builds up a picture of the complete topology of the configuration and then performs a routing calculation. This approach also has problems if used in an exterior routing protocol:

1. Again, different autonomous systems may use different metrics and have different restrictions. Although the link-state protocol does allow a router to build up a picture of the entire topology, the metrics used may vary from one autonomous system to another, making it impossible to perform a consistent routing algorithm.
2. The flooding of link-state information to all routers implementing an exterior routing protocol across multiple autonomous systems may be unmanageable.

An alternative is to dispense with routing metrics and simply provide information about which networks can be reached by a given router and the autonomous systems that must be crossed to get there. The approach differs from a distance-vector algorithm in two respects: First, the path-vector approach does not include a distance or cost estimate. Second, each block of routing information lists all of the autonomous systems visited in order to reach the destination network by this route.

Because a path vector lists the ASs that a datagram must traverse if it follows this route, the path information enables a router to perform policy routing. That is, a router may decide to avoid a particular path in order to avoid transiting a particular AS. For example, information that is confidential may be limited to certain kinds of ASs. Or a router may have information about the performance or quality of the portion of the internet that is included in an AS that leads the router to avoid that AS. Examples of performance or quality metrics include link speed, capacity, tendency to become congested, and overall quality of operation. Another criterion that could be used is minimizing the number of transit ASs.

Border Gateway Protocol

BGP[5] was designed to allow routers, called gateways in the standard, in different autonomous systems to cooperate in the exchange of routing information. The protocol operates in terms of messages, which are sent over TCP connections. The repertoire of messages is summarized in Table 14.3. The current version of BGP is known as BGP-4.

---

[5] RFC 1771, *A Border Gateway Protocol (BGP-4)*, March 1995.

TABLE 14.3   BGP-4 MESSAGES

Open	Used to open a neighbor relationship with another router.
Update	Used to (1) transmit information about a single route and/or (2) list multiple routes to be withdrawn.
Keepalive	Used to (1) acknowledge an Open message and (2) periodically confirm the neighbor relationship.
Notification	Send when an error condition is detected.

Three functional procedures are involved in BGP:

- Neighbor acquisition
- Neighbor reachability
- Network reachability.

Two routers are considered to be neighbors if they are attached to the same subnetwork. If the two routers are in different autonomous systems, they may wish to exchange routing information. For this purpose, it is necessary to first perform **neighbor acquisition**. In essence, neighbor acquisition occurs when two neighboring routers in different autonomous systems agree to exchange routing information regularly. A formal acquisition procedure is needed because one of the routers may not wish to participate. For example, the router may be overburdened and does not want to be responsible for traffic coming in from outside the system. In the neighbor acquisition process, one router sends a request message to the other, which may either accept or refuse the offer. The protocol does not address the issue of how one router knows the address or even the existence of another router, nor how it decides that it needs to exchange routing information with that particular router. These issues must be dealt with at configuration time or by active intervention of a network manager.

To perform neighbor acquisition, one router sends an Open message to another. If the target router accepts the request, it returns a Keepalive message in response.

Once a neighbor relationship is established, the **neighbor reachability** procedure is used to maintain the relationship. Each partner needs to be assured that the other partner still exists and is still engaged in the neighbor relationship. For this purpose, the two routers periodically issue Keepalive messages to each other.

The final procedure specified by BGP is **network reachability**. Each router maintains a database of the subnetworks that it can reach and the preferred route for reaching that subnetwork. Whenever a change is made to this database, the router issues an Update message that is provided to other routers that implement BGP. By the broadcasting of these Update message, all of the BGP routers can build up and maintain routing information.

BGP Messages

Figure 14.12 illustrates the formats of all of the BGP messages. Each message begins with a 19-octet header containing three fields, as indicated by the shaded portion of each message in the figure:

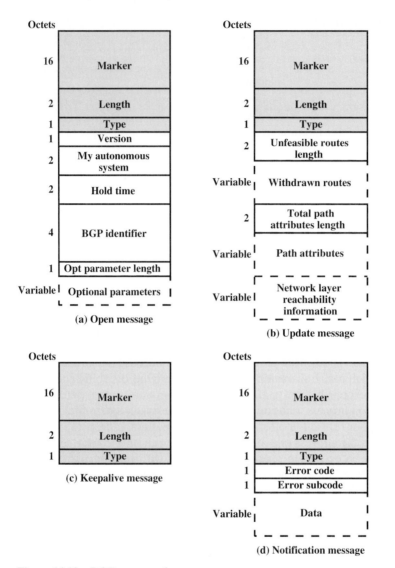

Figure 14.12 BGP message formats.

- **Marker:** Reserved for authentication. The sender may insert a value in this field that would be used as part of an authentication mechanism to enable the recipient to verify the identity of the sender.
- **Length:** Length of message in octets.
- **Type:** Type of message: Open, Update, Keepalive, Notification

To acquire a neighbor, a router first opens a TCP connection to the neighbor router of interest. It then sends an Open message. This message identifies the AS to which the sender belongs and provides the IP address of the router. It also includes a Hold Time parameter, which indicates the number of seconds that the sender proposes for the value of the Hold Timer. If the recipient is prepared to open a neighbor relationship, it calculates a value of Hold Timer that is the minimum of its Hold Time and the Hold Time in the Open message. This calculated value is the maximum number of seconds that may elapse between the receipt of successive Keepalive and/or Update messages by the sender.

The Keepalive message consists simply of the header. Each router issues these messages to each of its peers often enough to prevent the Hold Time from expiring.

The Update message communicates two types of information:

1. Information about a single route through the internet. This information is available to be added to the database of any recipient router.
2. A list of routes previously advertised by this router that are being withdrawn.

An Update message may contain one or both types of information. Let us consider the first type of information first. Information about a single route through the network involves three fields: the Network Layer Reachability Information (NLRI) field, the Total Path Attributes Length field, and the Path Attributes field. The NLRI field consists of a list of identifiers of subnetworks that can be reached by this route. Each subnetwork is identified by its IP address, which is actually a portion of a full IP address. As was mentioned in Section 11.1, an IP address is a 32-bit quantity of the form {network, end system}. The left-hand or prefix portion of this quantity identifies a particular subnetwork.

The Path Attributes field contains a list of attributes that apply to this particular route. The following are the defined attributes:

- **Origin:** Indicates whether this information was generated by an interior routing protocol (e.g., OSPF) or an exterior routing protocol (in particular, BGP).
- **AS_Path:** A list of the ASs that are traversed for this route.
- **Next_Hop:** The IP address of the border router that should be used as the next hop to the destinations listed in the NLRI field.
- **Multi_Exit_Disc:** Used to communicate some information about routes internal to an AS. This is described later in this section.
- **Local_Pref:** Used by a router to inform other routers within the same AS of its degree of preference for a particular route. It has no significance to routers in other ASs.
- **Atomic_Aggregate, Aggregator:** These two fields implement the concept of route aggregation. In essence, an internet and its corresponding address space can be organized hierarchically, or as a tree. In this case, subnetwork addresses are structured in two or more parts. All of the subnetworks of a given subtree share a common partial internet address. Using this common partial address, the amount of information that must be communicated in NLRI can be significantly reduced.

The reader may wonder about the purpose of the Next_Hop attribute. The requesting router will necessarily want to know which networks are reachable via the responding router, but why provide information about other routers? This is best explained with reference to Figure 14.4. In this example, router R1 in autonomous system 1 and router R5 in autonomous system 2 implement BGP and acquire a neighbor relationship. R1 issues Update messages to R5 indicating which networks it could reach and the distances (network hops) involved. R1 also provides the same information on behalf of R2. That is, R1 tells R5 what networks are reachable via R2. In this example, R2 does not implement BGP. Typically, most of the routers in an autonomous system will not implement BGP. Only a few routers will be assigned responsibility for communicating with routers in other autonomous systems. A final point: R1 is in possession of the necessary information about R2, because R1 and R2 share an interior routing protocol.

The second type of update information is the withdrawal of one or more routes. In each case, the route is identified by the IP address of the destination subnetwork.

Finally, the Notification Message is sent when an error condition is detected. The following errors may be reported:

- **Message header error:** Includes authentication and syntax errors.
- **Open message error:** Includes syntax errors and options not recognized in an Open message. This message can also be used to indicate that a proposed Hold Time in an Open message is unacceptable.
- **Update message error:** Includes syntax and validity errors in an Update message.
- **Hold timer expired:** If the sending router has not received successive Keepalive and/or Update and/or Notification messages within the Hold Time period, then this error is communicated and the connection is closed.
- **Finite state machine error:** Includes any procedural error.
- **Cease:** Used by a router to close a connection with another router in the absence of any other error.

BGP Routing Information Exchange

The essence of BGP is the exchange of routing information among participating routers in multiple ASs. This process can be quite complex. In what follows, we provide a simplified overview.

Let us consider router R1 in autonomous system 1 (AS1) in Figure 14.4. To begin, a router that implements BGP will also implement an internal routing protocol such as OSPF. Using OSPF, R1 can exchange routing information with other routers within AS1, build up a picture of the topology of the subnetworks and routers in AS1, and construct a routing table. Next, R1 can issue an Update message to R5 in AS2. The Update message could include the following:

- **AS_Path:** The identity of AS1
- **Next_Hop:** The IP address of R1
- **NLRI:** A list of all of the subnetworks in AS1.

This message informs R5 that all of the subnetworks listed in NLRI are reachable via R1 and that the only autonomous system traversed is AS1.

Suppose now that R5 also has a neighbor relationship with another router in another autonomous system (say, R9 in AS3). R5 will forward the information just received from R1 to R9 in a new Update message. This message includes the following:

- **AS_Path:** The list of identifiers {AS2, AS1}
- **Next_Hop:** The IP address of R5
- **NLRI:** A list of all of the subnetworks in AS1.

This message informs R9 that all of the subnetworks listed in NLRI are reachable via R5 and that the autonomous systems traversed are AS2 and AS1. R9 must now decide if this is its preferred route to the subnetworks listed. It may have knowledge of an alternate route to some or all of these subnetworks that it prefers for reasons of performance or some other policy metric. If R9 decides that the route provided in R5's Update message is preferable, then R9 incorporates that routing information into its routing database and forwards this new routing information to other neighbors. This new message will include an AS_Path field of {AS1, AS2, AS3}.

In this fashion, routing update information is propagated through the larger internet consisting of a number of interconnected autonomous systems. The AS_Path field is used to assure that such messages do not circulate indefinitely: If an Update message is received by a router in an AS that is included in the AS_Path field, that router will not forward the update information to other routers, preventing looping of messages.

The preceding discussion leaves out several details that are briefly summarized here. Routers within the same AS, called internal neighbors, may exchange BGP information. In this case, the sending router does not add the identifier of the common AS to the AS_Path field. When a router has selected a preferred route to an external destination, it transmits this route to all of its internal neighbors. Each of these routers then decides if the new route is preferred—in which case, the new route is added to its database and a new Update message goes out.

When there are multiple entry points into an AS that are available to a border router in another AS, the Multi_Exit_Disc attribute may be used to choose among them. This attribute contains a number that reflects some internal metric for reaching destinations within an AS. For example, suppose in Figure 14.4 that both R1 and R2 implemented BGP and both had a neighbor relationship with R5. Each provides an Update message to R5 for subnetwork 1.3 that includes a routing metric used internal to AS1, such as a routing metric associated with the OSPF internal router protocol. R5 could then use these two metrics as the basis for choosing between the two routes.

Inter-Domain Routing Protocol

The Inter-Domain Routing Protocol (IDRP)[6] is an exterior routing protocol that has been designated for use with IPv6. IDRP is an ISO standard defined within the OSI family of protocols. However, it is not dependent on OSI networking or on the use of the OSI internet protocol. Instead, IDRP can be used with any other internet protocol and in an internet with a mixture of internet protocols.

Like BGP, IDRP is based on path-vector routing and represents a superset of BGP's functions. The key differences are as follows:

---

[6] ISO 10747, *Protocol for Exchange of Inter-Domain Routing Information among Intermediate Systems to Support Forwarding of ISO 8473 PDUs.*

- BGP operates over TCP, whereas IDRP operates over the internet protocol used in the configuration. IDRP includes its own handshaking exchanges to guarantee delivery of messages.
- BGP uses 16-bit autonomous system numbers. IDRP uses variable-length identifiers.
- IDRP can deal with multiple internet protocols and multiple internet address schemes. Indeed, in a single route advisory, an IDRP message can carry different network address formats.
- BGP communicates a path by specifying the complete list of autonomous systems that a path visits. IDRP is able to aggregate this information using the concept of routing domain confederations.

The last point is perhaps the most important difference between BGP-4 and IDRP. In IDRP, a set of connected autonomous systems may be grouped together to form a confederation. A system administrator may configure autonomous systems into a confederation so that they appear to the outside world as a single autonomous system. Therefore, any path that terminates in or passes through the confederation is identified by a single entry in the path vector, rather than one entry for each autonomous system that is visited. This process is recursive, so that groups of connected confederations can be aggregated into a single confederation. The result is a routing strategy that scales effectively with increasing size and complexity of the internet environment.

14.5 RECOMMENDED READING

Detailed coverage of OSPF and other routing algorithms is provided by [HUIT95]; these topics are also treated in [STEE95] and [PERL92]. For more information on IDRP, see [REKH93] and [THOM96].

HUIT95 Huitema, C. *Routing in the Internet.* Englewood Cliffs, NJ: Prentice Hall, 1995.

PERL92 Perlman, R. *Interconnections: Bridges and Routers.* Reading, MA: Addison-Wesley, 1992.

REKH93 Rekhter, Y. "Inter-Domain Routing Protocol (IDRP)." *Interneworking: Research and Experience*, June 1993.

STEE95 Steenstrup, M. *Routing in Communications Networks.* Englewood Cliffs, NJ: Prentice Hall, 1995.

THOM96 Thomas, S. *IPng and the TCP/IP Protocols.* New York: Wiley, 1996.

14.6 PROBLEMS

14.1 Should internet routing be concerned with a network's internal routing? Why or why not?

14.2 One would expect the loss of some segments during network link failures for TCP connections. If a link fails and segments are lost, TCP cuts down its window size after detecting the loss. Unicast routing adapts to the failed link (that was on the shortest path) by routing through another path (longer than the failed path). Describe the behavior of the TCP connection when the old route becomes available again. (Consider the case where TCP window size is such that the communication pipe between the sender and receiver on the longer path is filled with segments. Assume the same data rate on all links.)

14.3 Draw a weighted digraph corresponding to Figure 14.1.

14.4 For each of the entries in each of the vectors of Figure 14.5b, show the path that produces the path cost.

14.5 Show the routing table for router A for Figure 14.1. Now assume that within a 30-second period, both link costs from E become 1, and both link costs from F become 1 and that the updated distance vectors from E and F arrive at A. Further assume that updated distance vectors have not yet arrived from any other router. Show the result after A has updated its routing table on the basis of the new information from E and F.

14.6 In discussing the distance-vector routing algorithm used in RIP, it was stated that "it would be difficult to coordinate the activities of all routers so that the algorithm could be executed synchronously." State two problems that create the difficulty.

14.7 The counting-to-infinity problem discussed with reference to Figure 14.6 can occur without a network becoming unreachable. Add a WAN to Figure 14.6 that connects C and D, with a link cost of 10 in each direction.

    a. Show the distance ($L(x, 5)$) and next hop ($R(x, 5)$) to network 5 for each router.

    b. Now assume that network 3 fails. The routes should now adjust to use the link from C to D. The routing changes start when B notices that the route to D is no longer usable. Show the values of $L(x, 5)$ and ($R(x, 5)$) for each router over time until stable new values are reached.

14.8 In RIP, the split horizon with poisoned reverse rule clearly works for a point-to-point link between two routers. But on a broadcast network, such as Ethernet, RIP messages are broadcast to all other nodes implementing RIP; they are not addressed to a specific node. Suppose that A, B, and C are routers on the same Ethernet and that A sends a poisoned reverse message to C because A has a route that goes through C. The same message will also go to B. Will this cause a problem? If not, why not?

CHAPTER 15

ROUTING FOR HIGH-SPEED AND MULTIMEDIA TRAFFIC

The organization for the control and guidance of the trade should therefore be of so complete a character that the trade may be either dispersed about the ocean or concentrated along particular routes; or in some places dispersed and in others concentrated; and that changes from one policy to the other can be made when necessary at any time.

—*The World Crisis,* **Winston Churchill**

As this book has stressed, the demands on data networks continue their relentless rise. Traditional data-oriented applications, such as file transfer, electronic mail, USENET news, and client-server systems, place an increasing load on LANs, the Internet, and private internets. This increasing load is due not just to the number of users and the increased amount of time of their use, but also to increasing reliance on image as well as text and numerical data. At the same time, there is increasing use of video and audio. One option for multimedia applications is to use a combination of dedicated circuits and ATM technology. But the timing of the demand has outrun any hope of installing a desktop-to-desktop ATM infrastructure. On the Internet and corporate intranets, there is an explosive growth in the use of audio and video on Web pages. In addition, these networks are being used for audio/video teleconferencing and other multicast "radio" and video applications.

Thus, the burden of meeting this new demands falls on the TCP/IP architecture over a packet-based network infrastructure. The central issues that must be addressed are capacity and burstiness. Audio and video applications generate huge numbers of bits per second, and the traffic has to be streamed, or transmitted in a smooth continuous flow rather than in bursts. This contrasts with conventional types of data as text, files, and graphics, for which the uneven flow typical of packet transmission is acceptable.

In the absence of a universal ATM service, designers have looked for ways to accommodate both bursty and stream traffic within the TCP/IP architecture. The problem has been attacked with a number of complementary techniques:

1. Increased capacity. Corporate LANs and WANs, as well as the Internet backbone structure and corporate internets, have been upgraded to higher data rates, with high-performance switches and routers. However, it is uneconomical and, indeed, given the self-similar nature of much of the traffic (see Chapter 8), virtually impossible to size the network infrastructure to handle the peak busy period traffic. Accordingly, intelligent routing policies (Chapter 14) coupled with end-to-end flow control techniques (Chapter 10) are vital in dealing with the high volume such networks support.

2. A transport protocol appropriate for the streaming requirements of video and other real-time data is needed. The real-time transport protocol discussed in Chapter 10 is designed for this purpose.

3. Multimedia applications inevitably imply multicast transmission. Efficient techniques for multicasting over an internet are needed.

4. Users need to be able to reserve network capacity and assign priorities to various traffic types.

The first two items have been addressed in other chapters. This chapter begins with a discussion of internet multicasting and examines the routing protocols needed to support multicasting. Then capacity reservation is discussed, and a reservation protocol is introduced. Finally, this chapter looks at an intriguing and important area of network design: the effective use of a mixed ATM/internet environment. One promising approach, IP switching, is examined in detail.

15.1 MULTICASTING

Typically, an IP address refers to an individual host on a particular network. IP also accommodates addresses that refer to a group hosts on one or more networks. Such addresses are referred to as **multicast addresses**, and the act of sending a packet from a source to the members of a multicast group is referred to as **multicasting**.

Multicasting has a number of practical applications, including the following:

- **Multimedia:** A number of users "tune in" to a video or audio transmission from a multimedia source station.
- **Teleconferencing:** A group of workstations form a multicast group such that a transmission from any member is received by all other group members.

- **Database:** All copies of a replicated file or database are updated at the same time.
- **Distributed computation:** Intermediate results are sent to all participants.
- **Real-time workgroup:** Files, graphics, and messages are exchanged among active group members in real time.

Multicasting done within the scope of a single LAN segment is simplicity itself. IEEE 802 and other LAN protocols include a provision for MAC-level multicast addresses. A packet with a multicast address is transmitted on a LAN segment. Those stations that are members of the corresponding multicast group recognize the multicast address and accept the packet. In this case, only a single copy of the packet is ever transmitted. This technique works because of the broadcast nature of a LAN: A transmission from any one station is received by all other stations on the LAN.

In an internet environment, multicasting is a far more difficult undertaking. To see this, consider the configuration of Figure 15.1; a number of LANs are interconnected by routers. Routers connect to each other either over high-speed links or across a wide area network (network N4). Suppose that the multicast server on network N1 is transmitting packets to a multicast address that represents the workstations indicated on networks N3, N5, N6. Suppose that the server does not know the location of the members of the multicast group. Then one way to assure that the packet is received by all members of the group is to **broadcast** a copy of each packet to each network in the configuration, over the least-cost route for each network. For

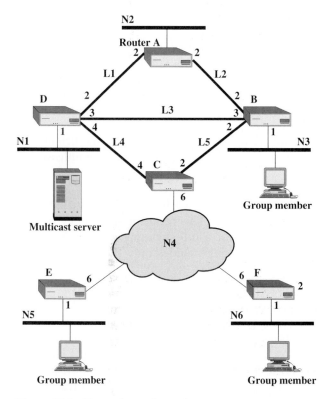

Figure 15.1   Example configuration.

TABLE 15.1   TRAFFIC GENERATED BY VARIOUS MULTICASTING STRATEGIES

	Broadcast					Multiple Unicast				Multicast
	S → N2	S → N3	S → N5	S → N6	Total	S → N3	S → N5	S → N6	Total	
N1	1	1	1	1	4	1	1	1	3	1
N2										
N3		1			1	1			1	1
N4			1	1	2		1	1	2	2
N5			1		1		1		1	1
N6				1	1			1	1	1
L1	1				1					
L2										
L3		1			1	1			1	1
L4			1	1	2		1	1	2	1
L5										
Total	2	3	4	4	13	3	4	4	11	8

example, one packet would be addressed to N3 and would traverse N1, link L3, and N3. Router B is responsible for translating the IP-level multicast address to a MAC-level multicast address before transmitting the MAC frame onto N3. Table 15.1 summarizes the number of packets generated on the various links and networks in order to transmit one packet to a multicast group by this method. A total of 13 copies of the packet are required.

Now suppose the source system knows the location of each member of the multicast group. That is, the source has a table that maps a multicast address into a list of networks that contain members of that multicast group. In that case, the source need only send packets to those networks that contain members of the group. We could refer to this as the **multiple unicast** strategy. Table 15.1 shows that in this case, 11 packets are required.

Both the broadcast and multiple unicast strategies are inefficient because they generate unnecessary copies of the source packet. In a true **multicast** strategy, the following method is used:

1. The least-cost path from the source to each network that includes members of the multicast group is determined. This results in a spanning tree of the configuration. Note that this is not a full spanning tree of the configuration. Rather, it is a spanning tree that includes only those networks containing group members.
2. The source transmits a single packet along the spanning tree.
3. The packet is replicated by routers only at branch points of the spanning tree.

Figure 15.2a shows the spanning tree for transmissions from the source to the multicast group, and Figure 15.2b shows this method in action. The source transmits a single packet over N1 to router D. D makes two copies of the packet, to transmit over links L3 and L4. B receives the packet from L3 and transmits it on N3, where it is read by members of the multicast group on the network. Meanwhile, C

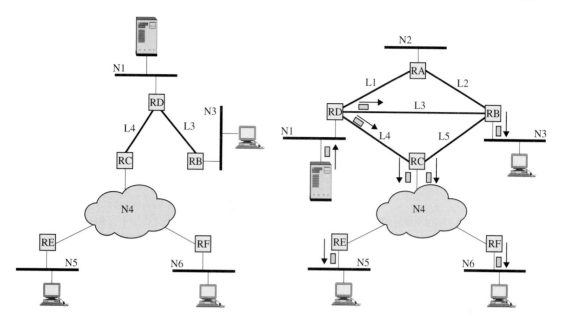

(a) Spanning tree from source to multicast group

(b) Packets generated for multicast transmission

Figure 15.2 Multicast transmission example.

receives the packet sent on L4. It must now deliver that packet to both E and F. If network N4 were a broadcast network (e.g., an Ethernet LAN), then C would only need to transmit one instance of the packet for both routers to read. If N4 is a packet-switching WAN, then C must make two copies of the packet and address one to E and one to F. Each of these routers, in turn, retransmits the received packet on N5 and N6, respectively. As Table 15.1 shows, the multicast technique requires only eight copies of the packet.

Requirements for Multicasting

In ordinary unicast transmission over an internet, in which each datagram has a unique destination network, the task of each router is to forward the datagram along the shortest path from that router to the destination network. With multicast transmission, the router may be required to forward two or more copies of an incoming datagram. In our example, routers D and C both must forward two copies of a single incoming datagram.

Thus, we might expect that the overall functionality of multicast routing is more complex than unicast routing. The following is a list of required functions:

1. A convention is needed for identifying a multicast address. In IPv4, Class D addresses are reserved for this purpose. These are 32-bit addresses with 1110 as their high-order 4 bits, followed by a 28-bit group identifier. In IPv6, a 128-bit multicast address consists of an 8-bit prefix of all ones, a 4-bit flags field, a 4-bit scope field, and a 112-bit group identifier. The flags field, currently, only indicates whether this address is permanently assigned or not. The scope field

indicates the scope of applicability of the address, ranging from a single sub-network to global.

2. Each node (router or source participating in the routing algorithm) must translate between an IP multicast address and a list of networks that contain members of this group. This information allows the node to construct a shortest-path spanning tree to all of the networks containing group members.

3. A router must translate between an IP multicast address and a subnetwork multicast address in order to deliver a multicast IP datagram on the destination network. For example, in IEEE 802 networks, including Ethernet, a MAC-level address is 16 or 48 bits long. In both cases, if the highest-order bit is 1, then it is a multicast address. Thus, for multicast delivery, a router attached to an IEEE 802 network must translate a 32-bit IPv4 or a 128-bit IPv6 multicast address into a 16-bit or 48-bit IEEE 802 MAC-level multicast address.

4. Although some multicast addresses may be assigned permanently, the more usual case is that multicast addresses are generated dynamically and that individual hosts may join and leave multicast groups dynamically. Thus, a mechanism is needed by which an individual host informs routers attached to the same network as itself of its inclusion in and exclusion from a multicast group.

5. Routers must exchange two sorts of information. First, routers need to know which subnetworks include members of a given multicast group. Second, routers need sufficient information to calculate the shortest path to each network containing group members. These requirements imply the need for a routing protocol.

6. A routing algorithm is needed to calculate shortest paths to all group members.

7. Each router must determine multicast routing paths on the basis of both source and destination addresses.

The last point is a subtle consequence of the use of multicast addresses. To illustrate the point, consider again Figure 15.1. If the multicast server transmits a unicast packet addressed to a host network N5, the packet is forwarded by router D to C, which then forwards the packet to E. Similarly, a packet addressed to a host on network N3 is forwarded by D to B. But now suppose that the server transmits a packet with a multicast address that includes hosts on N3, N5, and N6. As we have discussed, D makes two copies of the packet and send one to B and one to C. So far, so good. But what will C do when it receives a packet with such a multicast address? C knows that this packet is intended for networks N3, N5, and N6. A simple-minded approach would be for C to calculate the shortest path to each of these three networks. This produces the shortest-path spanning tree shown in Figure 15.3. As a result, C sends two copies of the packet out over N4, one intended for N5 and one intended for N6. But it also sends a copy of the packet to B for delivery on N3! Thus B will receive two copies of the packet, one from D and one from C. This is clearly not what was intended by the host on N1 when it launched the packet.

To avoid unnecessary duplication of packets, each router must route packets on the basis of both source and multicast destination. When C receives a packet intended for the multicast group from a source on N1, it must calculate the spanning tree with N1 as the root (shown in Figure 15.2a) and route on the basis of that spanning tree.

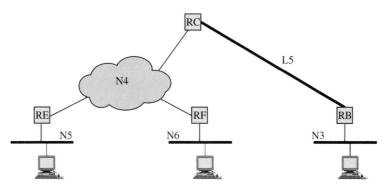

Figure 15.3   Spanning tree from router C to multicast group.

The remainder of this section examines three important protocols related to multicast routing. First, we look at IGMP, which is a protocol that enables hosts to join and leave multicast groups. Next, MOSPF is examined; this is an extension to the OSPF protocol discussed in Chapter 14 that enables multicast routing within an autonomous system. Finally, PIM is a protocol for interdomain multicast routing.

Internet Group Management Protocol (IGMP)

IGMP, defined in RFC 1112,[1] is used by hosts and routers to exchange multicast group membership information over a LAN. IGMP takes advantage of the broadcast nature of a LAN to provide an efficient technique for the exchange of information among multiple hosts and routers. All IGMP messages are transmitted in IP datagrams.

IGMP Message Format

All IGMP messages are transmitted in IP datagrams and have the format shown in Figure 15.4. The fields are as follows:

- **Version:** Protocol version, equal to 1.
- **Type:** There are two types. Type 1 specifies a query sent by a multicast router. Type 0 specifies a report sent by a host.
- **Checksum:** An error-detecting code, calculated as the 16-bit one's complement addition of the four 16-bit words in the message. For purposes of computation, the checksum field is itself initialized to a value of zero. This is the same checksum algorithm used in IPv4.

0   4   8   16   31

Version	Type	Unused	Checksum
Group address (Class D IPv4 address)			

Figure 15.4   IGMP message format.

---

[1]   RFC 1112, *Host Extensions for IP Multicasting*, August 1989.

- **Group address:** Zero in a request message, and a valid group address in a report message.

IGMP Operation

The objective of each host in using IGMP is to make itself known as a member of a group with a given multicast address to other hosts on the LAN and to all routers on the LAN. To join a group, a host sends an IGMP report message, in which the group address field is the multicast address of the group. This message is sent in an IP datagram with the same multicast destination address. In other words, the Group Address field of the IGMP message and the Destination Address field of the encapsulating IP header are the same. All hosts that are currently members of this multicast group will receive the message and learn of the new group member. Each router attached to the LAN must listen to all IP multicast addresses in order to hear all reports.

To maintain a valid current list of active group addresses, a multicast router periodically issues a IGMP query message, sent in an IP datagram with an *all-hosts* multicast address. Each host that still wishes to remain a member of one or more multicast groups must read datagrams with the all-hosts address. When such a host receives the query, it must respond with a report message for each group to which it claims membership.

Note that the multicast router does not need to know the identity of every host in a group. Rather, it needs to know that there is at least one group member still active. Therefore, each host in a group that receives a query sets a timer with a random delay. Any host that hears another host claim membership in the group will cancel its own report. If no other report is heard and the timer expires, a host sends a report. With this scheme, only one member of each group should provide a report to the multicast router.

Group Membership with IPv6

IGMP was defined for operation with IPv4 and makes use of 32-bit addresses. This same functionality is needed in IPv6 internets. Rather than define a separate version of IGMP for IPv6, its functions have been incorporated into the new version of the Internet Control Message Protocol (ICMPv6). ICMPv6 includes all of the functionality of ICMPv4 and IGMP. For multicast support, ICMPv6 includes both a group-membership query and a group-membership report message, which are used in the same fashion as in IGMP. In addition, there is a new group-membership termination message, which enables a host to announce that it is leaving a group.

Multicast Extensions to Open Shortest Path First (MOSPF)

MOSPF is an enhancement to OSPF (described in Chapter 14) that enables the routing of IP multicast datagrams. MOSPF is designed to operate within a single autonomous system.[2]

MOSPF follows the strategy outlined in the preceding general discussion of internet multicasting. Each router attached to a LAN uses IGMP to maintain a cur-

---

[2] RFC 1584, *Multicast Extensions to OSPF*, March 1994.

rent picture of local group membership. Periodically, each router floods information about local group membership to all other routers in its area. The result is that all routers in an area are able to build up a complete picture of the location of all group members for each multicast group. Using Dijkstra's algorithm, each router constructs the shortest-path spanning tree from a source network to all networks containing members of a multicast group. Because this source-destination calculation is time consuming, it is done only on demand. That is, a router does not construct a source-destination spanning tree for a given source and a given multicast destination until it receives a multicast IP datagram with that source and that multicast destination address.

When a router receives a multicast packet for forwarding or delivery, it will perform the following actions:

1. If the multicast address is not recognized, the datagram is discarded.
2. If the router attaches to a network containing at least one member of this group, it transmits a copy of the datagram on that network.
3. The router consults the spanning tree that it has calculated for this source-destination pair to determine if one or more copies of the datagram should be forwarded to other routers and performs the necessary transmission.

For any hop that is across a broadcast network such as a LAN, an IP multicast datagram is transmitted inside a MAC-level multicast frame addressed to all routers on the LAN.

MOSPF must deal with a number of special circumstances that complicate the algorithm just described. We examine each of these in turn.

Equal-cost Multipath Ambiguities

It may be that there are multiple paths between a given source and a given destination network of equal cost. Dijkstra's algorithm will generate a spanning tree that includes one of these paths. Which path is included depends on the order in which nodes are processed. In the case of unicast routing, it is not important that each router perform Dijkstra's algorithm in the same way to generate the same spanning tree, because each node is determining the shortest paths to all networks from itself. However, for multicast routing, each node determines the shortest paths to all destination networks that are covered by a multicast address from some other source network. Accordingly, it is important that all routers agree on a unique spanning tree for a given source node. To enforce this, MOSPF includes a tiebreaker rule that is deterministic so that all routers will agree.

Interarea Multicasting

Recall from Chapter 14 that OSPF incorporates the concept of area. An internet can be organized as a two-level hierarchy. At a top level is a backbone, and subordinate to the backbone are a number of areas. Each area is a contiguous set of networks and hosts, plus routers attached to any of those networks. The backbone is a contiguous set of networks and routers not contained in any area, plus routers that belong to multiple areas. The OSPF link-state algorithm is performed within each area. That is, the routers within an area have a detailed picture of the topology of their area and can perform Dijkstra's algorithm within the area. To reach a host outside the area, packets are routed to a border router, which forwards the datagrams through the backbone to the target area.

Multicasting complicates the use of areas, because a multicast group may contain members in more than one area. To minimize the size of the database that must be maintained by each router within an area, each such router only knows about the multicast groups that have members in its area. To achieve full connectivity, a subset of an area's border routers, called **interarea multicast forwarders**, forward group membership information and multicast datagrams between areas. The key functions are as follows:

1. Because each interarea multicast forwarders is attached to an area, it receives the multicast link status reports from that area and therefore knows all of the multicast groups in that area. Conversely, because each area includes at least one interarea multicast forwarder, its multicast group information is known to at least one router in the backbone.
2. Backbone routers exchange information about multicast groups so that all routers in the backbone know which areas contain members of each group.
3. Each interarea multicast forwarder also functions as a **wild-card multicast receiver**. Such routers automatically receive all multicast datagrams generated in an area, regardless of the destination multicast group. A wild-card multicast router will forward a multicast datagram if necessary and discard it otherwise. The wild-card multicast receiver guarantees that all multicast traffic originating in an area is delivered to its interarea multicast forwarder and then, if necessary, into the backbone.

Figures 15.5a and 15.5b illustrate the key concepts for interarea multicast routing. If the source of a multicast datagram resides in the same area as the router performing the spanning-tree calculation, that router must be sure that the spanning tree includes branches to subnetworks in the area with group members plus branches to each wild-card multicast receiver in the area. The local router does not know if there are group members residing in other areas and so must retain the wild-card multicast receivers.

If the source of a multicast datagram resides in a different area than the router performing the spanning-tree calculation, then the datagram has entered the area through an interarea multicast forwarder; this entry point is used as the base of the spanning tree by routers in the area in calculating the spanning tree.

Inter-AS Multicasting

OSPF and its extension, MOSPF, function within an autonomous system, or domain, of an internet. No detailed routing information is sent outside of the AS. In the case of unicast routing, we saw that some sort of interdomain routing protocol, such as BGP, is needed to route datagrams across multiple ASs. We would like to extend this capability to multicasting and, in the next subsection, we show an example of an interdomain routing protocol that supports multicasting—namely, Protocol Independent Multicast.

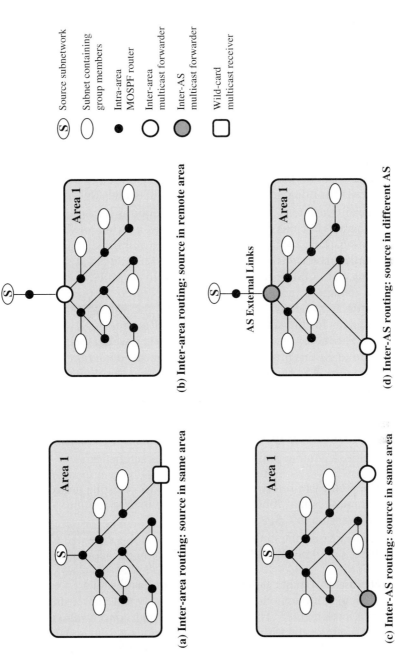

Legend:

(S) Source subnetwork

◯ Subnet containing group members

● Intra-area MOSPF router

◯ Inter-area multicast forwarder

⬤ Inter-AS multicast forwarder

▢ Wild-card multicast receiver

(a) Inter-area routing: source in same area

(b) Inter-area routing: source in remote area

(c) Inter-AS routing: source in same area

(d) Inter-AS routing: source in different AS

Figure 15.5 Illustrations of MOSPF routing [SEME96].

Although MOSPF has no responsibility for multicasting beyond its AS, it is responsible for providing multicast group information to outside entities and for accepting multicast datagrams for groups contained within its AS. MOSPF support inter-AS multicasting in the following ways:

1. Certain boundary routers (routers within this AS that are also a neighbor to a non-AS router) will be configured as **inter-AS multicast forwarders**. In addition to running MOSPF and OSPF, these routers also run an inter-AS multicast routing protocol.

2. MOSPF guarantees that the inter-AS multicast forwarders receive all multicast datagrams from within the AS; in other words, each inter-AS multicast forwarder functions as a wild-card multicast receiver. Each such router determines whether the datagram should be forwarded to other ASs, based on the inter-AS routing protocol. Figure 15.5c illustrates this feature.

3. Recall that internal multicast routing requires knowledge of the source of a datagram. For this purpose, MOSPF uses a technique known as reverse-path routing. This technique assumes that a multicast datagram originating at source X (outside the AS) will enter the MOSPF AS at the point that is advertising (into OSPF) the best route back to X. MOSPF calculates that path of the datagram through the MOSPF AS based on this assumption. In other words, suppose that a router internal to the MOSPF AS receives a multicast datagram for forwarding whose source IP address is X, which is external to the AS. The router first determines what route it would use to send a unicast datagram to X; this involves sending that unicast datagram to a boundary router within the AS. The router then assumes that this multicast datagram entered the AS at that particular boundary router and does its source-destination routing on that basis. Figure 15.5d illustrates this situation.

Protocol Independent Multicast

Most multicast routing protocols have two characteristics:

1. The multicast protocol is an extension to an existing unicast routing protocol and requires that routers implement the unicast routing protocol. MOSPF as an extension to OSPF is an example.

2. In most cases, the multicast routing protocol is designed to be efficient when there is a relatively high concentration of multicast group members.

The use of a multicast extension to a unicast routing protocol is appropriate within a single autonomous system where it is typical that a single unicast routing protocol is implemented. The assumption of a high concentration of multicast group members is often valid within a single autonomous system and for applications such as groupware. However, a different approach is needed to deal with a large internet of multiple autonomous systems and to deal with applications such as multimedia, in which the size of a given multicast group may be relatively small and widely scattered.

To provide a more general solution to multicast routing and new protocol has been developed, known as Protocol Independent Multicast (PIM). As the name suggests, PIM is a separate routing protocol, independent of any existing unicast routing protocol. PIM is designed to extract needed routing information from any unicast routing protocol and may work across multiple ASs with a number of different unicast routing protocols.

PIM Strategy

The design of PIM recognizes that a different approach may be needed to multicast routing depending on the concentration of multicast group members. When there are many multicast members and many subnetworks within a configuration have members of a given multicast group, then the frequent exchange of group membership information is justified. In such an environment, it is desirable to build shared spanning trees, such as we saw in Figure 15.2b, so that packet duplication occurs as infrequently as possible. However, when there are a few widely scattered members to a given multicast group, different considerations apply. First, flooding of multicast group information to all routers is inefficient, because most routers will not be along the path of any members of a given multicast group. Second, there will be relatively little opportunity for using shared spanning trees and therefore the focus should be on providing multiple shortest-path unicast routes.

To accommodate these differing requirements, PIM defines two modes of operation: dense-mode and sparse-mode operation. These are, in fact, two separate protocols. The dense-mode protocol is appropriate for inter-AS multicast routing and may be viewed as a potential alternative to MOSPF. The sparse-mode protocol is suited for inter-AS multicast routing. The remainder of this discussion concerns sparse-mode PIM.

Sparse-Mode PIM

The PIM specification defines a sparse group as one in which

- The number of networks/domains with group members present is significantly smaller than the number of networks/domains in the internet.
- The internet spanned by the group is not sufficiently resource rich to ignore the overhead of current multicast routing schemes.

Before proceeding, let us define a group destination router to be a router with local group members (members attached to a subnetwork interfaced by that router). A router becomes a destination router for a given group when at least one local host joins that group using IGMP or a similar protocol. A group source router is a router that attaches to a network with at least one host that is transmitting packets on the multicast group address via that router. For some group, a given router will be both a source and a destination router. However, for broadcast types of applications, such as video distribution, there may be one or a small number of source routers with many destination routers.

The approach taken for sparse-mode PIM has the following elements:

1. For a multicast group one router is designated as a *rendezvous point* (RP).

2. A group destination router sends a Join message toward the SP requesting that its members be added to the group. The requesting router uses a unicast shortest-path route to transmit the message toward the RP. The reverse of this path becomes part of the distribution tree from this RP to listeners in this group.

3. Any node that wishes to send to a multicast group sends packets toward the RP, using a shortest-path unicast route.

A transmission by this scheme, as defined so far, can be summarized as follows. A single packet follows the shortest unicast path from the sending node to the RP. From the RP, transmission occurs down the tree to the listeners, with each packet replicated at each split in the tree. This scheme minimizes the exchange of routing information, because routing information goes only from each router that supports group members to the RP. The scheme also provides reasonable efficiency. In particular, from the RP to the multicast receivers, a shared tree is used, minimizing the number of packets duplicated.

In a widely dispersed group, any RP will, of necessity, be remote from many of the group members, and paths for many group members will be much longer than the least-cost path. To help alleviate these drawbacks while maintaining the benefits of the PIM scheme, PIM allows a destination router to replace the group-shared tree with a shortest-path tree to any source. Once a destination router receives a multicast packet, it may elect to send a Join message back to the source router of that packet along a unicast shortest path. From then on, multicast packets between that source and all group members that are neighbors to that destination router follow the unicast shortest path.

Figure 15.6 illustrates the sequence of events. Once the destination begins to receive packets from the source by the shortest-path router, it sends a Prune message to the RP. This Prune message instructs the RP not to send any multicast packets from that source to this destination. The destination will continue to receive multicast packets from other sources via the RP-based tree, unless and until it prunes those sources. Any source router must continue to send multicast packets to the RP router for delivery to other multicast members.

The selection of an RP for a given multicast group is a dynamic process. The initiator of a multicast group selects a primary RP and a small ordered set of alternative RPs. In general, RP placement is not a critical issue because the RP-based tree will not be used for most receivers after shortest-path routers are followed.

15.2 RESOURCE RESERVATION: RSVP

A key task, perhaps the key task, of an internet is to deliver data from a source to one or more destinations with the desired quality of service (throughput, delay, delay variance, etc.). This task becomes increasingly difficult on any internet with increasing number of users, data rate of applications, and use of multicasting. We have seen that one tool for coping with a high demand is dynamic routing. A dynamic routing scheme, supported by protocols such as OSPF and BGP, can respond quickly to failures in the internet by routing around points of failure. More important, a dynamic routing scheme can, to some extent, cope with congestion, first

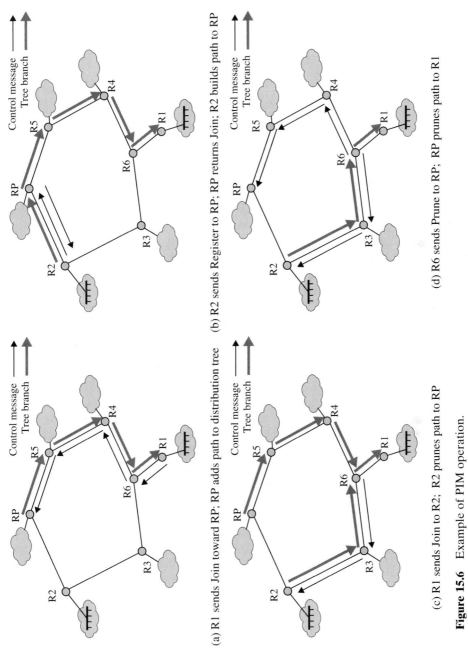

(a) R1 sends Join toward RP; RP adds path to distribution tree

(b) R2 sends Register to RP; RP returns Join; R2 builds path to RP

(c) R1 sends Join to R2; R2 prunes path to RP

(d) R6 sends Prune to RP; RP prunes path to R1

Figure 15.6 Example of PIM operation.

445

by load balancing to smooth out the load across the internet, and second by routing around areas of developing congestion using least-cost routing. In the case of multicasting, dynamic routing schemes have been supplemented with multicast routing capabilities that take advantage of shared paths from a source to multicast destinations to minimize the number of packet duplications.

Another tool available to routers is the ability to process packets on the basis of a QoS label. We have seen that routers can (1) use a queue discipline that gives preference to packets on the basis of QoS; (2) select among alternate routes on the basis of QoS characteristics of each path; and (3) when possible, invoke QoS treatment in the subnetwork of the next hop.

All of these techniques are means of coping with the traffic presented to the internet but are not preventive in any way. Based only on the use of dynamic routing and QoS, a router is unable to anticipate congestion and prevent applications from causing an overload. Instead, the router can simply supply a best-effort delivery service, in which some packets may be lost and others delivered with less than the requested quality of service.

As the demands on internets grow, it appears that prevention as well as reaction to congestion is needed. As this section shows, a means to implement a prevention strategy is resource reservation.

Preventive measures can be useful in both unicast and multicast transmission. For unicast, two applications agree on a specific quality of service for a session and expect the internet to support that quality of service. If the internet is heavily loaded, it may not provide the desired QoS and instead deliver packets at a reduced QoS. In that case, the applications may have preferred to wait before initiating the session or at least to have been alerted to the potential for reduced QoS. A way of dealing with this situation is to have the unicast applications reserve resources in order to meet a given quality of service. Routers along an intended path could then preallocate resources (queue space, outgoing capacity) to assure the desired QoS. If a router could not meet the resource reservation because of prior outstanding reservations, then the applications could be informed. The applications may then decide to try again at a reduced QoS reservation or may decide to try later.

Multicast transmission presents a much more compelling case for implementing resource reservation. A multicast transmission can generate a tremendous amount of internet traffic if either the application is high volume (e.g., video) or the group of multicast destinations is large and scattered, or both. What makes the case for multicast resource reservation is that much of the potential load generated by a multicast source may easily be prevented. This is so for two reasons:

1. Some members of an existing multicast group may not require delivery from a particular source over some given period of time. For example, there may be two "channels" (two multicast sources) broadcasting to a particular multicast group at the same time. A multicast destination may wish to "tune in" to only one channel at a time.

2. Some members of a group may only be able to handle a portion of the source transmission. For example, a video source may transmit a video stream that consists of two components: a basic component that provides a reduced pic-

ture quality, and an enhanced component.[3] Some receivers may not have the processing power to handle the enhanced component, or may be connected to the internet through a subnetwork or link that does not have the capacity for the full signal.

Thus, the use of resource reservation can enable routers to decide ahead of time if they can meet the requirement to deliver a multicast transmission to all designated multicast receivers and to reserve the appropriate resources if possible.

Internet resource reservation differs from the type of resource reservation that may be implemented in a connection-oriented network, such as ATM or frame relay. An internet resource reservation scheme must interact with a dynamic routing strategy that allows the route followed by packets of a given transmission to change. When the route changes, the resource reservations must be changed. To deal with this dynamic situation, the concept of *soft state* is used. A soft state is simply a set of state information at a router that expires unless regularly refreshed from the entity that requested the state. If a route for a given transmission changes, then some soft states will expire and new resource reservations will invoke the appropriate soft states on the new routers along the route. Thus, the end systems requesting resources must periodically renew their requests during the course of an application transmission.

We now turn to the protocol that has been developed for performing resource reservation in an internet environment: RSVP (Resource ReSerVation Protocol). [4]

RSVP Goals and Characteristics

Perhaps the best way to introduce RSVP is to list the design goals and characteristics. In [ZHAN93], the developers of RSVP list the following design goals:

1. Provide the ability of heterogeneous receivers to make reservations specifically tailored to their own needs. As was mentioned, some members of a multicast group may be able to handle or may want to handle only a portion of a multicast transmission, such as a low-resolution component of a video signal. Differing resource reservations among members of the same multicast group should be allowed.

2. Deal gracefully with changes in multicast group membership. Membership in a group can be dynamic. Thus, reservations must be dynamic, and again, this suggests that separate dynamic reservations are needed for each multicast group member.

3. Specify resource requirements in such a way that the aggregate resources reserved for a multicast group reflect the resources actually needed. Multicast routing takes place over a tree such that packet splitting is minimized. Therefore, when resources are reserved for individual multicast group members, these reservations must be aggregated to take into account the common path segments shared by the routes to different group members.

---

[3] For example, the MPEG video compression standard discussed in Chapter 18 provides this capability.

[4] RFC xxxx, *Resource ReSerVation Protocol (RSVP)—Version 1 Functional Specification.*

4. Enable receivers to select one source from among multiple sources transmitting to a multicast group. This is the channel-changing capability described earlier.

5. Deal gracefully with changes in routes, automatically reestablishing the resource reservation along the new paths as long as adequate resources are available. Because routes may change during the course of an application's transmission, the resource reservations must also change so that the routers actually on the current path receive the reservations.

6. Control protocol overhead. Just as resource reservations are aggregated to take advantage of common path segments among multiple multicast receivers, so the actual RSVP reservation request messages should be aggregated to minimize the amount of RSVP traffic in the internet.

7. Be independent of routing protocol. RSVP is not a routing protocol; its task is to establish and maintain resource reservations over a path or distribution tree, independent of how the path or tree was created.

Based on these design goals, the specification lists the following characteristics of RSVP:

- **Unicast and multicast:** RSVP makes reservations for both unicast and multicast transmissions, adapting dynamically to changing group membership as well as to changing routes, and reserving resources based on the individual requirements of multicast members.

- **Simplex:** RSVP makes reservations for unidirectional data flow. Data exchanges between two end systems require separate reservations in the two directions.

- **Receiver-initiated reservation:** The receiver of a data flow initiates and maintains the resource reservation for that flow.

- **Maintaining soft state in the internet:** RSVP maintains a soft state at intermediate routers and leaves the responsibility for maintaining these reservation states to end users.

- **Providing different reservation styles:** These allow RSVP users to specify how reservations for the same multicast group should be aggregated at the intermediate switches. This feature enables a more efficient use of internet resources.

- **Transparent operation through non-RSVP routers:** Because reservations and RSVP are independent of routing protocol, there is no fundamental conflict in a mixed environment in which some routers do not employ RSVP. These routers will simply use a best-effort delivery technique.

- **Support for IPv4 and IPv6:** RSVP can exploit the Type-of-Service field in the IPv4 header and the Flow Label field in the IPv6 header.

It is worth elaborating on two of these design characteristics: receiver-initiated reservations and soft state.

Receiver-initiated Reservation

In previous attempts at resource reservation, and in the approach taken in frame relay and ATM networks, the source of a data flow requests a given set of resources. In a strictly unicast environment, this approach is reasonable. A transmitting application is able to transmit data at a certain rate and has a given quality of service designed into the transmission scheme. However, this approach is inadequate for multicasting. As was mentioned, different members of the same multicast group may have different resource requirements. If the source transmission flow can be divided into component subflows, then some multicast members may only require a single subflow. If there are multiple sources transmitting to a multicast group, then a particular multicast receiver may want to select only one or a subset of all sources to receive. Finally, the QoS requirements of different receivers may differ depending on the output equipment, processing power, and link speed of the receiver.

It therefore makes sense for receivers rather than senders to make resource reservations. A sender needs to provide the routers with the traffic characteristics of the transmission (data rate, variability), but it is the receivers that must specify the desired QoS. Routers can then aggregate multicast resource reservations to take advantage of shared path segments along the distribution tree.

Soft State

RSVP makes use of the concept of a soft state. This concept was first introduced by David Clark in [CLAR88], and it is worth quoting his description:

> While the datagram has served very well in solving the most important goals of the Internet, the goals of resource management and accountability have proved difficult to achieve. Most datagrams are part of some sequence of packets from source to destination, rather than isolated units at the application level. However, the gateway[5] [footnote reference added] cannot directly see the existence of this sequence, because it is forced to deal with each packet in isolation. Therefore, resource management decisions or accounting must be done on each packet separately.
>
> This suggests that there may be a better building block than the datagram for the next generation of architecture. The general characteristic of this building block is that it would identify a sequence of packets traveling from source to destination. I have used the term *flow* to characterize this building block. It would be necessary for the gateways to have flow state in order to remember the nature of the flows which are passing through them, but the state information would not be critical in maintaining the described type of service associated with the flow. Instead, that type of service would be enforced by the end points, which would periodically send messages to ensure that the proper type of service was being associated with the flow. In this way, the state information associated with the flow could be lost in a crash without permanent disruption of the service features being used. I call this concept *soft state*.

In essence, a connection-oriented scheme takes a hard-state approach, in which the nature of the connection along a fixed route is defined by the state information in the intermediate switching nodes. RSVP takes a soft-state, or connectionless, approach, in which the reservation state is cached information in the routers that is installed and periodically refreshed by end systems. If a state is not refreshed within a required time limit, the router discards the state. If a new route becomes preferred for a given flow, the end systems provide the reservation to the new routers on the route.

---

[5] *Gateway* is the term used for *router* in most of the earlier RFCs and TCP/IP literature; it is still occasionally used today (e.g., Border Gateway Protocol).

Data Flows

Three concepts relating to data flows form the basis of RSVP operation: session, flow specification, and filter specification.

A session is a data flow identified by its destination. The reason for using the term *session* rather than simply *destination* is that it reflects the soft-state nature of RSVP operation. Once a reservation is made at a router by a particular destination, the router considers this as a session and allocates resources for the life of that session. In particular, a session is defined by the following:

Session:	Destination IP address
	IP protocol identifier
	Destination port.

The destination IP address may be unicast or multicast. The protocol identifier indicates the user of IP (e.g., TCP or UDP), and the destination port is the TCP or UDP port for the user of this transport-layer protocol. If the address is multicast, the destination port may not be necessary, because there is typically a different multicast address for different applications.

A reservation request issued by a destination end system is called a *flow descriptor*, and consists of a *flowspec* and a *filter spec*. The flowspec specifies a desired quality of service and is used to set parameters in a node's packet scheduler. That is, the router will transmit packets with a given set of preferences based on the current flowspecs. The filter spec defines the set of packets for which a reservation is requested. Thus, the filter spec together with the session define the set of packets, or flow, that are to receive the desired QoS. Any other packets addressed to the same destination are handled as best-effort traffic.

The content of the flowspec is beyond the scope of RSVP, which is merely a carrier of the request. In general, a flowspec contains the following elements:

Flow spec:	Service class
	Rspec
	Tspec.

The service class is an identifier of a type of service being requested; it includes information used by the router to merge requests. The other two parameters are sets of numeric values. The Rspec (R for reserve) parameter defines the desired quality of service, and the Tspec (T for traffic) parameter describes the data flow. The contents of Rspec and Tspec are opaque to RSVP.

In principle, the filter spec may designate an arbitrary subset of the packets of one session (i.e., the packets arriving with the destination specified by this session). For example, a filter spec could specify only specific sources, or specific source protocols, or in general only packets that have a match on certain fields in any of the protocol headers in the packet. The current RSVP version uses a restricted filter spec consisting of the following elements:

Filter spec:	Source address
	UDP/TCP source port.

Figure 15.7 indicates the relationship among session, flowspec, and filter spec. Each incoming packet is part of at most one session and is treated according to the logical flow indicated in the figure for that session. If a packet belongs to no session, it is given a best-effort delivery service.

RSVP Operation

Much of the complexity of RSVP has to do with dealing with multicast transmission. Unicast transmission is treated as a special case. In what follows, we examine the general operation of RSVP for multicast resource reservation. The internet configuration shown in Figure 15.8a is used in the discussion. This configuration consist of four routers connected as shown. The link between two routers, indicated by a line, could be a point-to-point link or a subnetwork. Three hosts, G1, G2, and G3, are members of a multicast group and can receive datagrams with the corresponding destination multicast address. Two hosts, S1 and S2, transmit data to this multicast address. The heavy black lines indicate the routing tree for source S1 and this multicast group, and the heavy gray lines indicate the routing tree for source S2 and this multicast group. The arrowed lines indicate packet transmission from S1 (black) and S2 (gray).

We can see that all four routers need to be aware of the resource reservations of each multicast destination. Thus, resource requests from the destinations must propagate backward through the routing trees toward each potential host.

Filtering

Figure 15.8b shows the case that G3 has set up a resource reservation with a filter spec that includes both S1 and S2, whereas G1 and G2 have requested transmissions from S1 only. R3 continues to deliver packets from S2 for this multicast address to G3 but does not forward such packets to R4 for delivery to G1 and G2. The reservation activity that produces this result is as follows. Both G1 and G2 send an RSVP request with a filter spec that excludes S2. Because G1 and G2 are the only members of the multicast group reachable from R4, R4 no longer needs to forward packets for this session. Therefore, it can merge the two filter spec requests and send these in an RSVP message to R3. Having received this message, R3 will no longer forward packets for this session to R4. However, it still needs to forward such packets to G3. Accordingly, R3 stores this reservation but does not propagate it back up to R2.

RSVP does not specify how filtered packets are to be handled. R3 could choose to forward such packets to R4 in a best-effort basis, or could simply drop the packets. The latter course is indicated in Figure 15.8b.

A more fine-grained example of filtering is illustrated in Figure 15.8c. Here we only consider transmissions from S1, for clarity. Suppose that two types of packets are transmitted to the same multicast address representing two substreams (e.g., two parts of a video signal). These are illustrated by black and gray arrowed lines. G1 and G2 have sent reservations with no restriction on the source, whereas G3 has used a filter spec that eliminates one of the two substreams. This request propagates from R3 to R2 to R1. R1 then blocks transmission of part of the stream to G3. This saves resources on the links from R1 to R2, R2 to R3, and R3 to G3, as well as resources in R2, R3, and G3.

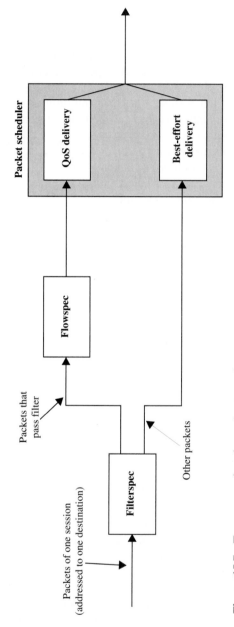

Figure 15.7 Treatment of packets of one session at one router.

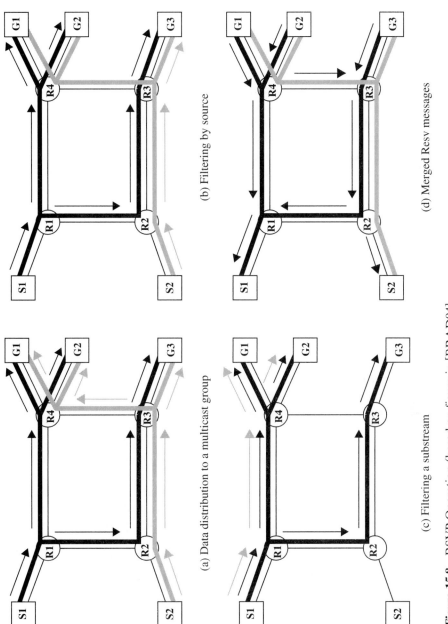

(a) Data distribution to a multicast group

(b) Filtering by source

(c) Filtering a substream

(d) Merged Resv messages

Figure 15.8 RSVP Operation (based on figure in [BRAD94]).

Reservation Styles

The manner in which resource requirements from multiple receivers in the same multicast group are aggregated is determined by the reservation style. These styles are, in turn, characterized by two different options in the reservation request:

- **Reservation attribute:** A receiver may specify a resource reservation that is to be shared among a number of senders (shared), or may specify a resource reservation that is to be allocated to each sender (distinct). In the former case, the receiver is characterizing the entire data flow that it is to receive on this multicast address from the combined transmission of all sources in the filter spec. In the latter case, the receiver is saying that it is simultaneously capable of receiving a given data flow from each sender characterized in its filter spec.
- **Sender selection:** A receiver may either provide a list of sources (explicit) or implicitly select all sources by providing no filter spec (wildcard).

Based on these two options, three reservation styles are defined in RSVP, as shown in Table 15.2. The **wild-card filter (WF) style** specifies a single resource reservation to be shared by all senders to this address. If all of the receivers use this style, then we can think of this style as a shared pipe whose capacity (or quality) is the largest of the resource requests from all receivers downstream from any point on the distribution tree. The size is independent of the number of senders using it. This type of reservation is propagated upstream to all senders. Symbolically, this style is represented in the form WF(*{Q}), where the asterisk represents wild-card sender selection and Q is the flowspec.

To see the effects of the WF style, we use the router configuration of Figure 15.9a, taken from the RSVP specification. This is a router along the distribution tree that forwards packets on port y for receiver R1 and on port z for receivers R2 and R3. Transmissions for this group arrive on port w from S1 and on port x from S2 and S3. Transmissions from all sources are forwarded to all destinations through this router.

Figure 15.9b shows the way in which the router handles WF requests. For simplicity, the flowspec is a one-dimensional quantity in multiples of some unit resource B. The *Receive* column shows the requests that arrive from the receivers. The *Reserve* column shows the resulting reservation state for each outgoing port. The *Send* column indicates the requests that are sent upstream to the previous-hop nodes. Note that the router must reserve a pipe of capacity 4B for port y and of

TABLE 15.2 RESERVATION ATTRIBUTES AND STYLES

	Reservation Attribute	
Sender Selection	Distinct	Shared
Explicit	Fixed-filter (FF) Style	Shared-explicit Style (SE)
Wildcard	—	Wilcard-filter (WF) Style

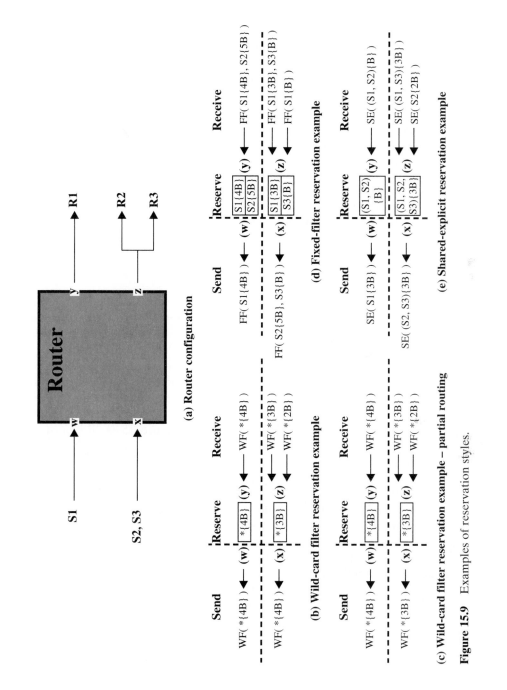

Figure 15.9 Examples of reservation styles.

455

capacity 3B for port z. In the latter case, the router has merged the requests from R2 and R3 to support the maximum requirement for that port. However, in passing requests upstream the router must merge all outgoing requests and send a request for 4B upstream on both ports w and x.

Now suppose that the distribution tree is such that this router forwards packets from S1 on both ports y and z but forwards packets from S2 and S3 only on port z, because the internet topology provides a shorter path from S2 and S3 to R1. Figure 15.9c indicates the way in which resource requests are merged in this case. The only change is that the request sent upstream on port x is for 3B. This is because packets arriving from this port are only to be forwarded on port z, which has a maximum flowspec request of 3B.

A good example of the use of the WF style is for an audio teleconference with multiple sites. Typically, only one person at a time speaks, so a shared capacity can be used by all senders.

The **fixed-filter (FF) style** specifies a distinct reservation for each sender and provides an explicit list of senders. Symbolically, this style is represented in the form FF(S1{Q1}, S2{Q2}, ...), where Si is a requested sender and Qi is the resource request for that sender. The total reservation on a link for a given session is the sum of the Qi for all requested senders.

Figure 15.9d illustrates the operation of the FF style. In the Reserve column, each box represents one reserved pipe on the outgoing link. All of the incoming requests for S1 are merged to send a request for 4B out on port w. The flow descriptors for senders S2 and S3 are packed (not merged) into the request sent of port x; for this request, the maximum requested flowspec amount for each source is used.

A good example of the use of the FF style is for video distribution. To receive video signals simultaneously from different sources requires a separate pipe for each of the streams. The merging and packing operations at the routers assure that adequate resources are available. For example, in Figure 15.8a, R3 must reserve resources for two distinct video streams going to G3, but it needs only a single pipe on the stream going to R4 even though that stream is feeding two destinations (G1 and G2). Thus, with FF style, it may be possible to share resources among multiple receivers but it is never possible to share resources among multiple senders.

The **shared-explicit (SE) style** specifies a single resource reservation to be shared among an explicit list of senders. Symbolically, this style is represented in the form SE(S1, S2, ... {Q}). Figure 15.9e illustrates the operation of this style. When SE-style reservations are merged, the resulting filter spec is the union of the original filter specs, and the resulting flowspec is the largest flowspec.

As with the WF style, the SE style is appropriate for multicast applications in which there are multiple data sources but they are unlikely to transmit simultaneously.

RSVP Protocol Mechanisms

RSVP uses two basic message types: Resv and Path. Resv messages originate at a multicast group receivers and propagate upstream through the distribution tree, being merged and packed when appropriate at each node along the way. These messages create soft states within the routers of the distribution tree that define the resources reserved for this session (this multicast address). Ultimately, the merged Resv messages reach the sending hosts, enabling the hosts to set up appropriate traffic control parameters for the first hop. Figure 15.8d indicates the flow of Resv messages. Note that messages are merged so that only a single message flows upstream along any branch of the combined distribution trees. However, these messages must be repeated periodically to maintain the soft states.

The Path message is used to provide upstream routing information. In all of the multicast routing protocols currently in use, only a downstream route, in the form of a distribution tree, is maintained. However, the Resv messages must propagate upstream through all intermediate routers and to all sending hosts. In the absence of reverse routing information from the routing protocol, RSVP provides this with the Path message. Each host that wishes to participate as a sender in a multicast group issues a Path message that is transmitted throughout the distribution tree to all multicast destination. Along the way, each router and each destination host creates a path state that indicates the reverse hop to be used for this source. Figure 15.8a indicates the paths taken by these messages, which is the same as the paths taken by data packets.

Figure 15.10 illustrates the operation of the protocol from the host perspective. The following events occur:

a. A receiver joins a multicast group by sending an IGMP join message to a neighboring router.
b. A potential sender issues a Path message to the multicast group address.
c. A receiver receives a Path message identifying a sender.
d. Now that the receiver has reverse path information, it may begin sending Resv messages, specifying the desired flow descriptors.
e. The Resv message propagates through the internet and is delivered to the sender.
f. The sender starts sending data packets.
g. The receiver starts receiving data packets.

Events a and b may happen in either order.

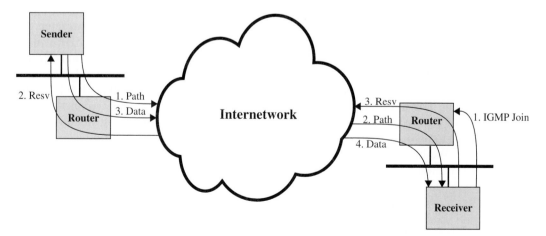

Figure 15.10   RSVP host model.

15.3 IP SWITCHING

Throughout this book, we have been looking at two important but very different technologies that are playing key roles in the evolving field of high-speed networks: ATM- and IP-based internetworking. ATM is a connection-oriented approach relying on high-performance hardware switches and the labeling of individual connections (virtual channels/virtual paths) on the basis of quality of service. Associated with ATM is relatively complex control signaling and network management software to manage the routing, creation, maintenance, and termination of logical connections. IP-based internetworking is a connectionless, or datagram, approach relying on software-controlled routers. The concept of flows with an associated quality of service is a relatively recent introduction to the realm. Routers make use of relatively simple routing protocols and avoid the overhead of control signaling involved in connection-oriented approaches. The connectionless nature of IP-based internets results in a robust architecture that responds well to localized congestion and to failures.

An attempt to marry these two technologies is needed. At the local level, moderate-speed shared-medium LANs, such as the 10-Mbps Ethernet and 16-Mbps token ring, are being replaced by high-speed switched LANs, such as switched Ethernet at 100 Mbps or even 1 Gbps and 155-Mbps ATM LANs. Such LANs, especially ATM LANs, can be easily hooked into an ATM WAN for wide area transmission. However, there remains a need to attach to the Internet and to wide area corporate internets. It seems unlikely that, even in the long run, the massive IP-based infrastructure currently in place will be replaced by a pure ATM solution. Therefore, IP-based internets must be evolved to handle the high loads generated by today's high-speed LANs and the growing multimedia application base.

Of course, the wide area links between routers can be enhanced to include point-to-point 155-Mbps links and the linking of routers across ATM networks. However, to handle a single full-duplex 155-Mbps port, a router must be able to process on the order of 100,000 packets per second. With the software processing required for datagrams, this is a significant load.

A number of approaches to streamlining the use of IP over ATM are currently being explored. The most promising approach, and the one that has attracted the most vendor support so far, is IP switching [MCQU96]. In its purest form, IP switching refers to the mapping of IP data flows onto connection-oriented virtual circuits, a technique designed to avoid the packet-by-packet processing overhead of routers.

In this section, we explore a particular approach to IP switching, developed by Ipsilon. This approach has been defined in a set of RFCs[6] and has attracted a number of significant corporate sponsors. This approach, or something similar to it, is likely to enjoy widespread use.

We begin with a discussion of the concept of flows, then look at the general approach for switching, and finally examine some of the details.

---

[6] RFC 1953, *Ipsilon Flow Management Protocol Specification for IPv4*, May 1996; RFC 1954, *Ipsilon Flow Labelled IPv4 on ATM Data Links*, May 1996; RFC 1987, *Ipsilon's General Switch Management Protocol Specification*, August 1996.

Flows

Any sustained traffic between end points across a network can be considered to consist of a collection of flows with different characteristics, including different traffic profiles (burstiness, magnitude) and different QoS requirements. Typically, the traffic breaks down into flows based on the applications running over TCP/IP, UDP/IP, or raw IP.

The requirement for IP switching is to determine which flows would benefit from delivery across ATM virtual channels, bypassing the router function, and which flows would generate more overhead than it is worth to perform such a mapping onto a virtual channel. An obvious way to do this is for the end application to declare the traffic profile and QoS requirements of the flow. However, IPv4 provides only limited capability for doing this, with its type-of-service field (Figure 11.2). The IPv6 flow label field (Figure 11.4) is well suited to this purpose but, as yet, IPv6 is not widely deployed. The RSVP protocol provides another way to achieve identification of specific flows but, again, RSVP is not widely implemented as yet.

Another alternative is to do flow analysis—namely, to classify traffic on the basis of its likely flow characteristics. A study of traffic over the Internet performed by Ipsilon [NEWM96] is instructive in this regard. In essence, the Ipsilon study found that a relatively small percentage of flows are of long duration and carry a high percentage of packets.

Figure 15.11 captures this pattern. This figure represents the results of examining 5 minutes of traffic. In this analysis, a flow is defined as the transfer of packets between a given source and destination address, subject to the restriction that an idle time of 60 seconds terminates the flow. The duration of the flow is defined as the time between the first packet that establishes the flow and the final packet transmitted on the flow. The figure shows the cumulative distribution function for flow duration. The figure also shows the cumulative distribution of packets within

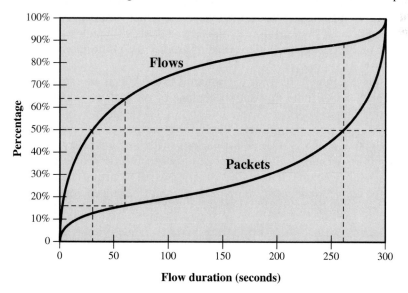

Figure 15.11 Cumulative distribution of flows and packets vs. flow duration (based on [NEWM96]).

these flows. To understand the figure, pick any point on the flow curve. This indicates what percentage of the total number of flows have a duration less than or equal to a given time value. The corresponding point on the packet curve directly below the flow curve gives the percentage of the total number of packets carried by that set of flows. For example, 64% of the flows have a duration of less than 60 seconds, but these flows account for only 16% of the packets. Conversely, 36% of the flows are longer than one minute, and these flows carry 84% of the packets. Two other data points worth noting: Half of the flows have a duration of less than about 30 seconds, whereas half of the packets are carried by flows with duration greater than 260 seconds.

The implication of these figures is that it should be possible to identify a relatively small number of flows that carry most of the traffic and last the longest. These flows warrant the extra effort needed to exploit ATM fully and to bypass the routing software. If these flows bypass the routing software and are forwarded by the more rapid ATM switching function, the load on routers is dramatically reduced. The remaining flows can be treated as individual datagrams to be handled by routers with little impact on overall performance.

In the absence of explicit guidance, such as the IPv6 flow label or an RSVP reservation, how would a node in the network determine which packets should be assigned to flows for the purpose of switching? The Ipsilon study looked at the flow characteristics of each protocol in the study's data set. If either TCP or UDP is running over IP, then the protocol is defined in the well-known port number from either the source or destination port field of the TCP or UDP header.[7] Otherwise, the protocol field in the header defines the protocol. Table 15.3 shows partial results from analyzing packet traffic in this fashion. In this case, a flow is defined as before (same source/destination, no longer than 60-second gap) with the additional restriction of same protocol. Again we see that the bulk of the packet traffic is concentrated on a relatively small number of long-duration flows. The shaded entries in the table indicate protocols with characteristics for which it appears worth establishing a switched flow. Ipsilon arbitrarily picked protocols with an average flow duration in excess of 20 seconds and an average of greater than 40 packets per flow for this assignment.

If this assignment of flows to protocols is used, then we can go back and look at the data set and find out what percentage of the traffic is carried in flows, and how many flows are defined. Table 15.4 shows this result and compares it to a decision to assign all packets to flows. That is, for every protocol between a given source and destination a flow is defined for packets, with a new flow started after any gap of one minute or more. The difference between the two columns illustrates the motivation for switching. If all traffic is carried in ATM virtual channels, then a large number of connections must be maintained and the rate of connection establishment/termination is high, all of which generates signaling overhead. However, if we

---

[7] Almost invariably, either the source port or the destination port of a TCP connection or UDP exchange is a well-known port number defining a particular application, such as FTP, TELNET, HTTP, etc. Without such a convention, it would be difficult to define a procedure whereby a remote application could set up an exchange with an application on a target machine.

TABLE 15.3   FLOW STATISTICS BY PROTOCOL (BASED ON [NEWM96])

Protocol	Packets/s	Flows/s	Flow Duration (s)	Packets/ Flow
News (NNTP in TCP)	1,096	0.7	177	627
Mbone(IP in IP)	456	0.1	173	2,307
X-Windows (TCP)	111	0.2	161	276
FTP-data (TCP)	2,018	2.2	118	525
Telnet (TCP)	803	4.2	114	114
Web (HTTP in UDP)	6,717	73.0	57	74
Mail (POP in TCP)	9	0.4	27	21
Mail (SMTP in TCP)	802	49.5	18	15
Management (SNMP in TCP)	43	6.1	18	6
Name Server (DNS in UDP)	929	216.6	15	4

TABLE 15.4   ASSIGNMENT OF PACKETS TO FLOWS

	Selected Protocols	All Packets
% of packets in flows	84%	100%
% of bytes in flows	91%	100%
Number of new flows/second	92	422
Average number of active flows	15,500	42,000

only assign high-usage flows to ATM channels, the bulk of the traffic is carried with greatly reduced control overhead; the remainder of the packets can be routed by with little impact on overall performance.

Ipsilon's Switching Scheme

The Ipsilon switching scheme functions in an environment in which the routers in an internet configuration are nodes that contain the routing function as well as ATM switching hardware. Each node connects to each of its neighbors (nodes that share the same network or that share a point-to-point link) by means of a point-to-point ATM virtual channel. That is, the two end points of the virtual channel are the two neighboring nodes. When a node begins to see traffic that can be assigned to a flow, it sends a message to the upstream node sending that traffic to request that it be switched to a new virtual channel dedicated to that flow. If the node then receives a similar request from the downstream node for this traffic, it creates a dedicated virtual channel to the downstream node and splices the two virtual channels together. From that point on, the packets on this flow are switched at the ATM hardware level and are not processed by this node's routing software.

The Switch

Figure 15.12 shows the general structure of an IP switch. The node includes an ATM switch, which implements the ATM logic in hardware. This switch has multiple 155-Mbps links to other nodes. There is a separate processor that runs the routing software and that connects to the ATM switch with a 155-Mbps link. In addition,

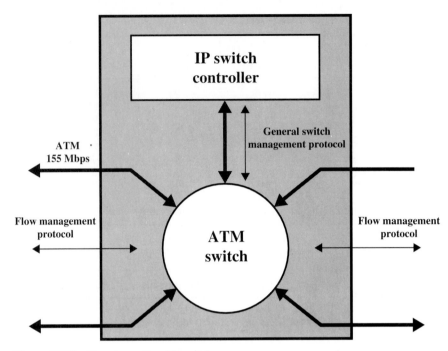

Figure 15.12   Structure of an IP switch.

two protocols are needed. The internet flow management protocol (IFMP) associates flows with ATM virtual channels and defines the format for flow-redirect messages and acknowledgments. The general switch management protocol (GSMP) is responsible for setting up, tearing down, and monitoring the status of the virtual channels defined for this ATM switch.

Figure 15.13 depicts the operation of the switch. At system startup, each node establishes a default virtual channel with each of its neighbors. Each virtual channel terminates at the switch controller. Initially, all traffic is carried on the default channels (1). An incoming datagram consists of a stream of ATM cells. These are delivered to the switch controller, which reassembles the datagram, performs the routing function, and then sends the datagram out on a different virtual channel on the downstream link. The controller also performs flow analysis on the datagrams in order to define flows for switching.

Once a flow is identified, the switch controller sends an IFMP message to the upstream node to request that this flow be transmitted over a new dedicated virtual channel (2). The flow is defined by the source and destination addresses, the upper-level protocol, and other characteristics, as explained in the next subsection. If the upstream node agrees, it begins to send packets for this flow over the new virtual channel (3). Independently, the node may receive a request from the downstream node to set up an outgoing virtual channel for this flow (4). When the flow is isolated to a particular input channel and a particular output channel (5), the switch controller uses GSMP to instruct its switch to make the appropriate port mapping in hardware to splice the two virtual channels together. Subsequently, the datagrams on this flow will pass through this node as a stream of switched ATM cells, bypassing the routing software.

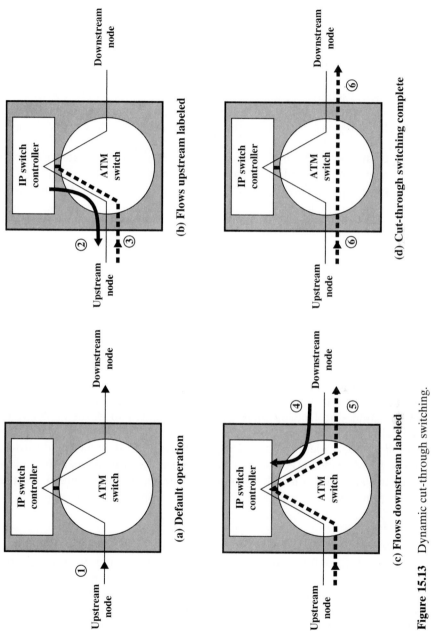

Figure 15.13 Dynamic cut-through switching.

463

Each switch maintains a timer for each virtual channel so that unused virtual channels may be destroyed. If no traffic arrives on a given channel during its time-out interval, then a message is issued to the upstream node to terminate that channel and return that stream to the default channel.

Mapping of Datagrams to ATM Cells

IP datagrams are transmitted over virtual channels using AAL Type 5. Recall from Chapter that the AAL-5 consists of a single sublayer, known as common-part convergence sublayer (CPCS), and that an AAL-5 CPCS PDU consists of a payload and an 8-octet trailer. The payload is used to carry a single datagram. The exact format of the payload depends on the type of flow. Three flow types are defined:

- **Flow type 0:** This is the default flow type that delivers datagrams to the switch controller. The entire datagram is encapsulated in the CPCS PDU.
- **Flow type 1:** This is a flow defined by the source and destination addresses, protocol (TCP or UDP), the type of service field, and the source and destination ports (TCP or UDP source and destination addresses).
- **Flow type 2:** This is a flow defined by the source and destination addresses.

In the latter two cases, some fields may be deleted for transmission. For flow type 1, the following fields of the IP header are not transmitted: version, internet header length, type of service, time to live, protocol, source address, and destination address. In addition, the first four octets immediately following the header are not transmitted; these correspond to the source and destination TCP or UDP ports. Figure 15.14 illustrates the resulting scheme. The CPCS payload consists of a reduced header, consisting of the total length, identification, flags, fragment offset, and checksum fields; followed by a reduced TCP or UDP segment in which the destination and source port fields are removed. The entire PDU is then segmented into 48-octet chunks and encapsulated into a sequence of 53-octet ATM cells. The virtual-path/virtual-channel fields of the ATM cells all contain the same value, which uniquely identifies this flow. These cells are then switched through one or more ATM switches. At the end of the spliced virtual channel, the cells are delivered to the switch controller, where the datagram is reassembled and the missing fields reinserted.

Multicast

A switch can support multicasting with no modification to the multicasting or routing software. If the router is at a point on the routing tree for a given multicast address that does not require splitting, then a single upstream virtual channel can be mapped to a single downstream virtual channel, as in the unicast case. If the router is at a split point, then a single upstream channel is mapped into multiple downstream virtual channels, and the ATM switch hardware replicates each cell for retransmission on multiple outgoing channels.

Mixed Configuration

The switching approach works without modification in a configuration that consists of a mixture of switches and traditional routers. Traffic that passes through

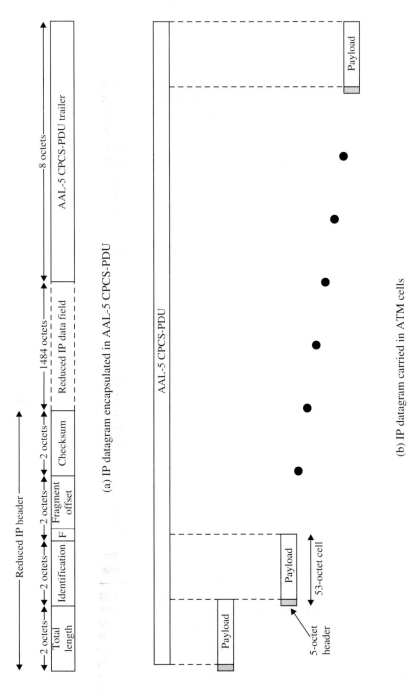

(a) IP datagram encapsulated in AAL-5 CPCS-PDU

(b) IP datagram carried in ATM cells

Figure 15.14 Flow-labeled IP over ATM (Flow Type 1).

465

two or more switches in sequence along a path from source to destination can be switched at the ATM level through such nodes. Traffic passing through a traditional router must be handled at the datagram level.

15.4 RECOMMENDED READING

[DEER90] is a seminal paper that describes the general approach and most of the mechanisms now in use for internet multicasting. [MOY94] describes the philosophy and general approach of MOSPF. [HUIT95] provides an overview of both dense- and sparse-mode PIM. [ZHAN93] is a good overview of the philosophy and functionality of RSVP, written by its developers. A more detailed discussion is provided in [THOM96]. [NEWM97] is a good overview of IP switching.

DEER90 Deering, S., and Cheriton, D. "Multicast Routing in Datagram Internetworks and Extended LANs." *ACM Transactions on Computer Systems*, May 1990.

HUIT95 Huitema, C. *Routing in the Internet.* Englewood Cliffs, NJ: Prentice Hall, 1995.

MOY94 Moy, J. "Multicast Routing Extensions for OSPF." *Communications of the ACM*, August 1994.

NEWM97 Newman, P., Minshall, G., Lyon, T., and Huston, L. "IP Switching and Gigabit Routers." *IEEE Communications Magazine*, January 1997.

THOM96 Thomas, S. *IPng and the TCP/ Protocols: Implementing the Next Generation Internet.* New York: Wiley, 1996.

ZHAN93 Zhang, L., Deering, S., Estrin, D., Shenker, S., and Zappala, D. "RSVP: A New Resource ReSerVation Protocol." *IEEE Network*, September 1993.

Recommended Web sites:

- http://www.ipmulticast.com: The IP Multicast Initiative is a multivendor group dedicated to the promotion of IP multicasting. Its Web site includes technical white papers, vendor and product information, and standardization activity status.

- http://www.isi.edu/div7/rsvp/rsvp-home.html: Home page for RSVP development.

- http://www.ipsilon.com: Information on IP switching.

15.5 PROBLEMS

15.1 In the discussion of Figure 15.1, three alternatives for transmitting a packet to a multicast address were discussed: broadcast, multiple unicast, and true multicast. Yet another alternative is flooding. The source transmits one packet to each neighboring router. Each router, when it receives a packet, retransmits the packet on all outgoing interfaces except the one on which the packet is received. Each packet is labeled with a unique identifier so that a router does not flood the same packet more than once. Fill out a matrix similar to those of Table 15.1 and comment on the results.

15.2 In a manner similar to Figure 15.3, show the spanning tree from router B to the multicast group.

15.3 Most multicast routing protocols, such as MOSPF, minimize the path cost to each group member, but they do not necessarily optimize the use of the internet as a whole. This problem demonstrates this fact.

    a. Sum the hop costs incurred by each packet involved in a multicast transmission of a source packet using the spanning tree of Figure 15.2a.

b. Design an alternative spanning tree that minimizes the total cost. Show the tree and the total cost.

15.4 Explain why MOSPF would be inefficient in a sparse multicast environment.

15.5 In sparse-node PIM, for the route between a given source and a given destination, the RP-based tree may be replaced with a path that is the shortest unicast path from source to destination. This statement is not quite accurate. What is wrong with the statement?

15.6 Some researchers argue that the optimal placement of the center of the shared tree (i.e., the rendezvous point in PIM) is crucial for achieving good delay characteristics for the multicast traffic. Argue for or against this statement.

15.7 In RSVP, because the UDP/TCP port numbers are used for packet classification, each router must be able to examine these fields. This requirement raises problems in the following areas:
a. IPv6 header processing
b. IP-level security.
Indicate the nature of the problem in each area, and suggest a solution.

15.8 Consider Figure 15.9a. This diagram appears to be a simplification, because each (source, destination) pair in a multicast routing scheme has a separate routing tree. Therefore, the output ports of the diagram should be labeled not just on the basis of destination but on the basis of (source, destination) pairs. Justify your agreement or disagreement.

15.9 Consider the description of the Type 1 flow in Ipsilon switching.
a. A number of fields are removed from the header and the TCP or UDP header. For each field of the original headers, justify its inclusion/exclusion from the transmitted datagram.
b. Suggest a security-related reason for removing the selected fields.

15.10 For Ipsilon IP switching, which fields should be included/excluded for Type 2 flows?

Compression

Despite the tremendous data rates found in contemporary networks and transmission systems, there is great interest in compressing data for transmission and storage. Regardless of the supply of network capacity available, demand always seems to catch up and surpass it. Compression provides a way of conserving network capacity and reducing the delays experienced by applications.

ROAD MAP FOR PART SEVEN

Chapter 16: Overview of Information Theory

This chapter provides an overview of concepts relevant to Part Three. For some readers, this material constitutes a review and refresher. For others, the chapter provides enough background to be able to follow the discussion in Chapters 17 and 18.

The first part of the chapter introduces the concepts of information and entropy and suggests that these concepts can form the basis for data compression. The remainder of the chapter discusses coding schemes that result in compression.

Chapter 17: Lossless Compression

Two forms of data compression are in widespread use: lossless and lossy. Lossless compression preserves all of the information in the original data so that, upon decompression, that data can be fully recovered. Lossless compression is appropriate for data files, messages, and other information in which bit errors are not tolerable. Chapter 17 discusses some of the most widely used lossless compression techniques, including run-length encoding, various facsimile compression techniques, arithmetic coding, and various string-matching algorithms.

Chapter 18: Lossy Compression

High compression ratios can be achieved if the requirement that no losses occur is dropped. Lossy compression techniques result in compressed files that, when decompressed, produce only an approximation of the original data. These techniques are useful in cases where some loss and distortion can be tolerated, such as voice, image, and video. Chapter 18 begins with a discussion of the discrete cosine transform, which is a basic technique used in many lossy compression algorithms. Then standardized approaches to image and video compression are examined. Techniques for compression of image and video have become critical in designing high-performance multimedia networks. Finally, the promising field of fractal image compression is surveyed.

CHAPTER 16

OVERVIEW
OF INFORMATION THEORY

The modern view is that messages having a high probability of occurrence contain little information, and that any mathematical definition adopted for "information" should conform to this idea—that the information conveyed by a sign, a message, a symbol, or an observation, in a set of such events, must decrease as their frequency of occurrence in the set increases.

—On Human Communication, Colin Cherry

Before beginning our study of data compression, we look at an important theoretical underpinning: information theory. Information theory was developed by Claude Shannon to provide a precise measure of the capacity of a data communications channel. The resulting theory has numerous applications. Of relevance to the present discussion is that information theory defines a limit to the amount of compression without loss that is possible for a given data stream.

This chapter begins with an overview of the relevant concepts from information theory, and then looks at the application of information theory to coding.

16.1 INFORMATION AND ENTROPY

At the heart of information theory are two mathematical concepts with names that can be misleading: information and entropy. Typically, one thinks of **information** as having something to do with meaning; **entropy** is a term familiar from the second law of thermodynamics. In the discipline of information theory, information has to do with the reduction in the uncertainty about an event and entropy is an averaging of information values that happens to have a mathematical form identical to that for thermodynamic entropy.

Let us approach this new definition of information by way of an example.[1] Imagine an investor who needs *information* (advice) about the status of certain securities, and who consults a broker with special *information* (knowledge) in that area. The broker *informs* (tells) the investor that, by coincidence, a federal investigator had come by just that morning seeking *information about* (evidence of) possible fraud by the corporation issuing that particular stock. In response to this *information* (data), the investor decides to sell, and so *informs* (notifies) the broker.

Put another way, being *uncertain* how to evaluate a portion of her portfolio, the client consults someone more *certain* than she about this side of the market. The broker relieves his client's *uncertainty* about relevant happenings by recounting the visit of the federal investigator, who had *uncertainties* to resolve of a professional nature. As an upshot of her increased *certainty* about the state of her securities, the client removes any *uncertainty* in the mind of the broker about her intention to sell.

Although the term *information* may signify notification, knowledge, or simply data, in each case the imparting of information is equivalent to the reduction in uncertainty. Information thus signifies the positive difference between two uncertainty levels.

Information

If we are to deal with information mathematically, then we need some quantity that is appropriate for measuring the amount of information. This problem was first raised, and solved, by Hartley in 1928 while studying telegraph communication. Hartley observed that if the probability that an event will occur is high (close to 1), then there is little uncertainty that it will occur. If we then learn that it has occurred, the amount of information gained is small. Thus, one plausible measure is the reciprocal of the probability of the occurrence of an event: $1/p$. For example, an event that has an initial probability of occurrence of 0.25 conveys more information by its occurrence than one with an initial probability of 0.5. If the measure of information is $1/p$, then the occurrence of the first event conveys an information value of 4 (1/0.25) and the occurrence of the second event conveys an information value of 2 (1/0.5). But there are two difficulties in using this measure of information:

1. This measure does not seem to "work" for sequences of events. Consider a binary source that issues a stream of ones and zeros with equal probability of a one or zero for each bit. Thus, each bit has an information value of 2: (1/0.5).

---

[1] This example appeared in [SAYR76].

But if bit b_1 conveys a value of 2, what is the information conveyed by the string of two bits $b_1 b_2$? This string can take on one of four possible outcomes, each with probability 0.25; therefore by the $1/p$ measure, an outcome conveys an information value of 4. Similarly, the information value of three bits $(b_1 b_2 b_3)$ is eight. This means that b_2 adds two units of information to the two of b_1, which is reasonable because the two bits have the same information value. But b_3 will add an additional four units of information. Extending the sequence, b_4 will add eight units of information, and so on. This does not seem reasonable as a measure of information.

2. Consider an event that gives rise to two or more independent variables. An example is a phase-shift-keying (PSK) signal that uses four possible phases and two amplitudes. A single signal element yields two units of information for the amplitude and four for the phase, for a total of six units by our measure. Yet each signal element is one of eight possible outcomes and hence ought to yield eight units of information by our measure.

Hartley overcame these problems by proposing that the measure of information for the occurrence on an event x be $\log(1/P(x))$. Formally,

$$I(x) = \log(1/P(x)) = -\log P(x) \tag{16.1}$$

This measure "works" and leads to many useful results. The base of the logarithm is arbitrary but is invariably taken to the base 2, in which case the unit of measure is referred to as the bit. The appropriateness of this designation should be obvious as we proceed. Base 2 logarithms are assumed in the rest of this discussion. We now can make the following observations:

1. A single bit that takes on the values 0 and 1 with equal probability conveys one bit of information $[\log(1/0.5) = 1]$. A string of two bits takes on one of four equally likely outcomes with probability 0.25 and conveys two bits of information $[\log(1/0.25) = 2]$. Therefore, the second bit adds one bit of information. In a sequence of three independent bits, the third bit also adds one bit of information $[\log(1/0.125) = 3]$, and so on.

2. In the example of the PSK signal, a single signal element yields one bit of information for the amplitude and two for the phase, for a total of three bits, which agrees with the observation that there are eight possible outcomes.

Figure 16.1 shows the information content for a single outcome as a function of the probability p of that outcome. As the outcome approaches certainty ($p = 1$), the information conveyed by its occurrence approaches zero. As the outcome approaches impossibility ($p = 0$), its information content approaches infinity.

Entropy

The other important concept in information theory is **entropy**, which was proposed in 1948 by Shannon, the founder of information theory. Shannon defined the entropy H as the average amount of information obtained from the value of a random variable. Suppose we have a random variable X, which may take on the values $x_1, x_2, \ldots, x_N$, and that the corresponding probabilities of each outcome are $P(x_1)$,

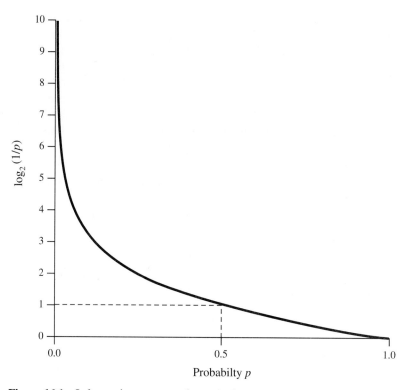

Figure 16.1 Information measure for a single outcome.

$P(x_2), \ldots, P(x_N)$. In a sequence of K occurrences of X, the outcome x_j will, on average, be selected $KP(x_j)$ times. Therefore, the average amount of information obtained from K outcomes is [using P_j as an abbreviation for $P(x_j)$]

$$KP_1 \log(1/P_1) + \ldots + KP_N \log(1/P_N)$$

Dividing by K yields the average amount of information per outcome for the random variable, referred to as the entropy of X, and designated by $H(X)$:

$$H(X) = \sum_{j=1}^{N} P_j \log(1/P_j) = -\sum_{j=1}^{N} P_j \log(P_j) \tag{16.2}$$

The function H is often expressed as an enumeration of the probabilities of the possible outcomes: $H(P_1, P_2, \ldots, P_N)$.

As an example, consider a random variable X that takes on two possible values with respective probabilities p and $1 - p$. The entropy associated with X is

$$H(p, 1 - p) = -p \log(p) - (1 - p) \log(1 - p)$$

Figure 16.2 plots $H(x)$ for this case as a function of p. Several important features of entropy are evident from this figure. First, if one of the two events is certain ($p = 1$ or $p = 0$), then the entropy is zero. One of the two events has to occur and no information is conveyed by its occurrence. Second, the maximum value of $H(X)$ is reached when the two outcomes are equally likely. This seems reasonable: The uncertainty of the outcome is maximum when the two outcomes are equally likely.

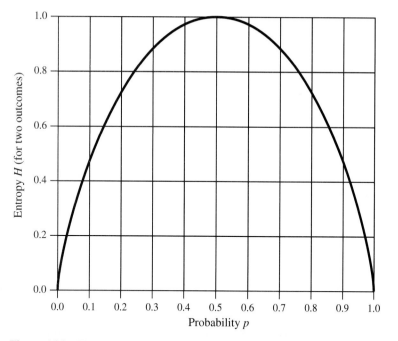

Figure 16.2   Entropy function for random variable with two equally likely outcomes.

This result generalizes to a random variable with N outcomes: Its entropy is maximum when the outcomes are equally likely:

$$\max \mathrm{H}(P_1, P_2, \ldots, P_N) = \mathrm{H}(1/N, 1/N, \ldots, 1/N)$$

For example,

$$\mathrm{H}(1/3, 1/3, 1/3) = 1/3 \log 3 + 1/3 \log 3 + 1/3 \log 3 = 1.585$$

whereas

$$\mathrm{H}(1/2, 1/3, 1/6) = 1/2 \log 2 + 1/3 \log 3 + 1/6 \log 6$$

$$= 0.5 + 0.528 + 0.43 = 1.458$$

Properties of the Entropy Function

We have developed the entropy formula $\mathrm{H}(X)$ by an intuitive line of reasoning. Another approach is to define the properties that an entropy function should have and then prove that the formula

$$-\sum_i p_i \log p_i$$

is the only form that has these properties. The properties, or axioms, can be stated as follows:

1. H is continuous over the range of probabilities. Thus, small changes in the probability of one of the occurrences only cause small changes in the uncertainty. This seems a reasonable requirement.

2. If there are N possible outcomes and they are equally likely, so that $P_i = 1/N$, then $H(X)$ is a monotonically increasing function of N. This is also a reasonable property because it says that the more equally likely outcomes, the larger the uncertainty.

3. If some of the outcomes of X are grouped, then H can be expressed as a weighted sum of entropies in the following fashion:

$$H(P_1, P_2, P_3, \dots, P_N) = H(P_1 + P_2, P_3, \dots, P_N) + (P_1 + P_2)H\left(\frac{P_1}{P_1 + P_2}, \frac{P_2}{P_1 + P_2}\right)$$

The reasoning is as follows. Before the outcome is known, the average uncertainty associated with the outcome is $H(P_1, P_2, P_3, \dots, P_N)$. If we reveal which outcome has occurred, except that the first two outcomes are grouped together, then the average amount of uncertainty removed is $H(P_1 + P_2, P_3, \dots, P_N)$. With probability $(P_1 + P_2)$, one of the first two outcomes occurs and the remaining uncertainty is $H[P_1/(P_1 + P_2) + P_2/(P_1 + P_2)]$.

The only definition of $H(X)$ that satisfies all three properties is the one that we have given. To see property (1), consider Figure 16.2, which is clearly continuous in p. It is more difficult to depict $H(X)$ when there are more than two possible outcomes, but the fact of continuity should be clear.

For property (2), if there are N equally likely outcomes, then $H(X)$ becomes

$$H(X) = -\sum_{j=1}^{N} \frac{1}{N} \log\left(\frac{1}{N}\right) = -\log\left(\frac{1}{N}\right) = \log(N)$$

We see that the function $\log(N)$ is a monotonically increasing function of N. Note that with four possible outcomes, the entropy is 2 bits; with eight possible outcomes, the entropy is 3 bits, and so on.

As a numerical example of property (3), we may write

$$H\left(\frac{1}{2}, \frac{1}{3}, \frac{1}{6}\right) = H\left(\frac{5}{6}, \frac{1}{6}\right) + \frac{5}{6}H\left(\frac{3}{5}, \frac{2}{5}\right)$$

$$1.458 = 0.219 + 0.43 + \frac{5}{6}(0.442 + 0.5288)$$

$$= 0.649 + 0.809$$

16.2 CODING

One of the important applications of entropy is the insight it provides into the design of data compression algorithms. The entropy of a random variable or message source determines a bound on the number of bits required to represent random variable outcomes or alternative messages without loss of information. Thus, in designing a compression algorithm, entropy is a measure of the best that it is possible to do.

We begin this section by looking at the Huffman code, which is a simple but effective code that illustrates the relationship between entropy and compression efficiency. Next, we present a general result about entropy and compression. Finally, we return to the Huffman code to illustrate some basic principles of compression.

Huffman Code

Consider a random variable X that takes on one of eight possible values $(x_1, x_2, \ldots, x_8)$ with the following probabilities:

$$
\begin{array}{ll}
P_1 = 0.512 & P_5 = 0.032 \\
P_2 = 0.128 & P_6 = 0.032 \\
P_3 = 0.128 & P_7 = 0.032 \\
P_4 = 0.128 & P_8 = 0.008
\end{array}
$$

where P_i is the probability of occurrence of x_i. Suppose a message consists of a sequence of occurrences of X and we wish to encode this in binary form. One obvious assignment is to use a fixed-length 3-bit code with one 3-bit value for each of the eight possible values of X. A better strategy is to use a variable-length code in which longer code words are assigned to less probable values of X and shorter code words are assigned to more probable values of X. This is the technique used in the Morse code and, more efficiently, in the Huffman code.

Suppose that messages are to be sent using an alphabet of N symbols. Each symbol is to be uniquely encoded as a binary sequence. What we are interested in is constructing an optimal code: one that gives the minimum average length for the encoded message. It is important to note that we are not seeking the minimum code length for one particular message or for all messages (the latter is impossible to find) but the minimum code length averaged over all possible messages.

Another way to look at the requirement is to consider that we are given a message that is already encoded using a fixed-length assignment of binary words to symbols. So if there are 8 symbols, each is encoded in 3 bits; if there are between 9 and 16 symbols, each is encoded in four bits, and so on. The requirement can then be stated that we are looking for an optimal variable-length coding scheme that gives the minimum average length for the compressed message.

Consider a binary code with code lengths $L_1, L_2, \ldots, L_N$ associated with an alphabet of N symbols with probabilities $P_1, P_2, \ldots, P_N$. For convenience, assume that the symbols are arranged in order of decreasing probability ($P_1 \geqslant P_2, \geqslant \ldots \geqslant P_N$) It can be shown that an optimal code should satisfy the following requirements:

1. No two messages consist of identical arrangements of bits.
2. No code word can be the prefix of another code word.
3. Higher-probability symbols have shorter code words. That is, $L_1 \leqslant L_2, \leqslant \ldots \leqslant L_N$.
4. The two least probable code words have equal length ($L_N = L_{N-1}$) and differ only in their final digit.

The first requirement ensures that any message is uniquely decipherable. The second requirement defines a code that is termed *instantaneous*. This requirement is not strictly necessary but is needed to ensure that a message can be decoded step by step. Proceeding left to right, as soon as a sequence of bits matches a given code word, the decoding algorithm can make the appropriate assignment. Here is an example of a code that violates requirements (1) and (2):

$$x_1 \quad 0$$
$$x_2 \quad 010$$
$$x_3 \quad 01$$
$$x_4 \quad 10$$

The binary sequence 010 could correspond to one of three messages: $x_2, x_3 x_1, x_1 x_4$.

Requirement (3) is easily seen by noting that if the condition is not met, you could exchange the two message codes and obtain a smaller average length.

To see requirement (4), suppose that $L_N > L_{N-1}$. By condition (2), code word $N - 1$ cannot be a prefix of code word N. Therefore, the first $N - 1$ digits of code word N constitute a unique code word and the excess digits can be dropped. If these two code words differ in some bit position other than the last, we can drop the last bit of each to obtain a better code.

These requirements suggest a method of constructing a code, called the Huffman code. Begin by ordering all of the symbols to be encoded in order of decreasing probability so that we have the symbols $(a_1, a_2, \ldots, a_N)$ with probabilities $Pa_1 \geq Pa_2 \geq \ldots \geq Pa_N$. Then combine the last two symbols into an equivalent symbol with probability $Pa_{N-1} + Pa_N$. The codes for these two symbols will be the same except for the last digit. We now have a new set of $N - 1$ symbols. If necessary, reorder the symbols so that we have $(b_1, b_2, \ldots, b_N)$ with probabilities $Pb_1 \geq Pb_2 \geq \ldots \geq Pb_{N-1}$. We can then repeat the process until only two symbols remain.

Figure 16.3 illustrates this process for the set of symbols with the probabilities defined at the beginning of this section. Consider each symbol to be a leaf node in a

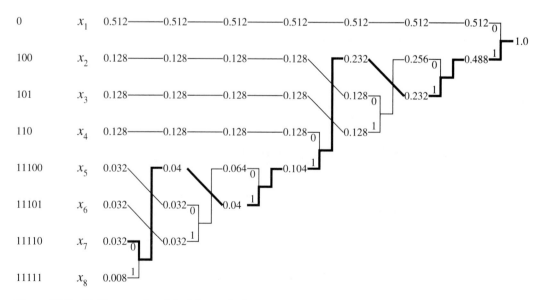

Figure 16.3 Huffman code with eight symbols.

TABLE 16.1 HUFFMAN CODE WITH EIGHT SYMBOLS

Symbol	Code	P_i	L_i	$P_i L_i$	$\log(1/P_i)$	$P_i \log(1/P_i)$
x_1	1	0.512	1	0.512	0.966	0.494
x_2	100	0.128	3	0.384	2.966	0.38
x_3	101	0.128	3	0.384	2.966	0.38
x_4	110	0.128	3	0.384	2.966	0.38
x_5	11100	0.032	5	0.16	4.966	0.159
x_6	11101	0.032	5	0.16	4.966	0.159
x_7	11110	0.032	5	0.16	4.966	0.159
x_8	11111	0.008	5	0.04	6.966	0.056
				Average Length = 2.184		Entropy = 2.167

tree to be constructed. Merge the two nodes of lowest probability into a node whose probability is the sum of the two constituent probabilities. At each step, repeat this process until one node remains. The result is a tree in which each node except the root has one branch from the right and two branches from the left. At each node, label the two branches on the left with 0 and 1, respectively. The code word for any symbol is the string of labels from the root node back to the original symbol; all of the resulting code words are shown along the left-hand side of the figure. For example, the construction of the code word for x_7 is indicated by the bold lines.

Table 16.1 summarizes the properties of the Huffman code for this example. The average length of a code word is just an expected value calculation:

$$E[L] = \sum_{i=1}^{8} L_i P_i = 2.184$$

where L_i is the length of code i. So, for example, for a message consisting of 1000 symbols, the average length of an encoded message is 2184 bits. If a straightforward assignment of 3 bits per symbol is used, then the fixed message length would be 3000 bits.

Entropy and Coding Efficiency

Consider a random variable with a set of outcomes $(x_1, x_2, \ldots, x_N)$ with probabilities $(P_1, P_2, \ldots, P_N)$; that is, P_i = probability of outcome x_i. Let us determine the lower bound on the average code length that can be achieved. We know from Equation 16.1 that the information measure for x_i is $\log(1/P_i)$. Therefore, ideally we would represent x_i with a code word of length $L_i = \log(1/P_i)$ bits. That is, because x_i conveys $\log(1/P_i)$ bits of information, the most efficient code is one in which each x_i is represented by a code word of $\log(1/P_i)$ bits. However, in most cases $\log(1/P_i)$ is not an integer, and the best that we can do is select the next larger integer, so that L_i satisfies

$$\log(1/P_i) \leq L_i < \log(1/P_i) + 1 \tag{16.3}$$

Multiplying by P_i and summing over all code words (using Equation 16.2), we have

$$\sum_{i=1}^{N} P_i \log(1/P_i) \leq \sum_{i=1}^{N} P_i L_i < \sum_{i=1}^{N} P_i \log(1/P_i) + \sum_{i=1}^{N} P_i$$

$$H(X) \leq E[L] < H(X) + 1$$

Therefore, an optimum code yields an average code length that is less than 1 bit greater than the entropy of the original symbol set. This leads to an interpretation of the entropy of X as being the minimum average number of bits needed to specify one outcome of X.

It can be shown that the Huffman code satisfies this inequality. Table 16.1 gives an example. The average code word length is 2.184 compared to an entropy of 2.167. Note that not all of the individual code words satisfy inequality 16.3. However, the overall inequality is satisfied.

Characteristics of the Huffman Code

Two observations concerning the Huffman code provide insight into the design of data compression algorithms. These observations relate to the blocking of symbols and to the use of dependencies.

Symbol Blocking

Suppose that we have a source that emits symbols from an alphabet X of just two symbols A and B that occur with probabilities 0.8 and 0.2. Then the entropy of this scheme is $0.8 \log(1.25) + 0.2 \log(5) = 0.722$ (see Figure 16.2). But the best we can do for coding is to use one bit for each code word (e.g., $A = 0, B = 1$). If we define the efficiency of a code as the ratio between the entropy of the source (average number of bits of information per symbol) and the average code word length (average number of bits used to encode a symbol), then the efficiency of this code is 0.722.

We can improve the efficiency of our code by taking blocks of symbols at one time and encoding these. For example, if we encode two symbols at a time, then we can consider that we are working with a new alphabet Y with four symbols (AA, AB, BA, BB). If successive instances of a symbol from X are independent, then the probabilities associated with Y are $P_{AA} = 0.64$; $P_{AB} = 0.16$; $P_{BA} = 0.16$; $P_{BB} = 0.04$. Figure 16.4a shows the Huffman code for this arrangement, and Table 16.2a shows the resulting statistics. We end up with an average code length of 1.56 versus an entropy of 1.444, for an efficiency of 0.926, considerably better than if we take the original symbols one at a time.

Note that the information content of the source has not changed. The entropy of X is 0.722 and the entropy of Y is $0.722 \times 2 = 1.444$, which is still 0.722 bits per single symbol.

Even better results are achieved by combining three symbols at a time. In that case, we end up with the probabilities shown in Table 16.1. That is, $P_{AAA} = 0.8 \times 0.8 \times 0.8 = 0.512$; $P_{AAB} = 0.8 \times 0.8 \times 0.2 = 0.128$; and so on. The efficiency in this case is $2.167/2.184 = 0.992$. Again, the entropy per single symbol is 0.722 ($2.167/3$, subject to rounding error).

It can be shown that the efficiency of an optimal code for independent sequences of symbols can be improved by means of blocking the symbols as described previously. For a block size of K symbols, the relationship is

TABLE 16.2 HUFFMAN CODE WITH FOUR SYMBOLS

(a) Independent Symbols

Symbol	Code	P_i	L_i	$P_i L_i$	$\log(1/P_i)$	$P_i \log(1/P_i)$
AA	0	0.64	1	0.64	0.644	0.412
AB	11	0.16	2	0.32	2.644	0.423
BA	100	0.16	3	0.48	2.644	0.423
BB	101	0.04	3	0.12	4.644	0.186
			Average Length = 1.56			Entropy = 1.444

(b) Dependent Symbols

Symbol	Code	P_i	L_i	$P_i L_i$	$\log(1/P_i)$	$P_i \log(1/P_i)$
AA	0	0.72	1	0.72	0.474	0.341
BB	11	0.12	2	0.24	3.059	0.367
AB	100	0.08	3	0.24	3.644	0.292
BA	101	0.08	3	0.24	3.644	0.292
			Average Length = 1.44			Entropy = 1.292

(c) Symbol Dependence Not Taken into Account

Symbol	Code	P_i	L_i	$P_i L_i$
AA	0	0.72	1	0.72
AB	11	0.08	2	0.16
BA	100	0.08	3	0.24
BB	101	0.12	3	0.36
			Average Length	1.48

$$H(X) \le \frac{E[L]}{K} < H(X) + \frac{1}{K}$$

Thus, the average number of bits per value of X can be made arbitrarily close to the entropy of X by choosing larger and larger block sizes.

Transition Dependencies

The analysis in the previous subsection assumed that the next symbol in sequence is independent of the previous symbols. If, however, there is such a dependence, then the probabilities associated with blocks of symbols change. For example, consider again the two-symbol alphabet X and suppose that the following transition probabilities apply:

	A	B
A	0.9	0.1
B	0.4	0.6

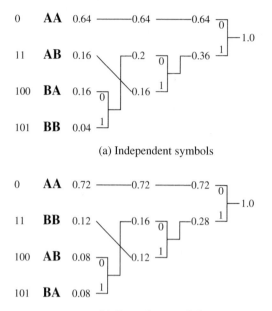

(a) Independent symbols

(b) Dependent symbols

Figure 16.4 Huffman Code with Four Symbols.

That is, the probability that an A follows an A is 0.9; the probability that a B follows an A is 0.1; and so on. This transition matrix is easily shown to be consistent with a probability of occurrence of a single A of 0.8 and of a single B of 0.2.

Now let us develop a code for the alphabet Y that combines two symbols at a time. We have

$$P_{AA} = \Pr(A/A)P_A = 0.9 \times 0.8 = 0.72$$

$$P_{AB} = \Pr(B/A)P_A = 0.1 \times 0.8 = 0.08$$

$$P_{BA} = \Pr(A/B)P_B = 0.4 \times 0.2 = 0.08$$

$$P_{BB} = \Pr(B/B)P_B = 0.6 \times 0.2 = 0.12$$

Figure 16.4b shows the Huffman code for this arrangement, and Table 16.2b shows the resulting statistics. Note first that the entropy of Y is less compared to the case when successive symbols are independent (1.292 versus 1.444). Since we still have the same single-symbol probabilities ($P_A = 0.8$, $P_B = 0.2$), how can this be? The answer is that the transition probabilities add prior information. Once the first of two symbols in a sequence is known, we have more information about which symbol will appear next. Therefore, the uncertainty is reduced and the overall entropy is less. Another way of putting this is to say that there is redundancy in the sequences. Similarly, there is considerable redundancy in English-language sequences.

Table 16.2b shows that the average code length is 1.44, for an efficiency of 1.292/1.44 = 0.897. Table 16.2c shows what happens if we ignore the transition probabilities and assume that successive symbols are independent even though they are not. In this case the same code assignment is used as in the independent case (AA = 0, AB = 11, BA = 100, BB = 101), and the average length of a code word is 1.48, longer than the average length of 1.44 produced by an optimal Huffman code.

The conclusion to be drawn from this discussion is that greater efficiency in data compression can be achieved by encoding larger blocks of data and by taking into account dependencies in the data.

16.3 RECOMMENDED READING

There are numerous books on information theory. The unsurpassed classic is [GALL68]. A more modern treatment, with emphasis on compression, is [COVE91]. A book suitable for self-study is [ASH90]. [SLEP74] contains reprints of many of the important papers in the field, including Shannon's seminal contributions.

ASH90   Ash, R. *Information Theory.* New York: Dover, 1990.

COVE91   Cover, T., and Thomas, J. *Elements of Information Theory.* New York: Wiley, 1991.

GALL68   Gallager, R. *Information Theory and Reliable Communication.* New York: Wiley, 1968.

SLEP74   Slepian, D., ed. *Key Papers in the Development of Information Theory.* New York: IEEE Press, 1974.

16.4 PROBLEMS

16.1 Verify that the relationship

$$H(P_1, P_2, P_3, \ldots, P_N) = H(P_1 + P_2, P_3, \ldots, P_N) + (P_1 + P_2)H\left(\frac{P_1}{P_1 + P_2}, \frac{P_2}{P_1 + P_2}\right)$$

is satisfied by the entropy function for a random variable with three possible outcomes, $H(P_1, P_2, P_3)$.

16.2 Is the following code uniquely decipherable?

x_1	010	x_3	0110	x_5	00011	x_7	11110
x_2	0001	x_4	1100	x_6	00110	x_8	101011

If not, construct an ambiguous sequence.

16.3 Construct Huffman codes for the following; in each case the symbols are enumerated together with their probability of occurrence:

a.		b.		c.		d.	
x_1	0.4	x_1	0.4	x_1	9/36	x_1	0.2
x_2	0.2	x_2	0.3	x_2	6/36	x_2	0.18
x_3	0.1	x_3	0.2	x_3	6/36	x_3	0.1
x_4	0.1	x_4	0.04	x_4	4/36	x_4	0.1
x_5	0.1	x_5	0.04	x_5	3/36	x_5	0.1
x_6	0.1	x_6	0.02	x_6	3/36	x_6	0.061
				x_7	2/36	x_7	0.059
				x_8	2/36	x_8	0.04
				x_9	1/36	x_9	0.04
						x_{10}	0.04
						x_{11}	0.04
						x_{12}	0.03
						x_{13}	0.01

16.4 One requirement for an optimal code was stated as $L_1 \leq L_2, \leq ... \leq L_N$. To prove this requirement, suppose we have a code C with $P_i > P_h$ and $L_i > L_k$. Now create code C' by interchanging code words i and k. Compute the difference between the average code-word length of C and C'.

16.5 For a two-symbol alphabet with symbols A and B and a transition matrix:

	A	B
A	0.9	0.1
B	0.4	0.6

Show that this matrix is consistent with $P_A = 0.8$, $P_B = 0.2$.

16.6 Given the following coding schemes for $\{x_1, x_2, x_3, x_4\}$, some of them could have been arrived at by Huffman's algorithm and some of them could not possibly be Huffman codes. For each of the schemes listed, state which is the case and justify your answer. For those coding schemes that could represent Huffman codes, give a probability distribution for which it could represent an optimal Huffman code.
   a. $\{x_1, x_2, x_3, x_4\} \rightarrow \{010, 011, 001, 10\}$
   b. $\{x_1, x_2, x_3, x_4\} \rightarrow \{0, 10, 110, 111\}$
   c. $\{x_1, x_2, x_3, x_4\} \rightarrow \{10, 0, 101, 11\}$
   d. $\{x_1, x_2, x_3, x_4\} \rightarrow \{00, 010, 011, 1\}$

CHAPTER 17

LOSSLESS COMPRESSION

One thing to be thankful for was that no more could get in. She had to revise this at Angel and again at Old Street. Perhaps a point was never reached where no more could get in, but they would be pushed and crushed until they died or the sides of the car burst with the pressure of them.

— *King Solomon's Carpet,* **Barbara Vine (Ruth Rendell)**

The principle of data compression is quite straightforward. Virtually all forms of data (text, numerical, image, video) contain redundant elements. The data can be compressed by eliminating these redundant elements. Compression is used for one of two purposes: to save storage space and to reduce communications capacity requirements. When compressed data are retrieved from storage or received over a communications link, it must be possible to expand the data back to the original form. For this purpose, when the data are compressed, some sort of code must be substituted for the eliminated elements so that the receiver can, based on the code, reconstruct the original data. As long as the coding scheme is such that the code is shorter than the eliminated data, compression will still occur.

Data compression falls into two broad categories: lossless and lossy. With **lossless compression**, no information is lost and the decompressed data are identical to the original uncompressed data. The efficiency of lossless compression is limited to the entropy of the data source, as we have seen in Chapter 16. With **lossy compression**, the decompressed data may be an acceptable approximation (according to some fidelity criterion) to the original uncompressed data. For example, for image or video compression, the criterion may be that the decompressed image is indistinguishable from the original to the human eye.

An important factor in the design and selection of data compression algorithms is the processing required for both compression and decompression. In general, there is a tradeoff between the amount of compression that can be achieved and how quickly and inexpensively the algorithm can be executed.

This chapter surveys some of the most important and widely used lossless compression schemes that are applicable in a number of contexts. Chapter 18 examines lossy schemes that are specifically designed for image and video compression.

This chapter begins with a very simple technique known as run-length encoding. Next, we show how this technique is incorporated into standards for facsimile compression. This is followed by a description of arithmetic encoding. Finally, the Liv-Zempel dictionary-based techniques are examined.

17.1 RUN-LENGTH ENCODING TECHNIQUES

Run-length encoding is a simple lossless compression technique that can be quite effective for text compression. It also finds use in facsimile compression, which is discussed in Section 17.2. This section begins with the even simpler null suppression technique and then describes run-length encoding, which is a generalization of null suppression.

Null Suppression

One of the oldest and simplest data compression techniques is known as null suppression or blank suppression. It is still used in the IBM 3780 BISYNC data link control protocol.

A common occurrence in text is the presence of a long string of blanks, or nulls, in the character stream. With the null suppression technique, the transmitter scans the data for strings of blanks and substitutes a two-character code for any string that is encountered. The code consists of a special control character followed by a count of the number of blanks. For example, the string of characters

$$\text{XYZbbbbbQRX}$$

is replaced by

$$\text{XYZS}_\text{c}\text{5QRX}$$

where S_c is a special compression indicator character and ƀ is the symbol for a blank space. This scheme will result in a savings for all strings of three or more blank characters.

When null suppression is in use, the receiver of a transmission scans the incoming characters for the special character used to indicate null suppression. Upon detection of that character, the receiver knows the next character contains the count of the number of blanks that were eliminated. From this information, the original data stream can be reconstructed.

While null suppression is a very primitive form of data compression, it has the advantage of being easy to implement. Furthermore, the payoff, even from this simple technique, can be substantial. For a number of computer installations that switched from the 2780 IBM protocol, which employs no data compression, to the 3780 protocol, which uses only null suppression, throughput gains of between 30 and 50% have been reported [HELD96].

Run-length Encoding

Run-length encoding is a generalization of the null suppression technique. Run-length encoding is used to compress any type of repeating data sequence. Figure 17.1 summarizes the technique when applied to character data and gives some examples. As with null suppression, the transmitter looks for sequences of repeating characters to replace. In this case, any sequence of repeating characters can be eliminated and replaced by a three-character code. The code consists of a special character that indicates suppression, followed by the character to be suppressed, followed by a count of the number of characters suppressed. Thus, any sequence of four or more identical characters can be suppressed with a net reduction in the total number of characters transmitted.

Run-length encoding efficiency depends on the number of repeated character occurrences in the data to be compressed and the average repeated character length. The standard measure of compression efficiency is the compression ratio, which is the ratio of the length of the uncompressed data to the compressed data (including any necessary codes). Table 17.1, from [HELD96], shows the compression ratio using run-length encoding on various inputs of 1000 characters. The table shows results by varying the number of occurrences of repeated characters from 10 to 50 and the average repeated character length from 4 to 10. The results show a compression ratio of from 1.01 to 1.538, depending on the characteristics of the input text. This table is a synthetic representation that reflects the wide divergence

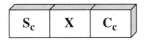

S_c = Special character indicating compression follows
X   = Any repeated data character
C_c = Character count; the number of times the compressed
      character is to be repeated

(a) Compression format

Original Data String	Encoded Data String
$*****55.72	$$S_c$*655.72
---------	S_c-9
GunsᵇᵇᵇᵇᵇᵇᵇᵇᵇᵇButter	GunsS$_c$ᵇ9Butter

(b) Examples

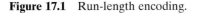

Figure 17.1   Run-length encoding.

TABLE 17.1 RUN-LENGTH ENCODING EFFICIENCY BASED ON ORIGINAL DATA STRING OF 1000 CHARACTERS [HELD96]

Number of Repeated Character Occurrences	Average Repeated Character Length	Compression Ratio
10	4	1.010
10	5	1.020
10	6	1.031
10	7	1.042
10	8	1.053
10	9	1.064
10	10	1.075
20	4	1.020
20	5	1.042
20	6	1.064
20	7	1.087
20	8	1.111
20	9	1.136
20	10	1.163
30	4	1.031
30	5	1.064
30	6	1.099
30	7	1.136
30	8	1.176
30	9	1.220
30	10	1.266
40	4	1.042
40	5	1.087
40	6	1.136
40	7	1.190
40	8	1.250
40	9	1.316
40	10	1.384
50	4	1.053
50	5	1.111
50	6	1.176
50	7	1.250
50	8	1.333
50	9	1.429
50	10	1.538

of actual text. It demonstrates that any compression scheme will have variable performance as the content of the input varies. However, in most text input, there will be sufficient character repetitions to warrant even as simple a technique as run-length encoding.

A variation on the scheme depicted in Figure 17.1 is used in the Microcom Networking Protocol (MNP), which is licensed for use by many switched network modem manufacturers. With an installed base of over one million modems, MNP is perhaps the most widely used implementation of character-based run-length encoding. With MNP, any string of three or more repeated characters is represented in the form CXXX, where C is the character count in excess of three and X is the character. For example,

Original Data	Compressed Data
AAA	0AAA
BBBB	1BBB
CCCCC	2CCC

17.2 FACSIMILE COMPRESSION

Compression techniques are essential to the widespread use of digital facsimile machines. To see this, consider that a typical page with 200 picture elements, or pels[1] (black or white points), per inch resolution (which is adequate but not high resolution) generates 3,740,000 bits (8.5 inches × 11 inches × 40,000 pels per square inch). At the basic ISDN rate of 64 kbps, a page would take about one minute to transmit. Ultimately, users will expect their systems to operate at a rate similar to that of a copier, or one page every few seconds. To meet this requirement without an inordinately high data rate requires the use of data compression techniques.

ITU-T has standardized two lossless compression techniques for facsimile: modified Huffman (MH) and modified READ (MR). MH is the default for Group 3 facsimile,[2] with MR an option. Group 4 facsimile[3] specifies MR. Briefly, these two facsimile standards are as follows:

- **Group 3:** This is the first digital facsimile standard. This system provides only black and white values, with sampling densities of 200 spots per inch horizontally across the paper and 100 or 200 lines per inch vertically down the page. Group 3 uses a digital encoding scheme and incorporates a means of reducing the redundant information in the document signal prior to modulation. It is assumed that Group 3 transmission is via a modem over an analog telephone network. Transmission time is speeded up by a factor of 3 or more compared to Group 2.

- **Group 4:** Group 4 is also a black-and-white digital facsimile standard. It is intended for use over digital networks at speeds of up to 64 kbps and with provision for error-free reception. Resolutions of from 200 to 400 pels per inch are specified. As with Group 3, compression techniques are used to reduce the

---

[1] A *picture element*, or *pel*, is the smallest discrete scanning-line sample of a facsimile system, which contains only black-white information (no gray scales). A *pixel* is a picture element that contains gray-scale information.

[2] *Standardization of Group 3 Facsimile Apparatus for Document Transmission.* Recommendation T.4, 1988.

[3] *Facsimile Coding Schemes and Coding Control Functions for Group 4 Facsimile Apparatus.* Recommendation T.6, 1988.

number of bits transmitted. With Group 4, transmission times drop to a few seconds rather than the minutes of earlier standards.

Modified Huffman Code

In a typical document, the black and white areas of the image tend to cluster. If we view the document as a sequence of lines and consider the pattern of black and white on a given line, we observe that there are long *runs* of black (B) and white (W) pels. This property suggests the value of compression based on run-length encoding. The two-valued input is converted to a many-valued run-length process, and this process is subsequently coded for transmission. In addition, because longer runs of black or white are, in general, less probable than shorter runs, variable-length coding can be employed to advantage.

The Huffman code, described in Chapter 16, could be used for the purpose of facsimile encoding. It could be applied to an image one horizontal line at a time to encode the sequence of black and white pels. For example, suppose that the scan of a single line of an image produces a sequence of W7, B7, W4, B8, W4, B7, W10. If we consider each of these elements as a symbol in a source alphabet, then Huffman encoding can be used to encode the source. However, since ITU-T standards require at least 1728 pels per line, the number of different codes and hence the average length of a code is very large.

An alternative is the modified Huffman (MH) encoding technique. MH regards a run-length N as the sum of two terms:

$$N = 64m + n; \quad m = 0, 1, 2, \ldots, 27; \quad n = 0, 1, 2, \ldots, 63$$

In words, each run of black or white pels consists of a multiple of 64 points plus a remainder.

Each run length can now be represented by two values, one for m and one for n, and these values can then be encoded using Huffman encoding. For example, a string of 200 black points in a row can be expressed as $64 \times 3 + 8$. For this purpose, ITU-T has defined eight representative documents and calculated the probabilities of the different run-length occurrences. As these probabilities are different for black and white, two sets of probabilities were calculated. From this information two code tables were developed, as shown in Table 17.2. The terminating code is used for run lengths of less than 64. For run lengths greater than 64, a combination of a terminating code (n) and a makeup code (m) is needed.

There are several additional details concerning this code. Each line ends with a unique code word for end of line (EOL). This is a code word that can never be found in a valid line of data; it therefore makes resynchronization after an error burst. Within a line, code words for black and white runs must alternate. However, note that different codes are used for the black and white runs; this provides an additional form of error checking. Finally, by convention, each line begins with a white run length. If, in fact, the first pel is black, then a white run length of zero is used.

Modified READ Code

The use of modified Huffman encoding significantly reduces the total number of bits that must be transmitted compared to a straightforward transmission of the bit-map image. Further gains in efficiency can be achieved by recognizing that there is a

TABLE 17.2   MODIFIED HUFFMAN CODE TABLE

Run Length	White	Black	Run Length	White	Black
			Terminating Code Words		
0	00110101	0000110111	32	00011011	000001101010
1	000111	010	33	00010010	000001101011
2	0111	11	34	00010011	000011010010
3	1000	10	35	00010100	000011010011
4	1011	011	36	00010101	000011010100
5	1100	0011	37	00010110	000011010101
6	1110	0010	38	00010111	000011010110
7	1111	00011	39	00101000	000011010111
8	10011	000101	40	00101001	000001101100
9	10100	000100	41	00101010	000001101101
10	00111	0000100	42	00101011	000011011010
11	01000	0000101	43	00101100	000011011011
12	001000	0000111	44	00101101	000001010100
13	000011	00000100	45	00000100	000001010101
14	110100	00000111	46	00000101	000001010110
15	110101	000011000	47	00001010	000001010111
16	101010	0000010111	48	00001011	000001100100
17	101011	0000011000	49	01010010	000001100101
18	0100111	0000001000	50	01010011	000001010010
19	0001100	00001100111	51	01010100	000001010011
20	0001000	00001101000	52	01010101	000000100100
21	0010111	00001101100	53	00100100	000000110111
22	0000011	00000110111	54	00100101	000000111000
23	0000100	00000101000	55	01011000	000000100111
24	0101000	00000010111	56	01011001	000000101000
25	0101011	00000011000	57	01011010	000001011000
26	0010011	000011001010	58	01011011	000001011001
27	0100100	000011001011	59	01001010	000000101011
28	0011000	000011001100	60	01001011	000000101100
29	00000010	000011001101	61	00110010	000001011010
30	00000011	000001101000	62	00110011	000001100110
31	00011010	000001101001	63	00110100	000001100111
			Make-up Code Words		
64	11011	0000001111	960	011010100	0000001110011
128	10010	000011001000	1024	011010101	0000001110100
192	010111	000011001001	1088	011010110	0000001110101
256	0110111	000001011011	1152	011010111	0000001110110
320	00110110	000000110011	1216	011011000	0000001110111
384	00110111	000000110100	1280	011011001	0000001010010
448	01100100	000000110101	1344	011011010	0000001010011
512	01100101	0000001101100	1408	011011011	0000001010100
576	01101000	0000001101101	1472	010011000	0000001010101
640	01100111	0000001001010	1536	010011001	0000001011010
704	011001100	0000001001011	1600	010011010	0000001011011
768	011001101	0000001001100	1664	011000	0000001100100
832	011010010	0000001001101	1728	010011011	0000001100101
896	011010011	0000001110010	EOL	000000000001	000000000001

strong correlation between the black-white patterns of two adjacent lines. In fact, for typical facsimile documents, approximately 50% of all the B-W and W-B transitions are directly underneath a transition on the previous line, and an additional 25% differ by only one pel [SILV87]. Therefore, approximately 75% of all transitions can be defined by a relationship that is plus or minus at most one pel from the line above it. This is the underlying basis of the Modified Relative Element Address Designate (MR) code.

In MR encoding, run lengths are encoded based on the position of changing elements. A **changing element** is defined as a pel of a different color from the immediately preceding pel on the same line. A changing element a_1 is coded in terms of its distance to one of two reference pels: either a preceding changing element a_0 on the same line or a changing element b_1 on the previous line. The selection of a_0 or b_1 depends on the exact configuration, as explained in the next paragraphs.

Figure 17.2 illustrates the five changing elements that are defined for this scheme, which are as follows:

a_0: The reference or starting changing element on the coding line. At the start of the coding line, it is set on an imaginary white changing element just to the left of the first element on the line. During the coding of a line, it is redefined after every encoding.

a_1: The next changing element to the right of a_0 on the coding line.

a_2: The next changing element to the right of a_1 on the coding line.

b_1: The first changing element on the reference line to the right of a_0 and of opposite color to a_0.

b_2: The next changing element to the right of b_1 on the reference line.

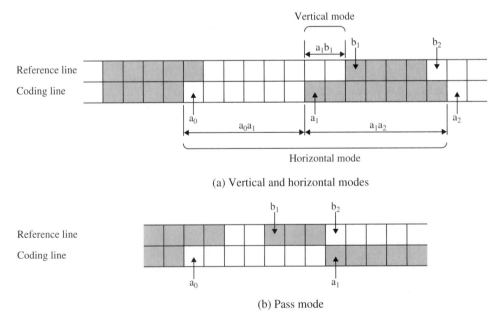

Figure 17.2 Changing picture elements for the MR technique.

TABLE 17.3 MR CODE TABLE

Mode	Elements to be Coded		Notation	Code Word
Pass	b_1, b_2		P	0001
Horizontal	$a_0 a_1, a_1 a_2$		H	$001 + M(a_0 a_1) + M(a_1 a_2)$
Vertical	a_1 just under b_1	$a_1 b_1 = 0$	$V(0)$	1
	a_1 to the right of b_1	$a_1 b_1 = 1$	$V_R(1)$	011
		$a_1 b_1 = 2$	$V_R(2)$	000011
		$a_1 b_1 = 3$	$V_R(3)$	0000011
	a_1 to the left of b_1	$a_1 b_1 = 1$	$V_L(1)$	010
		$a_1 b_1 = 2$	$V_L(2)$	000010
		$a_1 b_1 = 3$	$V_L(3)$	0000010

The encoding procedure is summarized in Table 17.3 and can be defined as follows:

Step 1:

a. If the position of b_2 lies to the left of a_1, this is coded using the word 0001. After this encoding, the position of a_1 is shifted to lie under b_2. This is referred to as pass mode. The algorithm resumes at Step 1.

b. If the condition in (a) is not satisfied, go to Step 2.

Step 2:

a. If the position of a_1 is within three of the position of b_1 ($|a_1 b_1| \leq 3$), then a_1 is coded in the vertical mode, after which the old position a_1 becomes the new position a_0, a_2 becomes a_1, and so on.

b. If the position of a_1 is not within three of the position of b_1, then a_1 is coded in the horizontal mode. Following the horizontal mode code 001, $a_0 a_1$ and $a_1 a_2$ are encoded by one-dimensional MH coding. After this, the old position a_2 becomes the new position a_0.

Step 1 is used to move the position of b_1 and b_2 along after the exercise of Step 2. Also, Step 1 has the effect of avoiding long run lengths. In Step 2, if the current changing element to be encoded is within three positions of the same transition in the previous line, then the position is encoded with one of seven possible values using MH. This situation will hold most of the time. In the few cases in which a transition in the current line is not within three positions of the same transition in the previous line, the next two runs are encoded using MH.

The MR scheme is more sensitive to an error than the MH scheme; the effects of an error could propagate for unpredictable distances. To avoid this, MH encoding is used for every Kth scanning line. ITU-T recommends a value of $K = 2$ for a resolution of 3.85 lines/mm and $K = 4$ for 7.7 lines/mm.

Modified Modified READ (MMR) Code

The MMR algorithm is defined for Group 4 facsimile in ITU-T Recommendation T.6. It differs from MR by removing the error protection feature. This maximizes the compression performance of the algorithm. Because Group 4 is intended to run on high-quality low-error lines, this seems a reasonable tradeoff.

Table 17.4 shows the performance of the MH and MR schemes against a representative set of pages; these results were reported in [ARPS94]. Similar results are also reported in [PRAT80] and [YASU80]. Included in the comparison is the Joint Bi-Level Image Experts Group Coding (JBIG) coding standard, defined in Recommendation T.82.[4] This standard for binary images includes both lossless and lossy algorithms and makes use of arithmetic coding.

The upper part of the table compares the compression algorithms on images of different resolutions. Three observations are readily made. First, all of the techniques achieve considerable compression. Second, MR is superior to MH and MMR is superior to MR, as would be expected. Third, the greater the image resolution and therefore the greater the detail, the more opportunity there is for compression. Thus, higher-resolution figures yield higher compression ratios. On a log-log plot, all of the algorithms show a roughly linear increase in compression ratios with spatial resolution.

The lower part of the table compares the compression algorithms on three standardized business documents defined by ITU-T. These are of increasing density of black pels on the page. Again, the relative performance shows MR superior to

TABLE 17.4 COMPARISON OF FACSIMILE COMPRESSION TECHNIQUES

(a) Compression Ratios for Different Image Resolutions

Image Resolution (pels/in)	Image Size (pels)	MH	MR	MMR	JBIG
12.5	272 × 192	2.34	2.32	3.43	6.69
25	544 × 384	3.56	3.94	5.68	10.07
50	1088 × 768	6.06	7.26	10.34	15.93
100	2176 × 1536	11.30	14.60	22.52	31.03
200	4352 × 3072	20.28	29.24	48.97	62.52
400	8704 × 6144	29.72	51.30	95.96	122.38

(b) Compression Ratios for Different Text Densities

Document Type	Image Size (pels)	MH	MR	MMR	JBIG
Letter	4352 × 3072	20.28	29.24	48.97	62.52
Sparse text	4352 × 3072	15.97	25.05	41.96	54.29
Dense text	4352 × 3072	3.08	3.95	4.54	5.91

---

[4] *Progressive Bi-Level Image Compression.* Recommendation T.82, 1993.

MH and MMR superior to MR. Note also that the denser the text, the less the compression. To account for this, consider that, in general, a data stream has higher entropy if the probabilities are unbalanced. With denser text, we approach a situation in which the probabilities of white and black sequences are more nearly equal.

17.3 ARITHMETIC CODING

Huffman coding, though simple to implement and relatively efficient to execute, does not achieve the maximum possible compression unless all of the probabilities involved are negative integer powers of 2. Arithmetic coding is designed to provide higher compression ratios by using probabilities that are closer to being all negative integer powers of 2, at the cost of greater computational complexity. Arithmetic coding is used in the JPEG and MPEG standards described in Chapter 18.

   We begin with a description of the basic concept behind arithmetic coding and then look at some of the details.

Basic Concept

Recall from the discussion of Huffman coding that if the individual symbols to be coded have probabilities P_i, then the best we can do in terms of coding efficiency is to use a code length for each symbol that satisfies

$$\log(1/P_i) \le L_i < \log(1/P_i) + 1$$

where P_i is the probability of occurrence of the ith symbol and L_i is the length of the binary code assigned to that symbol. From this, it can be shown that

$$H(X) \le E[L] < H(X) + 1$$

where $H(X)$ is the entropy of the set of symbols X and $E[L]$ is the average code length for X. For a lossless compression scheme, $H(X)$ will always be the lower bound because $H(X)$ defines the average amount of information contained in the symbol set.

   Finally, we saw that compression efficiency could be improved by blocking symbols, encoding groups of K symbols at a time. This results in the relationship

$$H(X) \le \frac{E[L]}{K} < H(X) + \frac{1}{K}$$

   This suggests a way of achieving the greatest possible efficiency. If we are to send a message of length N symbols, we could use a block length of N. In effect, we treat each message as a single outcome from an ensemble of M^N possible outcomes, where M is the number of atomic symbols and N is the message length. As an example, let us consider the case discussed in Chapter 16, in which there are two symbols, A and B, with probabilities of occurrence of 0.8 and 0.2. If we send a message of three symbols ($M = 2, N = 3$), then there are $2^3 = 8$ possible outcomes. If each symbol occurrence is independent of previous symbols occurrences, then we can write down the probabilities of all eight outcomes:

$$P_{AAA} = 0.512 \qquad P_{BAA} = 0.128$$

$$P_{AAB} = 0.128 \qquad P_{BAB} = 0.032$$

$$P_{ABA} = 0.128 \qquad P_{BBA} = 0.032$$

$$P_{ABB} = 0.032 \qquad P_{BBB} = 0.008$$

One possible approach is to proceed with Huffman coding, as was illustrated in Figure 16.3. For a message with eight possible outcomes this is reasonable, but for very long messages, the computational burden would be massive.

Arithmetic coding provides an ingenious alternative. Observe that the sum of the probabilities of all possible messages must equal 1.0. Therefore, it is possible to lay out all of the outcomes on the unit interval [0, 1], with each outcome having an interval length equal to its probability. The bottom part of Figure 17.3 shows this arrangement for our example message set. The figure also shows a simple method of generating the intervals one symbol at a time. The procedure is as follows:

1. Start with the first symbol position in the message and divide the unit interval according to the probabilities of the individual symbols. In this case, there are two symbols, A with probability 0.8 and B with probability 0.2. Therefore, the unit interval is divided into the subintervals [0, 0.8) and [0.8, 1). Arbitrarily, we assign the boundary between intervals to the subinterval on the left.

2. Divide each subinterval in the same fashion as step 1. That is, each subinterval is divided into 4/5 and 1/5 portions.

3. Repeat this process for all N symbol positions (message of length N).

Each message outcome now has associated with it an interval proportional to its probability. Therefore, each outcome could be represented by a binary fraction equal to some point in its interval. Let us use the lower bound of each interval for this purpose. The fifth column of Table 17.5 shows the results, using five significant digits to the right of the binary point. This amount of precision is sufficient to identify uniquely each interval and therefore each outcome. We could therefore use the fractional part of each value as the code for the corresponding outcome (e.g.,

TABLE 17.5   PROBABILITY INTERVALS FOR THREE-SYMBOL SEQUENCE

Sequence	P_i	Cumulative Probability	Interval	Binary Representation of Lower Bound[a]	Code	$P_i L_i$	$P_i \log(1/P_i)$
AAA	0.512	0.512	[0, 0.512)	0.00000	0	0.512	0.494
AAB	0.128	0.64	[0.512, 0.64)	0.10000	100	0.384	0.38
ABA	0.128	0.768	[0.64, 0.768)	0.10100	101	0.384	0.38
ABB	0.032	0.8	[0.768, 0.8)	0.11000	11000	0.16	0.159
BAA	0.128	0.928	[0.8, 0.928)	0.11001	11001	0.64	0.38
BAB	0.032	0.96	[0.928, 0.96)	0.11101	1110	0.128	0.159
BBA	0.032	0.992	[0.96, 0.992)	0.11110	11110	0.16	0.159
BBB	0.008	1.0	[0.992, 1.0)	0.11111	11111	0.04	0.056
						2.408	2.167

[a] to 5 significant digits.

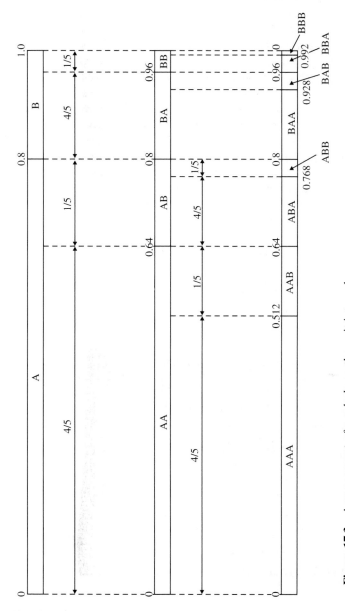

Figure 17.3 Arrangement of symbols on the unit interval.

ABA = 10100). We can do better than this, however. We can eliminate some digits as long as no code is the prefix of another code, resulting in the sixth column in the table. Notice that, in general, shorter intervals require more bits to identify. This is reasonable: A short interval has a lower bound that is close to the lower bound of the next interval. The binary fractions for these two boundaries will be identical for a number of bits; the smaller the interval, the more bits will be identical in their respective fractions.

Thus, we have developed a new technique for assigning codes to messages. The last two columns of Table 17.5 compare the average length of this new code to the entropy of the message set (also compare Table 16.1).

While the basic concept so far described appears attractive, it has two significant drawbacks;

1. If all possible intervals are computed ahead of time, a massive computational task is faced. For example, if a message consists of a sequence of 1000 characters, with an alphabet of 128 possible characters (e.g., the ASCII character set), then the number of possible messages is $128^{1000} \approx 10^{2107}$.
2. The scheme as described appears to require fixed-length messages.

Arithmetic coding overcomes both of these drawbacks.

Pure Arithmetic Coding

We begin with the simplest form of the arithmetic coding algorithm. While it overcomes the difficulties mentioned previously, it retains some computational difficulties. However, it is easier to understand the arithmetic coding approach if we look at this simple form first.

With arithmetic coding, it is not necessary to generate the intervals of all possible message outcomes ahead of time. Rather, the interval for a single message outcome is calculated symbol by symbol for that particular message. Thus, only one interval is calculated to send a single message. Furthermore, because the process is symbol by symbol, there is no need to fix the message length ahead of time: The calculation continues until the end of the message is reached.

Basic Algorithm

Each step of the algorithm begins with the half-open interval $[L, H)$, which is initialized to $[0, 1)$.

1. Subdivide the current interval into subintervals, one for each possible symbol. Each subinterval is proportional to the probability of the corresponding symbol.
2. Select the subinterval that corresponds to the symbol that actually occurs and make this the new current interval.

Steps 1 and 2 are repeated until the entire message is processed. The final steps are as follows:

3. Output enough bits to distinguish the final interval from the two adjacent intervals.
4. Output some special end-of-message code to alert the recipient.

In the first step, it is not necessary to compute all of the subintervals, but instead to compute only the subinterval that corresponds to the actual symbol. This can be concisely stated as follows. Define

X = the set of symbols $(x_1, x_2, \ldots, x_M)$

$X(k)$ = symbol that actually occurs in iteration k; the kth symbol in the message

$I(k)$ = index value of $X(k)$; e.g., if $X(k) = x_3$, then $I(k) = 3$

M = the number of possible symbols

$P_X(i) = \Pr[X = i] = P_i$ = probability density function for X

$F_X(i) = \displaystyle\sum_{j=1}^{i} P_i$ = cumulative probability distribution function for X

L_k = lower bound of subinterval after iteration k of the algorithm

H_k = upper bound of subinterval after iteration k of the algorithm

$W_k = H_k - L_k$ = width of subinterval after iteration k of the algorithm

Then each iteration involves the following calculations:

$$L_k = L_{k-1} + F_X(I(k) - 1) \times W_{k-1}$$
$$H_k = L_{k-1} + F_X(I(k)) \times W_{k-1}$$
$$W_k = H_k - L_k = \Pr[X = X(k)] \times W_{k-1}$$

The width of this final interval is equal to the product of the probability of each symbol encountered during the algorithm and hence is the probability that a given message m occurs out of the M^N possible messages. This can be expressed as

$$\Pr(m) = \prod_{k=1}^{N} \Pr[X = X(k)]$$

It can be shown that at most $2 + \log[1/\Pr(m)]$ bits are required to identify uniquely the interval of message m. To see this intuitively, let us consider the first two intervals, with respective lengths $\Pr(1)$ and $\Pr(2)$ and intervals $[0, \Pr(1))$ and $[\Pr(1), \Pr(1) - \Pr(2))$. Now suppose that we use the lower boundary of an interval to define the interval. Then the binary fraction that represents $\Pr(1)$ will be the code for the second interval. There is some number j such that 2^{-j} is the smallest value that satisfies $2^{-j} > \Pr(1)$. That number is a binary fraction beginning with $(\log[1/\Pr(m)] - 1)$ bits followed by a 1. If we use that value as the code for the second interval, we are assured that it is uniquely identified with respect to the first interval.

Note that this formulation makes no assumption about stationarity or transition independence.

Example

This example is taken from [HOWA94]. For this example, there are two symbols, a and b, whose probabilities depend on the position in the message, with a three-symbol message. The probabilities are

$$\Pr(a_1) = 2/3 \quad \Pr(b_1) = 1/3$$
$$\Pr(a_2) = 1/2 \quad \Pr(b_2) = 1/2$$
$$\Pr(a_3) = 3/5 \quad \Pr(b_3) = 2/5$$

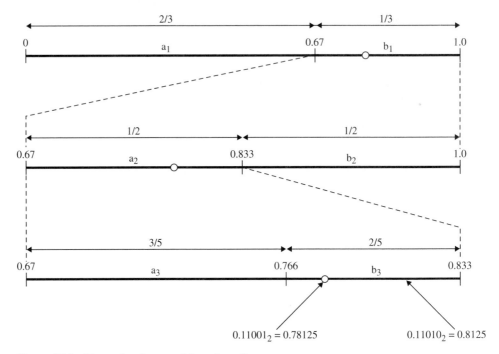

Figure 17.4 Example of pure arithmetic coding.

where $Pr(a_i)$ is the probability of occurrence of symbol a in the ith message position. The actual message is bab.

Figure 17.4 illustrates the arithmetic coding of this message. The final interval corresponding to the actual message is $[23/30, 5/6) \approx [0.766, 0.833)$. In binary, the final interval is $[0.110001 \ldots, 0.110101 \ldots)$. Note that all numbers beginning with 0.11001 are entirely within the interval, but that there are some numbers beginning with 0.1100 that are not in this interval (e.g., $0.1100001 < 23/30$). Therefore, the code 11001 is sufficient to identify uniquely the interval and therefore to identify uniquely the message. In general, the smaller the final interval (corresponding to a less probable message), the more code bits will be required to identify uniquely the interval.

Decoding

The decoding process follows the same general step-by-step scheme, this time discovering the successive subintervals that lead to the final interval and discovering the corresponding messages along the way.

The general rules are as follows. Again, begin with the interval [0, 1), Then

1. Subdivide the current interval into subintervals, one for each possible symbol. Each subinterval is proportional to the probability of the corresponding symbol.
2. Select the subinterval that contains the code, expressed as a binary fraction. Output the symbol that defines that code.

These two steps are repeated until the entire message is recovered. There are several ways in which this could be accomplished. An end-of-message symbol could be embedded in the original message; the decoding process would then stop when this symbol is encountered. Alternatively, the decoding process could test, after each step, whether all binary fractions beginning with the code are in a single interval and stop when this is false.

Figure 17.4 serves to illustrate the decoding process as well as the coding process. The numerical value of the final code ($0.78125 = 0.11001_2$) is indicated by a circle on each line of the process.

Interval Arithmetic Coding

There are two difficulties with the pure arithmetic coding algorithm just described. First, the shrinking size of the current interval requires the use of increasingly high-precision arithmetic. Second, the code cannot be sent until the entire message is processed.

Interval arithmetic coding overcomes both these problems. With this technique, the current interval is always blown up before the next step of the algorithm, and code bits are generated and each step and may be transmitted or stored after each step.

Description of Algorithm

Each step of the algorithm begins with the half-open interval $[L, H)$, which is initialized to $[0, 1)$; a **follow counter** is used and initialized to 0.

1. Subdivide the current interval into subintervals, one for each possible symbol. Each subinterval is proportional to the probability of the corresponding symbol.
2. Select the subinterval that corresponds to the symbol that actually occurs.
3. Execute the following steps repeatedly until an explicit loop-exit condition occurs:
   a. If the new subinterval is not entirely within one of the intervals $[0, 0.5)$, $[0.25, 0.75)$, or $[0.5, 1)$, exit the loop.
   b. If the new subinterval is in $[0, 0.5)$, output a **0** followed by zero or more **1**s corresponding to the value of the follow counter; set the follow counter to 0. Double the size of the subinterval by linearly expanding $[0, 0.5)$ to $[0, 1)$. That is, set $L = 2L$ and $H = 2H$.
   c. If the new subinterval is in $[0.5, 1.0)$, output a **1** followed by zero or more **0**s corresponding to the value of the follow counter; set the follow counter to 0. Double the size of the subinterval by linearly expanding $[0.5, 1)$ to $[0, 1)$. That is, set $L = 2(L - 0.5)$ and $H = 2(H - 0.5)$.
   d. If the new subinterval is in $[0.25, 0.75)$, increment the follow counter. Double the size of the subinterval by linearly expanding $[0.25, 0.75)$ to $[0, 1)$. That is, set $L = 2(L - 0.25)$ and $H = 2(H - 0.25)$.

Steps 1 through 3 are repeated until the entire message is processed.

Here, in essence, is what this algorithm is doing. If the current interval is wholly within $[0, 0.5)$ or $[0.5, 1)$, the algorithm produces a leading bit that indicates which half and then doubles the interval so that it reflects only the unknown part of the final interval. Let us see why this works. Suppose that the first step produces a subinterval in the upper half of the unit interval (e.g., Figure 17.4). Then we know that the final subinterval must also be in the upper half of the unit interval and therefore the most significant bit of the final code must be 1. Once this bit is known, the other half of the unit interval can be ignored and the subinterval can be doubled to determine the next bit in the code.

If the end points of the current interval are close to 0.5 but straddle 0.5, then it is not yet determined what the next output bit will be. However, whatever it is, the following bit will have the opposite value. The reader is invited to experiment with several values to see that this is so. Therefore, the algorithm keeps track of the following bit and expands the interval symmetrically around 0.5.

Example

Figure 17.5 illustrates the coding process, using the same *bab* message as before. In this example, interval expansion occurs once for each input symbol. This is not necessarily the case; there may be zero, one, or multiple doublings for a symbol. By the time the final symbol has been processed, the output is **110**. At this point, the final interval is [2/15, 2/3). Because all binary numbers in this interval begin with 0.01, an output of **01** is sufficient to identify uniquely this range. Therefore, we arrive at the same code as in the previous method (Figure 17.4). This will always be the case because the computations are essentially the same.

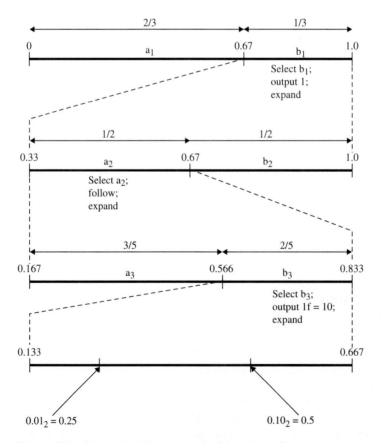

Figure 17.5   Example of incremental arithmetic coding.

17.4 STRING-MATCHING ALGORITHMS

Algorithms such as Huffman and arithmetic coding are based on knowing or estimating the statistics of the data to be compressed. These algorithms do not adapt to changes in the pattern of the data. In addition, storage constraints limit their ability to capture the higher-order relationships between words and phrases in text. A different approach, which has proved very effective, is a family of techniques known as string-matching algorithms.

Whereas Huffman and arithmetic coding map fixed-length sequences of input into variable-length codes, the string-matching algorithms map variable-length sequences of input into fixed-length codes. Further, the string-matching algorithms make no prior assumptions about the statistics of the data, but adapt to the changing patterns that they process.

All of the algorithms in this category stem from two important papers by two Israeli researchers Jacob Ziv and Abraham Lempel. In 1977, they described a technique based on a sliding-window buffer that holds the most recently processed text [ZIV77]. This algorithm is generally referred to as LZ77. A version of this algorithm is used in the zip compression scheme (PKZIP, gzip, zipit, etc.) that is popular on the Internet. In the following year, the same authors described an improved version of this technique based on a tree-structured dictionary [ZIV78]. This algorithm is referred to as LZ78. Terry Welch at Sperry devised an improvement on LZ78 that he termed LZW [WELC84]. Many compression programs are based on LZ78 and LZW, including the ITU-T V.42*bis* standard for voice-grade modems,[5] the popular image compression format GIF, and the UNIX compress program.

LZ77, LZ78, and their variants exploit the fact that words and phrases within a text stream (image patterns in the case of GIF) are likely to be repeated. When a repetition occurs, the repeated sequence can be replaced by a short code. The compression program scans for such repetitions and develops codes on the fly to replace the repeated sequence. Over time, codes are reused to capture new sequences. The algorithm must be defined in such a way that the decompression program is able to deduce the current mapping between codes and sequences of source data.

Another way of viewing the effectiveness of string-matching algorithms is to consider the entropy of input viewed as sequences of strings. Recall that the greater the level of aggregation of input symbols, the less the entropy. Therefore, we should expect that it is possible to achieve good compression ratios with string matching.

LZ77 Algorithm

Before looking at the details of LZ77, let us look at a simple example.[6] Consider the nonsense phrase

```
the brown fox jumped over the brown foxy jumping frog
```

---

[5]   *Data Compression Procedures for Data Circuit Terminating Equipment (DCE) Using Error Correction Procedures.* Recommendation V.42*bis*, 1990; described in [THOM92].

[6]   Based on an example in [WEIS93].

which is 53 octets = 424 bits long. The algorithm processes this text from left to right. Initially, each character is mapped into a 9-bit pattern consisting of a binary 1 followed by the 8-bit ASCII representation of the character. As the processing proceeds, the algorithm looks for repeated sequences. When a repetition is encountered, the algorithm continues scanning until the repetition ends. In other words, each time a repetition occurs, the algorithm includes as many characters as possible. The first such sequence encountered is the brown fox. This sequence is replaced by a pointer to the prior sequence and the length of the sequence. In this case the prior sequence of the brown fox occurs 26 character positions before and the length of the sequence is 13 characters. For this example, assume two options for encoding: an 8-bit pointer and a 4-bit length, or a 12-bit pointer and a 6-bit length. A 2-bit header indicates which option is chosen, with 00 indicating the first option and 01 the second option. Thus, the second occurrence of the brown fox is encoded as $<00_b><26_d><13_d>$, or 00 00011010 1101.

The remaining parts of the compressed message are the letter y; the sequence $<00_b><27_d><5_d>$, which replaces the sequence consisting of the space character followed by jump; and the character sequence ing frog.

Figure 17.6 illustrates the compression mapping. The compressed message consists of 35 9-bit characters and two codes, for a total of $35 \times 9 + 2 \times 14 = 343$ bits. This compares with 424 bits in the uncompressed message for a compression ratio of 1.24.

Compression Algorithm

The compression algorithm for LZ77 and its variants makes use of two buffers. A sliding-history buffer contains the last N characters of source that have been processed, and a look-ahead buffer contains the next L characters to be processed (Figure 17.7a). The algorithm attempts to match two or more characters from the beginning of the look-ahead buffer to a string in the sliding-history buffer. If no match is found, the first character in the look-ahead buffer is output as a 9-bit character and is also shifted into the sliding window, with the oldest character in the sliding window shifted out. If a match is found, the algorithm continues to scan for the longest match. Then the matched string is output as a triplet (indicator, pointer, length). For a K-character string, the K oldest characters in the sliding window are shifted out, and the K characters of the encoded string are shifted into the window.

Figure 17.7b shows the operation of this scheme on our example sequence. The illustration assumes a 39-character sliding window and a 13-character look-ahead buffer. In the upper part of the example, the first 40 characters have been processed and the uncompressed version of the most recent 39 of these characters is in the sliding window. The remaining source is in the look-ahead window. The

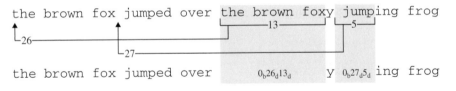

Figure 17.6 Example of LZ77 scheme.

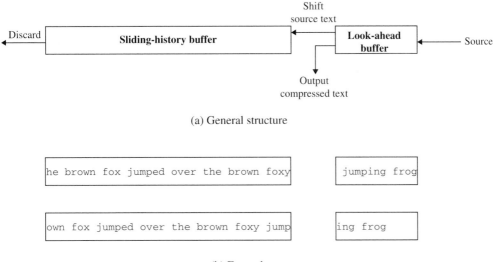

(a) General structure

(b) Example

Figure 17.7   LZ77 scheme.

compression algorithm determines the next match, shifts 5 characters from the look-ahead buffer into the sliding window, and outputs the code for this string. The state of the buffer after these operations is shown in the lower part of the example.

While LZ77 is effective and does adapt to the nature of the current input, it does have some drawbacks. The algorithm uses a finite window to look for matches in previous text. For a very long block of text, compared to the size of the window, many potential matches are eliminated. The window size can be increased, but this imposes two penalties: (1) The processing time of the algorithm increases because it must perform a string comparison against the look-ahead buffer for every position in the sliding window, and (2) the <pointer> field must be larger to accommodate the longer jumps.

Decompression Algorithm

Decompression of LZ77-compressed text is simple. The decompression algorithm must save the last N characters of decompressed output. When an encoded string is encountered, the decompression algorithm uses the <pointer> and <length> fields to replace the code with the actual text string.

LZ78 and LZW Algorithms

LZ78 and LZW attempt to overcome the limitations of LZ77 by abandoning the fixed-window approach and instead allowing dictionary entries to be created that may be available for future use over a long string of input.

Overview

As with LZ77, the LZW (and LZ78) algorithm maintains a dictionary of strings, with their codes, both for compression and decompression. When any of the strings in the dictionary appears in the input to the compressor, the code for that string is substituted; the decompressor, when it reads such a code, replaces it with the corresponding string from the dictionary. As compression occurs, new strings are added to the dictionary.

At any time, the dictionary contains all one-character strings plus some multiple-character strings. By the mechanism by which strings are added to the dictionary, for any multiple-character string in the dictionary, all of its leading substrings are also in the dictionary. Thus, if the string MEOW is in the dictionary, with a unique code word, then the strings MEO and ME are also in the dictionary, each with its own unique code word.

The dictionary can logically be represented as a set of trees, with each tree having a root corresponding to a character in the alphabet. So, in the default case, there are 256 trees (all possible 8-bit characters).

In the remainder of this section, we describe the algorithm in more detail using the V.42*bis* standard; this is, in most respects, the same as LZ78 and LZW.

Compression

Before describing the algorithm, we define the following quantities, using the notation in the standard:

C_1 = Next available unused code word
C_2 = Code word size; the default is 9 bits
N_2 = Maximum size of the dictionary = number of code words = 2^{C_2}
N_3 = Character size; the default is 8 bits
N_5 = First code word used to represent a string of more than one character
N_7 = Maximum string length that can be encoded

The compression algorithm consists of three main ingredients:

- String matching and encoding
- Addition of new strings to the dictionary
- Deletion of old strings from the dictionary.

The algorithm will always match the input to the longest matching string in the dictionary. The transmitter partitions the input into strings that are in the dictionary and converts each string into its corresponding code word. Since all one-character strings are always in the dictionary, all of the input can be partitioned into strings in the dictionary. The receiver accepts a stream of code words and converts each code word to its corresponding character string.

The algorithm is always seeking to add new strings to the dictionary, replacing older strings, which may not be as likely to appear in the future. The procedure is as follows:

1. Process incoming characters to produce the longest matching string.
2. If the matched string is of maximum length (N_7 characters), then transmit the code for this string and go to step 1.
3. Otherwise, append the next character to the matched string and add this string to the dictionary and assign a code to it. However, since this new string does

not yet exist in the receiver's dictionary, transmit the code for the original matched string and use the remaining character to begin again at step 1.

The procedure for adding a new string to the dictionary depends on whether the dictionary is full or not. In either case, the transmitter maintains a variable C_1, which is the value of the next available codeword. When the system is initialized, C_1 is initialized to have the value N_5, which is the first value after all one-character strings are assigned values. Thus, in the default, C_1 begins with a value of 256. As long as the dictionary remains empty, as each new string is defined, it is assigned the code value of C_1, and C_1 is incremented by 1.

When the dictionary is full, the following procedure is adopted. When a new string is defined, it is assigned the code value of C_1. Then

1. C_1 is incremented by 1.
2. If C_1 equals N_2, it is set equal to N_5. That is, once C_1 reaches its maximum value, it cycles back to its minimum value.
3. If the node identified by the value of C_1 is not a leaf node, then go to step 1.
4. If the node is a leaf node, then delete it from the dictionary.

At the end of this procedure, there is room for one new entry in the dictionary, and C_1 is the unused code to be assigned to that entry. The system is now ready to define the next new string for the dictionary.

Figure 17.8a illustrates the operation of the compression algorithm, using a three-character alphabet. Initially, only one-character strings are in the dictionary

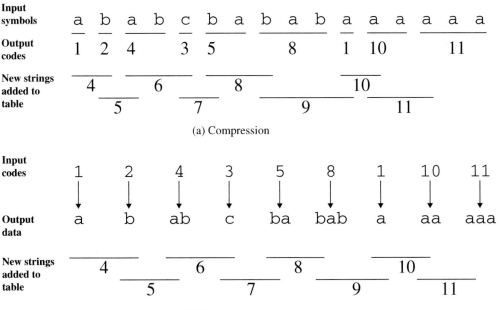

(a) Compression

(b) Decompression

Figure 17.8 LZW example.

TABLE 17.6 LZW DICTIONARY FOR EXAMPLE IN FIGURE 17.8

String Table		Alternate Table	
Symbol	Code	Symbol	Code
a	1	a	1
b	2	b	2
c	3	c	3
ab	4	1b	4
ba	5	2a	5
abc	6	4c	6
cb	7	3b	7
bab	8	5b	8
baba	9	8a	9
aa	10	1a	10
aaa	11	10a	11

(upper part of Table 17.6). The input data are read from left to right. Because no matching string longer than a exists in the table, the code 1 is output for this string and the new string ab is added to the table with code 4. Then b is used to start the next string. Because ba is not in the dictionary, it is added with code 5 and the code for b is output. The process continues in this manner.

Table 17.6 shows the dictionary resulting from this example. A more compact method of storage is shown in the right side of the table, in which each string is represented by its prefix string code and last character. In this representation, all multiple-character string entries are of equal length. This representation also suggests the multiple-tree structure of the dictionary, shown in Figure 17.9.

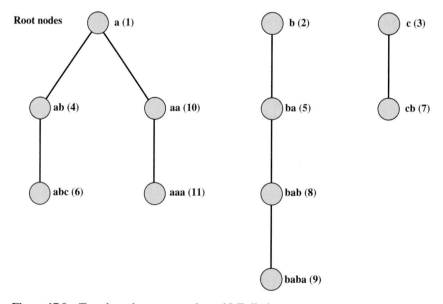

Figure 17.9 Tree-based representation of LZ dictionary.

Decompression

An interesting aspect of the LZ78 family of algorithms is that the dictionary is not communicated explicitly to the decompression algorithm. Rather, the decompression algorithm builds up the identical dictionary used by the compression algorithm while decompressing. What makes this possible is that on decompression a code is never encountered until the string corresponding to that code is encountered.

Figure 17.8b illustrates decompression. As each code is encountered it is translated into the corresponding character string to produce output. Meanwhile, following the same rules as the compression algorithm, the output is used to create new entries in the dictionary.

17.5 RECOMMENDED READING

A good technical treatment of the algorithms in this chapter is [SAYO96]. Two useful books on data compression are [NELS96] and [HELD96]. Both books contain a number of programs to compress and decompress data and to analyze the susceptibility of data to compression. These programs are also available on disk.

The June 1994 issue of the *Proceedings of the IEEE* contains 10 papers covering various compression algorithms, including the ones in this chapter.

HELD96   Held, G. *Data and Image Compression: Tools and Techniques.* New York: Wiley, 1996.

NELS96   Nelson, M., and Gailly, J. *The Data Compression Book.* New York: M&T Books, 1996.

SAYO96   Sayood, K. *Introduction to Data Compression.* San Francisco, CA: Morgan Kaufmann, 1996.

Recommended Web site:

- http://www.internz.com/compression-pointers.html: Good source of information on compression books, algorithms, products, etc.

17.6 PROBLEMS

17.1 List the advantages and disadvantages of the MNP technique for run-length encoding compared to that defined in Figure 17.1.

17.2 Construct an LZ77 code for the following sequence. Use a sliding-history buffer and look-ahead buffer of size 8 each.

01000100110100010100100000101000

17.3 Decode the sequence 0 0 1 3 5 2 with LZW coding and an initial dictionary (compare Figure 17.9) of a(0) b(1).

17.4 **a.** In a straight forward implementation of LZ77 coding, which step would be faster, compression or decompression? Why?
b. Answer the same questions for LZ78 coding.

17.5 Suppose you are given an input sequence of the form aaaa...aaa; that is, the symbol a repeated k times. Which string-matching encoding scheme, LZ77 or LZ78, would encode this more efficiently? Explain your answer and state the assumptions that you made, if any.

17.6 Consider the following character string, and assume that the relative probabilities of the symbols are reflected in this string [e.g., $\Pr(a) = 2/40$]:

```
aa bbb cccc ddddd eeeeee ffffffgggggggg
```

Show the code for this string for the following:
a. Huffman
b. LZW
c. Arithmetic

17.7 One way to improve compression efficiency is to preprocess the source data to place it in a form more suitable for compression. An example of this is the Burrows-Wheeler transform (BWT). BWT is performed on an entire block of data at once; the only limitation is storage size. For a string of length N, BWT generates an array of N different strings of length N, each character in the original being the start of a rotated version of the original string (this is a logical operation; the actual implementation will use pointers or some other space-saving technique). For example, if the original string is ESEP-AAT, then the logical matrix on the left is generated:

S0	E	S	E	P	A	A	T		S4	A	A	T	E	S	E	P
S1	S	E	P	A	A	T	E		S5	A	T	E	S	E	P	A
S2	E	P	A	A	T	E	S		S2	E	P	A	A	T	E	S
S3	P	A	A	T	E	S	E		S0	E	S	E	P	A	A	T
S4	A	A	T	E	S	E	P		S3	P	A	A	T	E	S	E
S5	A	T	E	S	E	P	A		S1	S	E	P	A	A	T	E
S6	T	E	S	E	P	A	A		S6	T	E	S	E	P	A	A

For convenience, the rows in the original matrix are labeled sequentially. Next, the rows of this matrix are sorted lexicographically, yielding the matrix on the right. Finally, the output of the transform is the final column of the sorted matrix (shaded) plus an integer that indicates which position (starting with 0) in the output string contains the original first character. In this example, the output is the string PASTEEA and the integer 5. This output can then be compressed by any common compression algorithm such as Huffman. To recover the original string, the output must be decompressed and then the original string recovered from the transform output.

a. At first glance, the transform may not seem to be reversible, but it is. Describe an algorithm for reversing the transform to recover the original input string.
b. How can the BWT algorithm improve compression performance?

CHAPTER **18**

LOSSY COMPRESSION

The reader who has persevered thus far in this account will realize the difficulties that were coped with, the hazards that were encountered, the mistakes that were made, and the work that was done.

—*The World Crisis*, Winston Churchill

L ossless data compression places a firm lower bound on the size of any file or message: the entropy of that file. With lossless data compression, it is possible to recover the original uncompressed data bit for bit. This characteristic is generally considered essential for text files, databases, binary object files, and so on. However, there are many types of files for which perfect recovery of the original data is not required. Examples are voice, image, and video. In these cases, some amount of error in reconstructing the original data is permissible, and lossy compression may be used.

A key issue with lossy compression is the tradeoff between compression ratio and fidelity. It should be clear that, in general, the greater the compression ratio for a given compression algorithm, the less the fidelity of the recovered data. The objective with any lossy compression algorithm is to use techniques that result in high compression ratios but that "sacrifice bits" in such a way that the reconstructed data are acceptably close to the original.

This chapter begins with a description of the discrete cosine transform; this transform is used in many compression applications. Next, a standard for still image compression known as JPEG is discussed. The following section deals with MPEG, which extends the techniques used in JPEG for video images. Finally, the promising area of fractal compression is examined.

18.1 DISCRETE COSINE TRANSFORM

The discrete cosine transform (DCT) is a one-to-one mapping of an array of pixel values into an array of values in the spatial frequency domain.[1] Subject to arithmetic rounding effects, the transform is reversible. The DCT does not provide any compression, but does put image information into a form that is more suitable for compression.

One-dimensional DCT

It is easier to understand the operation of the DCT in two dimensions, which is the form used in JPEG and MPEG, if we first explain the one-dimensional DCT.

Definition

Suppose that we have a one-dimensional image consisting of a linear array of N pixels, each of which has a gray-scale $p(x)$ ($0 \leq x < N$). Thus, $p(x)$ is a function that varies in space (rather than time). This image can be represented as the sum of spatial frequency components (see footnote 1) with frequencies ranging from 0 to $N - 1$:

$$p(x) = \sqrt{\frac{2}{N}} \sum_{f=0}^{N-1} C(f) S(f) \cos\left[\frac{(2x + 1)\pi f}{2N}\right] \tag{18.1}$$

$$= \frac{S(0)}{\sqrt{N}} + \sqrt{\frac{2}{N}} \sum_{f=1}^{N-1} S(f) \cos\left[\frac{(2x + 1)\pi f}{2N}\right]$$

where

$$C(f) = \begin{cases} 1/\sqrt{2} & f = 0 \\ 1 & f > 0 \end{cases}$$

This is reminiscent of a Fourier series representation of a continuous function. In this case, we are representing a discrete function $p(x)$, and the frequency components are defined only at discrete frequency values.

To arrive at the formulation of Equation 18.1, we need to calculate the coefficients $\{S(f), 0 \leq f < N\}$. Note that the first term of Equation 18.1 is the direct-current (dc), or zero-frequency component. This term must be equal to the average value of $p(x)$. Therefore,

---

[1]   A function of time can be expressed in the *time domain* by giving its value at each instant of time; it can also be represented by a Fourier series or Fourier transform that give the *frequency-domain representation* of the function. Similarly, a function that varies in space (in one, two, or three dimensions) can be represented as the sum or integral of frequency components, where each component is a sinusoid that varies in space rather than time. Hence the terms *space domain* and *spatial frequency domain*.

$$\frac{S(0)}{\sqrt{N}} = \frac{1}{N} \sum_{x=0}^{N-1} p(x)$$

$$S(0) = \frac{1}{\sqrt{N}} \sum_{x=0}^{N-1} p(x)$$

The general equation for $S(f)$ is

$$S(f) = \sqrt{\frac{2}{N}} C(f) \sum_{x=0}^{N-1} p(x) \cos\left[\frac{(2x+1)\pi f}{2N}\right] \qquad (18.2)$$

Equation 18.2 is called the one-dimensional DCT of $p(x)$, and Equation 18.1 is the inverse DCT of $S(f)$.

Example

We give an example in which a block of eight pixels from a monochrome image are transformed using DCT. Typically, the two-dimensional DCT works on blocks of 8×8 pixels, so this is a realistic one-dimensional version. The example uses an 8-bit value to designate the gray scale of a pixel, with 0 representing white and 255 representing black; again, this is typical of monochrome images.

Figure 18.1a shows the image to be transformed, and Figure 18.1b shows the vector of gray scale values for this image. For convenience, we subtract 128 from each value (an operation referred to as a **level shift**), so that the range of all possible gray scale values is symmetric around 0 (-128 to 127), yielding Figure 18.1c. The transform is then calculated:

$$S(f) = \frac{1}{2} C(f) \sum_{x=0}^{7} p(x) \cos\left[\frac{(2x+1)\pi f}{16}\right]$$

This calculation yields the DCT shown Figure 18.1d. To verify these values, one could calculate the inverse DCT:

$$p(x) = \frac{1}{2} \sum_{f=0}^{7} C(f) S(f) \cos\left[\frac{(2x+1)\pi f}{16}\right]$$

This yields Figure 18.1e, which is the original input to the DCT.

It is worth expanding the preceding equation to emphasize the nature of the DCT. We have

$$p(x) = \frac{1}{\sqrt{8}} S(0) \cos[0] + \frac{S(1)}{2} \cos[(2x+1)\pi/16] + \frac{S(2)}{2} \cos[(2x+1)2\pi/16]$$

$$+ \frac{S(3)}{2} \cos[(2x+1)3\pi/16] + \frac{S(4)}{2} \cos[(2x+1)4\pi/16] + \frac{S(5)}{2} \cos[(2x+1)5\pi/16]$$

$$+ \frac{S(6)}{2} \cos[(2x+1)6\pi/16] + \frac{S(7)}{2} \cos[(2x+1)7\pi/16]$$

(a) Image

43	138	148	183	208	254	248	148

(b) Gray-scale samples (scale 0:255)

p(0)	p(1)	p(2)	p(3)	p(4)	p(5)	p(6)	p(7)
−85	10	20	55	80	126	120	20

(c) Level shift of (b) by 128

S(0)	S(1)	S(2)	S(3)	S(4)	S(5)	S(6)	S(7)
122	−129	−95	26	−73	4	−31	−11

(d) DCT

−85	10	20	55	80	126	120	20

(e) Inverse DCT

Figure 18.1   Example of one-dimensional DCT.

Thus, $p(x)$ can be represented as a weighted sum of eight cosine functions. Figure 18.2 shows these eight functions, called basis cosine functions; each graph in the figure plots magnitude versus one-dimensional space (x). Each of these discrete functions is simply a continuous cosine function sampled at eight points. These functions have several important properties:

- **Complete:** A weighted sum of these eight functions can be found for any eight pixel sample values.
- **Minimal:** None of the eight waveforms can be represented by any weighted combination of the others, and all eight are required for completeness.

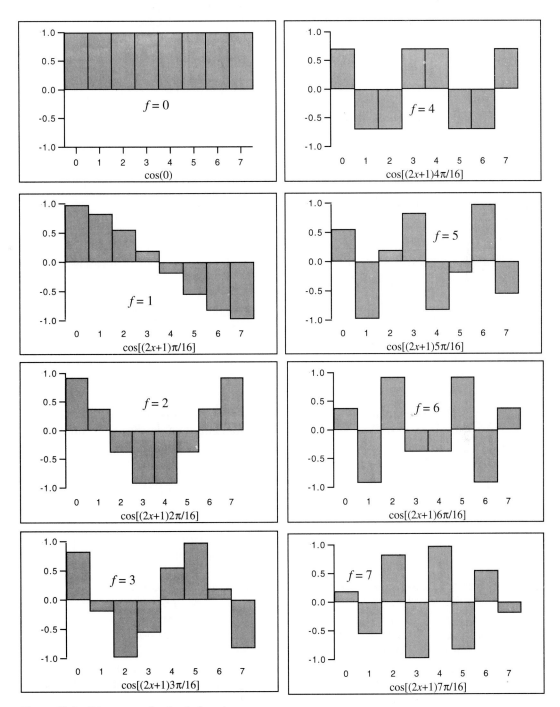

Figure 18.2 Discrete cosine basis functions.

- **Unique:** No other set of cosine waveforms, other than scaled versions of these eight waveforms, can be used to represent all possible sequences of eight pixel values.

These properties apply in the general case of using N cosine functions to represent a one-dimensional image of N pixels. That is, any discrete function $\{p(x), 0 \leqslant x < N\}$ can be represented by the set of discrete cosine functions $\{\cos[(2x + 1)\pi f/2N], 0 \leqslant f < N\}$.

Note that the DCT for this example has much of its magnitude concentrated at the lower frequencies, including dc (direct current; $f = 0$). This is common for images; typically, changes in lightness and darkness are gradual with few sharp edges. Accordingly, there is little or no contribution from higher spatial frequencies. The importance of the lower frequencies is illustrated in Figure 18.3, which shows a sequence of partial sums for this example. Each graph adds one more term to the summation, starting with just the zero-frequency component and ending with all eight weighted frequency components. After just the first three or four terms, the overall shape of the final function is apparent, and the final few frequency components add little. The graph in the lower right fully represents $p(x)$, as can be seen by comparing it with Figure 18.1c.

The significance of the frequency representation using the DCT is this: If, as is typically the case, the higher-frequency components add little to the image, then it is an easy matter to eliminate these components or to represent them with fewer bits. It would be difficult to achieve this type of compression dealing with the original image in the space domain rather than the DCT in the spatial frequency domain.

Two-dimensional DCT

The two-dimensional DCT is a key component of both JPEG and MPEG. As before, we begin with a mathematical definition and then provide an example.

Definition

Just as any linear array of N pixels can be represented by a weighted sum of N cosine functions at different frequencies, so a matrix of $N \times N$ pixels can be represented by a weighted sum of $N \times N$ cosine functions. The relationship is

$$p(x, y) = \frac{2}{N} \sum_{u=0}^{N-1} \sum_{v=0}^{N-1} C(u)C(v)S(u, v) \cos\left[\frac{(2x + 1)\pi u}{2N}\right] \cos\left[\frac{(2y + 1)\pi v}{2N}\right] \quad (18.3)$$

where

$$C(f) = \begin{cases} 1/\sqrt{2} & f = 0 \\ 1 & f > 0 \end{cases} \quad \text{for } f = u \text{ or } v$$

Equation 18.3 says that a two-dimensional array of pixels can be represented by the product of spatial frequency terms in the horizontal and vertical dimensions. The individual cosine factors are the same as in the one-dimensional case. So, for an 8×8 DCT, the cosine functions of Figure 18.3 are used.

As in the one-dimensional case, the zero-frequency term must equal the average value of $p(x)$. In this case, the term is $S(0, 0)/N$. Therefore,

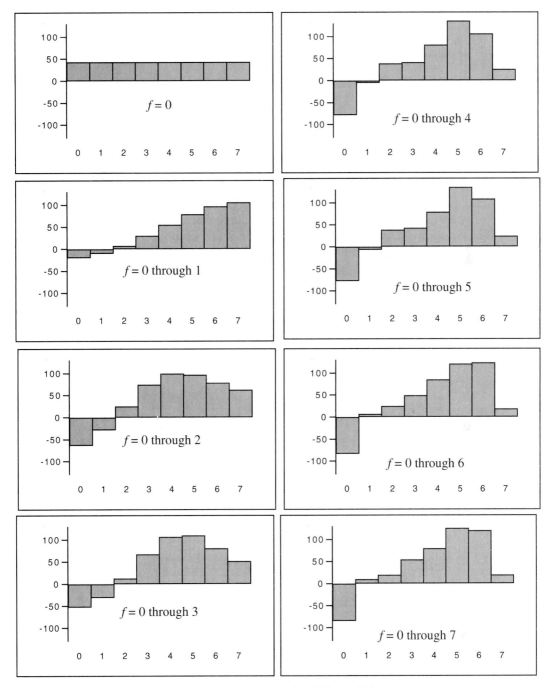

Figure 18.3 Summation of discrete cosines for example of Figure 18.1.

$$\frac{S(0,0)}{N} = \frac{1}{N^2} \sum_{x=0}^{N-1} \sum_{y=0}^{N-1} p(x,y)$$

$$S(0,0) = \frac{1}{N} \sum_{x=0}^{N-1} \sum_{y=0}^{N-1} p(x,y)$$

The general equation for $S(f)$ is

$$S(u,v) = \frac{2}{N} C(u)C(v) \sum_{x=0}^{N-1} \sum_{y=0}^{N-1} p(x,y) \cos\left[\frac{(2x+1)\pi u}{2N}\right] \cos\left[\frac{(2y+1)\pi v}{2N}\right] \quad (18.4)$$

Equation 18.4 is called the two-dimensional DCT of $p(x,y)$.

Example

We give an example (based on one in [ANDL96]) in which a square array of 64 pixels (8 × 8) from a monochrome image is transformed using DCT. In JPEG, images are processed in blocks of 8 × 8. This size was chosen for two reasons. First, the complexity of the computation grows rapidly with the size of the block being processed, and blocks larger than 8 × 8 appeared to impose an undue processing burden with current technology. Second, research on a variety of sample images indicates that little is lost in terms of fidelity by restricting the processing to this block size.

Figure 18.4a is matrix of gray-scale values, after a shift to a range of -128 to 127. Note that there is not a great deal of variation in the pixel values. This is typical of a large image: In any given 8 × 8 block, there is likely to be a small range of values. The transform is then calculated:

$$S(u,v) = \frac{C(u)C(v)}{4} \sum_{x=0}^{7} \sum_{y=0}^{7} p(x,y) \cos\left[\frac{(2x+1)\pi u}{16}\right] \cos\left[\frac{(2y+1)\pi v}{16}\right] \quad (18.5)$$

This calculation yields the DCT shown Figure 18.4b. The upper left entry (shaded) is $S(0,0)$, which corresponds to the average, or dc, value of the matrix multiplied by 8:

$$S(0,0) = \frac{1}{8} \sum_{x=0}^{7} \sum_{y=0}^{7} p(x,y) = 8 \times \frac{\displaystyle\sum_{x=0}^{7} \sum_{y=0}^{7} p(x,y)}{64}$$

79	75	79	82	82	86	94	94
76	78	76	82	83	86	85	94
72	75	67	78	80	78	74	82
74	76	75	75	86	80	81	79
73	70	75	67	78	78	79	85
69	63	68	69	75	78	82	80
76	76	71	71	67	79	80	83
72	77	78	69	75	75	78	78

619	−29	8	2	1	−3	0	1
22	−6	−4	0	7	0	−2	−3
11	0	5	−4	−3	4	0	−3
2	−10	5	0	0	7	3	2
6	2	−1	−1	−3	0	0	8
1	2	1	2	0	2	−2	−2
−8	−2	−4	1	2	1	−1	1
−3	1	5	−2	1	−1	1	−3

(a) Source pixel matrix $p(x,y)$ (b) DCT matrix $S(u,v)$

Figure 18.4 Example of two-dimensional DCT.

This has much greater magnitude than any of the others. The values of the other entries become smaller at higher frequencies (farther from the dc component). This will typically be the case. Another way of putting it is to say that most of the information in a typical image is at lower spatial frequencies. Still another way of putting it is that there are usually no sharp edges or abrupt changes in gray scale.

To verify these values, one could calculate the inverse DCT:

$$p(x, y) = \frac{1}{4} \sum_{u=0}^{7} \sum_{v=0}^{7} C(u) C(v) S(u, v) \cos\left[\frac{(2x + 1)\pi u}{16}\right] \cos\left[\frac{(2y + 1)\pi v}{16}\right] \quad (18.6)$$

This yields Figure 18.4a, which is the original input to the DCT.

18.2 JPEG IMAGE COMPRESSION

The Joint Photographic Experts Group (JPEG) is a collaborative standards-making effort between ISO and ITU-T. JPEG has developed a set of standards for the compression of continuous-tone still images, both gray scale and color. The JPEG standard is designed to be general purpose, meeting a variety of needs in such areas as desktop publishing, graphic arts, newspaper wire photo transmission, and medical imaging.

To get a feel for the need for image compression, consider the following data. A typical digital color image has 512 × 480 pixels. Each pixel is represented by 24 bits (8 bits each for the red, green, and blue components). This is a storage requirement of 737,280 octets. To transmit this image over a 64-kbps ISDN channel takes over a minute and a half. With JPEG, "excellent" image quality can be retained for a typical image at just one bit per pixel, which is a 24 to 1 compression ratio. At this compression ratio, the storage requirement is reduced to 30,720 octets and the 64-kbps transmission time is less than 4 seconds.

To satisfy the needs for a variety of image types, a single algorithm is inadequate. Accordingly, JPEG has defined four modes of operation (Figure 18.5):

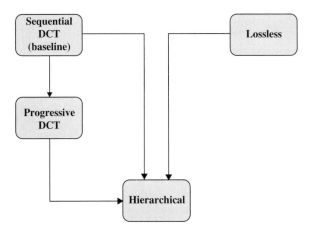

Figure 18.5 JPEG modes of operation.

- **Sequential DCT based:** Each image component is encoded in a single left-to-right, top-to-bottom scan.
- **Progressive DCT based:** The image is encoded in multiple scans for applications in which transmission time is long, and the viewer prefers to watch the image build up in multiple coarse-to-clear passes. The algorithm for this mode is derived from the sequential DCT-based algorithm.
- **Lossless:** The image is encoded to guarantee exact recovery of the source image.
- **Hierarchical:** The image is encoded at multiple resolutions, so that lower-resolution versions may be accessed without first having to decompress the image at full resolution. This mode may be used with any of the other three modes.

Sequential DCT–based Mode

The sequential DCT-based mode provides a combination of high compression ratios and good recovered image quality. Both compression and decompression phases consist of three major steps, as illustrated in Figure 18.6. This figure shows the sequence of steps for gray-scale, or single-component, image processing. The algorithm sequentially processes a stream of 8×8 gray-scale image blocks. Color image compression involves compression of each of the three components separately. When dealing with color images, the algorithm can either treat each component as a separate image and compress that, or can interleave 8×8 blocks from each component in turn.

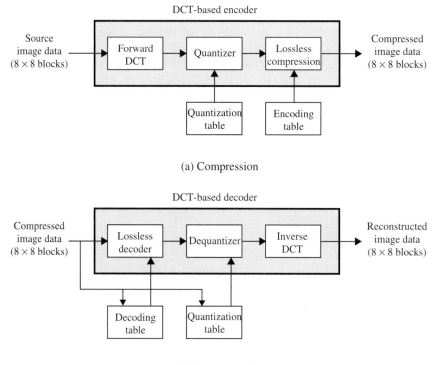

(a) Compression

(b) Decompression

Figure 18.6 JPEG sequential DCT-based algorithm.

Forward DCT

The compression algorithm begins the processing of each 8×8 block by level shifting the samples so that they range from -128 to 127. Then each block is mapped into the frequency domain using the DCT defined in Equation 18.5.

Quantization

The result of the DCT algorithm is to produce a matrix of coefficients. The input to the algorithm is a matrix of 8-bit values. Precise values of the DCT coefficients will generally require more bits. Quantization reduces the number of bits required to represent each DCT coefficient. In addition, quantization typically results in many zero-value coefficients in the DCT matrix, which leads to high compression ratios.

Quantization is applied independently to each of the 64 elements of the DCT matrix, and different amounts of quantization can be applied to the various elements. Invariably, the dc and lower-frequency coefficients are quantized to a lesser degree than higher-frequency coefficients. The reason for this is that changes in higher-frequency components are relatively less noticeable than changes in lower-frequency components.

The mechanism for quantization is an 8×8 quantization table, of which Figure 18.7a is a typical example. Given a quantization table with elements $Q(u, v)$ and a DCT matrix with elements $S(u, v)$, the following calculation is performed:

$$K(u, v) = \text{round}\left(\frac{S(u, v)}{Q(u, v)}\right) = \left\lfloor \frac{S(u, v)}{Q(u, v)} + 0.5 \right\rfloor$$

where $\lfloor x \rfloor$ is the largest integer smaller than x. This function rounds to the nearest integer. For example,

$$\text{round}(8/16) = \text{round}(0.5) = 1$$

$$\text{round}(7/16) = \text{round}(0.4375) = 0$$

$$\text{round}(8/15) = \text{round}(0.533) = 1$$

$$\text{round}(7/15) = \text{round}(0.466) = 0$$

16	11	10	16	24	40	51	61
12	12	14	19	26	58	60	55
14	13	16	24	40	57	69	56
14	17	22	29	51	87	80	62
18	22	37	56	68	109	103	77
24	35	55	64	81	104	113	92
49	64	78	87	103	121	120	101
72	92	95	98	112	100	103	99

(a) Quantization matrix $Q(u, v)$

39	−3	1	0	0	0	0	0
2	−1	0	0	0	0	0	0
1	0	0	0	0	0	0	0
0	−1	0	0	0	0	0	0
0	0	0	0	0	0	0	0
0	0	0	0	0	0	0	0
0	0	0	0	0	0	0	0
0	0	0	0	0	0	0	0

(b) Quantized DCT matrix $K(u, v)$

Figure 18.7   Effect of quantization.

If a number is less than half of the quantization term, then that number is rounded to zero.

If the quantization table entries are carefully selected, the result will produce high compression ratios with negligible distortion apparent to the human eye. JPEG does not dictate a specific quantization matrix but does provide a suggested set of matrices, of which Figure 18.7a is one.

Figure 18.7b shows the result of applying the quantization table of Figure 18.7a to the DCT matrix of Figure 18.4b. Many of the terms in the matrix are reduced to zero, which will enhance compression performance.

Lossless Compression

The final major phase of the compression process is a lossless compression algorithm. This algorithm involves two preparatory steps followed by the actual encoding. First, the quantized dc coefficient, which is the $(0, 0)$ entry in the quantized DCT matrix, is differentially encoded:

$$\text{DIFF} = \text{DC}_i - \text{PRED}$$

where DIFF is the resulting value, DC_i is the $(0, 0)$ entry for the ith 8×8 block, and PRED is the $(0, 0)$ entry for the preceding block. This differential encoding is effective for two reasons: (1) There is typically a strong correlation between the average or dc level of two adjacent 8×8 blocks, and (2) dc coefficients frequently contain a significant fraction of the total image value.

Next, the AC values from the matrix are ordered in a linear "zig-zag" sequence, as indicated in Figure 18.8 (the checkerboard shading is for clarity). Because many of the higher-frequency components are likely to be zero, this order-

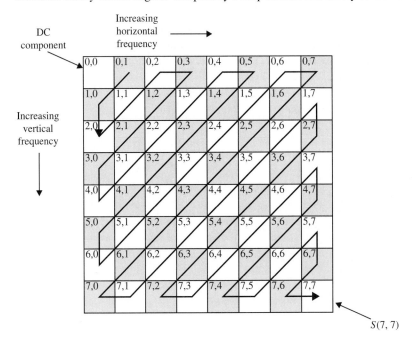

Figure 18.8 Zig-zag scan.

ing has the effect of creating long runs of zero components, which can be replaced by an end-of-block symbol. For example, the sequence for Figure 18.7b is

$$(\ 39 \ -3 \ 2 \ 1 \ -1 \ 0 \ 0 \ 0 \ 0 \ -1 \ EOB \ )$$

These two preparatory steps result in a string of integers, which are then encoded using an entropy encoding technique. Either Huffman or arithmetic coding may be used.

Decompression

Decompression follows the reverse sequence of steps (Figure 18.6). First, the entropy-encoded file is decoded and decompressed to recover a matrix of quantized DCT coefficients. This step is lossless and so the recovered matrix is the same as the original matrix.

The next step is to dequantize the matrix of quantized DCT coefficients to yield a matrix that approximates the original DCT matrix, using the equation

$$R(u, v) = K(u, v) \times Q(u, v)$$

This result will differ from the original $S(u, v)$ matrix because of rounding. Figure 18.9a shows the result of dequantizing the matrix of Figure 18.7b. Comparing the result to Figure 18.4b, we see noticeable differences, particularly in the lower right-hand portion of the matrix (higher frequencies).

Finally, the reconstructed DCT matrix is mapped into the space domain using the inverse DCT defined in Equation 18.6. Figure 18.9b shows the reconstructed

624	−33	10	0	0	0	0	0
24	−12	0	0	0	0	0	0
14	0	0	0	0	0	0	0
0	−17	0	0	0	0	0	0
0	0	0	0	0	0	0	0
0	0	0	0	0	0	0	0
0	0	0	0	0	0	0	0
0	0	0	0	0	0	0	0

(a) Dequantized DCT matrix $R(u, v)$

74	75	77	80	85	91	95	98
77	77	78	79	82	86	89	91
78	77	77	77	78	81	83	84
74	74	74	74	76	78	81	82
69	69	70	72	75	78	82	84
68	68	69	71	75	79	82	85
73	73	72	73	75	77	80	81
78	77	76	75	74	75	76	77

(b) Reconstructed pixel matrix $r(x, y)$

5	0	2	2	−3	−5	−1	−4
−1	1	−2	3	1	0	−4	3
−6	−2	−10	1	2	−3	−9	−2
0	2	1	1	10	2	0	−3
4	1	5	−5	3	0	−3	1
1	−5	−1	−2	0	−1	0	−5
3	3	−1	−2	−8	2	0	2
−6	0	2	−6	1	0	2	1

(c) Error matrix $E(x, y)$

Figure 18.9 Reconstruction of image.

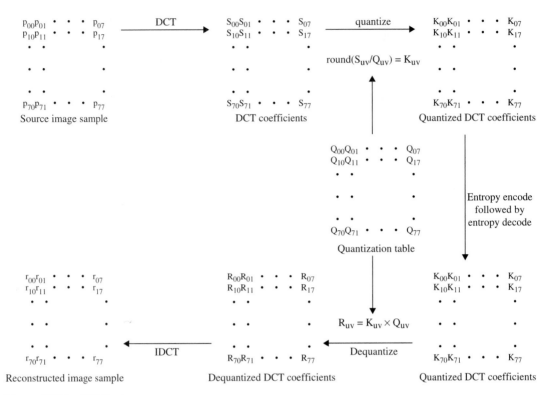

Figure 18.10 JPEG scheme.

pixel matrix for the source pixel matrix of Figure 18.4a, and Figure 18.9c is an error matrix that shows the difference between the two at each pixel position.

Figure 18.10 shows the relationships among the various matrices that we have been discussing.

Progressive DCT-based Mode

The progressive DCT-based mode is used to produce a quick approximate decoded image when the medium separating the coder and decoder has a low data rate. In this fashion, the viewer soon sees a rough approximation of the final image and then gradually sees a clearer and clearer version. This mode makes use of one or both of two techniques—spectral selection and successive approximation—and processes the image in multiple scans rather than a single scan.

For progressive DCT-based compression, the compression module must maintain an image-sized buffer at the output of the quantizer. The buffer must hold the quantized DCT matrix for each 8×8 pixel block in the original image. The coefficients in the buffer are then partially encoded in each of multiple scans.

Spectral Selection

Figure 18.11a illustrates the spectral selection technique. The first scan sends the dc component (0, 0 entry) from each of the blocks. On subsequent transmissions, some of the spectral components are sent in zig-zag order. In each scan a contigu-

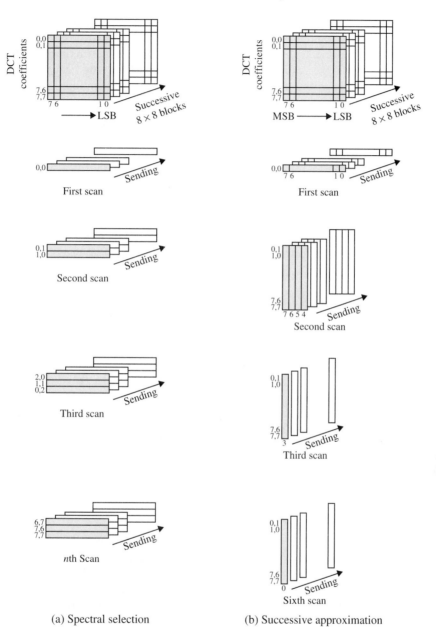

(a) Spectral selection (b) Successive approximation

Figure 18.11 Progressive DCT-based compression.

ous band of discrete frequencies is sent. Additional scans are used until all spatial frequency components are sent.

Successive Approximation

With this method, the precision of the coefficients is increased with each successive scan. Again, the dc coefficients are sent separately. Next, the N most significant bits of each coefficient are sent, where N is configurable. In subsequent scans, one additional bit of precision is sent (Figure 18.11b).

Both the spectral selection and the successive approximation techniques result in images that are initially rather coarse and become progressively crisper. For a discussion of the effects of each method and the combination of both methods, see [PENN93].

Lossless Mode

The JPEG standard includes a simple lossless mode of operation based on a predictive model. Compression ratios achieved with this method are typically about 2:1, which is much less than the ratios provided by the DCT-based methods [ARAV93].

Figure 18.12a shows the overall block diagram of this mode. In this case, an entire pixel matrix for an image is processed, rather than dealing with 8×8 blocks. As the image is scanned, each pixel value is replaced by a difference value according to the following formula:

$$\text{Difference} = \text{Pixel} - \text{Predictor}$$

where the predictor is based on the value of some previously scanned nearby pixels. The philosophy of this strategy is as follows. Typically, a pixel value will be close to the value of nearby pixels. Therefore, a prediction based on these nearby pixels should be close to the actual value and in many cases equal to the actual value. If

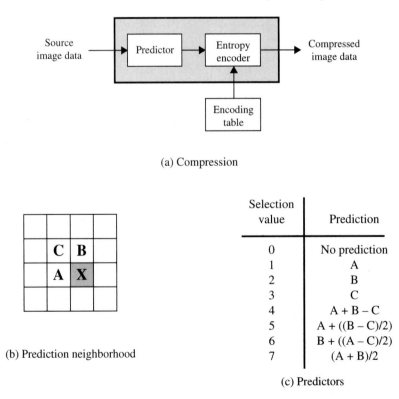

(a) Compression

(b) Prediction neighborhood

Selection value	Prediction
0	No prediction
1	A
2	B
3	C
4	A + B − C
5	A + ((B − C)/2)
6	B + ((A − C)/2)
7	(A + B)/2

(c) Predictors

Figure 18.12 JPEG lossless compression mode.

we transform a pixel matrix into a difference matrix based on the use of predictors, many of the entries will be zero and many others will be small values. The transformed image should encode more compactly.

The JPEG scheme allows for prediction based on some or all of the pixels that are adjacent to the current pixel but occur earlier in the left-to-right, top-to-bottom scanning process. As Figure 18.12b shows, there are three such pixels, labeled A, B, C for any pixel X. The only exceptions are pixels on the top row or left-hand column, which only have one preceding pixel neighbor.

The lossless algorithm can be configured to use any of the predictors listed in Figure 18.12c. Selections 1, 2, and 3 are one-dimensional predictors, while selections 4 through 7 are two-dimensional predictors. Which predictor to use is an implementation decision and must be communicated to the decompression module. The only exceptions to a given selection are as follows:

1. The predicted value for the top left pixel is 2^{P-1}, where P is the input precision.
2. The predictor for the other pixels in the top row is selection 1, which is the one-dimensional horizontal predictor.
3. The predictor for the other pixels in the leftmost column is selection 2, the one-dimensional vertical predictor.

Once the predictor matrix is generated, it can be encoded using either Huffman or arithmetic encoding.

Hierarchical Mode

In hierarchical mode, an image is coded in a set of increasingly higher-resolution frames. This mode can be used with any of the other three compression modes.

For this mode, the encoder begins by generating a set of successively lower-resolution images. Each successive image reduce the previous image by a power of 2 in one or both dimensions. For example, a 1024×1024 image could be reduced to a 512×512 image. This is a low-pass filtering operation that in essence averages the pixel values. This process continues down to the lowest-resolution image, which is set as a parameter of the algorithm. The encoding procedure then performs the following steps:

1. Compress the lowest-resolution image using one of the other three compression modes (sequential DCT, progressive DCT, lossless). The result is part of the compressed output but is also input to the next step.
2. Decode the result of the preceding step and then interpolate to produce the next higher resolution image.
3. Use the result of (2) as a prediction of the actual image at this resolution and generate a difference matrix. Compress this matrix using one of the other three compression modes. The result is added to the compressed output.
4. Repeat steps (2) and (3) until the full resolution of the image has been encoded.

Hierarchical resolution occurs when an image may be used by applications with a variety of resolution capabilities. In particular, an image may be used by a low-resolution device that does not have the buffer capacity to reconstruct an image at high resolution and then scale it down for the lower-resolution display.

18.3 MPEG VIDEO COMPRESSION

A moving picture is simply a succession of still pictures. Accordingly, one can achieve a degree of compression by independently compressing each still picture in the sequence that makes up the moving picture. But much more can be done. Even in a moving picture with a lot of action, the differences between adjacent still pictures are generally small compared to the amount of information in a single still picture. This suggests that an encoding of the differences between adjacent still pictures is a fruitful approach to compression; this is a tool used in MPEG.

Under the auspices of the ISO, the Moving Picture Experts Group (MPEG) has developed standards for video and associated audio in digital form, where the digital form may be stored on a variety of devices, such as CD-ROM, tapes, and writable optical disks, and transmitted on communications channels such as ISDN and LANs. The MPEG effort covers not only video compression, but also audio compression and associated system issues and formats. The premise of the MPEG effort is that a video signal can be compressed to a bit rate of about 1.5 Mbps with acceptable quality.

Overview of the Video Compression Algorithm

Much of the compression function performed in MPEG is very similar to that performed on JPEG. This can be seen in Figure 18.13. The input to the MPEG compression module is a sequence of video frames. Each frame is processed separately, being treated as a single still image. While operating on a single frame, the MPEG

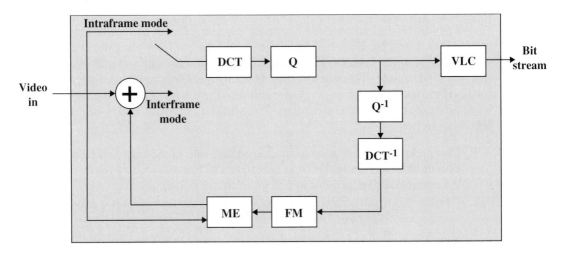

DCT: discrete cosine transform
Q: quantizer
VLC: variable length coder
FM: frame memory
ME: motion estimator

Figure 18.13   MPEG block diagram.

coder is in **intraframe mode**. In this mode, a frame is first transformed into the frequency domain using DCT, then quantized, and the result is encoded using Huffman coding.

Although significant compression can be achieved by simply processing a video signal as a sequence of still images, using a JPEG, this approach fails to exploit the considerable redundancy present in all video sequences. Typically, many of the pixels will change very little or not at all from one frame to the next, or the change simply involves the movement of a pattern of pixels from one location on a frame to a nearby location on the next frame. The MPEG studies indicate an additional compression on the order of a factor of 3 [GALL91] by exploiting these redundancies in an **interframe mode**.

For interframe mode, similar blocks of pixels common to two or more successive frames are replaced by a pointer that references one of the blocks. The major complication has to do with the order of the frames. Sometimes it is convenient to refer to a block in a preceding frame. At other times it is convenient to refer to a block in a future frame. In this latter case, the encoder replaces the block with a pointer and also reverses the order of the frame. The decompression routine must put the frames back in proper order prior to display.

Figure 18.13 shows the interframe technique in a very general way. After the DCT and quantization phases in the processing of a frame, the frame goes through the reverse process (dequantization, inverse DCT) in order to recover a frame that is identical to that which will be recovered by the decompression algorithm. This frame is then stored and used in the interframe mode to compare to succeeding frames.

In designing the video compression algorithm, the MPEG study group identified a number of features that are important in order to meet the range of applications of MPEG. Two of these are relevant to our discussion:

- **Random access:** A compressed video bit stream should be accessible at any point in the sequence of video frames, and any frame should be decodable in a limited amount of time. This implies the existence of access frames, which are frames coded only in intraframe mode and that therefore can be decoded without reference to other frames.

- **Fast forward/reverse searches:** It should be possible to scan a compressed bit stream and, using the appropriate access frames, display selected frames to obtain a fast forward or fast reverse effect. This feature is essentially a more demanding form of the random access feature.

Motion Compensation

The foundation of MPEG interframe compression is motion compensation. The idea behind motion compensation is that a portion of an image in one frame will be the same as or very similar to an equal-sized portion in a nearby frame. The MPEG scheme makes use of two forms of motion compensation: prediction and interpolation.

Prediction

MPEG makes use of blocks of 16×16 pixels, called **macroblocks** (in contrast to the smaller 8×8 blocks used in the DCT coding), for purposes of motion compensation. A frame processed in prediction mode is divided into its macroblocks, each of which is encoded separately. The encoding is done with reference to an **anchor frame** that precedes the current frame.

Each macroblock in the current frame is to be represented by a pointer, called the **motion vector**, to that macroblock in the anchor frame that most closely matches this macroblock. The motion vector gives the displacement of the macroblock in the current frame with respect to its match in the anchor frame. This is shown in the left two thirds of Figure 18.14. In this example, each video frame consist of 64×64 pixels grouped into 16 macroblocks. The shaded portion of the current frame is the macroblock whose upper left-hand pixel is in the x-y position $(16, 8)$. The match for this block in the previous frame is in position $(24, 4)$. The short arrowed line in the left-hand frame represents the motion vector, which in this case is $(8, -4)$.

Key aspects of predictive coding include the following:

1. The matching macroblock in the previous frame need not be on a 16-pixel boundary.
2. Matching is not done against a previous source video frame but rather against a video frame that has been through compression and decompression because the decompression module does not have access to the source video frames but only to decompressed versions of the original frames.

Having determined the matching block from the preceding frame, the MPEG algorithm records the motion vector and the prediction error, which is a 16×16 matrix of differences between the current macroblock, in frame c, and the reference macroblock, in frame r:

$$E_c(x, y) = I_c(x, y) - I_r[(x, y) + \mathbf{M}_{rc}]$$

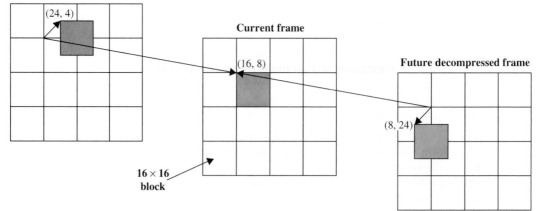

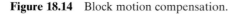

Figure 18.14 Block motion compensation.

where $E_c(x, y)$ is the prediction error, $I_i(x, y)$ is the value of the pixel located at position (x, y) in frame i, and $\mathbf{M}_{ij}$ is the motion vector for frame j relative to frame i.

Thus, the current frame is mapped into a matrix of prediction error values, one for each pixel position, and of motion vector values, one for each macroblock. The prediction error matrix will have many zero values. This matrix is encoded using the DCT-quantization technique and should yield a higher compression ratio than simply encoding the original pixel matrix.

The MPEG standard does not dictate how the matching process is to be done. Typically, the motion vector for a macroblock is obtained by minimizing a cost function that measures the difference between a macroblock and each predictor candidate. The calculation can be expressed as

$$\underset{m \in M}{\text{MIN}} \sum_{(x, y) \in B_i} C[I_c(x, y) - I_r((x, y) + m)]$$

where

$\quad B_i =$ a macroblock in the current frame I_c

$\quad m =$ the displacement vector with respect to the reference frame I_r

$\quad M =$ the search range in the reference frame

$\quad C =$ cost function

The value of m that minimizes the preceding expression is used as the motion vector $\mathbf{M}_{rc}$ for this block. The search range could encompass only small displacements or could range up to the entire frame size.

Interpolation

Although prediction results in higher compression ratios than a simple frame-by-frame JPEG compression, more can be done. In particular, MPEG allows some video frames to be encoded using two reference frames, one in the past and one in the future. This approach, called **bidirectional interpolation**, results in higher compression ratios than prediction based on one reference frame.

To see why bidirectional interpolation can improve results, consider a scene that is moving with respect to the picture frame at a rate of one half pixel per frame. If we attempt to predict a macroblock in the current frame based on the immediately preceding frame, no exact matching block will be found. Similarly, no exact match to the macroblock will be found in the immediately following frame. However, an average of the best match from the preceding and following frames provides an exact prediction, so that the error matrix is all zeroes.

Figure 18.14 illustrates the technique used in bidirectional interpolation. The current frame, referred to as a B frame, is processed against two reference frames, one before and one after this frame in time. Each macroblock can be encoded using a block from the preceding frame (forward prediction), the following frame (backward prediction), or one block from each reference frame (averaging), whichever gives the minimum error matrix. Table 18.1 summarizes the calculations for each option, with frame 1 being the current frame, frame 0 the preceding reference frame, and frame 2 the following reference frame.

In the case of bidirectional interpolation, more information must be encoded. As with predicted frames, a matrix of differences is produced and then encoded

TABLE 18.1 PREDICTION MODES FOR MACROBLOCK IN B PICTURE

Mode	Predictor
Forward Predicted	$\hat{I}_1(z) = \hat{I}_0(z + M_{01})$
Backward Predicted	$\hat{I}_1(z) = \hat{I}_2(z + M_{21})$
Average	$\hat{I}_1(z) = \dfrac{\hat{I}_0(z + M_{01}) + \hat{I}_2(z + M_{21})}{2}$

Note: z = the vector (x, y).

using DCT. In addition, each macroblock is encoded with an indication of the prediction mode (forward, backward, average), and one or two motion vectors.

Frame Ordering

Three types of frames are defined in MPEG:

- **Intraframe (I):** Encoded in JPEG style as an independent still image.
- **Predicted (P):** Encoded with reference to the preceding anchor frame.
- **Bidirectional interpolated (B):** Encoded with reference to the preceding and the following anchor frames.

The relative frequency of these types of frames within a video stream is a configurable parameter and must satisfy several tradeoffs. First, there is the need to satisfy the requirements for random access and fast forward/reverse searches, described earlier. These requirements place a lower bound on the fraction of I frames in the encoded stream. Second, there is a tradeoff between computational complexity and the number of B frames: More B frames means more computation. Finally, B frames can only be processed with respect to I and P frames; that is, one B frame can not serve as a reference frame for another B frame. Therefore, the higher the fraction of B frames, the greater the average distance between a B frame and its references, and the less the correlation between the B frame and its reference frames.

The rules for encoding are as follows. Each I frame is encoded using intraframe coding only. Each P frame is encoded based on the most recent preceding I or P frame, whichever is closest. Each B frame is encoded with the closest preceding and following I or P frames.

Picture frames in MPEG are organized into groups. Each group consists of a single I frame followed by a number of P frames and B frames. Because a B frame cannot be decoded until both its preceding and following reference frames are decoded, the members of a group are reorganized so that each B frame follows both of its reference frames. Figure 18.15 provides an example. The first six frames form a group. Frame 4 is stored after frame 1, because it is used as the forward prediction frame for B frames 2 and 3. Frames 5 and 6 are interchanged for the same reason. B frame 7 is recorded as part of the next group because it is encoded after I frame 8.

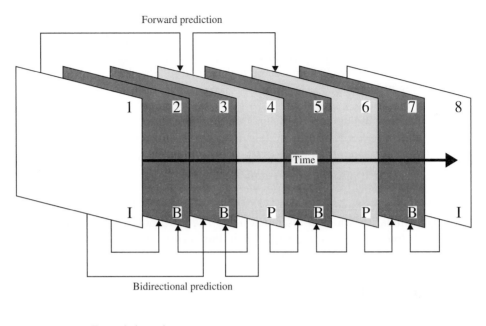

Forward prediction

Time

Bidirectional prediction

Transmission order

```
1  4  2  3  6  5 8  7 ...
I  P  B  B  P  B I  B ...
```

Group of pictures

Figure 18.15   Example of temporal picture structure.

18.4 FRACTAL IMAGE COMPRESSION

Perhaps the most intriguing approach to compression is the relatively new technique known as fractal image compression. All of the current approaches to fractal image compression can be traced back to work done by Michael Barnsley and his colleagues at Georgia Institute of Technology. Barnsley developed a scheme based on what he referred to as Iterated Function Systems (IFSs) and was co-founder of the company Iterated Systems, which exploits this technology. In the first article that documented the approach [BARN88], Barnsley claimed potential compression ratios of 10,000 to 1 or even higher. However, the initial approach required considerable human intervention as well as computational complexity. A modified scheme, known as the Partitioned Iterated Function System (PIFS), was developed as part of the work of one of Barnsley's students, Arnaud Jacquin [JACQ92]. The PIFS approach makes fractal image compression practical, although the compression ratios are in the range of 20:1 to 50:1, not the thousands to one that were originally claimed.

This topic can, and does, easily fill a book, so this section only provides an overview. We begin with two concepts that are needed to treat the subject: fractals and affine transformations.

Fractals

It is hard to find a clear definition of fractals that is universally accepted. It is easier to list the important features of fractals and proceed with our discussion from there. Fisher [FISH95] characterizes a fractal set F as having some or all of the following properties:

1. F has detail at every scale.
2. F is (exactly, approximately, or statistically) self-similar.
3. The fractal dimension of F is greater than its topological dimension.
4. There is a simple algorithmic description of F.

The first and second points are related and can be treated under the cover of self-similarity, which is discussed next. The third point requires a definition of the term *fractal dimension*, given later in this section. The fourth point suggests a way to develop fractal compression and is discussed later in this section.

Self-similarity

We first encountered the concept of self-similarity in Chapter 8, which dealt with self-similar data traffic. In that context, self-similarity was defined with respect to the time domain: A time function is self-similar if it has exactly or statistically the same appearance at various time scales. When dealing with fractals, we are concerned with self-similarity in the space domain of one, two, or three dimensions. In general terms, an object is spatially self-similar if it appears exactly or statistically the same under different levels of magnification.

The Cantor set is self-similar in one dimension (see Figure 8.2). If you examine a portion of the set and magnify it to the scale of the original set, you find that it has the same structure.

Self-similarity in two dimensions is more visually striking than one-dimensional self-similarity. One of the most popular examples used in books on fractals is the Sierpinski gasket.[2] The gasket is constructed as follows (Figure 18.16):

- **Start.** Begin with a solid black triangle.
- **Step 1.** Join the midpoints of the three sides of the triangle to form an enclosed triangle and remove the interior of the new triangle, leaving a triangular white hole and three black triangles.
- **Step 2.** Perform the same operation (create an enclosed triangle, remove its interior) on each of the three black triangles created in the preceding step. This results in nine black triangles and four triangular white holes.
- **Step N.** Repeat the process indefinitely. At step N, create a white triangular hole in all black triangles formed in step $N - 1$.

After infinitely many steps of this recursive construction, the Sierpinski gasket results. It is easy to see that this construct has self-similarity of scale. The gasket

---

[2] First suggested by the great Polish mathematician Waclaw Sierpinski (1882–1969) around 1915. He is one of the few mathematicians to have a lunar crater named after him.

Figure 18.16   The Sierpinski gasket.

includes one large white triangle in the center. Consider the portion of the gasket to the left of this large white triangle. Magnify this portion by a factor of 2 and you have the entire gasket. Furthermore, this self-similarity extends to all scales. No matter how many times you magnify the lower-left portion of the gasket, the result is always exactly the same as the entire gasket.

The Sierpinski gasket is a mathematical construct. In reality, it is impossible to draw the gasket because of the limited resolution of any printing or display medium. Further, our interest in fractals is not in mathematical constructs but in real images. A real image can be self-similar only over a finite range of magnitudes and, furthermore, will only be approximately or statistically self-similar. A good example is a mountain range. A photograph of an area that shows the top and part of the side of a mountain has a characteristic "peak and valley" appearance. If you zoom in on a portion of the mountain and enlarge it, it will have a similar appearance to the original, though it will not be an exact replica. This self-similar property is characteristic of many, if not most, natural images and is the basis for fractal compression.

Fractal Dimension

In geometry, we are familiar with the concept of dimension. A point has zero length and is considered zero dimensional. A line has an extent in one dimension, called the length, and is one dimensional. A line can also be viewed as in infinite number of contiguous points. Similarly, a rectangle has extent in two dimensions, called the area, and consists of an infinite number of contiguous lines.

How about fractal objects? Consider first the Cantor set defined on the unit interval. At the first step (Figure 8.2), the set has a length $L_1 = 2/3$. In the second step, one third of each portion of the set is removed, so that $L_2 = (2/3)(2/3) = (2/3)^2$. In general, after n steps, $L_n = (2/3)^n$. Because $L_n \to 0$ as $n \to \infty$, the Cantor set has a total length of zero. On the other hand, the Cantor set has infinitely many points.[3]

To see this latter point, consider that we only remove open intervals to form the next step of a Cantor set. So the end points of any interval at step K are still part of the set for step $K + 1$ and all subsequent steps. For example, the points 0, 1, 1/3, 2/3, 1/9, 2/9, 7/9, and 8//9 are all points in the Cantor set. However, the final Cantor set contains no intervals, because if it did, at some stage we would have removed its middle third.

A construct that contains an uncountably infinite number of points but zero length seems to be more than a zero-dimensional object yet less than a one-dimensional object. It makes mathematical sense to declare that this construct has a fractional dimension somewhere between zero and one.

The term *fractal dimension* is used to refer to the dimension of a fractal construct. A number of definitions have been proposed for this term. One of the easiest to understand is the box definition.

Let S be a subset of D-dimensional Euclidean space ($D = 1, 2, 3$), and let $N(r)$ be the minimum number of cubes with side r needed to cover S (e.g., Figure 18.17). On a two-dimensional space, how many such squares are needed to cover an object? For a smooth curve of length L, $N(r)$ is proportional to L/r. For a planar region bounded by a curve with area A, $N(r)$ is proportional to A/r^2. For a solid region in three-dimensional space with volume V, $N(r)$ is proportional to V/r^3. In all of these cases, the relationship involves an integer exponent with $N(r)$ proportional to $1/r^d$.

This power law holds for most fractal sets except that d is no longer an integer. In the fractal case, the fractal dimension d can be defined as

$$d = \lim_{r \to 0} \frac{\ln N(r)}{\ln(1/r)}$$

Let's see how this works on the fractal sets we have defined. For the Cantor set, at step n, there are 2^n intervals of length $(1/3)^n$ each. If we pick $r = (1/3)^n$, we need 2^n squares of side r to cover the Cantor set. Therefore, $N(r) = 2^n$ when $r = (1/3)^n$. Because $r \to 0$ as $n \to \infty$, we can write

$$d = \lim_{r \to 0} \frac{\ln N(r)}{\ln(1/r)} = \frac{\ln(2^n)}{\ln(3^n)} = \frac{n \ln(2)}{n \ln(3)} = \frac{\ln(2)}{\ln(3)} = 0.631$$

The dimension of the Cantor set is between 0 and 1, as expected.

For the Sierpinski gasket defined on the unit square (Figure 18.16c), it takes 3 boxes of side 1/2 to cover, 9 boxes of side 1/4, 27 boxes of side 1/8, and so on. In general, it takes 3^n boxes of side $1/2^n$, so the dimension is

---

[3] To be specific, the Cantor set has an uncountably infinite number of points; that is, there is a one-to-one correspondence between points in the Cantor set and *all* real numbers between 0 and 1.

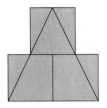 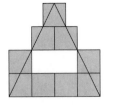 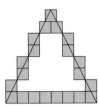

(a) Perimeter of triangle

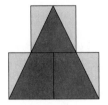 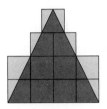 

(b) Solid triangle

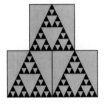 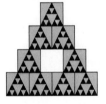 

(c) Sierpinski gasket

Figure 18.17   Demonstration of fractal dimension.

$$d = \frac{\ln(3^n)}{\ln(2^n)} = \frac{\ln(3)}{\ln(2)} = 1.585$$

Thus, it is possible to make an argument that the Sierpinski gasket is more than a one-dimensional object and less than a two-dimensional object. The construct has zero area (see Problem 18.5), like a one-dimensional object. Yet it consists of an infinite number of vanishingly small two-dimensional objects—namely, triangles.

Affine Transformations

The key to fractal image compression is to find a pattern in an image that is repeated at a different scale. In a natural image, it is rare for the repeated pattern to appear in exactly the same orientation and proportion. Instead, one may find a pattern that matches another pattern if the first pattern is rotated, stretched, reflected, or manipulated in some combination of ways. The transformations that are useful in this regard are called **affine transformations**.

The term *affine transformation* is used by mathematicians to refer to the same class of functions that are called linear functions in the engineering world. If w is a function in one dimension (of one variable) of the form $w(x) = ax + b$, where a and b are constants, then w is a linear function. When w is a function of n variables, then

w is linear if it is of the form $w(\mathbf{x}) = \mathbf{Ax} + \mathbf{k}$, where $\mathbf{x}$ is a vector of n variables, $\mathbf{A}$ is an $n \times n$ matrix of constants, and $\mathbf{k}$ is a vector of n constants. In two dimensions, w has the form

$$w(\mathbf{x}) = w\begin{pmatrix} x \\ y \end{pmatrix} = \begin{pmatrix} a & b \\ c & d \end{pmatrix}\begin{pmatrix} x \\ y \end{pmatrix} + \begin{pmatrix} e \\ f \end{pmatrix} = \begin{pmatrix} ax + by + e \\ cx + dy + f \end{pmatrix} \tag{18.7}$$

In this section, we look at the basic affine transformations in two dimensions and then describe the concept of a contractive mapping.

Basic Linear Transformations in Two Dimensions

A linear transformation takes a point $\mathbf{x}$ and maps it on the point $\mathbf{Ax} + \mathbf{k}$. In terms of images, such a transformation is interesting if we look at its effect on a set of points. In that case, any linear transformation can be constructed from a combination of the basic transformations illustrated in Figure 18.18 (based on a figure in [SCHE96]). The following transformations are of the form $f(\mathbf{x}) = \mathbf{Ax}$ and involve no translation:

- **Identity:** $\mathbf{A} = \begin{pmatrix} 1 & 0 \\ 0 & 1 \end{pmatrix}$ is the identity matrix, which leaves all points unmoved.

- **Axis rescaling:** The transformation $\mathbf{A} = \begin{pmatrix} a & 0 \\ 0 & b \end{pmatrix}$ expands or shrinks the image along one or both dimensions: by a factor of a on the x-axis and a factor of b on the y-axis. Figure 18.18b shows the result for $a = 0.5, b = 2$.

- **Rotation:** A rotation, defined by $\mathbf{A} = \begin{pmatrix} \cos\theta & -\sin\theta \\ \sin\theta & \cos\theta \end{pmatrix}$, moves points counterclockwise about the origin through an angle θ. Figure 18.18c illustrates a rotation for $\theta = \pi/6 = 30°$.

- **Reflection:** A reflection on the x-axis is defined by $\mathbf{A} = \begin{pmatrix} 1 & 0 \\ 0 & -1 \end{pmatrix}$, and a reflection on the y-axis is defined by $\mathbf{A} = \begin{pmatrix} -1 & 0 \\ 0 & 1 \end{pmatrix}$. A reflection through any other line can be made by combining a reflection on the x-axis with a rotation. A reflection on a line with an angle θ from the horizontal is defined by $\mathbf{A} = \begin{pmatrix} \cos\theta & -\sin\theta \\ -\sin\theta & -\cos\theta \end{pmatrix}$. Figure 18.18d illustrates a reflection for $\theta = 30°$.

- **Shearing:** This transformation leaves one of the two coordinates unchanged and is of the form $\mathbf{A} = \begin{pmatrix} 1 & a \\ 0 & 1 \end{pmatrix}$ for y-coordinate unchanged and $\mathbf{A} = \begin{pmatrix} 1 & 0 \\ b & 1 \end{pmatrix}$ for x-coordinate unchanged.

Figures 18.18e and 18.18f show the results for $a = -1$ and $b = 1$, respectively. Finally, a pure translation moves a set of points without changing the set itself and is of the form

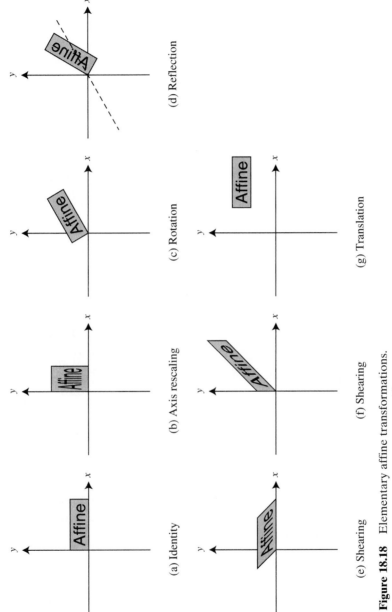

Figure 18.18 Elementary affine transformations.

(a) Identity

(b) Axis rescaling

(c) Rotation

(d) Reflection

(e) Shearing

(f) Shearing

(g) Translation

$$w(\mathbf{x}) = \begin{pmatrix} 1 & 0 \\ 0 & 1 \end{pmatrix}\begin{pmatrix} x \\ y \end{pmatrix} + \begin{pmatrix} e \\ f \end{pmatrix}.$$

Figure 18.18f shows the result for $e = f$.

Contraction Map

A contraction map is a linear transformation that "shrinks" the set being transformed. We state the definition for the case of two dimensions. In two dimensions, the distance $d(\mathbf{q}, \mathbf{r})$ between two points $\mathbf{q} = (x_1, y_1)$ and $\mathbf{r} = (x_2, y_2)$ is:

$$d(\mathbf{q}, \mathbf{r}) = \sqrt{(x_1 - x_2)^2 + (y_1 - y_2)^2}$$

A linear transformation w is a **contraction mapping** if for any vectors $\mathbf{q}$ and $\mathbf{r}$, there is a number $0 < s < 1$ such that

$$D[\, w(\mathbf{q}), w(\mathbf{r})] \leq s \times d(\mathbf{q}, \mathbf{r}) \tag{18.8}$$

Figure 18.19 shows an example of a contraction mapping (based on an example in [ITER95]). The mapping is defined by

$$w\begin{pmatrix} x \\ y \end{pmatrix} = \begin{pmatrix} 0.355 & 0.5733 \\ -0.355 & 0.1367 \end{pmatrix}\begin{pmatrix} x \\ y \end{pmatrix} + \begin{pmatrix} 2 \\ 5 \end{pmatrix}$$

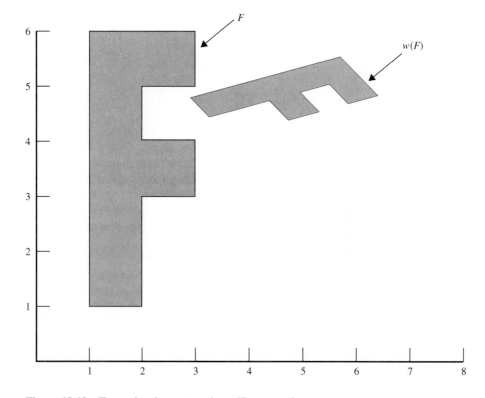

Figure 18.19 Example of a contraction affine mapping.

The figure shows the operation of this mapping on an F-shaped area. The mapping performs a shear of 30°, a rotation of 45°, a scaling of 0.5 in both dimensions, and a translation of 2 in the x-dimension and 5 in the y-dimension. Note that $w(F)$ is smaller in every dimension than F, so this is a contraction mapping.

Iterated Function Systems

Figure 18.19 shows that applying a contraction map to an area shrinks the area, as well as possibly moving, rotating, and distorting it. What happens if we apply the same contraction map repeatedly?

It can be shown that for a contraction mapping with parameter s as shown in Equation 18.8, the following relationship holds for any two areas, or sets, A and B:

$$\delta[w(A), w(B)] \leq s \times \delta[A, B] \tag{18.9}$$

In this case the function δ measures the difference between the two images using some suitable metric.[4] In any case, a contractive mapping applied to a set has the effect of reducing the distance between any two points in the set.

Figure 18.20 shows the result of repeatedly applying w to the set F. With each application, the set becomes smaller. Furthermore, $w^n(F)$ appears to be spiraling

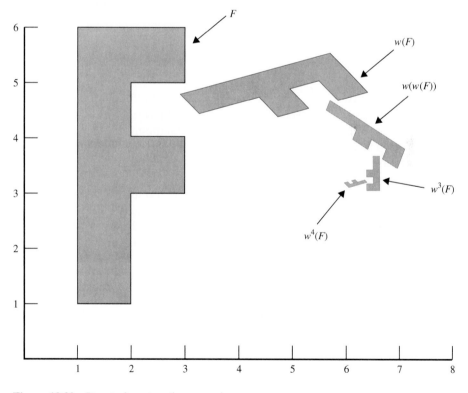

Figure 18.20 Iterated contraction mapping.

---

[4] A discussion of δ is beyond our scope. [SCHE96] and [BARN93] contain good discussions of this concept.

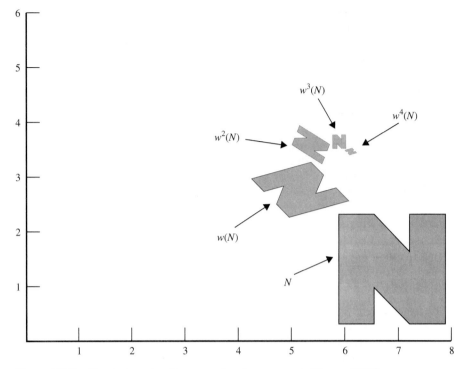

Figure 18.21 Iterated contraction mapping (same w as in Figure 18.20).

into a single fixed point. This is, in fact, the case. In this example, the fixed point of the mapping is approximately (5.94, 3.28). Furthermore, this fixed point is reached regardless of the initial set that is used in the mapping. Figure 18.21 shows the iterated application of w to the set N, and we have $w^{\infty}(F) = w^{\infty}(N) = (5.94, 3.28)$. It also follows that applying a contraction mapping to its fixed point produces that fixed point. In this case $w(5.94, 3.28) = (5.94, 3.28)$.

It follows that a point on the plane can be defined by the mapping w for which that point is its fixed point. This does not seem to get us very far. However, contractive mappings have a remarkable property that leads to a technique for compression: The union of a number of contractive mappings has as its fixed point, called an attractor, a set of points on the plane.

Suppose that w_1 and w_2 are both linear transformations. We can define a new transformation W by taking the union of w_1 and w_2, denoted $w_1 \cup w_2$, which is defined as

$$W(A) = (w_1 \cup w_2)(A) = w_1(A) \cup w_2(A)$$

where A is some set of points in N-dimensional space. It can be shown that if a mapping is formed from a union of contraction mappings, then it has a fixed attractor that is a set of points. Such mappings are called **iterated function systems** (IFSs).

Let us put this in general terms. Given a union of contractive mappings of the form

$$W(X) = \bigcup_{i=1}^{n} w_i(X)$$

then W has a fixed set F such that $W(F) = F$. Furthermore, repeated application of W to any set produces the fixed point; that is, $W^\infty(A) = F$ for arbitrary A. Finally, W itself is contractive and, if the contractivity parameter of w_i is s_i, then the contractivity parameter of W is $s = \max[s_i]$.

Examples

Let us define the following mappings in one dimension:

$$f(x) = \frac{1}{3}x \qquad g(x) = \frac{1}{3}x + \frac{2}{3}$$

The fixed point of f is 0 and the fixed point of g is 1. Define the union of f and g as $F = f \cup g$. Then we would expect that F has a fixed set A such that $F^\infty(X) = A$ for any set X and that $F(A) = A$.

Let's now determine the fixed point of F. Start with the interval $[0, 1]$. Then

$$F([0, 1]) = f([0, 1]) \cup g([0, 1]) = [0, 1/3] \cup [2/3, 1]$$
$$F^2([0, 1]) = f([0, 1/3]) \cup f([2/3, 1]) \cup g([0, 1/3]) \cup g([2/3, 1])$$
$$= [0, 1/9] \cup [2/3, 7/9] \cup [2/9, 1/3] \cup [8/9, 1]$$

Note that these are the first two steps in the construction of the Cantor set. If you continue, you will find that $F^3([0, 1])$ is the third step and that this mapping continues to converge to the Cantor set. Furthermore, this is true regardless of the initial set used in the mapping.

The use of this mapping to create a Cantor set is not as mysterious as it seems. In the Cantor set (Figure 8.2), the left one-third portion of the set is a one-third reproduction of the entire set and the right one-third portion of the set is a one-third reproduction of the entire set. So choose f to map the whole of the Cantor set onto the left portion and g to map the whole onto the right portion. The union of f and g then yields the entire set.

Now look at the following set of mappings:

$$w_1 \begin{pmatrix} x \\ y \end{pmatrix} = \begin{pmatrix} 0.5 & 0 \\ 0 & 0.5 \end{pmatrix} \begin{pmatrix} x \\ y \end{pmatrix}$$

$$w_2 \begin{pmatrix} x \\ y \end{pmatrix} = \begin{pmatrix} 0.5 & 0 \\ 0 & 0.5 \end{pmatrix} \begin{pmatrix} x \\ y \end{pmatrix} + \begin{pmatrix} 0.5 \\ 0 \end{pmatrix} \qquad (18.10)$$

$$w_3 \begin{pmatrix} x \\ y \end{pmatrix} = \begin{pmatrix} 0.5 & 0 \\ 0 & 0.5 \end{pmatrix} \begin{pmatrix} x \\ y \end{pmatrix} + \begin{pmatrix} 0.25 \\ 0.5 \end{pmatrix}$$

A careful study of this set of mappings shows that it produces a Sierpinski gasket (whose height equals its base). That is, the Sierpinski gasket is the fixed set for $W = w_1 \cup w_2 \cup w_3$. It follows that the Sierpinski gasket can be represented by the parameters of its constituent contractive mappings. Using the notation of Equation 18.7, Table 18.2 shows the IFS definition of the Sierpinski gasket.

Working Backward

Given a fractal image K, can we find an IFS for which K is the attractor? That is, can we find a mapping $W = w_1 \cup w_2 \ldots \cup f_n$ so that $W(K) = K$? Often this is the

TABLE 18.2 IFS FOR SIERPINSKI GASKET

Function	a	b	c	d	e	f
w_1	0.5	0	0	0.5	0	0
w_2	0.5	0	0	0.5	0.5	0
w_3	0.5	0	0	0.5	0.25	0.5

case, but it can be quite difficult to do so. For simple constructs such as the Cantor set and the Sierpinski gasket, the mapping is fairly obvious. In the general case, the mapping is not obvious and may involve rotation, shear, reflection, and scaling components. With the aid of computerized search techniques, such reverse mapping can be done, and this is the basis of fractal data compression.

Fractal Compression Concepts

Table 18.2 suggests a way to use IFSs to perform image compression. If we can come up with a set of transformations whose attractor is the image, then we can represent the image by that set of transformations. Although natural images typically have a fractal nature, in general it is not possible to find a set of transformations that exactly reproduce the image. Instead, we must look for ways to effectively approximate the image.

For an artificial image such as the Sierpinski gasket, it is possible to find a set of n transformations $\{w_i, 1 \leqslant i \leqslant n\}$ with a fixed point F that is equal to the desired image:

$$F = W(F) = \bigcup_{i=1}^{n} w_i(F) \qquad (18.11)$$

There are two important characteristics of Equation 18.11:

1. The set of transformations, applied iteratively to any initial image, reproduces F exactly.
2. The set W defines the entire image F.

For a realistic image, it is not possible, or at least not practical, to find a small set of transformations W that defines a fixed set (attractor) equal to that image. However, if both of the foregoing conditions are relaxed, then image compression is possible.

Approximation

If we cannot find a set of transformations that exactly reproduces some image A, perhaps we can find a set of transformations whose fixed point approximates A. Suppose that we found a set of mappings W such that $W(A)$ was close to the desired image A. Would W make a good approximate definition of A? The answer, embodied in the Collage theorem, is yes. This theorem states that if we have a contractive mapping W with contractivity s and fixed point F, then

$$\delta[F, A] \leqslant \frac{\delta[W(A), A]}{1 - s}$$

This inequality states that the closer $W(A)$ is to A, the closer the fixed attractor of W is to A, especially if W is strongly contractive (small s). This seems to suggest a promising approach to compression. If a small set of mappings w_i can be found such that $W = \cup w_i$ produces $W(A)$ close to A, then the image A can be represented by the parameters of W (as in Table 18.2). For decompression, the fixed point of W is calculated by beginning with an arbitrary image and applying W until convergence is achieved. The calculated fixed point should be close to the original image.

Partitioned Iterated Function System

Even if we allow for the use of mappings that produce an approximate image, it is not practical to find a set W whose fixed point approximates a given image. Instead, we need to rely on the observation that most natural images are fractal in nature and therefore exhibit self-similarity. Patterns within an image are repeated at different scales, perhaps with distortions that approach affine transformations.

Why is this important? If a full image is too complex to find a compact transformation set W that approximates it, then perhaps if we break the image up into smaller pieces, it will be possible to find a compact transformation set for each of these smaller pieces. However, we are still left with the problem of finding a particular set of transformations W whose fixed point approximates each small image. If the image exhibits self-similarity, then the task of finding such sets becomes more manageable, just as it was a relatively easy problem to find the transformation set for the Cantor set and the Sierpinski gasket.

The approach suggested by Jacquin [JACQ92] is the following. Partition the image to be compressed into a number of uniform blocks that are nonoverlapping and cover the entire image. For example, we could use blocks of 8×8 pixels; let us call these small blocks (SBs). For each SB, find a block of twice the size in each dimension (16×16) for which a simple affine transformation produces the best approximation to the SB. We will call these larger blocks big blocks (BBs)[5]; in doing the search, we could look at a grid of BBs that cover the image, or we could use a sliding-block technique so that any BB, not just those that align on 16-pixel boundaries, is allowed. For each SB, the position and transformation parameters of its corresponding BB are stored to represent the SB. This information represents the compressed version of the image. If the image exhibits self-similarity, then patterns should repeat at different scales and therefore it should be possible to find a BB that resembles an SB, subject to an affine transformation.

Figure 18.22 gives a general idea of the compression and decompression algorithms for this approach. Compression begins by partitioning the image into SBs. For each SB, the program chooses the BB that can be used to approximate most closely this SB using one of a small set of affine transformations. In a practical applications, the transformations may be limited to the form

$$w(\bullet) = 0.5A + m$$

---

[5] Jacquin and Barnsley use the terms *domain block* and *range block* for what we call *SB* and *BB*. Other authors interchange these meanings. The terms SB and BB, though not elegant, are at least unambiguous.

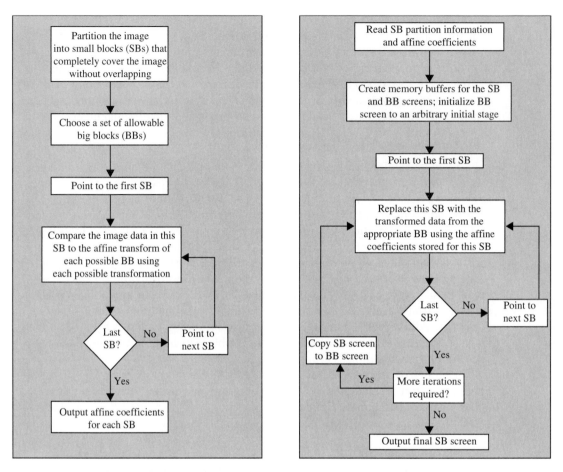

(a) Compression   (b) Decompression

Figure 18.22 Fractal compression decompression algorithms.

where m is the position of the BB relative to the origin and A is one of the following simple affine transformations:

0: Identity
1: Reflection in y-axis
2: Reflection in x-axis
3: 180° rotation
4: Reflection on diagonal $y = x$
5: 90° rotation
6: 270° rotation
7: Reflection on diagonal $y = -x$.

After all SBs are processed, the output consists of the identity of the BB and mapping information for each SB.

Decompression is initialized by assigning a memory buffer for two equal-size images, a target image to store the SB partition of the image and a source image that contains the BBs. Because of the fixed-point characteristic of the affine mappings, the initial content of the BB image is unimportant. The compression algorithm now makes a series of passes through the SB screen. On each pass, each SB is generated by locating the corresponding BB in the BB screen and mapping the contents of that BB onto the SB. For the second pass the entire contents of the SB screen are copied back to the BB screen, to serve as input for this pass. Then the mapping process for each SB is repeated. This process is repeated until the image converges; that is, until the differences between the two screens are indiscernible.

Example

Figure 18.23 is a simple example, based on one in [BARN93], that illustrates some of the basic principles of the PIFS approach. The image consists of three diagonal lines, and the resolution is 64×64 pixels. The image is partitioned into SBs of 8×8 pixels. Four of the SBs are not blank, and each of these can be approximated by a mapping from the 16×16 BB that begins at the lower left corner of the image. Figure 18.23c shows a compact encoding of the image.

Practical Details

A practical implementation of fractal image compression based on PIFS must include a number of considerations that we address only briefly here.

The size of the SB involves some tradeoffs. The larger the SBs, the fewer the number of transformations needed to model the image and the greater the compression ratio. But the larger an SB, the more difficult it is to find a BB that produces a good approximation.

The amount of time spent on determining the best fit for an SB can be varied. For a higher-quality result, a system can be configured to search a larger area for a suitable BB and can be configured to consider a larger collection of transformations.

The example shown in Figure 18.23 is of a black-and-white image. For practical image compression systems, gray-scale and color images must be processed. A gray-scale image can be treated as a three-dimensional image, with the gray-scale value being the third dimension. With gray scale, the transformations w_i are of the form

$$w \begin{bmatrix} x \\ y \\ z \end{bmatrix} = \begin{bmatrix} a & b & 0 \\ c & d & 0 \\ 0 & 0 & g \end{bmatrix} \begin{bmatrix} x \\ y \\ z \end{bmatrix} + \begin{bmatrix} e \\ f \\ h \end{bmatrix} \qquad (18.12)$$

where g controls the contrast and h the brightness of the transformation.

For color images, each of the three color components (red, green, blue) is treated as a separate gray-scale image.

18.5 RECOMMENDED READING

[WALL91] provides a good overview of JPEG, and [PENN93] covers the subject in exhaustive detail, including the full text of the standard. [GALL91] is a good overview of MPEG. Another good technical source for both JPEG and MPEG is [NETR95]. [RAO96] provides

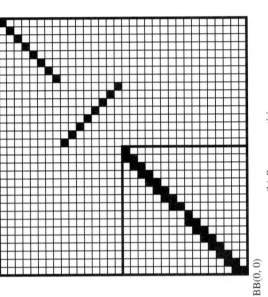

(a) Target partition

(b) Source partition

Small Block	Big Block	Transformation
SB₄	(0,0)	0
SB₇	(0,0)	2
SB₁₀	(0,0)	0
SB₁₃	(0,0)	0

(c) Mapping

Figure 18.23 Simplified example of PIFS.

a very detailed technical description of JPEG and MPEG as well as detailed discussions of implementation issues.

Many texts provide a discussion of the mathematics of fractals, affine transformations and iterated function systems; one of the clearest presentations is to be found in [SCHE96]. A more difficult but more thorough treatment is [BARN93], which includes a huge number of problems with solutions.

BARN93   Barnsley, M. *Fractals Everywhere*. Boston: Academic Press Professional, 1993.

GALL91   Gall, D. "MPEG: A Video Compression Standard for Multimedia Applications." *Communications of the ACM*, April 1991.

NETR95   Netravali, A., and Haskell, B. *Digital Pictures: Representation, Compression, and Standards*. New York; Plenum, 1995.

PENN93   Pennebaker, W., and Mitchell, J. *JPEG Still Image Data Compression Standard*. New York: Van Nostrand Reinhold, 1993.

RAO96   Rao, K., and Hwang, J. *Techniques and Standards for Image Video, and Audio Coding*. Upper Saddle River, NJ: Prentice Hall, 1996.

SCHE96   Scheinerman, E. *Invitation to Dynamical Systems*. Upper Saddle River, NJ: Prentice Hall, 1996.

WALL91   Wallace, G. "The JPEG Still Picture Compression Standard." *Communications of the ACM*, April 1991.

Recommended Web sites:

- http://www.mpeg.org/index.html: An exhaustive list of links to MPEG-related sites, including products, software, video files, announcements, FAQs, and technical information.
- http://inls3.ucsd.edu/y/Fractals: A site devoted to fractal compression, with pointers to a wide variety of Web and Internet resources on the subject.

18.6 PROBLEMS

18.1 For the example of Figure 18.1, determine the DCT for the gray scale samples (part b). Compare this to the DCT for part c.

18.2 Give a rationale for each of the lossless JPEG predictors in Figure 18.12c.

18.3 In the MPEG block diagram shown in Figure 18.13, interframe processing involves comparing the current frame to a processed copy of preceding frames $(DCT(Q(Q^{-1}(DCT^{-1}(F)))))$. Why not do the comparison between input frames?

18.4 Show that the Cantor set has zero length by summing the lengths of the intervals removed at each stage and showing that this sum converges to 1.

18.5 These questions refer to the Sierpinski gasket (Figure 18.16). Suppose the area of the enclosing triangle is X.
  a. Find the area of the black region at step N.
  b. Show that the area of the gasket at $N = \infty$ is zero.
  c. Find the number of white triangles and the number of black triangles at step N.
  d. Explain why the construction of the gasket does not end up in an all-white triangle.

18.6 The *Koch snowflake* is another classical self-similar set, constructed as follows:
  - Start with a solid (black) equilateral triangle of side length 1. There are three sides of length 1.
  - On the middle of each side, add a smaller equilateral triangle of side length 1/3. Now there are 12 sides of length 1/3.
  - On each successive step, on the middle of each side, add an equilateral triangle with side length 1/3 of the current side length. Continue indefinitely.
  Show that the length of the boundary is infinite.

18.7   Construct a new kind of Cantor set by removing the middle half of each subinterval, rather than the middle third. What is the fractal dimension of this set?

18.8   Find the fractal dimension of the following constructs defined in two dimensions:

   a. Sierpinski carpet: The closed unit square is divided into nine equal squares, and the open central square is deleted, giving the appearance of a square donut. This process is repeated for each of the eight remaining subboxes, and so on.

   b. Fractal cheese: A fractal slice of Swiss cheese is constructed as follows: The unit square is divided into p^2 squares, and m^2 squares are chosen at random and discarded ($p > m + 1$; p and m are positive integers). The process is repeated for each remaining square (side $= 1/p$). This process is repeated indefinitely.

18.9   The mapping in Figure 18.19 was described as a shear of 30°, a rotation of 45°, a scaling of 0.5 in both dimensions, and a translation of 2 in the x-dimension and 5 in the y-dimension. Demonstrate that this results in the value shown for w, namely

$$w(x, y) = (0.355x + 0.5733y + 2, -0.355x + 0.1367y + 5)$$

18.10   Find an affine transformation that takes the triangle with vertices at $(0, 0), (0, 1), (1, 0)$ to the triangle with vertices at $(4, 5), (-1, 2)$ and $(3, 0)$.

18.11   Demonstrate that the set of mappings defined in Equation 18.10 does produce the Sierpinski gasket.

18.12   In the discussion of PIFS, eight basic affine transformations are used. For two-dimension black-and-white images, show the matrix **A** for each transformation.

18.13   Explain why you would expect a better-looking result when you use more SBs in the PIFS compression algorithm. What happens in the limiting case where the number of SBs is equal to the number of pixels? What about when there are only four SBs?

18.14   Explain how the parameters g and h in Equation 18.12 control contrast and brightness.

GLOSSARY

In studying the Imperium, Arrakis, and the whole culture which produced Maud'Dib, many unfamiliar terms occur. To increase understanding is a laudable goal, hence the definitions and explanations given below.

—*Dune,* Frank Herbert

S ome of the definitions in this glossary are from the *American National Standard Dictionary of Information Technology*, ANSI Standard X3.172, 1995. These are marked with an asterisk.

Application layer   Layer 7 of the OSI model. This layer determines the interface of the system with the user.

Asynchronous transfer mode (ATM)   A form of packet transmission using fixed-size packets, called cells. ATM is the data transfer interface for B-ISDN. Unlike X.25, ATM does not provide error control and flow control mechanisms.

ATM adaptation layer (AAL)   The layer that maps information transfer protocols onto ATM.

Automatic repeat request (ARQ)   A feature that automatically initiates a request for retransmission when an error in transmission is detected.

Baseband   Transmission of signals without modulation. In a baseband local network, digital signals (1's and 0's) are inserted directly onto the cable as voltage pulses. The entire spectrum of the cable is consumed by the signal. This scheme does not allow frequency-division multiplexing.

Bit stuffing   The insertion of extra bits into a data stream to avoid the appearance of unintended control sequences.

Bridge*   A functional unit that interconnects two local area networks (LANs) that use the same logical link control protocol but may use different medium access control protocols.

Broadcast   The simultaneous transmission of data to a number of stations.

Broadcast address   An address that designates all entities within a domain (e.g., network, internet).

Broadcast communication network   A communication network in which a transmission from one station is broadcast to and received by all other stations.

Bus*   One or more conductors that serve as a common connection for a related group of devices.

Cell relay   The packet-switching mechanism used for the fixed-size packets called cells. ATM is based on cell relay technology.

Checksum   An error-detecting code based on a summation operation performed on the bits to be checked.

Collision   A condition in which two packets are being transmitted over a medium at the same time. Their interference makes both unintelligible.

Communication network   A collection of interconnected functional units that provides a data communications service among stations attached to the network.

Connectionless data transfer   A protocol for exchanging data in an unplanned fashion and without prior coordination (e.g., datagram).

Connection-oriented data transfer   A protocol for exchanging data in which a logical connection is established between the end points (e.g., virtual circuit).

Contention   The condition when two or more stations attempt to use the same channel at the same time.

CSMA (Carrier Sense Multiple Access)   A medium access control technique for multiple-access transmission media. A station wishing to transmit first senses the medium and transmits only if the medium is idle.

CSMA/CD (Carrier Sense Multiple Access with Collision Detection)   A refinement of CSMA in which a station ceases transmission if it detects a collision.

Cyclic redundancy check (CRC)   An error detecting code in which the code is the remainder resulting from dividing the bits to be checked by a predetermined binary number.

Data circuit-terminating equipment (DCE)   In a data station, the equipment that provides the signal conversion and coding between the data terminal equipment (DTE) and the line. The DCE may be separate equipment or an integral part of the DTE or of intermediate equipment. The DCE may perform other functions that are normally performed at the network end of the line.

Datagram* In packet switching, a packet, independent of other packets, that carries information sufficient for routing from the originating data terminal equipment to the destination DTE without the necessity of establishing a connection between the DTEs and the network.

Data link layer* In OSI, the layer that provides service to transfer data between network layer entities, usually in adjacent nodes. The data link layer detects and possibly corrects errors that may occur in the physical layer.

Data terminal equipment (DTE)* Equipment consisting of digital end instruments that convert the user information into data signals for transmission, or reconvert the received data signals into user information.

Encapsulation The addition of control information by a protocol entity to data obtained from a protocol user.

End system (ES) A device attached to one of the subnetworks of an internet that is used to support end-user applications or services.

Error-detecting code* A code in which each expression conforms to specific rules of construction, so that if certain errors occur in an expression, the resulting expression will not conform to the rules of construction and thus the presence of the errors is detected.

Error rate* The ratio of the number of data units in error to the total number of data units.

Flow control The function performed by a receiving entity to limit the amount or rate of data that is sent by a transmitting entity.

Frame A group of bits that includes data plus one or more addresses and other protocol control information. Generally refers to a link layer (OSI layer 2) protocol data unit.

Frame check sequence (FCS) An error-detecting code inserted as a field in a block of data to be transmitted. The code serves to check for errors upon reception of the data.

Frame relay A form of packet switching based on the use of variable-length link-layer frames. There is no network layer, and many of the basic functions have been streamlined or eliminated to provide for greater throughput.

Full-duplex transmission Data transmission in both directions at the same time.

Half-duplex transmission Data transmission in either direction, one direction at a time.

HDLC (high-level data link control) A very common bit-oriented data link protocol (OSI layer 2) issued by ISO. Similar protocols are LAPB, LAPD, and LLC.

Header System-defined control information that precedes user data.

Intermediate system (IS)   A device attached to two or more subnetworks in an internet and that performs routing and relaying of data between end systems. Examples of intermediate systems are bridges and routers.

Internet   A collection of packet-switching and broadcast networks that are connected together via routers. When used as a proper name (capatilized), the term refers to the worldwide internet based on TCP/IP that interconnects thousands of public and private networks and millions of users.

Internet protocol (IP)   An internetworking protocol that provides connectionless service across multiple packet-switching networks.

Internetworking   Communication among devices across multiple networks.

Intranet   A corporate internetwork that provides the key Internet applications, especially the World Wide Web. An intranet operates within the organization for internal purposes and can exist as an isolated, self-contained internet, or may have links to the Internet.

Layer*   A group of services, functions, and protocols that is complete from a conceptual point of view, that is one out of a set of hierarchically arranged groups, and that extends across all systems that conform to the network architecture.

Local area network (LAN)   A communication network that provides interconnection of a variety of data-communicating devices within a small area.

Logical connection*   An association established between functional units for conveying information.

Medium access control (MAC)   For broadcast networks, the method of determining which device has access to the transmission medium at any time. CSMA/CD and token are common access methods.

Multicast address   An address that designates a group of entities within a domain (e.g., network, internet).

Multiplexing   In data transmission, a function that permits two or more data sources to share a common transmission medium such that each data source has its own channel.

Network layer   Layer 3 of the OSI model. Responsible for routing data through a communication network.

Octet   A group of 8 bits, usually operated upon as an entity.

Open Systems Interconnection (OSI) Reference Model   A model of communications between cooperating devices. It defines a seven-layer architecture of communication functions.

Packet   A group of bits that includes data plus control information. Generally refers to a network layer (OSI layer 3) protocol data unit.

Packet switching   A method of transmitting messages through a communication network, in which long messages are subdivided into short packets. The packets are then transmitted as in message switching.

Parity bit*   A check bit appended to an array of binary digits to make the sum of all the binary digits, including the check bit, always odd or always even.

Physical layer   Layer 1 of the OSI model. Concerned with the electrical, mechanical, and timing aspects of signal transmission over a medium.

Piggybacking   The inclusion of an acknowledgment to a previously received packet in an outgoing data packet.

Pixel*   The smallest element of a digital image that can be assigned a gray level. Equivalently, a pixel is an individual dot in a dot-matrix representation of a picture.

Point-to-point   A configuration in which two stations share a transmission path.

Port   A means of identifying a user of the services of a protocol entity. A protocol entity provides one or more port numbers for use by higher-level entities. In OSI, the equivalent term is *service access point (SAP)*.

Presentation layer*   Layer 6 of the OSI model. Provides for the selection of a common syntax for representing data and for transformation of application data into and from the common syntax.

Propagation delay   The delay between the time a signal enters a channel and the time it is received.

Protocol   A set of rules that govern the operation of functional units to achieve communication.

Protocol architecture   The hardware and software structure that implements the communications function.

Protocol control information*   Information exchanged between entities of a given layer, via the service provided by the next lower layer, to coordinate their joint operation.

Protocol data unit (PDU)*   A set of data specified in a protocol of a given layer and consisting of protocol control information of that layer, and possibly user data of that layer.

Ring   A local network topology in which stations are attached to repeaters connected in a closed loop. Data are transmitted in one direction around the ring and can be read by all attached stations.

Router   An internetworking device that connects two computer networks. It makes use of an internet protocol and assumes that all of the attached devices on the networks use the same communications architecture and protocols. A router operates at OSI layer 3.

Routing   The determination of a path that a data unit (frame, packet, message) will traverse from source to destination.

Sequence number   A number contained in the header of a PDU that, either alone or with other header fields, serves to uniquely identify this PDU out of a sequence of PDUs.

Service access point   see *Port*.

Session layer Layer 5 of the OSI model. Manages a logical connection (session) between two communicating processes or applications.

Sliding-window technique A method of flow control in which a transmitting station may send numbered packets within a window of numbers. The window changes dynamically to allow additional packets to be sent.

Star A topology in which all stations are connected to a central switch. Two stations communicate via circuit switching.

Statistical time-division multiplexing A method of TDM in which time slots on a shared transmission line are allocated to I/O channels on demand.

Stop and wait A flow control protocol in which the sender transmits a block of data and then awaits an acknowledgment before transmitting the next block.

Subnetwork Refers to a constituent network of an internet. This avoids ambiguity because the entire internet, from a user's point of view, is a single network.

Switched communication network A communication network consisting of a network of nodes connected by point-to-point links. Data are transmitted from source to destination through intermediate nodes.

Synchronous time-division multiplexing A method of TDM in which time slots on a shared transmission line are assigned to I/O channels on a fixed, predetermined basis.

Time-division multiplexing (TDM) The division of a transmission facility into two or more channels by allotting the facility to several different information channels, one at a time.

Token ring A medium access control technique for rings. A token circulates around the ring. A station may transmit by seizing the token, inserting a packet onto the ring, and then retransmitting the token.

Topology The structure, consisting of paths and switches, that provides the communications interconnection among nodes of a network.

Transport layer Layer 4 of the OSI model. Provides reliable, transparent transfer of data between end points.

Virtual circuit A packet-switching service in which a connection (virtual circuit) is established between two stations at the start of transmission. All packets follow the same route, need not carry a complete address, and arrive in sequence.

World Wide Web A networked, graphically oriented hypermedia system. Information is stored on servers, exchanged between servers and browsers, and displayed on browsers in the form of pages of text and images.

REFERENCES

In matters of this kind everyone feels he is justified in writing and publishing the first thing that come into his head when he picks up a pen, and thinks his own idea as axiomatic as the fact that two and two make four. If critics would go to the trouble of thinking about the subject for years on end and testing each conclusion against the actual history of war, as I have done, they would undoubtedly be more careful of what they wrote.

—*On War,* Carl von Clausewitz

ABSX92   Apple Computer, Bellcore, Sun Microsystems and Xerox. *Network Compatible ATM for Local Network Applications, Version 1.01.* October 19, 1992 (available at parcftp.xerox.com/pub/latm).

ALLE80   Allen, A. "Queuing Models of Computer Systems." *Computer,* April 1980.

ANDL96   Andleigh, P., and Thakrar, K. *Multimedia Systems Design.* Upper Saddle River, NJ: Prentice Hall, 1996.

ARAS94   Aras, C., Kurose, J., Reeves, D., and Schulzrinne, H. "Real-time Communication in Packet-switched Networks." *Proceedings of the IEEE,* January 1994.

ARAV93   Aravind, R., et al. "Image and Video Coding Standards." *AT&T Technical Journal,* January/February, 1993.

ARMI93   Armitage, G., and Adams, K. "Packet Reassembly During Cell Loss." *IEEE Network,* September 1993.

ARPS94   Arps, R., and Truong, T. "Comparison of International Standards for Lossless Still Image Compression." *Proceedings of the IEEE*, June 1994.

ARUL96   Arulambalam, A., Chen, X., and Ansari, N. "Allocating Fair Rates for Available Bit Rate Service in ATM Networks." *IEEE Communications Magazine*, November 1996.

ASH90   Ash, R. *Information Theory.* New York: Dover, 1990.

ATM94   ATM Forum. *User-Network Interface (UNI) Specification Version 3.1.* September 1994.

ATM96   ATM Forum. *Traffic Management Specification Version 4.0.* April 1996.

BARN88   Barnsley, M., and Sloan, A. "A Better Way to Compress Images." *Byte*, January 1988.

BARN93   Barnsley, M. *Fractals Everywhere.* Boston: Academic Press Professional, 1993.

BENE64   Benice, R. "An Analysis of Retransmission Systems." *IEEE Transactions on Communication Technology*, December 1964.

BERA94   Beran, J. *Statistics for Long-memory Processes.* New York: Chapman & Hall, 1994.

BERA95   Beran, J., Sherman, M. Taqqu, S., and Willinger, W. "Long-range Dependence in Variable-bit-rate Video Traffic." *IEEE Transactions on Communications*, February 1995.

BERT92   Bertsekas, D. and Gallager, R. *Data Networks.* Upper Saddle River, NJ: Prentice Hall, 1992.

BONO95   Bonomi, F., and Fendick, K. "The Rate-based Flow Control Framework for the Available Bit Rate ATM Service." *IEEE Network*, March/April 1995.

BOX94   Box, G., Jenkins, G., and Riensel, G. *Time Series Analysis: Forecasting and Control.* Upper Saddle River, NJ: Prentice Hall, 1994.

BRAD94   Braden, B., and Zhang, L. "RSVP: A Resource ReSerVation Protocol." *Connexions*, August 1994.

BRAD96   Bradner, S., and Mankin, A. *IPng: Internet Protocol Next Generation.* Reading, MA: Addison-Wesley, 1996.

BREY95   Breyer, R., and Riley, S. *Switched and Fast Ethernet: How It Works and How to Use It.* Emeryville, CA: Ziff-Davis Press, 1995.

BRUN96   Bruna, C. "Internet Health Report: Condition Serious." *Network World*, September 1996.

BULM79   Bulmer, M. *Principles of Statistics.* New York: Dover, 1979.

BURG91   Burg, J., and Dorman, D. "Broadband ISDN Resource Management: The Role of Virtual Paths." *IEEE Communications Magazine*, September 1991.

BUX80   Bux, W.; Kummerle, K.; and Truong, H. "Balanced HDLC Procedures: A Performance Analysis." *IEEE Transactions on Communications*, November 1980.

CERF74   Cerf, V., and Kahn, R. "A Protocol for Packet Network Interconnection," *IEEE Transactions on Communications*, May 1974.

CHAR77   Chartrand, G. *Introductory Graph Theory.* New York: Dover, 1977.

CHEN96   Chen, T., Liu, S., and Samalam, V. "The Available Bit Rate Service for Data in ATM Networks." *IEEE Communications Magazine*, May 1996.

CLAR88   Clark, D. "The Design Philosophy of the DARPA Internet Protocols." *Proceedings, SIGCOMM '88, Computer Communication Review*, August 1988; reprinted in *Computer Communication Review*, January 1995.

CLAR90   Clark, D., and Tennenhouse, D. "Architectural Considerations for a New Generation of Protocols." *Proceedings, SIGCOMM '90, Computer Communication Review*, September 1990.

CLAR92   Clark, D., Shenker, S., and Zhang, L. "Supporting Real-time Applications in an Integrated Services Packet Network: Architecture and Mechanism" *Proceedings, SIGCOMM '92*, August 1992.

CLAR95   Clark, D. *Adding Service Discrimination to the Internet.* MIT Laboratory for Computer Science Technical Report, September 1995. Available at http://ana-www.lcs.mit.edu/anaweb/papers.html

COHE96   Cohen, J. "Rule Reversal: Old 80/20 LAN Traffic Model Is Getting Turned on Its Head." *Network World*, December 16, 1996.

COME94a   Comer, D., and Stevens, D. *Internetworking with TCP/IP, Volume II: Design Implementation, and Internals.* Upper Saddle River, NJ: Prentice Hall, 1994.

COME94b   Comer, D., and Stevens, D. *Internetworking with TCP/IP, Volume III: Client-Server Programming and Applications.* Upper Saddle River, NJ: Prentice Hall, 1994.

COME95a   Comer, D. *Internetworking with TCP/IP, Volume I: Principles, Protocols and Architecture.* Upper Saddle River, NJ: Prentice Hall, 1995.

COME95b   Comer, D., and Lin, J. "TCP Buffering and Performance Over an ATM Network." *Internetworking: Research and Experience*, March 1995.

CORM90   Cormen, T., Leiserson, C., and Rivest, R. *Introduction to Algorithms.* Cambridge, MA: MIT Press, 1990.

COVE91   Cover, T., and Thomas, J. *Elements of Information Theory.* New York: Wiley, 1991.

CROV96   Crovella, M., and Bestavros, A."Self-similarity in World-Wide Web Traffic: Evidence and Possible Causes." *Proceedings, ACM Sigmetrics Conference on Measurement and Modeling of Computer Systems*, May 1996.

CROW92   Crowcroft, J., Wakeman, I., Wang, Z., and Sirovica, D. "Is Layering Harmful?" *IEEE Network Magazine*, January 1992.

DEAN96   Deane, J., Smythe, C., and Jefferies, D. "Self-similarity in a Deterministic Model of Data Transfer." *International Journal of Electronics*, No. 5, 1996.

DEER90   Deering, S., and Cheriton, D. "Multicast Routing in Datagram Internetworks and Extended LANs." *ACM Transactions on Computer Systems*, May 1990.

DEME90   Demers, A., Keshav, S., and Shenker, S. "Analysis and Simulation of a Fair Queueing Algorithm." *Internetworking: Research and Experience*, September 1990.

DIJK59   Dijkstra, E. "A Note on Two Problems in Connection with Graphs." *Numerical Mathematics*, October 1959.

DUFF94   Duffy, D., McIntosh, A., Rosenstein, M., and Willinger, W. "Statistical Analysis of CCSN/SS7 Traffic Data from Working CCS Subnetworks." *IEEE Journal on Selected Areas in Communications*, April 1994.

ERRA94   Erramilli, A., Gordon, J., and Willinger, W. "Applications of Fractals in Engineering for Realistic Traffic Processes." *Proceedings, International Telecommunications Conference (ITC-14)*, Amsterdam: Elsevier, 1994.

ERRA95   Erramilli, A. (session organizer). "Performance Impact of Self-similarity in Traffic." *Proceedings, Sigmetrics '95/Performance '95*, May 1995.

ERRA96   Erramilli, A., Narayan, O., and Willinger, W. "Experimental Queueing Analysis with Long-range Dependent Packet Traffic." *IEEE/ACM Transactions on Networking*, April 1996.

FANG94   Fang. C., Chen, H., and Hutchins, J. "A Simulation Study of TCP Performance in ATM Networks." *Proceedings, GLOBECOM '94*, 1994.

FANG95   Fang, C., and Lin, A. *On TCP Performance of UBR with EPD and UBR-EPD with a Fair Buffer Allocation Scheme.* ATM Forum Contribution 95-1645, December 1995.

FANG97   Fang, C., and Lin, A. "TCP Performance in ATM Networks: ABR Parameter Tuning and ABR/UBR Comparisons." *Proceedings, IEEE Singapore International Conference on Networks*, April 1997.

FEDE88   Feder. J. *Fractals.* New York: Plenum Press, 1988.

FISH95   Fisher, Y., ed. *Fractal Image Compression.* New York: Springer-Verlag, 1995.

FLOY93   Floyd, S., and Jacobson, V. "Random Early Detection Gateways for Congestion Avoidance." *IEEE/ACM Transactions on Networking*, August 1993.

FLOY97   Floyd, S., and Fall, K. "Router Mechanisms to Support End-to-end Congestion Control." *Proceedings, SIGCOMM'97*, 1997.

FORD62   Ford, L., and Fulkerson, D. *Flows in Networks.* Princeton, NJ: Princeton University Press, 1962.

GALL68   Gallager, R. *Information Theory and Reliable Communication.* New York: Wiley, 1968.

GALL91   Gall, D. "MPEG: A Video Compression Standard for Multimedia Applications." *Communications of the ACM*, April 1991.

GARR94   Garrett, M., and Willinger, W. "Analysis, Modeling, and Generation of Self-similar VBR Video Traffic." *Proceedings, SIGCOMM 94*, August 1994.

GARR96   Garrett, M. "A Service Architecture for ATM: From Applications to Scheduling." *IEEE Network*, May/June 1996.

GERS91   Gersht, A., and Lee, K. "A Congestion Control Framework for ATM Networks." *IEEE Journal on Selected Areas in Communications*, September 1991.

GOLD87   Goldberg, S. *Probability: An Introduction.* New York: Dover, 1987.

GORA95   Goralski, W. *Introduction to ATM Networking.* New York: McGraw-Hill, 1995.

GOYA97   Goyal, R. et al. "UBR+: Improving Performance of TCP over ATM-UBR Service." *Proceedings, ICC '97*, June 1997.

GREE92   Greenberg, A., and Madras, N. "How Fair is Fair Queuing?" *Journal of the ACM*, July 1992.

GRIM92   Grimmett, G., and Stirzaker, D. *Probability and Random Processes.* Oxford: Oxford University Press, 1992.

GROS96   Grossglauser, M., and Bolot, J. "On the Relevance of Long-range Dependence in Network Traffic." *Proceeding, SIGCOMM'96*, August 1996.

HAFN96   Hafner, K., and Lyon, M. *Where Wizards Stay up Late*, New York: Simon & Schuster, 1996.

HAMM91   Hamming, R. *The Art of Probability: For Scientists and Engineers.* Reading, MA: Addison-Wesley, 1991.

HAND94   Handel, R., Huber, N., and Schroder, S. *ATM Networks: Concepts, Protocols, Applications.* Reading, MA: Addison-Wesley, 1994.

HARB92   Harbison, R. "Frame Relay: Technology for Our Time." *LAN Technology*, December 1992.

HELD96   Held, G. *Data and Image Compression: Tools and Techniques.* New York: Wiley, 1996.

HOE96   Hoe, J. "Improving the Start-up Behavior of a Congestion Control Scheme for TCP." *Proceedings, SIGCOMM '96*, August 1996.

HOWA94   Howard, P., and Vitter, J. "Arithmetic Coding for Data Compression." *Proceedings of the IEEE*, June 1994.

HUIT95   Huitema, C. *Routing in the Internet.* Englewood Cliffs, NJ: Prentice Hall, 1995.

HUIT96   Huitema, C. *IPv6: The New Internet Protocol.* Upper Saddle River, NJ: Prentice-Hall, 1996.

HURS65   Hurst, H., Black, R., and Simaika, Y. *Long-term Storage: An Experimental Study.* London: Constable, 1965.

ITER95   Iterated Systems, Inc. *Welcome to Fractals and Imaging.* On-line document at http://www.iterated.com, 1995.

JACO88   Jacobson, V. "Congestion Avoidance and Control." *Proceedings, SIG-COMM '88, Computer Communication Review*, August 1988; reprinted in *Computer Communication Review*, January 1995, a slightly revised version is available at ftp.ee.lbl.gov/papers/congavoid.ps.Z.

JACO90a   Jacobson, V. "Berkeley TCP Evolution from 4.3 Tahoe to 4.3-Reno." *Proceedings of the Eighteenth Internet Engineering Task Force*, September 1990.

JACO90b   Jacobson, V. "Modified TCP Congestion Avoidance Algorithm." *end2end-interest mailing list*, 20, April 1990. Available at ftp://ftp.ee.lbl.gov/email/vanj.90apr30.txt.

JACQ92   Jacquin, A. "Image Coding Based on a Fractal Theory of Iterated Contractive Image Transformations." *IEEE Transactions on Image Processing*, January 1992.

JAIN90   Jain, R. "Congestion Control in Computer Networks: Issues and Trends." *IEEE Network Magazine*, May 1990.

JAIN91   Jain, R. *The Art of Computer Systems Performance Analysis: Techniques for Experimental Design, Measurement, Simulation, and Modeling*. New York: Wiley, 1991.

JAIN92   Jain, R. "Myths about Congestion Management in High-speed Networks." *Internetworking: Research and Experience*, Vol. 3, 1993.

JAIN96a   Jain, R. et al. "Source Behavior for ATM ABR Traffic Management: An Explanation." *IEEE Communications Magazine*, November 1996.

JAIN96b   Jain, R. et al. *ERICA Switch Algorithm: A Complete Description*. ATM Forum Contribution 96-1172, August 1996. Available at http://www.cis.ohio-state.edu/~jain.

JOHN96   Johnson, H. *Fast Ethernet: Dawn of New Network*. Upper Saddle River, NJ: Prentice Hall, 1996.

KALY97   Kalyanaraman, S. et al. "Performance and Buffering Requirements of Internet Protocols over ATM ABR and UBR Services." *IEEE Communications Magazine*, January 1997.

KAMA96   Kamal, A. "Performance Modeling of Partial packet Discarding Using the End-of-packet Indicator in AAL Type 5." *IEEE Transactions on Networking*, December 1996.

KARN91   Karn, P., and Partridge, C. "Improving Round-trip Estimates in Reliable Transport Protocols." *ACM Transactions on Computer Systems*, November 1991.

KAVA95   Kavak, N. "Data Communication in ATM Networks." *IEEE Network*, May/June 1995.

KLEI75   Kleinrock, L. *Queueing Systems, Volume I: Theory*. New York: Wiley, 1975.

KLEI76   Kleinrock, L. *Queueing Systems, Volume II: Computer Applications*. New York: Wiley, 1976.

KOHN80   Konheim, A. "A Queuing Analysis of Two ARQ Protocols." *IEEE Transactions on Communications,* July 1980.

LELA93   Leland, W., Taqqu, M., Willinger, W., and Wilson, D. "On the Self-similar Nature of Ethernet Traffic." *Proceedings, SIGCOMM '93*, September 1993.

LELA94   Leland, W., Taqqu, M., Willinger, W., and Wilson, D. "On the Self-similar Nature of Ethernet Traffic (Extended Version)." *IEEE/ACM Transactions on Networking*, February 1994.

LIN84   Lin, S.; Costello, D.; and Miller, M. "Automatic-Repeat-Request Error-Control Schemes." *IEEE Communications Magazine*, December 1984.

LIVN93   Livny, M., Melamed, B., and Tsiolis, A. "The Impact of Autocorrelation on Queuing Systems." *Management Science*, March 1993.

LURI94   Lurie, D., and Moore, R. *Applying Statistics.* U.S. Nuclear Regulatory Commission Report NUREG-1475. (Available from the Government Printing Office, GPO Stock Number 052-020-00390-4.)

MAND65   Mandelbrot, B. "Self-similar Error Clusters in Communications Systems and the Concept of Conditional Stationarity." *IEEE Transactions on Communications Technology*, Vol. 13, 1965.

MART93   Martine, R. *Basic Traffic Analysis.* Englewood Cliffs, NJ: Prentice Hall, 1993.

MCDY95   McDysan, D., and Spohn, D. *ATM: Theory and Application.* New York: McGraw-Hill, 1995.

MCQU96   McQuillan, J. "The Arrival of IP Switching." *Business Communications Review*, June 1996.

MOLD95   Moldeklev, K., and Gunningberg, P. "How a Large ATM MTU Causes Deadlocks in TCP Data Transfers." *IEEE/ACM Transactions on Networking*, August 1995.

MOLL89   Molloy, M. *Fundamentals of Performance Modeling.* New York: Macmillan, 1989.

MOY94   Moy, J. "Multicast Routing Extensions for OSPF." *Communications of the ACM*, August 1994.

MURP95   Murphy, E., Hayes, S., and Enders, M. *TCP/IP: Tutorial and Technical Overview.* Upper Saddle River: NJ: Prentice Hall, 1995.

NAGL87   Nagle, J. "On Packet Switches with Infinite Storage." *IEEE Transactions on Communciations*, April 1987.

NBS63   National Bureau of Standards. *Experimental Statistics.* NBS Handbook 91, 1963. (Available from the Government Printing Office, GPO Stock Number 003-003-00135-0.)

NELS96   Nelson, M., and Gailly, J. *The Data Compression Book.* New York: M&T Books, 1996.

NETR95   Netravali, A., and Haskell, B. *Digital Pictures: Representation, Compression, and Standards.* New York: Plenum, 1995.

NEWM94   Newman, P. "ATM Local Area Networks." *IEEE Communications Magazine*, March 1994.

NEWM96   Newman, P., Lyon, T., and Minshall, G. "Flow Labelled IP: Connectionless ATM Under IP." *Proceedings, Networld+Interop*, April 1996.

NEWM97   Newman, P., Minshall, G., Lyon, T., and Huston, L. "IP Switching and Gigabit Routers." *IEEE Communications Magazine*, January 1997.

NORR94   Norros, I. "A Storage Model with Self-similar Input." *Queueing Systems*, Vol. 16, 1994.

NORR95   Norros, I. "On the Use of Fractional Brownian Motion in the Theory of Connectionless Networks." *IEEE Journal on Selected Areas in Communications*, August 1995.

ORE90   Ore, O., and Wilson, R. *Graphs and Their Uses.* Washington, DC: The Mathematical Association of America, 1990.

OSHA95   Oshaki, H., et al. "Rate-based Congestion Control for ATM Networks." *Computer Communication Review*, April 1995.

PAPO91   Papoulis, A. *Probability, Random Variables, and Stochastic Processes.* New York: McGraw-Hill, 1991.

PARE93   Parekh, A., and Gallager, G. "A Generalized Processor Sharing Approach to Flow Control in Integrated Services Networks: The Single-node Case." *IEEE/ACM Transactions on Networking*, June 1993.

PARE94   Parekh, A., and Gallager, G. "A Generalized Processor Sharing Approach to Flow Control in Integrated Services Networks: The Multiple Node Case." *IEEE/ACM Transactions on Networking*, April 1994.

PAXS95   Paxson, V., and Floyd, S. "Wide Area Traffic: The Failure of Poisson Modeling." *IEEE/ACM Transactions on Networking*, June 1995.

PAXS96   Paxson, V. "End-to-end Routing Behavior in the Internet." *Proceedings, SIGCOMM'96*, August 1996.

PENN93   Pennebaker, W., and Mitchell, J. *JPEG Still Image Data Compression Standard.* New York: Van Nostrand Reinhold, 1993.

PERL92   Perlman, R. *Interconnections: Bridges and Routers.* Reading, MA: Addison-Wesley, 1992.

PERL95   Perloff, M., and Reiss, K. "Improvements to TCP Performance in High-speed ATM Networks." *Communications of the ACM*, February 1995.

PHIL92   Phillips, J. *How to Think about Statistics.* New York: Freeman, 1992.

PITT96   Pitts, J., and Schormans, J. *Introduction to ATM Design and Performance.* New York: Wiley, 1996.

PRAT80 Pratt, W. et al. "Combined Symbol Matching Facsimile Data Compression Sysetms." *Proceedings of the IEEE*, July 1980.

PRYC96 Prycker, M. *Asynchronous Transfer Mode: Solutions for Broadband ISDN.* New York: Ellis Horwood, 1996.

RAO96 Rao, K., and Hwang, J. *Techniques and Standards for Image Video and Audio Coding.* Upper Saddle River, NJ: Prentice Hall 1996.

REKH93 Rekhter, Y. "Inter-domain Routing Protocol (IDRP)." *Interneworking: Research and Experience*, June 1993.

ROMA95 Romanow, A., and Floyd. S. "Dynamics of TCP Traffic Over ATM Networks." *IEEE Journal on Selected Areas in Communications*, May 1995.

RYU96 Ryu, B., and Elwalid, A. "The Importance of Long-range Dependence of VBR Video Traffic in ATM Traffic Engineering: Myths and Realities." *Proceeding, SIGCOMM'96*, August 1996.

RYU97 Ryu, B., and Lowen, S. "Point Process Approaches for Modeling and Analysis of Self-Similar Traffic, Part II—Applications." *Proceedings, International Conference on Telecommunications Systems, Modeling, and Analysis*, March 1997.

SAIT96 Saito, J. et al. "Performance Issues in Public ABR Service." *IEEE Communications Magazine*, November 1996.

SATO90 Sato, K., Ohta, S., and Tokizawa, I. "Broad-band ATM Network Architecture Based on Virtual Paths." *IEEE Transactions on Communications*, August 1990.

SATO91 Sato, K., Ueda, H., and Yoshikai, M. "The Role of Virtual Path Cross-connection." *IEEE LTS,* August 1991.

SAUN96 Saunders, S. *The McGraw-Hill High-speed LANs Handbook.* New York: McGraw-Hill, 1996.

SAYO96 Sayood, K. *Introduction to Data Compression.* San Francisco, CA: Morgan Kaufmann, 1996.

SAYR76 Sayre, K. *Cybernetics and the Philosophy of Mind.* Atlantic Highlands, NJ: Humanities Press, 1976.

SCHE96 Scheinerman, E. *Invitation to Dynamical Systems.* Upper Saddle River, NJ: Prentice Hall, 1996.

SCHR91 Schroeder, M. *Fractals, Chaos, Power Laws: Minutes from an Infinite Paradise.* New York: Freeman, 1991.

SCHW77 Schwartz, M. *Computer-Communication Network Design and Analysis.* Englewood Cliffs, NJ: Prentice Hall, 1977.

SCHW80 Schwartz, M., and Stern, T. "Routing Techniques Used in Computer Communication Networks." *IEEE Transactions on Communications*, April 1980.

SCHW96 Schwartz, M. *Broadband Integrated Networks.* Upper Saddle River, NJ: Prentice Hall PTR, 1996.

SCIU96   Sciuto, A. "TCP over ATM Performance in NASA NREN and CTI." \
1996. Available at http://www.tisl.ukans.edu/Workshops/ATM_Performance

SEME96   Semeria, C., and Maufer, T. *Introduction to Multicast Routing.* 3Com
Corp. http://www.3com.com/nsc/501303.html, October 1996.

SHEN95   Shenker, S. "Fundamental Design Issues for the Future Internet." *IEEE
Journal on Selected Areas in Communications*, September 1995.

SILV87   Silver, D., and Williamson, J. "Data-compression Chip Eases Document-
processing design." *Computer Design*, November 15, 1987.

SLEP74   Slepian, D., ed. *Key Papers in the Development of Information Theory.*
New York: IEEE Press, 1974.

SPOH93   Spohn, D. *Data Network Design.* New York: McGraw-Hill, 1994.

SPRA91   Spragins, J., Hammond, J., and Pawlikowski, K. *Telecommunications
Protocols and Design.* Reading, MA.: Addison-Wesley, 1991.

STAL95   Stallings, W. *ISDN and Broadband ISDN, with Frame Relay and ATM.*
Upper Saddle River, NJ: Prentice Hall, 1995.

STAL97a   Stallings, W. *Data and Computer Communications, 5th ed.* Upper Saddle River, NJ: Prentice Hall, 1997.

STAL97b   Stallings, W. *Local and Metropolitan Area Networks, 5th ed.* Upper Saddle River, NJ: Prentice Hall, 1997.

STAR94   Stark, H., and Woods, J. *Probability, Random Processes, and Estimation
Theory for Engineers.* Upper Saddle River, NJ: Prentice Hall, 1994.

STEE95   Steenstrup, M. *Routing in Communications Networks.* Englewood Cliffs,
NJ: Prentice Hall, 1995.

STEV94   Stevens, W. *TCP/IP Illustrated, Volume 1: The Protocols.* Reading, MA:
Addison-Wesley, 1994.

STEV96   Stevens, W. *TCP/IP Illustrated, Volume 3: TCP for Transactions,
HTTP, NNTP, and the UNIX(R) Domain Protocol.* Reading, MA: Addison-
Wesley, 1996.

STUC85   Stuck, B., and Arthurs, E. *A Computer and Communications Network
Performance Analysis Primer.* Englewood Cliffs, NJ: Prentice Hall, 1985.

SUZU94   Suzuki, T. "ATM Adaptation Layer Protocol." *IEEE Communications
Magazine*, April 1994.

TANN95   Tanner, M. *Practical Queueing Analysis.* New York: McGraw-Hill, 1995.

THOM92   Thomborson, C. "The V.42bis Standard for Data-compressing
Modems." *IEEE Micro*, October 1992.

THOM96   Thomas, S. *IPng and the TCP/IP Protocols: Implementing the Next Generation Internet.* New York: Wiley, 1996.

TIPP95   Tipper, C., and Daigle, J. "ATM Cell Delay and Loss for Best-effort TCP in the Presence of Isochronous Traffic." *IEEE Journal on Selected Areas in Communications*, October 1995.

VAUG59   Vaughan, H. "Research Model for Time Separation Integrated Communication." *Bell System Technical Journal*, July 1959.

WALL91   Wallace, G. "The JPEG Still Picture Compression Standard." *Communications of the ACM*, April 1991.

WALR91   Walrand, J. *Communication Networks: A First Course*. Homewood, IL: Asken Associates, 1991.

WANG92   Wang, Z., and Crowcroft, J. "SEAL Detects Cell Misordering." *IEEE Network,* July 1992.

WEIS93   Weiss, J., and Schremp, D. "Putting Data on a Diet." *IEEE Spectrum*, August 1993.

WELC84   Welch, T. "A Technique for High-performance Data Compression." *Computer*, June 1984.

WILL94   Willinger, W., Wilson, D., Wilson, D., and Taqqu, M. "Self-similar Traffic Modeling for High-Speed Networks." *ConneXions*, November 1994.

WILL97   Willinger, W., Taqqu, M., Sherman, R., and Wilson, D. "Self-similarity through High Variability: Statistical Analysis of Ethernet LAN Traffic at the Source Level." *IEEE/ACM Transactions on Networking*, February 1997.

WORN96   Wornell, G. *Signal Processing with Fractals: A Wavelet-based Approach.* Upper Saddle River, NJ: Prentice Hall, 1996.

WRIG95   Wright, G., and Stevens, W. *TCP/IP Illustrated, Volume 2: The Implementation.* Reading, MA: Addison-Wesley, 1995.

YANG95   Yang, C., and Reddy, A. "A Taxonomy for Congestion Control Algorithms in Packet Switching Networks." *IEEE Network*, July/August 1995.

YASU80   Yasuda, Y. "Overview of Digital Facsimile Coding Techniques in Japan." *Proceedings of the IEEE*, July 1980.

ZHAN86   Zhang, L. "Why TCP Timers Don't Work Well." *Proceedings, SIGCOMM '86 Symposium*, August 1986.

ZHAN93   Zhang, L., Deering, S., Estrin, D., Shenker, S., and Zappala, D. "RSVP: A New Resource ReSerVation Protocol." *IEEE Network*, September 1993.

ZHAN95   Zhang, H. "Service Disciplines for Guaranteed Performance Service in Packet-switching Networks." *Proceedings of the IEEE*, October 1995.

ZIV77   Ziv, J., and Lempel, A. "A Universal Algorithm for Sequential Data Compression." *IEEE Transactions on Information Theory,* May 1977.

ZIV78   Ziv, J., and Lempel, A. "Compression of Individual Sequences via Variable-rate Coding." *IEEE Transactions on Information Theory,* September 1978.

ZORZ96   Zorzi, M., and Rao, R. "On the Use of Renewal Theory in the Analysis of ARQ Projects." *IEEE Transactions on Communications*, September 1996.

INDEX

Acronyms

AAL	ATM Adaptation Layer
ABR	Available Bit Rate
ARQ	Automatic Repeat Request
ATM	Asynchronous Transfer Mode
CBR	Constant Bit Rate
CIR	Committed Information Rate
CRC	Cyclic Redundancy Check
CSMA/CD	Carrier Sense Multiple Access with Collision Detection
DCE	Data Circuit-terminating Equipment
DTE	Data Terminal Equipment
FCS	Frame Check Sequence
FTP	File Transfer Protocol
HDLC	High-level Data Link Control
IAB	Internet Architecture Board
ICMP	Internet Control Message Protocol
IEEE	Institute of Electrical and Electronics Engineers
IETF	Internet Engineering Task Force
IP	Internet Protocol
IPng	Internet Protocol—Next Generation
ISA	Integrated Services Architecture
ISO	International Organization for Standardization
ITU	International Telecommunication Union
ITU-T	ITU Telecommunication Standardization Sector
LAN	Local Area Network
LAPB	Link Access Procedure—Balanced
LAPF	Link Access Procedure for Frame Mode Bearer Services
LLC	Logical Link Control
MAC	Medium Access Control
nrt-VBR	Non-real-time Variable Bit Rate
OSI	Open Systems Interconnection
OSPF	Open Shortest Path First
PDU	Protocol Data Unit
QoS	Quality of Service
RSVP	Resource ReSerVation Protocol
RTP	Real-time Transport Protocol
rt-VBR	Real-time Variable Bit Rate
SDH	Synchronous Digital Hierarchy
SDU	Service Data Unit
SMTP	Simple Mail Transfer Protocol
TCP	Transmission Control Protocol
UBR	Unspecified Bit Rate
UDP	User Datagram Protocol
UNI	User-Network Interface
VBR	Variable Bit Rate
VCC	Virtual Channel Connection
VPC	Virtual Path Connection
WWW	World Wide Web